THOMAS WOLFE

A Biography

Ossip Garber

THOMAS WOLFE

Thomas Wolfe

A BIOGRAPHY

BY

Elizabeth Nowell

GARDEN CITY, NEW YORK

Doubleday & Company, Inc.

1960

Permission to reprint selections from the following material is acknowledged with thanks:

Look Homeward, Angel, by Thomas Wolfe, reprinted by permission of Charles Scribner's Sons; copyright 1929 Charles Scribner's Sons, renewal © 1957 Edward C. Aswell, as Administrator C.T.A. of the Estate of Thomas Wolfe, and/or Fred W. Wolfe.

Of Time and the River, by Thomas Wolfe, reprinted by permission of Charles Scribner's Sons; copyright 1935 Charles Scribner's Sons.

The Story of a Novel, by Thomas Wolfe, copyright 1936 Charles Scribner's Sons.

Editor to Author: The Letters of Maxwell E. Perkins, selected and edited by John Hall Wheelock; copyright 1950 Charles Scribner's Sons.

The Marble Man's Wife, by Hayden Norwood, reprinted by permission of Charles Scribner's Sons.

Thomas Wolfe's Letters to His Mother, edited by John Skally Terry, reprinted by permission of Charles Scribner's Sons.

You Can't Go Home Again, by Thomas Wolfe, reprinted by permission of Harper & Brothers; copyright 1934, 1937, 1938, 1939, 1940 by Maxwell E. Perkins as Executor of the Estate of Thomas Wolfe.

The Web and the Rock, by Thomas Wolfe, reprinted by permission of Harper & Brothers; copyright 1937, 1938, 1939 by Maxwell E. Perkins as Executor of the Estate of Thomas Wolfe.

Through Embassy Eyes, by Martha Dodd, copyright 1939 by Harcourt, Brace & Company, Inc., and Victor Gollancz, Ltd.

The Journey Down, by Aline Bernstein, reprinted by permission of Alfred A. Knopf, Inc., and Mrs. Edna Cusick.

Three Blue Suits, by Aline Bernstein, reprinted by permission of Mrs. Edna Cusick.

TO

John Hall Wheelock

ACKNOWLEDGMENTS

Grateful acknowledgment is here made

To William B. Wisdom for making available the major portion of the source material in this book, drawn from The Thomas Wolfe Collection of William B. Wisdom in the Harvard College Library; and also for the use of his unpublished personal reminiscences of Wolfe;

To Houghton Library, Harvard University, and to the following members of its staff: William A. Jackson, William H. Bond, Carolyn E. Jakeman, Mary Shea Goulart, Jean Briggs, Mary K. Daehler, Julie P. Johnson, Marilyn S. Schultz, Winifred Cadbury Beer, Arnold Weinberger, W. B. Van Lennep, Mary J. Reardon, George W. Cottrell, Leslie M. Oliver, and Thomas Mathews; also to Widener Library and Thomas Little, and to the Poetry Room of Lamont Library and Mrs. Lydia Roberts and Robert O'Clair;

To the late Mabel Wolfe Wheaton and to Fred W. Wolfe for making available letters written by Wolfe to them and other members of the family, for permitting quotations from letters of their own and from Mrs. Wheaton's recorded interview made for the Library of Congress, and, in general, for their tireless and devoted aid;

To the University of North Carolina Library for making available the letters and other material by or about Wolfe in its possession; also to the late Charles E. Rush, Director, and to Mary L. Thornton, Librarian of the North Carolina Collection;

To Charles Scribner's Sons for permission to quote from the published writings of Wolfe, for permission to reprint letters from Maxwell E. Perkins to John S. Terry, Madeleine Boyd, Ernest Hemingway, Thomas Beer, and Charles Scribner III, and for making available their own correspondence with Wolfe and their records concerning him; also to the following Scribner employees, past or present: Irma Wyckoff Muench, Marion Ives, W. Gilman Low, S. Elizabeth De Voy, Whitney Darrow, Robert Cross, George Merz, David Randall, Wallace Meyer, Elizabeth Youngstrom, and Fidelia Stark; and to John Hall Wheelock and the late Charles Scribner III for their sympathetic encouragement and affectionate paternalism;

To the late Aline Bernstein for making available certain letters written to her by Wolfe, for providing much background material, and for giving unstintedly of her own recollections concerning Wolfe; and to her daughter, Mrs. Edna Cusick, for giving permission to quote from her mother's letters and published writings;

To Mrs. Maxwell E. Perkins for permission to quote from the letters and articles of Maxwell E. Perkins;

To Belinda Jelliffe for permission to read and quote from her excellent unpublished reminiscences of Wolfe and Perkins;

To James and Theresa Stevens and to Dr. E. C. Ruge for permission to read and quote from their reminiscences concerning Wolfe's last illness;

To Harold Ober Associates for permission to reprint a letter from F. Scott Fitzgerald to Thomas Wolfe; copyright 1960 by Frances Lanahan;

To Pack Memorial Public Library, Asheville, and to Myra Champion of the Reference Department for her energetic and enthusiastic help;

To the New York Public Library and to Paul North Rice, Chief of the Reference Department; to Southworth Library, South Dartmouth, Massachusetts, and to Dorothy Martin, Mary Wilson, Phoebe Winterbottom, Lititia Pettway, and Virginia Morrison;

To Newberry Library, Chicago, and to Stanley Pargellis, Librarian, and Amy Nyholm, Manuscript Cataloguer;

To Mrs. Sherwood Anderson for allowing quotation from the diary of Sherwood Anderson and his letters to Thomas Wolfe and for supplying background material; also to R. L. Sergel;

To New York University for making available the correspondence between Wolfe and Homer A. Watt, the reminiscences of Wolfe's students, and other material from *Thomas Wolfe at Washington Square*, and the records concerning Wolfe's employment at the University; also to Thomas Clark Pollock, Oscar Cargill, A. Gerald Doyle, LeRoy Kimball, and Jean Webster;

To the Princeton Library and to Julian Boyd, Alexander Clark, and Alexander D. Wainwright;

To Mrs. George P. Baker for allowing the author to examine Professor Baker's own correspondence and for supplying background material;

To Miss Margaret R. Roberts for allowing the quotation from her mother's unpublished manuscript;

To Melville H. Cane for his encouragement and advice;

To Richard S. Kennedy for allowing the author to read his "Thomas Wolfe at Harvard" and other writings concerning Wolfe before their publication and, in general, for making available to her the results of his own research;

To Harper & Brothers for permission to quote from Wolfe's published writings and from a publicity release written by Edward C. Aswell;

To Vardis Fisher for permission to quote from his article "My Experiences with Thomas Wolfe";

To Kathleen Hoagland, the *Carolina Quarterly*, and the National Broadcasting Company, Inc., for permission to quote from "Thomas Wolfe: Biography in Sound";

And to the late Edward C. Aswell, Administrator C.T.A. of the Estate of Thomas Wolfe, for permission to quote freely from the unpublished writings of Wolfe, for his loyalty and devotion, and for his self-sacrificing expenditure of patience, strength, and time.

Grateful acknowledgment is also made to the following for information about Wolfe, for permission to quote from their own writings about him, or for help of other kinds.

Milton A. Abernethy, George Matthew Adams, Phoebe Adams, Walter S. Adams, Mrs. Charles S. Albert, Ruth and Maxwell Aley, Elizabeth Ames, Anne W. Armstrong; the *Atlantic Monthly*: Edward Weeks and Charles W. Morton; Caroline Bancroft, LeBaron R. Barker, Jr., Stringfellow Barr, Hamilton Basso, Ralph A. Beals, Gweneth P. Beam, Alice Beer, Richard C. Beer, Alladine Bell, Pincus Berner, Arthur F. Blanchard, Rose and Sanford Brown, LeGette Blythe, Charles S. Boesen, Dr. Walter Bonime, Hilda Westall Bottomley, Mrs. James Boyd, Nancy Hale Bowers, the late Donald Brace, E. N. Brandt, William Braswell, Joseph Brewer, the late Herschel Brickell, H. Tatnall Brown, Jr., John Mason Brown, Mr. and Mrs. Struthers Burt, Witter Bynner, Gwen Jassinoff Campbell, Henry Seidel Canby, Henry Fisk Carlton, William D. Carmichael, Jr., Mrs. D. D. Carroll, John Carswell, Lenoir Chambers, Harry Woodburn Chase, John W. Chase; The Chatham and Fred F. Holsten, General Manager; Richard S. Childs, Albert Coates, William J. Cocke, Allan C. Collins, Benjamin Cone, Pascal Covici, Ray Conway, Kyle Crichton; The North Carolina Historical Society and Christopher Crittenden, Secretary; E. A. Cross, B. Crystal and Son, Mina Curtiss, Jonathan Daniels, Alfred S. Dashiell, Edward Davison, Mrs. Clarence Day, Frederic L. Day, L. Effingham de Forest, George V. Denny, Jr., Byron Dexter, Robert B. Dow, Olin Dows, Dr. A. Wilbur Duryee, Dr. Eugene F. Du Bois, Max Eastman, Duncan Emrich, Morris L. Ernst, Evangelical United Brethren Church, W. Ney Evans, Mrs. Raymond C. Everitt, Mrs. Marjorie C. Fairbanks, Dr. Achilles Fang, Thomas Hornsby Ferril, Mrs. Arthur Davison Ficke, Kimball Flaccus, Dr. John G. Frothingham, A. S. Frere, Daniel Fuchs, Charles Garside; Genealogical Society of Pennsylvania and John Goodwin Herndon, Executive Director; General Alumni Association of the University of North Carolina: J. Maryon Saunders and William M. Shuford; Charles Goetz, J. Lesser Goldman, Henry Gollomb, Edward Goodnow, Mack Gorham, Mr. and Mrs. Douglas W. Gorsline, Elaine Westall Gould, Frank P. Graham, Hans J. Gottlieb, Mrs. W. W. Grant, Paul Green, Kent Roberts Greenfield, Ferris Greenslet; The John Simon Guggenheim Memorial Foundation: Henry Allen Moe, Josephine Leighton, and James F. Mathias; James J. Hankins, William E. Harris, Henry M. Hart, Jr., Rupert Hart-Davis, Harvard University Appointment Office; Harvard University Archives: Thelma Laird, Miss Florence K. Leetch, and Clifford K. Shipton; Charles M. Hazlehurst, George W. Healy, Jr., Theresa Helburn, Dorothy Kuhns Heyward, Greta Hilb, Betsy Hatch Hill, Helen Train Hilles, Clayton and Kathleen Hoagland, Mr. and Mrs. Terence Holliday; Houghton Mifflin Company: Paul Brooks and Mrs. Dorothy de Santillana; James S. Howell,

Arthur Palmer Hudson, Louis C. Hunter, Katherine Gauss Jackson, Dr. A. C. Jacobson, Edith Walton Jones, The Reverend Arthur Ketchum, Donald W. Keyes, Kenneth J. Kindley, Freda Kirchwey, Mary Mathews Kittinger, T. Skinner Kittrell, Blanche Knopf, Mrs. Frederick H. Koch, Charlotte Kohler, Eleanor Lake, Dr. Else K. La Roe, H. M. Ledig-Rowohlt, Dr. Russel V. Lee, Elizabeth H. Lemmon, Edgar Lentz, Dr. Isaiah Libin, G. Linnemann, Louis Lipinsky, Marian Smith Lowndes, Mabel Dodge Luhan, Ralph E. Lum, Percy Mackaye, Dr. J. Donald MacRae, George and Lola McCoy, Thomas McGreevy, Lura Thomas McNair, Gertrude Macy, J. Carroll Malloy, Arthur Mann, Sam Marx, Mrs. Edgar Lee Masters, Robert D. Meade, Nina Melville, Mr. and Mrs. Edward M. Miller, Fred B. Millett, Cornelius Mitchell, Nathan Mobley, Doris Moskowitz, Anne Armeill Mueller, Herbert J. Muller, James Buell Munn, Hugo Münsterberg; National Institute of Arts and Letters and Felicia Geffen, Secretary; *New Directions*, the New York *Times*, the *New Yorker* and Mrs. E. B. White, Marcus C. S. Noble, Jr., Paul Nordhoff; Northwestern University Alumni Association and G. Willard King, Executive Director; the *Observer*, Donald Olyphant, Paul Palmer, Hortense Roberts Pattison, Wendell L. Patton, Charles A. Pearce, Marjorie N. Pearson, Norman H. Pearson, Bessie Peretz, Mrs. Maxwell E. Perkins, Frances Phillips, James Poling, William T. Polk, Garland Porter, Desmond Powell, George R. Preston, Henry F. Pringle; the Raleigh *News and Observer* and Mrs. Harry W. McGalliard, Librarian; Dr. James G. Ramsay, Burton Rascoe, Mr. and Mrs. Robert Raynolds, Filomena Ricciardi, Mrs. Lillian W. Richards, Mrs. Lennox Robinson, Barnet B. Ruder, Phillips Russell, Thomas Sancton, Mrs. Dorothy Greenlaw Sapp, the *Saturday Review*, Mrs. A. P. Saunders, Mrs. Bradley Saunders, Mark Schorer, Edgar Scott, George Seldes, Mrs. Mary Shuford, Luise M. Sillcox, Mrs. Lora French Simmons, Beverly Smith, Harrison Smith, Mrs. Stella Brewster Spear, Mrs. Catherine Brett Spencer, Corydon P. Spruill, Stanford Alumni Association, Marion L. Starkey, George M. Stephens, Mrs. Martha Dodd Stern, George Stevens, Donald Ogden Stewart, James Stokely, Edward Stone, Jesse Stuart, Mr. and Mrs. James Sykes, Nathan R. Teitel, Arthur Thornhill, William Y. Tindall, Perry Tomlin, Mrs. Susan Hyde Tonetti, Jean Toomer, William Troy, S. Marion Tucker, U. B. Publishing Estab., Inc., the late Carl Van Doren, Mark Van Doren, Willard Van Dyke, Henry Volkening, Frank K. Wallace, Mrs. George Wallace, Margaret Wallace, Nathan Wallack, William W. Watt, the late Dixon Wecter, Mrs. Emily MacRae West, Bruce William Westall, Mr. and Mrs. Charles Westall, Mr. and Mrs. James Westall, Caroline Whiting, Mrs. Dorothy F. Wiley, Mrs. Jeannie Colvin White, Mrs. Lenore Powell Whitfield, Max Whitson, John Hay Whitney, James Southall Wilson, Ella Winter, Edgar E. Wolf, Olivia Saunders Wood; Yale School of Fine Arts and Maude K. Riley, Registrar; Stark Young.

INTRODUCTION

IN JULY 1935, when *Of Time and the River* was at the height of its success, Maxwell Perkins called me up and asked me to have a drink with him after work. Wolfe was at the Writers' Conference in Boulder, Colorado, and Perkins was so full of his affairs that he wanted to talk with somebody about him. As Wolfe's agent, I was a logical person for him to confide in. Mr. Perkins took a drink from his martini. "There's this man," he said, "who's written in to Scribners. He wants to do a biography of Tom, but I'm going to tell him no." He cocked his head at me like a wise cockatoo. "For one thing," he went on, "it's much too soon. And for another——" Suddenly his face lit up with mirth. "Well, you know, Miss Nowell, if there ever *was* a writer who didn't need a biographer, that writer is Thomas Wolfe." He chuckled gleefully, then sobered to reflection. "But it would be hard to get Tom right," he said.

Since then things have changed. Wolfe died only three years later, and there has been a real need of a biography of him ever since. Also, in spite of his humorous remark to me, Perkins knew better than anyone that Wolfe's novels cannot be taken as straight autobiography: they suddenly depart into the realm of pure fiction just when a reader is inclined to accept everything in them as the gospel truth. Wolfe himself has told how some residents of Asheville not only swear that certain occurrences are true but that they witnessed them themselves—when the incidents were really invented out of whole cloth by Wolfe. In 1943 Perkins arranged with John S. Terry, the editor of *Thomas Wolfe's Letters to His Mother*, for the writing of a biography. However, when Terry died in 1953, no trace of any such manuscript was to be found among his belongings. Meanwhile Perkins himself had died, in 1947, but when I was approached about writing the biography, I remembered him lost in sober meditation over his martini after saying, "It would be hard to get Tom right."

This was one of the chief criteria by which Wolfe and Perkins judged a piece of writing. They would sit down together at their favorite table, by the second window in the Chatham bar, and sooner or later some writer or new book would be mentioned in the course of conversation. If it was about an actual occurrence or real people or had a background that was based on life, they would look at each other meditatively; then one would say, "I think old So-and-so [the author] got it right," or "Of course old So-and-so *means well*, but I don't think he got it right!"

What Mr. Perkins meant about Wolfe himself was that he had a complex, almost contradictory character.

In a way, Mark Twain's remark about the weather in New England, "If you don't like it, wait a minute," could be applied to Wolfe. It wasn't that his character was contradictory, but that it was so terribly complex that certain traits offset each other, like facets of a diamond, though they all came from one unchanging central core. He had his mother's penny-pinching frugality, but his father's lavish love of spending. He could never bring himself to throw things away, but he lost things—hats, coats, manuscripts, and uncashed checks—continually. He had a gourmet's passion for good food, but he starved himself day after day, with only cigarettes and strong black coffee to sustain him. He had a tendency toward alcoholism, but he put in more long, sober, grueling hours than anyone on earth. He loved women and was somewhat over-sexed, but he resented any trickery or possessiveness from them and preferred the good companionship of men.

He was completely ignorant of how to shape a piece of writing and make it publishable, but he had a deep instinctive feeling for his work which rarely played him false. He was fascinated by the concept of time in all its aspects, but he always was an hour or more late to his appointments. He loved to ride on boats and trains, but he had the greatest difficulty in catching them. He loved baseball and read all the dope about it in the New York papers, but he seldom found the time to watch a game. He had what he called "a mountaineer's suspicion of people from outside," which sometimes made him accuse even his best friends of "betraying" him, but he was the most naïve and trusting man on earth and wanted everyone to be his friend. He had "black moods" so deep that he sometimes was afraid of going crazy, but he also had periods of the greatest hope and joy. He had a humorless self-pity, but a sense of humor that was superb. He had the greatest difficulty in making decisions, but when he made one, he did it utterly, ir-revocably, and with a bang. He had a ruthlessness in breaking free from too smothering relationships, but he had depths of loyalty which never changed. He was driven wild with exasperation at his family, but he worried endlessly about them and gave them hundreds of his own much-needed dollars during hard times. He was in many ways an adolescent boy, but he had the philosophy, the hope, the resignation of a great man. Even his physical appearance varied greatly: when he saw a nice thick sirloin steak, a bottle of good wine, or a pretty woman, he would crow and ogle like a suckling babe, and when he told his comic stories and tall tales, he would roll his eyes and grin like Wordsworth's idiot boy: but in repose of meditation, his face had the grandeur and the genius of the Höfel Beethoven, and his eyes were always dark and sad with a knowledge of the strangeness and the tragedy of life.

The strongest impulse in Wolfe's life was his compulsion to pour out the history of his experience in talk, in letters, diaries, and most of all, in creative fiction. He described it as a storm, a flood, a river, an elemental force which had to find release; "and if energy of this kind is not used, if it keeps boiling over and is given no way of getting out," he said, "then it will eventually destroy and smother the person who has it." Whenever he was distracted from his work, he would get into one of his black moods and would do nothing but brood and drink and pace the streets all night and telephone his friends and accuse them of betraying him. He had a list of favorite accusations against many of his friends which would have caused a lot of outraged feelings if they hadn't been so ludicrous. For instance, John Hall Wheelock, the editor at Scribners who had changed *Of Time and the River* from the first person, in which it was originally written, to the third person, would be awakened by the ringing of the phone at 2 or 3 A.M. to hear Wolfe's deep, sepulchral voice say, "Look at line 37 on page 487 of *Of Time and the River*. Do you see that 'I'? You should have changed that 'I' to 'he.' You betrayed me, and I thought you were my friend!" Or I myself, who had told Wolfe before publication of *Of Time and the River* that I thought some of the left-wing reviewers might criticize him but that he must pay them no attention if they did, would answer the phone in the middle of the night to hear Wolfe say, "You—said—my—book—would—fail!" The next day he would again telephone his friends and apologize abjectly. "The effort of writing or creating something seems to start up a strange and bewildering conflict in the man who does it," he wrote to Alfred Dashiell, "and this conflict at times almost takes on physical proportions so that he feels he is struggling not only with his own work but also with the whole world around him, and he is so beset with demons, nightmares, delusions and bewilderments that he lashes out at everyone and everything, not only people he dislikes and mistrusts, but sorrowfully enough, even against the people that he knows in his innermost heart are his true friends. I cannot tell you how completely and deeply conscious I have been of this thing and how much bloody anguish I have sweat and suffered when I have exorcised these monstrous phantoms and seen clearly into what kind of folly and madness they have led me. . . . But I live constantly in the hope, and I have never lost it, that a man can make his life better and cure himself of some of his grievous errors. In my good moments I do not believe any man on earth values the friendship and affection of his friends more than I, and desires more earnestly to be worthy of their belief and is more cruelly tormented when he thinks he has misused them."

"If I can only keep on writing, everything will be all right," Wolfe often said, and he meant it, not only for the sake of his literary output but also for that of his own peace of mind. Writing hell for leather as he always did left him utterly exhausted and yet so keyed up that he couldn't sleep at night, but it was the thing which he excelled at, and the thing he had to do. One early morning, Nancy Hale, who lived on East Forty-ninth Street a few doors up from the Perkinses' house, heard a deep and distant chant out on the street; as it grew louder and nearer she went to her window and looked out. There was Tom, in his battered black fedora and long dark-blue raincoat, swinging along at his tremendous stride and chanting over and over, "I wrote ten thousand words today. I wrote ten thousand words today." He was as happy then as he could ever be.

Wolfe's daily life was governed almost wholly by this need to write. He was the most completely un-mechanical of men and never knew how to operate a typewriter, although on at least two occasions he got machines and swore that he would learn. He rented a Dictaphone in 1936, in the hope that he could recite his work into it and have it typed up later, but the only thing he ever actually dictated was a few remarks on the ancestry and character of his most unfavorable critic, Bernard De Voto. He would sometimes play this back and listen to it, grinning.

At any rate, because of his inability to type, he hired a stenographer for twenty-five dollars a week, who came each day and transcribed his longhand as fast as he could get it down on paper. When she arrived in the morning, he was usually still asleep, but he would leap up, stuttering apologies and assurances that he'd "be with you in a minute." He hastily would dress, gulp down cup after cup of vile black coffee, and light the first of the endless chain of cigarettes which dangled from his lips or smoked unnoticed in a butt-filled ash tray or on the burn-scarred edge of his beloved writing table with the good solid Doric-column legs. But before he could start writing, he must first pour out to his secretary an account of the latest difficulty in which he was involved. Perhaps it was a lawsuit that had been brought against him, or some difficulty with his publishers or friends or family, or with the women who were always desperately in love with him. He always had to talk about it, endlessly, to everyone he happened to encounter, from virtual strangers to his father-substitute and arbiter, Maxwell Perkins. He had to get it off his chest and to win their sympathy and approval, and somehow, in the repeated telling of it, he would manage to digest it and store it in his memory, from where it might emerge, years later, transmuted into fiction.

Finally, after perhaps an hour of striding up and down and talking to his secretary, he'd pull a chair up to his table, roll up his sleeves, select a stub of pencil from the coffee can in which he kept them, light still another cigarette, and start to write, pursing up his lips with concentration and occasionally running his fingers through his hair. From then on, almost without interruption, the sheets of yellow paper covered with his scrawl would fall like autumn leaves upon the floor, while his secretary scurried back and forth to pick them up and copy them.

Sometimes, when he struck a difficult passage, he would seek out the seclusion of the bedroom, or of the kitchenette, where he would write quite comfortably standing up, with the top of the refrigerator for a table. Sometimes, especially in his later years, he would stride up and down the length of his apartment dictating directly to his secretary. He always wrote in iambic pentameter, and he would pace in time to his words, with one hand thrust, Napoleon-wise, between the buttons of his shirt to rub his chest, or with his hands hanging loosely at his sides while he clenched and unclenched his fingers with a sort of snapping noise. But no matter where he wrote or how he wrote, the main thing was: *he wrote*—with no time out for lunch or rest or recreation from the middle of the morning till late afternoon, when his exhausted secretary would finally insist on going home.

The rest of the day he might spend in a variety of ways. Perhaps he'd have a date with one of his best girls or would dine with one or two old friends and talk to them till dawn (he was always surprised and offended if they "threw him out" to get some sleep). Perhaps he'd go out to a restaurant alone, or, if we were going to work on stories, he might eat with me. He was ravenously hungry by dinnertime and didn't care who knew it, and after having a drink or two, "to relax," as he explained, he would attack his food. I remember once when he was served a plate of wonderful thick split-pea soup. He looked challengingly at the diners near him, then picked up the soup plate in both hands and drank its entire contents from the rim in two great gulps. He hated what he called "Nice Nellyism," in table manners as well as in literature.

However, the thing that Wolfe did oftenest and liked to do the most was to meet Perkins at Scribners around closing time and then go somewhere with him for a drink. They went usually to the Chatham, to the bar, or, in summer, to the outdoor café called Chatham Walk, which Wolfe especially liked because he could sometimes hear and feel the rumble of a train on the Grand Central tracks beneath him. There they would sit for hours, and all the time Wolfe would pour out to Perkins the story of his latest difficulties and of every detail of his life in the day or two since he'd seen him last. A great deal has been written, both by Wolfe and other people, of his "search for a father," for an "image of a strength and wisdom external to his need and superior to his hunger, to which the belief and power of his life could be united." However, during eight of the nine years between Look Homeward, Angel and Wolfe's death, he never made a decision of any importance without first consulting Perkins. He was simply too unsure of himself, too hemmed in by doubt and contradictions, and too immature. "Max thinks" or "Max says" was a frequent prefix to Wolfe's statements, even to things which "Max" had not exactly said but only tacitly agreed with, just as "my father says" or "my mother says" is a constant phrase used by a child.

Nowadays, from a vantage point of twenty years, people are inclined to think of Wolfe as someone fixed, immutable, historic. Actually he was always changing, always growing, like an adolescent boy, and one could no more hold him back than one could grow a mighty oak tree under glass. In the last year of his life he found himself: he reached maturity, outgrew his need for a father-substitute, and lost his intense preoccupation with himself in a love for all of mankind. "I had derived . . . a new sense of life, a newer and, it seems to me, a better hope," he wrote in the speech he delivered at Purdue in 1938. "For . . . I had begun to see and understand and feel the common heart of man, and finally, I had come to see that this, no matter how much it gets corrupted, is the thing that finally can never be corrupted; no matter how much it gets defeated, is the thing that never can be defeated—the thing that is rock bottom at the end. . . ." "I have not felt such hope and confidence in many years," he wrote to me on May 12, 1938. "It may be that I have come through a kind of transition period in my life—I believe this is the truth—and have now, after a lot of blood-sweat and anguish, found a kind of belief and hope and faith I never had before."

Because of all these things, when I was first approached about writing the biography, I was reluctant to undertake the responsibility. In the meanwhile, however, I was collecting and editing *The Letters of Thomas Wolfe*, which was published in 1956, and as the flood of Wolfe's correspondence came pouring in, I began to combine and paraphrase Perkins' two remarks to me and to tell myself that if there ever was a writer who didn't need to be "got right," who had done it himself in hundreds of thousands of his own words, that writer was Thomas Wolfe.

Thus, in writing this biography I have drawn heavily upon Wolfe's interpretation of himself—in his novels, in his strictly autobiographical writings such as *The Story of a Novel*, the Purdue speech, his letters, and his pocket notebooks. It would be ridiculous not to. And I hope that he and Perkins, sitting at a favorite table next the second window in some Theresien Chatham bar, will take a drink and nod their heads and say I've "got Tom right." But if they don't, I think they'll say I "meant well" anyway.

THOMAS WOLFE
A Biography

I

THOMAS CLAYTON WOLFE was born on October 3, 1900, at 92 Woodfin Street, Asheville, North Carolina. The son of William Oliver and Julia Elizabeth (Westall) Wolfe, he was of mixed Pennsylvania-German, English, and Scotch-Irish stock. Through his mother he was descended from several of the oldest and best-known Scotch-Irish families, notably the Penlands and the Pattons, who had settled in western North Carolina before the Revolution. One of his ancestors, Peter Penland, was a captain in the Colonial Army under George Washington during the French and Indian War. Two others, Robert and Aaron Patton, served under General Charles McDowell in the Revolution and took part in the campaigns culminating in the battle of Kings Mountain in October 1780. His great-great-grandfather and great-great-grandmother, George and Nancy Patton, the children respectively of Robert and Aaron Patton and hence cousins as well as husband and wife, were prominent landowners on the Swannanoa River, nine miles from what was later to become Asheville. His great-great-grandaunt Elizabeth Patton, the sister of George Patton, was the second wife of David Crockett.

The Westalls were of English stock, one of them reputedly having been a dean of the Church of England and another a member of the Royal Academy. They came to America before the Revolution and settled in Winchester, Virginia, but remained loyal to the King. After the Revolution, Wolfe's great-great-grandfather Thomas Westall came from Winchester to western North Carolina, where for twenty-five or thirty years he owned and farmed six hundred acres of land four and a half miles east of what later became Asheville. Around 1820 he sold his land and moved to Winchester, Tennessee, which he named after his birthplace in Virginia; then, in 1821, he accompanied Steven and J. B. Austin to Texas, where in 1828 or 1829 his daughter Eliza married J. B. Austin. His first wife and former children remained in North Carolina, however, settling in Burnsville, Yancey County. His grandson Thomas Casey Westall married Martha Anne Penland, the daughter of Leander and Marilda (Patton) Penland, served in the

Civil War as a captain and then major under General Robert B. Vance, and lived at Swannanoa, where Tom's mother, Julia Elizabeth Westall, was born in 1860.[1]

Concerning Wolfe's paternal ancestors comparatively little is known, probably because they were unpretentious Pennsylvania farmers with little or no interest in genealogy. They were perhaps descended from Hans Georg Wolff and Hans Bernhard Wolff, Palatinate Germans who came to Philadelphia in 1727 on the ship *William and Sarah*. However, nothing definite is known about the family until 1806 or 1807, when Wolfe's paternal grandfather, Jacob Wolf, was born at Gardners Church, York Springs, Pennsylvania, about seventeen miles from Gettysburg. He married Eleanor Jane Heikes, who was of Dutch descent, and had six children, of whom Wolfe's father, William Oliver Wolf, was the fifth. In recent years the genealogy of Eleanor Jane (Heikes) Wolf has been traced back to William Wierman and Gertrude (Seitman or Sateman) Wierman, who came to Pennsylvania from either Germany or Holland in 1720.[2] However, this was not done until after Wolfe's death, and he knew little about his grandmother except that she was reportedly of "Holland Dutch" descent and died at the age of ninety-nine, a highly honored old lady, who had lived all her life in the vicinity of York Springs. During his adult life Tom made earnest if sporadic attempts to trace the genealogy of his grandfather Jacob Wolf but never met with any success.

William Oliver Wolf was only twelve years old at the time of the battle of Gettysburg, although his older brother George and his sister's husband, Jacob Lentz, were soldiers in the Union Army. George Wolf was killed at Chancellorsville and Lentz at Gettysburg, and in 1865, William Oliver, who was then fourteen, went to work with his brother Wesley in the Union mule camps at Harrisburg. Soon after the close of the war the two boys went to Baltimore, and William Oliver became a stonecutter's apprentice. He worked there and in York until 1871, when he went to Raleigh, North Carolina, where he worked as a mason and stonecutter on the construction of the new state penitentiary and

[1] For the information concerning Wolfe's maternal ancestry the author is indebted to the genealogical notes compiled by the late Henry A. Westall and now in the possession of his daughter, Hilda Westall Bottomley; the author is also grateful for the genealogies supplied her by Wendell L. Patton and his family.

[2] This family line was traced by the genealogist William Perry Johnson of Raleigh, North Carolina, who is himself a descendant of William and Gertrude Wierman.

later set up his own marble shop. At some time during this period he adopted the more usual spelling of Wolfe for his name. While in Raleigh he was married twice, first to Hattie Watson, who divorced him; then to Cynthia Hill. When his second wife's health began to fail, they moved to Asheville, where she died a year later. By this time the Westalls had moved into Asheville from Swannanoa, and in 1885 he married Julia Elizabeth and brought her to the house he had built not long before at 92 Woodfin Street, where, fifteen years later, Thomas Wolfe was born.

Wolfe was named Thomas after his grandfather Thomas Casey Westall, and his great-great-grandfather as well, but his middle name, Clayton, was in honor of William Clayton Bowman, an Asheville clergyman and friend of Thomas Casey Westall's, who was greatly admired by Mrs. Wolfe when she was a young girl. Tom was the youngest of eight children, the others being, in order of their birth, Leslie, who died of cholera infantum at the age of nine months, Effie, Frank, Mabel, Grover Cleveland and Benjamin Harrison, the twins, and Fred. Tom was almost six years younger than Fred and thirteen years younger than Effie and accordingly was treated as a baby by the entire family. He was also the object of the exaggerated possessiveness which a mother often feels for her last child. In her interview with John S. Terry quoted in the introduction to *Thomas Wolfe's Letters to His Mother*, Mrs. Wolfe says:

"He being the baby I kept him a baby. I think he has written it up himself that he slept with me until he was a great big boy. He wasn't weaned until he was three and a half years old. . . . I think we just weaned Tom off by the other children laughing at him and talking to him about being just a baby. He still nursed. But it was a habit with him, that was all: he didn't really need it. . . . Tom . . . had beautiful curls, beautiful brown hair . . . I kept it curled every day. It struck him around his shoulders. He often said they called him a girl because he had curls and wanted his hair cut off. I told him, 'Oh no, I want to keep it long, you know.' . . . So I kept putting him off until it had to be cut off. . . . But the sad part to me—my baby was gone—he was getting away from me."[3]

This abnormally prolonged infantile relationship affected Wolfe's entire character and life. He was always trying to escape from it, and yet was always reverting to it, either with his mother herself, as in his early years, or to substitutes for her, as in his later ones. His letters to her, which she saved and had published with such touching pride, make

[3] From *Thomas Wolfe's Letters to His Mother*, Scribners, 1943.

uncomfortable reading, especially those written up to the time when he was twenty-five. Until then, her domination of him was almost complete, since it was financial as well as psychological. Over and over he asked her for more money with which to further his development and his career, or tried, unhappily, to justify the fact that she had already given him more than she thought justified. And over and over again he complained that she "didn't understand" him and the kind of life that he felt himself destined to lead. It was this lack of understanding that made him turn as a young boy to his schoolteacher, Margaret Roberts, and make her what he called "the mother of his spirit." And later, when at the age of twenty-five he met and fell in love with a forty-four-year-old married woman, Aline Bernstein, he was again repeating the old filial pattern with another mother-substitute. It was not till he found a father-substitute in Maxwell Perkins that Wolfe achieved a permanent measure of freedom from and tolerance for his mother. And it was not until the last two years of his life that he emerged as an adult who could stand and face the world alone.

Tom's relationship with his father was a happier one. Mr. Wolfe was a periodic drinker who indulged in epic sprees which both terrified and outraged his teetotaler wife and caused a lot of headshaking in the still-small town of Asheville. But children adjust to such things very easily, and Tom and all the others worshiped him, both because of his genuine paternal warmth toward them and by their fascination for his character—of what Wolfe called "the enormous beating color of his life." As Mabel Wolfe Wheaton puts it, "It was Papa who made the grass green for us." Or, as Wolfe says in Look Homeward, Angel,[4] "The family was at the very core and ripeness of its life together. Gant lavished upon it his abuse, his affection, and his prodigal provisioning. They came to look forward eagerly to his entrance, for he brought with him the great gusto of living, of ritual. They would watch him in the evening as he turned the corner below with eager strides, follow carefully the processional of his movements from the time he flung his provisions upon the kitchen table to the re-kindling of his fire . . . on to which he poured wood, coal and kerosene lavishly. . . . The children grew to await his return in the evening with a kind of exhilaration." Years later, Wolfe told how, when he was five years old, he looked out of the window and saw "the most perfect frost-golden moon

---

[4] The story of Eugene Gant's relationship with his family in Look Homeward, Angel is so obviously autobiographical that it has been used as a main source for information concerning Wolfe's early life, but with the qualification that parts of it may be fictional, as are other large portions of Look Homeward, Angel.

that ever rode the sky." "See that?" he asked excitedly. "Papa brought that!"[5]

It was also through his father that Wolfe got his first taste of literature. In *The Story of a Novel* he says: "I don't know how I became a writer, but I think it was because of a certain force in me that had to write and that finally burst through and found a channel. My people were of the working class of people. My father, a stonecutter, was a man with a great respect and veneration for literature. He had a tremendous memory, and he loved poetry, and the poetry that he loved best was naturally of the rhetorical kind that such a man would like. Nevertheless it was good poetry, Hamlet's Soliloquy, *Macbeth*, Mark Antony's Funeral Oration, Gray's 'Elegy,' and all the rest of it. I heard it all as a child; I memorized and learned it all." Wolfe got from his father the richness, the rhetoric, and the sonority of his prose: also his "great gusto of living," his high-strung nerves, and his fits of brooding suspicion when he imagined that the world was in conspiracy against him. From his mother he got his garrulity, which in his books became excessive length, his mysticism, his enormously retentive memory, and his dogged will power for long-sustained, exhausting work.

To readers of *Look Homeward, Angel,* the story of Wolfe's childhood and of the conflicts and relationships in his "nervous brawling family group" is a familiar one. The chief conflict was that between his father and his mother—"the one with an inbred and also an instinctive terror and hatred of property; the other with a growling mounting lust for ownership that finally is tinged with mania." As Wolfe explains in the *Angel*, "The four oldest [Westall] children . . . had passed their childhood in the years following the [Civil] war. The poverty and privation of these years had been so terrible that none of them ever spoke of it now, but the bitter steel had sheared into their hearts, leaving scars that would not heal. The effect of these years upon the oldest children was to develop in them an insane niggardliness, an insatiate love of property . . ." Several of Mrs. Wolfe's brothers had become wealthy men in Asheville, and she was never one to be outdone. She was a little woman, almost childlike in stature, but gifted with limitless energy, great native canniness, and an indomitable will. Her life with Mr. Wolfe would have brought a weaker person to the limit of endurance, but as Wolfe says in the *Angel*, she "came through stolidly . . . to

[5] This anecdote is repeated by L. Ruth Middlebrook in her article "Further Memories of Thomas Wolfe," in the April 1947 issue of the *American Mercury*.

victorious strength." "Year by year, above his howl of protest . . . they gathered in small bits of earth, paid the hated taxes, and put the money that remained into more land. Over the wife, over the mother, the woman of property, who was like a man, walked slowly forth."

Mrs. Wolfe's first step toward independence was made in 1904, when she took all the children to St. Louis, with the exception of her oldest daughter, Effie, whom she left at home to keep house for Mr. Wolfe. In St. Louis she rented a house at the corner of Fairmount Avenue and Academy Street, named it The North Carolina, and ran it as a boarding-house for visitors to the World's Fair. The venture ended tragically in the death of Grover from typhoid, contracted at the fairgrounds, where he worked. The family returned to Asheville with Grover's body and settled down again at Woodfin Street. In *Look Homeward, Angel* Wolfe says that the death of Grover gave his mother "the most terrible wound of her life." This probably was true: thirty-four years later, when she was told that Tom himself was going to die, she reverted to the death of Grover and described it almost word for word as Wolfe had quoted her in his story "The Lost Boy." But Grover's death had other consequences. As Mabel Wolfe Wheaton says, "Ben was the twin alone —Tom was coming along then—Ben was alone, Tom was alone."[6] And in this way began the close relationship between Ben and Tom.

In 1906 Mrs. Wolfe made a decisive move which virtually broke up the family and deeply affected Tom. In August of that year she bought the large rambling Victorian house at 48 Spruce Street, Asheville, which is now preserved as a memorial to Wolfe, and began to operate it as her boardinghouse, the Old Kentucky Home. Mr. Wolfe remained at Woodfin Street, with his devoted daughter Mabel keeping house for him. The other children were, as Wolfe says in the *Angel*, left vaguely "floating in limbo," living at one house or the other as they preferred. But Tom, as the youngest, had no choice—he was taken to Spruce Street by his mother. "He was the last tie that bound her to all the weary life of breast and cradle; he still slept with her of nights . . . He was riven into her flesh. Forgetful of him during the day's press, she summoned him at night over the telephone, demanding his return . . . There was a bitter submerged struggle over him between Eliza and her daughter." For, as Mabel Wolfe Wheaton says, "he always wanted to live back home—we always left the doors unlocked,"[7] and

[6] From Mrs. Wheaton's recorded interview with Duncan Emrich of the Library of Congress: "Mrs. Wheaton, Sister of Thomas Wolfe, Chronologically Telling His Life History, ⚹1300, February 23, 1947."

[7] Ibid.

he spent much of his time there. He hated "the great chill tomb" of the Old Kentucky Home: he also was ashamed of it and of his mother's career as a frugal boardinghouse keeper. And so, as he later wrote to his teacher, Margaret Roberts, "I was without a home—a vagabond since I was seven—with two roofs and no home. I moved inward on that house of death and tumult from room to little room, as the boarders came with their dollar a day, and their constant rocking on the porch. My overloaded heart . . . was strangling, without speech, without articulation, in my own secretions."

It would be difficult to say just when and from what causes Tom first began to think of himself as weighted down with "loneliness and terror" and began to seek an escape in self-dramatization and fantasy, but it was evidently around the time when the family's life at Woodfin Street was broken up and he "lost forever the tumultuous, unhappy, warm center of his home." And it was probably because he felt that he had lost this center that he began "the search for a father" which motivated his entire life. Over and over again, in both his books and letters, he describes this endless quest and the bitter disillusionment it inevitably led to. In *Look Homeward, Angel* he says: "In the cruel volcano of the boy's mind, the little brier moths of his idolatry wavered in to their strange marriage and were consumed. One by one the merciless years reaped down his gods and captains. What had lived up to hope? What had withstood the scourge of growth and memory? Why had the gold become so dim? All his life, it seemed, his blazing loyalties began with men and ended with images; the life he leaned on melted below his weight, and looking down, he saw he clasped a statue . . ."

This search became the main theme of *Of Time and the River* six years later. "From the beginning . . . ," he says in *The Story of a Novel*, "the idea, the central legend that I wished my book to express had not changed. And this central idea was this: The deepest search in life, it seemed to me, the thing that in one way or another was central to all living, was man's search to find a father, not merely the father of his flesh, not merely the lost father of his youth, but the image of a strength and wisdom external to his need and superior to his hunger, to which the belief and power of his own life could be united."

And so he went through life, seizing upon first one person and then another as "the image of strength and wisdom . . . to which the belief and power of his own life could be united." First there was his childhood teacher, Margaret Roberts; then the first arbiter of his literary career, Professor George P. Baker of the Harvard 47 Workshop. Then there was Aline Bernstein, who made it possible, materially and spiritually, for him to write *Look Homeward, Angel* and who for six years guided and transformed his life. Then, finally, there was Maxwell Perkins, his editor at Scribners, who shaped his literary career and whom he idolized for seven years. And as each of these idols was in turn "levelled down" by change and time and too idealistic, too exacting scrutiny, Wolfe's disillusionment and his "desire to escape" became so agonizing that it "turned his feeling almost into hatred." As he said in an unpublished passage from *Of Time and the River*, "I see every wart and sore upon them, every meanness, pettiness, and triviality . . . and I hate these mutilations in them ten times more cruelly and bitterly than if I saw them in people that I did not know, or cared nothing for."

By 1937 he knew that the quest was hopeless. "We never perhaps give up the wonderful image of our youth—that we will find someone external to our life and superior to our need who knows the answer," he wrote to Sherwood Anderson. "It does not happen—'is not my strength in me?'—but it comes, I think, from the deepest need in life, and all religiousness is in it." Students of Wolfe have pointed out that this final statement throws a new and different light upon Wolfe's search for a father, as not merely an attempt to find a parental substitute but to find the God-the-Father of a religion which he, intellectually, could not accept but for which he still felt a need. As a result, he tried to make each of his father-substitutes into a God, and when he found that they were only fallible and human after all, he felt a bitter disillusionment and a sense of having been betrayed.

Between the ages of five and eleven Tom went to the Orange Street Public School, as did his older brothers and sisters. After school he would go to his old home on Woodfin Street, or to his father's marble shop on Pack Square, or to the public library, where he reportedly read every book, good or bad, that it contained. However, this escape into reading and fantasy was soon broken into by his family. Under the direction of his brother Fred, who held the local agency for the sale of the *Saturday Evening Post*, Tom was sent out on the streets to sell copies of that magazine. In a letter to his sister Effie, who had married Fred W. Gambrell and moved to Anderson, South Carolina, he boasts gleefully of selling more copies than any other Asheville boy, but according to *Look Homeward, Angel*, he "loathed the work with a deadly, an inexplicable loathing. . . . He writhed with shame and humiliation, but he stuck desperately to his task, a queer curly-headed passionate little creature, who raced along by the side of an astonished captive, pouring out of his dark eager face a hurricane of language. And men, fascinated somehow by this strange eloquence from a little boy, bought."

Meanwhile his mother, who had had severe attacks of rheumatism, began going away for her health every winter, when the boardinghouse season was at its ebb. She always took Tom with her, either hiring a tutor for him, teaching him herself, or enrolling him in public school wherever they might be. Between 1907 and 1913 he went to New Orleans; to St. Petersburg, Jacksonville, St. Augustine, Daytona, and Palm Beach, Florida; to Knoxville, Tennessee; to Hot Springs, Arkansas; and finally to Washington, D.C., to witness the inauguration of Woodrow Wilson. In this way began the habit of wandering which became so marked in Wolfe's adult life. As he says in *Look Homeward, Angel,* "Thus did he see first, he the hill-bound, the sky-girt, of whom the mountains were his masters, the fabulous South. The picture of flashing field, of wood, and hill, stayed in his heart forever . . . he dreamed of the quiet roads, the moonlit woodlands, and he thought that some day he would come to them on foot, and find them there unchanged, in all the wonder of recognition."

In the fall of 1912 Tom became a pupil of Margaret Roberts, the first of the parental substitutes who were to influence him and be idolized by him at different periods throughout his life. Her husband, J. M. Roberts, had been principal of the Orange Street Public School and had resigned to organize the private North State School, which he and Mrs. Roberts conducted in an old house on Buxton Hill, on the outskirts of Asheville. According to Mr. Roberts' recollection, he had taken home a batch of compositions from the Orange Street School and had asked his wife to help him read them. She had never seen or heard of Tom, but when she read his paper she asked who he was, and then said, "Well, he is a genius."[8]

When the North State School was founded the following year, Tom enrolled for the first term and continued there, for four years, until he went to the University of North Carolina. Mrs. Roberts taught him history and English literature and composition and was the first to shape his literary taste and to encourage him to write. Up to that time he had read everything he could get his hands on, with no power of selection,

[8] This anecdote, like many others concerning Wolfe, has become a legend in Asheville. Some versions of it represent Mrs. Roberts as only saying, "We want this boy," but that she did recognize his talent earlier than anyone else is incontrovertible.

but, as he said later, "it was through her that I first developed a taste for good literature which opened up a shining Eldorado for me." He described her as "one of the three great teachers who have ever taught me," but she was much more than a mere teacher: as he said, her influence was "inestimable on almost every particular of my life and thought." "I was . . . groping like a blind sea-thing with no eyes and a thousand feelers toward light, toward life, toward beauty and order," he wrote to her in 1927. "And then I found you, . . . you mother of my spirit who fed me with light. Do you think that I have forgotten? Do you think I ever will?"

During his four years at the North State School, Tom changed from a child into an adolescent boy. His description of Eugene at this point in *Look Homeward, Angel* is a very good one of himself:

"The prison walls of self had closed entirely round him; he was walled completely by the esymplastic power of his imagination—he had learned by now to project mechanically, before the world, an acceptable counterfeit of himself which would protect him from intrusion. . . . His hair had been cut when he was nine years old, after a bitter siege against Eliza's obstinacy. He no longer suffered because of the curls. But he had grown like a weed, he already topped his mother by an inch or two; his body was big-boned but very thin and fragile, with no meat on it; his legs were absurdly long, thin, and straight, giving him a curious scissored look as he walked with long bounding strides. Stuck on a thin undeveloped neck beneath a big wide-browed head covered thickly by curling hair which had changed, since his infancy, from a light maple to dark brown-black, was a face so small, and so delicately sculptured, that it seemed not to belong to its body. The strangeness, the remote quality of this face was enhanced by its brooding fabulous concentration, by its passionate dark intensity, across which every splinter of thought or sensation flashed like a streak of light across a pool. The mouth was full, sensual, extraordinarily mobile, the lower lip deeply scooped and pouting. His rapt dreaming intensity set the face usually in an expression of almost sullen contemplation; he smiled, oftener than he laughed, inwardly, at some extravagant invention, or some recollection of the absurd, now fully appreciated for the first time." He also had a tendency to stammer whenever nervous or excited, but stammer or not, his words flowed with a garrulous intensity which was like "an elemental flood."

Mrs. Roberts worried about his health and saw to it that he took part in outdoor athletics with the other boys instead of reading inside the school all afternoon, but "he became nervous, highly excited, and erratic in team-play" and "shrank from the physical conflict of boy life." She also urged him to get nine hours of sleep every night, but by the time he was fourteen he had taken a paper route in accordance with his mother's admonitions that he was "big enough to do a little work." For the remainder of his boyhood in Asheville he got up before dawn every morning and went out to deliver his copies of the Asheville *Citizen* in Niggertown, finishing just in time for breakfast before school. But in spite of this drain upon his adolescent strength, he was an exceptionally brilliant pupil, and he completed the college preparatory course in June 1916, when he still was only fifteen years old.

It was during his last term at the North State School that Tom wrote his essay "Shakespeare the Man" for the contest sponsored by the *Independent Magazine* in celebration of the Shakespeare Tercentenary. In *Look Homeward, Angel* he tells how, full of inspiration, Eugene tacked up a copy of the Chandos portrait of the Bard upon his wall, with "the great echoing paean of Ben Jonson's . . . 'My Shakespeare, rise!'" scrawled below it in large, trembling letters, and how for weeks afterward he was teased unmercifully about it by Ben and Helen.

"Thereafter, he was called poetically to table, to the telephone, to go an errand.

"'My Shakespeare, rise!'

"With red resentful face, he rose.

"'Will My Shakespeare pass the biscuits?' or 'Could I trouble My Shakespeare for the butter?' . . . 'My Shakespeare! My Shakespeare! Do you want another piece of pie!'"

It is therefore with a sense of mirth and familiarity that one finds Tom's actual essay ending with Jonson's stirring exhortation. However, it was a good ending, and the essay itself was far above the average—boyish and rhetorical, but showing real admiration for Shakespeare and studded heavily with quotations from his plays which showed that Tom had read them all and virtually knew them by heart. As the judges proudly wrote upon the essay, "Among these ten essays on Shakespeare, each of which we have now read several times, there are some which possess certain special merits in a degree greater than is exhibited by this essay. Others are neater in form and show a cast of mind more accurate in detail. Several give the facts of Shakespeare's life, or characterize and illustrate certain features of his works, as this essay does not attempt to do. But because of its *symmetry*, because of the internal evidence it betrays of wide, sympathetic and appreciative reading, and *especially* because of its *appreciation* of the genius and spirit of 'Shakespeare the Man,' we give the first place to this essay."

Tom won the bronze medal offered by the *Independent* for the best essay written in the North State School, and he later read the piece aloud in the school declamation contest, thus winning another prize, in spite of his tendency to stammer. As Mrs. Wolfe wrote afterward, "I was proud and happy, and so was Tom." To them it seemed a fitting climax to the four years during which Mrs. Roberts had carefully nurtured Tom's talent as a writer. As the twig was bent, the tree would grow, and from then on writing was to be the foremost interest in Wolfe's life.

II

DURING the summer of 1916 there was a great deal of discussion in the Wolfe family about Tom's future. All his life he had heard "the thunder of the great flanged wheels, the long retreating whistle wail" of trains going out from Asheville, and had "dreamed and hungered for the proud unknown North with that wild ecstasy, that intolerable and wordless joy of longing and desire, which only a Southerner can feel." As Maxwell Perkins later said, "No one could understand Thomas Wolfe who had not seen or properly imagined the place in which he was born and grew up. Asheville . . . is encircled by mountains. The trains wind in and out through labyrinths of passes. A boy of Wolfe's imagination imprisoned there could think that what was beyond was all wonderful—different from what it was there where there was not for him enough of anything."[1] And now that Tom was old enough to go away to college, he had set his heart on attending one in the outside world—Princeton or the University of Virginia—almost any college as long as it was far away from home. But his father, who wanted him to be a lawyer and eventually go into politics, would not consent to this. "No," he said. "You belong to North Carolina and you must go to Chapel Hill." Mrs. Wolfe was too absorbed with running the Old Kentucky Home to take much part in the discussions, but she, too, urged Tom to go to the University of North Carolina, at least for the first year. The older children were somewhat jealous and resentful, and had been ever since Tom had been going to the private North State School. Only Ben, his guardian angel, urged him to "take everything you can get. The rest of us never had anything, but I want to see you get all that's coming to you."

Mrs. Roberts argued for the University of Virginia, but Mr. Wolfe had the final word. He was to pay for Tom's tuition, and he was already suffering from the cancer which eventually caused his death. Gant's ultimatum in *Look Homeward, Angel* is very similar to Mr. Wolfe's as described by Mabel Wolfe Wheaton and by Henry A. Westall, who discussed the matter with his brother-in-law: "In his youngest son he

[1] From Perkins' article "Thomas Wolfe," in the Autumn 1947 issue of the *Harvard Library Bulletin*.

saw the last hope of his name's survival in laurels—in the political laurels he so valued. . . . 'He's ready to go,' said Gant, 'and he's going to the State University, and nowhere else. He'll be given as good an education there as he can get anywhere. Furthermore, he will make friends there who will stand by him the rest of his life.' He turned upon his son a glance of bitter reproach. 'There are very few boys who have had your chance,' said he, 'and you ought to be grateful instead of turning up your nose at it. . . . Now, I've given you my last word: you'll go where I send you or you'll go nowhere at all.'"

In a letter written to his college classmate, Benjamin Cone, in 1929, Wolfe said: "I don't suppose you remember me very well my first year at Chapel Hill, but I made history. It was I who made the speech of acceptance when elected to the Literary Society. I took the catalogue exam, went to Chapel Saturday and let a Sophomore lead me in prayer at noon. I made half the places on the Booloo Club that year . . ."[2] This same experience is attributed to Eugene Gant in *Look Homeward, Angel*: "Eugene's first year at the university was filled for him with loneliness, pain, and failure. Within three weeks of his matriculation, he had been made the dupe of a half-dozen classic jokes . . . He was the greenest of all green freshmen, past and present: he had listened attentively to a sermon in chapel by a sophomore with false whiskers; he had prepared studiously for an examination on the contents of the college catalogue; and he had been guilty of the inexcusable blunder of making a speech of acceptance on his election, with fifty others, to the literary society. And these buffooneries—a little cruel, but only with the cruelty of vacant laughter, and a part of the schedule of rough humor in an American college— . . . opened deep wounds in him, which his companions hardly suspected. . . . There was no one to whom he could turn: he had no friends. . . . No one had given him even the rudimentary data of the somewhat rudimentary life of an American university. . . . Thus, he had come greenly on his new life, unprepared, as he came ever thereafter on all new life, save for his opium visions of himself a stranger in Arcadias."

In spite of his unhappiness and his tendency to stammer, he was always a great talker, took active part in the debates of the Dialectic Literary Society, and was elected vice-president of the Freshman Debating Club. But on the whole his first year was a miserable one. "It

[2] The *Carolina Magazine* satirically describes the Booloo Club as "a group of freshmen whose wit and sharply defined personalities had singled them out for special honor by the sophomores." Wolfe was "president" of it during his first year.

seemed to him that . . . he had stamped the beginning of his university life with folly that would never be forgotten, and that the best thing he could do would be to seek out obscurity for the next four years. . . . He finished the year living alone in a big bare carpetless room— an existence rare at Pulpit Hill, where the students, with very few exceptions, lived two or three to a room. In that room began a physical isolation, hard enough to bear at first, which later became indispensable to him, mind and body." And so, at the end of his freshman year, Wolfe went home to Asheville more firmly resolved than ever to persuade his father to let him go to Princeton.

But his summer was a miserable one too. The United States had declared war on Germany in April, and the tension of the war affected everyone and everything. Fred had joined the Navy, but Ben had been rejected by the draft because of his weak lungs. Mabel had married Ralph H. Wheaton but had returned with him to Woodfin Street and was wearing herself out in caring for her slowly dying father. Mrs. Wolfe, as usual, was absorbed in running the Old Kentucky Home. Tom was left to his own devices and fell hopelessly in love with one of the boarders at the Old Kentucky Home, a twenty-one-year-old girl named Clara Paul. In *Look Homeward, Angel* he describes a love affair between Eugene and a girl named Laura James and indicates that the love was reciprocal until the girl suddenly went away and married someone else; but if this refers to Clara Paul it is evidently one of the most fictional portions of the book. In actuality Clara Paul seems to have made no secret of the fact that she was planning to be married as soon as she went home. However, her younger brother, to whom she was devoted, was convalescing from an illness, and on doctor's orders she had brought him to Asheville for his health. Mabel Wolfe Wheaton remembers her as a nice, happy-go-lucky girl with freckles, a slightly turned-up nose, and a boyish haircut "like Amelia Earhart's" who became friendly with the entire family. "I can't remember anything except the best about Clara Paul," she says. "She was grateful for all kindness done for her and she fitted into the boarding house business which I had learned to hate. To her it seemed fun to help Mama—to cooperate." The Wheatons took her and her brother on a trip to the summit of Mount Mitchell, leaving Tom home all day to tend Ralph Wheaton's office. "At the time I didn't dream of Tom's love for the girl," says Mrs. Wheaton. "But he was pleased to see us doing something for them and it strengthened his cause to know I liked the girl."[3]

[3] From a letter written by Mabel Wolfe Wheaton to Elizabeth Nowell.

Mrs. Wolfe's recollection of the affair is even more forthright and unromantic: "This girl Clara Paul was the Laura James in the book," she is quoted as saying in *The Marble Man's Wife*. "She came up here and made no secret she had her trousseau. Her little brother had had a sick spell, and she brought him up here, and I told Tom to go with them everywhere. I considered Tom a child. I don't suppose he was over fourteen or fifteen years old. I never thought about it. They went to Riverside Park—took trips to the mountains. The little boy went with them. I was perfectly honest in trying to treat a stranger well. She had said, 'If Tom will go, I'll pay his fare everywhere.' One day out on the porch, I went around the porch and Mabel was out there, and Clara and this little boy and Tom. Tom was sitting on the railing. Mabel said, 'Mama, did you know your baby has fallen in love?' I saw how red Tom's face had gone, and I said, 'Don't tease him, he isn't thinking anything about the girls.' Tom had often told Mabel, 'Mama never expects me to grow up. I'm just the baby.' Well, I never thought about Mabel talking about him falling in love with Clara. Clara was to be married in two weeks after she left here. . . . It was just a fascination. He knew she was going to be married at that time. She was ready. She brought the boy up here, this little boy . . . Tom built it all up in imagination. He tells about Mabel fixing up a lunch for them. I remember, the little boy must have been nine or ten years old. Tom left him out of the book . . ."[4]

But even if Tom's love for Clara was only unreciprocated calf love, it was very real for him; and it was made all the more tragic by the fact that after she had married and gone to live in Norfolk, she died of influenza during the epidemic of 1918. "Did you know I fell in love when I was sixteen with a girl who was twenty-one?" he wrote in 1924 to Mrs. Roberts. "Yes, honestly—desperately in love. And I've never quite got over it. The girl married, you know: she died of influenza a year or two later. I've forgotten what she looked like, except that her hair was corn-colored. A woman five years older can make putty of a boy . . . In one way, she is as old as she will ever be, and a great deal depends upon her own quality."

As a climax to the entire tragic summer, Mr. Wolfe's illness became much more pronounced, and it was decided that he must be taken by Ben and Mabel to Johns Hopkins Hospital for radium treatments. Tom had secretly been corresponding with the registrar at Princeton about the possibility of transferring there and had persuaded his

[4] From *The Marble Man's Wife*, by Hayden Norwood, Scribners, 1947.

English professor at Chapel Hill, James Holly Hanford, to recommend him for the transfer. Before Mr. Wolfe left for Baltimore, Tom broached the subject to him and was told for once and for all that he must go back to the University of North Carolina or give up college altogether. And so, defeated on all sides, he went back to Chapel Hill in late September 1917.

And then—surprisingly—began three of the happiest and most successful years of Tom's entire life. In *Look Homeward, Angel* he implies that the chief reason for Eugene's happiness was that life at Pulpit Hill was so much pleasanter than that at home: "His escape from the bleak horror of disease and hysteria and death impending, that hung above his crouched family, left him with a sense of aerial buoyancy, drunken freedom." That was undoubtedly true of Tom himself, but the more obvious reason was that he was now a sophomore and was beginning to be recognized as a successful man on the campus. "He was happier than he had ever been in his life . . . He greeted everyone with enthusiastic gusto. . . . He began to join. He joined everything. He had never 'belonged' to any group before, but now all groups were beckoning him. He had without much trouble won a place for himself on the staff of the college paper and the magazine. The small beginning trickle of distinctions widened into a gushet. . . . He was initiated into literary fraternities, dramatic fraternities, and in the Spring into a social fraternity. He . . . went about . . . more pleased than a child or a savage, with colored ribbons in his coat lapel, and a waistcoat plastered with pins, badges, symbols, and Greek letterings."

It may surprise readers of Wolfe's work who identify him too literally with his hero, Eugene Gant, to know that his chief claim to fame at Chapel Hill was as a humorist. As he says in *Look Homeward, Angel*, the entire family had "a spirit of vulgar mirth . . . a great comic intelligence," which "was shaken daily" by their father. Wolfe's own sense of humor was a fine one: he seldom revealed it to strangers, with whom he was almost always ill at ease, but it was one of his strongest and most endearing qualities in his relationships with his close friends. His teen-age humor consisted chiefly of broad burlesque and adolescent clowning, but it made history at Chapel Hill. His college friends still love to tell how one day, in Professor Edwin Greenlaw's English class, he began to read his theme from sheets of yellow paper dug out from one pocket, then paused dramatically in the middle of a sentence, dug with mock wildness in his other pockets, drew out a single sheet of white paper, read from that, dug around some more, read a few lines from the back of an old brown envelope, and in final triumph, to the gleeful howls of his classmates, produced the last installment on folds of toilet paper. "Mr. Wolfe," said Professor Greenlaw, "are we to judge the quality of your essay by the paper on which it is written?"[5]

Tom was in constant demand for skits and speeches at smokers and class banquets, where he recounted burlesque thrillers with titles such as "The Fall of Swine Castle," "The Last of the Profiteers," and "Sam Hole Brow's Departure," and in the college newspaper, the *Tar Heel*, he poked fun at himself as well as everyone else:

Fresh: It sure is a great pity and loss to the Varsity that Tom Wolfe doesn't play football.
Campbell [the football coach]: Why?
Fresh: He could fall down with the ball and make a touchdown every time.

Or

Thomas Clayton Wolfe, editor of the *Tar Heel*, was on the Hill a few fleeting hours last Wednesday. Mr. Wolfe is taking a rest cure in Raleigh and Greensboro following a week of strenuous and nerve-wracking exams. It is thought he is taking the Keeley cure.

Perhaps some of these short squibs were written by his associates, but in view of the fact that he is known to have written almost the entire contents of the *Tar Heel* by himself, most of them must have been his own.

However, Wolfe's college writing was by no means limited to humor. In fact, as editor of the *Tar Heel* during his junior and senior years, he covered nearly every phase of life at Chapel Hill and did a remarkably good job of it. There was a good deal of straight reporting, earnest editorials on college morale or needed reforms, a series of informal essays called "With Apologies to Pepys," into which Wolfe managed to cram almost everything that fitted nowhere else, and a good many special features which were far above the average. Some of these, such as an article called "Ye Who Have Been There Only Know," about the invasion of Richmond by the University of North Carolina and the

[5] For this anecdote the author is indebted to "The Thomas Wolfe I Knew," by LeGette Blythe, in the August 25, 1945, issue of the *Saturday Review of Literature*; to "Tom Wolfe as a Student," by Don Bishop, in the March 1942 issue of the *Carolina Magazine*; and to *Thomas Wolfe: Carolina Student*, by Agatha Boyd Adams, University of North Carolina Library, 1950.

University of Virginia for their annual Thanksgiving football game,[6] contain the seeds of Wolfe's later writing in his novels. Others, such as "Useful Advice to Candidates," an admonition to the political office seeker that "the student body is interested in you the man . . . and not in party politics," were outstanding enough to cause comment in adult newspapers throughout the state. Wolfe's best-known journalistic tour de force, however, was not published in the *Tar Heel*, but in the April 20, 1920, issue of the college humor magazine, the *Tar Baby*, and was a burlesque of Josephus Daniels' famous Raleigh *News and Observer*. Characteristically, he put off writing this until the night before it was to go to press; then sat up all night and wrote the entire forty-four pages of the issue, including the satiric "drammer" "The Streets of Durham, or Dirty Work at the Crossroads; A Tragedy in Three Muddy Acts."

Meanwhile Wolfe was also associate editor and assistant editor-in-chief of the *Carolina Magazine*, in which appeared his poetry, stories, and other purely literary work. When some of the earliest of these were published in the March 1918 issue, he proudly sent a copy to his father, but twenty years later, in a speech he made at Purdue University, he describes them humorously: "The War was going on then; I was too young to be in service, and I suppose my first attempts creatively may be traced to the direct and patriotic inspiration of the War. I remember one in particular—a poem . . . which was aimed directly at the luckless head of Kaiser Bill. The poem was called defiantly 'The Challenge' and . . . was written in the style . . . of 'The Present Crisis' by James Russell Lowell. . . . In the name of embattled democracy, I let the Kaiser have the works, and I remember two lines in particular that seemed to me to have a very ringing tone: 'Thou hast given us the challenge— Pay, now dog, the cost, and go!' . . . I also remember a short story—my first—which was called 'A Cullenden of Virginia'— which was about the recreant son of an old family who recovers his courage and vindicates his tarnished honor in the last charge over the top that takes his life." But at any rate, Wolfe was making a beginning. As he said later in *The Story of a Novel*, "The desire to write, which had been strong during all my days in high school, grew stronger still. I was . . . still thinking I would become a lawyer or a newspaperman, never daring to believe I could seriously become a writer."

Moreover, in his classes under Professor Greenlaw, Wolfe was getting a strong antidote to the sentimental post-Victorian kind of writing

---

[6] In those days this was played at Richmond, not at Charlottesville.

which he imitated in the *Magazine*. Greenlaw recognized that he was "an exceedingly able writer . . . and a man of interesting personality"[7] and gave him the mixture of guidance and freedom that he needed. In the reminiscences which Wolfe jotted down in 1926 as a preliminary to writing *Look Homeward, Angel*, he wrote that in the Advanced Composition class "Greenlaw said I had achieved 'style'—what most men don't get till forty." But more important was the thorough soaking in Elizabethan literature which Wolfe got in Greenlaw's courses on Elizabethan drama and on the non-dramatic literature of the Renaissance. As some of Wolfe's more discerning critics pointed out years later, he was in many ways an Elizabethan, and that quality is one of the richest and most enduring in his work. Of course, it had to be— and was—inherent in Wolfe himself, but it was nourished in him at just the right impressionable age by Greenlaw and was refreshed from time to time all through his life by his habit of reading and rereading Burton's *Anatomy of Melancholy*, Shakespeare, Donne, and the other great writers of the English Renaissance.

As a student at the university, Wolfe already had many of the characteristics which marked him in his adult life. He was so tall that people constantly asked him "How's the weather up there?" He didn't have an ounce of fat on his bones, and his legs and arms stuck out beyond his clothes inches farther than they should. As one of his friends said later, "Tom seemed to buy his clothes from the skin out. He apparently bought an entire outfit and wore it till it had to be removed." Another says: "It is true that most of the time Tom was absolutely dirty. No one seemed to know when he took a bath and apparently he never changed his shirt. Very seldom did he get a haircut and I don't think he ever pressed his trousers, which almost invariably were too short and very baggy in the knees. I remember Tom packing to go home for Christmas: from underneath the bed, dresser, and out of dresser drawers he pulled all sorts of dirty clothes, threw them in the trunk, stood on them, stamped up and down, and closed the trunk and was ready to go. Upon his return, Tom would look comparatively dressed up, but within a week it was the same old Tom." There are some other stories of how, when he undressed, he would simply step out of his clothes and leave them scattered on the floor from one end of his room to the other, or how he would sit motionless and lost in

[7] From a letter recommending Wolfe which Greenlaw wrote in 1922 to the Harvard Appointment Office.

thought for half an hour or an hour with one sock on his foot and the other dangling from his hand. He simply couldn't bother with such a petty thing as neatness. However, the rumors that he was suspended from his fraternity, Pi Kappa Phi, because of this have been categorically denied by his fraternity brothers, including his old friend Corydon P. Spruill, who is now dean at the university.[8]

Tom was his mother's son and would always rather talk than eat or sleep. He spent hours in what he called "delightful bull sessions" in students' rooms or at the Young Men's Christian Association, where he often went in the evening. One well-known anecdote about him tells how at the latter place, after talking about everything under the sun till 3 A.M. with the Y.M.C.A. secretary and a group of students, he suddenly leaped dramatically to the middle of the floor, exclaiming, "My God, gentlemen, I've had nothing to eat since breakfast!"—whereupon he hurried out to Gooch's Café for his first square meal that day. He ate at Gooch's almost every night, but as soon as the aching void inside of him was filled, he went right back to talking, pouring out a compulsive flood of words to the waiters or the taxi drivers there, or prowling around the college campus in hopes of finding some of his friends still up and ready to start another bull session.

He also had the hopeless inability to keep track of time which was chronic with him all his life. He was late to meetings and to classes, and late with work assignments and copy for the *Tar Heel*, except on the epic occasions when he sat up all night and wrote an entire issue just in time to meet the deadline. Finally he would catch the early morning bus to Durham, where the paper was printed at Seeman's Printing Shop, but even there he would continue to rewrite the issue, throwing out ads without the slightest hesitation to make room for news or editorials, or changing the entire layout of page one just as the paper was about to go to press. As the business manager of the *Tar Heel* said despairingly, "He was one of the most impractical persons I ever saw." His general reputation on the campus was that of a humorous, happy-go-lucky boy whose very eccentricities made him all the funnier and better loved, but underneath he still had the supersensitivity and intense emotionalism which were basic to his character. If any of his teachers tried to criticize his serious creative work, he

[8] The author is indebted to Don Bishop for this and other material about Wolfe at Chapel Hill, contained in the notes and correspondence which he compiled for his article "Tom Wolfe as a Student," in the March 1942 issue of the *Carolina Magazine*.

would weep with mortification or leap up and rush wildly from the
room. He simply could not bear adverse criticism, either then or at
any time in his entire life.

In the spring of 1918 Tom's life at college was touched with
tragedy. His roommate, an Asheville boy named Edmund Burdick,
who had been managing editor of the *Tar Heel* that year, died of a heart
attack, and the shock of his death so affected Tom that for days he
refused to eat or to go back to the room which they had shared together.
Tom never did sleep there again, but at least two sets of his good friends
who roomed together had cots put in their rooms for him, where he
camped out for the remainder of the term. However, it was lucky that
this was in his sophomore year, when he had good friends to take him
in; if it had happened when he was a freshman, the emotional shock
and added loneliness would have been almost unbearable.[9]

During all this time Tom had been struggling to maintain his freedom from his family. He went home for Christmas 1917, but he spent
the summer of 1918 doing war work in Norfolk, Virginia. In a letter
written to his mother from Norfolk in July, he represents himself as
happy and successful, but according to *Look Homeward, Angel*, his
summer was "filled with terror and hunger." At first he simply roamed
the streets, drinking in the life of the great wartime embarkation port,
sleeping on a dormitory cot at the Y.M.C.A., on deserted piers, or on
the Portsmouth ferry, and brooding constantly about Clara Paul, who
was living with her husband there. When his money was gone and he
was almost starving, he found a job as a time checker over gangs of
laborers at Langley Flying Field in Hampton. He got eighty dollars a
month salary and all living expenses, but he quit the job after a month.
He then began to starve again, tried unsuccessfully to qualify as a carpenter for the building of a quartermaster terminal, and finally got work
as a government checker of supplies and ammunition on the docks
at Newport News. For this he received a hundred and sixty dollars a
month, but he went home in September with little or no money and
without ever having dared to look up Clara Paul.

He had been back at Chapel Hill for only a few weeks when he
received a telegram from his mother: "Come home at once. Ben has
pneumonia." The great influenza epidemic of 1918 was at its height,

---

[9] Incidentally, the death of the Carolina student who cut his jugular vein on
a bottle, which Wolfe describes in *You Can't Go Home Again*, actually occurred
in September 1912, four years before Wolfe ever went to Chapel Hill.

and Effie Wolfe Gambrell's children, who had come to visit their grandmother at the Old Kentucky Home, had spread the infection in the
family. Ben's "weak lungs"—probably arrested tuberculosis—had made
his case a dangerous one from the beginning, but he had received little
or no proper care, for which the other children blamed their mother.
Now pneumonia had developed in both lungs, and he was dying: as
the family doctor says in Look Homeward, Angel, "Not all the doctors
and nurses in the world can help him now. . . . He's drowning!
Drowning!" Wolfe's description of Ben's death in Look Homeward,
Angel is perhaps the finest thing he ever wrote. In it, there is not only
the tragedy of Ben's own wasted life, and of his loss to Tom, the
younger brother whom he always championed: there is also the revelation of the entire family with all of its complex relationships, each
heightened by intense anxiety and grief in "the last terrible congress
before death."

"Then, over the ugly clamor of their dissension, over the rasp and
snarl of their nerves, they heard the low mutter of Ben's expiring breath.
The light had been re-shaded: he lay, like his own shadow, in all his
fierce gray lonely beauty. And as they looked and saw his bright eyes
already blurred with death, and saw the feeble beating flutter of his
poor thin breast, the strange wonder, the dark rich miracle of his life
surged over them its enormous loveliness. They grew quiet and calm,
they plunged below all the splintered wreckage of their lives, they drew
together in a superb communion of love and valiance, beyond horror
and confusion, beyond death. And Eugene's eyes grew blind with love
and wonder: an enormous organ-music sounded in his heart, he
possessed them for a moment, he was a part of their loveliness, his life
soared magnificently out of the slough of pain and ugliness. He
thought: 'That was not all! That really was not all!' . . . The rattling
in the wasted body, which seemed for hours to have given over to death
all of life that is worth saving, had now ceased. The body appeared to
grow rigid before them. . . . But suddenly, marvellously, as if his
resurrection and rebirth had come upon him, Ben drew upon the air in
a long and powerful respiration; his gray eyes opened. Filled with a
terrible vision of all life in the one moment, he seemed to rise forward
bodilessly from his pillows without support—a flame, a light, a glory—
joined at length in death to the dark spirit who had brooded upon
each footstep of his lonely adventure on earth; and, casting the fierce
sword of his glance with utter and final comprehension upon the room
haunted with its gray pageantry of cheap loves and dull consciences

and on all those uncertain mummers of waste and confusion fading now from the bright window of his eyes, he passed instantly, scornful and unafraid, as he had lived, into the shades of death."

Wolfe always referred to Ben's death as the most tragic experience of his entire life, but Ben had always urged him to "get away" from home and now he realized more strongly than ever that he must go. "The great wild pattern of the family had been broken forever. The partial discipline that had held them together had been destroyed by the death of their brother: the nightmare of waste and loss had destroyed their hope."

In *Look Homeward, Angel* Wolfe describes his realization that he must break away from home and from his mother. "Eliza sat before the fire at Dixieland with hands folded, reliving a past of tenderness and love that never had been. And as the wind howled in the bleak street, and Eliza wove a thousand fables of that lost and bitter spirit, the bright and stricken thing in the boy twisted about in horror, looking for escape from the house of death. No more! No more! (it said). You are alone now. You are lost. Go find yourself, lost boy, beyond the hills. . . .

"O but I can't go now, said Eugene to it. (Why not? it whispered.) Because her face is so white, and her forehead is so broad and high, with the black hair drawn back from it, and when she sat there at the bed she looked like a little child. I can't go now and leave her here alone. (She is alone, it said, and so are you. . . . You must escape, or you will die.) It is all like death: she fed me at her breast, I slept in the same bed with her, she took me on her trips. All of that is over now, and each time it was like a death. (And like a life, it said to him. Each time that you die, you will be born again. And you will die a hundred times before you become a man.) I can't! I can't! Not now—later, more slowly. (No. Now, it said.) I am afraid. I have nowhere to go. (You must find the place, it said.) I am lost. (You must hunt for yourself, it said.) . . .

"Then, as the bright thing twisted about in him, Eugene heard the whine of the bleak wind about the house that he must leave, and the voice of Eliza calling up from the past the beautiful lost things that never happened.

" '—and I said, "Why, what on earth, boy, you want to dress up warm around your neck or you'll catch your death of cold." '

"Eugene caught at his throat, and plunged for the door.

" 'Here, boy! Where are you going?' said Eliza, looking up quickly.

" 'I've got to go,' he said in a choking voice. 'I've got to get away from here.'

"Then he saw the fear in her eyes, and the grave troubled child's stare. He rushed to where she sat and grasped her hand. She held him tightly and laid her face against his arm.

" 'Don't go yet,' she said. 'You've all your life ahead of you. Stay with me just a day or two.'

" 'Yes, mama,' he said, falling to his knees. 'Yes, mama.' He hugged her to him frantically. 'Yes, mama. God bless you, mama. It's all right, mama. It's all right.'

"Eliza wept bitterly.

" 'I'm an old woman,' she said, 'and one by one I've lost you all. He's dead now, and I never got to know him. O son, don't leave me yet. You're the only one that's left: you were my baby. Don't go! Don't go.' She laid her white face against his sleeve.

"It is not hard to go (he thought). But when can we forget?"

A few days later he went back to Chapel Hill. He fell automatically into the pattern of his busy life there, was managing editor of the *Tar Heel* and associate editor of the *Magazine,* and distinguished himself in the philosophy classes of Horace Williams, who was his favorite teacher and who later described Wolfe as "one of six remarkable students in my thirty years experience."[10] In June 1919 Wolfe won the Worth Prize for Philosophy with an essay written on "The Crisis in Industry," in which he examined the labor problems that had followed the signing of the Armistice in November, and offered as his solution "industrial democracy—a system of democratic cooperation in industry with equal rights and responsibilities for capital and labor." The essay is about what would be expected of an eighteen-year-old boy, but as Professor Williams pointed out in his introduction to the pamphletized edition of it, it was a refreshing change from the usual prize-winning essays on collegiate philosophical abstractions.

In the speech which Wolfe made at Purdue in 1938, he said that Williams' philosophy had no lasting influence upon him, but then went on: "But what was most important was the man himself; he was a great teacher, and . . . he supplied the many of us, for the first time in our lives, the inspiration of a questioning intelligence. He taught us not to be afraid to think, to question; to examine critically the most

[10] From a letter recommending Wolfe which Williams wrote in 1922 to the Harvard Appointment Bureau.

venerable of our native superstitions, our local prejudices, to look hide-bound conventions in the eye and challenge them. . . . And the seed he planted grew." Wolfe's "questioning intelligence" stood him in good stead all through his adult life. Because of it, he was quick to detect the false and the superficial, and stanch in withstanding the transitory literary and political vogues of the period from 1920 to 1938. The seed that Williams planted grew, and its fruit was ripening in 1938, when Wolfe's development was broken off by his untimely death.

Meanwhile Wolfe had embarked upon the career as a dramatist which was to mislead him and almost break his heart for eight long years. In September 1918, a few weeks before Ben's death, Professor Frederick H. Koch had come to Chapel Hill and had begun to organize the Carolina Playmakers. Wolfe, who was always ready to try any form of writing, had been the first male pupil to sign up for his class, which boasted seven coed members and was called "The Ladies Aid Society." But Koch—and Wolfe—went ahead with boundless enthusiasm and soon enrolled six more men students, including the future dramatist Paul Green. On March 14 and 15, 1919, the first program of the Play-makers was put on at the Chapel Hill High School auditorium, with *The Return of Buck Gavin, A Tragedy of the Mountain People*, by Thomas Wolfe, as one of the three plays. The play was based on an actual incident in the life of one Patrick Lavin, known in Texas as the bank robber Cyclone Pat, but in accordance with Koch's chief dictate, Wolfe wrote it with the "folk" characters and background of the North Carolina mountaineers, even though he himself had lived all his life in Asheville and knew the mountaineer life only secondhand.

He also played the part of Buck in the production. As Koch wrote later, "We couldn't find anyone to play the part and I said to him, 'I guess you'll have to play it yourself, Tom. You may not know it, but you really wrote that part for yourself!' 'But I can't act, Prof, I've never acted.' 'You're a born actor . . . and you *are* Buck Gavin.' I shall never forget his first performance. With free mountain stride, his dark eyes blazing, he became the hunted outlaw of the Great Smokies. There was something uncanny in his acting of the part—something of the pent-up fury of his highland forbears."[11]

For the rest of his time at Chapel Hill, Wolfe kept on enthusiastically writing one-act plays. A second play, *Deferred Payment*, was published

[11] From "Thomas Wolfe: Playmaker," in the March–June 1943 issue of the *Carolina Playbook*.

in the June 1919 issue of the *Magazine*. A third, *The Third Night, A Mountain Play of the Supernatural*, was produced by the Playmakers on December 12 and 13, 1919. A fourth, *Concerning Honest Bob*, which satirized college elections, was published in the May 1920 issue of the *Magazine*. In later years Wolfe was ashamed of these—as he wrote in the application for a Guggenheim fellowship which he made in 1930, "I was at this time young and lazy; I scribbled constantly and at random; I had not learned to work, and what I wrote did not represent the best in me"—but his playwriting was an important step in his career, even though it turned out to be one in a wrong direction.

He spent the summer of 1919 at home in Asheville, then returned for his senior year at Chapel Hill as "a great man on the campus."[12] In June his father was too sick to attend his graduation, but Mrs. Wolfe came and proudly saw the honors heaped upon her son. In *Look Homeward, Angel* Eliza Gant is similarly elated. " 'Well, son, . . . I want you to go ahead now and try to be Somebody. None of the others ever had your opportunity, and I hope you do something with it. . . . Have you thought yet of what you're going to do?' . . . 'I'll talk to you in a few days when I see you at home,' said Eugene. 'I'll tell you about it then.' . . . He had nothing to tell them. He was nineteen; he had completed his college course; but he did not know what he was going to do. His father's plan that he should study law and 'enter politics' had been forgotten since his sophomore year, when it became apparent that the impulse of his life was not toward law. . . . No one saw very clearly what he was going to do—he, surely, least of all—but his family, following the tack of his comrades, spoke vaguely and glibly of 'a career in journalism.' This meant newspaper work. And, however unsatisfactory this may have been, their inevitable question was drugged for the moment by the glitter of success that had surrounded his life at the university."

But the inevitable question was argued back and forth by the entire family during the summer of 1920, as it had been four years earlier, when Wolfe had enrolled at Chapel Hill. This time, however, Mr. Wolfe refused to pay the bills. "You've got to shift for yourself from now on," Gant says in *Look Homeward, Angel*. "You've had the best education money can buy. The rest is up to you." Meanwhile Wolfe was offered jobs on several newspapers and also a position as an English teacher at the Bingham School, a military academy in Asheville. His

[12] From the editorial on Wolfe in the October 1938 issue of the *Carolina Magazine*.

parents evidently pressed him to accept the latter so that he could
be at home, but he vehemently refused. As the summer wore on, his
somewhat vague desire to do graduate study at Harvard grew more
definite and strong. The possibility of his going there had been mentioned as early as 1914, when his uncle Henry A. Westall, who had
attended the Harvard Divinity School, had discussed it with Mr.
Wolfe but had advised that he go to the University of North Carolina
first. More recently, at Chapel Hill, Wolfe had been urged to go to
Harvard by Horace Williams, who had also studied at the Divinity
School, and especially by Frederick Koch, who had first become a playmaker under Professor George Pierce Baker in the 47 Workshop. To
Wolfe, the possibility of continuing his work as a dramatist under Baker
offered realization of all of his desires to become a writer, to escape
from home, and to visit "the proud fierce North with all its shining
cities, and its tides of life."

August came, and nothing definite had been decided. Mr. Wolfe
was due to go back to Johns Hopkins for more radium treatments.
At this point in *Look Homeward, Angel* Gant says wearily, "Let him
do as he likes. I can't pay out any more money on his education. If
he wants to go, his mother must send him." Wolfe besieged his
mother with frantic pleas and wild suggestions that the money for his
further education could be deducted from his share of the inheritance
he was to receive under his father's will. In the *Angel* Eliza finally
makes a compromise. " 'Well,' she said, at length. 'I'll send you for
a year. Then we'll see.' "

And so, at last, Wolfe won his release from home, even though only
on a temporary one-year basis. On August 16 he wrote to Harvard
applying for admission to the Graduate School of Arts and Sciences;
he sent to the University of North Carolina for the records of his
work there and for certification that he had received his bachelor's
degree; and as late as September 9 he forwarded this necessary information to Harvard, asking the dean of the Graduate School of Arts and
Sciences to wire him collect if he was accepted, so that he could come
to Cambridge and try to find a room. Finally he was accepted in a
letter dated September 13, and he began making frantic preparations
for departure. A few days later he stood with his family on the station
platform, waiting for the train to Baltimore, where he was to say good-by
to his father at Johns Hopkins before going on to Boston.

In the first section of *Of Time and the River* he describes this great
moment in his life: "Now the train was coming. Down the powerful

shining tracks a half mile away, the huge black snout of the locomotive swung slowly round the magnificent bend and flare of the rails that went into the railway yards of Altamont two miles away, and with short explosive thunders of its squat funnel came barging slowly forward. Across the golden pollenated haze of the warm autumnal afternoon they watched it with numb lips and an empty hollowness of fear, delight, and sorrow in their hearts. . . . It was his train and it had come to take him to the strange and secret heart of the great North that he had never known, but whose austere and lonely image . . . had blazed in his vision since he was a child. . . . With a heart of fire, a brain possessed, . . . he had always known that some day he should find it—his heart's hope and his father's country, the lost but unforgotten half of his own soul—and take it for his own. And now that day had come . . . With a sudden feeling of release, a realization of the incredible escape that now impended for him, he knew that he was waiting for the train, and that the great life of the North, the road to freedom, solitude and the enchanted promise of the golden cities was now before him. Like a dream made real, a magic come to life, he knew that in another hour he would be speeding world-ward, life-ward, Northward out of the enchanted, time-far hills, out of the dark heart and mournful mystery of the South forever."

III

THE STORY of Thomas Wolfe at Harvard is like that of the Ugly Duckling, but it took Wolfe three and a half long years to realize that he had not been born to be a dramatist in the 47 Workshop's duckpond, and five years more before he emerged as a full-fledged novelist. He arrived at Cambridge late in September 1920, after a brief farewell visit with his father at Johns Hopkins and two days in New York "in the ecstasy of freedom at last." Over six thousand students were already enrolled for the fall term at Harvard, and the best and cheapest rooms had all been taken.[1] Fortunately for Wolfe, Professor N. A. Walker of the University of North Carolina had come to Harvard for a year of graduate work and with his wife and children had taken a house at 48 Buckingham Street. Wolfe rented a room in the Walkers' attic. He was already six feet three inches tall and was writing of himself in this room or a similar one when, in *Of Time and the River*, he says that the playwright Oswald Ten Eyck "had to manage his . . . stature carefully in order to keep from cracking his head upon the sloping white-washed walls that followed the steep pitch of the roof with painful fidelity. The central part of [the] room, which was the only place in which the . . . man could stand erect, was not over four feet wide: there was a single window at the front where stood his writing table. He had a couple of straight chairs, a white iron cot pushed in under the eave of the left side, a few bookshelves pushed in under the eave of the right. It could literally be said that the playwright crawled to bed, and when he read he had to approach the poets as a poet should—upon his knees." However, the habitual discomfort of cracking his head was more than made up for by the fact that Wolfe was surrounded by people he knew and liked and trusted. In the room next to his was William Polk and down the hall was Albert Coates, both of whom had been friends of his at Chapel Hill and were now studying at the Harvard Law School. Polk and Coates stood him in

[1] For information concerning Wolfe at Harvard the author is indebted to Richard S. Kennedy's "Thomas Wolfe at Harvard, 1920–1923," in the Spring and Autumn 1950 issues of the *Harvard Library Bulletin*.

good stead, for he felt more lost at Harvard than he had ever felt before.

During that first year, he also saw a great deal of his uncle Henry A. Westall. In *Of Time and the River* he says that "although he was living a life of the most savage conflict, the most blazing energy, . . . he would nevertheless spend a life of such utter loneliness that he would go for days at a time without seeing a face or hearing a voice that he knew, and until the sound of his own voice seemed strange and phantasmal to him. Then suddenly he . . . would feel an almost unbearable need to hear the voice and see the face again of some one he had known and . . . he would go to see his Uncle . . . , that strange and extraordinary man who, born like the others in the wilderness, the hills of home, had left these hills forever."

After many years as a Unitarian clergyman, Mr. Westall had left the ministry and become a real-estate conveyancer, with an office in downtown Boston. Tom went there often to seek his advice and also spent Sundays and holidays at the Westalls' house in Medford, where Mrs. Westall filled up his cadaverous frame with home-cooked food. The Westalls' children had all grown up, but as time went on, Tom went also to the homes of their two daughters, Elaine Westall Gould and Hilda Westall Bottomley. He had been more or less entrusted to the care of his uncle, and at first the relationship between them was a close one. When Tom, to his dismay, was charged well over a hundred dollars for the typing of one of his plays and was later sued for payment of this bill, Mr. Westall, with great relish, had himself appointed as his "guardian pro tem," and acting also as his attorney, pointed out that Tom was still a minor and that his contract was therefore "voidable, if not void ab initio."[2] The case accordingly was settled out of court, with Professor Baker acting as a referee.

Although Wolfe had written in his application to the Graduate School: "In considering this application you should know that I have decided on Journalism as my work," his chief ambition, fostered by Professor Koch, was to enroll in Professor George Pierce Baker's playwriting course, English 47, which was familiarly called the 47 Workshop. In a letter to his mother dated October 2, and one to Koch dated November 26, 1920, Wolfe described with jubilation how he was at first refused admission to the Workshop, which was restricted to twelve carefully selected members, and then how, on hearing that he had been a Carolina Playmaker, Baker let him join "the sacred circle." Meanwhile, in response to a frantic telegram from Wolfe, Koch had sent

[2] From a letter written by Henry A. Westall now in the possession of Hilda Westall Bottomley.

Baker copies of *The Return of Buck Gavin* and *The Third Night*. Baker heartily endorsed Wolfe's determination to go on with "the Carolina type of play" and encouraged him to write his one-act folk play *The Mountains*, which he had begun at Chapel Hill.

In return, Wolfe worshiped Baker with the exaggerated adoration which he always felt for the exceptional people who, one after another, were to influence his life. In a passage finally omitted from *Of Time and the River* he says: "I worshipped him for almost a year. He was the great man, the prophet, the infinitely wise and strong and gentle spirit who knew all, had seen all, could solve all problems by a word, release us of all the anguish, grief and error of our lives by a wave of his benevolent hand." Wolfe flung himself into his work as a dramatist. The 47 Workshop was "the rock to which his life was anchored, the rudder of his destiny, the sole and all-sufficient reason for his being here. It now seemed to him that there was only one work in life which he could possibly do, and that this work was writing plays, and that if he could not succeed in this work he had better die, since any other life than the life of the playwright and the theatre was not to be endured. Accordingly every interest and energy of his life was now fastened on this work with a madman's passion; he thought, felt, breathed, ate, drank, slept and lived completely in terms of plays."

His admiration for his fellow students in the Workshop was by no means as complete. In a letter written to Professor Koch he ridiculed their affectations, and his first reaction to them was his true and final one. On the other hand, their sophistication intensified his own eccentricities, which had been considered merely lovable at Chapel Hill. To put it frankly, these young men and women at Harvard considered him as something of a freak. He was still a tall, thin, gawky scarecrow of a youth, with a patch of what he called "the Westall tetter" (really a sort of eczema) upon his neck, which he rubbed or dug at with his nails when he was nervous or excited, as he usually was. His clothes were even dirtier, more ill-fitting, and more ragged than before, because he now had nobody to care for him and was constantly in desperate financial straits. Moreover, his chronic inability to keep track of time was an especially noticeable handicap in the theater, where everything is done on deadlines and the work of an entire company can be delayed by the tardiness of one.

As if conscious of his own shortcomings in the Workshop, he was very shy at first and spoke only in brief, painfully stammered phrases—or, if he really "got going," talked too long, too repetitiously, too intensely, and too exclusively about himself. He also had an unpleasant way of speech, connected with his stammer, which made spittle gather in the corners of his mouth and suddenly spray out into the face of whomever he was talking with. In spite of his shyness—or really because of it—he was very truculent at times. As he said later, in the speech he made at Purdue University, "Looking back, in an effort to see myself as I was in those days, I am afraid I was not always a very friendly or agreeable person. The plain truth of the matter is that I was carrying a chip on my shoulder, and I suppose I was daring the whole world to knock it off. The chip on my shoulder had, of course, to do with writing, and with the life I wanted to lead. And I suppose the reason I was outwardly so truculent at times and inclined to be arrogant and take a very high tone with people who, it seemed to me, doubted my ability to do the thing I wanted to do, was that inwardly I was by no means arrogantly sure that I could do it myself. It was a form of whistling to keep one's courage up."

Gradually, however, chiefly through his friendship with Professor Baker's assistant, Kenneth Raisbeck, Wolfe was more or less assimilated by the Workshop group and even came to share some of their aesthetic views.

He says in the Purdue speech: "I [went] through the stage of aesthetic preciosity, of talking about 'art' and 'beauty,' and about 'the artist'; of scorning 'the bourgeoisie,' 'the Philistines and Babbitts,' who were not only not artists, but who could never understand 'the artist,' but belonged to a completely different, separate world. . . . This was a time, I am afraid, in which I talked a great deal more about 'beauty' and 'art' than I created it; expended a great deal more time in scorning and ridiculing 'the bourgeoisie' than in trying to find out who they were and what they were like."

But even if Wolfe accepted some of the tenets of the cult, he was inclined to be a little wary of its members and had with them no friendships of lasting warmth except for those with Raisbeck, Henry Fisk Carlton, and George Wallace. Later, in *Of Time and the River*, he did a devastating burlesque of the entire group and summed it up as follows: "Instead of knowledge, the experience of hard work and patient living, they were given a formula for knowledge; a language that sounded very knowing, expert and assured, and yet that knew nothing, was experienced in nothing, was sure of nothing. It gave to people without talent and without sincerity of soul or integrity of purpose, with nothing, in fact, except a feeble incapacity for the shock and agony of life, and a desire to escape into a glamorous and unreal world of make

believe—a justification for their pitiable and base existence. It gave to
people who had no power in themselves to create anything of merit or of
beauty—people who were the true Philistines and enemies of art and of
the artist's living spirit—the language to talk with glib knowingness
of things they knew nothing of—to prate of 'settings,' 'tempo,' 'pace,'
and 'rhythm,' of 'boldly stylized conventions,' and the wonderful way
some actress 'used her hands.' And in the end, it led to nothing but
falseness and triviality, to the ghosts of passion, and the spectres of
sincerity, to the shoddy appearances of conviction and belief in people
who . . . were just the disloyal apes of fashion and the arts. . . . False,
trivial, glib, dishonest, empty, without substance, lacking faith—is it
any wonder that among [these] young men few birds sang?"

But, for the first year at any rate, Wolfe's work in English 47
"gripped" him "heart and soul." He also took as many courses in the
history of the drama and of literature as he could squeeze into his
schedule, both to earn points toward his master's degree and to "stock
up with materials the same as a carpenter carries a mouthful of nails."
He took a course on the drama from the Greeks to modern times under
Baker, one on American literature under Professor Chester Greenough,
and sat in on one on Shakespeare under Professor G. L. Kittredge; but
the course which, after the 47 Workshop, had the deepest effect on him
was one on the Romantic poets under Professor John Livingston Lowes.
In a letter written in the spring of 1922 to Professor Greenlaw of
Chapel Hill, Wolfe says that "Professor Lowes' book on Coleridge
[published later as *The Road to Xanadu*] had a great effect on me. In
that book he shows conclusively how retentive of all it reads is the mind
and how, at almost any moment, that mass of material may be fused
and resurrected in new and magic forms. That is wonderful, I think. So
I'm reading, not so analytically as voraciously."

Lowes' studies of Coleridge's reading and how it had become transmuted into his poetry were read aloud in class in 1920–21, and they
gave Wolfe a justification and an impetus for a compulsion of his own.
Ever since the days when he had reportedly read every book in the
Asheville library, he had had a hunger for knowledge: it had gained
in strength as his ambition to become a writer had grown more definite,
and it now went far beyond all rationality. In *Of Time and the River*
he calls it "fury," saying: "Now mad fury gripped his life, and he was
haunted by the dream of time. . . . What is the fury which this youth
will feel, which will lash him on against the great earth forever? It is
the brain that maddens with its own excess, the heart that breaks from

the anguish of its own frustration. . . . It is to see a million men, a million faces and to be a stranger and an alien to them always. It is to prowl the stacks of an enormous library at night, to tear the books out of a thousand shelves . . . The thought of these vast stacks of books would drive him mad: . . . the greater the number of books he read, the greater the immense uncountable number of those which he could never read would seem to be. Within a period of ten years he read at least 20,000 volumes[3] . . . and opened the pages and looked through many times that number. . . . He pictured himself as tearing the entrails from a book as from a fowl. . . . Walking at night among the vast piled shelves of the library, he would read, watch in hand, muttering to himself in triumph or anger at the timing of each page: 'Fifty seconds to do that one. Damn you, we'll see!' . . .—and he would tear through the next page in twenty seconds.

"This fury which drove him on to read so many books had nothing to do with . . . formal learning. . . . He simply wanted to know about everything on earth . . . And it was the same with everything he did. In the midst of a furious burst of reading in the enormous library, the thought of the streets outside and the great city all around him would drive through his body like a sword. It would now seem to him that every second that he passed among the books was being wasted—that at this moment something priceless, irrecoverable was happening in the streets, and that if he could only get to it in time and see it, he would somehow get the knowledge of the whole thing in him—the source, the well, the spring from which all men and words and actions, and every design upon this earth proceeds. And he would rush out in the streets to find it, be hurled through the tunnel into Boston and then spend hours in driving himself savagely through a hundred streets, looking into the faces of a million people . . . until bone and brain and blood could stand no more . . . and his heart sank down beneath its weight of desolation and despair. . . .

"Yet a furious hope, a wild extravagant belief, was burning in him all the time. . . . He would get up in the middle of the night to scrawl down insane catalogs of all that he had seen and done: . . . the number of people he had known, the number of women he had slept with, the number of meals he had eaten, the number of towns he had visited, the number of states he had been in. And at one moment he would gloat and chuckle over these stupendous lists like a miser gloating over his hoard, only to groan bitterly with despair the next moment, and to

[3] Wolfe's estimates were always exaggerated by his intense emotionalism.

beat his head against the wall, as he remembered the overwhelming amount of all he had not seen or done, or known. Then he would begin another list filled with enormous catalogs of all the books he had not read, all the food he had not eaten, all the women that he had not slept with, all the states he had not been in, all the towns he had not visited. Then he would write down plans and programs whereby all these things must be accomplished, how many years it would take to do it all, and how old he would be when he had finished. An enormous wave of hope and joy would surge up in him, because it now looked easy, and he had no doubt at all that he could do it."

Some of these lists are still to be found among Wolfe's papers, scrawled in pencil on loose sheets or on the pages of the greasy, battered little notebooks that he carried in his pocket. They showed that his "insatiate reading" ended around the time when he began working on *Look Homeward, Angel,* but that his more general "hunger to devour the earth" lasted unabated until publication of that novel and continued to some extent until the day he died. It drove him to cross the Atlantic and wander over Europe seven times in eleven years and finally, in 1938, to undertake the exhausting "Western journey" which ended in his fatal illness.

One factor in this compulsive hunger was undoubtedly Wolfe's half-repressed fear that he might not live long enough to accomplish everything he had set out to do. It is false to examine a person's life in the light of his death, but Wolfe's "fury" did become strongest in him just after his first intimation that he might have tuberculosis. He describes his first frightening symptom in a letter to his mother evidently written in the early fall of 1920: "On the train coming up I developed a heavy cold, which hung on most persistently after I got here. The thing got down into my chest and a week or two ago, I began to cough—at first a dry cough—then a rattling, tearing, sort of cough, full of phlegm. I became worried. My right lung was sore. . . . One night I started coughing here, in my room, and I put my handkerchief to my mouth. When I drew it away there was a tiny spot of blood on it. I was half sick with horror and I tried not to think of it. Thereafter when I coughed I kept my mouth closed and coughed in my throat. I swallowed pneumonia salve at night in huge balls, and rubbed my chest with the stuff. I ate cough drops. The cold got better, the cough subsided, it has gone now—and the soreness has disappeared from my lung. But that is not the important thing; when this thing happened—which, I think, meant little—I . . . saw the sure destruction . . . of my dreams and my poetry

—and myself—and I couldn't face it. And then, almost in a miraculous fashion, I steadied, my mind cleared, and the old fear left me. . . . There is a new fatalism in my beliefs and I feel ready for whatever may come, but, whatever it be, I mean to express myself to the last ounce, meanwhile." From this time on Wolfe's letters often express this fear of his: they also often tell of bad colds with persistent fever, which may or may not have been symptomatic of the tubercular lesion found on his right lung in 1938.

Of course, a more immediate and pressing reason for the frenzy with which Wolfe threw himself into his work at Harvard was the knowledge that his mother had only consented to his going there "to try it for a year." His letters to her make painful reading. In them he apologizes constantly for his expenditures, gives would-be impressive accounts of his progress in his studies, reiterates his arguments that to return to Asheville would ruin his life, and repeatedly professes the great obligation he is under to her and Mr. Wolfe. "From now on I will practice strict economy. I have not been extravagant but I know I have wasted some money, which has worried me considerably, and which I will try to profit by. The rest of the family hold it against me, I know, that I have been to school so much and spent so much, and there is much truth in what they are saying about me. But . . . I will try to return home some day justified in the eyes of all." Or, "I am in a delicate, trying position before you and the family and I am trying to meet and solve the problem as honestly and courageously as I can. Of one thing I earnestly entreat you never to doubt: That is the sense of gratitude and loyalty I feel to you and Papa. That is stronger now in me than it ever was, stronger than, when as a little boy, we occupied the same room, stronger than when you took me on your trips to Florida and elsewhere. When I retire at night, when I wake in the morning, I am conscious of the weight of my gratitude; it is the spur that drives me on." From the first day when Wolfe arrived at Harvard to the final bitter one when he left there to become a teacher, his life was a constant struggle to win recognition as a dramatist and thus justify himself in his mother's eyes.

By November 1920 Wolfe was working on *The Mountains* in a state of "pure exaltation." The plot and characters were fictitious, but Wolfe could easily project himself into the leading character of the young Carolina doctor who returned from medical school to the mountains and reverted to the ways and feuds of his forebears. As he wrote somewhat pointedly to his mother, "The tragedy of the play is the tragedy of this fine young man fighting against conditions that overcome him and destroy him in the end. When you read this play, I hope you will be aware of this tragedy, and the tragedy of the lot of those poor oppressed mountain people, old and worn-out at middle age by their terrific hopeless battle with the mountain. . . . And always in the background of this story is the picture of those monsters, the Mountains, racing like hounds across the horizon, shutting these people eternally away from the world, hemming them in, guarding them, and finally killing them. I not only believe this is the truth but I know it . . ." On January 25, 1921, the play was given a trial performance in the Workshop rehearsal room before the members of the class. It was too long, too wordy, and too lacking in dramatic action, but Professor Baker promised Wolfe that, after revision, it would be given regular Workshop production before the public.

It was also at some time during this first year that Wolfe got the idea for the full-length play which he was to write and rewrite at intervals for the next four years, and which he called first *The Heirs* or *The Wasters*, then *The House*, and finally *Mannerhouse*, under which title it was published in 1948. Again, he chose a southern theme, which he described as follows in a letter to his mother: "I heard Papa tell one time about a family of aristocrats in W. N. Carolina who owned a vast quantity of Mountain land. . . . They owned 500,000 acres and sold it for 20¢ an acre to lumber people simply because they were impoverished by the War. They died in want. I am using this as a basis for my story." Again, too, Wolfe projected himself into the character of his hero: Eugene, the younger son, was a mouthpiece for his own views, and also, like himself at that time, was "a fellow who concealed his dark and tender poetry under the mask of a sardonic humor." Wolfe considered this play his best, but it was not as good and did not come as close to success as his other long play, *Welcome to Our City*, and by 1933 he was able to give the following correct evaluation of it in *Of Time and the River*: "It was a play called 'Mannerhouse,' a title which itself might reveal the whole nature of his error—and its subject was the decline and fall . . . of a proud old family of the Southern aristocracy . . . and the final acquisition of its proud estate, the grand old columned house that gave the play its name, by a vulgar, coarse and mean, but immensely able member of the rising 'lower class.' This theme—which . . . was probably influenced a good deal by *The Cherry Orchard* of Chekhov—was written in a somewhat mixed mood of romantic sentiment, Byronic irony, and sardonic realism. . . . The hero's final return 'years later,' a lonely and nameless wanderer, . . . to the old ruined house in which already the rasping note of the wrecker's crew was audible, was tempered by the romantic gallantry of Cyrano. . . . The final scene, in which the gigantic faithful negro slave . . . wraps his great arms around the rotting central column of the old ruined house, snaps it in two . . . and brings the whole ruined temple thundering down to bury his beloved master, his hated 'poor white' enemy the new owner, and himself beneath its ruins—was obviously a product of the Samson legend.[4] In spite of this, there was good stuff in the play, dramatic conflict, moving pageantry. The character of the hard, grasping but immensely able materialist of 'the lower class' . . . had been derived from the character of the youth's own uncle, William Pentland. . . . The speech of Porter was the plain, rich, pungent, earthy, strongly colored speech of his mother, of his uncle William Pentland, and of the Pentland tribe. . . . From this description, it will be seen how the young man's play was made up both of good and bad, how strongly it was marked by the varied influence of his reading and idolatry . . . and how he had also already begun to use some of the materials of his own life and feeling and experience . . . Thus the play . . . really did illustrate . . . the confused incertitude and the flashes of blind but powerful intuition, which mark the artist's early life here in America, and for this reason chiefly the play was interesting."

At the end of the college year in May 1921 Wolfe had completed with high grades three of the four courses required and had to take one more course and pass the elementary French and German examinations with a grade not lower than C. He took the French exam on May 20, but he received a mark of only 60 and thenceforth referred to this as "the accursed French requirement" until he passed it satisfactorily a year later.

With the closing of the term the members of the 47 Workshop and all the other people Wolfe had known at Harvard went home for the summer holidays. Professor Walker and his family moved out of the house on Buckingham Street, and Wolfe was left alone, having persuaded the new tenants to let him stay for a few days because of his French examination. In one of his pocket notebooks he describes his state of mind as follows: "An extraordinary thing happened. He suffered from one of those astounding suspensions of the will which were to be frequent in his life. . . . For six weeks he found himself powerless to do a single act which would relieve him from the limbo of this

[4] In the published edition the column is pulled down by Eugene himself.

terrible inaction in which his life was held. The year had ended—the Harvard year that was to have been the limit of his mother's gift. Now he found himself unable to move or act. Why could he not go home? His shoes in ragged holes and tatters—a feeling of horrible insecurity— the two old maids who fed him. . . ." He was abysmally lonely, completely broke, and very close to hungry, but he did not dare go home to Asheville for fear that he would not be allowed to come back to Harvard in the fall.

By July, after some inconclusive attempts to get a job as an iceman in Cambridge or as a stoker on a transatlantic liner, he had settled down in a new room at 42 Kirkland Street and had enrolled in summer school for a half course in English history. He continued his "merciless dissection of books" in Widener Library, began thinking of rewriting *The Mountains* as a three-act play, and probably also made his first rough notes for a play about his own family which finally, in 1929, became his novel *Look Homeward, Angel.* One fragment of this play shows the older children of a family dressing before a roaring fire in a living room similar to the Wolfes' at Woodfin Street: the father then brings down the youngest child, a little boy, and tells the others to make room for him before the fire.

All summer long Wolfe had intended to see Professor Baker's Pilgrim Tercentenary Pageant in Plymouth, but with his customary obliviousness to the passage of time, he had put it off until the day of the last performance, when he hastily persuaded Louis Hunter, a graduate student in history, to hitchhike to Plymouth with him. The two boys had difficulty in getting rides, however, and finally had to sprint for several miles along a dusty road to catch the last train for Plymouth at a country way station. Wolfe, with his long hair and long legs flying, easily outdistanced Hunter and gave the natives quite a start: one farmer dropped his hoe and shouted after him: "Hey there! Slow down a bit and give the little feller a chance!"[5] At any rate, they reached Plymouth in time for the last performance of the pageant, and Wolfe was able to write to Baker that he had seen it and "was greatly thrilled by it."

Meanwhile, after the close of summer school in August, Wolfe had become more desperately homesick, but also more frantically anxious lest his parents should refuse to let him spend another year at Harvard.

[5] The author is indebted for this anecdote to Louis C. Hunter, who is now on the faculties of the Industrial College of the Armed Forces and the American University in Washington, D.C.

In September he wrote to Mrs. Roberts: "I want to go home. I've *got* to go somewhere, but I'm afraid they won't want me to come back next year and I've got to do that also." He began besieging his mother with letters, but she was evidently too busy with the Old Kentucky Home to answer. Finally, on September 19, he wrote to her again: "I have waited from day to day for some answer to my special delivery letter. Your last letter is five weeks old. In three and a half months I have heard twice from you. . . . I am deeply sensible of my obligation to you and of your generosity but how am I to interpret your failure to write me? . . . If the time has come for me to go out on my own, so be it, but please try not to treat me with the indifference while I am alone and far away that has characterized your correspondence, or lack of it, for the last year. . . . You didn't want me at home, you said nothing about my returning and I shall see that your desires and those of the family are satisfied. . . . I am being put out of my room here Thursday—it is leased for next year. I have nowhere to go. I have heard nothing from you. You are the only one with whom I can discuss my plans and you have denied me even that connection. I cannot, I will not write any more. I am too deeply stirred, too grieved and disillusioned to add anything to what I have written." Just as the fall term was about to start he heard from her: she had taken Mr. Wolfe to Johns Hopkins for more radium treatments and suggested that Tom come and meet them there. He went immediately to Baltimore, spent two weeks with his parents, and returned triumphant, although late, to enroll at Harvard for another year.

IV

F O R his second year at Harvard, Wolfe signed up for a course with Professor Lowes on the literature of the Renaissance and for one on the drama in England with Professor A. N. Murray. However, the thing on which his life and hopes were centered was the advanced course in the 47 Workshop. On October 21 and 22 *The Mountains* was produced at Radcliffe's Agassiz Theatre with two other one-act plays by members of the Workshop, but it was not at all successful. Wolfe spent hours in composing angry retorts to the criticisms of it written, in accordance with Workshop custom, by the audience. Moreover, even thirteen years later, he bitterly described his disillusionment about it to a would-be writer who had asked him for advice: "Although the play read well in class, it was a complete and dismal failure when it was put on. No one thought it was any good, and most people took pains to tell me so. It was a very desperate occasion for me. It seemed to me that my whole life and future depended upon it, and in this state of mind I went to see a man on whose judgment, honesty and critical ability I relied to the utmost. I asked him what he thought of my abilities as a writer, and if he thought I would ever succeed in doing the thing I most wanted to do; and although he tried at first, out of the kindness of his heart, to evade the issue, he finally told me point-blank that he did not think I would ever become a writer and that he thought my abilities were critical rather than creative and therefore advised me to devote my time to graduate study in the University, leading to a Ph.D. degree and a position in the teaching profession. . . . I will never forget the almost inconceivable anguish and despair that his words caused me."[1]

This man "on whose judgment, honesty and critical ability" Wolfe "relied to the utmost" was probably an older member of the Workshop who had befriended Wolfe at Baker's request. A passage in one of Wolfe's notebooks remarks on the "generous enthusiasm" of both this friend and Baker when he first read his play to them, but then goes on

[1] From Wolfe's letter of November 18, 1934, to Elizabeth Cattelle.

to say: "But how they turn on you when it fails—the coldness and neglect." In his supersensitivity and extreme depression, he evidently misinterpreted both men's attitudes. At any rate, if this anonymous friend did advise Wolfe to become a teacher—and there is serious doubt that he actually did—he was certainly not the first to broach the subject. Wolfe probably suggested it himself, since he had been worrying about the eventual necessity of teaching ever since he had graduated from the University of North Carolina. Moreover, it had been urged upon him during his first Harvard year by Professor Lowes, who had highly praised his thesis on "The Supernatural in the Poetry and Philosophy of Coleridge" and had said (according to what Wolfe wrote his mother) that "it was one in a thousand, and that I ought to lose no time in completing my training for teaching." But to Wolfe, becoming a teacher meant failure in the one thing his entire life was set upon— to be a dramatist. So he fought against it constantly for the next two years, until economic necessity finally forced him to admit defeat.

It may seem strange that after the failure of the one-act version of *The Mountains* Wolfe spent a good part of his second year at Harvard in expanding it into a three-act play. But that was typical of him: he never was satisfied with a thing until he had achieved fullness of expression: he always felt that if he could only "get it all in" and "say everything he had to say," the work he was doing would be good. By midyears he had written a prologue and two new acts and had also completed all the necessary work for his M.A. except for passing the elementary French examination with a sufficiently high grade. However, he brooded constantly over the failure of *The Mountains* and the possibility that Baker thought he was "no good." His longed-for success as a dramatist seemed more remote than when he had first come to Harvard; the second year that he had wrung from his reluctant mother was now drawing to a close; and the necessity of earning his living as a teacher became more inevitable every day.

On March 24, in desperation, he filed with the Harvard Appointment Office an application for a position as a teacher of English, preferably at a college in the North or Middle West. It was probably soon after this that he wrote to Baker to notify him of his withdrawal from the Workshop, saying, "The conviction has grown on me that I shall never express myself dramatically. I am therefore ending the agony by the shortest way." However, he may never have sent this note to Baker but simply written it in a fit of deep despondency to blow off steam. If he did actually send it, Baker must have given him the sympathy he so badly wanted, because he continued in the Workshop in a final desperate burst of hope. From then until the end of the spring term he was given much encouragement. Baker read his prologue to the long version of *The Mountains* to the class and, according to what Wolfe wrote his mother, "pronounced it the best prolog ever written here."[2] He urged Wolfe to complete the third act of *The Mountains* and to finish *The Heirs* for the annual climax of the Workshop course, when the New York producer Richard Herndon awarded to the best students' play the Belmont Prize of a $500 cash award and a guarantee of production in New York. Baker also wrote a letter, recommending Wolfe, to be used by the Harvard Appointment Office in finding him a job. This letter gives a hint of the conflict that was to develop between him and Wolfe, but on the whole it is very flattering: Mr. Wolfe is "one of the promising students in English 47A, the advanced course in playwriting. Whether he will be a successful playwright some day depends, I think, entirely upon himself. He is intelligent, ambitious and well-equipped. I much want him to return for special work another year."

Meanwhile the Appointment Office was working on Wolfe's application for a position as a teacher. At the suggestion of Miss Louisa McCrady, the head of that office, he applied to the University College of Arts and Sciences of New York University, but failed to get employment.

Then, on May 23, he applied to Northwestern University and shortly afterward was offered an instructorship in the English Department there. He now was forced to come to a decision: if he refused the offer he might have great difficulty in getting another later, but if he accepted he would have failed in the one thing on which his heart was set. Characteristically, he postponed making up his mind: by June 19 he still had failed to write Northwestern in answer to their offer. Then, late at night, while he was reading in his room, a telegram arrived. His father was dying: he must come home at once.

An hour later he was on the train for New York, where before going on to Asheville he mailed a hasty postcard to Miss McCrady asking her to write Northwestern and "explain the circumstances." "In this way," he says in *Of Time and the River*, "he left Cambridge and a life he had known for two years; instantly re-called, drawn back by the hand of death into the immediacy of a former life that had grown strange as dreams. That year he had been informed of his eligibility for

[2] In *Thomas Wolfe's Letters to His Mother* this letter is erroneously dated May 16, 1921 instead of 1922.

the Master's degree . . . and, at the time he had received the telegram, he had been waiting for the formal exercises at which he would receive the degree—a wait prompted more by his total indecision as to his future purpose than by any other cause. Now, with explosive suddenness, his purpose had been shaped, decided for him, and with the old feeling of groping bewilderment, he surveyed the history of the last two years and wondered why he had come, . . . toward what blind goal he had been tending: all that he had to 'show' for these years of fury, struggle, homelessness and hunger was an academic distinction which he had not aimed at, and on which he placed small value."

Meanwhile, at midnight, Mr. Wolfe had died.

When Tom's train stopped at Morganton and he bought a copy of the early edition of the Asheville paper, the announcement of his father's death stared up at him from the printed page. He got off at Biltmore Station on the outskirts of Asheville and ran weeping along the platform to Mabel, saying, "You don't have to tell me. I read it in the paper."

In the days immediately following, Tom heard from Mabel and his mother many times the story of his father's death, which later became the finest and most moving section in *Of Time and the River*. He had always worshiped him and now, in his grief and loss, he intensified "the search for a father," which was one of the dominant themes of his work and life. In *Of Time and the River* he says: "His father was dead, and now it seemed to him that he had never found him. His father was dead, and yet he sought him everywhere, and could not believe that he was dead, and was sure that he would find him. . . . He thought he heard his great voice ringing in the street again, and that he would see him striding toward him across the Square with his gaunt earth-devouring stride, or find him waiting every time he turned the corner, or lunging toward the house bearing the tremendous provender of his food and meat, bringing to them all the deathless security of his strength and power and passion, bringing to them all again the roaring message of his fires that shook the fire-full chimney throat with their terrific blast, giving to them all again the exultant knowledge that the good days, the magic days, the golden weather of their lives would come again . . . 'Come to us, Father, in the watches of the night, come to us as you always came, bringing to us the invincible sustenance of your strength, the limitless treasure of your bounty, the tremendous structure of your life that will shape all lost and broken things on earth again into a golden pattern of exultancy and joy. Come to us, Father, while the winds howl in the darkness . . . For we are ruined, lost, and broken if you do not come, and our lives, like rotten chips, are whirled about us onward in darkness to the sea.'"

In his will Mr. Wolfe had left five thousand dollars to each of his five children, and the rest of his estate to Mrs. Wolfe. However, the expenses of his seven-year illness had been such a drain upon his savings that when he died, his estate was found to amount to only an approximate eleven thousand dollars in Liberty Bonds and cash. His executors, Fred Wolfe and Ralph Wheaton, Mabel's husband, were at a loss as to what to do, but they finally made a settlement, which is best described in an exchange of letters between Tom and Fred in January 1938:

"Just to get the matter straight for the record here and now about what happened, so far as I was concerned, in its connection to Papa's estate, the facts are these," Tom wrote to Fred on January 22 of that year. "When I was graduated from Chapel Hill in 1920, I was nineteen years old. As you know, I decided then to go to Harvard and do graduate work. It was my intention to go to Harvard for a year, but as it eventually turned out I stayed three. Papa, of course, was still alive in 1920, but very feeble and very ill, and no longer able to take an active interest in what was going on around him. When I decided to go to Harvard I went to Mama and talked to her about it. We all knew, even at that time, that Papa had made a will, and that according to the terms of the will each of the children was to receive the sum of five thousand dollars, and that the remainder of the estate would go to Mama. I proposed to her, as I remember it, that I be allowed to go to Harvard for a year, and that the expenses of this year at Harvard should be deducted from my share in the estate. At the time, I believe that the matter rested there, but, as you know, I remained at Harvard for three years instead of one. Papa died in 1922: When the question of settlement finally came up, somewhere around 1923, which was my last year at Harvard, or shortly after that, it was proposed to me that I cancel any claim I had in the estate in recognition of the expenses of my three years. To this I readily agreed, and for that matter, have never made any objection to that arrangement since. But Mama did object. She said, as I recall it, that it was fair to deduct the expenses of one year from my share, but that she had herself agreed to bear the expense of the additional two years, and that she did not think it was fair to charge me the whole amount.

"I certainly do remember signing a document at about this period which you and Ralph gave me in your capacity as executors to the estate and that document, as I remember it, was a release to the estate of my share in the inheritance. . . .

"Now, Fred, I've gone into all this just to go upon the record, and to make my own part in the whole business as clear as I can. I know you understand that I make absolutely no claim to anything besides what I have received. But this is what happened. From a technical point of view, I suppose I really did not receive a full share in the estate. But I always consider that I actually did, since the help I received at Harvard during the three years I was there was approximately equivalent to what a full share would have been."

To this, Fred answered on January 26: "I have read your letter carefully. Your statements are all correct about the papers signed etc. with the exception that you are wrong, that the signing of said paper signed away your right to your supposed inheritance. Your paper was merely acknowledgment of having received $5000 cash on account by terms of will, but not 'all your inheritance.' At that time I also signed one for $5000. I beat you by $240. This amount was left, I got it. I lacked $4760 of getting $5000. You lacked $5000 of getting $5000. It all was merely the juggling of two inexperienced people, Ralph and I, to attempt to make $11,000 in cash and Liberty Bonds cover the grounds in terms of $25,000 (5 x $5000) as set forth by the will."

However, according to Fred Wolfe's recollection, Mrs. Wolfe then gave Tom her definite promise to pay for his longed-for third year with the 47 Workshop. He had never answered Northwestern University in either acceptance or refusal of their offer of a teaching job, but finally, on August 26, he wrote to Miss McCrady of the Harvard Appointment Office, apologizing for his delay and saying: "My finances are now in such a condition as will permit me to return for another year to Harvard. Professor Baker has been so unfailingly kind and encouraging that I believe this extra year which is now made possible will be of the utmost importance to me."

Late in September 1922 he went back to Cambridge, got a room at 21 Trowbridge Street, and flung himself into writing for the Workshop with the exuberance that was typical of him. In one of his notebooks he describes this last year as follows: "I lived in a kind of dream . . . —in a radiance—drunken with joy and with power." According to the recollection of William E. Harris, who was a member of the 47 Workshop at this time, Wolfe began the year by submitting to Professor Baker the first acts of six different plays. For the most part, these seem to have been expressions of abstract ideas rather than truly dramatic material, but he finally hit upon a good strong subject and began his play *Niggertown*, which was later retitled *Welcome to Our City*.

The idea for this play had first come to him during the summer in Asheville. In a letter to Mrs. Roberts, written in early September, he said: "Coming home this last time I have gathered enough additional material to write a new play—the second fusillade of the battle. . . . There is a spirit of world-old evil that broods about us . . . Greed, greed, greed—deliberate, crafty, motivated—masking under the guise of civic associations for municipal betterment. . . . The knave, the toady, and the hog-rich flourish. There are three ways, and only three, to gain distinction: (1) Money, (2) more money, (3) a great deal of money. And the manner of getting it is immaterial."

Welcome to Our City is by far the best play Wolfe ever wrote, and it came much closer to success than any of the others. Its central incident concerns the efforts of a group of real-estate men to improve the city by reclaiming from the Negroes a certain section of it, including a fine old house owned by a Negro doctor named Johnson. The town becomes bitterly divided on this issue and finally, when the Negroes resist eviction, a race riot breaks out in which Johnson is killed and the Negroes' houses set on fire.

However, Wolfe did not limit himself to this one central theme, but tried to represent the life of the entire town and all the local manifestations of "the booster spirit." When various critics pointed out that the play was too diffuse, he defended it vehemently. To his cousin Elaine Westall Gould he wrote: "I want to impress the fact that the play is not about any problem—least of all about the negro problem. . . . My play is concerned with giving a picture about a certain section of life, a certain civilization, a certain society. I am content with nothing but the whole picture, I am concerned with nothing else." And to Professor Baker: "I would be sorry to think that a close eye on the relevancy, the direct bearing of each scene and incident on the main problem, that of the negro, would conceal from you the fact that I knew what I wanted to do from the beginning to the end. . . . Will you please remember this: a play about the negro, a play in which each scene bore directly upon the negro, a play in which the negro was kept ever before you, might be a better play: it would not be the play I started to write. . . . I have written this play with thirty-odd *named* characters because it required it, not because I didn't know how to save paint. Some day I'm going to write a play with fifty, eighty, a hundred people—a whole town, a whole race, a whole epoch—for my soul's ease and comfort." In a way, both Wolfe's critics and Wolfe himself were right: the play was much too sprawling and unwieldy, but the story of the Negro, Johnson, seems not clearly focused or defined, whereas the satiric description of the town and its booster spirit is strong, real, salty, and original. In some ways it is reminiscent of Wolfe's Chapel Hill burlesques: in others, it foreshadows his more mature satire, such as "Boom Town" and other sections of *You Can't Go Home Again*.

By the middle of January he had written a complete rough draft of *Welcome to Our City* and read it to the Workshop class. By the end of spring vacation he wrote to an unidentified friend, who perhaps was William Polk: "I am getting my leviathan of a ten scene, three hour play in shape. . . . Poor dear Professor Baker will never live and learn as regards me. He's going to try it again: this time in the last production of the year, barely three weeks off." Rehearsals began on April 23 but progressed with the greatest difficulty and confusion. Wolfe had been asked by Baker to make some cuts and changes in the play and had agreed to do so, but either because he would and could not cut, or because he was characteristically unconscious of the passage of time, he had failed to produce the revised script by as late as April 18. As Professor Baker's secretary wrote to him, "Absolutely nothing makes an impression upon him, threats, tears of rage, or smiles of kindness." Finally Professor Baker cut the play himself, and they began rehearsals of it, but whenever the actors came for the first time to a section which had been cut, poor Wolfe would begin "weaving back and forth in his chair like a polar bear suffering from the heat,"[3] and finally losing control of himself despite his desperate efforts not to, would leap to his feet with a roar of agony and dash out into the night. Half an hour later he would reappear as if nothing had happened, but every time the actors struck another cut, he would be off again. It is said by some of his fellow members in the Workshop that he occasionally lost his temper entirely and threatened to withdraw the play, but if he did so, it must have been under extreme duress. He knew quite well that this production of *Welcome to Our City* was his one big chance—and probably his last—of becoming a successful dramatist, and he was desperately anxious about its success. "Mama: get down and pray for me," he wrote to Mrs. Wolfe on March 31. "Prof. Baker is having Richard Herndon, the New York producer, up here to see the play when it goes on. Of

[3] The story of Wolfe's outbursts is well known among his fellow members in the 47 Workshop. However, the author is indebted for the polar-bear simile to Philip W. Barber's "Tom Wolfe Writes a Play," in the May 1958 issue of *Harper's Magazine*.

course this means nothing more than that he's sufficiently interested to come and look it over with an eye to New York production. As I may have told you Mr. Herndon is the man who gives the prize every year for the best play written in the Workshop. The prize is small, $500, but it carries with it a contract for a New York production within six months. . . . I try not to build my hopes too high, but I can't help feeling I've more than a good chance."

But as the weeks dragged on and it became more and more evident, even to Wolfe, that the play was too unwieldy, his hopes sank, and in one of his diarylike passages, written just before the first performance, he recorded his premonition of its failure. "Friday, May 11, at 5:55 in the afternoon, with the first Workshop performance of my play less than two and one-quarter hours distant, I want to record here, for my personal satisfaction, my belief that the play which I have written has no better show than that of the snowball in the infernal regions. I can only hope that the cast and producing organization will give a performance superlatively better than any they have previously given. And even then? And even then?? 'Hope springs eternal'—but let me resolutely abandon it now and henceforth."

His fears were justified. The play had, on his insistence, a cast of forty-four people, of whom thirty-one had speaking parts. It called for seven changes of scene, and these were very slow in being made: the performance dragged on and on from 8 P.M. till midnight and left the audience exhausted. The crowning defeat came when Richard Herndon failed to select *Welcome to Our City* for the Belmont Prize, but chose instead another Workshop play, *Nancy Ann*, by Dorothy Kuhns (now Dorothy Kuhns Heyward).

Nevertheless, Professor Baker had great faith in *Welcome to Our City* and in Wolfe. He took him to his summer home at Silver Lake, New Hampshire, for the weekend immediately after the performance and told him (according to what Wolfe wrote his mother) that "he thought it had a much better chance of success than *The Adding Machine*—a play, like mine, written in scenes, which went off in New York last week after 3 months' run." The following week Baker went to New York and personally recommended *Welcome to Our City* to the Theatre Guild, who wrote to Wolfe asking if they could read it. Wolfe's hopes soared again: he stayed in Cambridge for the summer and revised the play before submitting it to the Guild. His intention was to cut it down "to the usual two and a half hours before I send it to them," but when he got to work on it he seems to have succumbed to the temptation to lengthen it instead, by restoring the cuts which Baker had made. Finally, in late August, he took the revised play to New York, where he had it retyped, and submitted it to the Guild.

For the next four months Wolfe was on tenterhooks, waiting for a decision from the Guild. On August 31 he wrote to his mother: "Everything I have is staked on this play . . . I dare not think of failure. What I want—what would satisfy me—seems so little. If my play were not wonderful—if it were put on and ran for only six or eight weeks—it would be enough to start me." In the meanwhile, he had no fixed living place, no money, and no plans. He wandered feverishly back and forth, first visiting various friends in and around New York, then going to Henry Fisk Carlton's house in New Hampshire, then back to New York again, then home to Asheville and on to his sister Effie's in Anderson, South Carolina. Finally, in early November, he came back to New York, where he shared an apartment at 439 West 123rd Street with Lacey Meredith and William Folger, two college friends from Chapel Hill, and had a temporary job soliciting contributions from University of North Carolina alumni for the completion of the Graham Memorial building there. In *Of Time and the River* he says that the Theatre Guild declined his play in October, when he was still in Asheville, but this does not seem to have been true, although the succeeding episode in that novel, in which Eugene is arrested for drunkenness on his way to Anderson, was evidently based on fact. The Theatre Guild's decision was not given him until late November or early December and was not an outright refusal of the play, but a request for its revision and resubmission to them.

In a letter written to his mother from New York at Christmas time Wolfe describes his conference with Courtenay Lemon and Lawrence Langner of the Guild as follows: "The Guild has returned my play— but they first told me I was the best man the Workshop had yet turned out and the coming young man in the theatre. This was their playreader, Lemon. . . . He told me . . . that Langner . . . was 'crazy about my play' and wanted to see me . . . He called Langner and *he* suggested that I come right up. . . . I talked to him two hours. . . . The sum total was this: If I would . . . work a week on the play— cutting it down thirty minutes, and from ten scenes to eight, and 'tightening' it up—that is, making the main thread of the story . . . more plain in every scene—he would . . . put it before the Guild for me, and if they couldn't produce it this season, he knew other producers here that he felt would . . . give it production. Well, I will take one more chance and give him what he wants, in spite of the fact that Professor Baker will throw up his hands and say that I have 'prostituted my art,' and so on, when I see him. Well, 'my art' has kept me ragged, and driven me half mad;—I will see now if prostitution can put a few decent garments on my back and keep me housed."

In this determined state of mind Tom went back to Cambridge and told Baker of his plans. Baker protested much in the way Wolfe had prophesied he would, and Wolfe answered that a man must eat. He tried to revise the play to meet Langner's requirements, but again only ended by making it still longer!

But even before he had left New York, Wolfe had come to the final, desperate realization that he must be a teacher. In the letter written from there to his mother he says: "This is what I have decided to do. Several of my old Harvard friends are here in New York—one, in particular—a young man named Dow[4]—is an instructor here at New York University—an instructor in English. He informed me recently that they would need a new man the second semester . . . I'm going up to Cambridge and get the Harvard Teachers' Bureau—which once before, you may remember, got me a job at Northwestern, to send all my letters of recommendation, and my scholastic records, and so on, to N.Y.U." On January 10, 1924, Wolfe applied to Professor Homer A. Watt, chairman of the English Department at the Washington Square College of New York University, and was offered an assistant-instructorship in English there, at a yearly salary of $1800. He went to New York for a brief interview, returned to Cambridge, and wired his acceptance of the job from there on January 21. On February 1 he reported for the beginning of the spring term at New York University.

He never said good-by to Baker or told him of his decision. He had tried to make him into a god, a father, "the great man, the prophet, the infinitely wise and strong and gentle spirit who knew all, had seen all, could solve all problems by a word, release us of all the anguish, grief and error of our lives." But gradually, painfully, he had come to realize that Baker was fallible and mortal.

In a letter written soon after this to Mrs. Roberts he said: "I began to understand—a bitter draught it was—that Professor Baker was an excellent friend, a true critic, but a bad counsellor. I knew that, from this time on, the disposition of my life was mainly in my own hands." And in his disillusionment, he turned against Baker with great bitterness. In the unpublished portion of Of Time and the River which at

[4] Robert Bruce Dow was an instructor in English at the University College of New York University at this time. He is now associate professor of English at the Washington Square College and assistant director of admissions.

first described his idolatry of Baker, he wrote: "And then I saw that half the man was sawdust—that he was lacking in warmth, in greatness and humanity. He knew a great deal and understood almost nothing. He was unable to see the genuine quality in a man, and he lavished his benefits on buffoons, aesthetes, feeble weaklings, and let most of the good people—the people with a spark of life and talent—go to hell." The "joy and power" of the last Harvard year had turned to ashes in Wolfe's mouth, and smarting with defeat and disillusionment, he entered "the odious bondage of teaching," which was to last for six long years.

V

Wolfe's first year at New York University was probably the most miserable and most difficult he ever spent. In the speech he delivered at Purdue in 1938 he explains the reasons why:

"I left Harvard and for several years I lived and worked in New York, supporting my body by teaching school in the daytime, and my soul by writing plays at night. During this time I cannot say that things got better with me in my relation to my work and to the world. If anything, I think I became more truculent, for I was up against it now—I no longer had the soothing assurance of support from home, or the comforting agreements of sophisticated colleagues in the Harvard Yard. I was living all alone in the big city, earning my living, and trying to make my own way; and for the first time in my life, as far as my work and my ambitions were concerned, I was right up against it. In blunt phrase, I had to 'put up or shut up'—not only to justify myself in the eyes of the world, but to justify myself in my own belief and faith and conviction and self-respect. That is certainly a hard time in the life of any young man—particularly of any young man who is trying to create. . . . The man is right up against the naked facts of self and work—there is nothing beyond himself that can help him, his strength is in himself, and he has to pull it from himself; and if he cannot, there is no other hope for him. But it does explain also a good deal of the truculence and the arrogance of youth; its furious distemper, its conflict with the world.

"With me, the period was a time of stress and torment, for I had now committed myself utterly—there was no going back, no compromise, and my position was a desperate one. The result was I had pulled up my roots bodily; broken almost utterly away from my old life— from my family, my native town, my earlier associations—there was nothing for me now except myself and work. I suppose the almost religious belief I have in work may date from just this period; for I think it was the fact that I could work that saved me. The fact also was, I wanted to work, and felt that I had work to do; and I think that was also a fact of great importance. . . . So that period, although still a confused and tormented one, and in some respects a mistaken one, was not by any means a wasted one; for in that time, I began to learn the great necessity of work."

However, during at least his first year at the university Wolfe was able to do very little work: the hated job of teaching took up all his time and strength. In his letter of application for employment to Professor Watt he had made no secret of the fact that writing plays was the one and only thing he wanted to do, saying:

"I have had no experience as a teacher. It is only fair to tell you that my interests are centred in the drama, and that someday I hope to write successfully for the theatre and to do nothing but that. My play is at present in the hands of a producer in New York but, even in the fortunate event of its acceptance, I feel the necessity of finding immediate employment.

"I am twenty-three years old and a native of Asheville, North Carolina. I do not know what impression of maturity my appearance may convey but it is hardly in excess of my age. In addition, my height is four or five inches over six feet, producing an effect on a stranger that is sometimes startling. I think you should know so much in advance, as the consideration may justly enter into any estimates of my qualifications.

"If New York University feels justified in offering me employment as an instructor in English, and if I am satisfied with the offer, I promise to give the most faithful and efficient service of which I am capable."

The disarming frankness of this letter had made a favorable impression on Professor Watt, which he later described in an unfinished recollection about Wolfe, on which he was working shortly before his death:

"Certain elements in his letter struck me at once. It was direct, it was frank, it was honest. This Thomas Wolfe—whoever he was—did not try to conceal his inexperience as a teacher. He did not even pretend that he wanted to make teaching a lifelong profession but asserted almost bluntly that his chief goal was to write successful plays. He showed a penetrating awareness that if he were to join a college department of English his personal appearance might very 'justly enter into any estimates' of his qualifications. His own consciousness of his unusual stature I came to know later as a very sensitive point with him.

"I was pleased by his promise at the end of his letter that, if appointed, he would 'give the most faithful and efficient service' of which he was capable. Here the applicant did not 'protest too much,' and his assertion was simple and rang true. When Tom finally left the department just six years after he made this promise, I could agree with him that not once had he failed to carry out his initial pledge."[1]

In this way Wolfe got off to a good start with his superiors, which lasted during his entire time at New York University. Again and again, during those six years, he wrote to Professor Watt with almost shocking frankness that he would accept re-employment if he failed to sell his play, or later, his novel; and again and again, both Professor Watt and his associate, Professor James B. Munn, accepted this with remarkable sympathy and forbearance. However, the Washington Square branch of New York University was growing like Jack's mythical beanstalk at this time, and Wolfe, like every other instructor there, was forced to carry a heavy teaching load. In the three sections in Elementary Composition which he taught during that first year, he had a hundred and four students, which, in the words of the present dean of New York University and chairman of the English Department, was "a tremendous load involving about twenty-six hours a week of theme reading. . . . Unless he cut corners, he had a 54-hour week in prospect to fulfill his obligation to the College, and much less time than he anticipated for writing."[2] For an older, more experienced man, this would have been none too easy, but for Wolfe, on top of the necessity of adjusting his entire life, it was almost unbearable.

In *Of Time and the River* he describes the agonies he went through: "Although his position as instructor had been given to him in one of the usual ways, through the recommendation of the teachers' bureau at Harvard University, and the letters of some of the professors there, he was tortured constantly by the thought of his inadequacy and ignorance, and by the horrible fear that his incompetence would be discovered and that one day he would be suddenly, peremptorily, ruinously, and disgracefully discharged. At night, when he went to bed in his little cell at the cheap little hotel nearby where he lived, the thought of the class he had to meet the next day fed at his heart and bowels with cold poisonous mouths of fear, and as the hour for a class drew nigh he would begin to shake and tremble as if he had an ague; . . . the successive stages of a journey to . . . the electric chair . . . Thus, while a thousand . . . images of disgrace and terror swarmed

[1] From "Tom Wolfe, Teacher," an unfinished article by Homer A. Watt.
[2] From *Thomas Wolfe at Washington Square*, edited by Thomas Clark Pollock and Oscar Cargill, New York University Press, 1954.

through his mind, he stood before each class on a small raised platform, . . . staring at the faces that seethed and swarmed below him, . . . nauseous, and sick, and palsied, left only with something clear and small and shining at the bottom of his mind, one pure small note of conviction and belief . . . Then, in a voice that was remote, unreal, and hollow in his throat and ears, he would attempt to silence them, he would begin to speak to them, and one by one, each in his accustomed place he would see the dark, ugly, grinning faces in their seats below him . . . And then, faint and far, . . . fantastic and unreal at first . . . , the old words, the undying words, the deathless bird-song in the city street returned, and he spoke to them again out of the lips of Herrick, Donne, and Shakespeare, of all the things that never change, of all the things that would abide forever. . . .

"Never before had Eugene been driven through desperation to such exhausting intensities of work: night by night he sweated blood over great stacks and sheaves of their dull, careless, trivial papers—he read, re-read, and triple-read them, putting in all commas, colons, periods, correcting all faults of spelling, grammar, punctuation that he knew, writing long, laborious comments and criticisms on the back and rising suddenly out of a haunted tortured sleep to change a grade. . . .

"Under the furious goad of desperation, a fear of failure and disgrace, a sense of loneliness and desolation, and a grim determination to go down into the dust of ruin only when he could no longer lift a hand or draw a breath, he learned his job, and found his life again, he did the labor of a titan, the flesh wasted from his bones, he became a mad, driven zealot, but he was a good teacher, and the day came when he knew he need no longer draw his breath in fear or shame, that he had paid his way and earned his wage and could meet them eye to eye. He took those swarthy swarming classes and looted his life clean for them: he bent over them, prayed, sweated, and exhorted like a prophet, a poet, and a priest—he poured upon them the whole deposit of his living, feeling, reading, the whole store of poetry, passion and belief . . ."

The fact that Wolfe did what he describes here has been attested to by several of his pupils, although some of his fellow instructors felt that he read aloud too much. A. Gerald Doyle, who was in his class in literature in 1929–30, says: "We were reading aloud, a stanza per pupil from 'St. Agnes' Eve,' and it was my lot to read the lovely one about the 'silver, snarling trumpets 'gan to chide.' I sensed the beauty of the words and the clangor of the words cued by the opening door, but

I was too timid to 'read with expression.' He shook his head impatiently and re-read the stanza as it should be read, with hot and cadenced vigor. It was a lasting lesson in poetry. Wolfe was by long odds the most interesting instructor I ever had at NYU. The impact of the man was terrific. He often appeared to be bored with the prosiness of the syllabus, and bored with the members of the class, too. But he made the great writers live when they challenged his imagination."[3]

Theodore G. Ehrsam, who was a student in Wolfe's English 35-36 in 1927–28, is not quite as complimentary: "When he spoke to the class on poetry, for instance, . . . whether about *Beowulf* or Thomas Hardy's 'Hap,' he seemed to be entranced, intrigued with the beauty of language, of literature, of love. Up and down the front of the long room would he stride in long, jerky steps, holding the bulky volume in one of his huge hands while he recited poetry; though he held the book open, he rarely had to read, for many of the poems he knew by heart. . . . On some days in class, Mr. Wolfe would be more than usually enthusiastic. Then his eyes would shine, his cheeks would flush, his voice would quiver with emotion, his head would toss almost wildly in emphasis of his words and his lower lip would, in his sheer excitement, become flecked with bits of foamy white saliva. At moments like these, when he wasn't looking directly at us, a few of us students would nod sagely to each other, wink, and whisper, in our crude lack of understanding. 'He's off again on another one of his sprees!' But we didn't dare interrupt his almost magical flow of words; we had an uncomfortable feeling that inspiration of some sort had seized hold of him, though we were never articulate enough to say this to each other."[4]

And James Mandel, who was a student in Dean Munn's Bible course, for which Wolfe read and corrected papers in 1929–30, and who was employed by Wolfe to type a good deal of *Look Homeward, Angel,* says: "Teaching composition and an appreciation of literature to the pre-meds, pre-dents, and pre-laws at the Square was no easy task for any teacher; but for Wolfe the job was almost an impossible one. He was too conscientious about his work. He tried to make every one of his students respond to the beauty of a Shelley, but how could he when they were thinking of the rats they had just dissected, or the ether they were going to prepare in the organic chemistry lab the next hour?

[3] From a letter written by Doyle to Professor Oscar Cargill, reprinted in the "Memorabilia" section of *Thomas Wolfe at Washington Square.*

[4] From "I Knew Thomas Wolfe," in *Fact Digest* V, reprinted in *Thomas Wolfe at Washington Square.*

This period for them was the time to relax. Wolfe fought to gain their interest. He fumed and sputtered. He shouted at them to stop talking. He read poetry against a wall of constant murmur. He grew hoarse in a period and they wondered how long his voice would last under the strain. At the end of the lesson, he would leave the room perspiring, exhausted. Viewed from the present, it is remarkable that he did not become discouraged and resign his position at the college before he had achieved his success as a writer. But he stubbornly persisted in his efforts to train his students to appreciate a poem or an essay; and by the end of the term, in fairness to him, it must be said that he had succeeded to a large extent where a more experienced teacher might have failed. . . .

"It may be the popular notion that Wolfe was so much interested in his writing that he neglected much of his work at the school. Nothing could be further from the truth. Though he dreaded the mountains of compositions he had to read each week, he could not rest before he had conscientiously corrected each theme. He felt that it was work worth doing. He sympathized with the creative agonies of his students; he was sorry for the difficulties many of them experienced in expressing themselves. He hurled himself into the job of correcting papers because he honestly realized that it was something which should and must be done. Certainly, he was not a shirker. Tom would go through each theme reading every word. He would underline every poorly chosen phrase, insert punctuation marks, remove others. He became so efficient in judging themes that he could determine the sex of the writer, for '. . . a girl's paper is easily recognized by its detailed punctuation and its careful wording . . . the man is careless, but it is from him that one expects flashes of strength and individuality.'

"On the back of every theme he marked, Tom wrote a long and critical essay where the average instructor would have merely indicated the grade and a word of damnation or praise. Critics have thought Wolfe incapable of rendering judgment on a piece of writing, but these numerous and extensive criticisms which he wrote on every composition seem to prove otherwise. He could not leave a paper before he had dissected every creative impulse of the writer."[5]

[5] From "Thomas Wolfe, a Reminiscence," by James Mandel, in the "Memorabilia" section of *Thomas Wolfe at Washington Square*. At the conclusion of his reminiscence Mandel tells an anecdote that is very characteristic of Wolfe. "He was extremely sensitive about his awkwardly long body. . . . One day, after I had told him of the torture I had suffered as a youth because of my lame leg, he revealed how touchy he was about his own incongruous figure.

During his first few weeks at N.Y.U., Wolfe had reported hopefully to his mother that "there is some time to write" and "I have had very little time to write so far—but I have written a little." But by early April he realized what he was up against and wrote to her: "You can't serve two masters; I have elected to serve one, and I must see it through. . . . My life is like water which has passed the mill; it turns no wheel. . . . The great play is yet unwritten; the great novel beats with futile hands against the portals of my brain. . . . There is not time! If I but had a hundred years there might be some realization of my dream. But I shall not live so long . . ."

Wolfe had a strong compulsive force in him that had to find release in writing. When it couldn't, he went through agonies of repression—was nervous, surly, suspicious, given to brooding, to drinking, to violent outbursts, sometimes even to fears that he was "going mad." From 1924 to 1926 this force was bottled up inside him until it reached explosive strength. However, "it was something that had to come out sooner or later, as a pent flood bursts above a dam." And finally, in 1926, it did come out. "The force in [him] that had to write sought out its channel" and became *Look Homeward, Angel*.

In a way, it seems strange that Wolfe could and did deny the urge to write so long. He had to a marked degree what he called "the writer's conscience": in other words, the unshakable conviction that his first and highest duty was to his creative work. In *Of Time and the River* he describes "the reason why the artist works and lives and has his being—the reward he seeks—the only reward he really cares about, without which there is nothing. It is to snare the spirits of mankind in nets of magic, to make his life prevail through his creation, to wreak the vision of his life, the rude and painful substance of his own experience, into the congruence of blazing and enchanted images that are themselves the core of life, the essential pattern whence all other things proceed, the kernel of eternity. . . . This is the artist, then—life's hungry man, the glutton of eternity, beauty's miser, glory's slave—and to do these things, to get the reward for which he thirsts, with his own immortality to beat and conquer life, enslave mankind, utterly to possess and capture beauty he will do anything, use anything, destroy anything—be ruthless, murderous and destructive, cold and cruel and

---

. . . 'It's because many people are so close to the baseline of the primitive themselves that they chuckle and laugh at us,' he said. . . . 'And there's nothing we can do about it.' Trying to make a joke of the whole matter, he sputtered, 'Well, you're lame, I'm an elephant, and they're crazy!' "

merciless as hell to get the thing he wants, achieve the thing he values and must do or die."

But, as he wrote his mother, he also had "a great deal of my Presbyterian conscience left, and I can't shirk the job." And in 1928, when he was thinking of resigning his instructorship, he was able to write to Professor Watt: "Within my limits I have given you honest and faithful service. It is perhaps childish for me to mention this, but I am childishly proud of this—that being notorious for a lack of discipline and regularity when I first came here, I have, in my three years, missed only one class. That happened my first year, and was caused by the lateness of a boat returning from Boston. And I think I have never put a grade on a student's paper without trying to add a few lines of sensible and honest criticism. . . . Within the trap of my nature I have done all things I could to fulfill my obligation to you."

The only thing that made life bearable for Wolfe during that first grim year at New York University was the prospect of five months' vacation, from September 1924 till February 1925. He had accepted his instructorship with the understanding that he would teach the summer term as well as the spring one and would therefore have the fall term off as his vacation. During this time off he would receive his regular salary of $150 a month: he was even given some assurance that he could get the entire five months' wages in advance as of September first. So, from the very beginning of his life at New York University, he began counting the days till he could get the money, go abroad, and "write and write until I'm broke or my fortune's made."

He believed that traveling in Europe and absorbing its centuries-old culture was a necessary part of his education to be a writer. He had first thought of working his way over on a steamer in 1920, but he had been too bewildered about his future to act decisively about it then. In 1923 he had argued with Professor Baker about the advisability of his going but had been persuaded to stay at Harvard and continue in the Workshop. Later, when Baker realized that Wolfe was determined to leave the Workshop anyway, he seems to have advised him to go abroad as a last resort, but by then Wolfe's finances would not permit it. Now he had resolved to put it off no longer. It had now become a great deal more than just an educational trip: it had become an actual obsession with him. It meant getting away from New York University and "the deep damnation of Freshman Composition." It meant the longed-for opportunity to "write" his "heart out" until a catharsis of his pent-up emotions had taken place. And in some vague way, it also meant the chance to escape forever from "the odious bondage of teaching" and to get his life back again on its true creative course. Wolfe had no very definite idea as to how his "fortune" would be "made." He had great hopes for the completion and production of *The House*, and at any rate, he had the firm conviction that he was "inevitable" and that somehow, some day soon, he would achieve success.

Meanwhile his efforts to sell *Welcome to Our City* had brought no definite results. The Theatre Guild had turned it down but continued their proprietary interest in his work. As he wrote to Mrs. Roberts, "Everyone . . . is enthusiastic, but I notice that *I* earn my own living. The Theatre Guild is cordial. When am I going to bring my new play in? Their officials want to know me. Will I have lunch? Their play reader, Lemon, trumpets my name abroad. He told me recently he had spoken of me at the banquet of some dramatic association. I am grateful, but how I wish someone would *produce* one of my plays."

In January he had sent *Welcome to Our City* to the Provincetown Theatre, and all that spring he waited hopefully for a decision, only to have them decline it after five long months' delay. He then submitted it to the Neighborhood Playhouse through Miss Ann MacDonald, the play reader and translator there, who happened to live at his hotel, the Albert. After some time he received an encouraging letter, evidently written by Miss Alice Lewisohn, one of the directors of the Playhouse. He described this in a letter to his mother: "God knows what I shall do, unless I sell my play—my new or my old one, or both. The old one went to Europe with a wealthy woman producer, and she wrote back very enthusiastically, saying it was 'unusually fine,' 'promised well for your America,' and did I have another with not so many characters. What she intends to do I don't know. I'm sick of praise; I want money."

Little did he know that his submission of *Welcome to Our City* to the Playhouse had been his first introduction to the next exceptional person who was to transform his entire life and to sustain him all through the writing of *Look Homeward, Angel*. Aline Bernstein, who was the stage designer for the Playhouse and also one of its directors, had read the play and taken it to Europe to recommend it to Miss Lewisohn. But at this time Wolfe had never heard of her, nor she of him except as the promising young author of the play.

Ironically enough, the only definite offers Wolfe received in 1924 were from book publishers. At the suggestion of the Theatre Guild, the editors of D. Appleton & Company wrote him to ask if they could read *Welcome to Our City* with the idea of publishing it in book form, but he was reluctant to allow this—he still had his heart set on getting it produced. Meanwhile Professor Koch had come to New York for a few days and had asked Wolfe's permission to reprint *The Return of Buck Gavin* in the second series of *Carolina Folk Plays*, which he was editing for Henry Holt & Company. Wolfe was very much opposed to this; as he explained to Koch, "I am desperately afraid to have that one-act play published. I was so young, so raw, so green. . . . I . . . wrote that play at one sitting, on a rainy October afternoon when I was seventeen or eighteen. And I knew nothing of the theatre at the time." But Wolfe had a reluctance to hurt people's feelings that sometimes came close to moral cowardice: he would let people "talk him into" things, and then brood over what he had done for weeks, or months, or even years. In the face of his old professor's boundless enthusiasm, he could not bring himself to make a definite refusal. *The Return of Buck Gavin* was finally included in *Carolina Folk Plays, Second Series*, and Wolfe brooded about it off and on for nine whole years until, in 1933, he finally made a clean breast of it and asked Koch to refuse permission thenceforth for any productions of either *The Return of Buck Gavin* or *The Third Night*, saying: "I should like to be remembered as a Playmaker and as one who had the honor to be a member of that pioneer first group, but I do not want to be remembered for the work which a careless boy did."

Meanwhile the spring term at New York University was slowly dragging to a close. In the four days' Easter vacation Wolfe had the temporary satisfaction of getting "almost an entire act done on my new play" (*The House*). Again, in the ten days' examination period in May, he tried to complete the play but gave it up as "impossible" and began expressing hopes that he could finish it "before September." But during the time when he was actually teaching, he could do no work: he was "so worn out by nightfall" that he slept "as though drugged" in his little room at the Hotel Albert. If he was not completely exhausted, he would go out for dinner with George Wallace, an advertising man who was at that time taking writing courses at Columbia, or with one of his two friends who, at one time or another, had taken rooms at the Albert: first, Henry Stevens,[6] who had grown up with Wolfe at Asheville and the University of North Carolina, and later, Olin Dows, who

[6] Stevens accidentally set fire to his room at the Albert, but he and Wolfe managed to put it out with fire extinguishers from the corridor without having to call the fire department. Stevens committed suicide in 1933.

had known him at Harvard and had begun to paint his portrait there. Or he would spend hours reading at the New York Public Library, or go over to Broadway to see a play, with the Workshopper's firm conviction that it would help him in his own work. For the most part, however, his life was completely solitary. As time went on and he became adjusted to his new profession, he made warm and lasting friendships with some of his fellow instructors at the university, especially Desmond Powell, Vardis Fisher, and Henry T. Volkening; but during the first year he had neither time, nor nervous strength, nor inclination for such close relationships. Fisher's description of him is based on the latter's first contact with him in 1928, but it was probably even more true of him in 1924: "One morning . . . there entered a man who, I observed at once, attracted instant and, in some of his colleagues, critical attention. . . . He was so huge, his stride was so long and aggressive, his dark hair was so long and uncombed, his dark eyes were so unhappy and suspicious, and his whole bearing was so obviously that of a man who felt himself called to an uncommon destiny that I stared at him, fascinated. . . . For a few moments I slyly studied the man; then, at last, turning to Hal White I asked in a whisper: 'Who is that?' and in a whisper Hal answered, 'Tom Wolfe.' I had heard the name from our chairman, . . . but I was not prepared for the response of our colleagues. Several of them round about were also slyly observing Wolfe and in some of the faces I saw unmistakable distaste. . . .

"He was not often at his desk. It was not his habit, as it was with most of us, to read class papers at his desk or to prepare his lecture notes there or to consult with his students there. Every time he came to his desk I perceived that he was restless, impatient, suspicious, eager to be off. . . . He had prodigious contempt for pedants, even for college teachers; his contempt for those around him was so plain, yet so childlike in its defensive pose, that I was amused and delighted . . . He never, so far as I observed him, said hello to anyone in that office. He simply strode in, sprawled at his desk and brooded, his eyes flickering with spite, scorn, contempt, malice, anxiety, fear; and after a few minutes he would rise and go away. . . . I knew . . . that here was an extraordinary person, an extraordinary child, lonely, lost, obsessed, embittered, in the great hulking form of a man. . . . For I was another child, lonely and lost, and I recognized my kin."[7]

The truth was, Wolfe disliked most of his associates and the entire

[7] From "My Experiences with Thomas Wolfe," by Vardis Fisher, in the April 1951 issue of *Tomorrow*.

atmosphere around them. With a morbid exaggeration which came chiefly from his own sense of insecurity, he felt that the people at the university and the entire population of New York were poisoned by the "hate and fear and venom in the city's life." "It got into the faces of the people," he says in *Of Time and the River*, ". . . it glittered in the eyes of the instructors at the university, their flesh got green and yellow with its poisons, the air about them was webbed, cross-webbed, and counter-webbed with the dense fabric of their million spites and hatreds. They wasted and grew sick with hate and poison because another man received promotion, because another man had got his poem printed, because another man had eaten food and swallowed drink and lain with women, and lived and would not die; they sweltered with hate and fear against the professors who employed them—they grew pale and trembled, and spoke obsequiously when their employer passed, but when the man had gone, they whispered with trembling lips: 'Has he spoken to you yet? . . . Has he said anything to you yet about next year?' . . . They greeted him with sly humility and a servile glance, but they snickered obscenely at him when his back was turned. And they smiled and sneered at one another with eyes that glittered with their hate: they never struck a blow but they spoke lying words of barbed ambiguity, they lied, cheated, and betrayed, and they sweltered in the poisons of their hate and fear, they breathed the weary hatred-laden air about them into their poisoned lungs."

When *Of Time and the River* was published, this passage, together with Wolfe's entire depiction of life at the university, caused a great deal of bitterness at N.Y.U. As Dean Pollock and Professor Cargill wrote nineteen years later in *Thomas Wolfe at Washington Square*, "It was received with incredulity, astonishment, anger, and grief at Washington Square. How could he who had broken bread amongst us, who had shared our limited fare and small rewards, treat us as he had done? Had he no sense of the betrayal of an enterprise to which he had committed so much of himself—a measure, at least, of others' commitment?"

They then explained that "Wolfe was genius, he had been dominated by mood when he had written, he had not been conscious of conferring injury, he had meant to transmute what he had reported beyond recognition, the report was surely inconsequential beside the fiction. William Faulkner has written of 'the consuming unsleeping appeaseless thirst for glory for which any normal artist would destroy his aged mother,' and Wolfe clearly felt that awful thirst. It is understandable that, in the grip of it, friends and acquaintances, students and colleagues, kinfolk and his beloved, became simply materials, like sticks and stones, and were so used." However, the resentment against Wolfe is still bitter, both among individuals and collectively, at New York University, even though almost a quarter of a century has now elapsed.

It must be remembered that during his first year at New York University Wolfe was still only twenty-three, whereas most of the instructors were older men, and in spite of his three years at Harvard, he was still in some ways a small-town southern boy. He had the villager's dread and dislike of urban Jews, which, when he expressed it in *Of Time and the River*, was branded as a more vicious kind of anti-Semitism, and he still had at least vestiges of traditional southern feeling about Negroes; when a Negro elevator boy "told off" white people, even white women, Wolfe was so outraged that he walked up and down the seven flights of stairs to his classroom, swearing never again to use "any elevator operated by that blankety-blank nigger."[8] He still was markedly eccentric in general appearance,[9] size, and mannerisms, and when people stared at him in restaurants or on the street, he went through agonies of self-consciousness. "Why do I become so angry when people stare at me?" he wrote in one of his pocket diaries, and a few pages later: "Fear—fear—like a cold oil around my heart—of what I do not know. Always carry in your heart this war on fear, fear, fear. When a man wearing glasses watches you, you are not always sure." And some time later he admonished himself: "Looking hard at people, trying to outstare them—foolish and common." But this sort of thing bothered him for a long time.

The very act of living in the city was a psychological strain on him: he was at once repelled and fascinated by it, and night after night he tramped the streets in exploration of it. "The sense of drowning daily in the man-swarm returned to him," he wrote in *Of Time and the River*. "Each day there began anew one of the most ancient and fatal struggles that was ever waged—the struggle of man against the multitude: each

[8] The author is indebted for this anecdote to L. Ruth Middlebrook's "Reminiscences of Thomas Wolfe," in the November 1946 issue of the *American Mercury*. Professor Watt refers to the incident in his letter of February 24, 1925: "Please do come back, Wolfe. Since you left we have had no one to keep the elevator boys in their proper places and we miss your diminutive form in the faculty room."

[9] Just before going to New York University he had bought new clothes, but according to the prices which he dutifully itemized to his mother—$35 for the suit and $34.50 for an overcoat—they must have been cheap and ill fitting, as were all his clothes at this time.

day like a man who is going into battle, he would brace himself with
savage resolution, and gird his spirit to the sticking point each time
he went out in the streets, and each day, beaten, driven, trembling
and inchoate, drowned in horror and oblivion, he would at length re-
treat into the four walls of his cell again, conscious only of having
passed through a maelstrom of sound, movement, violence, and living
tissue . . . which flowed constantly back and forth along the beaten
pavement in a lava-like tide of tallowy flesh, dark dead eyes, and gray
felt hats. . . .

"But if he retreated daily, out of this savage and unequal struggle
with the Herculean forces of the city, . . . his pride and fury grew
from every beating that they got . . . And every night, the merciful
anodyne of dark restored him; sunk deep, at length, in midnight,
beastwise aprowl in all the brooding silence of the night, his spirit
swept out through the fields of sleep, he heard the heartbeats of six
million men . . . He saw the city with the great giant webbing of its
thousand streets, he heard the long deep notes of warning and departure, from the great ships in the harbor; and then he saw the city as
a whole, six million sleepers celled in sleep and walled in night, and
girdled by the bracelet of two flashing sea-borne tides that isled them
round: he held them legible as minted gold within his hand, he saw
them plain as apples in the adyts of his brain. Exultant certitude and
joy welled up in him, and he knew that his hunger could eat the earth,
his eye and brain gulp down the vision of ten thousand streets, ten
million faces, he knew he should beat and eat them all one day, and
that a man was more than a million, stronger than a wall, and greater
than a door, and taller than a ninety-storey tower."

Finally the spring term ended and the summer one began. Wolfe had
smaller classes and fewer papers to correct, but he suffered from the
city heat and kept complaining that "my brains are baked." Fortunately
for him, his Harvard friend Olin Dows began inviting him to
spend weekends at Rhinebeck on the Hudson. With naïve volubility,
Wolfe described his first weekend there in a letter written to his mother
in July: "I have had a wonderful experience. In June a young fellow
I knew at Harvard—by name of Olin Dows—wrote from Cambridge
and asked me if I could get a room for him here in the hotel near me.
I knew the boy slightly—he's just twenty—and he saw my play at
Harvard, and was enthusiastic and painted me—he's studying art. So he
came, and we've been together a great deal. . . . He invited me up
to his father's country place up the Hudson two weeks ago—at a colony
for millionaires, a very old Dutch place, called Rhinebeck. His people

are fabulously wealthy . . . They live in a great estate of 2000 acres overlooking the Hudson, with gatekeeper's lodges, and a wonderful colonial house. Next door are the Roosevelts—Franklin D.—and the Astors and Delanos are farther up. . . . His people are wonderful— left me absolutely free to do as I pleased—put me at ease. . . . I think they understand my position—but they liked me and insisted that I come back as often as possible."

Wolfe was not a social climber: in his pride, he leaned far back the other way. However, he was fascinated by the chance to study firsthand the way the wealthy Hudson River people lived: to use a favorite expression of his, it was "all grist to" his "mill." Moreover, the friendship between him and Dows was a real and lasting one, and for the next five years Rhinebeck was a sort of haven where he could escape from the turmoil of his life at New York University and rest and read.

VI

O<small>N SEPTEMBER</small> 5 Wolfe met his last classes for the summer term and received from them a farewell present of a Dunhill pipe. He was urged by Professor Watt to come back and resume teaching in the spring, at a yearly salary of two thousand dollars, or two hundred dollars more than he had had. However, he was so convinced that he might "make his fortune" at any moment by his writing that he hesitated to accept. Finally, with great patience and understanding, Professor Watt told him that he need not decide until December. He certainly was in no proper frame of mind for an acceptance of another term at N.Y.U: all his hopes and thoughts were bent on going abroad and writing to his heart's content. "Heaven and Hell shall not prevent me," he wrote his mother. "I have become like some mad beast who sees through famished eyes a pool of forest water; I have only one thought in mind, to get away—anywhere, anywhere out of this world about me . . . I must go, Mama; my life has turned to dust and ashes in my mouth, and I find myself unable to do the only thing I care for—the only thing I ever shall."

Both his financial and psychological dependence on his mother were still very strong, and instead of sailing immediately for Europe, he went home to Asheville for a visit and stayed there for several weeks, during which time the question of his finances was endlessly discussed. During his months at New York University he had found it almost impossible to live on his monthly salary of $150, and with many apologies and promises that "next month I'll do it or bust," he had obtained money from his mother at least four times. He could now repay her out of the advance money due him for his vacation, but he asked her to wait, saying, "I can barely get along this winter on what I have." She seems to have agreed to this and also to have helped pay for his trip. "When I left home . . . ," he wrote her later, "the understanding was that I should go as far as I could on my own, and that I should ask you for help when that was gone."

And so, at last, he sailed—on the *Lancastria* on October 25—with about four hundred dollars in his pocket and the unfinished play, *The*

House, in his battered suitcase. To him the trip was "Jason's Voyage": "I am going . . . like a discoverer": he wrote repeatedly to his friends, "The world is opening before me like an oyster, and valiant deeds are in me." However, he was still far too immature and unsophisticated to adjust himself to a strange new life abroad. His entire year there was a series of endless difficulties, tragedies, and confusions such as he had always had a talent for, but now increased and magnified by the fact that he was, for the most part, alone, without advice or guidance, in a foreign land. As he wrote four years later to his old friend at Chapel Hill, Ben Cone, "I wandered around Europe for about a year . . . and what mistakes I failed to make in Paris, I managed to make in various other parts of the continent before I was through. I seem to have been born a Freshman—and in many ways I'm afraid I'll continue to be one." It was like taking Rousseau's Natural Man and setting him down in the complexities of modern civilization.

But no matter what mistakes he made later on in Europe, this first voyage of his upon a transatlantic liner was a wonderful and inspiring experience for him. During the remaining thirteen years of his short life he made the voyage twelve more times, or six round trips. It was an unfailing source of rest and recreation for him, a means of getting away and beginning over that was even better than a trip on one of his beloved trains. Some of his most inspired lyric writing is about great ships upon the ocean, and he never heard them "baying at the harbor's mouth" without being moved to an ecstasy of love and longing to be on board one, putting out to sea.

He was hardly past Nantucket Lightship before he started writing: not on his play or on anything that would be apt to make his fortune, but on a hodgepodge journal of the voyage, which he called "A Passage to England." As he wrote two weeks later to his good friend George McCoy of the Asheville *Citizen*, "I put it all on paper from day to day; I let nothing escape me, and even when the sea made me feel a bit sorry for myself I put it down. Now that voyage—the poignant emotion of it all, and the astonishing differences in habit and custom and opinion of different races, English and American—is recorded hastily, it is true; sometimes clumsily. But it is there. I don't know what to do with it. I might send it to some American magazine, but it is a conglomerate of so many things—drama, comment, incident, opinion—that I scarcely know what to call it."

There are only a few fragments of the journal left among Wolfe's papers now. Most of them record, with great perspicuity, the conversations and relationships between two passengers who sat at Wolfe's table, a Cockney and a British peer. However, one brief fragment describes a storm at sea and a wild young man with a strong resemblance to the autobiographical character known as Eugene Gant. For the most part, the journal was evidently random, diarylike jottings, similar to the little pocket notebooks which Wolfe kept on similar trips abroad.

He knew nothing about writing articles or stories that would sell: he only followed his compulsion to pour everything out on paper, with the vague and optimistic idea that he might get some money for it from the Asheville *Citizen*. In his letters to McCoy he said repeatedly that he was "sending the manuscript tomorrow," but he actually did not get around to sending it until five months later. Then, in March 1925, when both his time abroad and his money were running very short, he mailed his journal to Mrs. Roberts, asking her to give it to McCoy for the *Citizen* if she thought best. By this time he had given it the subtitle "Log of a Voyage That Was Never Made" and had written a long, whimsical prologue to go with it, in which he represented himself as only imagining that he was on a ship. "This occurred to me at first purely as a device to escape libel . . . ," he explained to Mrs. Roberts. "Then I remembered that I had not sailed on the day I had originally planned—that I had remained in Asheville a week longer, and that during that time I had had a queer feeling that I was or should be on the Atlantic."

Finally, in their Sunday, July 19, 1925, issue, the *Citizen* published one short piece by Wolfe, "London Tower," which was probably an excerpt from his journal. It began by describing the instruments of torture on exhibition at the Tower and then launched into a humorous burlesque, similar to those which Wolfe had written at Chapel Hill, concerning the life and character of a fictitious Asheville sadist,

> "John the Sheriff
> Who shot the Nigger Reece
> And kept his skull for company
> Upon the mantelpiece."

Wolfe landed in England on November 5 and spent a month exploring London, then took a hasty trip to Bath and Bristol, from where he sent his mother a postcard of the monument to Thomas Chatterton, explaining rather pointedly that he was "a great poet and a great genius who could make no way in the world and killed himself at the age of seventeen." Then he went to Paris, with about $275 left on which to "settle down and write." As he said later in *The Story of a Novel*, he was "filled with all the romantic faith and foolishness which many young men at that time felt when they saw Paris. I had come there . . . , so I told myself, to work, and so glamorous was the magic name of Paris . . . that I really thought one could work far better there than anywhere on earth; that it was a place where the very air was impregnated with the energies of art; where the artist was bound to find a more fortunate and happy life than he could possibly find in America."

He did work, and harder than he had ever worked before, during his first month in Paris, but that was caused by the first of the calamities which were to befall him, the theft of one of his suitcases, which contained the manuscript of his play *The House*. He described this in great detail in a letter to his mother, and more briefly in another to Professor Watt: "I . . . settled in a small hotel in the Latin Quarter. I went to this place with my bags very late at night—one o'clock—the concierge who admitted me had been wounded in the war, and gave a great groan when he saw the baggage, and when I told him my room was five flights up. He pointed to his crippled leg, and hobbled around painfully; I suggested that he keep one of the bags until morning; I would take the other two myself, he agreed to this gladly. The story is that during the night a man entered, asked for a woman formerly resident of the hotel, and on the way out, stole my bag. The bag was old and battered, the articles in it were not of great value; what it did contain that could not be replaced was the prologue and two acts in a manuscript of the play I had lived with for more than a year. I know this sounds silly, but nothing has hit me like this since the death of my brother Ben six years ago."

In great excitement, Wolfe went to the police, having first persuaded the only person he knew in Paris, George Stevens, who had been at Harvard with him, to act as his interpreter. The case came up before the Justice of the arrondissement in January, and Wolfe finally accepted a settlement from the hotel proprietor of five hundred francs. Meanwhile he had moved to a new hotel, the Hôtel d'Alsace, in the Rue des Beaux Arts, where Oscar Wilde had died. As he wrote to Professor Watt, "I bought paper and swore that I should rewrite the play . . . by New Year's—and on January third I had not only recreated what was lost, but completed an entire first draft." In the process of rewriting, Wolfe gave the play a new title, *Mannerhouse*, under which it finally was published in 1948.

Except for a short trip to the battlefields of World War I with friends of his from Chapel Hill, Benjamin Cone, Marcus Noble, and Frank P. Graham, Wolfe went nowhere and saw no one all December, and

was abysmally homesick. Then he met his old friend Kenneth Raisbeck, Professor Baker's assistant in the 47 Workshop, and through
him, two Boston girls who had a studio in Paris. Immediately Wolfe's
entire life was changed: he now had the guidance and companionship
which he so desperately needed, and he was swept up in a festive round
of "doing Paris" with his friends. For three weeks everything went
beautifully, so much so that the quartet planned to rent a car and go
on a long motor trip through France. Meanwhile Professor Watt had
written Wolfe urging him to come back to New York University in
early February and accept the teaching appointment that had been
offered him for the spring term, but he was so engrossed in his new life
in France that he wrote Watt and declined it, saying, "Although my
own money is nearly gone, I feel that everything that is happening
to me now is too important to be checked violently." Gradually, however, disagreements arose between Wolfe and Raisbeck and his friends.
Wolfe had fallen desperately in love with the younger of the Boston
girls; he was jealous of Raisbeck and thoroughly disillusioned with him;
he was suspicious of the arrangements for the sharing of expenses on
the motor trip; and at any rate, he was by now almost completely
without money. Finally he quarreled violently with Raisbeck, gave up
the motor trip with him and the Boston girls, and cut himself off
from them entirely.

The next few weeks were bitter ones for Wolfe. In late December
or early January he had appealed to his mother for financial help and
had received a check from her for $100, only to find that it had been
erroneously made out to her instead of to himself and could not be
cashed without her endorsement. In vain he went to the American
Express and Morgan Harjes in an attempt to cash it; then, characteristically, he postponed doing anything more about it and lost it,
probably in the sea of papers which always filled his room. Finally, he
had cabled his mother and had received new checks, totaling $124,
from her and his brother Fred, but since then he had spent most of
this amount with Raisbeck and the Boston girls. He now found himself
deep in debt and unable to leave Paris. He had been invited by
Professor D. D. Carroll of the University of North Carolina to join
him and his family in St. Raphaël, but he could not afford a railroad
ticket to the South of France, nor could he leave the Hôtel d'Alsace
till he had paid his bill there.

Meanwhile he had received a letter from his brother Fred suggesting
that it was about time he came home. He brooded constantly over
this and over his quarrel with Raisbeck and his friends: he spent a

good deal of time in writing the younger girl deeply hurt, defensive letters, most of which he never mailed but carried around with him. Later he reread these and wrote of them: "I almost choked with shame when I came to the fine and flowery phrases, when I struck up a high and mighty attitude, and ranted about to impress myself or others. . . . In those old letters I was always passionate about something I thought at the time mattered: love, anger, honor, and so on, and I tried to express it in fine phrases. In those old letters I saw an honest and excited child, full of books and poetry, who wanted beauty and heroism and glory from life. I still want them. The fancy phrases were bad, but the thing that caused them was good."

In spite of all his troubles and his persistent homesickness, Wolfe was still determined to stay in Europe and "settle down to the business of writing stories." Accordingly he wrote a painful and humiliating letter to his mother, saying: "It is a matter of deep regret that I should have to ask you for anything, but if, within the next five or six months you could let me have as much as $500, I could see Southern France, Italy, and do my work. . . . I want you to understand, Mama, that I am giving myself one last desperate chance before I return to teaching. . . . *Please*, if you are able, stand by me a little longer." Finally, toward the end of February, he received another $125 from his mother in answer to his appeal.

With great jubilation he paid his hotel bill and left Paris, with the vague intention of going South and "stopping at interesting places on the way down." But instead of going to St. Raphaël, he went to Chartres, to Orléans, where he was befriended by an aged countess very similar to the one described in *Of Time and the River*, and finally to Tours, where he at last began to write. He describes this in the final portion of *Of Time and the River*: "An astounding—an almost incredible thing—now happened. He had come to Tours, telling himself that now at last, at last, he was going 'to settle down and write,' that he was going to justify his voyage by the high purpose of creation. In his mind there swarmed various projects, cloudy, vague, and grandiose in their conception, of plays, books, stories, essays he must write: with desperate resolve he sat down grimly now to shape these grand designs into the stern and toilsome masonry of words. A few impatient, fragmentary beginnings, the opening pages of a story, the beginning speeches of a play—all crumpled in a wad and impatiently tossed aside— were the final results of this ambitious purpose.

"And yet, write he did. Useless, fragmentary, and inchoate as were these first abortive efforts, he began to write now like a madman—

. . . tranced in a hypnosis by whose fatal and insatiate compulsions he was forced, without will, to act. . . . Seated at a table in his cold, little room that overlooked the old cobbled court of the hotel, he wrote ceaselessly from dawn to dark, sometimes from darkness on to dawn again—hurling himself upon the bed to dream . . . strange sleeping-wakeful visions, dreams mad and terrible as the blinding imagery that now swept constantly across his brain its blaze of fire. The words were wrung out of him in a kind of bloody sweat . . . ; he wrote them with his heart, his brain, his sweat, his guts; he wrote them with his blood, his spirit; they were wrenched out of the last secret source and substance of his life. And in those words was packed the whole image of his bitter homelessness, his intolerable desire, his maddened longing for return . . . all the impossible and unutterable homesickness that the American, or any man on earth, can know. They were all there—without coherence, scheme, or reason—flung down on paper like figures blasted by the spirit's lightning stroke, and in them was the huge chronicle of the billion forms, the million names, the huge, single, and incomparable substance of America."

Finally, in the second week of March, he realized that his money again was almost gone. He managed to get back to Paris and, luckily, found another check from his mother waiting for him there. He also found a letter from Professor Watt asking him to come back to New York University for the fall term, and after a few weeks' hesitation, he answered in acceptance, "hoping," as he wrote to Mrs. Roberts, "that the heavens may rain manna before." Meanwhile he had arrived in St. Raphaël just in time to help the Carrolls pack and start for home, but he stayed on alone until late May. He then went to northern Italy for three weeks, then back to Paris and immediately to England, where for three more weeks he was "a great deal more dead than alive" with one of his feverish colds, and he hinted that he had received "serious and disquieting news" about his health. He may have been warned about the possibility of tuberculosis, which had so frightened him during his first weeks at Harvard in 1920, but if so, there is no definite proof of it now.

His "Jason's Voyage" was drawing to a close: he would have to sail for home in August to arrive at New York University in time for the fall term. He had not made his fortune: he had not even written anything that he could sell: during the next winter, *Mannerhouse* was to be considered by the Theatre Guild, the Provincetown Theatre, and the Neighborhood Playhouse, only to be declined: *Welcome to Our City*, too, was to be reconsidered by those three theaters but rejected for a second time. However, he had gained a great deal in experience and had found the thing which was his own, the thing which would shape his whole career in years to come and would set him apart from any other writer. As he said later in *The Story of a Novel*, he had "discovered America . . . out of my very need for her." In a letter written to his mother on July 27 he summed up the whole trip: "I have come alone, wandered alone, almost without plan—indeed, in an insane fashion—but it has been right *for me*. . . . I have known some sadness, a great deal of loneliness, but I am older, more matured—I believe, more of a man. . . . Presently, I think, I shall come partly into my own kingdom. I know that I have something to say now; it twists at my brain and heart for expression. If God would only give me a hundred hands to write it down."

The second week in August he sailed for home on the *Olympic*. When the ship put in at Cherbourg, Aline Bernstein was among the passengers who came on board. Wolfe did not actually meet Mrs. Bernstein till the ship had reached New York, but he always considered the fact that they sailed together on the *Olympic* a miracle of fate. Three years later he wrote: "My life has been a strange and miraculous thing. . . . In a thousand places the miracle has happened to me. Because I was penniless and took one ship instead of another, I met the great and beautiful friend who has stood by me through all the torture, struggle and madness of my nature." And ten years later, when he sent her one of the first copies of *Of Time and the River*, he marked for her the concluding passage of the book, in which Eugene sees an unknown woman waiting to embark at Cherbourg:

"He turned, and saw her then, and so finding her, was lost, and so losing self, was found, and so seeing her, saw for a fading moment only the pleasant image of the woman that perhaps she was, and that life saw. He never knew: he only knew that from that moment his spirit was impaled upon the knife of love. From that moment on he never was again to lose her utterly, never to wholly re-possess unto himself the lonely, wild integrity of youth which had been his. At that instant of their meeting, that proud inviolability of youth was broken, not to be restored. At that moment of their meeting she got into his life by some dark magic, and before he knew it, he had her beating in the pulses of his blood—somehow thereafter—how he never knew—to steal into the conduits of his heart, and to inhabit the lone, inviolable tenement of his one life; so, like love's great thief, to steal through all the adyts of his soul, and to become a part of all he did and said and was—through this invasion so to touch all loveliness that he might touch, through this strange and subtle stealth of love henceforth to share all that he might feel or make or dream, until there was for him no beauty that she did not share, no music that did not have her being in it, no horror, madness, hatred, sickness of the soul, or grief unutterable, that was not somehow consonant to her single image and her million forms—and no final freedom and release, bought through the incalculable expenditure of blood and anguish and despair, that would not bear upon its brow forever the deep scar, upon its sinews the old mangling chains, of love.

"After all the blind, tormented wanderings of youth, that woman would become his heart's centre and the target of his life, the image of immortal one-ness that again collected him to one, and hurled the whole collected passion, power and might of his one life into the blazing certitude, the immortal governance and unity, of love.

"Set me as a seal upon thine heart, as a seal upon thine arm: for love is strong as death; jealousy is cruel as the grave: the coals thereof are coals of fire, which hath a most vehement flame."

VII

WOLFE'S relationship with Aline Bernstein was the one great love affair of his entire life, and the influence she had on him was incalculably great—second only to that of his parents and of his father-substitute and editor, Maxwell Perkins. When he met Mrs. Bernstein in September 1925, he was still a frustrated, wild, eccentric boy: when their relationship came virtually to an end in 1931, he still had some eccentricities, but he had become a man, with a great deal more wisdom, maturity, and self-control, and with the achievement of his greatest dream—the successful publication of a book —behind him. All these things he owed to her. It is true that with his compulsive genius he was "inevitable" as a writer, but without her un-wavering belief in him and her financial aid, he never would or could have written *Look Homeward, Angel* when he did.

From the very beginning there were serious obstacles to their relationship. She was forty-four years old when he first met her, nine-teen years older than himself, or, as he later repeatedly pointed out, "old enough to be my mother." Moreover, she had two grown children and a husband, with whom she lived on the most amicable terms for all her life. The daughter of the Shakespearean actor Joseph Frankau, she was of half-Jewish blood and more than half-Jewish background and sympathy: in her letters to Wolfe there are some passages in which she stanchly extols the merits of the Hebraic way of life and thought as against the Gentile. Wolfe, however, had a provincial kind of anti-Semitism for at least the first thirty years of his life, which was probably derived from his mother and her people. He never could for-get the Jewish blood that ran in Mrs. Bernstein's veins, and his habit of referring to her as "my Jew," both in his diaries and to her face, was not a pretty one. She was a brilliantly successful stage designer and one of the directors of the Neighborhood Playhouse, and by the time he met her, he had come to have a strong revulsion against the theater, caused partly by his own failure there and perhaps partly by his early Presbyterian puritanism. He felt that the entire theatrical world was "tainted," and sometimes he would half convince himself that the taint must have touched her too. In her own book, *The Journey Down*, she describes his first outburst to her on this subject, made only a few hours after he had met her on board the *Olympic:* "Then it came, the storm, the violence, he caught her upper arms and shook her, her head bobbed back and forth until it ached, her upper and lower teeth hit together until she thought they would break. 'Where did you get your face, raised in that dung-heap the theatre, among evil and rotten people, people bloated and foul and vile, people without the decency to keep in their own homes, strutting and showing their bodies; answer me, where did you get your eyes of love, your mouth of love, your flower face, did your mother cheat and lie with an angel? Answer me!' "[1]

And yet, in spite of all these difficulties, he and Mrs. Bernstein had a deep and wonderful relationship that enriched their lives for six entire years and left its mark upon them till the day they died. Or, as she described it twenty-five years later, "It was a supreme experience, the most wonderful thing in the world." "The most important thing between us was our feeling for each other. It was a deep passionate love, added to a clear fine friendship. Personal things were always coming between us, his intense jealousy of me, one thing and another. Our real companionship was beyond anything anyone can imagine, often so gay and filled with laughter. We shared a sense of beauty in poetry and painting that enriched our lives, brought everything to twice its value. This is what remains to me of Tom."[2]

Mrs. Bernstein was a fascinating woman, with more character and charm in her little finger than most people have altogether. She was a little woman, ridiculously short in comparison with Wolfe's great height, with a brisk and firmly rounded figure and a lovely ruddy face, over which expressions played with swiftness and variety. Even when Wolfe first knew her, she was somewhat deaf, but this almost added to her charm and gave her face what he called "a kind of lovely *listening* quality," saying: "I think it is something like this that gives your . . . face its indefinable loveliness. I believe there is a deep and glorious music in the hearts of all of us which very few of us ever come to hear in all the savage jargon of this world. You are strong and beautiful because there is a great deal of it in you, and because you have been able to hear it."[3]

[1] From *The Journey Down*, by Aline Bernstein, Knopf, 1938.
[2] From two undated letters written by Mrs. Bernstein to Elizabeth Nowell in 1950.
[3] From a letter written by Wolfe to Mrs. Bernstein on August 27, 1928.

As she said later, with disarming frankness, "I was in the real flower
of my physical self, I was beautiful. Please do not take it ill that I say
this, it is not a boast, only a corroborative detail. He thought I was
the most beautiful woman in the world."[4] However, it was not so much
sheer physical beauty that gave her her chief charm as it was the richness of her personality. She had a tremendous emotional sincerity, so
intense that it had an almost hypnotic effect on people with whom she
talked. However, she also had a never failing sense of humor and a
most endearing trick of suddenly breaking off when she was at her most
intense, and making a humorous, flippant, even slangy remark about
herself. She was a hard worker, with a degree of worldly sophistication,
an almost inexhaustible supply of energy, and a large supply of will
power and plain old-fashioned common sense. In contrast to Wolfe's
doubts and hesitations and psychic blocks, she went directly to the
point of any matter and dealt with it both promptly and efficiently.
Or, as he wrote to Henry Carlton, "She is a very exceptional person—
with the grit, determination and executive capacity that men are mistakenly supposed to have, but good-humored and kindly always."
Later, he complained to Mr. Perkins that she boasted that "she always
got what she wanted," and even though this was not invariably true,
it was often so, and no wonder. However, she was far from selfish: she
loved people and had a warmth and loyalty that rewarded her with
friendships that endured for her entire life.

She also loved life and had a tremendous capacity for sensuous enjoyment. She was a wonderful cook, with a true gourmet's feeling for
good food, and she would labor in Wolfe's hot, dirty little kitchens for
hours at a time to make delicious meals for him. Because of her prowess
in this field, he evolved a theory that being a good cook was an indica-
tion of a capacity for sensuous enjoyment of all kinds, and in later years,
when he was interested in other women, he would peer earnestly into
their faces and ask suddenly, to their surprise, "Are you a good cook?"
But he never found anyone with the richness and the love of life of
Mrs. Bernstein. Moreover, it was this same capacity that gave her her
artist's sense of beauty in all things, from the poetry of John Donne
and the great paintings of the Flemish Renaissance to the freshness
of a dewy rose picked in the early morning in her garden, or the gaudy
color of the paper on a five-cent candy bar. This was one of the strongest
and most sustaining forces of her life. Another was her work: the fact

---

[4] From another undated letter written by Mrs. Bernstein to Elizabeth Nowell
in 1950.

that she had found herself and was happy and successful in her chosen field, largely because of this same sensuous richness and sensitivity. Even though Wolfe had turned against the theater and found it "limited," he could not help but admire this quality in Mrs. Bernstein. "My dear," he wrote to her in a mood of contrition, "if only I had a little of your calm certitude, your wisdom, your beautiful vision. . . . In your own work you have been so certain: you have so fine a talent and you have found the thing you like best and for which you are the best fitted. Dear happy darling Aline—I would give my crooked nose and my weak eye for a little of your strength and ability."[5]

Immediately after his first meeting with Mrs. Bernstein on the *Olympic* Wolfe went to Asheville for a visit, and then came back and plunged into the ordeal of another year at N.Y.U.; but he evidently could not get her out of his mind, and he wrote to her immediately on returning to New York. Soon they were seeing each other constantly and had fallen deeply and utterly in love. In a letter written to Mr. Perkins in 1931 Wolfe says that at first his relationship with her began "lightly and exultantly": after all the loneliness and frustration of his first year at N.Y.U., he had got himself a girl, and no ordinary one at that, but "an elegant and fashionable woman," and that he was "pleased about it." "Then," he went on, "without knowing how, when or why, I was desperately in love with the woman; then the thought of her began to possess and dominate every moment of my life." One of his associates in the English Department at the university remembers him as pacing up and down the faculty room ecstatically exclaiming, "I'm in love! I'm in love!"[6] But for the most part, he tried to keep his new-found happiness a secret, making constant but oblique references to Mrs. Bernstein as "the best friend I've ever had" or "a very great lady" to his family and his friends. However, by the end of that first winter he had confided to Mrs. Roberts about his love affair, and when she wrote him predicting that it would end unhappily, he answered: "If, in this affair, you see only consequences of future unhappiness for me—what, pray, should unhappiness mean to me who called for wine, and was given the sponge, and whose bread as a child was soaked in his grief? Am I so rich, then, that I can strike love in the

[5] From Wolfe's letter to Mrs. Bernstein of October 27, 1928. This was just after he had been injured in the fight at the October Fair; hence the reference to his crooked nose and weak eye.

[6] From a conversation between Professor Waldo Buckham and Professor Oscar Cargill, quoted in *Thomas Wolfe at Washington Square*.

face, drive away the only comfort, security, and repose I have ever known, and destroy myself just as my mind and heart, aflame with hope and maturity, as they have never been before, promise me at length release?" Encouraged by Mrs. Bernstein's loyal sympathy for the woes of his childhood and his youth, he had entered upon the period of bitterness against his mother which was to find expression in *Look Homeward, Angel.* Mrs. Wolfe's "baby was getting away from" her with a vengeance now: her complete financial and psychological domination of him had ended, and the relationship between them, although still strong, never would be quite the same again.

Moreover, Wolfe had not only found someone with whom to be in love: he had also found a new "superior being," another "image of a strength and wisdom external to his need and superior to his hunger, to which the belief and power of his own life could be united." "We are strangers and exiles here," he wrote to Mrs. Bernstein later. "I feel it now more certainly than ever—and the only home a man ever has on earth, the only moment when he escapes from the prisms of loneliness, is when he enters into the heart of another person. In all the enormous darkness of living and dying, I see these brave little lights go up—the only hope and reason for it all. . . . I believe in love, and in its power to redeem and save our lives. I believe in the loved one, the redeemer and saviour."

By the summer of 1926, after seven months of trying in vain to sell *Mannerhouse* and *Welcome to Our City,* Wolfe was forced to admit that he would never be a successful dramatist. He was undoubtedly helped to this realization by Mrs. Bernstein, who understood the theater as few people did and who knew that neither his plays nor his temperament was suited to it. In his Purdue speech he says that his youthful conviction that he must be a playwright was "not only wrong— it was as fantastically wrong as anything could be. Whatever other talents I had for playwriting—and I think I had some—the specific requirements of the theatre for condensation, limited characterization, and selected focus were really not especially for me. Even my plays at that time showed unmistakably the evidence of my real desire—for they abounded in scenes and characters, a great variety of places and of people, too great a variety, in fact, for the economic and commercial enterprise of the theatre profitably to produce. Something in me very strong and powerful was groping toward a more full, expansive, and abundant expression of the great theatre of life than the stage itself could physically compass: it was something that had to come out sooner or later, as a pent flood bursts above a dam—and in 1926 I found it—and another cycle had been passed, another period of development begun."

Meanwhile he had taught the fall and spring terms at New York University: another vacation with pay now was due him, and again he planned to go to Europe "with maddening eagerness to return" there. He sailed on the *Berengaria* on June 23 and went to Paris with the intention of starting work upon a novel. There, as he says in his Purdue speech, "the beginnings of my plan now working in me, I bought a tablet and began to jot notations down. I simply jotted down on the pages of this tablet—without plot or plan, and often without order—a sequence of the things I wanted to put into a book." These things were all the incidents he could remember from his youth. They were the first rough outline of *Look Homeward, Angel,* and they were also the beginnings of the one enormous book which all his books composed—the "enormous task of excavation" into his own experience which absorbed him all his life.

After about ten days in France, Wolfe joined Mrs. Bernstein in England, where she had been working on a production of *The Dybbuk* in Manchester. He then went with her to Ilkley, in the Lake Country, to settle down and work. She had bought him some huge ledgers in which to write, and she says that he actually began *Look Homeward, Angel* sitting out on a green hillside with her one warm July afternoon. It was a moment of intense and solemn inspiration for him, and he told her that he would be a great writer and that long after she was dead people would know about her because she would be "entombed in his work."[7] She stayed with him in Ilkley for two weeks while he brought the outline of the *Angel* almost to completion, then went to Glasgow with him, and in August, sailed for home, leaving him to write the book alone in London. In a moving passage in her own book, *The Journey Down,* she tells how, after they spent a day touring the Lake Country with two close associates of hers in the theater, he wept and begged her never to desert him for her "fine successful friends." She promised that she never would: she never did. As it finally turned out, it was the other way around.

In *The Story of a Novel* Wolfe says: "I began to write my . . . book in London. I was living all alone at that time. . . . and in a foreign country. I did not know why I was there or what the direction of my

[7] From a letter written by Mrs. Bernstein to Elizabeth Nowell.

life should be, and that was the way I began to write my book. I think that is one of the hardest times a writer goes through. There is no standard, no outward judgment, by which he can measure what he has done. By day I would write for hours in big ledgers which I had bought for the purpose; then at night I would lie in bed and fold my hands behind my head and think of what I had done that day and hear the solid, leather footbeat of the London bobby as he came by my window, and remember that I was born in North Carolina and wonder why the hell I was now in London lying in the darkened bed, and thinking about words I had that day put down on paper. I would get a great, hollow, utterly futile feeling inside me, and then I would get up and switch on the light and read the words I had written that day, and then I would wonder: why am I here now? why have I come?"

On September 12 he suddenly left London for a two weeks' trip to Belgium, where by sheer and happy accident he toured the battlefield of Waterloo on the same sight-seeing bus with James Joyce and his family. If Mrs. Bernstein's recollection is correct, Wolfe had been introduced to Joyce by her a month before. She had known Joyce when his play *Exiles* had been put on by the Neighborhood Playhouse, and before she had sailed for home in August 1926, she had gone to call on him in London to pay him his royalties from this production, in American dollars. As she remembers it, Wolfe called for her at Joyce's house and was introduced hastily to him in the dimly lighted hallway just as she was leaving: if this was so, he probably could not clearly see Joyce's face. In any case, he was too overcome with shyness to speak to him at Waterloo, in spite of being given every opportunity to do so. Even when he met him two years later on another sight-seeing tour in Frankfurt, his diffidence prevented him from exchanging more than a few words with him and from accepting the suggestion, made by Joyce with equal diffidence, that they explore the Old Town together.

Only a Beerbohm could do justice to the picture of Joyce and Wolfe careening through the forest on the sight-seeing bus from Waterloo, with Joyce in the front seat wrapped theatrically in his overcoat as if it were a cape, and Wolfe in the back, "making idiot noises" in his throat and "crooning" with sheer mirth; or of the two men walking down opposite sides of the street in the Old Town of Frankfurt, covertly glancing at each other's reflections in shopwindows. But perhaps Wolfe was right in thinking that "it was too good to spoil" by familiar conversations. At this time he worshiped Joyce and wrote *Look Homeward, Angel* so much under his influence that he later sometimes called it "my *Ulysses* book." He acknowledges this debt more correctly in *The Story of a Novel*: "Like every young man, I was strongly under the influence of writers I admired. One of the chief writers at that time was Mr. James Joyce with his book *Ulysses*. The book that I was writing was much influenced, I believe, by his own book, and yet the powerful energy and fire of my own youth played over and, I think, possessed it all."

Wolfe went back to London early in October and almost immediately moved to Oxford, where he rented a bedroom and sitting room at Hilltop Farm, a large house on the outskirts of the town. He was not as lonely here as he had been in London: he spent a good deal of time with William Cocke, an Asheville boy who was a Rhodes scholar at Merton College, and through him met various other scholars. He also spent many pleasant hours drinking beer at his favorite Oxford pub: on one occasion he struck up an acquaintance with a poacher, a sailor, and a busman there, and when the pub closed, insisted on riding the sailor's bicycle down Cowley Road. Strangely enough, he had never ridden one before: he fell repeatedly, tearing his trousers, straining his left knee, and bruising and skinning his face and hands: but he finally succeeded in riding, to the applause of the crowd which had gathered to laugh at his wild gyrations.

However, these were only interludes between the five or six hours a day he spent working on his book before the coal fire in his little sitting room. Mrs. Bernstein had generously undertaken to finance his stay in England while he wrote his novel. It was his golden opportunity to write, free from the necessity of teaching and from financial worries. Moreover, "the force" in him "that had to write" was sweeping him along. As he said later, in *The Story of a Novel*, "I was very young at the time, and I had the kind of wild, exultant vigor which a man has at that period of his life. The book took hold of me and possessed me. In a way, I think it shaped itself. . . . I wrote about things that I had known, the immediate life and experience that had been familiar to me in my childhood. . . . I had never had anything published before. My feeling towards writers, publishers, books, that whole fabulous faraway world, was almost as romantically unreal as when I was a child. And yet my book, the characters with which I had peopled it, the color and the weather of the universe which I had created, had possessed me, and so I wrote and wrote with that bright flame with which a young man writes who never has been published, and who yet is sure all will be good and must go well."

By October 28 he was writing a report to Mrs. Bernstein of how much he had accomplished: "The book stands thus: I work five or six hours every day on it now—I see my way through the first three books as straight as a string. I brood constantly over the fourth and last— the book lifts into a soaring fantasy of a Voyage, and I want to put my utmost, my most passionate into it. The prefatory action to these four books I can write down in ten days. I am confident now I can get the central body on paper by Christmas—that is, the first three books. I am also confident I can *not* get the last book done by that time." And again, on November 8, he wrote to her: "I shall stay here two weeks longer and try to get as much of the second book on paper as I can. The first is done, the third almost done. I shall finish the last one in New York. I have written 100,000 words, or almost that, since you left—it is an immense quantity of writing, and however bad it may be, I have said a great number of things I have always wanted to say. It is going to be for you, I think, if for no one else, an exciting book: I have somehow recovered innocency—I have written it almost with a child's heart: the thing has come from me with a child's wonder, and my pages are engraved not only with what is simple and plain but with monstrous evil, as if the devil were speaking with a child's tongue. The great fish, those sealed with evil, horribly incandescent, hoary with elvish light, have swum upwards."

He did not realize that his childhood memories would continue to "swim upwards" and keep the book coming from him for almost two years more—keep it coming from him till it utterly exhausted him and reached a length of 350,000 words, three times the length of the average publishable novel. But there was nothing he could do about it. Creation always had to run its course with him: he had to "pour it out, boil it out, flood it out" till he had realized himself "through a process of torrential production." And although *Look Homeward, Angel* had to be cut before it could be published, he brought it to its conclusion without help from anyone. In later years he pointed, with great pride, to the fact that he had done so. It was the best and only way for him to work, although it always seemed as if he never would live through it.

It was always harder than he thought it would be, and by November 13, only five days after he had confidently predicted that he could get the first three "books" of his novel done by Christmas, his first creative streak had petered out and he was writing to Mrs. Bernstein: "I have gone dead and flat. . . . My mind has gone to pieces these last three days. It is scattered and cannot follow either reading or writing. It will all come back in a week or so, I am sure." "You will not tell me, after

I get home, will you, that I have had my chance and that I should have finished my book before I came back?" he went on. "That would be a bestial and unfair thing. Somehow or other, you must see that I finish it there. I have failed at the other thing, I shall never attempt another play: this is the end, perhaps." However, he did not seriously think she would withdraw her support, and he was right, for by November 14 he had gone back to London, where he found a cable from her and more money, which enabled him to have one last fling of seeing Europe before he sailed for home. "Must get home by Jan 1 now," he wrote in his pocket notebook. "Finish book. The grey weather, heavy food, depression of spirits—can't work." And again, "I am depressed and weary. Want no more of England for a long time. I'll see if the Germans are better."

He went to Paris, then to Strasbourg, Stuttgart, and Munich for two weeks, then back to Paris by way of Switzerland and Alsace-Lorraine. Finally he sailed for home on the *Majestic*, arriving in New York on December 28. He was still in love with Mrs. Bernstein: before leaving him in London she had exacted a promise of chastity from him and he now noted in his diary with surprise and some amusement: "By God, I kept the faith," but now that he was going back to her, he felt some qualms about the continuance of their relationship. "How shall the years pass, Jew?" he had written in his diary just before going to Paris, and finally, as the *Majestic* hove in sight of the coast line of America, "What rut of life with the Jew now? Is this a new beginning or a final ending? Get the book done." However, when the ship finally docked at eight o'clock on the morning of December 29, after being anchored in New York Harbor for an entire day and night because of a thick fog, Mrs. Bernstein was standing at the end of the wharf and began dancing up and down with joy when she saw him. Her certitude dispelled his doubts, as it so often did, although they would keep recurring with increasing strength and frequency as time went on.

Mrs. Bernstein had a surprise for him. She had rented a loft on the top floor of an old building at 13 East Eighth Street and planned for him to live there while he finished writing his book. It was filthy and ramshackle, but it cost only thirty-five dollars a month, and she undertook to pay this, with the excuse that she was going to fix it up and use it as a workroom for her stage designing. Meanwhile the people at New York University had welcomed him "with open arms" and tried to sign him up to teach the spring and summer terms at a salary of $2200, but Mrs. Bernstein insisted that he must finish his book first

and promised to support him for the remainder of that year. For a week
he was in an agony of indecision. "I moved into Eighth Street last
night," he wrote in his diary on January 5. "Very nervous, trying to
work. Offer from N.Y.U.—anxious for me. Want to write—but nervous.
Must decide what. Must finish book. I am weary of the old forms—
the old language—it has come to me quite simply these past three days
that we must mine deeper—find language again in its primitive sinews—
like the young man, Conrad. Joyce gets it at times in *Ulysses*. It is
quite simple but terrific. Build the book, brick by brick."

Finally he yielded to Mrs. Bernstein's arguments and to his own compulsion to write the book. By the second week in January he was settled
down at Eighth Street and making notes for the famous lunchroom
scene in *Look Homeward, Angel*, as well as the scene in which Gant
returns from California in 1906. He hoped to "get" the book "on paper
by April," but the more he worked on it, the more he was impelled to
write. His description of George Webber's difficulties with this sort of
thing in *The Web and the Rock* is most revealing: "He worked feverishly, furiously, day by day, week by week, and month by month . . . —
and at the end . . . there was nothing done, nothing really accomplished, nothing finished, in all that plan of writing which, begun so
modestly the year before, had spread and flowered like a cancerous
growth until now it had engulfed him. From his childhood he could
remember all that people said or did, but as he tried to set it down his
memory opened up enormous vistas and associations, going from
depth to limitless depth, until the simplest incident conjured up a
buried continent of experience, and he was overwhelmed by a project
of discovery and revelation that would have broken the strength and
used up the lives of a regiment of men.

"The thing that drove him on was nothing new. Even in early childhood some stern compulsion, a burning thirst to know just how things
were, had made him go about a duty of observing people with such
fanatical devotion that they had often looked at him resentfully, wondering what was wrong with him, or them. And in his years at college,
under the same relentless drive, he had grown so mad and all-observing
that he had tried to read ten thousand books, and finally had begun
to stare straight through language like a man who, from the very fury of
his looking, gains a superhuman intensity of vision, so that he no longer
sees merely the surfaces of things but seems to look straight through
a wall. . . . Words—even the words of the greatest poets—lost all the
magic and the mystery they had had for him, and what the poet said
seemed only a shallow and meager figuration of what he might have

said, had some superhuman energy and desperation of his soul, greater than any man had ever known or attempted, driven him on to empty out the content of the ocean in him."

The winter of 1927 dragged along. Wolfe wrote almost every night from midnight until 6 A.M., then slept and woke to write again, goading himself on by drinking twelve to eighteen cups a day of the vile strong coffee which he made himself and which, as he put it, "gets me simply crazy with nerves but . . . keeps me alive and cursing." He usually took time off for only one real meal a day, cooked for him by the devoted Mrs. Bernstein or eaten in a restaurant in the vicinity of N.Y.U. or of the Harvard Club, where, for the sake of keeping Eighth Street free from intrusion, he received his mail. There are many stories about his "gargantuan appetite," but it takes a large amount of food to satisfy a whole day's hunger.

Sometimes Mrs. Bernstein took him to literary parties, thinking it would help him to meet people in the publishing world. However, as he wrote to Mrs. Roberts, "I'm somewhat afraid of people, and sometimes conceal my fear by being arrogant and sneering magnificently." In spite of Mrs. Bernstein's unwavering belief in him, the "chip on his shoulder" was still there, and its size and precariousness increased in direct ratio to every ounce of liquor he drank. He was not an outright alcoholic, though he had a tendency toward being one which he fought against with varying degrees of success for all his adult life. However, if he was sick or mentally upset or having trouble with his work, he often would use liquor as a kind of cure-all or escape. Also, if he were obliged to go to parties or to meet new people, both of which he dreaded, he would "fortify himself with copious drafts of raw gin" (or later, after the repeal of Prohibition, whisky). The results were ludicrously lamentable. He was painfully polite and eager to be friends with everyone, so much so that he was constantly imposed upon, but he also had a trait which Maxwell Perkins later called "Tom's mountaineer suspicion." If he had much to drink, he would suddenly take offense at some innocently meant remark, or burst out with some wild and all-inclusive condemnation of the people he was with, or give vent to his pathological jealousy over Mrs. Bernstein. He describes a typical example of the latter in his diary for New Year's Eve 1927, only two days after his return from Europe: "Met Jew at 11 o'clock. Waited till after New Year's in Eighth Street. Went then to Webster Hall, 11th Street, Fine Arts Ball. Danced with her. Floor crowded—nearly everybody drunk. . . . Went upstairs to Neighborhood Playhouse box. . . .

Young men and women come in. Young man drunk, gives me a drink, tells me he likes me, later puts arms around her. . . . I ask her if she minds. He questions me challengingly about that. I throw him back in his seat. Excitement and disorder. Presently he says if I want physical satisfaction (although he likes me) he will give it to me. I will give you all you want, I said. I get up and face him, and they all surround me. She insists that I come below to dance. When we get there, says we must go. We walk to Eighth Street, very sad. She weeps for an hour and says my attack was unnecessary—that he was 'just a kid.' I am cut to the heart—she says 'No heroics,' but I talk to her plainly. I say I have acted badly but like myself—I am no better than I was to-night—I do not want them to put their hands on her. I told the young man so—I did what I felt like doing at the moment—I am no better, no worse—and I am not a belligerent person. She says we must never go out among people again. I am terribly sad. 'I'm sorry, but you mustn't put your hands on her,' I said."

The spring of 1927 came, and with it a new burst of inspiration. "The room was littered now with great piles and heaps of finished manuscript, and still he wrote," Wolfe said later of George Webber in *The Web and the Rock.* "His mind was ablaze with a stream of swarming images, stamping a thousand brilliant pictures on his brain with the speed of light, the flare of a soaring rocket. And in each of these flaming and instant pictures there was buried entire and whole the fruit of every long and painful ardor of his mind and memory. . . . He yielded stubbornly and irritably to snatches of fevered sleep, where the whole enormous weight of time and memory worked constantly, unrestingly, shaping itself into a vast, congruent structure of experience. The heightened activities of his mind fed always at repose and energy with a vulture's beak, so that he woke exhausted in the morning, only to hurl himself into his work again."

In July, Wolfe and Mrs. Bernstein went abroad again: this time to Paris, Strasbourg, Munich, Vienna, Prague, and Nuremberg. He stayed alone in Paris for a week or two after she had sailed for home: then he came back and resumed teaching at New York University. Mrs. Bernstein still stood by him with occasional financial aid and rented with him the second floor of an old house at 263 West Eleventh Street, using the big front room as her studio and leaving the rest for him. Here he plunged into work again, writing the last section of the book and also dictating the already finished portions of it from the illegible longhand in his ledgers to James Mandel, the student from N.Y.U. who at this time was typing for him. The day after Christmas he wrote his mother: "I am almost at the end of my book (and of my strength!). If I hold out I should finish by Jan 1, or a little later. I am writing the 'big scene' at the end now." But, as usual, he was too optimistic—he did not actually finish until three months later.

Meanwhile he had been trying to find a title for the book. In July 1926, when he had first begun to write it, he had thought of calling it *The Building of a Wall*, to symbolize the struggle of his hero to find "an essential isolation; a creative solitude; a secret life." A few months later, in November, he jotted down a list of "Possible Titles": *The Building of a Wall*; *Young Poseidon*, *Poseidon's Harbor*, or *Theseus* (allegories which he later tried again to use for *Of Time and the River* and finally discarded); and *The Hills Beyond Pentland* (a title which he later gave to his projected book about his mother's people). By June 1927 he was considering *Alone*, *Alone*, "from the poem I love best, *The Rime of the Ancient Mariner*." But by September of that year he had written his refrain "O lost, and by the wind grieved, ghost, come back again." Gradually he began to weave this into his narrative, as a recurrent theme, and to call the entire book *O, Lost!* It was not until the spring of 1929, when Scribners asked him to find a better title, that he finally hit upon *Look Homeward, Angel*, from the lines in Milton's "Lycidas": "Look homeward, Angel, now, and melt with ruth."

The last week in March 1928, Wolfe finally finished his book and wrote his apology for it (in the true sense of the word) in his "Note for the Publisher's Reader": "A book of this length from an unknown writer no doubt is rashly experimental, and shows his ignorance of the mechanics of publishing. . . . But I believe it would be unfair to assume that because this is a very long book it is too long a book. . . . There are some pages here which were compelled by a need for fullness of expression, and which . . . may now be excised. But their excision would not make a short book. . . . The book may be lacking in plot but it is not lacking in plan. The plan is rigid and densely woven. There are two essential movements—one outward and one downward. The outward movement describes the effort of a . . . youth for release, freedom, and loneliness in new lands. . . . The downward movement is represented by a constant excavation into the buried life of a group of people, and describes the cyclic curve of a family's life—genesis, union, decay, and dissolution. To me, who was joined so passionately with the people in this book, it seemed that they were the greatest people I had ever known . . . If I could get my magnificent people on paper as they were, . . . I believed that no one would object to my 250,000 words . . . If I have failed, . . . the fault lies not in my people—who could make an epic—but in me. . . .

"But that is what I wanted to do and tried to do. . . . When I began to write the book twenty months ago I got back something of a child's innocency and wonder. You may question this later when you come to the dirty words. But the dirty words can come out quickly—if the book has any chance of publication, they will come out without conscience or compunction. . . .

"It is, of course, obvious, that the book is 'autobiographical.' But in a literal sense, it is probably no more autobiographical than 'Gulliver's Travels.' . . . The book is a fiction—it is loaded with invention: story, fantasy, vision. But it is a fiction that is, I believe, more true than fact—a fiction that grew out of a life completely digested in my spirit . . . —which tries to comprehend people, in short, not by telling what people did, but what they should have done."

Wolfe ended his long apologia with the plea which all new writers make or want to make, and which is the despair of editorial readers: "I have written all this, not to propitiate you, . . . but to entreat you, if you spend the many hours necessary for a careful reading, to spend a little more time in giving me an opinion. If it is not publishable, could it be made so? . . . I need a little honest help. If you are interested enough to finish the book, won't you give it to me?"

He sent a carbon copy of the manuscript to Professor James B. Munn, who, as dean of New York University, had helped him both materially and with his unfailing understanding. The original typed copy he gave to Mrs. Bernstein, who had undertaken to show it to publishers for him. He had been unbusinesslike, to say the least, in trying to market his plays. As he wrote to his sister Mabel, "My greatest deficiency is a total lack of salesmanship . . . I never sent my plays to more than two or three managers and if I got no answer within a month I wrote insulting letters demanding their return. I have never known where to go, where to turn, or what to do." He concluded with relief: "This time, certain friends [by which he meant Mrs. Bernstein] will probably attend to that part of it for me."

Mrs. Bernstein first took the manuscript to Boni & Liveright, but after five weeks' consideration, their editor declined it, saying: "It is so long—so terribly long—that it is most difficult for a reader to sustain an interest to the end. One cannot deny that much of it has quality, if not originality—on the whole it is a pattern—the autobiography of a young man—and so much of it has been done, and so often, that we hesitate to take another chance. . . ." Wolfe went into one of his fits of deep depression. In his ignorance of publishing, he had thought that the book would be accepted by the first editor who read it: now he swung too far the other way and became convinced that he was "no good." But Mrs. Bernstein was undaunted. She next took the manuscript to Melville Cane, who was attorney for Harcourt, Brace, hoping that he would recommend it to that firm. Cane did not do so because he felt that its enormous size and chaotic condition would discourage any publisher.[8] However, he was most sympathetic and friendly to Wolfe and urged him to cut the manuscript before showing it elsewhere so that it would stand a better chance. This, Wolfe could not and would not do.

Meanwhile Mrs. Bernstein had given a carbon copy of the book to Ernest Boyd, the writer and critic. Boyd evidently did not find time to read the entire manuscript, but when Mrs. Bernstein phoned him to ask about it, he offered to give it to his wife, Madeleine Boyd, who at that time was starting her literary agency. Mrs. Boyd was very much interested in it and sent word to Wolfe that she would like to try to sell it as his agent. He was only too relieved to turn over the marketing of it to her—as he naïvely put it in his first letter to her of May 18, "I know very few writing and publicity people—and I am in great need of someone who will talk to me and advise me."

Mrs. Boyd first submitted *Look Homeward, Angel* to the newly founded firm of Covici, Friede. They, too, rejected it but asked for an option on Wolfe's next book, saying that if it was shorter than the first and as well written, they would publish it. Wolfe, of course, refused to give them this: he wanted to sell the *Angel*. However, he had grown discouraged about the possibility of doing so and had begun referring to it as "the Monster." "The illusion of creation which had sustained" him "for two and a half years had . . . worn off." Moreover, as he said later, "a writer writes a book in order to forget it. For that reason, a writer, after he has got the whole thing off his chest, wants to forget it utterly." And so he left the marketing of the manuscript entirely in the hands of Mrs. Boyd and began making plans to go abroad.

With the completion of his book he had come to a definite turning point in his career and, as he wrote to Dean Munn, he felt "as if my life were beginning again." Instinctively he turned away from the *Angel*, and from many other things in his life as well. His turnings away

[8] From a letter written by Melville Cane to Richard S. Kennedy.

were not decisive at this time—they were only a series of tentative steps, followed by reversions to his former ways—but they came from a deep impulse inside him, and they marked the way his life would go during the next three years.

Only four days after finishing his book he resigned from New York University, explaining in his letter to Professor Watt: "I think the time has come when I must make a bold venture with my life: in some way—not, I am afraid, very clearly defined yet—I want to get the energy of my life directed towards the thing it desires most. In short, I am going to try to support myself by writing—if necessary, by hack writing of any sort, stories, advertising, articles—but *writing* of a sort." For over a year he had thought of trying some radio shows for the free-lance programs which his friend Henry Carlton was then doing over WJZ and WEBF. He had also talked vaguely of doing free-lance synopses for the movies, but he never actually tried either, and his talent was even less suited to these kinds of work than it had been for writing plays. He also considered working as an advertising writer for J. Walter Thompson. Mrs. Bernstein had shown parts of *Look Homeward, Angel* to Mrs. Helen Resor of that firm, who had promptly offered Wolfe a job but had stipulated that he must promise to keep it for three years. He was tempted by the generous salary but, as he wrote his mother, "I don't like the three year business." He asked "for a month or two leeway" before giving Mrs. Resor a definite answer, went abroad, and then lost interest in the job. Finally, in January 1929, he went back to New York University and taught there for another year. However, this was only an economic stopgap while he waited to see whether the Scribners publication of the *Angel* would be a success: he had already decided that he was through with teaching, and in January 1930 he resigned again, for good.

It was also at this time that Wolfe yielded to his compulsion to be free from Mrs. Bernstein and made his first definite attempt to break off his relationship with her. For the past two years they had had quarrels of increasing frequency and bitterness, and during the spring of 1928 these had mounted to such a pitch that they were both at the end of their endurance. In his notes Wolfe called his trip abroad that summer "The Grand Tour of Renunciation" and said that that year came the parting of the ways between himself and Mrs. Bernstein, "after a long and bitter war of separation." Although she, too, was traveling in Europe that summer and at one time was only 160 miles away from him, they did not see each other, but the truth was that, after his first taste of freedom, he missed her dreadfully and sent her the finest and most deeply affectionate letters that he ever was to write. Finally, after being injured in a drunken brawl at the October Fair in Munich, he again surrendered to her, in a fit of deep remorse at all the error of his ways. When he arrived back in America in January 1929, they resumed their old relationship and maintained it for another year. However, his decision to break away from her had been irrevocably made: in spite of all his vacillations, the die was cast, and finally, in the early 1930s, he made the severance complete. It was a cruel, a heartbreaking thing, which cost him years of bitterness and brooding and which drove her to attempted suicide, but he could not possibly deny his deep compulsion to be free.

VIII

THE REASONS for Wolfe's quarrels with Mrs. Bernstein and his final rejection of her are far too numerous and too complex for any glib accounting. But, for one thing, he undoubtedly was swayed by the normal masculine urge for freedom: as he wrote later to Maxwell Perkins, "I think the desire for wandering is more common to men, and for fixity . . . to women." For another, he was still too young—too immature emotionally—to settle down to any permanent relationship: he felt that he must regain "the lonely wild integrity of youth which had been his" before he met her, and in this he undoubtedly was right.

For still another thing, she was much too old for him, and too much his mother in every way. His subconscious resentment against maternal domination undoubtedly repeated itself in his attitude toward her, as it did toward any woman and every woman, and made him think of each of them as "the author of his doom."[1]

For another, his compulsion to search for a "superior being" had made him subject her to the most intense and searching examination of her life and character, and led to his discovery of human weaknesses in her which he brooded over with vindictive bitterness. In a revealing description of Monk Webber in *The Web and the Rock* he says: "Perhaps, although he did not know it, there was destruction in him too, for what he loved and got his hands on he squeezed dry, and it could not be otherwise with him. It was something that came from nature, from memory, from inheritance, from the blazing energies of youth, from something outside of him and external to him, yet within him, that drove him forever, and that he could not help."

In the letter which he wrote to Mr. Perkins in January 1931, Wolfe briefly outlined the different phases of his relationship with Mrs. Bernstein. After he fell desperately in love with her, he says that soon "the

[1] Vardis Fisher has examined Wolfe's entire life and work in the light of "his deep and tormenting attachment to his mother" in two articles, "My Experiences with Thomas Wolfe" and "Thomas Wolfe—Maxwell Perkins," in the April and July 1951 issues of *Tomorrow*.

thought of her began to possess and dominate every moment of my life, I wanted to own, possess and devour her; I became insanely jealous; I began to get horribly sick inside; and then all physical love, desire, passion, ended completely—but I still loved the woman, I could not endure her loving anyone else . . . and my madness and jealousy ate at me like a poison, like all horrible sterility and barrenness. Twice I got away from New York and came abroad in an effort to end it, but when I came back I would resume my life with the woman again." This pathological jealousy was the chief cause of their quarrels during the last years of their relationship together. At one time, probably when he was first in love with her, Wolfe had asked her to marry him[2] and she had very sensibly refused to desert her family for him. As a result, he was resentful of her family, but what tortured him most was a totally unfounded suspicion that she might become romantically involved with some unknown man. "I do not know whether you know how frightfully jealous he was," she wrote to Elizabeth Nowell later. "He could hardly bear to have me talk to another man. . . . It was a curse and caused me untold agony. . . . God in heaven will only know what I suffered from his jealousy, for years he would telephone me at two, three, or four in the morning to find out if I was home or out."[3]

He himself, in a remorseful letter written in August 1928, on finding that she had sailed for home without meeting him in Europe, blames their alienation upon this obsessive jealousy: "I have never felt so keenly the certainty of our parting as I do now, writing you on the ship that will take you thousands of miles away from me. Even when we left each other in New York, I think I told myself I should see you again in Europe, but even then I think I knew that I shouldn't. Because, dear Aline, it is not now that I am losing you—that happened a number of months ago, I saw it and knew it when it happened. I was obsessed with the work I was doing, driven on desperately to finish it, and unable to stop and try to save us both at the time. I was like a man engaged in some violent effort, who is yet conscious of all the sounds and movements around him. I think you must have seen and understood some of the agony of those months—my job to do, the horrible pain lengthening out day by day, and no escape—until I roamed the streets of New York by night, cursing like a madman, bolstering myself to face them

[2] This is according to what Wolfe told Edward C. Aswell in the spring of 1938 and to what Mrs. Bernstein told Aswell later.

[3] From an undated letter written by Mrs. Bernstein to Elizabeth Nowell in 1950.

with doses of raw gin, and so far losing myself as to call your house at unexpected times, day and night, in an effort to keep track of you. I am not very hopeful, Aline, about the future of my life, of our life—of anything at present. Love made me mad, and brought me down to the level of the beasts."

Even though he wrote this in a fit of real remorse, it is very characteristic of the indecision about his relationship with Mrs. Bernstein which he felt during that entire summer. In a letter written to her at Carlsbad in July, he had told her that he did not know whether he would ever see her again, but for the most part, he only dared to hint of the possibility of his breaking free from her. He simply could not get his courage up to tell her, let alone actually to leave her, and it is no wonder that when he finally did in 1930, she was shocked and outraged. If she could have simply let him go, instead of trying to hold him with such desperate tenacity and with such an unalterable conviction that she was being wronged, much of the bitterness and tragedy of their separation could have been avoided. But the harder she tried to hold him, and the more she heaped reproaches on him, the more determined he became to break away. As he said later, "A creative man . . . if he is going to live and grow, must change." His genius had to develop without interference, and if any person tried to hold him back, he felt a kind of claustrophobia, which made him struggle desperately to be free.

Before Wolfe sailed for Europe he went home to Asheville for a visit—his first since he had fallen in love with Mrs. Bernstein in 1925. During the writing of *Look Homeward, Angel* all his repressed resentment against his family had risen to the surface: he had written with great bitterness about them both in the book and in his letters, he had refused his mother's invitations to come home, and he had "broken almost utterly away from my old life—from my family, my native town, my earlier associations." Now the catharsis had been accomplished—he had "got the whole thing off his chest"—and he could "go home again." As he sat in the familiar Asheville Pullman car, K 19, on the 2:05 train out of Pennsylvania Station, he made a brief but emotional entry in his notebook: "Saturday, June 10, 1928. On this day I left New York for a few days in North Carolina where I was born."

He arrived to find "everyone very poor and the town flat on its back after the boom." The inflation of Asheville real estate had reached its peak in 1926 and had then gone into the long decline which ended in the complete financial collapse of the town in 1930. Wolfe's mother and some of the other members of his family had been involved in real-estate speculation both in Asheville and in Florida: they did not suffer serious losses until the crash of 1930, but they were already frightened and bewildered to see their paper profits vanish in thin air. Wolfe could not resist the temptation to crow over them a little—he had always been bitterly opposed to his mother's "real-estate mania"—but from this time forth the "chip on his shoulder" toward his family began to disappear and to be replaced by real solicitude for them.

Meanwhile he had started on another book, *The River People*. As he wrote to Dean Munn, "I've got a *new* book in mind. I thought I should not write again for several centuries, but there's no cure for my own kind of lunacy. I don't see how this one can fail—it has everything: rich people, swank, a poor but beautiful girl, romance, adventure, Vienna, New York, a big country house, and so on. Also, after a careful examination of 4,362 modern novels, I have decided to make it exactly 79,427 words long. Will you please order your copy now? But honestly, I'm excited about it. In spite of my summary, I've got stuff for a good and moving book—also, perhaps, stuff for a bad and trashy, but possibly successful book. Now what's a poor young guy to do, Dean Munn? I've got to do it one way or the other—straddling the fence is no good."

Influenced by the rejections of *Look Homeward, Angel*, Wolfe was trying to write a more popular kind of book. According to his notes and outlines, he first planned it as the story of a tragic love affair between a young artist, Joel Pierce, and a beautiful Viennese girl, Lili. Joel was to paint "one great picture of her, touched with love and madness," but his family was to oppose the romance and finally Lili was to "meet death at the hands of John," a cousin of Joel's. This plot was entirely fictitious and melodramatic, or, as Wolfe put it, "bad and trashy." Gradually he turned away from it and went back to describing the experiences of his favorite semi-autobiographical character, who had been introduced into the book as a friend of Joel's and who was sometimes called Eugene, sometimes Hugh or Oliver. By the time Wolfe reached Europe he had begun recounting all of his adventures there as those of Oliver. The book rambled off into these autobiographical fragments: it was never finished, but parts of it were later included in *Of Time and the River* and *The Web and the Rock*.

He sailed for Europe on June 30, spent two weeks in Paris, two in Brussels, and then set out for Cologne by way of Antwerp and Malines. In the latter town he had a close escape from being set upon and robbed in his room at 3 A.M., but he let out a bloodcurdling rebel yell and hurled his size-13 shoe against the door, making such a terrifying noise that the thieves fled back in panic to the next room down the hall.

However, to be on the safe side, he spent the remainder of the night in singing at the top of his lungs, pounding thunderously with his walking stick against the wall, and bursting into sudden fits of insane laughter. The thieves were evidently nonplused by this strange behavior and did not bother him again.

Wolfe felt strongly drawn to Germany as "his father's country"—the place from which his paternal ancestors had come. He wanted to see it and absorb it because it was a part of his own roots. However, he was uneasy about going there because of the aftermath of the First World War. In one of his notebooks he says: "I was afraid to enter far into the country—for a long time I hung upon its borders. I visited the cities along the Rhine, . . . I went into Bavaria. During all the time I had been in Germany, I had always been placed so that freedom and escape lay not over four hours away by train."

From Cologne he went up the Rhine by boat to Bonn, where he visited Beethoven's birthplace. In one of the autobiographical fragments written for *The River People* he describes the deep effect this visit had upon him: "Oliver went up the narrow crooked stairs. . . . In a little dark room at the end of the hall so low he had to stoop to enter, all the music and all the glory had been born. There was little furniture—a bust of Beethoven with a faded wreath at its base; a glass case with a few scraps of yellowed paper in it. . . . And in one cabinet there were several enormous ear horns of brass—great clumsy devices of the early eighteenth century. Oliver looked for a moment, remembering suddenly what he had forgotten—that all this magic which had enchanted the ears of the world had fallen on its own deaf ones. Something like a hand was clenched around his heart; his eyes were blind for a moment. He moved on. He began to look at the paintings and drawings of the composer which covered the walls, . . . staring for minutes at that wild and stormy face in which music was flowing like a wind. And always there was that sense of listening, of seclusion within the fortress of one's self that he had come to notice on the faces of the deaf. There was one picture in which Beethoven came stamping across uneven ground, with a great wrack of cloud behind him and his wild hair blown in the wind, and a tempest gathered in his stormy face. And it was evident from this picture that this man was a world complete unto himself—the earth around him did not matter, the storm behind him did not matter, nothing human or divine or earthly could touch him—a storm wilder than any in heaven was gathering within him: in him were all the elements of creation. . . .

"Oliver moved on, again and again around the room, with the thousand shapes of that immortal face before him. And presently he, too, had forgotten the world; and the million sounds of life: he felt the all-inclusive power of that great face: he was entrenched within the ramparts of his own soul, and he felt the elements of a world within him. Presently he stood again before the case where the ear horns were, and as he looked at their great clumsy shapes, a gate swung open suddenly in his heart, his senses seemed to drown, and a smothering flood of passion and of joy rose up and smote him in the throat. His eyes went blind and he began suddenly to weep. Great hoarse cries were wrenched from him, great tearless sobs that filled the house of music with their harsh pain . . . and yet he did not know he wept: he only knew that a gate had opened in his heart and he had found release."

Perhaps Wolfe did not actually weep, but at any rate he was so deeply moved that for the following week he kept his ears stuffed with cotton in order to experience deafness and to feel "entrenched within the ramparts of his own soul." He was taking one groping step forward in his struggle to overcome his "hunger to devour the earth," "to find some sense of peace, certitude and direction in my own life." Wolfe had a striking resemblance to Beethoven, especially to the Höfel portrait, and was like him, too, in his highly emotional nature, his sudden outbursts of anger, his subsequent fits of remorse, and his basically deep affection and pity for his fellow men. As Desmond Powell said in his article on Wolfe,[4] "Like Beethoven he knew all the agonies. But the resolution of all agonies into surety or strength or resignation he did not know."

After a week in Bonn he went on up the Rhine to Mainz, Wiesbaden, and Frankfurt, where he had his second chance encounter with James Joyce. Then, finally, on September 8, he went to Munich. By the sixteenth of that month he had settled down there in a pension and was writing in his diary one of his typical exhortations to himself to work: "If I can write 50,000 words—2500 a day—for the three weeks I shall stay here, I shall consider my stay here not useless." But he could not settle down and write—he still was trying to "devour too much of the world"—too much of "his father's country." In *The Web and the Rock* he attributes this "hunger" of his to Monk Webber and describes it at great length: "He was hungry all the time, ravenous as he had never been in his whole life before, and nothing that he did or ate could stop or diminish it. . . . It was a hunger not only of the belly, but a hunger of the mind and heart and spirit, which got translated in the most

[4] "Of Thomas Wolfe," in the Spring 1945 issue of the *Arizona Quarterly*.

astounding and appalling way to all the appetites of sense and flesh. . . . It was like some enormous consumption of the soul and body for which there is no cure, for which there is no end.

"In the morning he would go out . . . and pass along the Theresien-strasse . . . and a dozen times along the way he would be halted by the temptations of this agonizing hunger and this thirst. . . . The windows of the 'Feinkost' shops were maddening. They were crammed with the most astounding variety of appetizing foods, sausages of every shape and kind that fairly made his mouth water when he looked at them, cheeses, roasts of meat, smoked hams, tall, slender bottles of fine wine, . . . a gourmet's treasure house, that exerted over him an irresistible hypnotic fascination. Whenever he approached one of these places . . . he would turn his eyes away, lower his head, and try to hurry past—but it was no use. . . . It was impossible to go by them without stopping. . . . And if he got by one, there was always another. . . . It was the same way with the pastry shops with their cherry, plum, and peach, and apple cakes, their crusty miracles of bakery, covered with whipped cream. So, too, with all the sweet and candy stores. There were the chocolates and bonbons, the candies and the crystal fruits, the glacéed plums and cherries and the cubes of pineapple, the brandied chocolates and the fragrant gums.

"It was the same with everything he saw, with everything he did. . . . He wanted to eat up everything, to drink up everything, to read up everything, to remember and to look up everything, to get his hands upon the palpable and impossible body, the magnificent plenitude, of a whole groaning earth, to devour it, to consume it, to have and hold it for his own forever. . . .

"He went to the museums, those crowded and innumerable granaries into which they had collected the enormous treasures of their art. . . . He tried to feed upon the very pigments of the canvas, he tried to print each picture in his brain and on his memory with such voracious eagerness that it seemed as if the very color had gone out of them and had sunk through into his eyes. Day after day he walked the crowded galleries of the Old Pinakothek until the guards were fearful of his purpose and followed him from room to room. He almost pulled Mathias Grünewald from the wall; he walked straight out of there carrying those lovely naked girls of Lucas Cranach in his brain. He pulled every ounce of rose-hued flesh, every swirling universe of heaven and of earth, out of the swarming canvases of Rubens, and every canvas in that whole enormous gallery, from Grünewald to Rubens, from Lucas Cranach to Hans Holbein, from Breughel to 'The Apostles' of

Albrecht Dürer, and from Teniers to the Master of 'The Life of Mary.'
He had them all enlisted in his brain, printed in his heart, painted
on the canvas of his soul.

"He haunted bookshops with the same insatiate and unreasoning
desire. He spent hours before the crowded windows of the book stores,
memorizing the names of countless books, written in a language he
could scarcely read. . . . That staggering superflux of German culture
maddened him with an intolerable and impossible hunger for possession. . . . He was horribly involved, caught up, entangled, in the
Laocoön coils of his own madness. . . . He wanted to possess in its
entirety, fathom in its profundity, utter in its finality, that which was
in itself unpossessable, unfathomable, and unutterable—the old Germanic and swarm-haunted mind of man. . . .

"At night he walked the streets. He went into the crowded places. He
sought the beer-fogged flash and roar, the enormous restaurants. He
plunged into the roaring tumult of the Hofbrau Haus, swung to the
rhythm of that roaring life, breathed the air, felt the warmth, the surge,
the powerful communion of those enormous bodies, gulped down from
stone mugs liter after liter of the cold and powerful dark beer. He
swung and swayed and roared and sang and shouted in the swaying
mass, felt a terrible jubilation, a mad lust, the unsated hunger filling
him, and still could find no end and seek no rest."

Then the October Fair began, in celebration of the dark October
beer, which was twice as strong as the usual variety. On his third visit
to the fair Wolfe got in a drunken brawl, from which he emerged
with a broken nose, a slight concussion, and four deep lacerations of
the scalp. He describes this best in his long letter of October 4 to Mrs.
Bernstein: "The place was closing for the night . . . I talked to the
people at my table, drank my beer, and got up to go. I had had seven or
eight liters—this would mean almost a quart of alcohol. I was quite
drunk from the beer. I started down one of the aisles toward a side
entrance. There I met several men—and perhaps a woman, although
I did not see her until later. . . . They spoke to me—I was too drunk
to understand what they said, but I am sure it was friendly enough.
. . . One of them, it seems to me, grasped me by the arm—I moved
away, he held on, and although I was not angry, but rather in an excess
of exuberance, I knocked him over a table. Then I rushed out of the
place exultantly, feeling like a child who has thrown a stone through a
window.

". . . Outside it was raining hard; I found myself in an enclosure
behind some of the fair buildings . . . I heard shouts and cries behind

me, and turning, I saw several men running down upon me. One of them was carrying one of the fold-up chairs of the beer hall . . . I saw that he intended to hit me with this, and I remember that this angered me. I stopped and turned and in that horrible slippery mudhole, I had a bloody fight with these people. I remember the thing now with horror as a kind of hell of slippery mud, and blood, and darkness, with the rain falling upon us several maniacs who were trying to kill. At that time I was too wild, too insane, to be afraid, but I seemed to be drowning in mud—it was really the blood that came pouring from my head into my eyes. . . . I felt the heavy bodies on top of me, snarling, grunting, smashing at my face and back. I rose up under them as if coming out of some horrible quicksand—then my feet slipped again in the mud, and I went down again into the bottomless mud. . . .

"Somehow—I do not know how it came about—I was on my feet again, and moving towards the dark forms that swept in towards me. . . . From this time on I can remember fighting with only two men, and later there was a woman who clawed my face. The smaller figure —the smaller man—rushed towards me, and I struck it with my fist. It went diving away into the slime. I was choking in blood and cared for nothing now but to end it finally—to kill this other thing or be killed. So with all my strength I threw it to the earth: I could not see, but I fastened my fingers and hand in its eyes and face—it was choking me, but presently it stopped. . . . The woman was now on my back, screaming, beating me over the head, gouging at my face and eyes. She was screaming out 'Leave my man alone!' . . . Some people came and pulled me from him—the man and woman screamed and jabbered at me, but I could not make out what they said, except her cry of 'Leave my man alone,' which I remember touched me deeply. . . .

"These people went away—where or how I don't know—but I saw them later in the police station, so I judge they had gone there. . . . Some German people gathered around me yelling and gesticulating, and one man kept crying 'Ein Arzt! Ein Arzt!' ('A Doctor! A Doctor!') I felt my head all wet, but thought it was the rain, until I put my hand there and brought it away all bloody. At this moment, three or four policemen rushed up, seized me, and hustled me off to the station. First they took me to the police surgeons—I was taken into a room with a white, hard light. The woman was lying on a table with wheels below it. The light fell upon her face—her eyes were closed. I think this is the most horrible moment of my life . . . I thought she was dead, and that I would never be able to remember how it happened. The surgeons . . . dressed my head wounds. Then one of them looked at my nose, and said it was broken, and that I must go the next day to a doctor. When I got up and looked around, the woman and the wheeled table was gone. I am writing this . . . six days later: if she were dead, surely by this time I would know. . . .

"From the doctors I was taken before the police next door where they asked me many questions which I did not answer. They also had two of the other men there, looking very bloody, also—and perhaps others I did not see. Then they let me go, when they could get nothing out of me."

Wolfe spent the rest of the night at his pension and in the morning went to an American physician, Dr. Eugene F. Du Bois of Cornell Medical College, who at that time was working as a volunteer in a Munich clinic. Dr. Du Bois immediately put him in the hospital under the care of the leading head surgeon of Munich, where he remained four days. His stay there was not a peaceful one. He was questioned further by the police, and he became obsessed with fear that the woman or one of the men he had fought with might have died: he thought he would be arrested for murder as soon as he was well enough to leave the hospital. Furthermore, he had an inborn fear of sickness and of hospitals which, at first, kept him on the verge of hysteria. One of his scalp wounds was a small one far back on his head which the German surgeon either had not discovered or had left to heal by itself. Wolfe kept worrying about it and shouting for the nuns who served as nurses in the hospital until it finally was treated to his satisfaction.

But as the days dragged by, he grew more calm and began solemnly to reflect about himself. His remorse was deep, not only for the brawl at the October Fair but for all his frenzy of the past few months; and he resolved on a complete reconciliation with Mrs. Bernstein. In a moving letter he wrote to her: "In several of your letters you have begged me to make use of 'this precious time'—not to waste it—to make something of my life now while I have the chance. Every one of these words stabs me—I know how right you are, and how little I have made of my chances—how I have wasted everything most precious—paramountly yourself—and made a wreck of everything I wanted to make beautiful. I do not know the reason for it. It seems to me that the people who lose all reason in this world are the people who try most desperately to find it. I know I have always been after the reason of things—I am now more than ever—my brain is weary and wants rest and cannot get it. It is like something that hunts round and round inside an iron cylinder, trying to find some way out when there is none. . . . My dear, I am coming back to America and get some kind of paying work, and then perhaps, if you want it, we can have some kind of life together again. . . .

"I am going through a horrible struggle of the spirit, and unless I find some way out, I am done for. It is not new—it has gone on now for several years. You have seen it, and I do not think you have ever understood it very well. . . . We can do nothing until we know our limits—I have never found mine, I don't know what they are—and at present I am spiritually a grovelling worm, wondering why some useful catastrophe can not erase this constructive-less, light-less, nothing-less life."

On October 4, the day after his twenty-eighth birthday, Wolfe left the hospital and, a few days later, went to Oberammergau to visit the Passion Players with an elderly American woman who wanted him to write a book about them. But one of his head wounds had broken open and become infected, and it had to be dressed by the Oberammergau doctor and famous Passion Player Anton Lang. Wolfe came back to Munich for another week, but he still lived in constant terror lest he be arrested, and to make things worse, he came down with one of his severe feverish colds. Finally he "escaped" across the border into Austria, arriving at Vienna on October 19. It was here that he received a cablegram from Mrs. Bernstein and a letter from Mrs. Boyd saying that Maxwell Perkins, the head editor of Scribners, had read the manuscript of Look Homeward, Angel and was interested in it.

Strangely enough, Wolfe refused to be excited by this news. He explains this as the attitude of Monk Webber in You Can't Go Home Again: "All the time he was abroad it nauseated him to think of his manuscript, of the years of work and sleepless nights he had put into it, and of the high hopes that had sustained him through it; and he had tried not to think of it, convinced now that it was no good, that he himself was no good, and that all his hot ambitions and his dreams of fame were the vaporings of a shoddy aesthete without talent. . . . But now . . . the Rodney people were interested. Well, they had taken their time about it. And what did 'interested' mean? Very likely they would tell him they had detected in the book some slight traces of a talent which, with careful nursing, could be schooled to produce, in time, a publishable book. He had heard that publishers sometimes had a weather eye for this sort of thing and that they would often string an aspiring author along for years, giving him just the necessary degree of encouragement to keep him from abandoning hope altogether and to make him think that they had faith in his great future if only he would go on writing book after rejected book until he 'found himself.' Well, he'd show them that he was not their fool! Not by so much as a flicker of an eyelash would he betray his disappointment, and he would commit himself to nothing!"

Moreover, he was sunk so deep in remorse over the fight at the October Fair, and involved so completely in the struggle with his own soul, that he could concentrate on nothing else. In reply to Mrs. Bernstein's excited cablegram telling him of Scribners' interest he wrote: "In my present state, Scribners does not make even a dull echo in me. I have seen so much print that I feel it is criminal to add to it. Perhaps you can help me to get back a little vanity, a little self-belief, a little boastfulness. God knows we all ought to have some, and all my egoism has plunged downwards and left me stuck in the mud."

In this frame of mind, he wandered around Vienna for five more days, then went to Budapest, where, except for a brief trip to the picturesque village of Mezö-Kövesd, he stayed two weeks. It was not until he got back to Vienna that he found the letter which had been written to him on October 22 by Mr. Perkins:

Dear Mr. Wolfe:

Mrs. Ernest Boyd left with us, some weeks ago, the manuscript of your novel, "O, Lost!" I do not know whether it would be possible to work out a plan by which it might be worked into a form publishable by us, but I do know that, setting the practical aspects of the matter aside, it is a very remarkable thing, and that no editor could read it without being excited by it and filled with admiration by many passages in it and sections of it.

Your letter, that came with it, shows that you realize what difficulties it presents, so that I need not enlarge upon this side of the question. What we should like to know is whether you will be in New York in a fairly near future, when we can see you and discuss the manuscript. We should certainly look forward to such an interview with very great interest.

Wolfe's answer was written in his new and humble mood. It had no trace of the "proud and vaunting speech" which had made his letters to producers so offensive, but was simple, boyish, and confiding. He began by telling Mr. Perkins of his fight at the October Fair, "which," as he wrote to Mrs. Roberts, "was beginning early with a stranger." He then went on to explain: "I had indigestion from seeing and trying to take in too much, and I was depressed at my failure to settle down to work. Now I feel better. I have decided to come back to New York in December, and I shall come to see you very soon after my arrival.

"I have not looked at my book since I gave a copy to Mrs. Boyd. At the time I realized the justice of all people said—particularly the impossibility of printing it in its present form and length. But at that time I was 'written out' on it—I could not go back and revise. Now I believe I can come back to it with a much fresher and more critical feeling. I have no right to expect others to do for me what I should do for myself, but, although I am able to criticize wordiness and over-abundance in others, I am not able practically to criticize it in myself. The business of selection and of revision is simply hell for me—my efforts to cut out 50,000 words may sometimes result in my adding 75,000.

"As for the obscene passages and the dirty words, I know perfectly well that no publisher could print them. Yet, I swear to you, it all seemed to me very easy and practical when I wrote them. But I already have begun to write a long letter to you, when all I should do is to thank you for your letter and say when I am coming back. Then the other things can come out when I see you. . . .

"I am looking forward to meeting you, and I am still youthful enough to hope that something may come of it. It will be a strange thing indeed to me if at last I shall manage to make a connection with such a firm as Scribners which, in my profound ignorance of all publishing matters, I had always thought vaguely was a solid and some-what conservative house. But it may be that I am a conservative and at bottom very correct person. . . ." It was altogether a strange letter to write to an unknown editor who might be persuaded to publish his first book, but it really was a good one to write to Maxwell Perkins, who always meditated deeply and with fascination on his authors' characters and who reacted to their wildest escapades with a mixture of fatherly anxiety and vicarious excitement. Moreover, every word of it showed that Wolfe was what in editorial parlance is known as "a real writer." But he did not stop to consider what effect his letter might have: he still had not the slightest hope that his book would be accepted, and he took Mr. Perkins' letter with so little seriousness that in the first draft of his reply he mistakenly addressed him "Dear Mr. Peters."

After mailing his reply, Wolfe seems to have put the whole thing out of his mind and relapsed into the trancelike state in which he had wandered over Europe for the past five months, trying to absorb it all. He spent two more weeks in Vienna, going to the festivities of Schubert Week, to the theater, to the coffeehouses, and to the museums, especially the Kunsthistorisches and the Albertina. Then, early in December, he started home, but on the way spent three more weeks exploring Italy before finally, on December 21, he sailed on the

Vulcania from Naples. In the little pocket diary which he kept during the stormy voyage across, he tried to sum things up: "Of what I shall find in New York, of what life I shall lead there, nothing yet. That must wait. . . . I have lived deeply, intensely, vividly, on the whole unhappily, for six months. Some people say that is all that matters. I do not think it is. But things can not be tallied up so easily. I am wondering in a vast *vague* about her. I love her, I think of seeing her again with a sense of strangeness and wonder; but I have no sort of idea what it will be like, or what has happened. Why can we not remember the face of anyone we love? This is true: Their faces melt into a thousand shades and shapes and images of faces, the moment we try to fix them in our memory. It is only the face of a stranger we remember there. Why? . . . Never has the many-ness and much-ness of things caused me such trouble as in the past six months. But never have I had so firm a conviction that our lives can live upon only a few things, that we must find them, and begin to build our fences. All creation is the building of a fence. But deeper study always, sharper senses, profounder living; *never* an end to curiosity! The fruit of all this comes later—I must think. I must mix it all with myself and with America. I have caught much of it on paper. But infinitely the greater part is in the mesh of my brain and blood."[5]

Then, as the ship approached New York, he cried out wildly in his diary: "What now! What now!" He did not dream that the next two weeks would be, as he said later, "the most glorious I have ever known . . . like all the fantasies I had as a child of recognition and success— only more wonderful." He did not know that in this same battered little pocket diary he would write in great elation: "January 7, 1929. On this day Charles Scribner and Son, Pub., accepted the *mss* of my first book." And again: "January 9, 1929. On this day I got letter from Scribners confirming their acceptance of my book." Beneath these momentous entries he inscribed two names:

Aline Bernstein   Thomas Wolfe

[5] This entry was later used in Eugene's diary in *Of Time and the River*.

IX

IN HIS article in the *Harvard Library Bulletin* Maxwell Perkins describes the beginning of his relationship with Wolfe: "The first time I heard of Thomas Wolfe I had a sense of foreboding. I who loved the man say this. Every good thing that comes is accompanied by trouble. It was in 1928 when Madeleine Boyd, a literary agent, came in. She talked of several manuscripts which did not much interest me, but frequently interrupted herself to tell of a wonderful novel about an American boy. I several times said to her, 'Why don't you bring it here, Madeleine?' and she seemed to evade the question. But finally she said, 'I will bring it, if you promise to read every word of it.' I did promise, but she told me other things that made me realize that Wolfe was a turbulent spirit, and that we were in for turbulence. When the manuscript came, I was fascinated by the first scene where Eugene's father, W. Oliver Gant, with his brother, two little boys, stood by a roadside in Pennsylvania and saw a division of Lee's Army on the march to Gettysburg.

"But then there came some ninety-odd pages about Oliver Gant's life in Newport News, and Baltimore, and elsewhere. All this was what Wolfe had heard, and had no actual association with which to reconcile it, and it was inferior to the first episode, and in fact to all the rest of the book. I was turned off to other work and gave the manuscript to Wallace Meyer, thinking, 'Here is another promising novel that will probably come to nothing.' Then Meyer showed me that wonderful night scene in the cafe where Ben was with the Doctors, and Horse Hines, the undertaker, came in. I dropped everything and began to read again, and all of us were reading the book simultaneously, you might say, including John Hall Wheelock, and there never was the slightest disagreement among us as to its importance."[1]

It was at this point that Perkins had written his letter of October 22 to Wolfe at Munich. He had already virtually decided to accept the

[1] From "Thomas Wolfe," by Maxwell E. Perkins, in the Autumn 1947 issue of the *Harvard Library Bulletin*.

book and had discussed it with Charles Scribner III, the president of the firm; but with characteristic conscientiousness, he was careful not to commit Scribners too hastily or to raise the author's hopes too high until every detail could be discussed and agreed upon. As he said later, "I never had a shadow of a doubt about the values of the book when I had finished it. I did know, though, that such a book would be resented by a good many people here, that it was very strong meat. I therefore did not try to get us committed to it immediately because I wanted first to find out what the author was like, and how difficult modifying it would be, on account of his temperament. Then, too, it obviously needed considerable reorganization—that even more than cutting. I had no right to get us committed to a book that was full of dangers and did require revision, until I knew whether these things could be accomplished. I really was determined that we should publish it from the start, and if I had been a publisher on my own, would have been ready to say so instantly. I did suspect that the writer of such a book would be a difficult man to deal with, as the best writers generally are, and I could foresee plenty of trouble when some time later Mrs. Boyd told me of a letter she received in which Tom said he was in a hospital in Germany as the result of that terrible fight he had. That, together with the book which I knew was autobiographical, showed me what was ahead."[2]

In his article in the *Harvard Library Bulletin* Perkins goes on to tell of his first impression upon meeting Wolfe: "After some correspondence between me and Wolfe, and between him and Madeleine Boyd—Wolfe arrived in New York and stood in the doorway of my boxstall of an office, leaning against the door jamb. When I looked up and saw his wild hair and bright countenance—although he was so altogether different physically—I thought of Shelley. *He* was fair, but his hair was wild, and his head disproportionately small."

Wolfe himself described the interview that followed in his letter of January 12, 1929, to Mrs. Roberts: "Mr. Perkins is not at all 'Perkinsy'—name sounds Midwestern, but he is a Harvard man, probably New England family, early forties, but looks younger, very elegant and gentle in dress and manner. He saw I was nervous and excited, spoke to me quietly, told me to take my coat off and sit down. He began by asking certain general questions about the book and people (these weren't important—he was simply feeling his way around, sizing me up, I suppose). Then he mentioned a certain short scene in the book, and in my eagerness and excitement I burst out, 'I know you

[2] From Perkins' letter of October 22, 1945, to John S. Terry.

can't print that! I'll take it out at once, Mr. Perkins.' 'Take it out?' he said. 'It's one of the greatest short stories I have ever read.' He said he had been reading it to Hemingway a week before. Then he asked me if I could write a short introduction for it to explain the people—he was sure *Scribner's Magazine* would take it; if they didn't someone else would. I said I would. I was at once elated and depressed—I thought now that this little bit was all they wanted of it.[3]

"Then he began cautiously on the book. Of course, he said, he didn't know about its present form—somewhat incoherent and very long. When I saw now that he was really interested, I burst out wildly saying that I would throw out this, that, and the other—at every point he stopped me quickly saying, 'No, no—you must let that stay word for word—that scene's simply magnificent.' It became apparent at once that these people were willing to go far farther than I had dared hope—that, in fact, they were afraid I would injure the book by doing too much to it. I saw now that Perkins had a great batch of notes in his hand and that on the desk was a great stack of handwritten paper—a complete summary of my whole enormous book. I was so moved and touched to think that someone at length had thought enough of my work to sweat over it in this way that I almost wept. When I spoke to him of this, he smiled and said everyone in the place had read it. Then he went over the book scene by scene . . . For the first time in my life I was getting criticism I could really use. The scenes he wanted cut or changed were invariably the least essential and the least interesting; all the scenes I had thought too coarse, vulgar, profane, or obscene for publication he forbade me to touch save for a word or two. . . . He said the book was new and original, and because of its form could have no formal and orthodox unity, but that what unity it did have came from the strange wild people—the family—it wrote about, as seen through the eyes of a strange wild boy. These people, with relatives, friends, townspeople, he said were 'magnificent'—as real as any people he had ever read of. He wanted me to keep these people and the boy at all times foremost—other business, such as courses at state university, etc., to be shortened and subordinated. Said finally if I was hard up he thought Scribners would advance money.

"By this time I was wild with excitement—this really seemed something at last—in spite of his caution and restrained manner, I saw now

[3] This scene was the one in Chapter XIX of *Look Homeward, Angel,* in which "Queen" Elizabeth buys from W. O. Gant his marble angel and has it erected as a tombstone for one of her prostitutes. It was published as a short story, "An Angel on the Porch," in the August 1929 issue of *Scribner's Magazine.*

that Perkins really was excited about my book, and had said some tremendous things about it. He saw how wild I was—I told him I had to go out and think—he told me to take two or three days—but before I left he went out and brought in another member of the firm, John Hall Wheelock, who spoke gently and quietly—he is a poet—and said my book was one of the most interesting he had read for years. I then went out and tried to pull myself together. A few days later, the second meeting—I brought notes along as to how I proposed to set to work, and so on. I agreed to deliver one hundred pages of corrected manuscript, if possible, every week. He listened, and then when I asked him if I could say something definite to a dear friend, smiled and said he thought so; that their minds were practically made up; that I should get to work immediately; and that I should have a letter from him in a few days. As I went prancing out I met Mr. Wheelock, who took me by the hand and said: 'I hope you have a good place to work in—you have a big job ahead.' I knew then that it was all magnificently true. I rushed out drunk with glory."

In *The Story of a Novel* Wolfe says: "It was the first time, so far as I can remember, that anyone had concretely suggested to me that anything I had written was worth as much as fifteen cents, and . . . I left the publisher's office that day and entered into the great swarm of men and women who passed constantly along Fifth Avenue at Forty-eighth Street and presently I found myself at 110th Street, and from that day to this I have never known how I got there." He continued in this transport of joy for at least a week, during which time the contract for publication of the book was drawn and signed, and the advance of five hundred dollars paid to him through Mrs. Boyd, who received fifty dollars of this sum as her commission. But slowly he began to realize that he must get to work upon the cutting and revision of the manuscript. In his pocket notebook he had jotted down the "notes as to how I proposed to set to work" which he had suggested to Mr. Perkins at their second conference:

"I propose to correct and revise the mss. 100 pages at a time, and if possible, to deliver 100 pages every week.
"*Proposal for Condensation.*
"First, to cut out of every page every word that is not essential to the meaning or emphasis of the writing. If I can find even 10 words in every page, this will be 10,000 words or more in entire mss.
"Then, to cut out the introductory part and write a new beginning.

"To shorten the child-in-cradle scenes.

"To shorten St. Louis scene save for Grover's death.

"To correct all unnecessary coarseness in language and to cut out unnecessary pages and passages scattered through the book.

"To revise Newport News scenes, and to omit scene with woman on the boat.

"To shorten State University part as much as possible. And further, in the University scenes, to keep Eugene's relations with his family uppermost.

"*Questions.*

"What about several pages that list all the smells and odors?

"What about child's fantasies?

"What about the seduction scene . . . in Charleston?

"What about paper-boy scenes, and especially the one with negress?

"Scribners suggests unity of scene so far as possible. What about Julia's various trips to Hot Springs, Florida, New Orleans, and so on?

"*Propose to Scribners.*

"If I can get some definite assurance of their willingness to publish the book—if revised—I will set to work immediately. The first thing I will do will be to write new introduction and omit the present beginning. I can have this ready and delivered one week from the present interview."

Wolfe's intentions were of the best, but he was prevented from carrying them out by his chronic inability to cut. As he wrote to Mrs. Boyd on February 15, "I stare for hours at the manuscript before cutting out a few sentences: sometimes I want to rip in blindly and slash, but unless I know *where* the result would be disastrous." During his entire life he was almost totally lacking in the ability to "know *where*" to cut. He would begin to reread a piece of manuscript in an attempt to find things which could be omitted, but he would be completely blind to them: instead, he would invariably be reminded of other things he could and should have said, and enthusiastically would begin to write in long additions and digressions. As he wrote to Scott Fitzgerald in 1937, he was "a putter-inner" rather than "a taker-outer." Moreover, his mother and her people had been "putter-inners" long before him: he was simply made that way.

He had, moreover, gone quite stale upon *Look Homeward, Angel:* creatively, he had been through with it for almost an entire year. He was also through with his second, and unsuccessful, novel, *The River People,* and was now starting on a third one, which he called *The*

Fast Express. This was a continuation of his own life story, beginning where *Look Homeward, Angel* had left off, with his first year at Harvard, and ending with his return home for his father's funeral. At one time, Wolfe had intended to include this in *Look Homeward, Angel,* thus ending the book with the death of Gant instead of that of Ben. He had finally omitted it from the *Angel,* but now, acting under his old compulsion, had resumed its telling in another book. As he wrote to Mrs. Boyd, "my new book fills my mind," and instead of completing the revision of *Look Homeward, Angel,* he kept making notes and outlines for *The Fast Express.* He continued to do so till late in 1929 or early in 1930, when, by a process of inevitable expansion, it became the first part of the book he called *The October Fair.* This book, in turn, kept expanding and expanding until, in 1933, it was divided into halves by Perkins. The first half became *Of Time and the River*: the second half was still called *The October Fair* until it was finally rewritten and included in *The Web and the Rock.*

By the end of March, Perkins realized that if *Look Homeward, Angel* was to be published in the fall, he himself would have to take a hand in cutting and revising it. He accordingly wrote and asked Wolfe to come and see him, saying: "I want to arrange to go over the manuscript thus far, in order to show cuts I would like to suggest, and to consider others;—and this might take an hour or two. Besides, we ought to get on now as rapidly as we possibly can with the book." It was in this way that he began working with Wolfe at night, after a long and busy day at Scribners. It was an exhausting and nerve-racking chore which probably no other editor-in-chief would have undertaken, but during this first year at least, he did it with great enjoyment and enthusiasm. By April 12 he had written to Mrs. Boyd: "We are making progress with Wolfe's book. I believe we shall soon have it short enough to be got into one volume form. And the more I see of it, the more I think of it." By May he was working with Wolfe every night and was cutting the manuscript hard. He now was sure enough of completing the revisions to put the book on the fall list and to have dummies made up for the Scribner salesmen, with the finally selected title of *Look Homeward, Angel.* And by early June he had sent the manuscript to press.

Just what this cutting and revision amounted to is described by Perkins in the *Harvard Library Bulletin*: "We then began to work upon the book and the first thing we did, to give it unity, was to cut out that wonderful scene it began with and the ninety-odd pages that followed, because it seemed to me, and he agreed, that the whole tale should be unfolded through the memories and senses of the boy, Eugene, who was born in Asheville. We both thought that the story was compassed by that child's realization; that it was life and the world as he came to realize them. When he had tried to go back into the life of his father before he arrived in Asheville, without the inherent memory of events, the reality and the poignance were diminished—but for years it was on my conscience that I had persuaded Tom to cut out that first scene of the two little boys on the roadside with Gettysburg impending.

"And then what happened? In *Of Time and the River* he brought the scene back to greater effect when old Gant was dying on the gallery of the hospital in Baltimore and in memory recalled his olden days. After that I felt much less anxiety in suggesting cuts: I began to realize that nothing Wolfe wrote was ever lost, that omissions from one book were restored in a later one. . . . But most, and perhaps almost all, of those early incidents of Gant's life were worked into *The Web and the Rock* and *You Can't Go Home Again*. . . .

"In truth, the extent of cutting in that book has somehow come to be greatly exaggerated. Really, it was more a matter of reorganization. For instance, Tom had that wonderful episode when Gant came back from his far-wandering and rode in early morning on the trolley car through the town and heard about who had died and who had been born and saw all the scenes that were so familiar to Tom or Eugene, as the old trolley rumbled along. This was immediately followed by an episode of a similar kind where Eugene, with his friends, walked home from school through the town of Asheville.[4] That was presented in a Joycean way, but it was the same sort of thing—someone going through the town and through his perceptions revealing it to the reader. By putting these episodes next to each other the effect of each was diminished, and I think we gave both much greater value by separating them. We did a great deal of detailed cutting, but it was such things as those I speak of that constituted perhaps the greater part of the work."

Wolfe himself, in "My Record as a Writer," written when he applied for a Guggenheim fellowship in late 1929, says that he and Perkins "cut out over 100,000 words." As he wrote to his sister Mabel, "We are cutting out big chunks, and my heart bleeds to see it go, but it's die dog or eat the hatchet. . . . This man Perkins is a fine fellow and perhaps the best publishing editor in America. I have great confidence

[4] John Hall Wheelock's recollection of the original manuscript differs from Perkins'. He thinks the section following Gant's return was what now appears as Chapter XIV.

in him and I usually yield to his judgment." In these early days he deferred to Perkins almost completely, and it was very fortunate that he did. Certainly the work that Perkins did upon *Look Homeward, Angel* was entirely responsible for transforming it from an amateurish, too long, too inchoate, and virtually unpublishable novel into the great book that it basically was.

It was at this time that Perkins almost inadvertently suggested to Wolfe the theme of the "search for a father," which became the central one of his next book. "In the . . . summer before 'The Angel' was published, I was in New York for quite awhile at the Harvard Club," he wrote later. "Tom came there in the evenings five or six times, and we took long walks, once all the way around Central Park. . . . It was on one of those walks that I told Tom I had always thought a wonderful novel could be written (but I was thinking of a sort of picaresque novel where the wanderings are toward a goal) about a young man who for some reason has never known his father and goes in search of him. Tom seemed to consider this as if it were a serious matter and finally said: 'I think I could use that . . .' I was puzzled because my idea was merely a superficial story of adventure far below Tom's talents. I was even a little worried that he should take it. I think this is significant of Tom. He was taking the search for a father in a profound sense, and that is what he was bound to write about, as I later discovered."[5]

In the meanwhile Wolfe was beginning to worry about the nakedly autobiographical quality of his book, and how it would be received, especially in his native town. As early as January 1929 he had expressed this anxiety in a letter to Mrs. Roberts: "This book dredges up from the inwards of people pain, terror, cruelty, lust, ugliness, as well, I think, as beauty, tenderness, mercy. . . . I wrote this book in a white heat, simply and passionately, with no idea of being either ugly, obscene, tender, cruel, beautiful, or anything else—only of saying what I had to say because I had to. The only morality I had was in me; the only master I had was in me and stronger than me. I went into myself more mercilessly than into anyone else—but I am afraid there is much in this book which will wound and anger people deeply, particularly those at home. . . . Scribners told me people would cry out against this, because people are unable to realize that that spirit which is sensitive to beauty is also sensitive to pain and ugliness. . . . I will soften all I can but I cannot take out all the sting—without lying to myself and destroying the book. . . . The people of Asheville, I fear,

[5] From Perkins' letter of October 29, 1945, to John S. Terry.

may not understand me after this book and may speak of me only with a curse—but some day, if I write other books, they will."

Judging from this letter, he and Perkins had discussed the nakedly truthful quality of the book when it was first accepted, but Perkins evidently did not realize how completely autobiographical it was till three months later. In his article in the *Harvard Library Bulletin* he says: "I had realized, for Tom had prefaced his manuscript with a statement to that effect, that *Look Homeward, Angel* was autobiographical, but I had come to think of it as being so in the sense that *David Copperfield* is, or *War and Peace*, or *Pendennis*. But when we were working together, I suddenly saw that it was often almost literally autobiographical—that these people in it were his people. I am sure my face took on a look of alarm, and Tom saw it and he said, 'But Mr. Perkins, you don't understand. I think these people are *great* people and that they should be told about.' He was right. He had written a great book, and it had to be taken substantially as it was."

Yet from that time on Wolfe became increasingly worried about the effect his book would have in Asheville. On the back of pages of manuscript and in his pocket diaries, beginning in April and recurring as late as September, he wrote fragmentary drafts of a letter to the editor of the Asheville *Citizen:* "Thank you very much for your friendly and courteous invitation to contribute an article to your columns answering critics of my book *O, Lost!* I must decline to do so for several reasons, the most important of which are as follows: at the beginning of my career as a novelist I have determined, so far as possible, to let my books speak for me. If the Asheville critics of my work infer from this that I am anxious to avoid controversy, they are certainly right. But if . . . they believe that my book is a 'bitter attack' against the town, the state, the South, they are certainly wrong. One does not attack life any more than he curses the wind; shakes his fist at the storm; spits angrily at the ocean."

At first glance, it would seem that Wolfe had actually been invited by the *Citizen* to defend his novel. But the chronological position of the various drafts in his diaries and the fact that he calls the book *O, Lost!* instead of *Look Homeward, Angel* indicate that he wrote this letter long before the book was published, before it could have been criticized, and before the *Citizen* could have invited him to defend it. Furthermore, there is no record at the *Citizen* that he was ever asked to write such a defense, or that he ever sent one to the editor. He evidently was anticipating, far ahead of time, the reaction of Asheville people to his book and was writing his defensive letter simply to relieve his mind. In one version he even entertained himself by writing: "As to the implied criticisms of my personal life, I again have nothing to say. . . . If the indignant Methodist ladies and gentlemen suspect me of fleshly carnalities, let them suspect no more. I am enthusiastically guilty. I have eaten and drunk with sensual ecstasy in ten countries. I have performed the male function with the assistance of several attractive females, a few of whom were devout members of the Methodist Church." After these very typical remarks, the letter breaks off short, as was no doubt just as well.

All that spring Wolfe had been teaching half time at New York University as well as working on his book. Now, with the end of the college year and the completion of revisions on the book, he was anxious to leave New York before the onset of hot weather. He first went to Rhinebeck, where he spent his time reading Defoe, Smollett, Dickens, and the poems of Swift, and arguing violently with Olin Dows about the Astors. "I suppose it is wrong to say one cannot believe in the Astors and enter the kingdom of Heaven," he wrote to Mrs. Bernstein, "but I think it is true—I don't even believe one can go to Hell by believing in them. One gets what he deserves—if he believes in the Astors, it ends up by the Astors believing in him."

By this time the galleys of *Look Homeward, Angel* had started coming from the press. Wolfe wanted to settle down and read these in some cool and restful place, so he rented a cottage for two weeks at Ocean Point, Boothbay Harbor, Maine. The letters he sent back with the corrected proofs to John Hall Wheelock show how he reacted to work which had been cut for him by other people. He had an unfailing instinct for spotting passages which, in cutting, had become too thin, too jerky, or "not quite right," or which now lacked some detail needed to make sense, or did not preserve the iambic pentameter in which he usually wrote. He would smooth and round things out till they were deeper, better, truer to himself, and one would have to recognize that fact, even though in so doing he had made the manuscript too long again. He made so many changes and additions on the proofs that the bill from the printer for alterations was approximately seven hundred dollars. According to his contract, he was supposed to pay all such charges in excess of 20 per cent of the total cost of composition, but because Perkins and Wheelock had had a hand in the revision of the manuscript, Scribners assumed the whole expense themselves.

Except for the daily chore of reading proofs, his stay in Maine was quite idyllic. Mrs. Bernstein joined him there, and together they read Proust and Donne, choosing for his dedication to her in *Look Homeward, Angel* the fifth verse from Donne's "A Valediction: Of His Name in the Window":

> Then, as all my soules bee,
> Emparadis'd in you, (in whom alone
> I understand, and grow and see,)
> The rafters of my body, bone
> Being still with you, the Muscle, Sinew, and Veine,
> Which tile this house, will come againe.

For the rest, he fished from an old deserted pier, took long midnight walks along the shore, and dreamed of someday buying an island like the little spruce-grown one that he could see from his cottage porch. Except for visits to Florida in his childhood, he had never lived upon the ocean, and it filled him with a lyric eloquence. "I am more full of strength and power and hope than I have been in years," he wrote to Wheelock. ". . . In this wild and lovely place, all America stretches below me like a vast plain: the million forms that spend themselves in the city, and torture us so by their confusion and number, have been fused into a calmer temper—I am filled with a kind of tragic joy. . . . The other night I walked along the road. The little farmhouses slept below the moon, the gnarled apple trees full of apples getting ripe leaned over the hedges, and on the walls the wild wood lilies grew. You would not say along that road the sea was there behind the houses, behind the fir trees and the hedge, and the apples getting ripe—and yet you round a bend, and the sea is there. I thought there would be vast lengthenings into the sea, slow stoppages of land and rock, drear marshy vacancies, slow lapse and waste relinquishment of earth, but when you round the bend of the road the sea is there—he has entered at one stride into the land. This union of the vast and lonely . . . made a great music in me. I could not tell you all it meant but it was like Milton standing by a little door. And I thought that if one came into this place on a ship from open sea it would be with the suddenness of a dream."

Meanwhile "An Angel on the Porch," the story made from Chapter XIX of *Look Homeward, Angel*, was published in the August issue of *Scribner's Magazine*. Wolfe wrote to his friend Henry Volkening: "I had expected convulsions of the earth, falling meteors, suspension of traffic, and a general strike when the story appeared—but nothing happened. I was in Maine." However, something was beginning to happen—something which he had anticipated and which would exile him from his native town for seven long years. Evidently his story was not widely read in Asheville, despite an announcement in the *Citizen* that it had appeared. But one of his most devoted friends, Margaret Roberts, had read it and had written him expressing grave concern for the effect it would have on his own family. When he returned to New York after his two weeks in Maine and a brief trip to Canada, he found her letter waiting for him, became terribly upset, and began writing draft after draft of his reply:

"I hope you may be wrong in thinking what I have written may distress members of my family, or anyone else. Certainly, I would do anything to avoid causing anyone pain—except to destroy the fundamental substance of my book. I am afraid, however, that if anyone is distressed by what seemed to me a very simple and unoffending story, their feeling when the book comes out will be much stronger. And the thought of that distresses *me* more than I can tell you. Nothing, however, may now be done about this. Everything that could reasonably be done to soften impressions that might needlessly wound any reader has been done by my publishers and me. Now, the only apology I have to make for my book is that it is not better—and by 'better' I mean that it does not represent by any means the best that is in me. But I hope I shall feel this way about my work for many years to come, although there is much in this first book about which I hope I shall continue to feel affection and pride.

"A thousand words leap to my tongue—words of explanation, persuasion, and faith—but they had better rest unsaid. Silence is best. More and more I know that the grievous and complex web of human relationship may not be solved by words. However our motives or our acts may be judged or misjudged, our works must speak for us, and we can ultimately only trust to the belief of other men that we are of good will. I can not explain the creative act here. That has been done much better than I could hope to do it, by other people. I can only assure you that my book is a work of fiction, and that no person, act, or event has been deliberately and consciously described. The creative spirit hates pain more, perhaps, than it does anything else on earth, and it is not likely it should try to inflict on other people what it loathes itself. Certainly the artist is not a traducer or libeler of mankind—his main concern when he creates is to give his creation life, form, beauty. This dominates him, and it is doubtful if he thinks very much of the effect his work will have on given persons, although he may think of its effect on a general public. But I think you know that fiction is not spun out of the air; it is made from the solid stuff of human experience —any other way is unthinkable.

"Dr. Johnson said a man would turn over half a library to make a single book; so may a novelist turn over half a town to make a single figure in his novel. . . . The world a writer creates is his own world— but it is molded out of the fabric of life, what he has known and felt— in short, out of himself. How in God's name can it be otherwise? This is all I can say—I think you will understand it. Having said this, I can but add that at the last ditch, the writer must say this: 'I have tried only to do a good piece of work. I have not wished nor intended to hurt anyone. Now I can go no farther. I will not destroy nor mutilate my work, it represents what is best and deepest in me, and I shall stand by it and defend it even if the whole world would turn against me.' That, it seems to me, is the only answer he can make. Perhaps there are two sides to this question but this, at any rate, is my side, and the one I believe in with all my heart."

By this time *Look Homeward, Angel* was going into page proofs and was scheduled for publication in October. In *The Story of a Novel* Wolfe says: "The awful, utter nakedness of print, that thing which is for all of us so namelessly akin to shame, came closer day by day. That I had wanted this exposure, I could not believe. It seemed to me that I had shamelessly exposed myself and yet that subtle drug of my desire and my creating held me with a serpent's eye and I could do no other." In his anxiety, he began another draft of his defensive letter to the Asheville *Citizen* but gave it up as hopeless after writing a few paragraphs. He also wrote his note "To the Reader," which appears at the beginning of *Look Homeward, Angel* and which contains parts of his letter to Mrs. Roberts, parts of his "Note to the Publisher's Reader," and several new paragraphs:

"This note, however, is addressed principally to those persons whom the writer may have known in the period covered by these pages. To these persons, he would say what he believes they understand already: that this book was written in innocence and nakedness of spirit, and that the writer's main concern was to give fulness, life, and intensity to the actions and people in the book he was creating. Now that it is to be published, he would insist that this book is a fiction, and that he meditated no man's portrait here.

"But we are the sum of all the moments of our lives—all that is ours is in them: we cannot escape or conceal it. If the writer has used the clay of life to make his book, he has only used what all men must, what none can keep from using. Fiction is not fact, but fiction is fact selected and understood, fiction is fact arranged and charged with purpose."

Early in September he went to Asheville, with the strong premonition that this would be the last visit he would have there for a long, long time. He went home with a desperate resolve to warn his family as to what *Look Homeward, Angel* was about, but the two weeks of his visit passed and he still had failed to get his courage up to do any more than hint it to them. In a postcard written from Asheville to Mr. Perkins on September 14 he said: "My family knows what it is all about and I think is pleased about it—and also a little apprehensive." But the account given by his sister Mabel contradicts this: "When Tom left Asheville in September, 1929, he had been much entertained by friends. . . . by Mrs. Roberts and by us (Ralph and me). It had already been announced that Thomas Wolfe's forthcoming novel, *Look Homeward, Angel,* would soon be released. I didn't think then that people in the town would read it. Tom's sensitivity and withdrawal from talking *about it* made me fear it was one of those boring philosophies or criticisms, or a book on the negro-mulatto subject. . . . I had a party at my beautiful home, 98 Kimberly Avenue, . . . for Tom the night before he left. . . . The next day at three o'clock, we (Ralph and I) went for him and Mama, rode around and then to Biltmore, N.C., where we always took trains east or north. . . . Tom and I walked down the tracks and he clutched my arm and said: 'Now Mabel, when I come again I may have to come incognito or wear false whiskers.' I gasped at such a remark, and he explained: 'I've said a few things in this book coming out that some of them are not going to like. I hope you will understand and know I tried to do my best.' He frightened me, fearing the negro subject or sex. I never dreamed—and this opinion I voice for my family: Mama, Fred, Effie, Frank—what would be in the book."[6]

Then the train came in, and Wolfe boarded it for "the great life of the North . . . and the enchanted promise of the golden cities . . . now before him." The scene and the participants in it were the same as that of his first departure from home in 1920, but he now had realized the great ambition which he had hardly dared to hint before— to be a writer. The "song of triumph, joy and victory" should have

[6] From a letter written to Elizabeth Nowell.

welled up in him now, but instead his heart was heavy with anxiety and grief. And as the train rushed northward, he pulled his greasy, dog-eared little notebook from his pocket and wrote down one question: "Shall I ever come back to my home, ever again?"

X

I T H A S seemed to me . . . that there is a kind of significance in the fact that my first book appeared in October, 1929," Wolfe says in his Purdue speech. "For me, it seemed that in a way my life—my working life—had just begun; but in so many different ways I did not know about . . . so many things that I believed in, or thought that I believed in, were ending. Many people see in the last great war a kind of dividing line in their own lives—a kind of great tale of two worlds, a world before the war, and a world after the war; but in my own experience, if I had to write my own tale of two worlds, I think I should be more inclined to use 1929 as the dividing line. Certainly that has been the most memorable division in my own life that I can now recall.

"Before that, as we have seen, my experience as a man and as a writer had passed through certain well-defined stages, all of which were very familiar to the times and to the lives of many other young men of the times. The son of an average small-town family, I had in the early Twenties embarked upon a writing career—had decided to be a writer— a fact which was not only in complete variance with the lives of all my other people before me, but was also symptomatic of a marked social tendency of the time—the desire of thousands of young men everywhere to write. I had passed through progressive stages of change and of development which were also characteristic of the time: I had gone through the stage of aesthetic preciosity, of talking about 'art' and 'beauty,' and about 'the artist'; of scorning 'the bourgeoisie,' 'the Philistines and Babbitts,' who not only were not artists, but who could never understand 'the artist,' but belonged to a completely different separate world. From this . . . I passed into the period when I had to go to work, and where I learned for the first time what work—hard, creative work—was like; and where at last I began to spend more time in an effort to create 'art' and 'beauty' than in talking about it. And now finally, I had reached the stage of first accomplishment—where at last I had accomplished something, got it completed, accepted, printed, and put between the covers of a book. . . .

"This is certainly a definite and closely linked chain of clear development, and for me it marked the end of one great cycle. Although perhaps I did not know much in 1929, I did know a good deal more than I knew in 1920. I knew, first of all, that writing was hard work—desperately hard work—and whoever accomplishes a good piece of writing must work hard and constantly, with exhausting concentration, and not depend upon sporadic flashes of casual inspiration to do the job for him. I knew furthermore . . . that I could write—that I was able to see a job through to the end, and able to get it published by a good publisher. It is not necessary to point out what an inestimable comfort this knowledge was to me, for it had served to establish some confidence in my own abilities, which I had never had before, and to restore my self-respect and my belief in myself and in what I wanted to do, which had been shaken by years of failure and frustration.

"I was certainly a wiser man in 1929 than I was in 1920, and I think I was also a stronger and surer one. I no longer had so big a chip upon my shoulder, I was no longer so truculent and occasionally arrogant in my relations to other people, because I no longer felt such inner need to prove to myself that I could do what I wanted to do. But I suppose a good deal of the old foolishness still remained: I would have smiled in 1929 at some of the aesthetic snobberies and preciosities of the young men at Harvard in 1923, but if anyone had asked me why I wrote, why I wanted to be a writer . . . , I would have said some of the same things that I had said years before: I would have talked about 'the artist,' and I suppose I might still have had a romantic and fanciful notion of him, and of his relation to society. I am afraid I might also have talked a good deal about 'art' and 'beauty'—perhaps I shouldn't have been so hard on 'the Babbitts and the Philistines' and as arrogantly scornful of 'the bourgeoisie' as I had been in 1923, but I would have still looked down on them from a kind of aesthetic altitude and felt that they belonged to a separate order of things, in a different world.

"I was a lot closer to life, to people, to the world around me, to America in 1929, than I had ever been before; although I was still too detached from it, not nearly close enough. But the experience of the last few years—the experience of work—. . . had now brought me much closer to life, much closer to an understanding of the lives of people, as I think work always does. And for the last three years . . . the work I had been doing had taught me much—that work, in substance, had demanded a kind of spiritual and emotional excavation of the deepest and intensest sort into the life I had known and of which I had been a part—the life of my home town, of my family, of the people I had

come from, of the whole structure and frame of things that had produced me. I knew more about all of this than I had ever known before,
but, as I was to discover, I did not know enough.

"For one thing, the book still showed unmistakably the evidence of
the stages I had gone through, . . . the special aesthetic faiths and
creeds of the time. It is what is called an autobiographical novel—
a definition with which I have never agreed, simply because it seems
to me every novel . . . is autobiographical. Nevertheless, it is true that
this book was autobiographical in the personal and special sense: it
was possible, for example, to identify the life of the hero with the life of
the author, . . . and . . . I believe that in this sense of the word—in
this special autobiographical sense—was the book's greatest weakness.
I believe the character of the hero was the weakest and least convincing
one in the whole book, because he had been derived not only from
experience but colored a good deal by the romantic aestheticism of
the period. He was, in short, 'the artist' in pretty much the Harvard
Forty-seven Workshop sense of the word—the wounded, sensitive, the
extraordinary creature, in conflict with his environment, with the
Babbitt, the Philistine, the small town, the family. I know that I was
not satisfied with this character even at the time: he seemed to me
to be uneasy and self-conscious, probably because I was myself uneasy
and self-conscious about him. . . .

"So there I was in 1929, at the end of one route, at the beginning
of another, at the end and the beginning of so many different things
I then did not know or suspect, that, looking back now, I seem to
have been a guileless innocent. On the whole, my view of things was
pretty hopeful, pretty cheerful, for although I did have the desolating
and rather desperate sense of exile, of having pulled up my roots completely as far as the old life was concerned, I had a feeling now of new
beginning, too—of being launched at last, of having before me the
happy prospect of an established and productive career.

"At that time, among the many other things I did not know, I did
not know that for a man who wants to continue with the creative life,
to keep on growing and developing, this cheerful idea of happy estab-
lishment, of continuing now as one has started, is nothing but a delusion
and a snare. I did not know that if a man really has in him the desire
and the capacity to create, the power of further growth and further
development, there can be no such thing as an easy road. I did not
know that so far from having found out about writing, I had really
found out almost nothing. . . . I had made a first and simple utterance; but I did not know that each succeeding one would not only be

. . . more difficult than the last, but would be completely different—
that with each new effort would come new desperation, the new, and
old, sense of having to begin from the beginning all over again; of being
face to face again with the old naked facts of self and work; of realizing
again that there is no help anywhere save the help and strength that
one can find within himself."

Look Homeward, Angel was published on October 18, 1929. Shortly
before that day, in his intense excitement and anxiety, Wolfe asked
Perkins if he could foretell what success the book would have. In *The
Story of a Novel* he quotes Perkins' reply: "All that I know is that
they cannot let it go, they cannot ignore it. The book will find its way."
And as usual, Perkins' deep conviction was right. The book started
rather slowly. It had had a promising advance sale of 1600 copies, but
because it was a first novel by an unknown writer, it was not widely
reviewed in the daily press. Moreover, what reviews it had were not too
favorable. For instance, the first important review in a New York newspaper, Harry Hansen's in the *World*, on Saturday, October 26, was
sardonically titled "Ah, Life! Life!" and while saying that the book
gave "an impression of strength and promise. . . . There is rich emotion in it, there is understanding and sympathy in it," went on to
ridicule Wolfe's "Meredithian prose" and "musings over destiny, fate,
love, ah me! ah me!"

But the following day, this lukewarm reception was completely can-
celed out by an extremely favorable review in the most important
publication of them all, the Sunday New York *Times* Book Review.
The reviewer, Margaret Wallace, had the rare courage and conviction
to praise Wolfe's work unreservedly, although he was totally unknown,
and the fact that she did so was a first and important step toward
his success. Her review is too long to be quoted in its entirety here, but
the first and final paragraphs are indicative of its completely eulogistic
tone: "Here is a novel of the sort one is too seldom privileged to
welcome. It is a book of great drive and vigor, of profound originality,
of rich and variant color. Its material is the material of everyday life, its
scene is a small provincial Southern city, its characters are the ordinary
persons who come and go in our daily lives. Yet the color of the book is
not borrowed; it is native and essential. Mr. Wolfe has a very great
gift—the ability to find in simple events and in humble, unpromising
lives the whole meaning and poetry of human existence. He reveals to
us facets of observation and depths of reality hitherto unsuspected, but
he does so without outraging our notions of truth and order. His

revelations do not startle. We come upon them, instead, with an almost electric sense of recognition. . . .

"*Look Homeward, Angel* is as interesting and powerful a book as has ever been made out of the drab circumstances of provincial American life. It is at once enormously sensuous, full of the joy and gusto of life, and shrinkingly sensitive, torn with revulsion and disgust. Mr. Wolfe's style is sprawling, fecund, subtly rhythmic and amazingly vital. He twists language masterfully to his own uses, heeding neither the decency of a word nor its licensed existence, so long as he secures his sought for and instantaneous effect. Assuredly, this is a book to be savored slowly and re-read, and the final decision upon it, in all probability, rests with another generation than ours."

One week later the second most important review, that in the New York *Herald Tribune* Books, was equally glowing in its praise. By some good fortune, the reviewer for the *Herald Tribune* was Margery Latimer, a fine creative writer herself, who reacted to Wolfe's genius as only a kindred soul could do; in a letter written to him soon afterward, she summed up this complete sympathy in a longhand postscript: "Are you my brother? Yes!" Her review, like Miss Wallace's, is too long to quote entirely, but its first and last paragraphs are as follows:

"Sometimes an intense shock or a pain that has to be endured will give you a monstrous delight in life, as if the cautious habitual self in you had had its death blow and you were thrown out of yourself into the universe. This book is like that. There is such mammoth appreciation of experience and of living that the intention of the novel cannot be articulated. It comes through to you like fumes or like one supreme mood of courage that you can never forget, and with it all the awe, the defilement and grandeur of actual life. Mr. Wolfe makes you experience a family through twenty years of its existence. He gives the disharmony, the joy, the hideous wastefulness and the needless suffering, and yet not once do you dare shrink from life and not once are you plastered with resentment and loathing for reality and experience. The author has stated in his introduction that he wrote this book with strong joy, not counting the costs, and I believe it. . . .

"The story is always present. There is always the tremendous excitement of the life of this family, of what they will do and say and feel. . . . The author proudly and naively says 'It sometimes seems to me that this book presents a picture of American life that I have never seen elsewhere.' I agree with him, and if I could create now one magic word that would make everyone want to read the book, I would write it down and be utterly satisfied."

These two reviews completely turned the tide, and by November 6
Look Homeward, Angel had sold another thousand copies, making
2600 in all. The first printing of it had been 5540 copies, but Perkins
now anticipated its success and ordered a second printing of 3000 more.
As he wrote to Madeleine Boyd, "The book seems to have aroused a
good deal of interest, and its prospects are distinctly favorable."

Wolfe's elation at this first success was, however, completely overshadowed by the news from home. The reaction of the town of Asheville to *Look Homeward, Angel* was far more violent than even he
had ever dreamed: as Mabel Wolfe Wheaton said in her recorded
interview made for the Library of Congress, its publication "caused
more excitement, gossip, and talk and distress in Asheville than when
the banks failed. The only reason we weren't tarred and feathered was
because Tom didn't spare us in the book." She goes on to describe the
first reception of the book, both by the family and by the town: "Mama
phoned—said, 'Mabel, I have Tom's book. You'd better come by here
on your way home.' I said, 'Is it good?' She said, 'You'd better read
some of it yourself, and you can be the judge.' . . . We went by the
house, and Mama was sitting in front of her fireplace in her living
room, just as calm and collected as could be—but of course she was
some shocked by what she had been reading. . . . So much that was
in the book was true and so much was only fiction, of course. So she
read us a portion of the book and my husband's mother jumped up . . .
She always . . . walked with a cane, and she threw her cane up in the
air. 'Don't read me another line! Don't read me another line if he says
anything about my son!' The phone was ringing all the time from
these well-meaning people who were sympathizing with us, saying what
did the boy mean: they'd known us all our lives and we were decent
people. They were denouncing him from the roofs and the corners and
the housetops."[1]

This outraged protest was quickly echoed by many of the southern
newspapers, which judged the book from a purely local viewpoint
rather than from a literary one. The review in the Asheville *Citizen*
by Lola Love (who soon afterward became Mrs. George McCoy) was
extremely sympathetic: "This first novel by Thomas Wolfe, of Asheville, is, according to those who have been already privileged to read it,
destined to be the sensation of the fall literary season. . . . The book
is a genius' combination of reality, which will not shrink from even

[1] From "Mrs. Wheaton, Sister of Thomas Wolfe, Chronologically Telling
His Life History, ⅍1302, February 23, 1947."

the most sordid details of everyday life, and of a child-like expression of
the most delightful fantasy." However, the one by Walter S. Adams
in the Asheville *Times* gave further impetus to the already spreading
scandal: "An amazing new novel is just off the press which is of great
and unique interest to Asheville. This community, in fact, is going to
be astounded by it. Some few well known residents may be shocked
into chills. Others will probably be severely annoyed. Many others will
snicker and laugh. The reason is that the book is written about Asheville and Asheville people in the plainest of plain language. . . . The
author paints himself and his home circle, as well as neighbors, friends
and acquaintances with bold daring lines, sparing nothing and shield-
ing nothing. . . . Most of the Asheville people who appear in the novel
wear their most unpleasant guises. If there attaches to them any scandal which has enjoyed only a subterranean circulation, it is dragged
forth into the light. If they have any weaknesses which more tolerant
friends are considerate enough to overlook, these defects are faithfully
described. In describing them, the author must often convey the impression to the unknowing that these weaknesses were the distinguish-
ing characteristics of the persons. The novel will be acclaimed to
literary critics as a work of real distinction. But the suspicion is strong
that Asheville people will read it not because of its literary worth but
rather . . . because it is the story, told with bitterness and without
compassion, of many Asheville people."

Moreover, the review in the Raleigh *News and Observer* by Jonathan Daniels, Wolfe's fellow student at Chapel Hill, expressed an almost personal sense of betrayal. Under the headline "Wolfe's First Is
Novel of Revolt: Former Asheville Writer Turns in Fury upon North
Carolina and the South," Daniels wrote: ". . . Tom Wolfe, once of
Asheville, has gone the way of rebels and in a sense this first novel of
his is the reign of terror of his talent. Against the Victorian morality
and the Bourbon aristocracy of the South, he has turned in all his fury,
and the result is not a book that will please the South in general and
North Carolina in particular. Here is a young man, hurt by something
that he loved, turning in his sensitive fury and spitting on that thing.
In *Look Homeward, Angel*, North Carolina and the South are spat
upon.

"In this novel, which is admittedly autobiographical in some parts,
the author Wolfe says of his hero, who is easily identifiable with Wolfe:
'His feeling for the South was not so much historic as it was of the
core and desire of dark romanticism . . . And this desire of his was unquestionably enhanced by all he had read and visioned, by the romantic

halo that his school history cast over the section, by the whole fantastic distortion of that period where people were said to live in "mansions," and slavery was a benevolent institution, conducted to a constant banjo-strumming, the strewn largesses of the colonel and the shuffle-dance of his happy dependents, where all women were pure, gentle, and beautiful, all men chivalrous and brave, and the Rebel horde a company of swagger, death-mocking cavaliers. Years later, when he could no longer think of the barren spiritual wilderness, the hostile and murderous intrenchment against all new life—when their cheap mythology, their legend of the charm of their manner, the aristocratic culture of their lives, the quaint sweetness of their drawl, made him writhe—when he could think of no return to their life and its swarming superstition without weariness and horror, so great was his fear of the legend, his fear of their antagonism, that he still pretended the most fanatic devotion to them, excusing his Northern residence on grounds of necessity rather than desire. Finally, it occurred to him that these people had given him nothing, that neither their love nor their hatred could injure him, that he owed them nothing, and he determined that he would say so, and repay their insolence with a curse. And he did.'

"*Look Homeward, Angel* is that curse. And in just so far as the curse has entered into the creation, his work has been injured, but it is a novel fine enough to show that once Mr. Wolfe has got this little score paid off to his own country he should be able to move on in greater serenity of spirit. . . ."

Wolfe was completely stunned and shocked by all of this. In spite of his long-standing anxiety about the effect the book would have at home, he had never thought that the reaction to it would be so widespread. As he says in *The Story of a Novel*, "I had thought there might be a hundred people in that town who would read the book, but if there were a hundred outside of the Negro population, the blind, and the positively illiterate who did not read it, I do not know where they are. For months the town seethed with a fury of resentment which I had not believed possible. . . . I received anonymous letters full of vilification and abuse, one which threatened to kill me if I came back home, others which were merely obscene. One venerable old lady, whom I had known all my life, wrote me that although she had never believed in lynch law, she would do nothing to prevent a mob from dragging my 'big overgroan karkus' across the public square. She informed me further, that my mother had taken to her bed 'as white as a ghost' and would 'never rise from it again.' There were many other venomous attacks from my home town and for the first time I learned another lesson which every young writer has got to learn. And that lesson is the naked, blazing power of print. At that time it was for me a bewildering and almost overwhelming situation."

Mrs. Wolfe did not "take to her bed" never to "rise from it again": she was made of stronger, smarter stuff than that, and she met the situation by refusing to admit that she was the original of Eliza Gant. All the members of Wolfe's immediate family stood by him loyally, but life was very difficult for them at home, and they were human enough to mention this in letters to him. His replies to them are on the defensive all through 1929 and the spring of 1930. "It has never occurred to anyone with whom I have spoken here that Eliza was anything but a very strong, resourceful, and courageous woman, who showed great character and determination in her struggle against the odds of life," he wrote to his mother in November 1929. "That is certainly the way I felt and feel about her, and since I wrote the book my opinion ought to be as good as anyone's." Again, in April 1930: "I am sorry that my book was any kind of shock to you—I did not want it to be or intend it to be; and I shall try to write other ones which I hope will seem grander and more beautiful to you. I am very sorry to know that anyone in Asheville looks at you with 'inquiring looks'; but I should not pay any attention to them—you are a much more remarkable person than any of them, as the world perhaps may someday know." And, more bitterly, to his sister Mabel: "You say that women in clubs have called you up and lectured you or sympathized with you. Very well, let them. You are bigger than any of them and they cannot hurt you. I suppose the sympathy was because you had a brother like me. Very well. That's all right, too. Apparently you can rob banks, be a crooked lawyer, swill corn whiskey, commit adultery with your neighbor's wife—and be considered a fine, lovable, misunderstood fellow; but if you try to make something true and beautiful, you are 'viciously insane' and your 'big overgrown body' ought to be dragged through the streets by a lynching mob. . . . Well, they can not hurt us. I do not believe one fine person, worthy of being a friend, would ever turn either on you or me because I have written a book—and anyone who would is probably not worth knowing."

But although the publication of *Look Homeward, Angel* did not shake his family's loyalty to him, it did disturb others among the local people, and it caused a breach between him and "the mother of his spirit," Mrs. Roberts, which lasted for six years. She had known, in advance, as much about the book as anyone in Asheville and had protested repeatedly against his treatment of his family in it; but when she actually read it, she felt also that his portrayal of Mr. Leonard of the Altamont Fitting School was a shocking misrepresentation of her husband's character. And her loyalty to *him* was naturally even greater than her loyalty to Wolfe.

In the unpublished commentary on Wolfe's letters to her, which she wrote in 1940, she describes how their estrangement came about: "By October 17, 1929, . . . I was . . . in bed with what was to prove a long and desperate illness. I chanced to be alone in the house for a few minutes when I heard the postman slip what I instinctively knew was The Book inside the screen door. If my heart had pounded on reading Tom's long letter of the previous January telling of 'the publishers' glorious letter of acceptance' of *Look Homeward, Angel,* it fairly galloped now as I crept weakly to the door, and excitedly back to bed with the book in my hand. By some bitter irony, the book opened exactly at the chapter on the North State School. With natural curiosity I read those pages first, numb with misery as I read. Then, as I laid the book aside, feeling hurt and helpless, as a further bit of irony, my eye fell upon his so-familiar scrawl upon the fly-leaf: To Margaret Roberts, who was the Mother of my Spirit, I present this copy of my first book with hope and with devotion. Thomas Wolfe, October 15, 1929.

"I had a brief but significant and moving letter from him in answer to one I wrote him after finishing *Look Homeward, Angel.* In this letter of mine, brief because I had so little strength, I tried to be objective in my comments on the quality of the book. The only sentence I can remember is the closing one: 'You have crucified your family and devastated mine.'

"I continued very ill until March, and then followed many weeks of slow convalescence after a serious operation. With painful effort of mind and body I wrote him a comprehensive letter, a few sentences at a time, as strength permitted. But somehow I could never get it finished. The days went by, and it never got mailed, not because of deliberate intention, but—— It may be noted in his letter to me of February 2, 1930, that he says 'Two or three months ago I wrote you a very long letter in reply to your own [this written to him just after having received *Look Homeward, Angel*], but that letter still remains folded and unfinished in my notebook.' Neither of us was wise enough to untangle what he speaks of in a previous letter as 'the grievous and complex web of human relationship.' Here again was 'the unfound door.'"

Nine years later, in his Purdue speech, Wolfe was able to describe with more perspective the effect upon himself of Asheville's reception of *Look Homeward, Angel:* "Briefly, the people of the town read the book as if it had been the pages of the World Almanac; and seeing that some things were true, they became almost immediately convinced that everything was literally true and literally intended. . . . Their outrage and anger, although mistaken, were unmistakable: there is no doubt that from the moment of the book's publication, I became an exile from my native town. I could not have come back at that time, and it was seven years, in fact, before I wanted to come back, and did return.

"This was bewildering and overwhelming: it was all so different from what I had expected—so different from the reception that I had hoped to have in my home town—that for a time my own sense of grief, disappointment and chagrin were very great: for one of the things it is hard to lose is the desire for the approbation and applause of one's own neighbors—the knowledge that one has succeeded in the estimation of the people of his own town. Moreover, it did do something to strengthen me in a further belief in what was perhaps the fundamental theme of the whole book—the story of the sensitive young man in conflict with his environment, driven out at last, forced to flee and escape from his own town. For now that had happened to me, and if that had been all that had happened, it might have embittered me into a further belief and confirmation of my earlier error."

But in the meanwhile, *Look Homeward, Angel* was continuing to "find its way." The monthly magazines were now coming out with their reviews, and these were for the most part very favorable. John Chamberlain in the *Bookman* said: "It is a rich, positive grappling with life. . . . No more sensuous . . . novel has been written in the United States." Robert Raynolds in *Scribner's Magazine* said: "If we were to label Wolfe, we would put him with Melville and Whitman." Geoffrey T. Hellman in the *New Republic* said: "Mr. Wolfe has a quality that is rare enough in itself and is practically never found (as it is here) combined with literary ability, taste, and a scholarly background: relish." Basil Davenport in the *Saturday Review of Literature* said: "Mr. Wolfe, like Rabelais, . . . is happily able to devour sensations with an enormous vigor; his perceptions have a rare combination of fineness and largeness." And Carl Van Doren said in *Wings:* "Mr. Wolfe with much that is heroic in his constitution, has had the courage of his heroism. He has dared to lift his characters up above the average meanness of mankind, to let them live by their profounder impulses, and to tell about them the things which smooth, urbane novelists insist on leaving untold about men and women."

Moreover, as Wolfe says of *Look Homeward, Angel* in *The Story of a Novel,* "what was best of all, as time went on, it continued to make friends among people who read books." The list of people who volunteered their praise of it is a surprising one. Sinclair Lewis wrote to Wolfe: "I wish there hadn't been quite so many brisk blurb-writers these past twenty years, . . . so that I might have some fresh phrase with which to express my profound delight in *Look Homeward, Angel!* There is, you needn't be told, authentic greatness in it. It and *Farewell to Arms* seem to me to have more spacious power in them than any book for years, American OR foreign. . . . God, your book is good!" Robert Norwood wrote: "It is a remarkable book, not far from *The Brothers Karamazov.* . . . I have the feeling of an archangel with broken wings trying to regain the heights he has lost." Thomas Beer said: "It is the most important contribution to American letters since Glenway Wescott's *The Grandmothers.*" James Boyd said: "It has the simple and undebatable merit of containing elements of greatness, and all of the formidable vigor of life." And Hugh Walpole was quoted in a newspaper interview as saying of Wolfe: "His novel is as nearly perfect as a novel can be. I feel it a duty as a literary man to say something in his favor."

This, of course, is only a partial list of the people whom Wolfe considered as "friends of my book." Except for Beer and Boyd, they were all total strangers to him at this time, and they all spoke out voluntarily from sheer enthusiasm. But more important than these prominent people were the thousands of unknown men and women who read *Look Homeward, Angel,* and still read it, for what it means to them. The play *Look Homeward, Angel,* adapted by Ketti Frings from the novel, has been awarded the New York Drama Critics Circle Award and the Pulitzer Prize for 1958, and ran for 554 performances on Broadway.

And so, as Wolfe says in *The Story of a Novel,* "I found myself with a position as a writer." The day before Christmas 1929 he summed it all up in a note to Mr. Perkins:

"One year ago I had little hope for my work, and I did not know you. What has happened since may seem to be only a modest success to many people; but to me it is touched with strangeness and wonder. It is a miracle.

"You are now mixed with my book in such a way that I can never separate the two of you. I can no longer think clearly of the time I wrote it, but rather of the time when you first talked to me about it, and when you worked upon it. . . . You have done what I had ceased to believe one person could do for another—you have created liberty and hope for me.

"Young men sometimes believe in the existence of heroic figures, stronger and wiser than themselves, to whom they can turn for an answer to all their vexation and grief. Later, they must discover that such answers have to come out of their own hearts; but the powerful desire to believe in such figures persists. You are for me such a figure: you are one of the rocks to which my life is anchored.

"I have taken the publication of my first book very hard—all the happy and successful part of it as well as the unhappy part: a great deal of the glory and joy and glamour with which in my fantasy I surrounded such an event has vanished. But, as usual, life and reality supplant the imaginary thing with another glory that is finer and more substantial than the visionary one.

"I should have counted this past year a great one, if it had allowed me only to know about you. I am honored to think I may call you my friend, and I wish to send to you on Christmas Day this statement of my loyal affection."

He had found in Perkins a new person on whom to fix his father image, and on whom to keep it fixed for the greater part of his creative life.

XI

FOR SEVEN months after the publication of *Look Homeward, Angel* Wolfe was too keyed up and too distracted to get back to work. As he wrote to Arthur Davison Ficke, "Having a book published has happened to millions of other people, but it's the first time it ever happened to me, and, thank God, I took it hard—letters, excitement, reviews good or bad, sales, invitations, telephone calls, everything." All through his life Wolfe's reaction to reviews was abnormally intense. "He read the notices avidly, feverishly," he says of Monk Webber in *You Can't Go Home Again*, "and sooner or later he must have seen them all, for his publisher showed him the clippings as they came in from every section of the country. He would take great bunches of them home to devour. When his eager eye ran upon a word of praise it was like magic to him, and he would stride about his room in a delirium of joy. When he read a savage, harsh, unfavorable review, he felt crushed: even though it came from some little rural paper in the South, his fingers would tremble, his face turn pale, and he would wad it up in his hand and curse it bitterly.

"Whenever a notice of his work appeared in one of the best magazines or weekly journals, he could hardly bring himself to read it; neither could he go away from it and leave it unread. He would approach it as a man creeps stealthily to pick a snake up by the tail, his heart leaping at the sight of his name. He would scan the last line first, then with a rush of blood to his face he would plunge into it at once, devouring the whole of it as quickly as he could. And if he saw that it was going to be 'good,' a feeling of such powerful joy and exultancy would well up in his throat that he would want to shout his triumph from the windows. If he saw that the verdict was going to be 'thumbs down,' he would read on with agonized fascination, and his despair would be so great that he would feel he was done for, that he had been exposed to the world as a fool and a failure, and that he would never be able to write another line.

"After the more important reviews appeared, his mail gradually took

on a different complexion. Not that the flood of damning letters from
home had ceased, but now, along with them, began to come messages
of another kind, from utter strangers who had read his novel and liked
it. . . . Soon his box was stuffed with fan mail, and the telephone
jingled merrily all day long with invitations from wealthy and cultivated
people who wanted him for lunch, for tea, for dinner, for theatre parties, for week-ends in the country—for anything at all if he would only
come.

"Was this Fame at last? It looked so, and in the first flush of his
eager belief, he . . . rushed headlong into the welcoming arms of
people he had never seen before. He accepted invitations right and
left, and they kept him pretty busy. And each time he went out it
seemed to him that he was on the very point of capturing all the gold
and magic he had ever dreamed of finding, and that now he was really
going to take a place of honor among the great ones of the city, in a
life more fortunate and good than he had ever known. He went to each
encounter with each new friend as though some wonderful and intoxicating happiness were impending for him. But he never found it. For,
in spite of all the years he had lived in New York, he was still a country
boy, and he did not know about the lion hunters."

Wolfe's work always had a direct emotional effect upon his readers—
so direct and so emotional that many of them sought him out. He
received many letters from people who confided that their experiences
and emotions were almost identical with his and who expressed a compulsive eagerness to meet him and tell him all about themselves. He
had also a great appeal for high-strung, emotional women, who fell in
love with him through his books and almost literally threw themselves
at him. His files are full of letters from these women: he would meet
them and often have brief love affairs with them, only to end up by
insulting them with a vindictive bitterness that came from deep within
him. He received also, of course, many letters of genuine appreciation
of his work from both men and women; and the usual mail which every
well-known writer gets: the crank letters, the invitations, the overtures
from other publishers, the requests that he autograph copies of his book,
that he recommend someone or something, that he compose a greeting
for a Christmas-card company, and so on. In later years he learned to
accept all this with equanimity—sometimes with great amusement; but
at the time of the publication of *Look Homeward, Angel* he took it very
seriously and let it "get him down."

"Month was passing into month," Wolfe says in *The Story of a*

Novel. "I had had a success. The way was opened to me. There was only one thing for me to do and that was work, and I was spending my time consuming myself with anger, grief, and useless passion about the reception the book had had in my native town, or wasting myself again in exuberant elation because of the critics' and the readers' praise, or in anguish and bitterness because of their ridicule. For the first time, I realized the nature of one of the artist's greatest conflicts, and was faced with the need of meeting it. For the first time I saw not only that the artist must live and sweat and love and suffer and enjoy as other men, but that the artist must also work as other men and that, furthermore, he must work even while these common events of life are going on. It seems a simple and banal assertion, but I learned it hardly, and in one of the worst moments of my life. There is no such thing as an artistic vacuum; there is no such thing as a time when the artist may work in a delightful atmosphere, free of agony that other men must know, or if the artist ever does find such a time, it is something not to be hoped for, something not to be sought for indefinitely. At any rate, while my life and energy were absorbed in the emotional vortex which my first book had created, I was getting almost no work done on the second. . . . I realized suddenly with a sense of definite shock that I had let six months go by since the publication of my first book and that, save for a great many notes and fragments, I had done nothing."

Wolfe was suffering from what publishers call "second book trouble," and he would continue to suffer from it, more and more, for five long years, until Perkins mercifully put a stop to it by taking his manuscript away from him and publishing the first part of it as *Of Time and the River.* First and foremost, he was under the great mental disadvantage of finding his talent as a writer taken very seriously. He explains this in *The Story of a Novel:* "I had been a writer in hope and in desire before and now I was a writer in fact. I would read about myself, for example, as one of the 'younger American writers.' I was a person who, some of the critics said, was to be watched. They were looking forward to my future book with interest and with a certain amount of apprehension. Here, too, my education as a writer was increasing all the time. Now, indeed, I could hear myself discussed, and somehow the fact was far more formidable than I had dreamed that it could be. It worried me, confused me, gave me a strange feeling of guilt and responsibility. I was a young American writer, and they had hopes and fears about my future, and what would I do, or would it be anything, nothing, much or little? Would the faults which they had found in my work grow worse or would I conquer them? Was I another flash in the pan? Would I come through? What would happen to me?

"I let it worry me. I would go home at night and look around my room and see that morning's coffeecup still unwashed and books on the floor and a shirt where I had thrown it the night before and great stacks of manuscript and everything so common and familiar-looking and so disorderly, and then I would think that I was now 'a young American writer'; that somehow I was practising an imposture on my readers and my critics because my shirt looked the way it did and my books and my bed—not, you understand, because they were disorderly, common, familiar, but just because they looked the way they did. . . .

"The critics had begun to ask questions about the second book, and so now I had to think about the second one as well. I had always wanted to think about the second one and the thirty-second one and the fifty-second one. I had been sure that I had a hundred books in me, that all of them would be good, that each of them would make me famous. But here again was a strange and jolting transition from wild hope and exultant conviction; and plain, blazing fact remained. Now that I had actually written one book and *they*, the actual readers and critics who had read it, were looking for a second, I was up against it. I was not up against it the way I dreaded, I was just up against it cold and hard as one comes up against a wall. I was a writer. I had made the writer's life my life; there was no going back; I had to go on. What could I do? After the first book there had to be a second book. What was the second book to be about? Where would it come from?"

There was also, of course, the immediate and practical problem of how Wolfe was to support himself while he wrote the second book. He had agreed to teach at New York University for the entire academic year of 1929–30, but he was now more anxious than ever to be wholly free to write. Accordingly, at Perkins' suggestion, he had applied in December 1929 for a Guggenheim fellowship. He was very highly recommended for it by Perkins, Robert Norwood, James Boyd, and Professor Watt; and because of the unquestionable talent shown in *Look Homeward, Angel,* he stood a very good chance of being chosen by the Guggenheim committee. However, the fellowships would not be awarded until March, and both he and Perkins were anxious to have him start on his new book immediately. Therefore, on December 18, 1929, after consultation with Charles Scribner III, Perkins had written Wolfe a letter offering to subsidize him:

Dear Mr. Wolfe:

We are deeply interested in your writing, and have confidence in your future, and we wish to cooperate with you so far as possible toward the production of a new novel. We think you would be able to write it to much greater advantage if you were free from the necessity of earning money at the same time, and we should be glad to undertake to pay you, as an advance on the earnings of the next novel, forty-five hundred dollars ($4500.) in installments, at the rate of two hundred and fifty dollars a month, beginning with February 1st. . . .

On the strength of this letter, Wolfe jubilantly sent New York University his resignation, to become effective with the beginning of the spring term in February 1930. He began drawing his monthly subsidy of $250 from Scribners in that month and continued to do so until June. By that time he had been granted his Guggenheim fellowship of $2500; moreover, *Look Homeward, Angel* had by then earned $3500 worth of royalties in excess of the advance. Wolfe therefore stopped drawing the monthly subsidies against his second book. He did not draw against it any more until the summer of 1933, and the contract for the book was not signed until that time.

His application for the Guggenheim fellowship brought the "long and bitter war of separation" between him and Mrs. Bernstein to its final phase. In spite of his reconciliation with her in 1929, his old compulsion for freedom had been only temporarily suppressed, and he now felt more strongly than ever that he must follow without encumbrance his destiny as a writer. Moreover, the "heroic figure, stronger and wiser" than himself, from whom he now sought guidance toward that destiny, was no longer she, but Mr. Perkins.

Mrs. Bernstein was quick to sense this, and she was inclined to blame Wolfe's desertion of her entirely on Perkins. Moreover, Wolfe seems to have done nothing to correct this notion, but to have actually encouraged it. In all good faith, he often quoted the opinions of his parental substitutes and even put into their mouths advice which was an echo of his own convictions more than anything that they had definitely said. According to what Perkins wrote later, Wolfe did this now. "The first time I ever heard of Aline Bernstein was shortly before the publication of *The Angel*," Perkins wrote in 1945 to John S. Terry. "And then I did not know her name. Tom told me of his relationship with a woman twenty years older than himself whom he greatly admired but no longer loved in the modern sense of the word. He asked my advice, but I, naively thinking at that time that such a matter was not one for an editor, evaded the question on several separate occasions. Finally I said that in the circumstances, I did not see how the relationship could continue and that since she was so very much older, it would certainly eventually have to end. That is as far as I went. But according to Aline, Tom told her he had consulted me and that I had advised him to break off with her."[1]

The whole thing was brought to a climax by the fact that, if Wolfe should receive a Guggenheim fellowship, he must spend it in work and study abroad. Mrs. Bernstein, with deep devotion and perfect willingness to subsidize him whenever he might need it, begged him not to leave her, but he was adamant. "Aline was very clever about people . . . ," he says in one of his notebooks. "Could do what she liked with me, but we can not be clever about the fundamental structure of life—that settles itself and us." She herself, in the chapter called "Eugene" in her book *Three Blue Suits*, describes the scene that took place between them when he returned from lunch with his editor, Mr. Watkins, and told her of his application for the fellowship:

"There was something the matter, his voice was different. She turned towards him.

" 'Eugene, what is the matter, tell me at once. . . .'

" 'Watkins suggested,' he cleared his throat. 'You see it will be six months before anything comes in from the book, even if it is a success, they all thought it would be a good idea—' He got up from his chair and went to her. 'Watkins thought it would be a good idea if I went abroad on a Guggenheim Fellowship, it would give me a year on the new one, quiet now, my dear.'

"The plates fell crashing to the floor, her hands caught at her throat, she moved a step away.

" 'How much?'

" 'Twenty-five hundred for the year, away from America, no more teaching—'

" 'So you'd let me down, sell me out for twenty-five hundred, would you!' Black wings beat freezing air upon her. 'Darling, no, you can't mean it. . . . How can you live and do such a thing, how can you take your food or breathe the air?' She could barely speak, sobs choked her. 'How can you deny the Eugene I have loved? You promised you would never leave me, darling, you said as long as we both lived you would never—remember, remember all the times you have said it.' Her sobs, her tears in great streams were on his shoulder. . . .

[1] From Perkins' letter of October 22, 1945, to John S. Terry.

"It seemed to Eugene as though she would weep an ocean full. It was terrible. He tried to comfort her, but there was no comforting in this situation. Either he must stay or go, and his resolve was to go. She was becoming a little more quiet, but she was holding so tight to him that he could scarcely move. He hated it, he wished with all his heart that things could be always just the way he wanted them. He wanted a world where he could wander at his own sweet will, he wished that he could write in thought, he wished that his books would spring full printed from his brain, without the drudgery of pencil guided by his hand on paper, typing, cutting, revising. He wished that he could tell her of his deep love, and still make her see the necessity of his going. He wished he could do all this without having to do it. . . . There was so much in his mind, he tried to reach his note book. It was in the pocket of his coat. He moved and looked down at her face. The beauty was obliterated, sobs and tears and grief had made it red and swollen. It was like a battlefield, plowed with the harrow of her pain. He wanted none of her grief, no pain but his own. He pulled his arm free, and wrenched the note book from his pocket, tearing a long gash in the coat. He wrote in the book 'Can there be no revolution without bloodshed?'

"She looked at what he had written. 'No, no,' she cried, and her helpless hands beat upon his head and chest."

And so the struggle began again: she tried desperately to hold him, and the more she tried, the more he became obsessed with the necessity of breaking free. He began quarreling violently with her, and in general treated her so badly that several of her friends remonstrated with him. One of them evidently urged a severance for her sake, and Wolfe immediately seized upon this as justification for what he had wanted all along. Characteristically, he brooded over this incident and exaggerated it until he half convinced himself that he was leaving her against his will because her friends insisted on it. "Being born, living, dying—and we waste ourselves in petty squabbles," he wrote in his notebook at the time of his acceptance of the fellowship, when the struggle between him and Mrs. Bernstein had reached its crucial stage. "I am now in such a mood that the littlest things possess and harrow my soul. . . . This is courage, to screw and rivet every jerking nerve together by the supremest effort of the will, to conquer the nausea around the heart, the weakness in the bowels, and to strike hardest when most afraid. This is courage, and we must learn to do it—men like me—to beat life to this extent unless we are to let it beat us entirely. . . .

Now, keep hold: strike hard—keep your breath cool and calm, and endure. Do all that can be done with calmness and with decency—if you are forced to leave, leave because you are forced by things outside of your control—and leave without fear or shame."

This sort of emotional distortion occurred increasingly in his notebooks and his letters during his ten months' stay abroad. He repeated again and again that "I did not want to come, but I yielded to what her friends wanted for her, and what it seemed to me would be best"; or that "I have never betrayed or deserted anyone—in the end, if anyone gets betrayed or deserted, it will be me." But contradictorily, and in almost the same breath, he insisted that Mrs. Bernstein and her friends were "spying on" him and "conspiring" against him, either to force him to go back to her or to "ruin" him as punishment for having left her. The whole thing became a terrible obsession with him, or, as he described it, a "disease of the spirit"; and at the bottom of it were the two emotions he had told himself he must not have—fear and shame. But there was also the inescapable conviction that he must be free to live and work alone.

Wolfe was awarded his Guggenheim fellowship in March, but he did not actually sail for Europe until May. He would normally have gone home to see his mother before leaving, but the scandal in Asheville over *Look Homeward, Angel* now made that impossible. He was nervous and upset and could not work, so he gratified his old childish love of riding on fast trains. "I have been . . . to Atlantic City," he wrote to James Boyd, ". . . riding in the engine cab of the fastest train in America—83 miles an hour on a steel cyclone—and I have soaked up the power and the glory until it's oozing out." On the way back he gratified another deeply rooted impulse—to visit the country of southern Pennsylvania from which his father had come. On this first trip he did not actually reach York Springs, his father's birthplace, but only went as far as Lancaster, "a town I have heard him speak of many times. There I saw where half of me came from," he wrote his mother. "It is the richest, fattest farming country you ever looked at, and the Dutch people were out in the great fields behind teams of four big horses abreast. The barns were painted red and were four times as big as the houses and everything was neat as a pin: although I had never been there before it was like something you see in a dream come true, for it was all exactly as he had described it. One half of me is great fields and mighty barns, and one half of me is the great hills of North Carolina." Because of his exile from the hills of home, he had found his other half—"his father's world."

He sailed on the *Volendam* on the tenth of May, and just before he left, he gave to Mrs. Bernstein the carbon copy of the manuscript of *Look Homeward, Angel*, the book he had written "because of her."[2] He also drew a will, naming her and his mother as equal beneficiaries. He had never been able to repay any of the money which Mrs. Bernstein had given him, and this weighed heavily upon his conscience. And now that he had virtually won the battle to be free of her, he felt a sudden rush of tenderness and pity and regret. He wrote her a brief but very affectionate note on shipboard and another when he arrived in Paris. Then, when she continued to write him letters of desperation and resentment, he abruptly cut off all communication with her and became obsessively suspicious of her desperate attempts to get some word from him.

"I was conscious now of the fatal impingement of time," Wolfe says in his Purdue speech, "a sense of pressure and the knowledge that I must get to work at once, make good use of my year abroad, . . . and have a new book finished, if I could, by the time I came back." But during his entire time abroad he was distracted from his work by a succession of misfortunes and emotional upheavals. For the first two weeks in Paris he failed completely to begin his book. Paris was for him the worst place in the world in which to work. He disliked the French, whom he felt were crafty, avaricious, and "cats, with the mews of cats," and the gaiety of the city increased his natural weakness for drinking, whoring, and wandering restlessly about all night. It was probably because of this mistrust and these excesses that he complained again and again in his Paris diaries of being "in a crucifixion of nervousness and fear." "To-day has been a horrible one," he wrote there on May 24. "I was able to sleep only the most diseased and distressed sleep (the worst sort of American-in-Europe sleep) last night . . . and I got up sick and with the *shakes* this morning. . . . The day was of

[2] Wolfe's longhand inscription in the copy of *Look Homeward, Angel* which he had given to Mrs. Bernstein says: "To Aline Bernstein. On my twenty-ninth birthday, I present her with this, the first copy of my first book. This book was written because of her, and is dedicated to her. At a time when my life seemed desolate, and when I had little faith in myself, I met her. She brought me friendship, material and spiritual relief, and love such as I had never had before. I hope therefore that readers of my book will find at least a part of it worthy of such a woman. Thomas Wolfe. Oct. 3, 1929." In comparison with the beautiful verse from Donne in the printed dedication to her, this inscription seems somewhat formal and self-conscious.

the most horrible European sort—something that passes understand-ing—the wet, heavy air that deadens the soul, puts a lump of indigestible lead in the solar plexus, depresses and fatigues the flesh until one seems to lift himself leadenly through the thick, wet, steaming air. With this a kind of terrible fear—an excitement that is without hope—that waits only the news of some further grief, failure, humiliation, and torture. There is a lassitude that enters the fold and lappings of the brain, that makes one hope for better things and better work to-morrow, but hope without belief or conviction."

Once a day he went to the Guaranty Trust to get his mail, but it usually upset him. In the first batch he received on reaching Paris, he found a bill for $535 from two New York dentists who had removed some of his back teeth and replaced them with bridgework just before he had sailed. The amount was over one fifth of his entire Guggenheim allowance: he became terribly incensed, wrote Scribners not to pay it, and wasted many hours scrawling down insulting letters to the dentists, which he never mailed. The cables and letters which he received from Mrs. Bernstein invariably plunged him into fits of brooding, and to cap it all, his brother Fred, with the best intentions in the world, sent him the news of the latest scandal which *Look Homeward, Angel* had caused in Asheville.

Just before he sailed he had been interviewed by Lee Cooper for the Asheville *Times*. The interview itself he found no fault with, but he took violent exception to its headline: "Wolfe Denies Having Betrayed Asheville." The new scandal, however, was caused by a photograph of a stone angel printed with the interview, with a title explaining that it was the angel which had given Wolfe's book its name. According to the book, this angel had been sold by Gant to "Queen" Elizabeth for the grave of one of her prostitutes. As Wolfe said later in *The Story of a Novel*, "The unfortunate part of this proceeding was that I had never seen or heard of this angel before, and that this angel was, in fact, erected over the grave of a well-known Methodist lady who had died a few years before, and that her indignant family had im-mediately written the paper to demand a retraction of its story, saying that their mother had been in no way connected with the infamous book or the infamous angel which had given the infamous book its name."

Meanwhile he had been sought out by a wealthy woman friend of Mrs. Bernstein's, but he felt that "on May 31, . . . after many letters to me," she had "conspired that I be insulted at her apartment." This was evidently the final straw: he left Paris the next morning and went to Rouen for three days of rest and sight-seeing. He was by now abysmally homesick for America. "The soft air that entered in easy flows into his lungs heavied and drowsied him," he wrote in his little notebook. "They recalled to him two hundred other reeking days in Europe—two hundred days upon that soft, wet continent. He missed the sharp burning oxygen of America. Around the tower of Jeanne d'Arc, the light green grass of France was growing. The sight of that kept nature, so old, so cloying, filled him with sadness and despair. He wanted the old piercing hope and agony of Spring in his native land." And so, at last, his longing for America impelled him to begin to write. He filled page after page of his notebook with outlines for his book and with lyric chants and phrases: "And in America the chinquapins are falling. The corn sticks out in hard and yellow rows upon dried ears, fit for a winter's barn and the big yellow teeth of crunching horses; and the leaves are turning, turning, up in Maine."[3]

He went back to Paris on June 4 and moved to a new hotel to escape from Mrs. Bernstein's wealthy woman friend. He was anxious to begin work on his book immediately, but he was also anxious to see his English editor, A. S. Frere of William Heinemann, Ltd., who was going to publish the *Angel* in England in July. He had met Frere in New York, in January, and had written to him when he first arrived in Paris, saying: "I am a little terrified at the idea of complete isolation. I used to be able to do it when I came abroad, but I want someone to talk to once in a while now." Frere had immediately got Thomas McGreevy, the Irish poet, to look Wolfe up, and he himself now flew to Paris and introduced Wolfe to Michael Arlen, Richard Aldington, and Mrs. Brigit Patmore. But although Wolfe was genuinely fond of Frere, he felt alien and uneasy with the English writers. "I was no good with people," he said later, "and I did not go back to see them." He was "still getting over New York" and felt "all beaten and bloody inside"; and he was by now "in a very bad state" about his failure to begin his book.

It was at this point that he made what seemed to him a very important discovery. "After two weeks of casting around, moving from one hotel to another," he wrote to John Hall Wheelock, "I suddenly decided that we spend too much of our lives looking for ideal conditions to work in, and that what we are after is an ideal condition of the soul which almost never comes. So I got tired and disgusted with myself . . .

[3] This is the first seed of the famous "October" passage, which became the first part of Section XXXIX, in "Telemachus," *Of Time and the River*.

and set to work." For the next two weeks he saw practically no one except three young Americans, Susan and Robert Hyde and Marian Smith. He bought himself "the most beautiful book to write in, . . . over 700 pages and strongly bound and a foot broad," and by July 23 he was able to report jubilantly to Frere: "I am working six to ten hours a day. Paris has no more interest for me than Sauk Center."

"I was in Paris for a couple of months, until the middle of July," Wolfe says in *The Story of a Novel*, "and although I now compelled myself to work for four or five hours a day, my effort at composition was still confused and broken, and there was nothing yet that had the structural form and unity of a book. The life of the great city fascinated me as it had always done, but also aroused all the old feelings of naked homelessness, rootlessness, and loneliness which I have always felt there. It was, and has always remained for me, at least, the most homesick city in the world . . . During that summer in Paris, I think I felt this great homesickness more than ever before, and I really believe that from this emotion, this constant and almost intolerable effort of memory and desire, the material and the structure of the books I now began to write were derived. The quality of my memory is characterized, I believe, in a more than ordinary degree by the intensity of its sense impressions, its power to evoke and bring back the odors, sounds, colors, shapes, and feel of things with concrete vividness. Now my memory was at work night and day, in a way that I could at first neither check nor control and that swarmed unbidden in a stream of blazing pageantry across my mind, with the million forms and substances of the life that I had left, which was my own, America. I would be sitting, for example, on the terrace of a café watching the flash and play of life before me on the Avenue de l'Opéra, and suddenly I would remember the iron railing that goes along the boardwalk at Atlantic City. I could see it instantly just the way it was, the heavy iron pipe; its raw, galvanized look; the way the joints were fitted together. It was all so vivid and concrete that I could feel my hand upon it and know the exact dimensions, its size and weight and shape. And suddenly I would realize that I had never seen any railing that looked like this in Europe. And this utterly familiar, common thing would suddenly be revealed to me with all the wonder with which we discover a thing which we have seen all our life and yet have never known before.

"Or again, it would be a bridge, the look of an old iron bridge across an American river, the sound the train makes as it goes across it; the spoke-and-hollow rumble of the ties below; the look of the muddy banks; the slow, thick, yellow wash of an American river; an old flat-bottomed boat half-filled with water stogged in the muddy bank; or it would be, most lonely and haunting of all the sounds I know, the sound of a milk wagon as it entered an American street just at the first grey of the morning, the slow and lonely clopping of the hoof upon the street, the jink of bottles, the sudden rattle of a battered old milk can, the swift and hurried footsteps of the milkman, and again the jink of bottles, a low word spoken to his horse, and then the great, slow, clopping hoof receding into silence, and then quietness and a bird song rising in the street again. . . .

"Or again, it would be an American street with all its jumble of a thousand ugly architectures. It would be Montague Street or Fulton Street in Brooklyn, or Eleventh Street in New York, or other streets where I had lived; and suddenly I would see the gaunt and savage webbing of the elevated structure along Fulton Street, and how the light swarmed through in dusty, broken bars, and I could remember the old, familiar rusty color, that incomparable rusty color that gets into so many things here in America. And this also would be like something I had seen a million times and lived with all my life.

"I would sit there, looking out upon the Avenue de l'Opéra, and my life would ache with the whole memory of it; the desire to see it again; somehow to find a word for it; a language that would tell its shape, its color, the way we have all known and felt and seen it. And when I understood this thing, I saw that I must find for myself the tongue to utter what I knew but could not say. And from the moment of that discovery, the line and purpose of my life was shaped. The end towards which every energy of my life and talent would be henceforth directed was in such a way as this defined."

Late in June, at Perkins' suggestion, Wolfe met Scott Fitzgerald, who was to be his bête noire for the next two months. Fitzgerald's playboy manner immediately put Wolfe on the defensive, although he at first tried hard to like him. "He has not yet graduated from Princeton," he wrote to Henry Volkening in July. "He has good qualities and I am sorry for him, probably without cause." "I like him, he is kind and generous," he wrote to Frere, "but I have not yet learned how to drink longer than twelve hours at a stretch, and he apparently can keep it up for at least twenty-four without flushing." And, more earnestly, to Perkins: "When I am with someone like Scott, I feel that I am morose and sullen—and violent in my speech and movement part of the time. Later I feel that I have repelled them."

Soon he began to suspect that Fitzgerald was giving information about him to the wealthy woman who had "insulted" him in Paris, and that she, in turn, was relaying it back to Mrs. Bernstein in New York. He describes this at great length in an unmailed letter written to Henry Volkening from Freiburg in September: "I must explain to you that Mr. F. had discovered the day I saw him in Paris that I knew a very notorious young lady, now resident in Paris . . . Mr. F. immediately broke out in a sweat on finding I knew the lady and damned near broke his neck getting around there: he insisted that I come ('Every writer,' this great philosopher said, 'is a social climber.') and when I told him very positively I would not go to see the lady, this poet of the passions at once began to see all the elements of a romance—the cruel and dissolute society beauty playing with the tortured heart of the sensitive young writer, etc.: he eagerly demanded my reasons for staying away. . . . I told Mr. F., the great analyst of the soul, to tell the woman nothing about me, to give no information at all about me or what I was doing, or where I was. I told him this in Paris, I told him again in Switzerland, and on both occasions the man got to her as fast as he could. . . . She immediately sent all the information back to America—and the heart-rending letters, cables, etc., with threats of coming to find me, going mad, dying, etc. began to come directly to my hotel."

By this time Wolfe had cut himself off completely from Mrs. Bernstein. He had vowed to stay in Paris until he had finished the first section of Part I of his book—"It does me so much good to show myself that it can be done in Paris," he explained to Frere—but now he hastily packed up and went to Switzerland. "Silence! Silence! Silence!" he wrote in his notebook on the way. "Do not let them see you! Do not let them spy upon you! Go to the wilderness and live alone in silence, silence. Do things that they can not share in or be a part of. Live a life that they can not feed upon. When they ask you, lie: say other things. 'Deal out your honest heart in tricks,' and keep silence, silence, silence!"

By July 11 he had settled down in Montreux. "I had a room in a small but very clean hotel . . . ," he said later in his Purdue speech, "and my room had a large stone balcony, and down below there was a lawn that was a sheet of velvet, and flowers that seemed to have been embroidered there, and all this stretched directly to the lake, which was fifty yards or so away, and of a blue incredible; and across the lake, on the French side, were the Alps that you had to look at twice before you believed they were there, and even then you didn't quite believe it; and it was very quiet, a few casual and intimate voices of people down below, and of the kitchen help, and every now and then the great fast thrash of the paddles as the lake steamers, white and clean as swans, came into the landing down below, disgorged and took on, and then, with startling speed, were on their way again." It seemed like an ideal place in which to work, and for several weeks he wrote and wrote like one possessed.

"An extraordinary image remains to me from that year . . . ," Wolfe says in *The Story of a Novel.* "It seemed that I had inside me, swelling and gathering all the time, a huge black cloud, and that this cloud was loaded with electricity, pregnant, crested, with a kind of hurricane violence that could not be held in check much longer; that the moment was approaching fast when it must break. Well, all I can say is that the storm did break. It broke that summer while I was in Switzerland. It came in torrents, and it is not over yet.

"I cannot really say the book was written. It was something that took hold of me and possessed me, and before I was done with it . . . it seemed to me that it had done for me. It was exactly as if this great black storm cloud . . . had opened up and, mid flashes of lightning, was pouring from its depth a torrential and ungovernable flood. . . . There was nothing at first which could be called a novel. I wrote about night and darkness in America, and the faces of the sleepers in ten thousand little towns; and of the tides of sleep and how the rivers flowed forever in the darkness. I wrote about the hissing glut of tides upon ten thousand miles of coast; of how the moonlight blazed down on the wilderness and filled the cat's cold eye with blazing yellow. I wrote about death and sleep, and of that enfabled rock of life we call the city. I wrote about October, of great trains that thundered through the night, of ships and stations in the morning; of men in harbors and the traffic of the ships."

His letters to Perkins and Wheelock about the book are more explicit. What he was doing was playing variations on his theme, "of wandering forever and the earth again." "I am working on the part called 'Antaeus' now, which is like a symphony of many voices run through with the beginning thread of story . . . ," he wrote to Perkins. "The book has to do with what seem to me two of the profoundest impulses in man—Wordsworth, in one of his poems, 'To a Skylark,' I think, calls it 'heaven and home' and I called it in the first line of my book 'of wandering forever and the earth again.' By 'the earth again'

I mean simply the everlasting earth, a home, a place for the heart to come to, and earthly mortal love, the love of a woman, who, it seems to me, belongs to the earth and is a force opposed to that other great force that makes men wander, that makes them search, that makes them lonely, and that makes them both hate and love their loneliness. . . . In the first part—'Antaeus'—. . . everything moves, everything moves across the enormous earth, except the earth itself, and except for the voices of the women crying out 'Don't go! Stay! Return, return!"

"There are these scenes," he wrote to Wheelock, "a woman talking of the river, the ever-moving river, coming through the levee at night, . . . and of how she feels the house break loose and go with the tide, then of living on the roof-top with Furman and the children, and of other houses and people—tragedy, pity, humor, bravery, and the great wild savagery of American nature. Then the pioneer telling of 'the perty little gal' he liked, but moving on because the wilderness was getting too crowded; then the hoboes waiting quietly at evening by the water tower for the coming of the fast express; then a rich American girl moving on from husband to husband, from drink to dope to opium, from white lovers to black ones, from New York to Paris to California; then the engineer at the throttle of the fast train. Then a modest little couple from 123rd St. . . . cruising in their cheap little car through Virginia and Kentucky in autumn . . . Then a school teacher from Ohio taking University Art Pilgrimage No. 36 . . . Then Lee coming through Virginia in the night on his great white horse; then the skull of a pioneer in the desert, a rusted gun stock and a horse's skull . . . And more, and more, and more!"[4]

Wolfe was anxious to avoid having his new book called autobiographical as *Look Homeward, Angel* had been, and this was probably

[4] Many of these episodes were omitted from *Of Time and the River* and were published elsewhere: the incident of the woman describing her experience in the flood was never published, except for her words about the river, which "goes by me, by me, by me, to the sea." This was changed to "flows by us, by us, by us, to the sea" and repeated as a lyrical refrain in various places in *Of Time and the River*; the scene of the hobos waiting for the fast train became "The Bums at Sunset" in *Vanity Fair* and *From Death to Morning*; the episode of the schoolteacher taking "University Art Pilgrimage No. 36" became "One of the Girls in Our Party" in *Scribner's Magazine* and *From Death to Morning*; and the story of the "rich American girl moving on from husband to husband" became that of Amy Carleton in "The Party at Jack's," which first appeared in *Scribner's Magazine* and was then used as a section of *You Can't Go Home Again*. And so it went: as Perkins said, "Nothing Wolfe wrote was ever lost."

one of the reasons why he spent so much time writing introductory material instead of plunging into the main body of the book. "By God, Jack," he had written to Wheelock from Paris late in June, "I have not written a word directly about myself yet." But when, in his letter of July 17 to Perkins, he attempted to describe what his book would be about, the autobiographical quality of it began to be evident. "I told you that the book begins with 'of wandering forever, and the earth again,' and that these two opposing elements seem to me to be fundamental in people. . . . I think you have sometimes been puzzled when I have talked to you about parts of this book—about the train as it thunders through the dark, and about the love for another person— . . . but I think you can get some idea of it now: the great train . . . is rushing across the everlasting and silent earth—here the two ideas of wandering and eternal repose . . . Also, the love theme, the male and female love, represent this again . . .

"There is no doubt at all what the book is about, what course it will take, and I think the seething process, the final set of combinations, has been reached. . . . The four parts of the book as they now stand are:

(1) 'Antaeus' or 'Immortal earth' . . .
(2) 'Antaeus' or 'The Fast Express'
(3) 'Faust and Helen'
(4) 'The October Fair.' . . .

"Now the general movement of the book is from the universal to the individual: in Part I . . . we have a symphony of many voices, . . . through which the thread of the particular story begins to run. . . . We have a character called David . . . but this character appears at first only as a window, an eye, a wandering seer . . . , who makes us very briefly conscious of his presence from time to time by saying, 'I have heard,' or 'it has been told me.' Thus . . . in the chapter called 'The River,' the woman telling the story of the river in flood refers to him once by name. In the chapter 'Pioneers, O Pioneers,' we understand that David is a member of an American family, two or three hundred of whose members are buried in different parts of the American earth, and we get the stories and wanderings of some of these people. In the letter of the tourist from Prague he is referred to by name; in the chapter 'On the Rails,' we know that he is on the train, although the story is that of the engineer; in the chapter 'The Bums at Sunset,' we know he has seen them waiting for the train at the water-tower; in the chapter called 'The Congo,' the wandering negro who goes crazy and kills people and is finally killed by the posse as he crosses a creek,[5] is known to David, the boy—etc.

"So much for some of the general movement: now among the twenty chapters of this first part are interspersed the first elements of the particular story—the figure of David . . . begins to emerge as an individual from what is told about him by other people . . . —but in this first part, not to tell about him, but to tell about his country, the seed that produced him, etc. It will be seen in the particular story that the desire and longing of David is also the desire and longing of the race—'wandering forever and the earth again.' . . .

"Now, if you will follow me a little farther in this, here is another development. . . . Contained in the book like a kernel from the beginning, but unrevealed until much later, is the idea of a man's quest for his father. The idea becomes very early apparent that when a man returns he returns always to the *female* principle—he returns . . . to the womb of earthly creation, to the earth itself, to a woman, to fixity. But I dare go so far as to believe that the other pole—the pole of wandering—is not only a masculine thing, but that in some way it represents the quest of a man for his father. . . . This last theme . . . does not become fully revealed until the very end of the book: under the present plan I have called the final chapter of the fourth and last part ('The October Fair') 'Telemachus.' . . .

"One final thing: please understand . . . that my new book will make use of experience, things I have known and felt, as the first one did—but that now I have created fables and legends and that there will be no question of identification (certainly not in the first two parts) as there was in the first. The David I have referred to is part of me, . . . but nothing like, in appearance or anything else, what people think me. . . . In making the character of David, I have made him out of the *inside* of me, of what I have always believed the inside was like: he is about five feet nine, with the long arms and the prowl of an ape, and a little angel in his face. He is part beast, part spirit—a mixture of the ape and the angel. There is a touch of the monster in him. But no matter about this—at first he is the bard and, I pray God, that is what I can be."

It will be apparent to readers of Wolfe's novels that "the final set of combinations" for his book had by no means been reached. The

[5] This, too, was omitted from *Of Time and the River*. It was rewritten and published as "The Child by Tiger" in the *Saturday Evening Post* and used as Chapter VIII in *The Web and the Rock*.

entire first section was finally omitted from *Of Time and the River*, except for the brief lyrical passage in italics which serves as an introduction to the book, and a few sections which were woven into the story proper. David himself reassumed the name and physical characteristics of Eugene Gant for six more years—until *The Web and the Rock* and *You Can't Go Home Again*—and *Of Time and the River* began exactly where *Look Homeward, Angel* had left off, with Eugene's departure from home in 1920. Moreover, the four parts outlined by Wolfe grew and grew and were changed and rearranged until *Of Time and the River* finally had eight parts: "Orestes: Flight before Fury," "Young Faustus," "Telemachus," "Proteus: The City," "Jason's Voyage," "Antaeus: Earth Again," "Kronos and Rhea: The Dream of Time," and "Faust and Helen." These titles, however, did not finally apply to the material originally planned for them, but only to introductions to it. For instance, "Telemachus" described the death of Gant and the beginning of Eugene's "search for a father" rather than its end; "Antaeus: Earth Again" merely told of Eugene's adventures in the château country during his first trip abroad; and "Faust and Helen" described only his first glimpse of the woman with whom he was to fall in love. In this sense, *Of Time and the River* was really only a long introduction to what Wolfe thought of as the main part of his story. For the remainder of his life, in spite of delays, vicissitudes, and changes of intention, he struggled to tell the rest of it, and his exhaustion from too protracted work on it was one of the main causes of his death in 1938.

XII

FOR two weeks Wolfe lived and worked in peace in his hotel room overlooking Lake Geneva. "I shall not try to conceal from you the fact that at times now I have hard sledding," he wrote to Perkins. "My life is divided between just two things:—thought of my book, and thought of an event in my life which is now, *objectivally,* finished. I do not write any more to anyone concerned in that event —I received several letters, but since none have come for some time I assume no more will come." But a week later he began receiving directly at his hotel cablegrams and letters from Mrs. Bernstein, in which she threatened to come abroad and find him if she did not hear from him immediately that he was all right. He became terribly upset again, and when a writer who was a client of Mrs. Boyd's dropped in to see him, he suspected that the man had been sent by Mrs. Bernstein to "spy" upon him. "This woman is of course behind it," he wrote in his diary, with the irrationality of helpless rage. "She wrecked me, maddened me, and betrayed my love, constantly, but she will not leave me alone now."

He had met Scott Fitzgerald by chance at the Montreux casino and had later gone to call on him in Vevey, and he now again suspected him of having disclosed his whereabouts to Mrs. Bernstein through her friend in Paris. "That ended Montreux for me," he wrote in his unmailed letter of September to Henry Volkening. ". . . The hotel people, who had been very kind to me, charged me three francs extra because I had brought a bottle of wine from outside into the hotel. They have a right in Switzerland to do this, but I took my rage out on them, told them I was leaving next day, went on a spree, broke windows, plumbing fixtures, etc. in the town, and came back to the hotel at 2 A.M., pounded on the door of the director and on the doors of two English spinsters, rushed howling with laughter up and down the halls, cursing and singing—and, in short, *had* to leave."

He went immediately to Geneva and was still there, brooding over his difficulties with Mrs. Bernstein, when he received two very unfavorable reviews of the English edition of *Look Homeward, Angel.* Heinemann had published the book on July 4, and at first Wolfe had refused to read reviews of it, saying that they "would bother me—good or bad—and I'm at work and can't fool with it." But the first of them, led off by high praise from Richard Aldington in the *Sunday Referee,* were unanimously favorable. Even the *Times Literary Supplement* went so far as to say: "Such native force is rare in England now; and it is impossible to regard this unstinting output of magnificent, raw vigour without a thrill and a hope that it will be channelled to great art. The present book is not great art; but its promise and its power are so extraordinary that we dwell upon them rather than upon the details of its story. . . . What is going to be done with this great talent, so hard, so sensual, so unsentimental, so easily comprehending and describing every sordidness of the flesh and spirit, so proudly rising to the heights? Knowing the times and the temptations of the times, we may well watch its fresh emergence with anxiety; for if Mr. Wolfe can be wasted, there is no hope for to-day."[1]

By the end of July the English edition was selling a thousand copies every four or five days: Frere was impelled to write to Wolfe of its success, and he enclosed the clippings which had come in up to that date, saying, "Read these reviews—you have nothing to be afraid of."[2] Wolfe read them and, as he said later, "got in a very excited condition about a book I should have left behind me months ago." But on August 8 the London *Evening News* published a very unfavorable review by Frank Swinnerton: "Personally I found Mr. Wolfe's *Look Homeward, Angel* very long indeed," it said in part. "Mr. Wolfe has a very dangerous fluency. He is almost glib, particularly in his improvisations of bar-room scenes, domestic scenes in which a ranting father performs mechanically, and scenes of coquetry; and to my mind he is intolerable in his passages of ecstatic apostrophe. Here, amid the squalor of a disagreeable family life, he suddenly begins crying 'O this' and 'O that,' as if he were parodying the Greek Anthology as a last resort. The book is a great jumble of good and bad. It is laboured with adjectives and adverbs . . . It is emotional without feeling, crowded with violences and blasphemies, and to one reader appears incoherent, not from strength or intensity, but from over-excited verbosity. For these reasons, I am unable to praise *Look Homeward, Angel* as highly as some

[1] From the unsigned review in the July 24, 1930, issue of the London *Times Literary Supplement.*

[2] These words are quoted from Wolfe's letter of September to Henry Volkening. Frere's own letter has been lost.

have done. I do not see just what contribution it makes to justify such enthusiasm as has been shown, to the art of the novel."

Then, on August 17, the London *Observer* published another unfavorable review, by Gerald Gould. Gould begins by quoting the passage from Chapter XXII of *Look Homeward, Angel:* "'A voice, sleep-strange and loud, forever far-near spoke: Eugene! Spoke, ceased, continued without speaking, to speak. In him spoke. Where darkness, son, is light . . . ,'" and then goes on to ridicule it: "That is the way in which Mr. Thomas Wolfe writes at his most ecstatic! I can see no reason why anybody should abstain from writing like that if he wants to write like that: I can see no reason why anybody should read the result. A voice, sleep-strange indeed, and very loud, but forever fast-loose. Spoke, never ceased for six hundred pages, continued, without saying anything, to speak. . . . Where light ought to be, son, is darkness. I cannot form the remotest conception of what *Look Homeward, Angel* is about, though I have been humbly gnawing at it for weeks. There is an untidy American family which, for the six hundred pages already mentioned, manages to continue in a state of almost unbroken excitement about everything and nothing. To scream, to leap, to whine, to roar, is for these persons the work of an odd moment: and all their moments are extremely odd. Eugene is the hero, and is perhaps by a shade more violently silly than the others: we are taken through his childhood and adolescence, I know not why. . . ."

Wolfe had evidently got over the first shock of Swinnerton's review and was writing Frere a long and humorous retort to it when he by chance bought a copy of the *Observer* in Geneva and read the Gould review. This was the final straw. He was plunged immediately into a fit of desperate despondency. He managed to write to Frere with some restraint: then he composed a brief but melodramatic note to Perkins: "Will you please have Mr. Darrow send me, at his convenience, a statement of whatever money is due me? I shall not write any more books, and since I must begin to make other plans for the future, I should like to know how much money I will have. . . ." But it was to Wheelock, of whom he stood less in awe than of Perkins, that he poured out all his grief and bitterness at the reviews, with which his obsession about Mrs. Bernstein was inextricably mixed: "There is very little that I can say to you except that (1) I have stopped writing and do not want ever to write again. The place that I had found to stay—Montreux—did not remain private very long: (2) Fitzgerald told a woman in Paris where I was, and she cabled the news to America—I have had all kinds of letters and cables speaking of death and agony, from people who are perfectly well, and leading a comfortable and luxurious life among their friends at home. . . .

(3) "The English edition has been a catastrophe: some of the reviews . . . have said things that I shall never be able to forget—dirty, unfair, distorted, and full of mockery. . . . There is no life in this world worth living, there is no air worth breathing, there is nothing but agony and the drawing of the breath in nausea and labor, until I get the best of this tumult and sickness inside me. . . . What reward in the world can compensate the man who tries to create something? My book caused hate and rancor at home, venom and malice among literary tricksters in New York, and mockery and abuse over here. I hoped that that book, with all its imperfections, would mark a beginning: instead it has marked an ending. Life is not worth the pounding I have taken both from public and private sources these last two years. But if there is some other life . . . I am going to find it. I am not thirty yet, and if these things have not devoured me, I shall find a way out yet. . . . I have cut off all mail by wiring Paris, and I am going to stay alone for some time to come. I know that that is the only way."

He immediately packed his bags, rushed to the Geneva airport, and boarded the first plane out, which happened to be going to Lyons and Marseilles. He had never flown before, and he found it "magnificent— there's nothing like it to ease a distressed spirit." Almost immediately he began to feel more cheerful. "The beautiful little farms of the Rhone Valley appeared below me," he wrote later to Volkening. "I saw a little dot shovelling manure in a field and recognized a critic." For the next three weeks he flew here and there in France—from Lyons to Marseilles, to Arles and Provence, then finally back to Geneva. "The point of going into oblivion and exile as I have is, of course, not to brood or wonder what they're thinking or who will write and how often when one returns," he exhorted himself in his pocket diary. "The point is solely and simply to *get a piece of work done* at the rate of 1000 or 1500 words a day. If you do that—then brood, grieve, mourn, curse God, the world, everyone and everything all you please. *But get the work done.*"

But now, in spite of the flying start which he had made in "Antaeus," he found himself in a state of complete indecision as to what to write. "I have started three books and written twenty or thirty thousand words on each," he wrote in his pocket notebook. "I must finish one. Which?"

It is difficult to tell which three books he meant, because his notebook at this time is filled with lists of books or portions of books. Chief among these were *The Fast Express,* or a part of it which he called "K 19"; "Antaeus," or "The Immortal Earth," and other sections of his long book, *The October Fair.* There was also *The River People,* which he evidently still thought of as a separate book. There was *The Good Child's River,* which was to describe the early life of Mrs. Bernstein and which he sometimes thought of as a separate book, sometimes as a part of *The October Fair.* There was a book to be called *Hunger,* which was evidently based on the life of a fellow instructor of his at New York University: "A young man who lives life intensely discovers he has diabetes," he wrote in his summary of this. "Three years later he develops tuberculosis. Question: does he try to prolong his life in the hope of an almost impossible cure, or does he live freely and fully until death ends it?" And there were also many lists of titles, such as *Early Sorrow, Early Harvest, Delicate Death, Delicate Time, The Deep River, Call for the Robin,* which he may have intended for *Hunger* or *The Good Child's River,* or for both. Most of these books were basically parts of Wolfe's own long story, in spite of his attempt to divide them into separate units. Probably he was driven to do this by the realization that it was now September and that only seven months of his Guggenheim year were left in which to complete a publishable book. However, his own explanation for it is a different one: "I am all broken up in fragments myself at present and all that I can write is fragments. The man is his work: if the work is whole, the man must be whole."

Wolfe went back to Geneva to pick up his heavy baggage, which he had left there, and once more ran into his bête noire, Fitzgerald. By now he had half convinced himself not only that Fitzgerald had revealed his whereabouts to Mrs. Bernstein but that he had done it in a deliberate attempt to hurt his work. "I am sorry I ever met him," he wrote in his unmailed letter to Volkening. ". . . His conduct to me was mixed with malice and generosity; he read my book and was very fine about it: then his bitterness began to qualify him; he is sterile and impotent and alcoholic now, and unable to finish his book, and I think he wanted to injure my own work. This is base, . . . but I trusted him and I think he played a shabby trick by telling tales on me." He left Geneva immediately and headed straight for the Black Forest. "The inside of me was like a Black Forest," he wrote to Volkening, "and I think the name kept having its unconscious effect on me." But he was actually coming out of his depression, and the great batch of solicitous letters from Frere, Wheelock, and Perkins which were now forwarded to him by the Guaranty Trust did a great deal to make him feel more optimistic. His first attempt to answer his mail shows the half-reluctant, half-humorous frame of mind he now was in:

"Dear Mr. Perkins: I got your note in Geneva, Switzerland. Yours."

"Dear Jack: I got your letter the other day. It is a fine letter. I wish I could answer it. I am all right now and will write you later."

"Dear Mama: I died in Marseilles on Aug. 22. I am buried in a good Christian churchyard there, and I hope you will come to see me."

"To Mr. Ezra P'd. Dear Mr. P'd: I r'd a p'm of y'rs once. K.M.R.A.A. Y'rs Tr'ly."

To readers of *Ulysses* it will be evident that Wolfe was inviting Pound to "kiss my royal American arse." His sense of humor had come back, and he was mentally, if not physically, "out of the Black Forest."

"I know it's going to be all right now," he wrote in his unmailed letter from Freiburg to Volkening. "I believe I'm out of the woods at last. Nobody is going to die on account of me; nobody is going to suffer any more than I have suffered: the force of these dire threats gets a little weaker after a while, and I know now, no matter what anyone may ever say, that in one situation I have acted fairly and kept my head up. . . . I did all that was asked of me; I came away here when I did not want to come; I have fought it out alone; and now I am done with it. I do not think it will be possible for me to live in New York for a year or two, and when I come back I may go elsewhere to live. As for the incredible passion that possessed me when I was twenty-five years old and that brought me to madness and, I think, almost to destruction—that is over: that fire can never be kindled again."

But it was at this point that he broke off in the writing of his letter, never to finish it or to mail it. The truth was, he was none too sure that "that fire" could "never be kindled again" and his fear that he might succumb to it was at the bottom of his cruelest attempts to break free. "I sweated out great drops of agony," he wrote soon afterward in his pocket notebook. "At night in Europe I tossed upon a thousand distressful beds: I slept, yet through the night I heard the thousand sad and tortured sounds of time, . . . the ten million moments of my life were moving in my sleep in tortured restlessness and *all* the time I knew that she was living in the world." A few entries later he began exhorting himself again to "Silence! Silence! And Patience!" Then he scrawled down: "My life is bitter with your loveliness: you slay me and my senses burn." As he wrote later in *Of Time and the River*, there could be "no final freedom and release . . . that would not bear upon its brow forever the deep scar, upon its sinews the old mangling chains, of love."

After a few days in Strasbourg and Colmar, where he wrote the description of Grünewald's Isenheim altar which appears in *Of Time and the River*, Wolfe went to London and settled down to work in a service flat at 15 Ebury Street, which Frere had found for him. "I spent the winter of that year in England . . . ," he says in *The Story of a Novel*, "and here perhaps because of the homely familiarity of the English life, the sense of order and repose which such a life can give one, my work moved forward still another step from this flood-tide chaos of creation. For the first time the work began to take on the lineaments of design. These lineaments were still confused and broken, sometimes utterly lost, but now I really did get the sense at last that I was working on a great block of marble, shaping a figure which no one but its maker could as yet define, but which was emerging more and more into the sinewy lines of composition. . . .

"Yet I was terribly far away from the actual accomplishment of a book—how far away I could not at that time foresee. . . . But I was still sustained by the exuberant optimism of youth. My temperament, which is pessimistic about many things, has always been a curiously sanguine one concerning time, and although more than a year had now gone by and I had done no more than write great chants on death and sleep, prepare countless notes and trace here and there the first dim outlines of a formal pattern, I was confident that by the spring or the fall of the next year my book would somehow miraculously be ready.

"So far as I can describe with any accuracy, the progress of that winter's work in England was not along the lines of planned design, but along this line that I have mentioned—writing some of the sections which I knew would have to be in the book. Meanwhile what was really going on in my whole creative consciousness, during all this time, although I did not realize it at the moment, was this: What I was really doing, what I had been doing all the time since my discovery of America in Paris the summer before, was to explore day by day and month by month with a fanatical intensity, the whole material domain of my resources as a man and as a writer. . . .

"In a way, during that period of my life, I think I was like the Ancient Mariner who told the Wedding Guest that his frame was wrenched by woeful agony which forced him to begin his tale before it left him free. In my own experience, my wedding guests were the great ledgers in which I wrote, and the tale which I told to them would have seemed, I am afraid, completely incoherent . . . had any reader seen them. . . . It included everything from gigantic and staggering lists of the towns, cities, counties, states, and countries I had been in, to minutely thorough, desperately evocative descriptions of the under-carriage, the springs, wheels, flanges, axle rods, color, weight, and quality of the day coach of an American railway train. There were lists of the rooms and houses in which I had lived or in which I had slept for at least a night, together with the most accurate and evocative descriptions of those rooms that I could write—their size, their shape, the color and design of the wallpaper, the way a towel hung down, the way a chair creaked, a streak of water rust upon the ceiling. There were countless charts, catalogues, descriptions that I can only classify here under the general heading of Amount and Number. What were the total combined populations of all the countries in Europe and America? In how many of those countries had I had some personal and vital experience? In the course of my . . . thirty years of living, how many people had I seen? How many had I passed by on the streets? . . . With how many had I actually had some vital and illuminating experience, whether of joy, pain, anger, pity, love, or simple casual companionship, however brief?

"In addition, one might come upon other sections under some such cryptic heading as 'Where now?' Under such a heading as this, there would be brief notations of those thousands of things which all of us have seen for just a flash, a moment in our lives, which seem to be of no consequence whatever at the moment that we see them, and which live in our minds and hearts forever, which are somehow pregnant with all the joy and sorrow of the human destiny, and which we know, somehow, are therefore more important than many things of more apparent consequence. 'Where now?' Some quiet steps that came and passed along a leafy nighttime street in summer in a little town down South long years ago; a woman's voice, her sudden burst of low and tender laughter; then the voices and the footsteps going, silence, the leafy rustle of the trees. 'Where now?' Two trains that met and paused at a little station at some little town at some unknown moment upon the huge body of the continent; a girl who looked and smiled from

the window of the other train; . . . the winter boarders in a little
boardinghouse down South twenty years ago; Miss Florrie Mangle, the
trained nurse; Miss Jessie Rimmer, the cashier at Reed's drugstore;
Doctor Richards, the clairvoyant; the pretty girl who cracked the whip
and thrust her head into the lion's mouth with Johnny J. Jones Carnival
and Combined Shows.

"'Where now?' It went beyond the limits of man's actual memory.
It went back to the farthest adyt of his childhood before conscious
memory had begun, the way he thought he must have felt the sun
one day and heard Peagram's cow next door wrenching the coarse grass
against the fence, or heard the streetcar stop upon the hill above his
father's house at noon; and Earnest Peagram coming home to lunch,
his hearty voice in midday greeting; and then the streetcar going, the
sudden lonely green-gold silence of the streetcar's absence and an iron
gate slamming, then the light of that lost day fades out. 'Where now?'
He can recall no more and does not know if what he has recalled is fact
or fable or a fusion of the two.

"Where now—in these great ledger books, month after month, I
wrote such things as this, not only the concrete, material record of
man's ordered memory, but all the things he scarcely dares to think he
has remembered; all the flicks and darts and haunting lights that flash
across the mind of man that will return unbidden at an unexpected
moment: a voice once heard; a face that vanished; the way the sunlight
came and went; the rustling of a leaf upon a bough; a stone, a leaf, a
door."

Wolfe settled down to the strange kind of regime he kept when
he was working. "I stay in from 6 o'clock on," he wrote Alfred
Dashiell, the editor of *Scribner's Magazine*, "read, eat the meal [my
charwoman] has left for me, . . . brew vast quantities of tea and coffee,
and at midnight, . . . when all outside is quiet save for the massive
footfalls of the bobby, . . . I set to work, and work, with time off
for tea, coffee, or beer, until broad daybreak. Then I see life awaken
in a London street, which is one of the nicest things I have seen: I
see the light come on the yellow walls and smoky brick: the milk
wagon comes through with the milkman making a funny cry, and I hear
the sound of a horse in the empty street—a sound that makes me think
of a thousand mornings in American streets."

But, as always, a succession of things began to happen to distract
him from his work. First of all, the New York dentists, whose bill
of the previous May he had never paid, wrote threatening to sue him.

He again became terribly incensed, and he was even more upset by a letter from Mrs. Bernstein, who had sent him to the dentists in the first place, in which she begged him to pay their bill, saying she could not afford to do so for him. "There is *no question of that*," Wolfe wrote to Perkins, "there must be no question of it"; but he himself was determined not to pay them either. He even went so far as to write a letter instructing Scribners "to pay over to my friend, Maxwell Evarts Perkins, all money that is due to me, or will be due to me, from the publication of any work of mine; said money to be used, administered, and governed by Maxwell Evarts Perkins as he sees fit." However, after discussing the matter with the dentists, Scribners got a reduction of the bill and made a settlement of it for Wolfe.

In the meanwhile, something far more serious had happened—the complete financial collapse of the town of Asheville and the impoverishment of Wolfe's entire family. He had been so absorbed in the publication of *Look Homeward, Angel* in the fall of 1929 that the Wall Street crash had made little or no impression on him, but now the depression was brought home to him "with explosive suddenness." "One morning in November," he says in his Purdue speech, "I awoke to look out on dumb yellow fog, and to find that . . . ruin had come at last to my home town. That morning there was a small item in the *Daily Mail* announcing that the bank at home had failed; and knowing this meant ruin to many people that I knew, I cabled. Soon I had a letter, giving fuller details of . . . the town's collapse. . . . The bank had gone down carrying with it the government, the business, the commercial and industrial life of the whole town. As the details poured in, there was revealed a picture of catastrophe—a picture of the whole corrupted web, the huge honeycomb of speculation, . . . inflation and deceit which . . . had mounted, mounted for ten years through all the successive stages of public drunkenness and hysteria. And now the whole thing was in ruins—not only the life of the town, but the lives of all its people."

Wolfe immediately wrote to Perkins, begging him to send $500 from his royalty account to Fred Wolfe, to be used as Fred thought best to help the various members of the family. The bitterness which he had expressed against them in *Look Homeward, Angel* was totally forgotten now. "Mr. Perkins," he wrote, "I know it's a bad year for everyone, but *if I've got it there* at Scribners, or even if I haven't got it, for God's sake get that money for the boy, and I will work my fingers to the bone. . . . Please understand my people have not asked me for a damned penny, . . . but . . . if I am able to help these people now, it is a Godsend for me, and if I don't do it, I shall regret it bitterly as long as I live. I think you understand how much joy it gives me to think I may be of a little help now in time of trouble—we have always stood together in trouble before, and I don't want to fail them now." During the remainder of his life he gave occasional financial help to some of the members of his family. He did it out of real affection and solicitude, but it was also very gratifying for him to be able to afford to do so, with the earnings of what his mother persisted in calling his "light, easy kind of work." "I can't tell you how good I feel about it," he wrote with disarming frankness to Volkening. "I've got the goods now on all these Big-hearted Boys who do unto others—they're a set of las-civious self-seeking sensualists: it's really a gratification that we must be careful of."

All this time *Look Homeward, Angel* had been selling slowly but steadily in the United States, and it now was given further impetus by the most important single recommendation Wolfe had ever re-ceived. Sinclair Lewis had just been awarded the Nobel Prize for Literature, and in the resulting newspaper interviews he praised *Look Homeward, Angel* in the highest terms. "If Mr. Wolfe keeps up the standard which he has set in this work," he said in the interview pub-lished in the New York *Times* on November 6, "he may have a chance to be the greatest American writer. In fact, I don't see why he should not be one of the greatest world writers. His first book is so deep and spacious that it deals with the whole of life." Moreover, in his formal speech of acceptance of the prize, delivered before the Swedish Acad-emy on December 12, he again praised Wolfe, together with the other young American writers: "There are young Americans to-day who are doing such passionate and authentic work that it makes me sick to see that I am a little too old to be one of them. There is Ernest Hemingway, a bitter youth, educated by the most intense experience, disciplined by his own high standards, an authentic artist whose home is in the whole of life: there is Thomas Wolfe, a child of, I believe, thirty or younger, whose one and only novel, *Look Homeward, Angel,* is worthy to be compared with the best in our literary production, a Gargantuan creature with great gusto of life. . . . I salute them, with a joy in being not yet too far removed from their determination to give to the America that has mountains and endless prairies, enormous cities and lost far cabins, billions of money and tons of faith, to an America that is as strange as Russia and as complex as China, a litera-ture worthy of her vastness."

After reading the New York *Times* interview, Wolfe wrote Lewis to thank him, and soon received an answer saying that Lewis would be in London in January and hoped to see him there. However, it was not till February 5 that Wolfe wrote jubilantly in his diary: "Red Lewis— Georgian House—I've seen him!" The long description in *You Can't Go Home Again* of their alcoholic jaunt together seems based entirely on fact except for two small details: one, their destination was actually Frere's house near Folkestone and, two, Wolfe was drunker than Lewis, or, if not, he showed it more. He has been accused of base ingratitude to Lewis for writing this Lloyd McHarg material, but in actuality he always had the greatest gratitude and admiration for him and would rise to his defense in towering rage if anybody criticized him or his work. The real trouble is that these chapters are too nakedly auto-biographical, too garrulous, too full of the zeal to "tell all about it" regardless of the consequences which characterizes so much of Wolfe's work—in short, too much of a first draft without enough transmutation into fiction. As it stands, the real importance of the incident, and the thing which ties it into the main theme of *You Can't Go Home Again*, is stated hastily in only two short paragraphs: "George could see what had happened to McHarg. He himself had gone through the same experience many times. McHarg, it is true, was a great man, a man famous throughout the world, a man who had now attained the highest pinnacle of success to which a writer could aspire. But on just this account his disillusionment and disappointment must have been so much the greater and the more crushing.

"And what disillusionment, what disappointment, was this? It was a disappointment that all men know—the artist most of all. The disappointment of reaching for the flower and having it fade the moment your fingers touch it. It was the disappointment that comes from the artist's invincible and unlearning youth, from the spirit of indomitable hope and unwavering adventure, the spirit that is defeated and cast down ten thousand times but that is lost beyond redemption never, the spirit that, so far from learning wisdom from despair, acceptance from defeat, cynicism from disillusionment, seems to grow stronger at every rebuff, more passionate in its convictions the older it grows, more assured of its ultimate triumphant fulfillment the more successive and conclusive its defeats."

By now the Guggenheim year was drawing to a close. Wolfe was faced with the prospect of going back to the United States: he was still determined to break away from Mrs. Bernstein, and after an interview with her sister, who happened to be in London, he became more upset about the whole affair than he had ever been before. He had always been ashamed to do much more than hint about it to Perkins, but now, in a long letter written to him on January 19, 1931, he poured out the entire story, with all the distorted sense of persecution which had been steadily growing in him during his eight months abroad:

"Here, bluntly and directly, is the cause of my present trouble, which I think you may help me with: when I was twenty-four years old I met a woman who was almost forty[3] and I fell in love with her. I cannot tell you here the long and complicated story of my relations with this woman—they extended over a period of five years. . . . Twice I got away from New York and came abroad in an effort to end it, but when I came back I would resume my life with the woman again. . . . I came away, finally, over eight months ago. I did not want to come, but I yielded to what her friends wanted for her, and what it seemed to me would be best. I wrote her from the boat but since then I have not written her. The woman wrote and cabled me often during the first five months, and then, quite properly, stopped. I cannot tell you what distress and torment these letters and cables caused me—I would get letters signed in her blood, and cables which said she was going to die. Finally, about three months ago, I got a cable which said: 'No word from you. Life impossible. Desperate. Cannot go on living like this. Are you willing to accept the consequences?' For a few days, I thought I would go mad. But I did not write or cable. Each day I would go for mail in the most horrible state of nerves, wondering if I should see some cable which carried the dreadful news . . . I would buy . . . the *Herald* and be afraid each day that it would contain news of her death by leaping from a window. I began to read the horrible mortuary columns of the New York *Times*, looking first in that dense double column for one that began with B.

"But then, in the theatrical columns of that same paper, at just about the date when I feared this tragic act had happened, I read an account of a great success she had scored in the theatre; I met a man who . . . said he had seen her, looking very radiant and happy at a party in New York several weeks before; other people wrote me telling me how well, happy and prosperous she was looking; in Paris people would seek out café tables next to me, and the women, whom I did not know, would begin discussing the lady and me, hinting new interests for her very loudly so that I would not lose the benefit; and finally about a month

[3] She was actually forty-four in 1924.

ago (the middle of December) her cables began again. There had been two months' silence, during which she had scored a great success—perhaps that had worn off again: anyway, she had decided to begin dying again, and I had done it. She said she was 'desperate, hold out your hand to me in my hour of need. Impossible to face New Year. I stood by you in bad years, why have you deserted me? I love you and am faithful unto death, pain I bear too great to endure,' etc. etc. There were eight or ten of these messages: I felt the most enormous relief to know she was still alive and kicking; I cabled back; I asked her if it was fair to cable such messages when I was alone in a foreign land trying to write; I told her not to speak of hard years, that none was harder than this, that I had no money, that her dentists and my family were getting it, and that if I didn't get peace and quiet to work now, I was done for. . . .

"You may wonder why I come to you with this: my answer is that if I cannot come to you with it, there is no one in the world I can come to. I cannot tell you what horrible pain and suffering this thing has caused me. I would wake up in the morning with a feeling of nausea in my guts, and my horror and fear would grow all day long until I went to the bank for mail—later, I would sometimes have to vomit from physical sickness. . . . But I am all right in spite of this weakness: during the past three months . . . I have written over 100,000 words on my book—I have made myself work sometimes in the most ghastly state, but I have worked—and it has taken guts . . . I shall always like myself for what I did here, and I hope you like me, too, for I honor and respect you, and I believe you can help me to save myself. Also, I tell you this: I want to save not only myself, but by doing so, to save something else that is part of me, and without which no one can be saved—I mean my utter and absolute belief in love and in human excellence. No matter what breach of faith, truth, or honesty this woman may be guilty of, I want to come out of this thing with a feeling of love and belief in her. I remember full well countless acts of beauty, loveliness, and tenderness in this woman; there is the most enormous beauty and loveliness in her yet, and if she has learned craft, cunning, and treachery from these rats of the spirit, that is a matter for grief and pity rather than hate. But in this, the most passionate and devastating event of my life, I shall not be devoured at the end by hatred and bitterness and finally by cynicism and indifference.

"That is what the rats of the world would like to see—it fits into all the traditions of sinister Van Vechtenism, etc.: the young fellow who comes to New York, falls in love with a worldly and experienced woman, is made a fool of, and then either destroys himself or becomes one of the rats' club, eagerly awaiting the delightful entry of another visitor into the Spider's Parlor. But this is not going to happen to me. I think, during the early years of this affair, her friends were quite amused at the spectacle of a kid of twenty-four going around like a madman, eaten up with love and desperation, getting drunk and violent over a woman of forty. But I broke the rules of the game by doing a piece of work that had some little success. At this, their amusement turned to venom, they said I was making the woman unhappy, how badly I treated her, etc.—and now, it seems they are willing to do any dirty trick to destroy my work for the future. If my next book is no good, I assure you they will be immensely pleased: they will then say it is because I left her, etc. . . .

"But it is not a fair fight. These people talk of fairness, but they are rich, cunning, and powerful—they are a hundred against one, and I have no money or influence. I have given this woman six of the best years of my life—madness, passion, good, bad—she had it all. Now it is a rotten thing to try to ruin me when I must go on and use the little success I have gained. . . . If I go back to her now, I am done for— it means real death—but I shall never go back, and I think she knows it.

"There are two courses left: one is a deep and abiding love and friendship, and the kind of relation I would like with her. I think this is possible and I am going to try to achieve it. The other to which her friends may counsel her is poison—the desire to 'get back,' to 'show me,' to see that rotten and malicious stories reach my ears, to launch out on new loves, to wound me through base trickery, and to bring the thing before me all they can. . . . If this is done, it will be a filthy thing, but I will not be made filthy by it: I am alone now, if I am brave and decent and have faith, and work, all will be well. I *must* not die. But I need help—such help as a man may hope to get from a friend. I turn to you for it now. . . . I must not be smashed this way at thirty—for God's sake stand by me now, and I will be all right. . . . This is the first appeal of this sort I have ever made. I do not know what to do, where to turn, but I want to live in my own country, and I want to forget this horrible business entirely. Someday, when we are both, I hope, better and calmer, I trust I can see her again and be her friend. . . ."

At the end of February, Wolfe sailed for home on the *Europa*. "Need no help now," he cabled Perkins. "Can help myself most. Work six months alone." He drew the last of his Guggenheim letter of credit just before he sailed: his year of grace in which to write a second book was over, and all he had to show for it was a vast mass of raw material[4] —"nothing that could be called a novel." But in his own way—in writing down his great catalogue of memories—he had accomplished a great deal. "I consider this experience on the whole the most valuable and practical in my whole writing life thus far," he said in *The Story of a Novel*. "With all the waste and error and confusion it led me into, it brought me closer to a concrete definition of my resources, a true estimate of my talents at this period of my life, and, most of all, toward a rudimentary, a just-beginning, but a living apprehension of the articulation I am looking for, the language I have got to have if, as an artist, my life is to proceed and grow, than any other thing that has ever happened to me. I know the door is not yet open. I know the tongue, the speech, the language that I seek is not yet found, but I believe with all my heart that I have found the way, have made a channel, am started on my first beginning. And I believe with all my heart, also, that each man for himself and in his own way, each man who ever hopes to make a living thing out of the substances of his one life, must find that way, that language, and that door—must find it for himself as I have tried to do."

It was this strange way of working which gave Wolfe's books their rich evocative quality—the quality that is most his own and most enduring. But it was also this which consumed more time and strength and sheer creative power than any ordinary writer could expend. With his usual blind optimism, he hoped to have his book completed in six months: it actually was to take him four long years of agonized, exhausted, hopeless, stubborn work before even the first portion of it could be edited and published.

[4] Wolfe's estimates of how much he had written at any given time were always emotional rather than arithmetical. In his letter of January 19, 1931, to Perkins he said, "I have written over 100,000 words on my book"; in his letter of February 25 to Henry Allen Moe he said, "I am bringing back six enormous book-keeping ledgers with about 200,000 words of manuscript and a great many notes"; in *The Story of a Novel* he estimates the notes and the written sections of the book together as "three or four hundred thousand words of material."

XIII

T H E tragic light of evening falls upon the huge and rusty jungle of South Brooklyn," Wolfe says in *You Can't Go Home Again.* "It falls without glare or warmth upon the faces of all the men with dead eyes and flesh of tallow-grey as they lean upon their window sills at the sad, hushed end of day. If at such a time you walk down this narrow street, between the mean and shabby houses, past the eyes of all the men who lean there quietly at their open windows in their shirt-sleeves, and turn in at the alley here and . . . go to the very last shabby house down at the end, and climb up the flight of worn steps to the front entrance, and knock loudly at the door . . . (the bell is out of order), and . . . ask whether Mr. George Webber lives here, you will be informed that he most certainly does, and that if you will just come in and go down this stairway to the basement and knock at the door there on your right, you will probably find him in. So you go down the stairway to the damp and gloomy basement hall, thread your way between the dusty old boxes, derelict furniture, and other lumber stored there in the passage, rap on the door that has been indicated to you, and Mr. Webber himself will open it and usher you right into his room, his home, his castle.

"The place may seem to you more like a dungeon than a room that a man would voluntarily elect to live in. It is long and narrow . . . and the only natural light that enters it comes through two small windows rather high up in the wall, facing each other at the opposite ends, and these are heavily guarded with iron bars, placed there by some past owner of the house to keep the South Brooklyn thugs from breaking in. The room is furnished adequately but not so luxuriously as to deprive it of a certain functional and Spartan simplicity. In the back half there is an iron bed with sagging springs, a broken-down dresser with a cracked mirror above it, two kitchen chairs, and a steamer trunk and some old suitcases that have seen much use. At the front end, under the yellow glow of an electric light suspended from the ceiling by a cord, there is a large desk, very much scarred and battered, with the handles missing on most of the drawers, and in front of it there is a straight-backed chair made out of some old, dark wood. In the center, ranged against the walls, . . . stand an ancient gate-legged table, so much of its dark green paint flaked off that the dainty pink complexion of its forgotten youth shows through all over, a tier of bookshelves, unpainted, and two large crates or packing cases, their thick top boards pried off to reveal great stacks of ledgers and of white and yellow manuscript within. On top of the desk, on the table, on the bookshelves, and all over the floor are scattered, like fallen leaves in autumn woods, immense masses of loose paper with writing on every sheet, and everywhere are books, piled up on their sides or leaning crazily against each other.

"This dark cellar is George Webber's abode and working quarters. Here, in winter, the walls, which sink four feet below the level of the ground, sweat continuously with clammy drops of water. Here, in summer, it is he who does the sweating. . . .

"To this place, then, George Webber has come, and here 'holed in' with a kind of dogged stubbornness touched with desperation. And you will not be far wrong if you surmise that he has come here deliberately, driven by a resolution to seek out the most forlorn and isolated hiding spot that he could find."

Here, at 40 Verandah Place, Wolfe went on with "that enormous task of excavation, of exploration and discovery" which he had begun in London. "I was crystallizing for myself the whole material picture of . . . the world around me," he says in his Purdue speech. "The great job now was just to dig it up and get it down, get it down—somehow record it, transform it into the objective record of manuscript—even upon thousands and thousands of pages that would never be printed, that no reader would ever see, that would never be framed into the sequence of a narrative—but at any rate, now would be *there* at last upon the record—worth all the labor of the effort just so long as I could get it down, get it down." This was his main intention for two more solid years of work. The fact that most of *Of Time and the River*, *The October Fair*, *From Death to Morning*, and also large sections of *The Web and the Rock* and *You Can't Go Home Again* were among the things which he "got down" was only secondary to him. He simply poured out whatever happened to be uppermost in his mind, in separate chunks of first-person narrative, regardless of chronology or order, and with no connective material. As Perkins wrote to Thomas Beer in March 1935, "No book was ever written in such an extraordinary fashion. It started almost backwards, and it came in sections that seemed to have no relation to each other. And yet it all did have a kind of unity in the mind of the author, even at the beginning." Wolfe was too completely absorbed in his "enormous task of excavation" to think of arranging his material as a book. "Having had this thing within me," he says in *The Story of a Novel*, "it was in no way possible for me to reason it out of me, no matter how cogently my reason worked against it. The only way I could meet it was to meet it squarely, not with reason but with life. . . . The only way I could get it out of me was to live it out of me. And that is what I did."

Wolfe had gone to live in Brooklyn with the express purpose of avoiding Mrs. Bernstein and her friends, but a brief note in the papers had announced his return from Europe, and upon seeing it, she had immediately sought him out. This time, however, he clung to his determination to break away from her. By the first of April she realized that she could never really win him back, and she did what she had always threatened to do: she attempted suicide by taking an overdose of sleeping pills. She was rushed from her house in Armonk to the White Plains hospital and for three days hovered between life and death: then, as a result of the suicide attempt, she contracted pleurisy and pneumonia and remained critically ill for several weeks. Wolfe went to visit her in the hospital, and after she recovered, he continued to see her occasionally for about a year. However, he persisted in his determination to be wholly free of her, and at last the severance between them became complete. The telegram which he sent her on first hearing of her suicide attempt was a strange mixture of anxiety, evasion, defensive truculence, merciless egoism, and the distorted sense of persecution which he had felt in Europe:

"Returned Washington to-night, found your letter," he wired her on April 9. "Saw mother and sister Washington, mother coming here next week for few days, perhaps you talk to her. Will help you all I can. You must help me. Had nothing to do with name in paper when I came back: you should not blame me. Your letter fine. You must try to live up to it, truth and fact. You can not blame me now for not believing everything at sight: you must see I have taken some little doses from you and your friends. We must get this straight first. If you do what you say in letter, everything will be all right. Tired. I must get some rest to think things over. You must put hysteria and coercion aside: it does irreparable harm. Think we can get somewhere now. I send you my love which does not change."

Perhaps the strangest thing of all in his strange message was his suggestion that she meet his mother and talk the whole thing over with her. He surely knew that his mother was, and always had been,

bitterly opposed to his relationship with Mrs. Bernstein, and he also
surely knew that for the past six years Mrs. Bernstein had been kept
in a state of indignation against his mother by his stories of how she
and the entire family had misunderstood and mistreated him. When
the two women actually met, Mrs. Wolfe proceeded to "tell off" Mrs.
Bernstein with a virulence that was compounded of anti-Semitism,
moral narrow-mindedness, and deep maternal jealousy. They were inevitable enemies, and they remained so all their lives. And the fact
that Wolfe, in turning away from Mrs. Bernstein, attempted to hide
behind his mother's skirts shows how strong his filial attachment still
remained.

As Wolfe's relationship with Mrs. Bernstein waned, his intimacy
with Perkins had increased until the latter had become his father,
friend, confessor, arbiter, in everything—the "superior being" who,
more than any other person in Wolfe's life, represented his "image
of a strength and wisdom external to his need and superior to his
hunger, to which the belief and power of his own life could be united."
"During all these desperate years in Brooklyn, when George lived and
worked alone," says Wolfe in *You Can't Go Home Again*, "he had
only one real friend, and this was his editor, Foxhall Edwards. They
spent many hours together, wonderful hours of endless talk, so free
and full that it combed the universe and bound the two of them together in bonds of closest friendship. It was a friendship founded on
many common tastes and interests, on mutual liking and admiration
of each for what the other was, and on an attitude of respect which
allowed unhampered expression of opinion even on those rare subjects
which aroused differences of views and of belief. It was, therefore, the
kind of friendship that can exist only between two men. It had in it
no element of that possessiveness which always threatens a woman's
relations with a man . . .

"The older man was not merely friend but father to the younger.
Webber, the hot-blooded Southerner, with his large capacity for sentiment and affection, had lost his own father many years before and
now had found a substitute in Edwards. And Edwards, the reserved
New Englander, with his deep sense of family and inheritance, had
always wanted a son but had had five daughters, and as time went on
he made of George a kind of foster son. Thus each, without quite
knowing that he did it, performed an act of spiritual adoption.

"So it was to Foxhall Edwards that George now turned whenever
his loneliness became unbearable. When his inner turmoil, confusion,

and self-doubts overwhelmed him, as they often did, and his life went dead and stale and empty till it sometimes seemed that all the barren desolation of the Brooklyn streets had soaked into his very blood and marrow—then he would seek out Edwards. And he never went to him in vain. Edwards, busy though he always was, would drop whatever he was doing and would take George out to lunch or dinner, and in his quiet, casual, oblique, and understanding way would talk to him and draw him out until he found out what it was that troubled him. And always in the end, because of Edwards' faith in him, George would be healed and find himself miraculously restored to self-belief."

The literary guidance which Wolfe received from Perkins was of great importance, but he depended on him, too, for guidance in every detail of his life. Day after day he would arrive at Scribners around five o'clock, when Perkins was getting ready to go home, and for an hour, or three, four, five hours, if Perkins could give him that much time, he would pour out to him an account of all the events and plans and thoughts and emotions in which he had been involved since he had seen him last. If Perkins approved of these, Wolfe could lose his torturing self-doubt and act with some decisiveness: if Perkins disapproved, he would brood and argue and rationalize until he could obtain from him some sort of makeshift half-approval. "Max says" became a frequent prefix to his statements—even to statements which were strictly more his own than Perkins'—just as a child constantly employs "my mother says" or "my father says" as its self-justification.

Each day would involve Wolfe in some new difficulties, some new emotional crises, and each day Perkins would endeavor to untangle them with a physical and nervous endurance which could only come from true devotion and enjoyment. He undoubtedly treated Wolfe as a son: he had a fatherly anxiety for all of Scribners' employees and writers, but this was markedly intensified for Wolfe as for no one else except his own five daughters. However, his attitude toward him was by no means patronizing: he looked upon him as an equal and a friend, and even, because he felt that creative genius was the rarest thing on earth, as a superior. Perkins had begun his adult life with the ambition to become a writer, but by gradual stages of newspaper reporting for the New York *Times* and work with the advertising department at Scribners, his talent had been diverted into editing. Wolfe represented the thing he might have been, exaggerated to the nth degree, and he got a pathetically strong vicarious excitement out of Wolfe's flamboyant personality, which contrasted so markedly with his own shy, inhibited, self-abnegating Yankee character. He loved to hear Wolfe talk and would sit and listen to him, in almost complete silence, for hours at a time. "His talk was beyond any I ever heard when he was not in the torment of his work," he wrote in the *Carolina Magazine*. "He would tell you of the river Cam in Cambridge, England, and the mist over it so that you knew the magic Tennyson felt; or of the tulip fields in Holland; or of the paintings he liked in the galleries of Europe so that if you knew them you saw them again and afresh; or of that ruined monastery, Fountains Abbey near York, in its old forest—and you knew it as it was when it was all alive."[1]

As an editor, Perkins felt that the highest function of his life was the discovery, the guidance, the bringing to fruition of great talent. "This, in his view," says John Hall Wheelock in his introduction to *Editor to Author*, "was a sacred task worth any amount of effort, of risk, of time expended." Wheelock goes on to tell how, when a certain eminent critic suggested to Perkins that Wolfe's work was not worth the amount of labor he was expending on it, Perkins retorted in a sudden flare of anger: "Well, then you just don't care about talent!" Perkins *did* "care about talent," and he cared about Wolfe's talent more than any other. Wolfe had been discovered by him in a completely unknown, unpublishable state: he depended on Perkins more completely than any other Scribner author; he had more markedly, in both his faults and virtues, the temperament of a "real writer": he had more raw, rich, unmined, constantly unfolding talent: and he cost an incalculable amount more of "effort, of risk, of time expended." And so, being the kind of man he was, Perkins felt a closer bond with Wolfe than with any other writer. "The plain truth is," he wrote to him in 1935, "that working on your writings, however it has turned out, for good or bad, has been the greatest pleasure, for all its pain, and the most interesting episode of my editorial life." And again, in 1936: "Your work has been the foremost interest in my life."

Wolfe had settled down to the routine of work which was to constitute his life for the four grim Brooklyn years. He would sleep late, usually waking only when his typist came to work, then leaping up guiltily to assure him or her (at first his typist was Abe Smith) that he'd "be with you in a minute." Then would follow his agonized effort to "get going," during which he would gulp down cup after cup of poisonously strong black coffee, smoke innumerable cigarettes, pace up and down, and pour out his endless flow of conversation. But the presence of the typist waiting there would finally impel him to begin

[1] From "Scribner's and Tom Wolfe," in the October 1938 issue of the *Carolina Magazine*.

to work, and once he had begun, he would write and write with the most intense, excited concentration, sprawling down the words on sheet after sheet of yellow paper so hastily and hugely that the pages often contained only about twenty words apiece. As each sheet was filled he would shove it to one side upon his table or drop it on the floor, from where the typist would retrieve it and endeavor to decipher it. In his haste he seldom took the time to form the separate letters of a word, but scrawled down the first letter and other salient letters and simply drew a straight line or a few random scribbles for the more ordinary letters in between. A typist had to have both practice and a vivid imagination to read what he had written, and most of them worked for him for only a short time. He was constantly distracted by this difficulty: "I can always find plenty of women to sleep with," he once blurted out, "but the kind of woman that is really hard for me to find is a typist who can read my writing."

Although he had difficulty in getting started on his daily stint of writing, he had even more difficulty in stopping once he had begun. Hour after hour he would fill up the yellow sheets of copy paper, seldom stopping to eat lunch, although he occasionally took time out for more black coffee. By late afternoon, when the typist was supposed to leave for home, he was always at the height of his creative power. Finally, with great reluctance, he would stop and let her go, and then, in the keyed-up, otherworldly frame of mind which is chronic with creative writers, he would stride like a wild, disheveled giant through the streets of Brooklyn. If he took the subway and went to Scribners, he would stay and talk with Perkins until the entire building was empty of employees: they would go out for cocktails and more talk. During the first part of Wolfe's relationship with Perkins, when they were working together on *Look Homeward, Angel,* they did not drink together: instead, Perkins would take Wolfe out to dinner and go with him on his habitual long walks, heroically keeping up with Wolfe's tremendous strides and inexhaustible supply of energy. In fact, the night in the summer of 1929 when they walked all the way around Central Park was, as Perkins said later, "the first time I ever had a drink with Tom, and it was on his suggestion. For I very seldom took a drink in those days, and never wanted to, only did it for the sake of convention. But we never drank to any quantity."[2] However, these long walks took up too much time and strength to be practicable at the end of the afternoon, so gradually the two men began going somewhere for a drink

[2] From Perkins' letter of October 29, 1945, to John S. Terry.

together. When Prohibition was repealed, they fell into the almost daily habit of having cocktails at the Chatham bar, sometimes with lamentable results. Perkins could drink four or five martinis with no visible result except a diminishment of his Vermont laconism, but Wolfe, with his empty stomach and wrought-up nerves, would be noticeably affected. He would talk more wildly than ever and would be subject to sudden fits of truculent suspicion, and the hours would fly past in excitement and confusion as they could only do with him. Finally Perkins would either catch a train home to New Canaan, Connecticut, or would stay in town and take Wolfe out to dinner. But no matter what time he left Perkins, or even if he did not see him, but stayed alone in Brooklyn, Wolfe never could relax enough to go to bed till dawn.

"At the end of the day of savage labor," he said in *The Story of a Novel*, "my mind was still blazing with its effort, could by no opiate of reading, poetry, music, alcohol, or any other pleasure, be put at rest. I was unable to sleep, unable to subdue the tumult of these creative energies, and as a result of this condition, for three years I prowled the streets, explored the swarming web of the million-footed city and came to know it as I had never done before." With his tremendous strides he would "eat up the pavements of New York" for miles on end, sometimes ending up far out in the Bronx, or down along the water front, or at the great wholesale markets, where he loved to watch the fresh vegetables and other produce coming in at dawn. Sometimes he would walk across the Brooklyn Bridge and roam around the toughest sections over there. It was a wonder that he never got held up or sandbagged: evidently his tremendous size and wild appearance intimidated even the Brooklyn thugs. Sometimes he would stop in at a bar and drink, or roam from bar to bar, or spend hours in a phone booth calling up his friends and accusing them, for minor and often ridiculous reasons, of having "betrayed" him. The next day he would be overcome with genuine remorse, would again phone his exhausted friends whose night's sleep he had so rudely interrupted, and would overwhelm them with stammered and abject apologies. Or, if he could not reach them on the phone, he would write them letters asking their forgiveness. His files were full of letters of this sort, many of which were agonizedly written and rewritten in many drafts, but which invariably ended with the protestation that "I am your friend and want you to be mine." However, even his wildest and most drunken condemnations usually had some grain of truth in them—some canny indictment of a basic flaw in a friend's character—and the truth would often stick and rankle, in spite of Wolfe's abject attempts to make amends. It was all a part of his "search for a superior being." He was always delving into his friends' characters in hopes of finding the perfection he was seeking, and when he found a flaw instead, however minor, he was totally unable to keep his disappointment to himself.

"The spring passed into the summer, the summer into autumn," Wolfe wrote in *The Story of a Novel*. "I was working hard, day after day, and still nothing that had the unity and design of a single work appeared. . . . I had still believed at the time of my return from Europe that I was writing a single book, which would be comprised within the limits of about 200,000 words. Now as scene followed scene, as character after character came into being, as my understanding of my material became more comprehensive, I discovered that it would be impossible to write the book I had planned within the limits I had thought would be sufficient.

"All of this time I was being baffled by a certain time element in the book, by a time relation which could not be escaped, and for which I was now desperately seeking some structural channel. There were three time elements inherent in the material. The first and most obvious was an element of actual present time, an element which carried the narrative forward, which represented characters and events as living in the present and moving forward into an immediate future. The second time element was of past time, one which represented these same characters as acting and being acted upon by all the accumulated impact of man's experience so that each moment of their lives was conditioned not only by what they experienced in that moment, but by all that they had experienced up to that moment. In addition to these two time elements, there was a third, which I conceived as being time immutable, the time of rivers, mountains, oceans, and the earth; a kind of eternal and unchanging universe of time against which would be projected the transience of man's life, the bitter briefness of his day. It was the tremendous problem of these three time elements that almost defeated me and that cost me countless hours of anguish in the years that were to follow.

"As I began to realize the true nature of the task I had set for myself, the image of the river began to haunt my mind. I actually felt that I had a great river thrusting for release inside of me and that I had to find a channel into which its flood-like power could pour. I knew I had to find it or I would be destroyed in the flood of my own creation, and I am sure that every artist who ever lived has had the same experience.

"Meanwhile, I was being baffled by a fixed and impossible idea whose error at the time I did not fully apprehend. I was convinced at that time that this whole gigantic plan had to be realized within the limits of a single book which would be called 'The October Fair.' It was not until more than a year had passed, when I realized finally that what I had to deal with was material which covered almost 150 years in history, demanded the action of more than 2000 characters, and would in its final design include almost every racial type and social class of American life, that I realized that even the pages of a book of 200,000 words were wholly inadequate for the purpose.

"How did I finally arrive at this conclusion? I think it is not too much to say that I simply wrote myself into it. During all that year, I was writing furiously, feeling now the full pressure of inexorable time, the need to finish something. I wrote like mad; I finished scene after scene, chapter after chapter. The characters began to come to life, to grow and multiply until they were numbered by the hundreds, but so huge was the extent of my design, as I now desperately realized, that I can liken these chapters only to a row of lights which one sometimes sees at night from the windows of a speeding train, strung out across the dark and lonely countryside.

"I would work furiously day after day until my creative energies were utterly exhausted, and although at the end of such a period I would have written perhaps as much as 200,000 words, enough in itself to make a very long book, I would realize with a feeling of horrible despair that what I had completed was only one small section of a single book."

Probably one reason for Wolfe's sense of bafflement was that during this summer and early autumn he had got sidetracked into writing "Death the Proud Brother," a sort of poetic narrative concerning the four deaths which he had witnessed on the streets of New York, which was finally published as a separate story in *From Death to Morning*. He also did some work on *The Good Child's River*: his pocket notebooks from March until November 1931 are full of notes and outlines for this book: he even did research for it at the Public Library, reading newspapers, theatrical notices, and illustrated magazines of the late 1800s and early 1900s, and looking up the addresses of Mrs. Bernstein's family in old directories as far back as the year she was born. Both "Death the Proud Brother" and *The Good Child's River* were fine material, but they were both digressions, and for months on end they diverted his time and strength from the writing of his main narrative.

By August, Wolfe was worn out by his labors and by the New York City heat, and he went to Orrs Island, Maine, for a brief and rather dreary vacation. "I'm taking my meals at a boarding-house," he wrote to Alfred Dashiell, "and the crowd of boarders is the same as it always was—they sit on the porch and rock—they never change." On his return to Brooklyn he received a letter from Perkins which said, with surprising optimism: "I think you ought to make every conceivable effort to have your manuscript completely finished by the end of September. . . . I hope you will come in soon and tell me what you think you can do." To this Wolfe replied: "I know you are not joking and that you mean *this* September, and not September four, five, or fifteen years from now. Well, there is no remote or possible chance that I will have a completed manuscript of anything that resembles a book this September, and whether I have anything that I would be willing to show anyone next September, or any succeeding one for the next 150 years, is at present a matter of the extremest and most painful doubt to me." Then, with the earnestness of desperation, he went on:

"I want you to know, Max, that the only thing I . . . care for now is whether I have lost the faith I once had in myself, whether I have lost the power I once felt in me, whether I have anything at all left—who once had no doubt that I had a treasury—that would justify me in going on. Do you think anything else matters to me? . . . No one can take anything from me now that I value, they can have their cheap, nauseous, seven-day notoriety back to give to other fools, but I am perfectly content to return to the obscurity in which I passed almost thirty years of my life without great difficulty. If anyone wants to know when I will have a new book out, I can answer without apology 'when I have finished writing one and found some one who wants to publish it.' . . .

"And please, Max, if you can tactfully and gently, without wounding anyone, suggest to whoever is responsible for these newspaper squibs about my having written 500,000 words, and more all the time, that he please for God's sake cut it out, I will be grateful. . . . I resent any effort to present me as a cheap and sensational person. In spite of my size, appetite, appearance, staying up all night, 500,000 words, etc., I am not a cheap and sensational person: if there is going to be publicity, why can't it tell the truth—that I work hard and live decently and quietly; that no one in the world had a higher or more serious feeling about writing; . . . that I do not know whether I will ever do the writing I want to do, or not, or whether I will be able to go on at all, . . . but that I work, ask nothing from anyone, and hope, for my own sake, that I have some talent and power in me. I say, I am not afraid of publicity like this, because it would be the truth, and it could not injure me save with fools. . . .

"Max, I have tried to tell you how I feel about all this, and now I want to sum it up in this way: Two years ago I was full of hope and confidence: I had complete within me the plans and ideas of at least a half dozen long books. To-day I still have all this material, but I have not the same hope and confidence: I have, on the contrary, a feeling of strong self-doubt and mistrust . . . Why this has happened I do not know. I think one reason is that I cannot work in a glare; I was disturbed and lost self-confidence because of the notice I had; I think my success may have hurt me. Also, I had a personal trouble of which I told you something. . . . I don't think I am unable to cope with the trial of life, but I think I may meet it clumsily and slowly, inexpertly, sweat blood and lose time. . . .

"I want to tell you finally that I am not in *despair* over the book I have worked on—I am in *doubt* about it—and I am not sure about anything: I think I will finish it, I think it may be valuable and fine— or it may be worthless. . . . I know that you want to see what I have done—to see if I had it in me to do more work after the first book, or whether everything burnt out in that one candle. Well, that is what I want to see, too, and my state of doubt and uneasiness is probably at least as great as your own. It seems to me that that is the best way to leave it now: . . . if I ever write anything else that I think worth printing, . . . I will bring it to you, and you can read it, accept it or reject it with the same freedom as with the first book. I ask for no more from anyone. The life that I desire, and that I am going to try to win for myself, is going to exist in complete indifference and independence to such of the literary life as I have seen . . . No one will match me as you match a cock or a prizefighter, no one will goad me to show smartness or brilliance against another's—the only standard I will compete against now is in me: if I can't reach it, I'll quit.

"It is words, words—I weary of the staleness of the words, the seas of print, the idiot repetition of trivial enthusiasms. I am weary of my own words but I have spoken the truth here. . . . I am tired with what I've seen . . . But did it mean nothing to you when I told you the beauty, exulting, joy, richness, and undying power that I had found in America, that I knew . . . to be the *real* truth, not the illusion, the thing we had never found the pattern for, the style for, the true words to express—or was it only words to you; did you just think I was trying to be Whitman again? I know what I know, it crushes the lies and staleness like a rotten shell, but . . . staleness and dullness has got into me— I look at it with grey dullness and will not say it—it's not enough to see it: you've got to feel the thick snake-wriggle in each sentence, the heavy living tug of the fish at the line.

"I'm out of the game—and it is a game—a racket: what I do now must be for myself. I don't care who 'gets ahead' of me— . . . I only care if I have disappointed you, but it's very much my own funeral, too. I don't ask you to 'give me a chance,' because I think you've given me one, but I don't want you to think this is a despairing letter, and that I've given up—I just say I don't know, I'm going to see: maybe it will come out right someday."

As Wolfe said later in *The Story of a Novel,* he had "reached that state of naked need and utter isolation which every artist has got to meet and conquer if he is to survive at all. Before this I had been sustained by that delightful illusion of success which we all have when we dream about the books we are going to write instead of actually doing them. Now I was face to face with it, and suddenly I realized that I had committed my life and my integrity so irrevocably to this struggle that I must conquer now or be destroyed. I was alone with my own work, and now I knew that I had to be alone with it, that no one could help me with it now no matter how anyone might wish to help. For the first time I realized another naked fact which every artist must know, and that is that in a man's work there are contained not only the seeds of life, but the seeds of death, and that that power of creation which sustains us will also destroy us like a leprosy if we let it rot stillborn in our vitals. I had to get it out of me somehow. I saw that now. And now for the first time a terrible doubt began to creep into my mind that I might not live long enough to get it out of me, that I had created a labor so large and so impossible that the energy of a dozen lifetimes would not suffice for its accomplishment."

It was at this crucial point in Wolfe's career that Perkins began the arduous vigil over him which he was to maintain for four and a half years, until the publication of *Of Time and the River*. "During this time," he wrote later in *The Story of a Novel,* ". . . I was sustained by one piece of inestimable good fortune. I had for a friend a man of immense and patient wisdom and a gentle but unyielding fortitude. I think that if I was not destroyed at this time by the sense of hopelessness which these gigantic labors had awakened in me, it was largely because of the courage and patience of this man. I did not give in because he would not let me give in, and I think it is also true that at this particular time he had the advantage of being in the position of a skilled observer at a battle. I was myself engaged in that battle, covered by its dust and sweat and exhausted by its struggle, and I understood far less clearly than my friend the nature and progress of the struggle in which I was engaged. At this time there was little that this man could do except observe, and in one way or another keep me at my task, and in many quiet and marvelous ways he succeeded in doing this. I was now at the place where I must produce, and even the greatest editor can do little for a writer until he has brought from the secret darkness of his own spirit into the common light of day the completed concrete accomplishment of his imagining. My friend, the editor, has likened his own function at this painful time to that of a man who is trying to hang on to the fin of a plunging whale, but hang on he did, and it is to his tenacity that I owe my final release."

Perhaps Wolfe would eventually have pulled himself out of his confusion and despondency unaided, made a whole fresh start, and finally emerged with a book as successful as *Look Homeward, Angel:* or perhaps he would simply have gone on writing his huge, formless catalogue of memories without ever producing anything that could be published. No one can say now, but at that time, he virtually forced Perkins' role upon him, both by his desperation and by his utter dependence on him for all things. Perkins knew, better than almost anyone, that it was dangerous to play Pygmalion to creative writers—that the more one did for them, the more they resented such interference later. But in this emergency he did not stop to think about himself or about the future: he only thought "this book *has* to be done,"[3] and when Wolfe asked for his help, was "glad and proud to give it,"[4] and in fuller measure than any other editor would have done.

[3] From "Scribner's and Tom Wolfe."
[4] From Perkins' letter to Wolfe of January 13, 1937.

XIV

WOLFE had formed the habit of recording his birthday every year in his little pocket diary and of writing a few sentences to sum up the progress of his life that far. Now, when October came around again, his entry was a very humble one: "October 2, 1931. 11:15 P.M. In forty-five minutes I will be 31 years old. I have made comments before. I know now there is no sense in pretentiousness. I have done very little—finished and published one book—know not where I am in the other. Three days ago K. Raisbeck either killed himself or died or was murdered. That ends one of the clinging threads."

On September 29 Kenneth Raisbeck had been found dead in the cemetery at Westport, Connecticut. He had bruises on his throat and a bloodstain on his shirt. The grass around him bore evidence of a struggle, and a trail of coins upon it seemed to have fallen from his pocket as he was dragged to where his body lay. He was thought to have been murdered, and the tabloid newspapers immediately published sensational accounts of the whole affair. However, after an autopsy, it was announced that he had died of an acute attack of meningitis and that the seeming evidence of violence had been caused by himself in his mortal spasm. Wolfe was deeply shocked by the whole thing and spent several days in talking with or writing to close friends of Raisbeck's. "He was a very brilliant young fellow who had many friends ready to help him," he wrote later to his brother Fred. "Everyone believed he had a great future; but he did nothing with it. . . . I have felt very depressed about it: I forget about the falling out we had and I remember the time we were both young fellows at Harvard full of hope, and what good friends we were. It seems a terrible thing that his life should end as it did."

"October came," Wolfe says in *The Story of a Novel*, "and with it a second full year since the publication of my first book. And now, for the first time, I was irrevocably committed so far as the publication of my book was concerned. I began to feel the sensation of pressure, and of naked desperation, which was to become almost maddeningly intolerable in the next three years." Up to this time Perkins had seen little of what Wolfe had been writing, but they now agreed that he should read each section of manuscript as it was finished. With this immediate goal to aim at, Wolfe made a whole new start: on November 1 he moved from Verandah Place to a larger, sunnier apartment at 111 Columbia Heights and began intensive work on the Bascom Hawke (later called Bascom Pentland) material for *Of Time and the River*. However, it ran to over thirty thousand words in length, and he did not finish it till January. Meanwhile he had been drawing constantly against his Scribner royalty account until there was now not enough left to last the month out. Aided by Sinclair Lewis' recommendation, *Look Homeward, Angel* had been sold by Mrs. Boyd to Bonnier in Sweden and Rowohlt in Germany and was also about to be brought out in a cheap five-shilling edition by Heinemann, but the money derived from these sales was not enough to keep Wolfe going. He was in desperate financial straits, and he was therefore overjoyed when Perkins not only praised the Bascom Hawke material as a section of the novel but also arranged for it to be bought by *Scribner's Magazine* for five hundred dollars.[1]

Wolfe now was seeing Perkins constantly, and being constantly sustained by him. "He has accomplished a great volume of work," Perkins wrote to Hemingway on January 14, 1932, "and what I have seen of it, not much, is as good as it could be. He keeps getting all upset, and he is so now, and I am to have an evening with him and try to make him think he is some good again. He is good all right." They spent another of their evenings together on January 26, and at the conclusion of it Wolfe walked with Perkins to Grand Central Station and, still talking, followed him on board the train he was taking for New Canaan. Perkins urged him to come along and spend the night at his house, and Wolfe at first agreed, but as the train started pulling out, he had a sudden change of heart and decided that he must go home to Brooklyn and write some more instead. He rushed down the aisle and jumped off the train, but it was by that time moving with considerable speed, and he was thrown violently to the concrete platform. The conductor pulled the emergency signal and brought the train to a sudden halt: then he and Perkins rushed to see if Wolfe was injured. His left elbow was bleeding copiously from a severed vein and also looked as if it had been fractured. Accompanied by the anxious Perkins, he was taken to

[1] Besides being head editor in the book department, Perkins had, at this time, the final say as to what should or should not be published in *Scribner's Magazine*.

the emergency hospital in Grand Central, where he received first aid and later had his arm X-rayed, and was persuaded to sign a statement absolving the New York, New Haven & Hartford Railroad from any responsibility for the accident. The X ray seemed to show a fracture, but two days later Wolfe's own physician had more X rays taken and found that there was no break. However, the laceration of Wolfe's elbow was so bad that it had to be kept dressed and bandaged for two weeks.[2] It was because of this injury that he began dictating letters to his typist instead of writing them out longhand as he had always done before. He did not dare to try it with his book—not at this time—but the gradual practice that he acquired finally led to his dictation of most of *The Web and the Rock* and *You Can't Go Home Again* five years later.

It was now over three years since Wolfe's last visit to Asheville, but in spite of his family's constant urgings, he persisted in his refusal to go home. "I am not afraid of any man living, nor do I apologize for my life to anyone," he had written to his brother Fred, "but I will not walk knowingly and willingly into any place where the population has threatened to attack me, unless there was something there I had to do, something to be gained by going. That is not the case: if I ever come home I want to be treated with the consideration and respect of any ordinary citizen—I don't care either for bouquets or lynching bees." Therefore, early in January, his mother had come again to visit him in Brooklyn. He went sight-seeing with the energetic old lady, but for the most part they did "nothing but talking," as he wrote to his sister Mabel. Wolfe was garrulous, but his mother could talk him to a standstill any day, and as he sat listening to her endless flood of reminiscences, an idea for a new story took shape in his mind. It was, as he explained later to his mother, a "story told completely in the words of one person, a woman, who starts out to tell her son about a single incident and in the course of telling it brings in memories, stories, and recollections that cover a period of seventy years. In the telling, the story weaves back and forth like a web and for that reason I have called it 'The Web of Earth.'"

At this time *Scribner's Magazine* was conducting a Best Short Novel Contest, which offered a $5000 prize. The contest closed on February 1, but with his strange optimism as to time, Wolfe plunged into the writing of his mother's story in hopes of finishing it before that date. But, as always, it took him much longer than he had anticipated. He was

[2] The author is indebted for this information to Dr. Arthur C. Jacobson of Brooklyn, who was Wolfe's physician at the time.

impeded by his injured arm and made "woozy" by one of his severe feverish colds, and he was interrupted by a second visit from his mother, who had gone to see her brother Henry Westall in Boston and stopped off again in Brooklyn before going back to Asheville. Furthermore, as "the web" wove back and forth, it grew and grew until the story ran close to 40,000 words. Wolfe did not finish it till March, a full month after the contest deadline. On January 28 Perkins had entered "A Portrait of Bascom Hawke" in the contest in its place, but everyone at Scribners felt great regret that "The Web of Earth" could not qualify. Technically, it was the most perfect thing that Wolfe ever wrote. As Perkins said later, it "had perfect form for all its intricacy. I remember saying to him, 'Not one word of this should be changed.'"[3]

"A Portrait of Bascom Hawke" was published in the April 1932 issue of *Scribner's Magazine* and immediately evoked outraged protests from the entire family of Wolfe's uncle Henry Westall. One of the Westall daughters, Hilda Bottomley, wrote to Mrs. Wolfe protesting that it ridiculed and misrepresented her father; the other daughter, Elaine Gould, wrote directly to Wolfe and took him to task for ridiculing and misrepresenting her mother; and Mr. Westall himself later wrote (but fortunately never mailed) a letter to Scribners in which he stated that he had "a clear case of libel against both the author and the publisher."[4] In a long answer to his cousin Elaine, Wolfe once more tried to justify the way he wrote: "That, after all, is a matter of personal vision, and in that respect the writer must be true to his own—he can do nothing else but be true to his own, whether it coincides with that of his friends or not. . . . If I was unfair to your mother . . . , as you say I was, it came not because I was meditating her portrait, but because I was not meditating her portrait. And neither, let me say, was I meditating the portrait of your father, because that is not the way the writer works— at least that is not the way I work. . . . In the end, a man's only explanation should be his work itself; and that explanation should cover the whole course of his life and appear in everything he does, and he should rest confident and certain in the conviction; and if his work is good or has any truth or living value in it, he has done thereby no real or lasting injury to any person, alive or dead; and this is a part of my faith and in this I shall try to live."

[3] From "Thomas Wolfe," in the Autumn 1947 issue of the *Harvard Library Bulletin*.

[4] The author is indebted to Hilda Westall Bottomley for making available a letter written by her father in which he describes his unmailed letter to Scribners.

By this time Wolfe and Perkins had decided that he could not possibly include all of his material in one single book. Accordingly, Wolfe went back to a variation of *The Fast Express* which he had started in 1929 and which he had later planned to use as the first section of *The October Fair*. This was by now as long as an entire book and bore the title *K 19*, after the number of the Asheville Pullman car on the fast express from New York to North Carolina. It told the story of Eugene's return to Altamont for a brief visit in the late 1920s and included most of the train scenes which were later used in *Of Time and the River* and *You Can't Go Home Again*: also a section called "The Passengers," which told the stories of the lives of Eugene's fellow travelers in car *K 19*. Its climax was the chapter "Boom Town," in which Eugene witnesses the real-estate boom which is sweeping his home town, and then returns to "the train, the city, and the unknown future" of the North.[5]

A great deal of this material was already written, and both Wolfe and Perkins felt confident that he could finish the whole thing in three months' time. Scribners accordingly sent out publicity releases saying that "Thomas Wolfe's novel, *K 19*, will be published this fall," and Wolfe went to work with a great new spurt of energy and optimism. "I have been working harder . . . and faster than I ever did before," he wrote to A. S. Frere on April 15. " 'The October Fair' will not be one novel, but a series of novels, and each, I hope, complete in itself but all related to a single thing. The section I am working on at present, and which I hope to have down on paper within three months, and which Scribners wants to publish in the autumn, is called 'K 19,' which is the name of a Pullman car on an American train. I cannot tell you very much more about it now save that it will be a very long book and it will have the lives and stories of a great many people in it, and I hope it will be full of interest and movement. I am writing at the rate of three, four, and occasionally five thousand words a day, which is more work than I have ever done before. . . . I get terribly tired, but I am also very happy to be getting something done at last, and I think everything is going to be all right now. I did a terrific amount of preparation and preliminary work on that book, and I am sure my time and labor was not wasted but what I was really doing apparently was getting the cement mixed for the building. . . . It has been a hell of a job. I

[5] This description of the contents of *K 19* is based on the author's recollection of the portions she read of it in 1934 and 1935; also on Richard S. Kennedy's study of the remaining fragments of the manuscript, which are now in the William B. Wisdom Collection at Harvard.

think I was deluded by some fantastic notion that I could say the final and ultimate word about everyone and everything all at once in a single huge and monstrous tome. I learned bitterly that it could not be done and I will have to write my books as other men have written theirs, one at a time."

Wolfe worked on the completion of K 19 from April till July 1932, but unfortunately he spent most of this time on one of the long digressions which always were his pitfalls. This was the life of Robert Weaver, which was entitled "The Man on the Wheel": it was intended to be the first part of the section called "The Passengers," but it ran away with Wolfe until it reached a total of approximately 80,000 words, or the length of an average novel. It was written very hastily and superficially and had none of the depth, the richness, or the compulsive personal emotion which usually characterized Wolfe's work. The better parts of it were later salvaged for *Of Time and the River*, but as a whole it simply was no good, and by its inferior quality and disproportionate length, it was the ruination of K 19. But even if "The Man on the Wheel" could have been greatly or entirely omitted, K 19 would not have been a successful book. Basically it was only a minor episode— a train trip and a brief visit at home—in the life of Eugene·Gant, and although Wolfe accidentally used over 200,000 words to describe it, the fact remained that it did not add up to enough to make a first-rate novel.

At the end of June, Perkins read the manuscript of K 19 and broke the news to Wolfe that he did not think it good enough to publish as a separate novel. It was, of course, a bitter blow, but Wolfe agreed with Perkins that his second book must be, if possible, as good or better than *Look Homeward, Angel*. For a week he did not work at all but, as he wrote to Robert Raynolds, did "nothing but loaf, sleep, and go to ball games and listen to the Democratic Convention." However, by July 12 he was back at work again and writing somewhat truculently to Henry Allen Moe: "I am going ahead daily with my book, or one section of it, which, no matter what publishers' announcements and statements say, will be published when I am done writing it and when I think it is fit to be published. That is all I can tell you at present because that is all I know myself."

Fortunately, just at this time, Wolfe learned that "A Portrait of Bascom Hawke" had tied for first place in the *Scribner's Magazine* contest. The three judges, Burton Rascoe, William Soskin, and Edmund Wilson, had voted a draw between "Bascom Hawke" and John Herrmann's novelette, "The Big Short Trip," and it was therefore decided that the

$5000 prize should be equally divided between the two. Wolfe forgot his disappointment over K 19 in his amazement and delight at having $2500 fall into his lap. "It was a totally unexpected windfall to me," he wrote his mother, "since at the time I wrote the story I did not even know that *Scribner's Magazine* was holding a contest. The award, therefore, was almost wholly unexpected and it was certainly welcome because I had begun to worry about money and this makes the immediate future considerably brighter and more secure."

With the prize money credited to his royalty account at Scribners, Wolfe settled down again to his "enormous task of excavation." "The only way I know of getting anything done is to do it my own way and as I want it," he wrote to Desmond Powell. "I have just begun to discover that publishing is a business and that publishers have dates and deadlines like other business men, but, although this is the way to *publish*, it is not the way to *write*." In late July he moved again—this time to 101 Columbia Heights—and worked stubbornly during all of August and September with no vacation except a three-day trip to Montreal for some non-Prohibition beer. But by October he was exhausted and depressed and began wandering restlessly about. First he went back to "his father's land" in southern Pennsylvania. This time he had obtained information about his relatives there from his mother and his brother Fred: he went directly to York Springs, his father's birthplace, and spent three days there with the son and widow of his father's brother Gilbert Wolf. It was a most rewarding visit: with his cousin Edgar Wolf he drove all over the countryside, seeing the houses where his father and his grandmother had lived, calling on various relatives, and re-creating in his mind the picture of his "other half." From this time on, his trips to Pennsylvania became almost annual events.

His next trip was to Bermuda in late October and was by no means so successful. "I went there to spend a vacation," he wrote afterward to Elaine Gould, "but I spent nothing but a lot of money and got madder and madder all the time at the island, the inhabitants and everything else they have there." He finally landed from the Bermuda boat in Boston, utterly exhausted and suffering from one of his severe feverish colds. His old friends the George Wallaces took him in at their house in Andover, and there he slept for four solid days, until he had recovered.

By the time he got back to Brooklyn his royalty account was down to $713—barely enough to last him until January. He lived simply but none too economically: in small things he was sometimes penurious, like his mother, but basically he had his father's love of lavish spending. His apartment cost him $65 a month, his food approximately $100, his typist another $100, and he also had expenses for stationery, supplies, liquor, telephone, clothes, doctors, traveling, and other items. If he could have learned to type, he would have saved over $1200 every year, but he never "got around to it," although he was presented with type-writers on two occasions: once by Professor Baker and his secretary and once by Belinda Jelliffe. His excuse for never learning was that his hands were too big, but the truth was that he was "nature's child" and totally alien to the operation of machinery of any sort. He felt intuitively that typing would hamper his creative flow, and so he wrote and wrote in longhand till he acquired not only expensive typists' bills but a large wart on his right index finger where it gripped the pencil.

Early in November 1932 he set to work on a series of stories which he hoped to sell to *Scribner's Magazine*. One of these was "Death the Proud Brother," on which he had worked during the summer of 1931, one was "The Train and the City," which had been a part of *K 19*, and one was "No Door," which was a more or less fictionalized account of his experiences in Brooklyn and New York since his return from the Guggenheim trip to Europe. All three of these were vaguely intended to be parts of his long book. "Death the Proud Brother" was, as has been noted, finally published as a separate story in *From Death to Morning*. "The Train and the City" appeared in *Of Time and the River*, except for the first part, which was scattered through *The Web and the Rock* and *You Can't Go Home Again*. And "No Door" was published partly in *Of Time and the River*, partly in *From Death to Morning*, and partly in *You Can't Go Home Again*. Wolfe was desperate for money and hoped to put the stories through as fast as possible, but, as always, he spent much more time than he had anticipated in rewriting and adding to them. He did not sell the first of them, "The Train and the City," to *Scribner's Magazine* till February 9, 1933, and during the last week in January he was literally "down to his last ten dollars."

It was at this time, when his finances were at their lowest, that he was invited to meet a Hollywood agent to discuss the possibility of his working as a script writer for the movies. The account of this interview later became one of his favorite funny stories and was improved with each retelling. One version represented him as actually going to meet the agent with an empty valise in which to put the vast amounts of money which he expected her to hand him after he had signed a motion-picture contract. However, the only assurance the agent could give him was that if he would come to Hollywood she felt sure she could find work for him there. "And how am I to get there, and who will pay my railroad fare?" he asked. "Well," she supposedly replied, "why don't you hitchhike?"

Meanwhile the fourth year since publication of *Look Homeward, Angel* had begun. Wolfe, according to his own estimate, had written well over "a half-million words," but he still had nothing that resembled a unified book, only great chunks of material which might go into one, or might be simply digressive. He was by now more desperate than ever. As he wrote to George Wallace, "I was in a horrible, ugly and furious temper . . . , because after all my bloody sweating in the last two years I seemed to have gotten nowhere, and in fact, the whole game seemed to be lost." Perkins knew that he was ready to admit defeat, and that something drastic must be done. He had arranged to go to Johns Hopkins for treatment for his rapidly increasing deafness and the violent hay fever which was a cause of it. He could not postpone his hospitalization, so he took Wolfe with him and, afterward, accompanied him to Washington to visit Mabel Wolfe Wheaton. All the way down and back on the train, and even while being treated in the hospital, Perkins discussed Wolfe's difficulties with him and, once again, he got him off to a new start.

"It is up to me to get the book done," Wolfe wrote to his mother in February, "not only for the sake of earning some money but for the sake of getting back my hope and belief and self-confidence again, without which everything will be lost for me. I believe and Perkins believes that I now have it, for I came back here . . . , plunged into work and did more work in one month than I had ever done before in my life in a similar period of time. Perkins says that I have the whole book in a nutshell, a very big nutshell it is true, for he already has over 100,000 words, and that if I can go ahead now and let nothing interfere with me until I finish, we will have a fine book, and will bring it out next autumn. . . . We also believe here, I mean the people at Scribners and myself, that all the sweating and working and writing I have done the last three years will not be lost but that it will fit into this book and the other books which are to follow. . . . I think things will . . . be all right, and that after all these months of desperate effort and confusion I have seemed to begin to unravel the knot and to have found the way to get started, which Perkins now thinks is where the trouble was, and the whole river now seems to be flowing."

It seems almost unbelievable that after four long years of intensive work, Wolfe had failed to do the one thing that was necessary—to "have found the way to get started," in other words, to have sat down and begun his book at the beginning and kept on working on it till he approached the end. The truth was, that in spite of all the long descriptions and outlines he had written to Perkins and Wheelock from abroad in 1930, he had little idea of what the chief point of the book or its main narrative was going to be. Also, his anxiety to avoid having this book criticized as being "autobiographical" had hampered him: he had his one story to tell—the story of Eugene Gant or George Webber or Thomas Wolfe—and his attempts to avoid telling it led to endless introductions, elaborate fictional disguises, and long digressions. Added to this was the fact that he had a bad case of "second book trouble." He had written out his chief compulsion in *Look Homeward, Angel*, and, as he explained to his sister Mabel, "the whole trouble seemed psychological rather than anything else. I think that I got afraid after the first book. I was afraid that I could never live up to the things they said about me." And finally, there was the fact that he was his mother's son, with all her talent for garrulity and digression. No other writer could have done what he did for four entire years without either running dry or realizing the error of his ways, but with Wolfe, as with his mother, the "web" wove back and forth forever, constantly renewing itself in variety and color and material: it never stopped as long as he or she drew breath. As a result of all these things, he had failed to come to grips with his new book, but had hedged and feinted all around it, writing hundreds of thousands of words of perfectly magnificent material, but material which, for the most part, had got him nowhere.

Perhaps Perkins should have realized sooner what Wolfe was doing, but he had only seen separate sections of the book, as Wolfe saw fit to show them to him, and had only done that for about a year. Moreover, as he said later, "no book was ever written in such an extraordinary fashion":[6] it had not occurred to him that anyone would or could write one in such a way. As Wolfe wrote to his sister Mabel, "Perkins . . . has been almost desperate about me, trying to figure what was wrong and how to get me out of it, but if he was desperate, you can imagine what my own state was." At any rate, Perkins had now put his finger on the trouble and Wolfe had got off to a whole new start, by beginning his book exactly where *Look Homeward, Angel* had left off, with

[6] From Perkins' letter of March 13, 1935, to Thomas Beer.

the departure of Eugene from Altamont for "the proud fierce North with all its shining cities and its tides of life." Once more he plunged into work, but this time with the joyful conviction that he was on the right track at last. According to his notebook, he wrote during February, March, and April "Return home, flight from home, 200,000 words," which, greatly cut, became "Telemachus," Book III of *Of Time and the River*. As he told George Wallace, it was now "all coming with a rush," and by April 18 Perkins was able to write an optimistic report about it to Charles Scribner III, who was at that time in London: "I do feel much encouraged about one thing . . . , although I can see unlimited work and struggle before it is fully accomplished;—that is Tom Wolfe's book. He brought me on Saturday something like 300,000 words of manuscript, considerable sections of which I had seen before. We already had here about 100 or 150,000 words. There is more to be done to fill in, but the book is really almost in existence now. There are many questions about it which will have to be argued out, and much revision and all that, just as was true of 'The Angel.' But I really think that this book has half a dozen chapters in it that are beyond anything even in 'The Angel'; and it may be a distinctly finer book than that. I had a sort of plan that after you come back, say in June or July, I might go off with Tom to the country and spend a couple of weeks, and get the book into shape."

But Perkins' hopes of being able to "get the book into shape" that summer were pathetically premature. Wolfe kept on writing it for an entire year—in fact, he really kept on till it was published and then complained to Perkins that he was "not through writing" even then. He would drive himself till he was utterly worn out and in one of his "black moods," whereupon he would lash out bitterly at someone— anyone—and then write them letters of abject apology. "The effort of writing or creating something seems to start up a strange and bewildering conflict in the man who does it," he wrote in one of these letters to Alfred Dashiell, "and this conflict at times almost takes on physical proportions so that he feels he is struggling not only with his own work but also with the whole world around him, and he is so beset with demons, nightmares, delusions and bewilderments that he lashes out at everyone and everything, not only people he dislikes and mistrusts, but sorrowfully enough, even against the people that he knows in his innermost heart are his true friends."

He had promised Perkins that he would stay in town and work all summer, but occasionally, when he was so exhausted that he could write no more, he took a few days' vacation. The first of these, in March, had been none too restful. He had promised his mother that he would meet her in Washington for Roosevelt's inauguration, and he had urged her to get a reserved seat for the parade and let him pay for it. But she either could not or would not get one, with the result that instead of seeing the parade, he "saw nothing but the back of my mother's shoulders for three hours and forty minutes." "But this was good enough," he wrote to Robert Raynolds, "for I was determined that she should miss nothing and I worked her down into the damnedest jammed crowd you ever saw, sent home to my sister's house for a chair, got Mama up in it and held her there. She saw the whole show and that was what we wanted."

His second trip was to York Springs and Gettysburg with his brother Fred in May, and his third was again to Gettysburg in July with Perkins, who had a weakness for going over the battlefield and reliving the entire Civil War. But for the most part, day after day and week after week, Wolfe simply worked and sweated in Brooklyn until, as he wrote to Mabel Wheaton, he felt "like that mule they tell about who ran himself to death trying to catch up with a bundle of hay that someone had tied a foot in front of his nose."

But unlike the mule, Wolfe did not concentrate on the single bundle of hay which represented the completion of his novel: he kept straying far afield after other and greener grass which he hoped somehow could be baled up into the book. By the first week in August he was writing to Perkins: "I am completing another section of my book which will be called 'The Hills Beyond Pentland,' and which, I think, in some ways may be as good as anything I have done." But when Perkins immediately wrote urging him to let him read this section, Wolfe answered that there was "still a great deal more writing to be done on it." And well there was: *The Hills Beyond Pentland* was to tell the history of Wolfe's maternal ancestors, the Westalls, Penlands, and Pattons, who had lived in the mountains of western North Carolina since the Revolution. Wolfe later realized that it must be a separate book, and although he lived to write only small portions of it, he always had a special feeling for it. "The book I am living for . . . ," he wrote in 1935 to Perkins, "is the Pentland book . . . and I feel if there is any chance of my doing anything good before I am forty it will be this book. I feel such a swelling and exultant sense of certitude and such a feeling of gathering power and fulfillment that I tremble when I think about it, and I hope to God that nothing happens to me or to my life . . . before I get to it."

By the end of August, Wolfe had broken off work on the Pentland material and had gone back to the main narrative of his book—to Eugene's first train ride North, which makes up the greater part of "Orestes: Flight before Fury," Book I of *Of Time and the River.* He had been making fragmentary notes for this ever since 1929, and even earlier, but he now was putting everything he had into the actual writing of it. "I am doing a very exciting piece of writing," he wrote to Robert Raynolds. "At least it's exciting to me, so much so that I'm in a delirious mental state and a horrible physical condition—a sort of cross between delirium tremens and Olympian calm. Sometimes when I'm working at it I think it's going to be so good I almost cry about it but when I'm not working at it I curse God, men, everything."

He kept at it until he was suffering from sheer exhaustion and colitis, then went with Raynolds on a short trip to Vermont. Raynolds had reviewed *Look Homeward, Angel* very favorably in 1929 and had later written Wolfe to praise "A Portrait of Bascom Hawke." The two writers had become good friends, and Wolfe had occasionally spent weekends at Raynolds' house in Connecticut: now they drove and walked in the Green Mountains until Wolfe felt "better than I have . . . in months." But by the end of September he was back in Brooklyn, moving into a cheaper apartment at 5 Montague Terrace, and desperately steeling himself for another long siege of work. "I'm thirty-three years old to-morrow," he wrote to his brother Fred on October 2, "but don't say anything about it. I feel that I have wasted much time and made many failures but still hope to do something with my life. Another year gone!"

"The early winter of 1933 arrived," he says in *The Story of a Novel,* "and with it, it seemed to me, the final doom of an abysmal failure. I still wrote and wrote, but blindly, hopelessly, like an old horse who trots around in the unending circle of a treadmill and knows no other end nor purpose for his life than this. If I slept at night, it was to sleep an unceasing nightmare of blazing visions that swept across my fevered and unresting mind. And when I woke, it was to wake exhausted, not knowing anything but work, lashing myself on into a hopeless labor, and so furiously at it through the day; and then night again, a frenzied prowling of a thousand streets, and so to bed and sleepless sleep again, the nightmare pageantry to which my consciousness lay chained a spectator.

"There was a kind of dream which I can only summarize as dreams of Guilt and Time. . . . My daily conflict with Amount and Number, the huge accumulations of my years of struggle with the forms of life, my brutal and unending efforts to record upon my memory each brick and paving stone of every street that I had ever walked upon, each face of every thronging crowd in every city, every country with which my spirit had contested its savage and uneven struggle for supremacy—they all returned now—each stone, each street, each town, each country— yes, even every book in the library whose loaded shelves I had tried vainly to devour at college—they returned upon the wings of these mighty, sad, and somehow quietly demented dreams—I saw and heard and knew them all at once, was instantly, . . . with the calm conscious- ness of God, master of the whole universe of life against whose ele- ments I had contended vainly for all-knowledge for so many years. . . .

"And *beyond, beyond*—forever *above, around, behind* the vast and tranquil consciousness of my spirit that now held the earth and all her elements in the huge clasp of its effortless subjection—there dwelt for- ever the fatal knowledge of my own inexpiable *guilt*.

"I did not know what I had done—I only knew that I had ruinously forgotten time, and by so doing had betrayed my brother men. . . . I had been long from home—I had grown old in some evil and enchanted place, I had allowed my life to waste and rot in the slothful and de- grading surfeits of Circean time. And now my life was lost—my work undone—I had betrayed my home, my friends, my people in the duties of some solemn and inviolable trust—and suddenly I was home again, and *silence* was my answer! . . . I walked among them, and they neither moved nor spoke until I passed, and if they looked at me, their eyes were blank with silence and no memory; there was no reproach, no grief, and no contempt, there was no bitterness and scorn—if I had died, there should at least have been the ghost of memory, but it was as if I never had been born. And so I passed them by, and everywhere I trod was death . . .

"Another and more pertinent variety of these dreams of Guilt and Time would take this form: It seemed to me that I had gone abroad, was living there, and yet was conscious that I was still employed as an instructor at the university. . . . I dreamed my life away in ancient Gothic towns, . . . my spirit slid from land to land, from one enchant- ment to another . . . —and yet I was forever haunted by a consciousness of Time and Guilt, the obscure gnawing of forsaken trust. And suddenly I would seem to wake into a full and frenzied consciousness: I had been gone from home a year—my classes at the university had been waiting on me . . . I saw them searching through the mazes of the corridors, prowling among the swarming myriads of their 30,000 fellow students, sitting in patient dejection . . . in classrooms where their absent teacher never entered. And finally—and most horrible of all—I saw the mounting pile of unmarked student themes—those accursed themes that . . . piled up in mountainous and hopeless accumulations—whose white backs were hideously innocent of the scrawled comment with which I had once—tormented by twin agonies of boredom and conscience—covered every scrap of their surface. And now it was too late! . . . It was the last day of the term, the last class ended, the last irrevocable moment of salvation had gone by. I found myself suddenly standing there in the offices of the English faculty, struck dumb with horror, confronted by the great white mountain of those unmarked themes. I turned, a ring of silent forms encircled me . . . My little Jews stood first, their dark eyes fixed on me with a dejected but unwavering reproach, and behind them stood the jury of my peers, the outer circle of instructors. They were all there—students, instructors, friends, enemies, and the huge damnation of that pile of unmarked themes—there was no word spoken, nothing but their quiet look of inflexible and unpardoning accusal. This dream returned to torture sleep a hundred times: Each time I would awake from it in a cold sweat of anguish and of horror . . . and lie for minutes in cold terror while my mind fought with the phantoms of my sleep to argue me back into reality.

"Nor were these dreams of Guilt and Time the only ones: my mind and memory in sleep blazed with a fiery river of unending images: . . . a million things, once seen and long forgotten, were restored and blazed across my vision in this stream of light—and a million million things unseen, the faces, cities, streets, and landscapes yet unseen and long imagined . . . all streamed across my fevered and unresting mind the flood of the unending pageantry—and suddenly I knew that it would never end.

"For sleep was dead forever, the merciful, dark, and sweet oblivions of childhood sleep. The worm had entered at my heart, the worm lay coiled and feeding at my brain, my spirit, and my memory—I knew that finally I had been caught in my own fire, consumed by my own hungers, impaled on the hook of that furious and insatiate desire that had absorbed my life for years. I knew, in short, that one bright cell in the brain or heart or memory would now blaze forever—by night, by day, through every waking, sleeping moment of my life, the worm would feed and the light be lit—that no anodyne of food or drink, or friendship, travel, sport or women could ever quench it, and that nevermore until death put its total and conclusive darkness on my life could I escape.

"I knew at last I had become a writer: I knew at last what happens to a man who makes the writer's life his own."

For several months Perkins had been anxiously observing Wolfe's keyed-up, increasingly exhausted state, and he now was beginning to consider the drastic and unheard-of step of "taking the book away from him." Characteristically, he began discussing it with his colleagues, although he was not so much asking their opinion as meditating out loud. First of all, he had always been convinced that Wolfe must publish a second book before the potential sales and general reputation built up by *Look Homeward, Angel* had been lost by the passage of too much time. In publishing, a novel by an unknown writer is a very difficult thing to sell: the only thing more difficult is a novel by a writer who has had some slight success and then, through failure to produce, has become a has-been. *Look Homeward, Angel* had done remarkably well for a first novel, and Perkins had taken an intense personal pride in its success. "The foremost interest in his life" was Wolfe's career, but he was powerless to further it until the second book was published, and after four long years of anxious waiting, he had set his will inflexibly on the conviction that it must be now or never.

Secondly, Perkins was impelled by the increasing fear that if Wolfe continued writing, his book would spread and spread until it could not be cut and edited into publishable form. It had by now reached a length of almost a million words, about four times the length of the uncut manuscript of *Look Homeward, Angel*[7] and ten times that of an average novel—and Wolfe was constantly adding to it at the rate of about 50,000 words a month. It was up to Perkins to achieve the miracle of getting all this into the covers of a book, and of a book which would be widely readable and salable. He had a deep intuitive confidence in his ability to keep a book in hand: he would give a writer all the leeway in the world and would then take an almost hopelessly chaotic manuscript and get it into shape with a knack which, deceptively, seemed casual. "It seems so easy when Fox does it," Wolfe wrote of him later in *You Can't Go Home Again*, "easy as a shoe, because he has had it from his birth. It is a genius." However, as Perkins wrote to Wolfe in 1937, "there are limitations of time, of space, and of human laws which cannot be treated as if they did not exist." And now, as Wolfe's

---

[7] These estimates are Wolfe's and are probably somewhat exaggerated.

book approached the million-word mark, Perkins' intuition told him that it was going dangerously far beyond those limitations, so far that he might not be able to bring it back.

Perkins often used to speculate as to what would happen if Wolfe should be allowed to write and write until he finally rounded out his huge design, and should then be published in a series of small volumes similar to those in which Dickens' novels first appeared. "Maybe it's the way Tom is. Maybe we should just publish him as he comes and in the end it will be all right,"[8] he quotes himself as having said to Wheelock as early as 1932, when Wolfe had written K 19. Later, when he was endeavoring to keep Wolfe on the Scribner list, he actually committed himself to trying this radical experiment: "Length could be dealt with by publishing in sections," he wrote to him in January 1937. This might have been barely possible in 1937, when Wolfe's reputation had been enhanced by publication of *Of Time and the River*; it would be a good deal more practicable now, approximately twenty-five years later, when his literary standing has become established; but in 1933 he still was only "a promising young writer" who might or might not live up to expectations. Publishing his work uncut and unedited, in sections, would have been almost suicidal, and, as Perkins wrote to him in 1937, "if we had, and the results had been bad at the moment, would you not have blamed me? Certainly I should have bitterly blamed myself."[9]

However, the immediately pressing reason for Perkins' decision to "take the book away" was Wolfe's increasing tension and fatigue. His nightmares and insomnia were by now so bad that he was in a state of trancelike exhaustion every day and of hopeless overstimulation every night: he insisted that he never really slept at all, and that he had not done so now for months. By November 1933 Perkins was expressing his anxiety about him to his colleagues. "He *can't* go on like that!" he repeatedly exclaimed. "If he does, something terrible is bound to happen!" He would pause and shake his head with wonder and concern, and then say, "I think I'll *have* to take the book away from him!" What he was afraid of was that Wolfe would have a breakdown, either physical or mental, or both together, or even, as he said later, that he might "go insane."[10] It is true that Wolfe himself occasionally expressed anxiety on the latter score, but never very seriously: in actuality, he was a prime example of the theory that neurotic people seldom, if ever, go

[8] From Perkins' letter to Wolfe of January 13, 1937.
[9] Ibid.
[10] From Perkins' letter to John S. Terry of December 19, 1945.

insane. The real cause for alarm was that his physical exhaustion might seriously undermine his health. However, at this time, Perkins' extreme anxiety about him seemed only an unnecessary exaggeration of his fatherly solicitude. It was not until Wolfe died in 1938 from an illness brought on by fatigue from insomnia and overwork that Perkins' fears proved to have been partly justified.

Wolfe's description of how Perkins finally took the book away is pathetic in its expression of the dependence which he had on him: "In the middle of December . . . ," he says in *The Story of a Novel*, "the editor . . . who, during all this tormented period, had kept a quiet watch upon me, called me to his home and calmly informed me that my book was finished. I could only look at him with stunned surprise, and finally I only could tell him out of the depth of my own hopelessness, that he was mistaken, that the book was not finished, that it could never be completed, that I could write no more. He answered with the same quiet finality that the book was finished whether I knew it or not, and then he told me to go to my room and spend the next week in collecting in its proper order the manuscript which had accumulated during the last two years.

"I followed his instructions, still without hope and without belief. I worked for six days sitting in the middle of the floor surrounded by mountainous stacks of typed manuscript on every side. At the end of a week I had the first part of it together, and just two days before Christmas, 1933, I delivered to him the manuscript of 'The October Fair' . . ."

Immediately after delivering his manuscript to Perkins, Wolfe sat down and wrote him a very characteristic letter:

"Dear Max: I was pretty tired last night when I delivered that last batch of manuscript to you, and could not say very much to you about it. There is not much to say except that to-day I feel conscious of a good many errors both of omission and commission and wish I had had more time to arrange and sort out the material, but think it is just as well that I have given it to you even in its present shape.

"I don't envy you the job before you: I know what a tough thing it is going to be to tackle, but I do think that even in the form in which the material has been given you, you ought to be able to make some kind of estimate of its value or lack of value and tell me about it. If you do feel on the whole I can now go ahead and complete it, I think I can go much faster than you realize. Moreover, when all the scenes have been completed and the narrative changed to a third person point of view,[11] I think there will be a much greater sense of unity than now seems possible, in spite of the mutilated, hacked-up form in which you have the manuscript; and I do feel decidedly hopeful, and hope your verdict will be for me to go ahead and complete the first draft as soon as I can; and in spite of all the rhythms, chants—what you call my dithyrambs—which are all through the manuscript, I think you will find when I get through that there is plenty of narrative—or should I say when *you* get through, because I must shamefacedly confess that I need your help now more than I ever did.

"You have often said that if I ever gave you something that you could get your hands on and weigh in its entirety from beginning to end, you could pitch in and help me to get out of the woods. Well, now here is your chance. I think a very desperate piece of work is ahead for both of us, but if you think it is worth doing and tell me to go ahead, I think there is literally nothing that I cannot accomplish. But you must be honest and straightforward in your criticism when you talk about it, even though what you say may be hard for me to accept after all this work, because that is the only fair way and the only good way in the end.

"I want to get back to work on it as soon as I can, and will probably go on anyway writing in the missing scenes and getting a complete manuscript as soon as I can. I wanted to write you this mainly to tell you that I am in a state of great trepidation and great hope also. Buried in that great pile of manuscript is some of the best writing I have ever done. Let's see to it that it does not go to waste."

In *The Story of a Novel* Wolfe goes on to describe Perkins' verdict on the manuscript: "He had seen most of it in its dismembered fragments during the three preceding years, but now, for the first time, he was seeing it in its sequential order, and once again his intuition was right; he had told me the truth when he said that I had finished the book.

"It was not finished in any way that was publishable or readable. It was really not a book so much as it was the skeleton of a book, but for the first time in four years the skeleton was all there. An enormous labor of revision, weaving together, shaping, and, above all, cutting

[11] Parts of the manuscript were still written in the first person. Wolfe never did get around to changing them to the third person, so finally Wheelock did it for him in the proofs.

remained, but I had the book now so that nothing, not even the despair of my own spirit, could take it from me. He told me so, and suddenly I saw that he was right.

"I was like a man who is drowning and who suddenly, at the last gasp of his dying effort, feels earth beneath his feet again. My spirit was borne upward by the greatest triumph it had ever known, and although my mind was tired, my body exhausted, from that moment on I felt equal to anything on earth."

It was not till later that he began to feel "a sense of irremediable loss" at having given up the manuscript so soon and a repressed resentment against Perkins for having made him do so.

XV

THE first thing Perkins did after reading the manuscript of *The October Fair* was to divide it into halves, each of which he planned to publish as a separate novel. The last half was still called *The October Fair*: the first half was given the alternate title of *Of Time and the River*, which Wolfe had occasionally considered for the entire book. "The book did describe two complete and separate cycles," Wolfe says in *The Story of a Novel*. "The first of these was a movement which described the period of wandering and hunger in a man's youth. The second cycle described the period of greater certitude, and was dominated by the unity of a single passion. It was obvious, therefore, that what we had in the two cyclic movements of this book was really the material of two completely different chronicles, and although the second of the two was by far the more finished, the first cycle, of course, was the one which logically we ought to complete and publish first, and we decided on this course."

All of this undeniably was true, but Perkins also had more cogent reasons for breaking off the book at the exact place where he did. Even at this early stage of the game, he was worried about *The October Fair* both from a literary and a legal point of view. "What seemed to me the very hardest part was that about his association with Esther," he wrote afterward. "This never seemed to me right, and I dreaded the struggle we would have over it. But then it occurred to me that we might end the book with the first meeting with Esther, in France."[1]

The job which had to be done upon the manuscript of *Of Time and the River* was a twofold and contradictory one: it needed drastic cutting, but it also needed the addition of the still unwritten parts. The result was a state of nerve-racking confusion, for as Perkins labored desperately to reduce the length, Wolfe kept increasing it by the addition of hundreds of thousands of new words. It was like trying to bail a sinking boat while the water kept pouring in through opened seams, and if Perkins seems sometimes to have seized the oars and rowed too frantically for the beach, it was because he feared the boat might be

[1] From Perkins' letter of October 29, 1945, to John S. Terry.

swamped completely. It would, of course, have been much easier for him to wait until Wolfe had completed the unwritten portions and then to take the whole thing and cut and edit it: but because of his conviction that the book must be published as soon as possible and his fear that Wolfe would keep on adding to it practically ad infinitum, he took things into his own hands. "We set to work," he wrote later in the *Carolina Magazine*. "I, who thought Tom a man of genius, and loved him too, and could not bear to see him fail, was almost as desperate as he, so much there was to do. . . . After I had read the manuscript and marked it up, we began a year of nights of work. The book was far from finished. It was in great fragments, and they were not in order. Large parts were missing. It was all disproportioned. Tom, who knew all this, would come in at eight or so, and I would point these things out, part by part. But I could tell Tom nothing, if it were right, that he did not easily see, and perhaps had already seen. But his whole natural impulse was outward, not inward—to express, not compress, or organize—and even though he realized that something had to be cut, as extrinsic, or otherwise superfluous, he could not easily bear to have it done. So every night we worked and argued in my boxstall of an office over Fifth Avenue, often accomplishing nothing, and strewed the floor with cigarettes and papers."[2]

Wolfe himself, in *The Story of a Novel*, gives a more detailed description of the kind of thing they did: "To give a few concrete illustrations of the difficulties that now confronted us: The opening section of the book describes the journey of a train across the State of Virginia at night. Its function in the book is simply to introduce some of the chief characters, to indicate a central situation, to give something of the background from which the book proceeds, and perhaps through the movement of the train across the stillness of the earth to establish a certain beat, evoke a certain emotion which is inherent to the nature of the book. Such a section, therefore, undoubtedly serves an important function, but in proportion to the whole purport of the book, its function is a secondary one and must be related to the whole book in a proportionate way.

"Now in the original version, the manuscript which described the journey of the train across Virginia at night was considerably longer than the average novel. What was needed was just an introductory chapter or two, and what I had written was over 100,000 words in

[2] From "Scribner's and Tom Wolfe," in the October 1938 issue of the *Carolina Magazine*.

length, and this same difficulty, this lack of proportion, was also evident
in other parts of the manuscript.

"What I had written about the great train was really good. But what
I had to face, the very bitter lesson that everyone who wants to write
has got to learn, was that a thing may in itself be the finest piece of
writing one has ever done, and yet have absolutely no place in the
manuscript one hopes to publish. . . . My spirit quivered at the
bloody execution. My soul recoiled before the carnage of so many lovely
things cut out upon which my heart was set. But it had to be done, and
we did it.

"The first chapter in the original manuscript, a chapter which the
editor, himself, admitted was as good a single piece of writing as I had
ever done,[3] was relentlessly kicked out, and the reason it was kicked out
was that it was really not a true beginning for the book but merely
something which led up to the true beginning; therefore it had to go.
And so it went all up and down the line. Chapters 50,000 words long
were reduced to ten or fifteen thousand words, and having faced this
inevitable necessity, I finally acquired a kind of ruthlessness of my
own, and once or twice, myself, did more cutting than my editor was
willing to allow.

"Another fault that has always troubled me in writing is that I have
often attempted to reproduce in its entirety the full flood and fabric
of a scene in life itself. Thus, in another section of the book,[4] four
people were represented as talking to each other for four hours without
a break or intermission. All were good talkers; often all talked, or tried
to talk, at the same time. The talk was wonderful and living talk because I knew the life and character and the vocabulary of all these
people from its living source, and I had forgotten nothing. Yet all the
time, all that was actually happening in this scene was that a young
woman had got out of her husband's motor car and gone into her
mother's house and kept calling to the impatient man outside every
time he honked his horn, 'All right. All right. I'll be with you in five

[3] Wolfe had written an introductory series of incidents which portrayed the
earliest history of North Carolina, but which had no bearing on his narrative
except that his leading characters were natives of that state. The first of these
was later published as "Polyphemus" in the June 1935 issue of the *North American Review* and the second as "Old Catawba" in the April 1935 issue of the
Virginia Quarterly Review; finally they were put back together and published
as "The Men of Old Catawba" in *From Death to Morning*.

[4] Section XL, the second section of "Telemachus," in *Of Time and the
River*.

minutes.' These five minutes really lengthened into four hours, while the unfortunate man outside honked upon his horn, and while the two women and two young men of the same family inside carried on a torrential discourse and discussed exhaustively the lives and histories of almost everyone in town, their memories of the past, adventures of the present, and speculations of the future. I put it all down in the original manuscript just as I had seen and known and lived it a thousand times, and even if I do say so myself, the nature of the . . . language, the utter naturalness, the flood-tide river of it all was wonderful, but I had made four people talk 80,000 words—200 printed pages of close type in a minor scene of an enormous book, and of course, good as it was, it was all wrong and had to go. . . .

"Meanwhile I was proceeding at full speed with the work of completing my design, finishing the unfinished parts and filling in the transition links which were essential. This in itself was an enormous job and kept me writing all day long as hard as I could go for a full year. Here again the nature of my chief fault was manifest. I wrote too much again. I not only wrote what was essential, but time and time again my enthusiasm for a good scene, one of those enchanting vistas which can open up so magically to a man in the full flow of his creation, would overpower me, and I would write thousands of words upon a scene which contributed nothing of vital importance to a book whose greatest need already was ruthless condensation. During the course of this year, I must have written well over a half million words of additional manuscript, of which, of course, only a small part was finally used.

"The nature of my method, the desire fully to explore my material, had led me into another error. The whole effect of those five years of incessant writing had been to make me feel not only that everything had to be used, but that everything had to be told, that nothing could be implied. Therefore, at the end, there were at least a dozen additional chapters which I felt had to be completed to give the book its final value. A thousand times I debated this question desperately with my editor. I told him that these chapters had to go in simply because I felt the book would not be complete without them, and with every argument he had, he tried to show me that I was wrong."

In *The Story of a Novel* Wolfe then goes on to make one of his frequent avowals that Perkins "on the whole was right about it," but actually, from the day when Perkins "took the book away from him" in December 1933 until the final day in January 1935 when it went into foundry proofs and could no longer be revised, he was torn between his utter trust in and complete dependence upon Perkins and his own unsuppressible conviction that the book was not yet ready to be published.

He hated to be hurried: he had to do things his own way, and any attempt to persuade him to a thing too hastily upset and angered him. His outbursts of protest against Perkins' pressure were both constant and violent, and even though they were succeeded by sincere protestations of devotion, his doubt and resentment kept on smoldering underneath. Sometimes his outbreaks were masked by a sardonic humor, as the famous one which Perkins describes in the *Carolina Magazine*: "Once I argued for a big deletion, late on a hot night, and then sat in silence. I knew he must agree to it, for the reasons were strong. Tom tossed his head about, and swayed in his chair, and his eyes roved over the office. I went on reading in the manuscript for not less than fifteen minutes, but I was aware of Tom's movements—aware at last that he was looking fixedly at one corner of the office. In that corner hung a winter hat and overcoat, and down from under the hat, along the coat hung a sinister rattlesnake skin with seven rattles—a present from Marjorie Rawlings. I looked at Tom. He was eyeing the group of objects, and the rattlesnake stood out. He waved his hand at them: 'Aha!' said Tom, 'the portrait of an editor.'"[5]

But sometimes the argument was in such deadly earnest that even Perkins lost his temper. "A couple of nights ago," he wrote to Hemingway in June 1934, "I told Tom that a whole lot of fine stuff he had in simply ought to come out because it resulted in blurring a very important effect. Literally, we sat here for an hour thereafter without saying a word, while Tom glowered and pondered and fidgeted in his chair. Then he said, 'Well, then will you take the responsibility?' And I said, 'I have simply got to take the responsibility. And what's more,' I said, 'I will be blamed, either way.'"[6] He knew that Wolfe made him a kind of repository not only of his successes but also of his errors, although he did not fully realize at this time that the errors would weigh more heavily with Wolfe—so heavily that they would finally result in his discarding the repository of them altogether. But there was nothing Perkins could have done about it anyway. Wolfe's relationships with people were on his own terms, colored and distorted by his own compulsions, and the extravagant devotion which he bestowed upon his

[5] From "Scribner's and Tom Wolfe."

[6] From Perkins' letter to Hemingway of June 28, 1934, reprinted in *Editor to Author: The Letters of Maxwell E. Perkins*, Scribners, 1950.

father-substitute was bound to be succeeded by violent disillusionment and rejection of him.

Wolfe had gone "into a slump of awful dejection for two or three
weeks" in January. As he explained to Robert Raynolds, "I was doing
little work except cutting and going over the manuscript with Perkins
every day. We really got a great deal accomplished, but I was not
getting on with my own work at home." But by February, with the
aid of one of the best typists he was ever to have, he was "going like
the wind" again, and from then on his life fell into a routine that lasted
for the remainder of the year. He would work at home until late afternoon, then begin the (for him) lengthy procedure of getting over to
Manhattan, eating dinner, and going to meet Perkins for their nightly
session with the manuscript. He was supposed to arrive at eight o'clock,
but he was often late, not only because of his chronic inability to be
on time but because his fatigue and reluctance often kept him brooding
over a drink in some restaurant or bar. Moreover, even when he did
reach Scribners, there was always a further delay while he poured out
to Perkins whatever might be on his mind: getting Wolfe to settle
down to work was always more exhausting than the work itself. But
finally they would get started and would work until about eleven; then
they would go for drinks at the Chatham, where, in warm weather,
they could sit outdoors. "During the summer we always went . . . to
Chatham Walk," Perkins wrote nostalgically later, "and sat out under
the sky. Tom liked that place because, for one thing, he could feel
the vibration as the trains went out or in.[7] It seems in recollection as
if it never rained, and we sat there often very late, always drinking,
but never too much. I don't think Tom was drinking greatly at that
time, because he felt as if he were advancing with the work. It was
when he was agonized over his writing that he drank so badly."[8]

Meanwhile the Perkins family had moved into town from New
Canaan to a house in the block of East Forty-ninth Street between
Second and Third Avenues, in the section known as Turtle Bay. It
had become a second home to Wolfe, and he usually walked there
with Perkins when the Chatham closed, then stayed and talked till
Perkins, as was his habit, went out to buy the first edition of the next
day's papers. It was pretty much the same routine as the two men had

[7] The tracks leading to and from Grand Central Station run underground in
the vicinity of the Chatham.

[8] From Perkins' letter of October 29, 1945, to John S. Terry.

followed earlier, but it was now constant and intense, seven nights a week, including holidays: Perkins had no opportunity to escape from it by going to New Canaan, and he aged noticeably under the strain of it on top of his exacting job at Scribners. When his old childhood friend Van Wyck Brooks protested that his nightly sessions with Wolfe would kill him,[9] he angrily denied it, but he did privately admit that it was "the most difficult work I ever was engaged in."[10]

Meanwhile Wolfe was still hard-pressed for money. The contract for *Of Time and the River* had been signed in May 1933, and he had begun drawing irregular amounts against it, which, by the time of the book's publication in March 1935, totaled $2050. He had also sold two more stories to *Scribner's Magazine*, "The Four Lost Men" and "Dark in the Forest, Strange as Time," which were published in the February and November 1934 issues. But he was dissatisfied with the price of $300 which Scribners paid him for each of them, and he began to think that if he could sell stories to other magazines as well, he could support himself more easily. He had broken off with Mrs. Boyd in January 1932 and had consulted another agent, Curtis Brown, in the spring of 1933, but nothing definite had come of this interview, chiefly because Wolfe had no idea of what constituted a salable short story. With the exception of "The Web of Earth," his stories had been picked out of his vast mass of manuscript by Perkins, accepted in rough draft by *Scribner's Magazine*, then reworked (and lengthened in the process) by Wolfe, and finally cut and edited by Alfred Dashiell.

There was also the constant difficulty of too great length: Wolfe never wrote a story under the usual limit of five thousand words in his entire life, with the exception of brief episodes which were lifted virtually untouched from his books, such as "The Sun and the Rain" and "The Far and the Near." His stories naturally came out somewhere between ten and thirty thousand words. In August 1933 he had sent out a form letter to the editors of *Harper's Magazine*, the *Forum*, the *American Mercury*, and the *Atlantic Monthly*, asking if they ever published stories of that length and if they would be interested in seeing some from him. Most of them had answered that such pieces would be too long for publication as short stories, although they might possibly be used as novelettes or serials. This had discouraged Wolfe, and he had done nothing further until finally Perkins had suggested that he

[9] From Perkins' letter of December 19, 1945, to John S. Terry.
[10] From Perkins' letter of February 1, 1934, to Marjorie Kinnan Rawlings.

try as agents Maxim Lieber and his assistant, Elizabeth Nowell, who had been on the editorial staff of *Scribner's Magazine* and had "learned to read Wolfe's writing" by typing revisions which he had made on stories there.

Wolfe was introduced to Lieber in Perkins' office and then went out to dinner with him and Miss Nowell to talk things over. He had no sooner reached Fifth Avenue with them than he turned to Lieber and launched into a recital of every dissatisfaction he had ever had with Scribners. Wolfe was still deeply devoted to Perkins and would spring furiously to his defense if anyone else criticized him, but the seeds of discontent had started growing in him: he was becoming vaguely conscious that publishing was a business instead of a philanthropic institution designed exclusively for him; he was harboring suppressed resentment at Perkins' pressure for the cutting and completion of his book; and he was beginning to chafe at the too close restriction of his benevolent paternalism.

Of the several sections of the manuscript which Wolfe showed them, Lieber and Miss Nowell chose the "Boom Town" chapter from *K 19* as the most salable, and after cutting it and sitting up nights with Wolfe while he revised it, they tried it with the higher-priced magazines. It was declined by all of them, chiefly because of its excessive length, and when it ended up by selling to the *American Mercury*, Wolfe was none too pleased. "My literary agents," he wrote wryly to Robert Raynolds in March 1934, ". . . finally succeeded in getting a hundred and ninety-two dollars out of the *American Mercury* for a 20,000 word story which I rewrote three times, and of the same length that *Scribner's* have paid me four hundred for." Later they sold a much-cut version of "Telemachus" from the *Of Time and the River* manuscript to *Redbook* for $750. However, it could not come out until the December 1934 issue of that magazine, and Perkins was still hoping against hope that *Of Time and the River* could be published late that fall. There was really only a slim chance of it, but he was holding that chance out to Wolfe as an incentive to push the book through to completion. "If he knows it can't be published till later than December," he told Miss Nowell, "he'll keep on writing new things into it and get it all messed up and much too long again." Finally Wolfe yielded to Perkins' opposition and, to his "unspeakable anguish," turned the *Redbook* offer down, "although," as he wrote to Raynolds, "at the present time so much money looks mountainous to me."

All through the spring of 1934 Wolfe continued to be worried about money. Independently of Lieber's office, he sold two more stories to

Scribner's Magazine, "The Sun and the Rain" and "The House of the Far and Lost," which came out in the May and August issues; he received an advance of $250 for the Modern Library edition of *Look Homeward, Angel*, and also an advance of £100 from Heinemann for the English edition of *Of Time and the River*; but he now had no big backlog of Scribner royalties to keep him going, and he was reluctant to draw too much in advance against *Of Time and the River*. In February he had applied to the Guggenheim Foundation for a renewal of his fellowship to enable him to complete his book, but he had been turned down.

Ironically enough, it was at this time that he was approached by another publisher,[11] who had heard rumors that he was "not happy" with Scribners. The various versions of this incident differ widely. Wolfe's version was that he went to meet the editor of the rival house after consulting Perkins and being told that he had every right to do so but that he should inform Scribners of any offer he might receive so that they could match or better it; and that the editor offered him an advance of $10,000 for his new book, sight unseen, but that when the man made some half-derogatory remarks about Perkins, Wolfe flew into a rage at him, shouted out that he was "so little, he *smelled* little" and how dared he speak that way of a great man like Perkins—whereupon he broke off the interview then and there. The editor's version was that he did talk with Wolfe, but only on an informal basis; that an advance of $10,000 was almost unheard of in those days; that he never offered or was authorized to offer any such terms to anyone at any time or under any circumstances; and that there was no quarrel between him and Wolfe at that time, although there was one on another, totally different occasion, when he and Wolfe were drinking at the Chatham bar.

At any rate, Wolfe told his version of the interview to Perkins the next day, with the result that Charles Scribner III wrote a letter of protest to the head of the rival publishing house, who, incidentally, was a close friend of his and had not known that his editor had talked with Wolfe. It was all a ludicrous misunderstanding and was straightened out to everybody's satisfaction. Moreover, Wolfe had signed the contract for *Of Time and the River* with Scribners a year earlier, so he could not have left them even if he'd wanted to. But from that time forth he referred to it as an example of his loyalty to Scribners. "If you are going to tell people that I turned my back and walked out on you,"

[11] The publisher remains anonymous here at the request of Charles Scribner III.

he wrote to Perkins in November 1937, when he had actually left, "why don't you also tell them that three years ago, when I didn't have a penny and was working on 'Of Time and the River,' I was approached by another publisher and offered what seemed to me a fortune. . . . You know when I did meet and talk with these people and heard their offer and rejected it on my own accord, and told you all about it, I never once asked you or Scribners to meet the offer, although most writers apparently, and even publishers, would have considered that entirely fair and businesslike. So if you are going to say now that I walked out on you, why not tell some of the rest of the story too, and admit that I not only never tried to hold you up about anything, but never made approaches to anybody else, and rejected all that were made to me, even when I didn't have a cent."

Meanwhile Wolfe and Perkins were working and arguing over the manuscript of *Of Time and the River* almost every night, and as Perkins slowly, stubbornly, got the book in shape, Wolfe's resentment steadily increased. At the end of March they had one of their bitter quarrels. "We have had another struggle here over the book," Perkins wrote to Frere, who was waiting for a set of proofs of *Of Time and the River* from which to print the English edition, "and the result is that I alone am to go through it all with a blue pencil, and the argument is to come later." Thus unimpeded, he went ahead. "I am cutting it hard now," he wrote to Frere on April 6, "and reducing it very greatly. Although there will, of course, be an argument later with Tom. Things are not going badly on the whole." But by May 12 Wolfe had had another outburst of rebellion. "Tom has been ranging around the country again," Perkins wrote to Frere, "and is in an unmanageable state, but I think he will soon calm down, and I hope we can get things into definite shape."

As a matter of fact, Wolfe's "ranging around the country" turned out to be a preparation for the writing of one of the finest things he ever did: the death of Gant in *Of Time and the River*. He had gone to the Brett School for defective children at Dingmans Ferry, Pennsylvania, where the principal, Catherine Brett, had a studio on the school grounds which she often lent to writers. Wolfe was touched and upset by the children—"It gives you a sick feeling," he wrote to his brother Fred—but in subsequent visits there he became devoted to them and even corresponded with one of them for several years. Moreover, even the northern part of Pennsylvania was to Wolfe "his father's land," and he was inspired and refreshed by the long drives into the countryside on which Miss Brett occasionally took him. He returned to

Brooklyn ready for a whole new start upon his work, and in the next two weeks wrote 50,000 words. He had written rough-draft sections of the death of Gant at least a year earlier, but he now plunged in and did the entire thing in one "terrific burst of work."

At first Perkins tried to prevent Wolfe from writing this. "When we came to the point where Eugene's father died," he wrote later in the *Carolina Magazine*, "I said that it must be written about, but that since Eugene was away at Harvard, Tom need only tell of the shock of the news, and of Eugene's return for the funeral—a matter of perhaps five thousand words. And Tom agreed. The next night he came in with some thousands of words about the life of the doctor who attended Gant. I said, 'This is good, Tom, but what has it to do with the book? You are telling the story of Eugene, of what *he* saw and experienced. We can't waste time with all this that is outside it.' Tom fully accepted this, but still, the next night, he brought in a long passage about Eugene's sister Helen, and her thoughts while shopping in Altamont, and then at night in bed when she heard the whistle of the train. I said, 'How in God's name will you get this book done this way, Tom? You have wasted two days already, and instead of reducing the length and doing what is essential, you are increasing it and adding what doesn't belong here.'

"Tom was penitent. He did not argue back as he almost always had done. He promised he would write only what was needed—and yet the next night he brought in thousands of words about Gant's illness, all outside of what I thought was wanted. But it was too good to let go. I said so. It was wrong, but it was right, and Tom went on, and the death of Gant is one of the finest things he ever wrote. Thank God I had sense enough to see it that early, even though it seemed to me to violate the principle of form. But I do not think I could have stopped Tom anyhow. He had agreed that I was right, but underneath he knew what he was doing and had to do it."[12]

Slowly, agonizedly, the work on the book progressed. By the first week in July, Wolfe was writing to Robert Raynolds: "It seems unbelievable, but Perkins and I finished getting the manuscript ready for the printer last night. There are still three full scenes to be written, and parts of a few other scenes to be completed, but he wants to start getting the stuff to the printer at once. As for myself, I am fighting against an overwhelming reluctance to let it go. There are so many things I want to go back over and fill in and revise, and all my beautiful notes I long to chink in somehow, and he is doing his best to restrain me

[12] From "Scribner's and Tom Wolfe."

in these designs. I had lunch with Perkins and Scott Fitzgerald yesterday, and Scott tried to console me about the cutting by saying that 'you never cut anything out of a book that you regret later.' I wonder if this is true. Anyway, I shall do all I can in what time is left to me, and then I suppose I will have to leave the matter on the lap of the gods and Maxwell Perkins. After all these years of bitter labor, and sometimes of despairing hope, I have come to have a strange and deep affection for this great hacked and battered creature of a manuscript as if it were my son—and now I hate to see it go. . . . I think Perkins' benevolently crafty design is to start giving this thing to the printer at once so that there will no longer be any possible drawing back on my part. He has already carefully impressed it upon my mind that the thing that costs is not so much the setting up into print but keeping the setters-up waiting once they have begun."

"The end came suddenly," Wolfe says almost ludicrously in *The Story of a Novel*, "—the end of those five years of torment and incessant productivity. In October I took a trip to Chicago, a two weeks' vacation, my first in over a year. When I returned I found that my editor had quietly and decisively sent the manuscript to the press, the printers were already at work on it, the proof was beginning to come in. I had not foreseen it; I was desperate, bewildered. 'You can't do it,' I told him, 'the book is not yet finished. I must have six months more on it.'

"To this he answered that the book was not only finished, but that if I took six months more on it, I would then demand another six months and six months more beyond that, and that I might very well become so obsessed with this one work that I would never get it published. He went on to say, and I think with complete justice, that such a course was wrong for me. I was not, he said, a Flaubert kind of writer. I was not a perfectionist. I had twenty, thirty, almost any number of books in me, and the important thing was to get them produced and not to spend the rest of my life in perfecting one book. He agreed that with six months' additional work upon the book, I might achieve a certain finish and completeness, but he did not think that the benefit would be nearly as great as I thought it would be, and his own deep conviction was that the book should be published at once without further delay, that I should get it out of me, forget about it, turn my life to the final completion of the work which was already prepared and ready, waiting for me. He told me, furthermore, exactly what the nature of the criticism would be, the criticism of its length, its adjectives, its overabundance, but he told me not to despair.

"He told me finally that I would go on and do better work, that I would learn to work without so much confusion, waste, and useless torment, that my future books would more and more achieve the unity, sureness, and finality that every artist wants his work to have, but that I had to learn in the way I had learned, groping, struggling, finding my own way for myself, that this was the only way to learn."

Wolfe's account of Perkins' exhortation to him is undoubtedly correct, but the manuscript of *Of Time and the River* actually went to press early in July instead of in October as he says. In a letter to Catherine Brett written on July 12 Wolfe said: "Mr. Perkins sent my huge manuscript to the press yesterday. It threw me into a kind of panic for a while." Moreover, on August 21 he wrote his mother that "the proofs of my book have begun to come in and we already have about half of it in type." When he wrote *The Story of a Novel* six months later, he evidently confused the date of the manuscript's being sent to press with that of Perkins' next decisive step—his returning the galley proofs to the press to be put into page proofs without waiting for Wolfe to read them.

For Wolfe, in his reluctance to let the book be published, failed completely to read his proofs. Instead, as Perkins says in the *Harvard Library Bulletin,* "he sat brooding over them for weeks in the Scribner library and not reading. John Wheelock read them and we sent them to the printer and told Tom it had been done. I could believe otherwise he might have clung to them to the end."[13] One week before the publication of the book, when Miss Nowell went to help Wolfe sort and pack his manuscript before he sailed for Europe, she found the floor, the mantelpiece, and most of the furniture of his apartment strewn with galleys, and asked him what they were. "Oh," he answered ruefully, "that's the reader's set of galleys for my book. I was supposed to read them, but I guess it's too late now."

Wolfe had also failed to read a great deal of his manuscript before he had given it to Perkins, with the result that many of his typists' errors in deciphering his writing went undetected through four stages of proofs until the book was published. Moreover, since parts of the manuscript were written in the first person, Wheelock was obliged to change them to third person all the way through. There was one "I" which might have been intended to mean "I, the author," and which Wheelock therefore did not change to "he." Wolfe discovered it after the book was published, and brooded over it for several years. When

[13] From "Thomas Wolfe," in the Autumn 1947 issue of the *Harvard Library Bulletin.*

in his alcohol-induced black moods, he would telephone to Wheelock in the middle of the night. "Look at line 37 on page 487[14] of *Of Time and the River*," he would snarl at the poor sleep-numbed man. "Do you see that 'I'? You *betrayed* me, and I thought you were my friend!"

All of these mistakes were caught in later printings of the book, but because Wolfe did not ask for the corrections until after publication, they had to be made by the costly process of patching the cast plates. The total bill for excess alterations came to $1180.60, and Wolfe was shocked and angered when this was deducted from his royalty account. He admitted that the deduction was not only customary but specifically agreed to in his contract: nevertheless, he nursed a deep conviction that because Scribners had read his proofs for him, they should also bear the staggering expense of the corrections which had to be made, and the fact that they had done so with *Look Homeward, Angel* made him resent the charge made against him even more. This rankled in his mind until a whole year later, when, in April 1936, he again complained bitterly about it to Perkins.

By August the first proofs of *Of Time and the River* had started coming from the press, and Perkins and Wheelock were endeavoring to persuade Wolfe to give up writing new material and, instead, to read his proofs. He seems to have made some attempt to read at least the first eleven galleys of Book I, for he wrote a note to Wheelock saying that he was "not wholly satisfied with the way it *flows*." But by the middle of September, Wheelock was still asking him: "When are you going to let me have back the first thirty-eight galleys which you and I went over together and which are, as I recall it, now ready for the printer?" Wolfe, however, was working desperately to complete "another big section" for his book while there still was time for it to be included. "The proofs of my book are now coming in," he wrote to his friends the L. Effingham de Forests, "and although a desperate struggle is being waged between the young author and his publisher, one to put in and the other to take out, I think the publisher may soon prevail. . . . From now on until they take the manuscript away from me finally and irrevocably, I have a tremendous job of work to do . . . There is something final and terrifying about print, even about proof, and I want to pull myself together for this big effort and keep at it if need be

---

[14] This is one of the places where an "I" appeared instead of a "he" in the first edition of *Of Time and the River*. Wheelock does not remember the exact line and page number that Wolfe used to complain about.

until I drop. My instinct prompts me to go away right now for several days and try to get myself in shape for this final struggle."

Ten days later, when he had reached a state of complete exhaustion, he boarded a train "on the spur of the moment" and rode by day coach all the way to Chicago to visit the World's Fair. But his "several days" were prolonged by his total disregard of time and his eagerness to explore America, and it was not till two weeks later, after stop-offs to see Ohio and Pittsburgh, that he returned. He was refreshed and ready for "the final struggle," but he had already lost it by his prolonged absence: Perkins had had the first 71 galleys read by Wheelock and had returned them to the press: moreover, he had resolved to follow this procedure till the entire book was set in pages, regardless of whether Wolfe read any of his proofs or not. "We finally told him," he wrote later to Frere, "that whatever came, we were going to send back twenty galleys a day to be put into pages." By October 31, 195 galleys had been sent back to the press. "Tom threatens to tear everything to pieces and put in a few hundred thousand more words," Perkins wrote to Frere on that date, "but I rather think the book will stand about as it is."

In the face of Perkins' determination, Wolfe gave in and went into a noncreative slump. "I'm just a bum and haven't done a thing—not written a line or done a lick of work for six weeks now," he wrote dejectedly to Elizabeth Lemmon on November 8, ". . . and I hadn't worked for almost a month when I went down there. I just led an eating sleeping drinking kind of life. All I know how to do now is work and if I don't do that I'm a bum." Miss Lemmon was a close friend of the Perkinses and had invited Wolfe to visit her beautiful old farm, Welbourne, in Middleburg, Virginia. Perkins had suggested it because, as Wolfe explained to her, "Max . . . thinks that if I saw your place my knowledge of American life would be greatly enlarged and deepened," and also because he wanted to prevent Wolfe from writing any more, or from interfering with the reading of his proofs. Wolfe arrived at Welbourne with a suitcaseful of unread galleys and explained that he had promised Perkins to correct them, whereupon he locked the bag and announced that he did not intend to open it. But at any rate, the last thing Perkins wanted was to have Wolfe make any changes in the galleys then, at that late date, when they had already been read by Wheelock and were being set in page proofs. Keeping the author otherwise engaged while his book was rushed through the press was a strange procedure, but Perkins now had definitely scheduled *Of Time and the River* for publication early in the spring of 1935, and he lived in dread lest Wolfe should somehow manage to delay it.

All through November, Perkins and Wheelock worked furiously to get the book set up in page proofs without Wolfe's interference, but in December they were forced to call on him to do some actual writing. "We . . . got not far from the end of the book, where something had to be done," Perkins wrote to Frere on December 18, "and for the last week he has been writing. I do not know what the result will be, but I suppose it will mean a very long passage which will need cutting. But it seems as though we ought to be able to send you complete page proof by the end of this month, or early in the next."

Finally, in the middle of January, the book was completely set in pages and began coming from the press in foundry proofs. "The battle seems nearly over, and I am still alive," Perkins wrote triumphantly to Frere on January 16. "I am sending you 766 pages in foundry, with the rest to follow soon." His jubilation was quite understandable, considering the strain he had been under for the past three and a half years, but Wolfe was still beset by doubts. "For better or for worse," he wrote to Robert Raynolds, "everything I can now do about my book has been done and ended. It has all now been taken out of my hands and put into pages and I cannot make a change or alteration now even if I would. Of course I continue to have regrets. I feel that I have been very lazy during the last two months and think of all the additional scenes I could have written. But Perkins and Wheelock both feel that these scenes would not contribute as much as I think they would and in fact might do more harm than good. I hope they are right. At any rate, it is over, done for, ended, and in this awful fatality of print I feel now, come what may, a kind of tremendous relief."

As Bernard De Voto later pointed out, it was a strange way to end a novel: "The end of a novel is, properly, dictated by the internal pressure, osmosis, metabolism—what you will—of the novel itself, of which only the novelist can have a first-hand knowledge. There comes a point where the necessities of the book are satisfied, where its organic processes have reached completion. It is hard to see how awareness of that point can manifest itself at an editor's desk."[15] Wolfe had not reached this point with *Of Time and the River*—as he himself said later, "I was not through *writing*"—but the trouble was that Perkins was afraid he never *would* get through, and so, for better or for worse, had been impelled to take things into his own hands.

[15] From De Voto's "Genius Is Not Enough," which first appeared in the April 25, 1936, issue of the *Saturday Review of Literature* and was later included in *Forays and Rebuttals*, published in 1936 by Little, Brown.

XVI

ALL through the summer and fall of 1934 Wolfe had been quarreling sporadically with Perkins. One of his outbursts in late August had been so violent that Mrs. Perkins had written him a letter of remonstrance, pointing out with complete correctness that if he ever heard anyone else talk to Perkins that way, he would fight him. The trouble was that the two men had found a whole new source of disagreement: Wolfe's slowly awakening social consciousness and his desire to express it in his book. The vogue for left-wing writing had begun as a result of the depression and by this time had reached its peak in New York literary circles. Wolfe had been disgusted by the way the literati had jumped upon the left-wing band wagon, but he had readily recognized the evils and suffering of the depression. As he said later in his Purdue speech, "The effrontery and what seemed to me also to be the bland dishonesty of these quick conversions disgusted and repelled me. But it was nevertheless manifest that something in the structure of the life around us was seriously amiss. I had seen the evidences of collapse in the collapse of my own town; and now new evidences were coming to me day by day. . . . Young men were writing manifestoes in the higher magazines of Manhattan, but the weather of man's life, the substance and the structure of the world in which he lives, was soaking in on me in those years in Brooklyn."

In *The Story of a Novel* he explains more specifically what these evidences of the depression were and how they "soaked in on him" during his long nocturnal wanderings: "In this endless quest and prowling of the night through the great web and jungle of the city, I . . . felt . . . the full weight of that horrible human calamity. I saw a man whose life had subsided into a mass of shapeless and filthy rags, devoured by vermin; wretches huddled together for a little warmth in freezing cold, squatting in doorless closets upon the foul seat of a public latrine within the very shadow, the cold shelter of palatial and stupendous monuments of wealth. I saw acts of sickening violence and cruelty, the menace of brute privilege, a cruel and corrupt authority trampling ruthlessly below its feet the lives of the poor, the weak, the wretched, and defenseless of the earth.

"And the staggering impact of this black picture of man's inhumanity to his fellow man, the unending repercussions of these scenes of suffering, violence, oppression, hunger, cold, and filth and poverty going on unheeded in a world in which the rich were still rotten with their wealth left a scar upon my life, a conviction in my soul which I shall never lose."

This new conviction was so strong that Wolfe began trying to impose it on his book by attributing it to Eugene Gant. But up to that point Eugene had been, in Wolfe's own words, "colored a good deal by the romantic aestheticism of the period" which had preceded the depression. "He was, in short," as Wolfe said in his Purdue speech, "'the artist' in pretty much the Harvard Forty-seven Workshop sense of the word—the wounded, sensitive, the extraordinary creature in conflict with his environment, with the Babbitt, the Philistine, the small town, the family." Perkins felt that Wolfe's new viewpoint was incongruous to Eugene's character and to the period in which the book was set, and he therefore fought against it on artistic grounds. "Old Tom has been trying to change his book into a kind of Marxian argument (having written most of it some years before he ever heard of Marx)" he wrote to Hemingway, "and I have been trying to express to him . . . that what convictions you hold on economic subjects will be in whatever you write, if they are really deep. So you don't have to drag them in."[1]

Among Wolfe's papers which are now at Harvard there is an astonishing typewritten announcement:

Thomas Wolfe, the author of Look Homeward, Angel, whose new novel Of Time and the River: A Legend of Man's Hunger in His Youth is in process of manufacture at the Scribner Press, has joined the Communist party. He took this step after long and serious thought and study. He is one of the very few who call themselves Communists who have actually been taken into the party itself into which admission is very difficult. His proletarian sympathies, though never directly expressed, are implicit in his new novel, as in some degree they were in his famous Look Homeward, Angel.

This is astonishing not only because Wolfe never was and never would have been a Communist, but also because some slight revisions in

[1] From Perkins' letter to Hemingway of November 28, 1934, reprinted in Editor to Author: The Letters of Maxwell E. Perkins.

the announcement and its final sentence are in the handwriting of Perkins, the last person on earth who would have wanted to announce Wolfe's joining of the party if he had ever done so. Actually, it was a joke which Perkins played on Wolfe when he was trying to persuade him against the injection of Marxian beliefs into his book. He showed it to him very casually one day, saying that it was a publicity note which Scribners was about to send out to the newspapers, and asking if he approved of it. As Perkins' former secretary, Irma Wyckoff Muench, who typed the announcement at his dictation, has pointed out, "That last handwritten sentence was what he tried so hard to have Tom understand—that his ideas need not be directly expressed—that they would come out indirectly in anything he wrote."[2]

Perkins finally won the argument to the extent that no Marxian beliefs were expressed in *Of Time and the River*. However, his victory was only temporary, and although Wolfe yielded to him on artistic grounds, he had a deep conviction that Perkins' attitude was colored by his innate conservatism. From this time forth the two men argued bitterly about politics and economics until the irreconcilable difference in their views became one of Wolfe's chief reasons for his final break with Perkins: in fact, the only reason which he considered important enough to discuss in his farewell to him at the conclusion of *You Can't Go Home Again*.

Now, however, in the early spring of 1935, all of Wolfe's resentment against Perkins was, for the time being, forgotten in the pleasure and excitement which he always felt when a book was on the verge of publication. Even his conviction that he had not been allowed to work long enough on *Of Time and the River* was temporarily allayed, and he felt a great new surge of gratitude to Perkins for having guided and supported him through the agony of writing it and brought him to his present delightful state of accomplishment and relief. He wanted to tell the entire world what he had done for him, and he began composing a dedication which expressed his gratitude with characteristic exaggeration and verbosity: the first version which he wrote was three entire pages long.

Perkins did not see this first version but was told of it by Wheelock, and he wrote to Wolfe to protest against it because of all the bitter disagreements they had had about the book: "Nothing could give me greater pleasure or greater pride as an editor than that the book of the

[2] From a letter written to the author by Mrs. Muench. Grateful acknowledgment is made to her for the details of this incident.

writer whom I have most greatly admired should be dedicated to me
if it were sincerely done. But you cannot, and should not, try to change
your conviction that I have deformed your book, or at least prevented it
from coming to perfection. It is therefore impossible for you sincerely
to dedicate it to me, and it ought not to be done. I know we are truly
friends and have gone through much in company, and this matter, for
my part, can have nothing to do with that, or ever shall. . . . The way
in which we are presenting this book must prove our (and my) belief
in it. But what I have done has destroyed *your* belief in it and you
must not act inconsistently with that fact."[3]

Finally Wolfe was persuaded by Wheelock to condense the dedication to the eight-line version which appears in *Of Time and the River*:

To Maxwell Evarts Perkins
A great editor and a brave and honest man, who stuck to the writer of this
book through times of bitter hopelessness and doubt and would not let
him give in to his own despair, a work to be known as *Of Time and the
River* is dedicated with the hope that all of it may be in some way worthy
of the loyal devotion and the patient care which a dauntless and unshaken
friend has given to each part of it, and without which none of it could have
been written.

Perkins did not see this dedication until the first bound copies of the
book came from the press in early February. He immediately wrote
and thanked Wolfe for it, but, as he said later in the *Harvard Library
Bulletin*, "though I was most grateful for it, I had forebodings when
I heard of his intention. . . . It gave shallow people the impression
that Wolfe could not function as a writer without collaboration, and
one critic even used some such phrase as 'Wolfe and Perkins—Perkins
and Wolfe, what way is that to write a novel.' "[4]

But if this was true of the dedication of *Of Time and the River*,
it was a great deal more so of Wolfe's proposed introduction to the
book. When Perkins read the latter, he advised against it: Wolfe
argued for it: and they had, as Perkins wrote to Frere, "quite a time
about it," in the course of which Wolfe accused Perkins of exerting
too dictatorial control upon his entire book. But Perkins remained

[3] From Perkins' letter to Wolfe of January 21, 1935, reprinted in *Editor to
Author: The Letters of Maxwell E. Perkins.*

[4] From "Thomas Wolfe," in the Autumn 1947 issue of the *Harvard Library
Bulletin.*

adamant. "As for your preface," he wrote to Wolfe, "there is this obstacle to it at the start: a reader is meant to enter into a novel as if it
were reality, and so to feel it, and a preface tends to break down that
illusion and to make him look at it in a literary way. But perhaps that is,
in some degree, a literary objection to a preface and when yours began
so finely I thought you might be right to have it. But when I read
more of it today, it seemed to me you did the very things you meant to
avoid doing in the novel: you made the book seem personal and autobiographical, and by showing resentment against those who objected
to the apparent reality (as the preface implied) of the characters of the
'Angel,' you opened yourself to the same charge against *this* book and
notified the whole public that it might rightly be brought. . . . In
these, and other ways, I thought, you bared yourself to all the enemies
you have and I told you so because I am your friend."[5]

With characteristic delicacy, Perkins did not say that one of the
"other ways" in which the preface laid Wolfe open to attack was its
admission of how much he himself had helped Wolfe in the writing of
the book. It described this guidance step by step, in seeming innocence
of the fact that writers usually do not have and do not need such aid,
and with a sort of naïve wonder, it attributed the miracle of the book's
completion to Perkins, and to him alone. When it finally was published
one year later as *The Story of a Novel*, it was seized upon as an admission of weakness by Wolfe's "enemies," who ridiculed him not only
for his method of writing but also for his frankness in describing it.
Chief among them was Bernard De Voto, who, in his review "Genius
Is Not Enough," declared that "one indispensable part of the artist
has existed not in Mr. Wolfe but in Maxwell Perkins" and went on
to criticize Wolfe's work as the product of "the assembly-line at
Scribners." Perkins had realized that there was danger of something
of this sort. However, he could not foresee the grave effect it would have
on Wolfe—the compulsion it would give him to sever his relationship
with Scribners and with himself to prove, as he said later, "that I could
write my books myself." From a vantage point of twelve years later,
Perkins was able to sum it up: "No writer could possibly tolerate the
assumption . . . that he was dependent as a writer upon anyone else.
He had to prove to himself and to the world that this was not so."[6]
And the irony of it was that Wolfe had started the whole thing himself,
out of sheer goodhearted gratitude to Perkins.

[5] From Perkins' letter to Wolfe of January 21, 1935.
[6] From "Thomas Wolfe."

Of Time and the River was scheduled to come out on March 8, 1935, but remembering how intensely Wolfe had reacted to the publication of *Look Homeward, Angel*, Perkins and he decided that this time he should go abroad to escape the excitement. He accordingly booked passage on the *Ile de France* for March 2, and it was lucky that he did: by the middle of February he was already becoming embroiled in the confusion and hysteria which seemed unavoidable for him at times like this. In order to help his book with a little advance publicity, Scribners arranged for him to be interviewed for the daily *Herald Tribune*, but when the piece was published it turned out to be written in ridicule of Wolfe.

Characteristically, he had forgotten all about the visit of the interviewer, Sanderson Vanderbilt, till the time when he was scheduled to arrive, and had then rushed out to eat lunch and buy a bottle of liquor with which to fortify himself for the ordeal, leaving a note for Vanderbilt to walk into his apartment and "make himself at home." During the hour which Wolfe kept him waiting, Vanderbilt wrote an on-the-spot description of his bachelor abode: the unwashed breakfast dishes, the empty icebox and the food set out to keep cool on the window sill, the piles of manuscripts and the clay jug full of stubby pencils, the broken furniture, the lamp devoid of shade and bulb, the unpaid telephone bill for $17.18 (which Wolfe explained was owed him by some neighbors who had used his phone to make long-distance calls), the hastily made bed, and the aged green alarm clock which would only run when laid flat on its face. The interview then proceeded to describe the entrance of Wolfe himself, "with a good two inches of blue shirt separating the bottom of his rumpled vest from the top of his unpressed pants," and to quote his discussion of his forthcoming book, interlarded with confidential asides to Vanderbilt such as "Now don't make that sound kind of fancy" and "You fix it up if it sounds like boasting because, damn it, I need some money and I want to sell this book." Finally it ended by saying: "Mr. Wolfe lit another cigarette and ran his fingers wildly through his hair. He said he was exhausted from the effort of bringing his novel into shape. He wants to rest and go away now. 'I'm a nut!' he cried."[7]

The piece could do no lasting harm, although it was not exactly the favorable build-up for Wolfe and his new novel which Scribners had intended it to be. However, the chief trouble with it was that it

[7] From Sanderson Vanderbilt's interview with Wolfe, in the February 18, 1935, *Herald Tribune*.

was so upsetting to poor Wolfe. He felt that Vanderbilt had "played a dirty trick" on him: he could talk of nothing else for days: and when the Asheville *Citizen* reprinted the piece a few weeks later, he had to run the gamut of rage and shame again, at being held up to ridicule in his own home town.

On top of this, one of the literary hangers-on who had tried to force his friendship upon Wolfe grew venomously angry when Wolfe failed to read his novel or to return a letter which he had sent him, and he wrote him saying that he had asked for *Of Time and the River* to review for the *Herald Tribune* Books section but had been told by them that Sinclair Lewis had already written a review of it and that it was unfavorable. Wolfe immediately went into a panic. "I almost got sick at the stomach," he wrote a little later to his sister Mabel, "not only because of the horrible display of venom . . . but also because I thought it was really true what he said about the *Tribune* and Sinclair Lewis and, after all these years of work, to have my book ruined at the beginning and to have a man like Lewis turn on me seemed about as rotten a break in luck as I could imagine. Well, I called up Max Perkins immediately and told him I had bad news for him . . . I was in a pretty excited state—in addition to the disappointment and bad luck of it, I thought that if a high class publication like the *Herald Tribune* could stoop to reveal the contents of an unfavorable review two weeks or more before publication and to run the book down two weeks before it was published, it was almost as rotten and unfair a trick as I had ever heard of. Max was very quiet and calm and told me to come in later in the day. When I got to Scribners later in the day, they had telephoned the *Herald Tribune*, explained the contents of the letter, and asked if it was true. The reply was this: That —— was known at the office as Public Nuisance and Bore Number 1; that he was constantly coming in and pestering them; that they never gave him books to review; that there was not the remotest possibility of his reviewing my book for the *Tribune*; that no one there had ever discussed my book with him; that it had *not* been given to Sinclair Lewis to review, but to Burton Rascoe, and that no one knew whether Rascoe's review was favorable or unfavorable."

In the meanwhile Wolfe had decided to move out of Brooklyn. He arranged to leave his crates of manuscript at Scribners and his furniture with his friends the Smith Ely Jelliffes, and Mrs. Jelliffe was now performing herculean labors to get him packed up and moved. First she threw out all of his broken furniture except a few good pieces, which she sent to be repaired; then she gave away all his clothes except the one good suit that he had on his back and the now-too-tight tuxedo which Mrs. Bernstein had got for him eight years before. Finally she sorted out the nondescript collection of old letters, laundry slips, and hotel bills dating back to 1920 which he kept jammed into battered suitcases: this took her a long time because he was in terror that she "might be throwing away part of a valuable manuscript" and insisted on examining each scrap of paper as she threw them in a pile in the middle of the floor.[8]

His actual manuscripts had already been sorted by himself and Miss Nowell and put carefully away in the big pine packing cases which he had especially for them: the day before he was to sail he delivered them to Scribners, except for the biggest, which, ostensibly because Scribners was closed for the night when he arrived there, he took to Perkins' house in Turtle Bay. "Tom and I and the taxi man carried it in and set it down," Perkins wrote later. "Then Tom said to the man: 'What is your name?' He said, 'Lucky.' 'Lucky!' said Tom—I think it was perhaps an Americanization of some Italian name—and grasped his hand. It seemed a good omen. We three had done something together. We were together for that moment. We all shook hands. But for days, that huge packing case blocked our hall until I got it removed to Scribners."[9]

Finally, owing to the valiant efforts of Mrs. Jelliffe, he got on board the *Ile de France*, together with his suitcases, books, newspaper, notebooks, a handful of unopened mail, his overcoat, an extra pair of shoes hung on one arm by their tied-together laces, a number of badly wrapped brown-paper parcels, the portable typewriter which he had bought but never learned to use, the huge paper bag of fruit which he had insisted on stopping to buy on the way to catch the boat although Mrs. Jelliffe had assured him that the French Line would serve him all the fruit he wanted, and the package of frayed shirts which he had left at his Brooklyn laundry and which had been delivered by a fat and frantic laundryman just as the ship was about to sail.[10]

But in spite of this fortunate departure and the good omen of Lucky the taxi driver, Wolfe was in a desperate frame of mind. "As the ship got farther and farther from the American shores," he says in *The Story of a Novel*, "my spirits sank lower and lower, reaching, I think, the lowest state of hopeless depression they had ever known. This, I believe, was largely a physical reaction, the inevitable effect of

[8] From Belinda Jelliffe's unpublished reminiscences of Wolfe.
[9] From "Thomas Wolfe."
[10] From Belinda Jelliffe's unpublished reminiscences of Wolfe.

relaxation upon a human organism which had for five years been strained to its utmost limit. My life seemed to me to be like a great spring which had been taut for years and which was now slowly uncoiling from its tension. I had the most extraordinary sense of desolation I had ever known when I thought about my book. I had never realized until now how close I had been to it, how much a part of me it had become, and now that it had been taken away from me, my life felt utterly futile, hollow as a shell. And now that the book was gone, now that there was nothing more that I could do about it, I felt the most abysmal sensation of failure. I have always been somewhat afraid of print, although print is a thing I have tried so hard to achieve. Yet it is literally true that with everything I have ever written, I have felt when the hour of naked print drew nigh a kind of desperation and have even entreated my publisher not only to defer the publication of my book until another season, but have asked the editors of magazines to put off the publication of a story for another month or two until I had a chance to work on it some more, do something to it, I was not always sure what.

"Now I had an overwhelming sense of shame greater than any I had felt before. I felt as if I had ruinously exposed myself as a pitiable fool who had no talent and who once and for all had completely vindicated the prophecies of the critics who had felt the first book was just a flash in the pan. It was in this frame of mind that I arrived in Paris on March 8, the day the book was to be published in America. I had come away to forget about it, and yet I thought about it all the time."

In Paris his condition went from bad to worse. For three days and nights he could not sleep; he walked the streets and drank continually. He was bothered by a persistent dizziness, which he considered the result of a very rough voyage over, but his real trouble was his intense anxiety about the success or failure of his book. It was not till March 11 that he nerved himself to go to the American Express for the cable which Perkins had agreed to send him on publication day telling him how the book had been received. "Monday. No lunch—no breakfast— facing 'great test' at the American Express Co. . . . ," he wrote in his pocket diary. "And if the news is horribly *bad?* And if there is no news— *nothing?*"

The cablegram was there all right, and it read: "Magnificent reviews, somewhat critical in ways expected, full of greatest praise." It was actually an understatement of the tremendous critical acclaim which *Of Time and the River* had received, and it was not enough to dispel

Wolfe's fears. "I read it the first time with a feeling of almost intolerable joy," he said later, in *The Story of a Novel*, "but as I continued to read and reread it, the old dark doubt began to creep across my mind and by the time night had come I was convinced that this wonderful cable was just a sentence of doom, and that my editor, out of the infinite compassion of his spirit, had taken this means of breaking the news to me that my book was a colossal failure." The more he became convinced of this, the more he drank, and the more he drank, the more he was convinced. For two days more he was, as he wrote afterward to Perkins, "in the worst shape I have ever been in in my life. All the pent-up strain and tension of the last few months seemed to explode and I will confess to *you* that there were times there when I really was horribly afraid I was going mad." Finally he cabled Perkins: "To-day if I mistake not is Wednesday March thirteenth. I can remember almost nothing of last six days. You are the best friend I have. I can face blunt fact better than damnable incertitude. Give me the straight plain truth."

Perkins' answer to this was unmistakable, even to Wolfe in his abnormal state: "Grand excited reception in reviews. Talked of everywhere as truly great book. All comparisons to greatest writers. Enjoy yourself with light heart." "To-day the grand wonderful beautiful news came," Wolfe wrote in his pocket diary. ". . . Already feel better and believe I'll be quieted down and all right in a day or two." By the time he left Paris for England ten days later, he was in a much calmer state of mind. Moreover, he was greatly reassured by the companionship of Frere, who met him at the Channel boat at Folkestone and took him to his country house in Aldington before driving him on up to London. Wolfe settled down again in London, in a service flat in Hanover Square, and here at last he received a heartening letter from Perkins enclosing excerpts from the chief American reviews of *Of Time and the River*. But he still was dubious about the book's success, and still bitterly regretful for his failure to have brought it to perfection, and in a long letter which he wrote to Perkins in installments from March 31 to April 7, he poured out his reaction to the entire thing:

"I hope to God it all really is true as you said—that we have had a genuine and great success and that when I come back I will find my position enormously enhanced. . . . If that is true—if it is true that we have successfully surmounted the terrible, soul-shaking, heart-rending barrier of the accursed 'second book'—I believe I can come back to work with the calm, the concentration, the collected force of my full power which I was unable to achieve in these frenzied, tormented, and soul-doubting last five years. More than ever before, I have come to realize during this past month when I have had time to look back on that period and take stock of it—more than ever before I have come to realize how much the making of a book becomes an affair of honor to its maker. The honor of the artist—his whole life, all his character and personal integrity, all that he hopes and wants and dreams of, everything that gives his life any value to him—is at stake each time he produces any work—and that is really what the whole business of creation amounts to in the end.

"I hope to God that you and I have come through this ordeal honorably—I hope that we have won a true and worthy victory. You, I think, have done so in your great labors with me as an editor and a man. As for myself, the victory, if I have really won it, while a precious one, is not entire and whole as I would make it. If I have made my stamp come through—if through the ordeal and the agony of that book, the main outline of my full intention is revealed—that is a victory. But I can not ease my heart with the thought that I came through unshaken—I was badly shaken, time and again I was driven to the verge of utter self-doubt and despair by the sense of pressure all around me—the questions asked, the doubts expressed about my ability to write another book, the criticisms of my style, my adjectives, verbs, nouns, pronouns, etc., my length and fullness, my lack of Marxian politics and my failure to expound a set position in my writings—by all this, and countless other evidences of this pressure, I allowed myself so seriously to be disturbed and shaken that once or twice I may have been upon the very brink of total failure and submission. And now, although, thanks to your great and patient efforts, I may have won through to a victory—and pray to God this may be so!—that victory, as I say, is but a partial one, the full sum and import of my purpose has not been revealed. I feel I have by no means begun to make a full and most effective use of my talent, and I hope this book will give me a position of some security, and freedom at last from the kind of perturbations that have tormented me these past five years, so that I may be able to achieve the concentration and totality I desire. . . .

"Now, as to those excerpts from the reviews you sent me. They were splendid, wonderfully heartening, and I hope they were not too *hand-picked*—i.e. I hope that, as you said, they were taken more or less at random, and if the reviews on the whole were, as you say, better than these excerpts would indicate, that would be wonderful. But even from these excerpts, good as they are, and from one or two indications in advance notices before I left New York, I think I can spot the trend of some of the enthusiasm. Max, Max, perhaps you think I hate all forms of criticism, but the sad truth is, how much more critical am I, who am generally supposed to be utterly lacking in the critical faculty, than most of these critics are. . . . I know for example that the great length of the book will be criticized, but the real, the tragic truth is that the book is not too long, but too short. I am not talking of page-length, word-length, or anything like that—as I told you many times, I did not care whether the final length of the book was 300, 500, or 1000 pages, so long as I had realized completely and finally my full intention—and that was not realized. I still sweat with anguish—with a sense of irremediable loss—at the thought of what another six months would have done to that book—how much more whole and perfect it would have been. Then there would have been no criticism of its episodic character—for, by God, in purpose and in spirit, that book was not episodic but a living whole and I could have made it so—the whole inwrought, inweaving sense of time and of man's past conjoined forever to each living present moment of his life could have been made manifest—the thing that I *must* and *will* get into the whole thing somehow.

"Again, people will talk of the book having taken five years to write, but the real truth of the matter was that it was written practically in the whole in a year—it was written too fast, with frenzied maddened haste, under a terrible sense of pressure after I had written two other antecedent books and found I had not got back to a true beginning. It is the work of frenzied, desperate, volcanic haste after too much time had slipped away, and no one will know that. Even now, I can not read the book, save for a page or two at a time—at every point the deficiency of my performance compared with the whole of my intent stares me in the face—the countless errors in wording and proof-reading —for which *I* alone am utterly to blame, but which in my frenzied state of mind I let pass by—stab me to the heart. I was not ready to read proof. I was not through *writing*—the fault is my own. I fell down on that final job, the book was written and typed and rushed in to you in such frantic haste day after day that I did not even catch the errors in wording the typist made in an effort to decipher my handwriting— there are *thousands* of them. . . .

"Max, Max, I cannot go on, but I am sick at heart—we should have waited six months longer—the book, like Caesar, was from its mother's womb untimely ripped—like King Richard, brought into the world 'scarce half made up.' Before I went away, you wrote me, in reference to the introduction I wanted to write, that you were trying to 'save me from my enemies.' Max, my enemies are so much more numerous than you expect . . . and I fear we have played directly into their hands by our carelessness and by our frenzied haste—our failure to *complete* just when completion was in our grasp. I gravely fear that by the time this reaches you the reaction will have set in—the enemy will have gathered itself together and the attack begun."

Wolfe's conviction about his book was an unshakable and true one, but fortunately the reviewers and the general reading public were not as critical of it as he. The "reaction" to the first favorable reception of it had not "set in": instead, it had been second or third on the best-seller lists ever since its publication, had gone into five printings, and sold 20,000 copies in its first six weeks. "The terrible, soul-shaking, heart-rending barrier of the accursed 'second book'" had been successfully surmounted, and Wolfe had become established as one of the foremost writers in America. As he said later in *You Can't Go Home Again*, "he was a famous man," but he was not to realize it until another month had passed.

XVII

THE first major review to turn the tide in favor of *Of Time and the River* was Henry Seidel Canby's "The River of Youth" in the March 9 issue of the *Saturday Review of Literature*. It was really a long essay on the American picaresque novel in general and Wolfe's book in particular, and cannot be adequately quoted here, but it said in part:

"*Of Time and the River* . . . is the epitome, after so many books, of the troublous and disintegrating years of the twenties when Mr. Wolfe was young. And those who wish to get in fullest and most impassioned form the spiritual record of those years, or who would see as in a newsreel the typical scenes of that period as youth saw them, will find, if they are persistent, what they want in this book, which is neither fiction nor autobiography, but both. . . .

"It is a wholly American book, one of the most American books of our time. It is in the direct tradition of those earlier anguished spirits and great seekers on our soil, Thoreau, Melville, Whitman. It is in the tradition, but with a momentous difference for which the break-up of the twenties and Mr. Wolfe's own idiosyncrasies are responsible. Yet if I should wish to know what these twenties meant to an American youth still asking the questions asked by his spiritual ancestors . . . I should go to this book. If I fail to give a clear account of Mr. Wolfe's thousand-page story . . . , forgive me. Have you ever tried to review the *Encyclopaedia Brittanica*?

"Mr. Wolfe's odd thousand pages are condensed but not adequately described in the paragraphs above. He calls them fiction, and fiction they are of the kind that he put into *Look Homeward, Angel*, but better organized, more poetical where poetical, more sharply realistic when realistic. . . . But fiction in the strict sense they are not, nor story, nor drama, but rather spiritual autobiography in which the thousand incidents, many of them trivial, and the dozens of characters, many of them extraordinary, have as their excuse for being that a youth met them on his way. Plot there is none. Structure in the ordinary narrative sense, there is none. It is a picaresque novel with the distraught mind of a poet of the twenties as *picaro,* and the incidents adventures in seeking a spiritual home.

"To be more precise, this book is a study of American dualism, and it is this which gives it poignancy. Leaf through it and you will see as in a moving picture successive moments of prose and poetry. Here are the fleshy people of an intensely actual Carolina, of a literal Boston, and of a photographic France. No reporter could have done them more vividly as news, and indeed Wolfe is a great reporter. . . . And between these flashes of intimate, literal humanity from the man-swarm, the novel leaves the literal entirely and in a poetic prose that owes much to Whitman and a little to Joyce, but has become Wolfe's own, rises into a chorus of anguish, perplexity, and delight, which chants the loneliness and the impotence and the beauty of this America, and struggles to break through to some solution which will satisfy the seeker, who is the youth Gant, the hero, and the excuse for all this profusion of words. . . .

"So much for the purpose of this novel. Its achievement is less. With all its richness of detail, its passion, its poetry, and its intense realism of contemporary life, there is an impotence in this book like the impotence Wolfe ascribes to his America. . . . I think that this novel, like many other fiery and ambitious American books—like Melville's *Pierre,* like many of Whitman's poems, like the now-forgotten romantic philosophic extravaganzas so common in the magazines of a century ago—is an artistic failure. And Mr. Wolfe's books, as wholes, will continue to be artistic failures until he finds and controls a medium in which the ego is sublimated into an imagination less involved in the immediate circumstances of his life. Yet it is an important book, and Mr. Wolfe is an important writer. He has more material, more vitality, more originality, more gusto than any two contemporary British novelists put together, even though they may be real novelists and he is not. He stands to them as Whitman stood to the wearied *Idylls of the King.* And he entirely escapes the sordid, whining defeatism of so many of his American contemporaries. I am not fool enough to try to teach him how to write. No one can do that. He can write like his own angel now, he can make speech that is a new speech in fiction and yet unmistakably authentic, he can strike off flashing pictures. . . .

"But he has not yet made his book. He has poured out his heart into a mould, over a mould, spilling through a thousand pages. He has tried to be philosopher, poet, journalist-observer, satirist, story teller, historian, and dreamer, not all at once, which is quite possible, but one after the other, which cannot be done in a book, which, like a man,

no matter how complex, should be integrated, harmonious, homogene-
ous, and unmistakably not many but one."

Dr. Canby's conclusion was far from favorable, but in arriving at it,
he had praised *Of Time and the River* so glowingly that the general
impression he created was astonishingly complimentary. Moreover, the
book was given importance by the fact that it was the subject of the
lead article by Canby himself, as editor of the *Saturday Review*: his
discussion of it occupied most of the first two pages of the issue and
was enhanced by a large front-page photograph of Wolfe, and also by
a cartoon which whimsically depicted the New York critics as picket-
ing Scribners in protest at the book's great length. And finally, in the
brief list of books especially recommended, *Of Time and the River*
was given first place, as "a monumental novel depicting the youth of a
creative artist." It seemed as if the editors of the *Saturday Review* had
outdone themselves to present the book as favorably as possible to the
public, in spite of Dr. Canby's reservations about it as a complete artistic success.

The daily newspaper reviews were for the most part favorable, but,
as usual, it was the Sunday New York *Times* Book Review and *Herald
Tribune* Books which definitely established *Of Time and the River* as
a great success. In the March 10 issue of the former, the review by
Peter Munro Jack entitled "Mr. Wolfe's Pilgrim Progresses" said in
part:

"The superabundance that Thomas Wolfe shares with the great writers . . . is in the very nature of this richest of young American writers.
Where other men write a sentence he writes a paragraph: where they
write books he writes libraries. . . . This is not to be dismissed as a
writing-mania. It is an essential belief in the richness and variety of
living, to which only a 'huge chronicle of the billion forms, the million
names [of] the huge, single, and incomparable substance of America'
can do justice. For this ambitious program Mr. Wolfe has been born
lucky.

"A backward glance at *Look Homeward, Angel* reminds us at once
that the driving power lay in the astonishing Gants and Pentlands of
North Carolina from whom Eugene sprang. In them was a living force
that exhausted the extremes of comedy and tragedy. The emotional
richness of their life, solidly and stubbornly maintained; their gross and
mountainous sensuality, their ever-rising fury, the oaths and the violence, the terror and the sudden pity; above all, the unappeasable
hunger for sensation—all this is an overflowing spring of life, as ungovernable as it is enriching. Mr. Wolfe's characteristic material is

continuous and dynamic where so much in contemporary fiction is
static: it expands where so much else contracts into a poverty of
spirit. . . . It is not surprising that Mr. Wolfe should write so much;
it is surprising that a portion of his illimitable material should find
itself within the manageable covers of a book. . . .

"The rich and powerful sense of life inherited from the Gants
and Pentlands is . . . a burden as well as a blessing to Eugene. He
looks for its counterpart and can match it nowhere in his travels. As
he wanders further away from it, to England and to France, the book
loses some of its zest in action and character, while it grows in the
poignancy of its longing for a lost integrity. . . . But by himself again,
in the train journey to Orléans (Wolfe has a genius for trains: there is
not a dull train journey in the book) . . . the book mounts to its old
height. It is coming nearer to terms with itself. Eugene is learning not
to be disappointed with people for not being what he is. He no longer
expects places and people automatically to educate him and help him
find himself. . . . He returns to Ben's wisdom in the remarkable last
chapter of *Look Homeward, Angel*: 'Where, Ben? Where is the world?'
'Nowhere,' Ben said. '*You* are your world.' . . .

"It will be seen that this book is only one movement in an enormous
machine for recapturing Wolfe's past and his present idealism. . . . It
has a continuing pattern of time that never comes to an end, and so it
has that sense of being constantly working itself out in the present
tense. This sense of immediacy is on every page. Mr. Wolfe's sensuous
perceptions are, as he describes Helen's, 'literal, physical, chemical, as-
toundingly acute.' . . . The reality of what he sees possesses him in
every part of his body and there is no peace until every part of it, every
least and peculiar aspect, is caught up in a welter of evocative words.
No American novelist is so vigilant in the perception of character or
so urgent in its expression. Nor is any one, except perhaps Dreiser, so
unafraid of the immensity of life. This tremendous capacity for living
and writing lifts *Of Time and the River* into the class of great books.
It is a triumphant demonstration that Thomas Wolfe has the stamina
to produce a magnificent epic of American life."

The review in the March 10 *Herald Tribune* Books by Burton Rascoe
was even more sympathetic. Under a headline of "The Ecstasy, Fury,
Pain and Beauty of Life: Thomas Wolfe Sings and Shouts in his
Gargantuan New Novel," Rascoe said in part: "Thomas Wolfe has
chaos in him and he is giving birth to a whirling nebula. Sometimes
he writes like an intoxicated Gargantua bestriding the world and bellowing of pain and beauty. Again he is like a normal, virile and elephantine

Proust roaring his minute remembrances of things past in the sententious and stentorian manner of the Victor Hugo of 'La Légende des Siècles' and 'Postscriptum de ma Vie.' . . .

"Thomas Wolfe has a magnificent malady: it may be called gigantism of the soul. All the conditions of his life have determined this malady and, because he is also lyrically and vociferously articulate, we have a voice in this novel which sounds as if it were from demons, gods and seraphim—in chorus—and, strangely, a voice speaking of intimate and common things. . . .

"While reading Thomas Wolfe it is requisite or advisable to suspend one's ordinary critical faculties, trained, sharpened, and selective as they may be by familiarity with the hard, clear image, the deft concision, the precise pattern of much of our modern writing; for Wolfe is lush and exuberant, word-drunk like an Elizabethan, with utterable and unutterable music pounding in his brain. To the calm, the phlegmatic, the insensitive, the sophisticated, the disillusioned or the imperturbable reader much of Thomas Wolfe's first and second novels . . . may appear like the rough draft of multitudinous notes from which a novel, in the more ordinary sense of the term, might be selected, edited, polished and builded. But like the novels of Rabelais, Sterne and Fielding these are not novels by any prosaic or academic definition. They are a deluge of intensity.

"Thomas Wolfe makes a frenzied and beautiful effort to arrest time and to catch in words not only beauty but the very evanescence of beauty. Every instant, every moment in life, however trivial appearing, is pregnantly important to him. . . .

"If you look for a plot, a story in the usual sense in *Of Time and the River* you will not find it; but you will find a hundred stories and five years of life, richly experienced, deeply felt, minutely and lyrically recorded. . . . In these days when some of our best writers are tired or short of breath it is thrilling to contemplate and to read the teeming novels of Thomas Wolfe. They furnish also another satisfaction; they so effectively give the lie to such solemn, half-persuasive essays as those of Burke, Wilson et al. which allege that literature is running down in bulk, beam, vitality and gusto because civilization itself is running down. Wolfe writes as though the Spanish Armada had not very long ago been sunk by Drake and the expansion of the North American continent had just begun, for all that he is Southern born, a Harvard graduate and a Brooklyn resident intent upon leaving vivid and candid testimony of his experience on this earth."

The prominent position given to all of these reviews, and the large photographs of Wolfe with which they were illustrated, were due somewhat to the fact that Scribners was promoting *Of Time and the River* as their major fiction title for the spring and summer publishing season, with an initial advertising appropriation of ten thousand dollars.[1] The New York literary critics, also, were undoubtedly impressed by the personal enthusiasm of Mr. Perkins, whose natural reticence and whose conviction that books would "find their way" usually kept him from committing himself about them. Moreover, Wolfe's reputation as a writer of great promise had been mounting steadily ever since the publication of *Look Homeward, Angel:* this was the first occasion since that time for widespread comment on his work, and the wave of admiration for it now came to a crest after six and a half years of slowly gathering momentum. But, after all, the book had to be judged for itself by every critic who reviewed it: if it had not had the qualities to justify and reassert Wolfe's claim to a tremendous talent, the reaction to it could not have been as emphatically favorable as it was.

Because of all these factors, *Of Time and the River* had got off to a flying start in the first two days after publication, and the reviews that followed—first in the daily newspapers all over the United States, then in the weekly magazines, the monthly magazines, and finally the quarterlies—kept it going all through the spring and summer.

There was, of course, some adverse comment. Many of the reviewers shared the opinion of Canby and Rascoe that the book was by no means a finished novel, and several of them attributed this failure to an immaturity in Wolfe's own attitude toward life. Wolfe himself was the first to agree (in private) that the book was far from a finished piece of work, but he took violent exception to some of the minor adverse criticisms. Chief among these was a statement made by Rascoe in his review: "He has no evident sense of humor; nor any true sense of comedy. Even when he attempts to be playful or funny the effect is the disconcerting and uncomfortable one of a rictus, an attack of giggles, or the fantastic laugh of 'L'homme qui rit.'" Wolfe also had a strong dislike for a paragraph which had been written by Isabel M. Paterson in her "Turns with a Book Worm" column in the *Herald Tribune* Books section as early as February 24, 1935: "Mr. Wolfe . . . steps up the scale of everything—all his principal characters are highly exaggerated. They are seven feet tall with megaphone voices. We don't mind; he

[1] This figure is based on the recollection of John Hall Wheelock and Whitney Darrow of Scribners, since the actual record of the advertising appropriation for *Of Time and the River* is no longer in existence.

does manage to keep up the excitement. But it might be an interesting experiment to take one of his chapters and eliminate all the superlatives, the adjectives indicating altitude, volume, and violence. Step it down again to life size and see what would remain." Also Wolfe objected to a passage from Clifton Fadiman's review in the March 9, 1935, *New Yorker*: "It is open to debate whether he is a master of language or language a master of him; but for decades we have not had eloquence like his in American writing. His declamations and apostrophes, such as the one to America on page 155, are astounding and even beautiful; and even when mere rhetoric, they are mere gorgeous rhetoric. . . . At their best, these tempests of poetic prose . . . are overwhelming, and at their worst they are startlingly bad . . . Thus it is impossible to say any one thing of Mr. Wolfe's style. At its best it is wondrous, Elizabethan. At its worst, it is hyperthyroid and afflicted with elephantiasis."

Wolfe's reaction to all this was very typical: in the years since the appearance of *Look Homeward, Angel* he had learned not to "waste" himself "in exuberant elation because of the critics' and the readers' praise," but he still could not fight off his "anguish and bitterness because of their ridicule," and in the letter which he wrote to Perkins between March 31 and April 7, he poured out the latter in a long impassioned tirade:

"For God's sake, try to kill false rumors when you hear them. Before I left, I saw that they were beginning to make another rubber stamp under the name of 'criticism.' Apparently they had discovered that I was six and a half feet tall, and very large: therefore it follows that all my characters are seven feet tall—bellow and roar when they talk—that I can create nothing but a race of gigantic monsters. Max, for Christ's sake, I beg and plead with you, don't let this horrible goddamned lie go unanswered. I have never created a monster in my life, none of my people are seven feet tall. The *fault*, the *fault* always, as *you* should know, is not that we exceed the vital energy of life but that we fall short of it—and that a horrible misbegotten race of anaemic critics whose lives have grown underneath a barrel call out 'monster' and 'exaggeration' at you the moment you begin to approach the energy of life. You yourself told me you took one of your daughters through the Grand Central Station and showed her twenty people who might have stepped out of the pages of Dickens, and not a day of my life passes—a day spent in the *anguish of intense and constant speculation* and not at *literary cocktail parties*—that I do not see a hundred—no, a thousand—who, if you put them in a book, would immediately bring down upon your head the sneers of the Patersons, the Benéts, the Van

Dorens, and all of their ilk, of 'monsters,' 'seven feet tall,' 'untrue to life,' etc.

"In Christ's name, Max, what is wrong with us in America? The whole world—not myself alone—wants to know. The English ask me, everyone asks me, why do we cry out that what we want is life, and then try to destroy and kill the best people that we have? Why do our best writers, poets, men of talent turn into drunkards, dipsomaniacs, charlatans, cocktail-cliquers, creators of Pop-eye horrors, pederasts, macabre distortions, etc? I tell you, it is not I alone who ask the question, but everyone here—all of Europe knows it. Why is it that we are burnt out to an empty shell by the time we are forty, that instead of growing in strength and power we are done for—empty, burnt-out wrecks at an age when men in other countries are just coming to their full maturity? Is it because . . . there is something in the American air, the weather of the American life that burns the lives of men to rust as quickly as it rusts iron and steel?

"Or is it perhaps that there is in us a sterile, perverse, and accursed love and lust for death that wishes to destroy the very people that we set up—the people who have something to give that may be of value and honor to our life? Is it because we take a young man of talent— a young man proud of spirit, and athirst for glory, and full with the urge to create and make his life prevail—praise him up to the skies at first, and then press in upon him from all sides with cynics' eyes and scornful faces, asking him if he can *ever do it again* or is done for, finished, no good, through forever? Is it because we deal this hand of death to young proud people, telling them they are the lords of the earth one year, and the glory of their nation's country, and the next year sneering, jeering, laughing, reviling, scorning and mocking them with the very tongues that sang their praises just a year before? Is this the reason why we fail—the reason that our finest artists are destroyed? Tell me, is this the reason—men in England also ask me; they all want to know. And then how easy for them all, when we *are* done for—when we have been driven mad, when we are drunkards, dipsomaniacs, perverts, charlatans, burnt-out shells—how easy it is for the whole pack to pull the face of pious regret, to sigh mournfully, to say: 'What a pity!— We had hoped once—He looked so promising at one time!—What a shame he had to go and waste it all!'

"I know your answer to these questions—that the strong man is as Gibraltar, that all these assaults will fall harmlessly against his iron front, the impregnable granite of his invincible soul—but, alas, no man is as strong as that—it is a pleasant fable—his great strength is needed, to be concentrated on the work he does, and while his brows and every sinew of his life is bent to the giant labor of creation, what shall protect him from these coward-hordes who come to destroy his life from every side? Why should the artist—who is life's strongest man, earth's greatest hero—have to endure this in America of all the countries of the earth, when his task alone is so cruel hard there: the need for a new language, the creation of a new form so stern and formidable? Why should he have to do this great work, and at the same time withstand the murderous attack of death-in-life when in every country in Europe the artist is honored, revered, and cherished as the proudest possession that a nation has?

"Take this for what it is worth. If you think it extravagant, then take it so, but see the core of truth in this as well. I have given my life to try to be an artist, an honor to my country, to create beauty, and to win fame and glory, and the honor of my people, for myself, and what has it got me? At the age of thirty-four I am weary, tired, dispirited, and worn out. I was a decent-looking boy six years ago—now I am a bald, gross, heavy, weary-looking man. I wanted fame—and I have had for the most part shame and agony. They continue to speak of me as a 'writer of promise'—and if I only do 197 impossible things—which they doubt that I *can* do—something may come of my work in the end. The Paterson woman says my people are all seven feet tall and talk in bellowing voices—she says take away his adjectives, nouns, verbs, pronouns, words of violence, height, altitude, colour, size, immensity—and *where* would he be? The Mark Van Dorens[2] say take away his own experience, the events of his own life, forbid him to write about what he has seen, known, felt, experienced—and where would he be? The Fadimans say take away his apostrophes, declamations, lyrics, dreams, incantations—and where would he be? The Rascoes say he has no sense of humour—this, to the man who created old Gant, wrote the lunch room scenes in the *Angel*, Bascom Hawke in the *River*, *The Web of Earth*, Oswald Ten Eyck, the Countess, the Englishmen at the inn and all the others. The Communists say he is a romantic sentimentalist of

[2] This reference to Mark Van Doren was not occasioned by any review of *Of Time and the River*, but dated back to an article which Van Doren had published in the *Nation* on April 25, 1934, in which he had said: "Thomas Wolfe's one novel to date, *Look Homeward, Angel*, needs to be followed by others before anybody can know whether Mr. Wolfe is an artist in anything beyond autobiography. . . . The public is justified in asking Mr. Wolfe whether he can keep himself out of the picture in books to come."

the old worn-out romantic school, with no Marxian code; and the Saturday Reviewers, a depicter of the sordid, grim, horribly unpleasant and surrealistic school—and so it goes—in Christ's name what do these people want?[3] Apparently, I would be a good writer if I would only correct 3,264 fundamental faults, which are absolutely, profoundly and utterly incurable and uncorrectable—so what in Christ's name am I to do?"

It was with this wild question that Wolfe concluded his letter to Perkins—his first since the news of *Of Time and the River*'s great success. The tenor of his complaint was similar to that which he had written to Wheelock because of the two unfavorable English reviews of *Look Homeward, Angel* in August 1930, but it was now longer, deeper, more mature, and more in the style of W. O. Gant. Also, it was now poured out directly upon Perkins, of whom Wolfe had stood too much in awe to write him in this vein in 1930. During the past five years, as they had grown more intimate, Wolfe had fallen more and more into the habit of subjecting Perkins to his outbursts: their intimacy was by now complete, and Perkins had become less of a venerated idol and more of a whipping boy for Wolfe's black moods.

Wolfe had come to London chiefly to see the Freres, and for the first few days he was with them constantly. But he was still tired and on edge, and when they invited him to a literary party to meet the two du Mauriers and several other English writers, he, as usual, resorted to drinking to give himself courage. "Was rude to Sir Somebody and told of 18,000 new airplanes in Peru," he wrote later in his diary. "Talked of Ruggles of Red Gap[4] to young man—liked woman with him.

[3] In this report to his critics Wolfe did not mention Malcolm Cowley, whose review in the March 20, 1935, issue of the *New Republic* was one of the most unfavorable. The reason is that he did not see this review till April 23. "So down George Street to Oddenino's where beheld the *New Republic*," he wrote in his diary on that night. "Made me tremble with despair and hopelessness and a feeling of 'the day the world is to be made safe for the Cowleys, Josephsons, etc. forever.' So what, you god damned bums, not Wolfe, Cowley and Josephson forever."

[4] This was Wolfe's nickname for the valet who took care of him at his service flat in Hanover Square. He repeated this anecdote about him when he returned to the United States, and it was quoted as follows in the July 15, 1935, issue of *Time*: "I had a service flat in London with an English butler that was such a prude he would make Ruggles of Red Gap look like a blacksmith. . . . One night I decided to find out just what kind of a fellow he was under his servant's mask. I gave him so many whiskeys and sodas that I got cockeyed drinking

Frere asked me to stay and I stayed when all had gone and acted badly toward Frere—was drunk—left in an atmosphere of tension—went to find something to eat." He apologized to Frere the following morning, but two days later, when again with him and Mrs. Frere, he had another fit of drunken irascibility and finally apologized to Mrs. Frere "for my conduct of two nights before, thanked her for all she had done and told her I would not see her again—and stalked away feeling like a callow over-sensitive damn fool who had acted badly." In his embarrassment and pride, he avoided them for the remaining three weeks of his month in London, and when he finally encountered Frere by chance in one of his favorite restaurants, it was on the eve of his departure and so too late to do any more than say good-by.

By this time, however, Wolfe felt quite at home in London, and during his self-imposed exile from the Freres, he passed the time quite pleasantly with Hugh Walpole, Henry Roberts of Heinemann, the Charles Scribners, who were then in England on their annual business trip, and his old friends Hester Dowden and Catherine Carswell and the London literary people who attended their salons in Hampstead Heath. But for the most part he led the kind of solitary life which had become habitual with him when abroad, striding like a Paul Bunyan through the crowded streets and spring-green parks of London, going to the National Gallery to see his favorites—Hogarth's "Servants" and Breughel's "Adoration of the Kings"—watching the Oxford-Cambridge boat race and filling his pocket notebook with an inspired but largely illegible account of the race, the river Thames, and the English poor who lined its banks to watch the crews go by. ("I think it's pretty good," he later used to say of this, "if I can only read it.")

But all the time he still was ruminating on his troubles of the past six years. At the National Gallery he saw a resemblance between one of the figures in Marinus' "The Usurers" and Robert Cross of Scribners, who had doled his money out to him in small amounts since 1929; and the sight of the huge Turners and Rubenses only reminded him of how his own enormous works had been edited and cut. "It is a curious thing how people of every kind and condition, whether they know anything about writing or not, are instantly convinced that the proper thing

---

with him. He wouldn't sit down and relax, but just stood there tossing off the drinks without a change in his tone, manner or posture. Finally I said, 'For God's sake, can't you be human and talk for once like a human being?' And what do you suppose this guy said, without changing his deadpan expression — 'Begging your pardon, sir, but here in England, we're all a bit of a snob.' So that was that."

to do with any piece of writing is to 'cut'—'cut ruthlessly'—'be relent-less'—'don't spare yourself,' etc.," he wrote in his pocket diary. "It seems to be taken as a fundamental axiom of artistic truth that any book which exceeds 300 pages should be 'cut to the bone' and the result will eventually be a marked improvement. Why is this? So far as I know, this conviction (about the necessity of 'cutting') applies only to the art of writing. A man who waded into the paintings of Turner, or to go to more enormous canvases, those of Rubens, say, or Paolo Veronese, with a 'blue pencil' and a pair of shears, saying 'You don't need this, old boy—much too much of that—slash!—out she comes—I assure you you'll be the better for it in the end,' etc.—such a man, I say, would be regarded as a maniac and a dangerous criminal, but when the same thing is done to a man's book—and in God's name, what in art is more long in art than a book, what has more life and sinew than man's living language—when such a thing is done to a man's book, I say, the act is represented as one of noble virtue—and the only pity is he didn't do more of it, etc."

Meanwhile he had been planning to go to Germany to spend the royalties which were due him there but which were prohibited by Nazi monetary restrictions from being sent out of the country. "It looks now as if I'm going to Berlin the end of this week or beginning of next," Wolfe had jocosely written to Perkins at the end of March, "from there to Copenhagen, and then on to Russia in time for the May Day cele-brations—this because I am now planning a monumental work in three volumes on The Success of Russian Communism, and following the example of some of my American colleagues, I figure I shall need at least a week in Russia to gather the necessary material. It looks as if I've got to go to Germany—it is apparently the only way of getting any money, if there is any—I understand it can not be taken out of the country, so I might as well go there and spend it. I wired the German publisher a week ago and asked him if he wanted the new book and what his intentions were, and said I was coming to Berlin. He wired back emphatically that he did want it, was 'enchanted' to welcome me to Berlin, and when would I arrive? To which I wired back, on Frere's cold business advice, that I was delighted, but was also hard up, and what sort of offer would he make. To which he answered that he was 'certain' I would be satisfied with his offer, and offered to pay the ex-penses of my trip. That's how the matter stands, so I suppose I'm going."

By the last week of April, Wolfe had had enough of London, and he set out for the eastern part of England with the intention of eventually going to the Continent by boat from Harwich to the Hook of Holland. For a week he explored the county of Norfolk, sleeping at inns in Norwich, Yarmouth, and small towns in that vicinity, taking long walks across the dunes and marshes and green countryside, drinking in little pubs with the common, unpretentious people there, and discovering "a real blunt and good England I had never seen before." Finally he took the Harwich boat for Holland: spring by now was at its peak and the entire country was "a blaze of flowers," but Wolfe was for the most part restless and discontented there. "I came away 'abroad' to be alone," he wrote in his pocket diary, "but what I am really tired of, what I am sick to death of, what I am exhausted and sickened and fed up to the roots of my soul with, is being *alone*. I am tired of myself, I am tired of being with myself, I am surfeited." It was like the old days when he had wandered across the face of Europe until his "aloneness had become a kind of terrible joke." He was more solitary, more humble, more completely anonymous than he had ever been since then—and all the time, unknown to him, his fame at home was steadily increasing. It was not until May 5, almost two months after the publication of *Of Time and the River*, that he took the train from Holland to Berlin and "found Fame waiting for him there."

XVIII

IN HIS Purdue speech Wolfe describes his triumphant arrival in
Berlin on May 7, 1935: "The circle goes full swing. The cycle
draws to its full close. For four months, emptied, hollow, worn
out, my life had marked time, while my exhausted spirit drew its breath.
And then the world came in again, upon the flood-tide of reviving
energy. . . . I had gone back for rest, for recreation, for oblivion to that
land which, of all the foreign lands that I had known, I have loved best.
I had gone back to it in hours of desperate confinement, of brain-fagged
searching, in retrospect, in imagination, and in longing, a thousand
times from the giant jungle web of Brooklyn. I had gone back to it a
thousand times, as men in prison pent, haltered by all the dusty shack-
les of the hour, the confused traffics of clamorous days, the wearying
greyness of inevitable Now, have longed for Cockaigne, for the haunted
woods, the enchanted meadows, and the faery flood, the cloven rock. I
had gone back to it in ten thousand dreams and memories of time
and of desire—the sunken bell, the Gothic town, the splash of waters
in the midnight fountain, the old place, the broken chime, and the
blond flesh of secret, lavish women. I had gone back so in my memory
and in desire a thousand times to Germany; and now that Spring I was
really there again—and no man ever had a happier or a more fortuitous
return.

"Byron, they say, awoke one morning at the age of twenty-four, and
found himself a famous man. Well, I had to wait some ten years longer,
but the day came when I walked at morning through the Brandenburger Gate, and into the enchanted avenues of the faery green Tiergarten, and found that fame—or so it seemed to me—had come to me.
For two months I had been away from home, had seen no papers and
read no letters, had sought to find some easement, some slow and merciful release of the great coiled spring that was my mind and heart and
very life that had been stretched to breaking point for years. And I had
found it now in a series of oblivious wanderings that had led from Paris
to Kent and from the Romney Marshes up to London, and from London to the flat fecundity of Norfolk, and from Norfolk to the small

and tidy smugness of the Dutch, and from Holland, as the train bore on, across the great and fertile tillage of Westphalia, to Hannover, old time-haunted town, and there across the kiefern-haunted forest of the North to vast Berlin—and now May had come again, and I walked below the mighty blossoms of the great horse-chestnut trees, and through the Brandenburger Gate, and through the arcades of enchanted green, and felt, like Tamerlane, that it was passing great to be a king, and ride in triumph through Persepolis—and be a famous man.

"After those long and weary years of Brooklyn, excavation, and brute labor—of desperation and the need for proof to give some easement to my tormented soul—it was the easement I had dreamed of, the impossible faery, so impossibly desired, and now brought magically to life. It was—it seemed to be—the triumphant and the glorious vindication of all that I had thought my life could be, that man could work for, or art achieve. The news of my success at home had come to Germany—where already I had been known for three years, and had achieved celebrity—and now, it seemed to me who had so often gone a stranger and unknown to the great cities of the world, that now the whole of it was mine. The great town, the whole world, was my oyster. Letters were there for me, and invitations: it seemed they had been waiting for me—and for three weeks there was a round of pleasure, celebration, the wonderful thrill of meeting in a foreign land and in a foreign tongue a hundred friends, now for the first time known and captured—and May, the cool nights, the glorious freshness of the air, the awakening of Spring, the enchanted brevity of northern darkness, and glorious wine in slender bottles, and morning, and green fields, and pretty women—all of it was mine now, it seemed to have been created for me, to have waited for me, to exist and live in all its loveliness for my possession.

"Three weeks passed so. By day there was the shining and the sapphire air, the horse-chestnut trees, the singing sparkle of exultant life that swept through me across the town, so that at noon among the great crowds thronging the Kurfürstendamm, I also was part of the green faery of the great Tiergarten park, and thence unto all crystal sparkles of Berlin, until I seemed to share it all, and all of it to be in me, as but a single, shining and exultant drop of water reflects and shares, and is a part of the million, million scallop shells of dancing light, and every lapping wave, and every white sail on the surface of the Wannsee. And there would be the singing of the air by day, the unheard singing of the blood, and the great crowds thronging the Kurfürstendamm, the gay and crowded terraces of the great cafés, and something half-heard, half-suspected, coming from afar, a few flung seeds of golden notes upon the air, the sudden music of the tootling fifes, and suddenly, the solid, liquid smack of booted feet, and young brown faces shaded under their steel helmets goose-stepping by beneath the green arcades of the Kurfürstendamm, the army lorries rolling past, each crowded with its regimented rows of young, formal, helmeted, arm-folded and ramrod bodies, and laughter, laughter in the crowd, and laughter rippling like a wave across the terraces of great cafés and bubbling like wine-sparkles from the lips of all the pretty women—and all the singing and the gold of it was mine."

This is, of course, a highly emotional account of Wolfe's visit to Berlin, but the important thing is that he felt that way about it, both at the time and for the remainder of his life. He already was well known in Germany: ever since Rowohlt Verlag's publication of *Look Homeward, Angel* in 1932,[1] he had been greatly admired as a writer there— more so than in his own United States or any other country—and now, although *Of Time and the River* was not to be published there till 1936, the news of its American success had reached Berlin ahead of him and added greatly to his reputation. Ernst Rowohlt accordingly seized upon his visit as the occasion for a celebration: he arranged for newspaper interviews with Wolfe, photographs of him, magazine articles both by him and about him, and parties, parties, parties in the lavish style for which he, Rowohlt, was well known.

Wolfe flung himself into the celebrative round with an eagerness which was only exceeded by his joy and his surprise. He went through the cafés and night life of Hitler's degenerate Berlin with the healthy gusto of a giant from a different world; he lived like a prince on his German royalties at the Hotel Am Zoo overlooking his beloved Tiergarten; and when he came back to his room, he "found it filled with magnificent flowers which beautiful women had brought there in his absence." It was in many ways the same sort of lionization which he had experienced in New York in 1929, but it was intensified now to the nth degree. Moreover, there was a change in his own attitude that made it all seem different: whereas he had been unsure of himself, gauche, suspicious, and tormented, he had now proved to himself and to the world that he was a writer of real talent. "All the confusion, fatigue, dark doubt, and bitter hopelessness that had afflicted him in times past had gone," he wrote of George Webber in *You Can't Go Home Again*, "and no shadow of any kind remained. . . . Fame was

[1] Wolfe was fortunate in having his books translated into German by Hans Schiebelhuth, who preserved their intrinsic poetry even while transposing them into a foreign tongue.

with him almost all the time, but even when he was alone without her, in places where he was not known and his name meant nothing, the aura which Fame had shed still clung to him and he was able to meet each new situation with a sense of power and confidence, of warmth, friendliness, and good fellowship. He had become the lord of life. There had been a time in his youth when he felt that people were always laughing at him, and he had been ill at ease with strangers and had gone to every new encounter with a chip on his shoulder. But now he was life's strong and light-hearted master, and everyone he met and talked to—waiters, taxi drivers, porters in hotels, elevator boys, casual acquaintances in trams and trains and on the street—felt at once the flood of happy and affectionate power within him, and responded to him eagerly, instinctively, with instant natural liking, as men respond to the clean and shining light of the young sun. And when Fame was with him, all this magic was increased."

Wolfe saw a good deal of Ernst Rowohlt and his son, Heinz Ledig-Rowohlt, who became for him the German counterpart of Frere in England and, to a lesser degree, of Perkins in America—the editor who especially loved and understood his work. However, the people who contributed even more to the success of his visit to Berlin were the American ambassador, William E. Dodd, and his family. Martha Dodd, the ambassador's daughter, had been assistant literary editor of the Chicago *Tribune*: ever since the publication of *Look Homeward, Angel* she had been especially sympathetic to Wolfe's work, and when she heard that he was coming to Berlin, she invited him to be the guest of honor at a literary party at the embassy. To Wolfe, this was a crowning glory—a symbol of recognition of him as a writer by the official representatives of his own country. He went to the party and was received so cordially by all the Dodds that he soon took to spending a great deal of his time with them, fell somewhat in love with Martha, and formed a great admiration for Ambassador Dodd himself. "I have felt a renewed pride and faith in America and a belief that somehow our great future still remains since I came here to Berlin and met some of the Americans here, particularly Ambassador Dodd," he wrote to Perkins. "He is a historian, a man who was born on a farm in my own state of North Carolina and who had spent his whole life before he came here in teaching and in the contemplation of history. He is, I believe, what is known as a Jeffersonian Democrat and believes in the society of free men and the idea of democracy which he thinks has never been given a fair and practical experiment anywhere on earth. I don't know whether he is right or wrong in this . . . but their home in Berlin has been a free and fearless harbor for people of all opinions, and people who live and walk in terror have been able to draw their breath there without fear, and to speak their minds. This I know to be true, and further, the dry, plain, homely unconcern with which the Ambassador observes all the pomp and glitter and decorations and the tramp of marching men would do your heart good to see. I wish you could have been there the other night in his house when he came back from attending Hitler's two hour and forty minute speech which was delivered to that group of automatic dummies that now bears the ironical title of the 'Reichstag,' and which was broadcast all over Germany. It was wonderful to hear him tell his wife 'the way the Jap looked and the way the Englishman looked and how the Frenchman looked pretty hot about it and how he himself shook hands with the Dutchman on the way out and said "very interesting but not entirely historical," and how the Dutchman grinned and agreed.' It was Emerson who said that if you heard the pop of a popgun not to believe it was anything else but a pop of a popgun, even if all the captains and kings of the earth told you it was the roar of a cannon—he said it better than this but that was the substance, and I always felt it was an American thing to say and was glad that an American said it. I think the Ambassador here is a man like this."

But in spite of his admiration for the ambassador and his long political discussions with Martha Dodd and her brother, William E. Dodd, Jr., Wolfe at first refused to recognize the evils of Hitlerism. In her book *Through Embassy Eyes* Martha Dodd describes his attitude from firsthand observation: "Wolfe came, strangely enough, with high enthusiasm about Germany. . . . He had studied and loved the great German writers and artists and felt more closely akin to the Germanic spirit than to any other. It took him some time to learn what was happening, as it does most people who have not been passionately interested in the political and economic developments in Europe. . . . The Germans, even the Nazis, loved Thomas Wolfe. He had long articles written about him, comparing him to a much-loved Bavarian poet of the people. His book, *Look Homeward, Angel*, had been acclaimed by pre-Hitler Germany, and his personality and later works by post-Hitler critics. . . . The fanatic Hitler-followers accepted and praised him, the enemies of Hitler were devoted to his personality, respected the power and lyricism of his prose. In fact, there actually seemed to be something Germanic about him which they all could claim. . . . In his short month or two there the first time, he became a legend around Berlin. For the first time since Hitler's coming to power, the famous Romanisches Café, formerly the center of literary lights, artists and intellectuals, took on life. He seemed to give a sort of animation to the streets and café. People began shyly to enter the almost deserted café. Tom, a huge man of six feet six, with the face of a great poet, strode the streets, oblivious of the sensation he created, with his long powerful strides, his head high, his posture free and full of a lumbering rhythm.

"To the desolateness of the intellectual life of Germany, Thomas Wolfe was like a symbol of the past, when great writers were great men. . . . He gave back to the intellectual and creative people of Berlin a sense of their past, of the dignity and power and freedom of a mind not under stress. Certainly he was the most vital experience literary Berlin had had in the Hitler years, and for months after, people would gather to talk of him. But when he had left, the famous café, no longer animated by his booming voice and reckless gestures, with his circle of friends and admirers around him, again was deserted and silent. I have heard that he attracted men to the café who had not been in such public places since Hitler; and that the Secret Police, aware of this, planted spies for weeks after in the café, to try to ferret out some free opinion that might have been less cautiously expressed after the sense of security and oblivion of terror that Wolfe's presence had given them.

"Part of Tom's uncritical attitude toward Nazism can be explained by his own state of delirium. He had just published his book, *Of Time and the River*, after five years of writing, during which time most of the critics said he was through, that he had written himself out in his first book and would never be able to repeat his success. . . . His book had been an overwhelming success immediately and was on the bestseller list in a few days, with the critics proclaiming him one of the greatest writers of his time. He was in a state of high nervous tension, wherein everything took on the proportions of a gigantic and infinitely beautiful dream. He loved everything and everyone, his high spirits flooded everything he did, thought, saw, or felt. And his moods of despair were equally terrifying in their intensity. He was mad with the music of his own personality and power, almost beside himself, and no one could come near him without feeling the charged atmosphere of his tremendous excitement. Several of us took a trip with him to Weimar, the home of Goethe in his adult and later years, and to the Wartburg. We tried futilely to show him that all was not unconditionally superb in Germany. He was to learn for himself; in the meantime, he was in a ferment, taking all of it in and waiting for the passion of the moment to become quieter."

Later, in a letter written to Elizabeth Nowell, Miss Dodd enlarged upon her memories of Wolfe at Weimar: "He proudly stood and measured himself against Goethe's statue and found himself to be taller! He was also fascinated by the way Goethe wrote either standing up or on a kind of saddle. . . . He stared at the room for a *very long time* and I had literally to pull him away. The Goethe business made a deep and wonderful impression on him—and he meditated solemnly on the nature of greatness. . . . Coming out of the gartenhouse, he stood under the magnificent trees and spoke like one possessed in a luminous, uniquely phrased, wild and ennobled flow of language. I stood almost dazed by his imagery. . . . Of all he said, I only recall one phrase, 'the demented music of the trees.' There *was* a strong wind blowing and it *did* sing wildly through the huge trees. But the way he talked! . . . He could rise to such incredible heights and then sink to such horrible depths."[2]

The trip to Weimar marked the climax of Wolfe's triumphant joy and of his gratitude to and love for Germany. It is no wonder that the efforts of Martha Dodd and her friends to convince him of the evils of Hitlerism were futile: he was not really living in Nazi Germany at all, but in a vivid emotional re-creation of the great cultural Germany of a hundred years before—of "the haunted woods, the enchanted meadows, and the faery flood, the cloven rock." "All through a wonderful sunlit day we drove down southwest through this magnificent, beautiful and enchanted country," he wrote to Perkins from the Wartburg on the second evening of the trip. "We spent the night in the old town of Weimar and today we went about the town and saw, first, Goethe's Gartenhaus in a wonderful green park and the rooms where he lived and worked and the saddle he sat on when he wrote, and his high old writing desk and many other things that he used and lived with, that made his life and work seem real and near to us. Then we went to the fine old house in Weimar where he lived later on and where all the evidences of his great and illimitably curious intelligence—his laboratories, his workshops, his great library, his rooms for his experiments in physics, chemistry, electricity and optics—have been exactly and truly preserved. Then we went about the town some more and visited the crypt where Goethe and Schiller are buried side by side, and finally with regret we left that wonderful and lovely old town that seems to me at least to hold in it so much of the spirit of the great Germany and the great and noble spirit of freedom, reverence and the high things of the spirit which all of us have loved. Then we came here through one of the most

[2] From a letter written by Martha Dodd Stern in April 1950.

indescribably lovely and magical landscapes I have ever seen. And to-night we are staying here in the Wartburg, a great legendary kind of hill from which came the legend that inspired Richard Wagner to write *Tannhäuser*. We are going back to Berlin to-morrow through the wonderful Harz Mountains, and I have not space or power enough here to tell you how beautiful and fine and magical this trip has been.

"I am telling you all this," he went on, "because you and I have often talked about Germany and the German people whom you do not like as much as I do and about what has happened here in recent years. But I want to tell you that I do not see how anyone who comes here as I have come could possibly fail to love the country, its noble Gothic beauty and its lyrical loveliness, or to like the German people who are, I think, the cleanest, the kindest, the warmest-hearted, and the most honorable people I have met in Europe. I tell you this because I think a full and generous recognition must be made of all these facts and because I have been told and felt things here which you and I can never live or stand for and which, if they are true, as by every reason of intuition and faith and belief in the people with whom I have talked I must believe, are damnable.

"Now I so much want to see you and tell you what I have seen and heard, all that has been wonderful and beautiful and exciting, and about those things that are so hard to explain because one feels they are so evil and yet cannot say so justly in so many words as a hostile press and propaganda would, because this evil is so curiously and inextricably woven into a kind of wonderful hope which flourishes and inspires millions of people who are themselves, as I have told you, certainly not evil, but one of the most child-like, kindly and susceptible people in the world. . . . More and more I feel that we are all of us bound up and tainted by whatever guilt and evil there may be in this whole world, and that we cannot accuse and condemn others without in the end coming back to an accusal of ourselves. We are all damned together, we are all tarred by the same stick, and for what has happened here we are all in some degree responsible. This nation to-day is beyond the shadow of a vestige of a doubt full of uniforms and a stamp of marching men—I saw it with my own eyes yesterday in one hundred towns and villages across two hundred miles of the most peaceful, lovely and friendly-looking country I have ever seen. A thousand groups, uncountable divisions of the people from children eight years old to men of fifty, all filled beyond a doubt with hope, enthusiasm and inspired belief in a fatal and destructive thing—and the sun was shining all day long and the fields the greenest, the woods the loveliest, the little towns the cleanest, and the faces and the voices of the people the most friendly of any I have ever seen or heard, so what is there to say?"

During the remainder of this visit to Germany, Wolfe failed to progress any further toward a definite conclusion about Nazism. It was not only that he was blinded by his love for the German people and their great cultural past: it was also because he, characteristically, had to "find his own way" through personal experience and emotion and meditation, instead of accepting at face value the arguments of other people. He had to come back to Germany again in 1936 before he made up his mind, and then his indecisive question "What is there to say?" was answered with strong personal conviction in "I Have a Thing to Tell You."

Wolfe returned to Berlin from Weimar and the Wartburg on May 26. By this time the success of *Of Time and the River* in America was a solidly established fact: he was not only a famous but a comparatively wealthy man, and one of the attendant circumstances of fame and wealth was coming now to plague him. In the batch of mail which he found waiting for him in Berlin was a letter from a New York attorney threatening suit against him on behalf of Madeleine Boyd for agent's commissions on the royalties earned by both *Look Homeward, Angel* and *Of Time and the River*.

The dispute between Mrs. Boyd and Wolfe now seems tedious and remote, but to him it was a stunning blow—and a sudden threat to the financial security and mental peace which he thought he had, at last, achieved. Now, in a postscript to the ecstatic letter which he had written to Perkins from the Wartburg, he poured out his first rage and shock at the threatened lawsuit and laid the blame on Perkins, although he was in no way responsible except as the father-substitute to whom Wolfe had insisted on turning for guidance in all things.

Wolfe stayed in Berlin for two more weeks, but the first ecstatic happiness of his success there had been dispelled by the threat of litigation with Mrs. Boyd. He was mentally depressed and, to add to all his difficulties, the excesses of his life in Berlin now also made him physically ill. He had originally planned to go to Russia, but instead he packed up hastily and left for Copenhagen, where he spent the next two weeks under the care of a physician. It was a disastrous ending for his triumphal tour, and he was in a chastened and reflective mood when he arrived at Hamburg on June 26 to board the *Bremen* for the voyage back to the United States.

"This is my last night in Europe," he wrote on a postcard to Robert Raynolds. ". . . I am sitting here on the terrace of a little hotel that overlooks the harbor of Hamburg. It is almost dark and I can see a great tangle of cranes and derricks against the sky—and big freighters all alight and lovely—and the rattling of a winch. Somehow it makes me think of Brooklyn and is comforting." Already in his pocket notebook he had started jotting down his endless lists of work completed and work to be done. "The circle" was beginning to "go full swing," and he was ready to come home again.

XIX

IN OUTLINES in his pocket notebooks Wolfe called his return to New York in 1935 "Return to Glory" or "Fame Exploding in the City." When he landed there on July 4, a blazing, unbearably hot day, he still was dubious about *Of Time and the River*'s complete success in the United States, and he was surprised and jubilant to find his "new won fame waiting at the boat" in the shape of newspaper reporters to interview him. Perkins, too, was waiting on the dock, but with news of trouble which would eventually cause Wolfe to abandon his entire *Of Time and the River* series. Just as Wolfe was leaving Berlin for Copenhagen, Mrs. Bernstein had come to call on Perkins at Scribners and had told him that she would do everything in her power to prevent the publication of *The October Fair* if she was represented as a character in it. "I thought this would trouble Tom greatly, and might block his future," Perkins wrote later, "and that was one reason why I . . . got a pass and went to the dock. I found Tom's baggage and waited . . . long after everyone else had come ashore, and when Tom finally arrived, I was sitting on one of his bags thinking about the Bernstein problem, and I didn't see him until he stood right before me. I was very much touched because of the completely sincere emotion of his first words when he leaned down toward me and said, 'Why, Max, you look so sad! What's the matter?' In fact, the matter was only the Bernstein affair, but I said that there was nothing the matter.

"When we got rid of Tom's baggage we went for lunch to a restaurant on the East River about 52nd Street, where you could sit out on the deck of a great barge converted from a coal barge. It was a wonderful place right there on the River, with boats going up and down. There Tom wanted me to tell him everything that concerned him, and I immediately told about Mrs. Bernstein. He did not seem to take this too seriously, and asked me if that was all. And when I assured him it was, he said: 'Well, then, now we can have a good time,' and a good time ended at about three or four in the morning, and reached from that restaurant to the Prince George Hotel in Brooklyn. It was from that roof that we looked down upon the City and the harbor at about sunset."[1]

Wolfe's celebrative happiness was momentarily marred by the appearance at the barge restaurant of his old bête noire, Scott Fitzgerald, but the latter had a girl with him and sat with Wolfe and Perkins for only a few minutes before going to a table of his own. Soon afterward Wolfe and Perkins left the barge and started on a round of all Wolfe's favorite places in New York. "I think we were on the way to the Lafayette," Perkins wrote, "when Tom stopped and said, 'There, Max, is the place where I lived in the attic and wrote *Look Homeward, Angel.* Let's go up and see if we can get in.' So we went and knocked on the door. There was no answer. While Tom was still knocking, I looked out the window at the rear and saw that a fire escape went right up to the open window of what Tom called the attic. I said, 'Well, Tom, if you really want to see the nest where the young eaglet mewed his mighty youth, it can be done,' and I started out on the fire escape. We went up to the window and in. You could call it an attic, for it was at the top of the house and there was a certain amount of slope to the upper halves of the walls, but it was magnificent—not the kind of attic you think of poets residing in at all. In fact, I would say it was the best place Tom ever did live in. I suppose we were guilty of some sort of crime or misdemeanor in going in there, but we did no harm. Tom scribbled on the wall of the vestibule: 'Thomas Wolfe lived here.' "[2]

Afterward they were like two gleeful schoolboys about their act of trespass, with Wolfe proudly telling everyone at Scribners of Perkins' surprising lack of dignity, and Perkins himself chuckling and saying, "I suppose we could have been arrested, but it was really perfectly all right."

After leaving Eighth Street the two men walked down to the Hotel Lafayette and had a drink in the café there. Then they went over to Brooklyn and up to the roof of the Prince George Hotel, where during his four desperate years of work on *Of Time and the River* Wolfe had often gone to stare down at New York spread out below him. In those years it had been "the invincible and unceasing city," the city of "no door," but now, through the completion of his book and its success, he felt that he had conquered it, and again, as in Berlin, "there beat in him . . . the pulse of Tamerlane, and he thought that it was passing

[1] From Perkins' letter to John S. Terry of November 1, 1945.
[2] Ibid.

great to be a king and ride in triumph through Persepolis." In *The
Web and the Rock* Wolfe ascribes an experience like this to George
Webber at an early point in his career, before he had published anything. However, there are phrases in his description, such as "the
triumphant knowledge of his own success" and the reference to Tamerlane, which seem to indicate that he was actually thinking of himself
after the success of *Of Time and the River*: "It was not merely that he
had been a stripling boy led mothwise, like a million others, from the
outer darkness of the province to the great blaze of this imperial light
. . . He was a poet, and the son of poets dead and gone, and a mighty
poet in his own domain, and in his wild, unuttered blood there sang
that night the wild, unuttered tongues of darkness and America. . . .
And he stood here on the lid of night, upon this shore of the immortal
dark, upon the undiscovered edge of all the brave new world of this
America; and knew that still the tide was coming in upon the full,
and that even yet the Muses . . . had not . . . reached their prime.

"That hour, that moment, and that place struck with a peerless
coincision upon . . . the crest and zenith of his own desire. . . . The
city blazed there in his vision in the frame of night, and for the first
time his vision phrased it as it had never done before. It was a cruel
city, but it was a lovely one; a savage city, yet it had such tenderness;
a bitter, harsh, and violent catacomb of stone and steel and tunneled
rock, slashed savagely with light, and roaring, fighting a constant cease-
less warfare of men and of machinery; and yet it was so sweetly and so
delicately pulsed, as full of warmth, of passion, and of love, as it was
full of hate. . . .

"It was a moment when the whole wine of life seemed to have been
distilled and poured into his veins, when his very blood was the wine
of life itself, when he possessed the whole of life—its power, beauty,
pity, tenderness, and love, and all its overwhelming poetry—when all
of it was his, fused to a perfect center in the white heat of his youth,
the triumphant knowledge of his own success."

As Wolfe looked down upon the city in this exalted sort of mood, his
"dauntless and unshaken friend" who had had so much to do with
his success stood quietly beside him, and suddenly Wolfe was overcome
with gratitude and love for him. It was the climax, the high point, of
the relationship between the two, who now were tragically to become
estranged. And three years later, when Wolfe had a premonition that
he was dying and wrote to make his peace with Perkins, he reminded
him of it in the last words that he ever was to write: "Whatever happens
—I had this 'hunch' and wanted to write you and tell you, no matter

what happens or has happened, I shall always think of you and feel about you the way it was that Fourth of July three years ago when you met me at the boat, and we went out on the café on the river and had a drink and later went on top of the tall building, and all the strangeness and the glory and the power of life and of the city was below."

When Scribners reopened on the Monday after the Fourth of July, Wolfe was further convinced of the success of *Of Time and the River* by the great stack of laudatory reviews and letters which had been accumulating for him ever since early March. "Last night I stayed up until five o'clock reading the hundreds and hundreds of reviews from all over the country," he wrote to Martha Dodd. "They took some nice, cheerful, wholehearted pokes at me, but they seemed to love me, and the total effect is overwhelming. The letters have been wonderfully moving and exciting. In addition to the regular sort of fan mail and autograph letters and flirty-girl kind of thing, there have been wonderful letters coming from people everywhere, all the way from hotel clerks to school teachers to ordinary men and women of all sorts, who said they had never written a writer before and don't want an answer and just wrote to tell me so the moment they finished the book. Among other things, I got a grand, generous letter from Sherwood Anderson who said he knew why he could never write a novel after finishing the book. The whole thing has made me pretty happy, and it also makes me feel a little guilty and ashamed. If they think this book is good, I know I am going to beat it forty ways with the next two. I failed in this book, not in the ways the critics said I did, but in another way that Max and I know about. In spite of their talk about its tremendous energy and so forth, I wrote it in less than a year before it was published, at a time when I was horribly tired and when I had exhausted myself in writing the two books which are to follow. Perhaps I should have taken another year, but so much time had gone by without publication that I agreed with Max that it was more important to get it out and to go on to all the work that awaits me than to spend more time perfecting this one.

"I feel grand. I am strong and happy and confident as I haven't been in several years, and if I failed last time, the time is coming when I may not fail. Anyway, I will use every energy of my life—and my life itself if need be—to justify what Max and my friends and some of the people in these letters have said and felt about what I do."

Wolfe had taken a room at a Lexington Avenue hotel, but for the first three weeks after his return from Europe he almost literally lived at Scribners. In fact, one morning he was even discovered sleeping soundly on the big table used for directors' meetings in the fifth-floor library. The library had been turned over to him for his stacks of fan mail. He hired a typist and started sorting it and dictating replies, but he was so brimming over with delight at the praise he had received that he could not keep it to himself. He kept wandering all over Scribners, beaming beatifically and talking to everyone from Perkins to the stenographers and the Spanish and Irish elevator men. Nobody got much work done and nobody really cared; they all were friends of Wolfe's and as delighted as he at *Of Time and the River*'s great success. As Perkins said later in the *Carolina Magazine*, "Tom was always one of them, the regular people. . . . He was lonely. He inspired fellow feeling, but it could not embrace him enough."[3]

Wolfe had been back in New York only a week when he had a dramatic encounter with Mrs. Bernstein, his first since his rejection of her in the early thirties. Just before sailing for Europe he had sent her an advance copy of *Of Time and the River*, with an ink line and the words "My dear" written in the margin beside the final passage of the book, where Eugene sees an unknown woman waiting on the dock at Cherbourg and knows "that from that moment his spirit was impaled upon the knife of love." He had found a letter in reply from her waiting for him on the *Ile de France*, and he had spent the better part of his first night at sea in writing her an answer:

"When I got your letter, I wept with joy and pride. I have kept silence, have not spoken or written to you in over five years—but not with an ugly stubbornness, only with a stubbornness that made me want to show you something that was worthy of me—and of you. My heart is full of affection and loyalty for you—it had always been: I am devoted to the memory of everything you ever said to me, of every kind or generous thing you ever did for me. Your proud words of faith and glory make a great music in me—I know your value, know the princely ore of which you're made. You are the best, the highest . . ."[4]

The way was thus opened for a reconciliation, and it was probably not by pure accident that Mrs. Bernstein appeared at the Chatham bar on Friday, July 12, just at the time when Wolfe and Perkins

[3] From "Scribner's and Tom Wolfe," in the October 1938 issue of the *Carolina Magazine*.

[4] This passage is quoted from a fragmentary rough draft found in Wolfe's own files, which Mrs. Bernstein confirmed as being identical or very similar to the copy which he actually sent her. That copy is no longer in existence.

habitually stopped there for a drink after the end of the business day at Scribners. Wolfe was so intent on talking with Perkins that at first he did not notice Mrs. Bernstein, who sat at a little table by the wall with her head bowed and her face half hidden by her hat; but almost unconsciously he kept glancing at the print from which her dress was made, thinking how beautiful it was and how similar to those she used to wear. It was Perkins, however, who actually recognized her and whispered to Wolfe that she was there. Wolfe then sprang to his feet and rushed across to speak to her, but he was too unnerved by this sudden meeting, and the Chatham was too public a place in which to talk with her. Accordingly, he and she and Perkins walked the two short blocks back to the Scribner Building and went up to the deserted fifth floor, where Perkins had his office. Wolfe was terribly upset and, as always, wanted Perkins' advice: he still had it on his conscience that he never had repaid the money which Mrs. Bernstein had given him, and he wanted to arrange to do so now, out of his *Of Time and the River* royalties. He asked her to wait in the railed-off receptionist's space by the elevator while he went and consulted privately with Perkins in the latter's office. Then he started back out to her—and, to his horror, found her in the act of putting a small vial of pills to her mouth. He lunged desperately toward her and knocked it from her hand, whereupon she collapsed into his arms. Both he and Perkins were terrified that she again had taken an overdose of sleeping pills in an attempt at suicide, and on the sacrosanct fifth floor of Scribners of all places! Perkins rang the elevator bell for Mr. Hinkson, the night watchman, and asked him to get a doctor—quick! Fortunately there was a woman doctor, a well-known dermatologist, who had an office in the Scribner Building and who was working late that night. She very calmly counted the pills in Mrs. Bernstein's bottle, phoned the pharmacy which had put up the prescription, and ascertained that all of them were still there.

This was the beginning of a reconciliation between Wolfe and Mrs. Bernstein which, however, lasted only a few months before he felt impelled to remind her that their relationship must now be one of friendship, pure and simple, with no ties or obligations. The five years' breach between them had gone too deep to heal, and gradually they became estranged again.

Wolfe stayed in New York only for the first part of July before starting out on two more months of wandering, this time in America. He had been invited to appear as a "visiting novelist" at the University of

Colorado's Writers' Conference, which was to be held at Boulder from July 22 until August 9, and he had accepted with alacrity: as he wrote his mother, "They will pay $250 which will cover my expenses and give me a chance to see a part of the country I want very much to see." He was still possessed by his old ambition to "know this country . . . as I know the palm of my hand," and he had never seen the West. This was a golden opportunity, and he decided to take advantage of it before settling down to another long, arduous siege of work upon a book.

Besides taking part in round-table discussions with other "visiting novelists" and interviewing students about their work, Wolfe was required to deliver one formal lecture at the conference, and for this he decided to use the preface which he had originally written for *Of Time and the River*. Although Perkins had persuaded him to omit it from that book, Wolfe had always been determined that it must be published somehow, somewhere; he had given a rough draft of the first part of it to his agent, Miss Nowell, in hopes that she could sell it to a magazine while he was abroad, but she had found that parts of it were missing and so had not done so. Now he got his copy out, began rewriting it, and gave it its title, *The Story of a Novel*. Moreover, Perkins now gave his consent to the use of it, thinking that it could no longer be very "harmful," since *Of Time and the River* had been published and was such a great success. In this he proved to be falsely optimistic, but he could not withstand Wolfe's enthusiasm; nor could he suppress forever so remarkable a piece of work.

On July 27 Wolfe started West with the boyish delight which he always felt on train trips. "The journey across the country was overwhelming—I've never begun to say what I ought to say about it," he wrote to Perkins on July 30 from Greeley, where he had stopped off to give an informal version of his lecture at the Colorado State College of Education before going on to Boulder. He arrived at the Writers' Conference the following day, and for the next twelve days was in a whirl of activity: he was wined and dined and lionized both in Boulder and in Denver, and a whole new batch of women fell in love with him; he was constantly exhilarated by the high atmosphere and by his own popularity; and he delivered his formal lecture with great success. "It took me the first fifteen minutes to quit stuttering, hemming and hawing, and fiddling around for an opening," he wrote later to William Polk, "but after that, if I do say so as shouldn't, I did the job up pretty brown. . . . It took one hour and forty minutes, and they were hanging on by their eyelids when I finished."

When the conference ended, Wolfe should by rights have started straight back East. Mrs. Boyd's attorneys had filed her suit against him with the Supreme Court of New York, and Wolfe's own lawyers were urgently requesting him to find various letters which he had received from her and which could now be used in his defense. Moreover, Perkins was anxiously waiting for him to give his approval to the collection of short stories, *From Death to Morning*, which Scribners wanted to publish in the fall, while his popularity still was at its peak. "I am very anxious to get this done rapidly," he had written to Wolfe in April while he was in London, "and we must tackle it as soon as you get back. The woman's story and 'Web of Earth' are entirely objective. And that is true of several of the other stories. You have completely imagined whole natures of people totally unlike yourself. I think these stories will show them a few things more you can do and will give them another surprise. This is the way to answer critics."[5]

Perkins had started getting the collection of stories together as early as July 1934, and he now had almost the whole book set in galley proofs and a dummy of it made up for the Scribner salesmen. However, Wolfe refused to let him go ahead with publication of it until he returned to New York, and returning there was the last thing he had in mind. Now that he had got as far west as Colorado, his thirst to see America had got complete possession of him, and he had resolved to go the entire way to the Pacific coast.

"You must not put the manuscript of a book of stories in final form until after my return to New York," he wrote with a new note of authority to Perkins. "If that means the book of stories will have to be deferred till next spring, then they will have to be deferred, but I will not consent this time to allow the book to be taken away from me and printed and published until I myself have had time to look at the proofs, and at any rate to talk to you about certain revisions, changes, excisions, or additions that ought to be made. I really mean this, Max. I have money enough to live on for a while now. I do not propose to trade upon the success of 'Of Time and the River.' I propose rather to prepare my work in every way possible to meet and refute, if I can, some of the very grave and serious criticisms that were made about the last book, and as my friend and the person whose judgment I trust most, you must help me to do this.

"I am coming back to New York in September. My mind is swarming with new material and the desire to get back and finish up 'The

[5] From Perkins' letter of April 20, 1935. "The woman's story" was "In the Park."

October Fair' as soon as possible, but before we do that, we must first do a thorough, honest and satisfactory job upon the book of stories, 'From Death to Morning'; we must get the Boyd matter settled; we must get the deck cleared for action; otherwise another shameful and revolting waste of talent right at the time of its greatest fertility and strength is likely to occur. . . .

"This is all for the present. I will be in the Southwest next week and then on to California, the Northwest, back through Idaho, Wyoming, and St. Louis and so back east again. And if they don't kill me out here with hospitality, or in New York with . . . lawsuits and so forth, I'll have some good stories to tell you and a lot of work to do in the winter."

Wolfe had got in touch with his old friend from New York University, Desmond Powell, who was teaching at Colorado College in Colorado Springs and who now met him in Denver and drove with him across the desert of New Mexico to Santa Fe.[6] It was from here that Wolfe set out upon his ludicrous expedition to call on Mabel Dodge Luhan in Taos. When Mrs. Luhan had written him to praise *Of Time and the River*, Wolfe had answered that he was coming West and hoped to see her. However, after she had invited him to come to Taos, he had been dubious about accepting until two young society women who met him at a party in his honor at Santa Fe offered to drive him there in their car. Characteristically, he was late in getting started, and it was not till well after midnight that he finally presented himself at Mrs. Luhan's door with the two attractive women, one on either arm. Mrs. Luhan had gone to bed, but her secretary opened the door, took Wolfe to task for arriving at such an hour of the night, and finally indicated by a wave of her arm that he could come in but that his feminine companions couldn't. Thereupon Wolfe delivered a few brief condemnatory remarks loudly enough to be heard by the recumbent Mrs. Luhan and departed into the night with his two companions. "I saw all this without seeing Mabel Dodge Luhan," he wrote gleefully to Alfred Dashiell on a picture postcard of the Pueblo of Taos. "Had a row with her the minute I entered her house —she had gone to bed—but I said my say anyway."

By August 28 Wolfe was on his way again, stopping off to see the Grand Canyon and again to feel convinced of the insufficiency of what he had written about America. "You can get no idea of this from a postcard, but it is stirring and incredible," he wrote to Perkins. "I begin

[6] Powell has described this trip in his article "Of Thomas Wolfe," in the Spring 1945 issue of the *Arizona Quarterly*.

to see how inadequate all I have said and written about this country really is." By August 31 he had reached the Pacific coast and was being shown around Hollywood by Joel Sayre, the author of *Rackety Rax*, and his wife. He was taken around the Metro-Goldwyn-Mayer studio by Mrs. Sayre, Sam Marx the story editor, and George Oppenheimer, and when asked if there was anything he was especially interested in, he said he'd like to meet Jean Harlow. He got on famously with her and spent most of his time at M-G-M in watching her on the set. Then he was taken by the Sayres to parties given by Gloria Stuart and Dorothy Parker, who, according to what he wrote to Perkins, "told a room of people that I was built on a heroic scale and that there was no one like me." "The liquor and hospitality flows like the Mississippi," he went on beseechingly to Perkins. ". . . I know I have stayed too long, but Max, Max, you *must* wait on me—I've *got* to see San Francisco—above all, I must see that wonderful town—in the end we shall not lose by it. Then, if you like, I'll cut it short and come straight home, only I'd hoped to see a little of Oregon, Salt Lake City, and stop off a day in St. Louis to see where Grover died on my way back. . . . Max, please wait on me—don't take the book away before I get back."

It was while being shown around the lot at M-G-M that Wolfe was approached about staying on there as a writer. Sam Marx, with the approval of the head of production, Irving Thalberg, made him the offer[7] but Wolfe replied quite candidly that he had a lot of books to write, and so could not accept. "They want me to stay, have offered me a job, and mentioned huge sums," he wrote to Perkins, "but perhaps I shall resist." And resist he did, for the reasons which he later explained in detail in his Purdue speech: "In the last few years I have rejected a number of offers that would have given me a great deal more money than I have ever had. . . . I counted up my total earnings over the past ten years, since I began to write professionally, the other day, and found that they did not exceed forty thousand dollars. That's a lot of money . . . and I certainly am not disappointed or depressed about it. But on at least one occasion, I could have earned more than that total sum in one year's time if I had accepted employment that was offered me in Hollywood. I didn't take it. Why? I hasten to assure you that it was not because I was being noble. I have listened to writers who had a book published shudder with horror at the very mention

---

[7] Since Wolfe immediately declined the offer, there is no record of it. However, according to Marx's recollection, it was either on a week-to-week basis at $1000 or $1500 a week, or on a yearly basis at $30,000 to $50,000.

of Hollywood—some of them have even asked me if I would ever listen
to an offer from Hollywood—if I could possibly submit my artistic
conscience to the prostitution by allowing anything I'd write to be
. . . made into a moving picture by Hollywood. My answer to this
has always been an enthusiastic and fervent yes. If Hollywood wants to
prostitute me by buying one of my books for the movies, I am not only
willing but eager for the seducers to make their first dastardly proposal.
In fact, my position in the matter is very much that of the Belgian
virgin the night the Germans took the town: 'When do the atrocities
begin?'

"But when I got an offer to go there and work, I did not take it,
although it would have paid me more money than I had ever earned
from writing in my whole life before; and I repeat again I have never
felt noble about it. I did not go because I did not want to go. I wanted
to write: I had work to do, I had writing, and still have, and I think
I will always have, that I wanted to get done. It meant more and it
means more to me than anything else I could do. And I think that is
the reason I am a writer."

Wolfe spent only a few days in Hollywood before going on to his
ultimate goal, San Francisco, which he had dreamed of seeing ever
since his father had gone there in 1908. Wolfe had met Dr. Russel Lee,
head of the Palo Alto Clinic, on board the *Bremen* on the voyage back
home from Germany in June, and he now spent ten days at the Lees'
house while he explored San Francisco to his heart's content. He was
especially fascinated by Chinatown and would go there almost every
evening, to roam through the back alleys and subterranean passages
till 3 or 4 A.M., finally coming back to the Lees' to sleep till noon.
Then, to the delight and amazement of the Lees' cook, he would
breakfast on a dozen eggs, two quarts of milk, and an entire loaf of
bread before starting out sight-seeing again. One day Dr. Lee drove
him to Big Basin, which contains one of the most magnificent groves
of redwoods in the world. Wolfe had not known where they were going,
and when Lee's car dropped down into the basin and stopped in the
gigantic grove of trees, he was literally dumfounded. He got out of the
car without a word, looked up at the great trees, immediately tried to
embrace one, then lay down on the pine needles underneath them and
gazed up at their tops. He spent an entire hour at this without saying a
single word. Then, as they drove back to Palo Alto, he launched into
one of the inspired rhapsodies which were characteristic of him when
deeply moved. The big trees, he said, were "the most satisfactory thing
he had ever seen in nature": for the first time in his life he had found

something that was built on an even more heroic scale than himself.

It was the middle of September before Wolfe headed back East, with a brief stopover at St. Louis to revisit the house where his brother Grover had died in 1904. He had had six months' vacation, and, as he wrote to Perkins, "that ought to be enough for any man." "But it has been a thrilling, wonderful experience," he continued. ". . . I have no words to tell you of the beauty, power and magnificence of this country. Thank God I have seen it at last!—and I know that I did not lie about it; I know I have not yet begun to put it down on paper: my store of wonderful subject matter has been enormously enriched." From this time forth he was more convinced than ever of his mission to "chronicle the . . . huge single and incomparable substance of America." "I have at last discovered my own America," he wrote to Perkins a year later. "I believe I have found my language, I think I know my way. And I shall wreak out my vision of this life, this world, and this America, to the top of my bent, to the height of my ability, but with an unswerving devotion, integrity and purity of purpose that shall not be menaced, altered or weakened by anyone." And as Perkins pointed out, "The trail he blazed is now open forever. American artists will follow, and widen it to express the things Americans only unconsciously know, to reveal America and Americans to Americans. That was at the heart of Tom's fierce life."[8]

[8] From "Scribner's and Tom Wolfe."

XX

I T W A S the last week of September before Wolfe got back to New York. His holiday was over; he had to settle down to work, but first he had to find a place to live. "I've been trying to move back to Manhattan," he had written earlier to Elizabeth Lemmon. "Am fed up with Brooklyn, have lived here long enough and finished a big job here, and now it's time to go—but find it hard to get a place in Manhattan that will fit my pocketbook, which is small, and my demands, which are pretty big—i.e. air, light, space and quiet, which in N.Y. have become capitalistic luxuries." In all but one of the apartments he had had in Brooklyn, he had lived on the wrong side of the street to get a view of the East River, though he had been able to get a tiny glimpse of it at Montague Terrace by leaning perilously out the window and craning down the street. Now, with sales of *Of Time and the River* at the 36,000 mark, he was determined to find a place on the East Side of New York from which he could actually see the river. With Mrs. Jelliffe, who still had his furniture stored at her house, he made the rounds of the real-estate agencies, only to find, to his infuriation, that a view of the river was indeed a "capitalistic luxury." When told the price of apartments such as he wanted, he would thrust out his lower lip, crouch menacingly, and say in a precise, staccato voice: "I see! Only the rich can see the river! Well, I'm poor and I damn well *will* see the river!" He would then stride out of the offending agency, only to whirl on Mrs. Jelliffe and exclaim: "What sort of a town *is* this, that a poor man can't see the river?"[1]

But finally, after days of fruitless searching, they found an ideal place for him, a three-room apartment on the fourteenth floor of 865 First Avenue, with a magnificent view, which he described in his unpublished story "No More Rivers": "Everything was touched with morning, and the river was flashing with all the ecstasy and movement of its thousand currents. . . . The tide was coming in upon the full. . . . It was a steady, flowing, crawling and impulsive surge—a welling

---

[1] From Belinda Jelliffe's unpublished reminiscences of Wolfe.

flood that would come on forever and knew no limit to the invasion
of its power. The river was not quiet; the tide was ruffled by the breath
of morning into a million scallop-shells of winking light—rose, golden,
silver, sapphire, pink—the whole polychrome of morning was reflected
in the stream, and within the channel of the river's life, the tide came
on. . . . A tug, set neatly in between two barges, each loaded with
twin rows of box-cars, backed out into the stream and quartered
slowly, steadily, with its enormous freight, then started head-on up
the stream. Thick water foamed against the blunt snouts of the barges,
as the little tug between them neatly forged ahead with its great cargo,
with a sense of limitless power, and with astonishing speed. The young
cool light of morning fell flat and cleanly on the rusty sides of the old
freight cars on the barges: everything began to blaze with thrilling
color. The excitement, the beauty, the feelings of wonder and recognition which all of the associations of the scene evoked, were intoxicating."

Besides the view which it commanded of the river, the apartment
had another thing to recommend it, the fact that it was only two blocks
away from the Perkinses' house. Wolfe had always been welcome there,
but now, for the next two years, he all but lived there as a member
of the family—or as Perkins' son, which to all intents and purposes
he was. Perkins never seemed to see enough of him, and Mrs. Perkins
fed him, cared for him, listened to his problems and entertained his
friends with the patience of a saint. However, the young Perkins girls
were not entirely enthusiastic about having their home invaded by this
garrulous giant who monopolized their father and who teased the
youngest of them in a way that they thought cruel, although it was no
doubt only an inept attempt at familiarity. At any rate, Wolfe came
and went so constantly between his house and the Perkinses' that
his huge figure soon became a familiar one on East Forty-ninth Street.
"The block between us and First Avenue was almost slumlike,"
Perkins wrote later. "Boys played some exciting adaptation of baseball,
and then of football, in the street, and the sidewalks were crowded
with children. They all knew Tom. When he went by in his long, slow,
country stride, looking at everything, they would call out, 'Hello, Mr.
Wolfe.' And the police all knew him too. Once my wife said, 'A flower
pot has disappeared from one of our window boxes. I can't understand
how it happened.' The window box was too high for anyone to reach,
you would think, and who would want a geranium? Long afterward, one
night Tom said: 'I meant to tell you, I took one of your geraniums.

I was coming in but the house was dark so I just took a flower pot, and a cop saw me and said, "What are you doing?" I said, "I'm taking it home to water it." He just laughed.' This was New York. Was the cop afraid of Tom and his great size? No, he knew him, and understood him: that human quality in Tom had made him friends with everyone around, and they knew he was one of them."

Wolfe was touchingly delighted with his new apartment. The rent was eighty dollars a month, which he considered highway robbery, but urged on by Mrs. Jelliffe, he had signed the lease and moved in on October 1. She had had his furniture repaired while he was abroad, and now she helped him to get settled, whereupon Mrs. Bernstein, not to be outdone, undertook to decorate the place for him, presenting him with a mirror for above the mantelpiece, a handsome old brass lamp, and best of all, a made-to-order bed, the first he'd ever had that was long enough and strong enough for his gigantic frame. She was jealous of Mrs. Jelliffe's able and disinterested management of his affairs, and when the latter suggested that he have venetian blinds, she strongly opposed their installation, adding that she had already found "some excellent material" for curtains. But Wolfe paid slight attention. He had asked the most important woman in his life—his mother— to come up and visit him, and he was intent on purchasing a comfortable day bed for the living room so that she could sleep there.

Wolfe's book of stories, *From Death to Morning*, was published on November 14, 1935, and was none too favorably received. As he wrote to Henry Volkening on the eve of publication, "I have a hunch the well-known 'reaction' has set in against me, and that I will take a pounding on this book." In other words, as is so often true after a writer has had a great success, the New York literary people were examining him more critically, to see what was so wonderful about him after all. "You know as well as I do, how quickly they can turn," he wrote later to Hamilton Basso. "How desperately hard it is to prevail when they make up their minds about you. . . . I am certainly not bitter about the reception of the stories. I am not sore about it. I'm only telling you that most of the criticism was as the minds made up in advance saw it. The things they'd begun to go for me for in 'Of Time and the River' were carried right over and plastered on my book of stories. The stories, it appeared, were not stories at all, but sections that Max Perkins and I had scissored out of the manuscript of 'Of Time and the River.' . . . The thing that made me tough, however, saved me from apoplectic strangulation, and, in fact, gave me a sort of haughty indifference, was the earnest and no doubt pigheaded belief shared in by Max Perkins and a few other people that the best single piece of writing, the truest, the most carefully planned, and in the end the most unassailable that I've ever done is in that book. I'm not going to tell you what it is.[2] Apparently, most of the critics didn't take the trouble to read it, and those that did, for the most part, dismissed it as chaotic, formless, a river of incondite and meaningless energy. Well, I'll stick to the piece and I'm willing to wait. I don't believe it's gone with the wind. I think the time will come when someone will really read it. So I don't feel bad about it or about the book."

Wolfe had come a long way from the supersensitivity to adverse reviews which in 1930 had made him threaten to give up writing. The "chip on his shoulder" which had come from his self-doubt had faded magically away before *Of Time and the River*'s great success, and not even the unfavorable reviews of *From Death to Morning* could mar his "knowledge that he had met the ordeal a second time, and finally had conquered."

By December 1935 *Of Time and the River* had sold 40,000 copies, and Wolfe was honored by a request from Whitney Darrow, the head of the sales department at Scribners, for an autographed photo to hang on Darrow's office wall, which was already crowded with the portraits of other best-selling Scribner authors. Wolfe went to a penny arcade on West Forty-second Street and enjoyed himself immensely sitting in a booth and making faces while he had a strip of inch-big pictures taken for a quarter. He chose the worst of these, which made him look like Wordsworth's idiot boy, had it mounted on a cardboard rectangle four feet by three, and solemnly presented it to Darrow.

He asked some of his old friends from Chapel Hill to a party on Christmas Eve, a belated housewarming of his new apartment and celebration of *Of Time and the River*'s sales success. He was always very sentimental about Christmas, and suddenly unable to control his happiness, he reached up to the ceiling of his living room with one of the expansive gestures typical of him and scrawled there with a big black crayon: "Merry Christmas to all my friends and love from Tom." The message stayed there on the ceiling for the two years that Wolfe lived at 865 First Avenue, and often, when he was pacing up and down, he'd glance up at it and smile. It was a symbol of his new-found happiness, his increasing freedom from the morbid supersensitivity of his own ego, and his greater love for all his fellow men.

[2] It was "The Web of Earth."

New Year's came, and now an entire year had passed since Wolfe had done any serious creative work on a book. He had planned to finish *The October Fair* and publish it as soon as possible. However, Perkins' anxiety about that book had been enormously increased by his interview with Mrs. Bernstein. "She said that she would do everything in her power to prevent the publication of that book with her as a figure in it," he wrote. "I was in the position of representing Tom, and so could not agree to any concession whatever. When she left, I held out my hand and she put hers behind her back, and said, 'I regard you as an enemy.' "[3] Later, Wolfe blamed Perkins for being too easily intimidated by Mrs. Bernstein's threat, but if he had insisted on finishing *The October Fair*, neither Perkins nor anybody else on earth could have stopped him. However, at that time he accepted Perkins' decision with very little protest. The truth was that he himself already had gone stale on the book during the two years that had elapsed since he had worked on it. To his way of thinking, it was part of *Of Time and the River*, and hence was far behind him. Feeling as he did about this, Wolfe could not overcome the inertia of his year's idleness and make the supreme effort of will required to get back to work. The full tide of his creative energy was dammed up by his reluctance to work on *The October Fair*: it would not flow till it could bypass that obstacle and find a whole new channel for itself.

During his trip to Boulder and the West he had already had one inspiration for a new and different book, one about nighttime in America, which he called at first *The Book of the Night* or *The Beast of the Night* and finally *The Hound of Darkness*. He had recorded the first germ of the idea for this in London four months earlier: "Frame of *The Hills Beyond Pentland*," he had written in his pocket notebook. "Chapter I, The Beast of the Night (America). A lion in the mouth sulfurous, in the maw ochreous—etc. Great medley of thoughts, scraps, darts, of a child's impressions." Then, in the course of his actual wanderings across "night-time America" all the way to the Pacific coast, he had expanded his conception of this material from a single chapter to an entire book. "At various times during the last month—at Boulder and elsewhere—I have discoursed very eloquently and persuasively about my book of the night, which is beginning to interest me more and more all the time," he wrote to Perkins from Reno on September 12. "I have told how much of my life has been lived by night, about the chemistry of darkness, the strange and

[3] From Perkins' letter of October 23, 1945, to John S. Terry.

magic thing it does to our lives, about America at night: the rivers, plains, mountains, rivers in the moon or darkness (last night, by the way, coming up here through the Sierra Nevadas there was blazing moonlight, the effect was incredibly beautiful)—and how the Americans are a night-time people, which I have found out everywhere is absolutely true. Now, I'm afraid I've talked too much—please don't think I'm fool enough to think anyone is going to, or can, 'steal my ideas,' but people have been immensely and instantly absorbed when I told about my book, and have at once agreed to the utter truth of it. I have got hold of an immense, rich, and absolutely true thing about ourselves, at once very simple, profound, and various—and I know a great and original book, unlike any other, can be written on it . . .

"It will be years before I do it, but it keeps gathering in me all the time. I don't know yet exactly what form it will take, or whether it can be called a 'novel' or not. I don't care—but I think it will be a great tone-symphony of night—railway yards, engines, freights, dynamos, bridges, men and women, the wilderness, plains, rivers, deserts, a clopping hoof, etc.—seen *not by a definite personality*, but haunted throughout by a consciousness *of personality*. In other words, I want to assert my divine right once and for all to be the *God Almighty* of a book— to be at once the spirit to move it, the spirit behind it, never to appear, to blast forever the charge of 'autobiography' while being triumphantly and impersonally autobiographical."

For the remainder of his life Wolfe would have moments of rhapsodic inspiration about "night-time in America," such as the one which he had at a little country railroad station with his friends Clayton and Kathleen Hoagland soon after his return from California. "One . . . beautiful moonlight night . . . about one o'clock in the morning, we decided we would walk down to the station with him," Mrs. Hoagland said years later. "He had just had about fifteen cups of tea (which he loved) and ten or eleven fish sandwiches (cold fish sandwiches, another of his pet things). . . . Anyway, we started out. We got down towards the station, which is . . . also where the bleachery has its loading platform and works, and they're built of yellow brick. . . . So Tom was coming along with his head thrown back, walking as if he owned the world and sniffing up everything . . . and there in front of us was this little station—a little wooden shack, one room. Behind it, silhouetted in the moonlight, was this great tree, and the rails were like silver ribbons, and the insects were going up-and-down (you know how they go in that chorus) and there was a freight car, two freight cars, one red, I remember, and one brown (one was the Virginia Railroad), and Tom looked, and you'd think he was sniffing fire like a Dalmatian or something when he saw a freight car, because he got all excited and his eyes came to light, everything came to light, and he threw his arms out and he looked at me and he said 'K-K-Kitty!' (You know he always spoke with a kind of stutter when he got excited and rapt over something.) 'K-K-Kitty! Look! This is America. All over the country there are little stations like this, with a tree, and there's a siding, with a factory, for loading freight cars. Look at the rails. Here,' he said. 'Come!' And he made us kneel down and feel the vibrations on the tracks of a train that might be coming. Then he said, 'Come along. I want to show you how you should write. See these walls. Feel them. You can't write except you feel them. Look at the color. They are yellow. They're a *faded* yellow. Feel those.' We all had to feel the wall. He said, 'Feel the ground. Put your hand on the ground,' he said. 'Listen to the insects. Look. The moon is shining over all this eastern part of America. It *will* be shining,' he said. 'This is America, Kitty.' Well, I came home and I sat down and I thought, 'Well, now I know why he writes like he does. He's in love with America.' "[4]

Wolfe never wrote his "book of the night," but during the last three years of his life he wrote great chunks of lyrical material for it. Some of these finally found a place in *The Web and the Rock* and *You Can't Go Home Again*, but the essence of the book was embodied in a short piece which appeared in the February 1, 1938, issue of *Vogue*. Wolfe called this piece "The Hound of Darkness," but because that number of *Vogue* was the "Americana issue," the editors changed his beloved title to one of their own: "Prologue of America."

January and February 1936 slipped by, and Wolfe still had not started on a book. However, as he wrote later to Hamilton Basso, "I had to get back to work, or I think I would have gone crazy . . . , and I finally found, as old Daniel Webster said, that the way to resumption was to resume." For years he had toyed with the idea of someday doing an objective and satiric book about a writer in the modern world. "I have been reading *Robinson Crusoe*," he had written in his notebook in August 1930. "Why not a book on Robinson in the modern world—the Crusoe in the desert island of this world. It would be hard to do." Again, in September of that year, an entry in his notebook shows that he tried and then discarded a combination of this objective book with his "search for a father" theme:

[4] From "Thomas Wolfe: Biography in Sound," first produced as an NBC radio broadcast and reprinted in the Fall 1956 issue of the *Carolina Quarterly*.

"Idea for
The Strange Life and Adventures of Mr. David Monkey Hawke,
A Gentleman of Good Family,
Of His Early Youth,
Of His Wanderings in America and Europe,
And of His Remarkable Search to Find His Father,
And How He Found Him.
As Compiled from the Original Manuscripts
And Edited by
Thomas Wolfe."

And again, in March 1932, he had written to George McCoy: "Some day I think I will write a book about what happens to a fellow who writes a book." The idea had been ripening inside him all the time, and now, in his reluctance to finish *The October Fair* and his anxiety to refute the criticism that he could write only autobiography, he was struck by it as if by a brand-new inspiration.

"It came boiling to the surface all of a sudden," he wrote to Basso. "Of course, it had been stewing around down there for a great many years, but when I told Max about it, he snapped his fingers and said at once, 'Do it, and do it now.' He then told me that he had known for years that I would have to write such a book, it was unquestionably a thing I ought to do now at this period of my life. He told me to get busy on it at once. I expressed doubts to him whether I would be able to achieve such a book, and he told me there was no doubt at all, if I would go at it and keep going, that I could undoubtedly do it and that I was the only person who could. Well, I hope the doctor is right. He has been right most of the time so far, and I hope he is right now. At any rate, we are both excited about it, and I am going to 'let 'er rip.' "

It was to Heinz Ledig-Rowohlt, the editor of Rowohlt Verlag who had always been most intimately concerned with Wolfe and with his work, that he wrote the fullest description of what he planned the book to be: "The general conception of the book is this: it is not one of the books that have been announced as part of the 'Of Time and the River' series, it is by far the most objective book I have ever written, although of course, like anything that is any good, it comes right out of my own experience, from everything I may have learned or found out during the course of my life. If I succeed in it, I want it to be a kind of tremendous fable, a kind of legend composed of all the materials of experience. The general idea, so far as I can tell you here in the limits of a letter, is the idea that so many of the great men of the past, each in his own way, has used as the fundamental idea of his book. That idea as I conceive it is the story of a good man abroad in the world—shall we say the naturally innocent man, the man who sets out in life with his own vision of what life is going to be like, what men and women are going to be like, what he is going to find, and then the story of what he really finds. It seems to me that this is the idea behind 'Don Quixote,' behind 'The Pickwick Papers,' behind 'Candide,' behind 'Gulliver,' and even, it seems to me, behind such works as 'Faust' and 'Wilhelm Meister.' I am putting everything into this book of mine. Of course, it has got to be the book of an American, since I am an American. Parts of it are going to be savage, parts fantastic, parts extravagant and grotesque, and some of it very coarse and very bawdy, and, I think, wonderfully comical and funny; and of course I also want the book to be full of faith and poetry and loveliness and my own vision of life and of America. . . . If I succeed, it ought to be a wonderfully exciting and interesting book to read. It will be another tremendously long book—God knows how long—longer perhaps even than 'Of Time and the River,' but I am not worrying about that at present. . . .

"Tentatively, I have called the book 'The Vision of Spangler's Paul.' It has a sub-title:

'The Story of His Birth, His Life,
His Going To and Fro in the Earth,
His Walking Up and Down in It:
His Vision also of the Lost, the
Never-Found, the Ever-Here America.

With an Introduction
by
A Friend.'

"The following quotation which I have taken from 'War and Peace' and which I intend to use as a kind of legend at the beginning of the book, may make it a little clearer:

'Prince Andrei . . . turned away . . . His heart was
heavy and full of melancholy. It was all so
strange, so unlike what he had anticipated.'

". . . There is a tendency here among the critics to assume the kind of writing I do best is what they call 'autobiographical,' and we hope through this book to show them once and for all that this is not true. Perkins says I can create freely, invent and tell a story as well as anyone in the country—and I hope he is right. . . . And really I think I am doing a very wise thing now to do this completely new kind of book at a time in my life when I am still young and full of energy and have the enthusiasm and the fire to do it."

It was on St. Patrick's Day, in 1936, that Wolfe actually began the writing of the book, while on a brief trip to Boston. "Wrote book beginning. Goes wonderfully. Full of hope," he wired to Perkins, and soon he had "begun to go again like a locomotive." One night soon afterward, Nancy Hale, who lived near the Perkinses on East Forty-ninth Street, heard at two or three in the morning a kind of deep and distant chant in the deserted street. As it grew louder and nearer she looked out of the window, and there was the unmistakably huge figure of Tom Wolfe, in his battered black fedora and long, dark, swaying raincoat, marching down the street with his tremendous strides, and chanting:

"I wrote ten thousand words today!
I wrote ten thousand words today!"

Another of Wolfe's great creative cycles had begun, the last one of his life. It would never be completed, but would be broken off halfway by his untimely death.

XXI

MEANWHILE, Wolfe's ill-fated preface from *Of Time and the River* had been published, after a series of typical vicissitudes. When he had been interviewed by Sanderson Vanderbilt for the *Herald Tribune* in February 1935, Wolfe had tried to explain the difficulties confronting the artist in America, and had suddenly grabbed up the manuscript of the preface from his table and handed a few pages of it to Vanderbilt, stammering earnestly: "H-h-here! T-t-take this! I've s-said it all in here m-much better than I can express it to you now." It was not till two weeks later, when on the eve of sailing for Europe he turned over the preface to Miss Nowell, that he realized he had given Vanderbilt part of the only copy in existence. "Well, try and get it back from him," he said to her. "And while you're at it, maybe you can bawl him out about that interview."

She had got back the missing pages from Vanderbilt, only to find that they did not fit onto the portion of the preface which she had received from Wolfe. Accordingly, she returned both fragments to him when he returned to New York in July, whereupon, after losing them in a bar where he had gone with Perkins and finally recovering them, he rewrote and expanded the entire thing into the speech which he was to deliver at the University of Colorado Writers' Conference. It was at this time that he gave the piece its title of *The Story of a Novel*. Again, just before his departure for Colorado, he gave a fragmentary copy to Miss Nowell, asking her to "try and get me some money for it from some magazine." She cut it from approximately 15,000 words to 7000, got Perkins to O.K. it during Wolfe's protracted absence, and sold it to the *Atlantic Monthly*. It was only when Wolfe returned to New York in late September and was asked to read her shortened version that he innocently said, "Oh, I forgot to give you the rest of this. This is only the first half."

"The rest" was another 15,000 words, which she again cut to approximately 7000, and sent to the editors of the *Atlantic* with an earnest message from Wolfe to the effect that if they would publish the second half as well as the first, they could have them both for the price originally offered. To this, however, they replied that the two halves made the piece too long for publication in one issue and that they still preferred the first without the second and wanted to carry out their plan of publishing just that. Wolfe, quite understandably, refused to let them do this. Accordingly, the manuscript was recalled from the *Atlantic* and for some weeks traveled around half in, half out of his coat pocket, like a baby kangaroo. On one occasion it fell out into the gutter at Broadway and 125th Street and lay there for about an hour till he missed it from his pocket. He went back and, miraculously, found it lying in the mud.

Finally he happened to see Nobel Cathcart and Henry Seidel Canby of the *Saturday Review of Literature*, who expressed an interest in the piece and ended up by publishing it in three installments, in the December 14, 21, and 28, 1935, issues of that magazine. It was unique, both as a human document and as a subjective description of the creative process, and it soon became recognized as one of the rare things which are of special value to other writers. And gradually, as praise of it was reported back to him, Perkins forgot his first anxiety about it, until he finally decided that Scribners ought to bring it out as a small book. It was published in book form on April 21, 1936, and four days later the "harmful reaction" which Perkins had originally feared found a strident and embittered voice in Bernard De Voto.

Ironically enough, De Voto's review appeared on the front page of the *Saturday Review*, where, four months earlier, *The Story of a Novel* had made its own debut. It was entitled "Genius Is Not Enough," and its malicious intent was emphasized by a photo of De Voto grinning vindictively from behind an upheld revolver. It was not the first time that he had gone gunning for Tom Wolfe. A year earlier, in the April 27, 1935, issue of the *Saturday Review*, he had begun a review of James Boyd's *Roll River* by saying: "There are a number of ways to write that undefined entity, the American novel. Mr. Wolfe has recently exhibited one way: to print the word 'America' ten thousand times, to depict young Faustus as a victim of manic-depressive insanity, to fill the stage with Mardi Gras grotesques who suffer from compulsion neuroses and walk on stilts and always speak as if firing by battery, to look at everything through the lens of an infantile regression . . . and to fluff up the material of fiction, one part, with ten parts of bastard blank verse ecstasy. I wonder if only an accident of the calendar led Scribners to hold *Roll River* till *Of Time and the River* was well launched, or whether capital investment may not have had something to do with the schedule. For Mr. Boyd now exhibits another way to write an American novel, and he wins by a number of Mormon blocks. . . . His book is only 600 pages long, it contains not a single goat-cry, and no one beats his head or knuckles to a bloody pulp on any wall within its covers. . . . There is no great hope that it will be widely acclaimed in the press. Mr. Boyd writes about individuals instead of classes, . . . so one half of the cheerleaders will find him lacking in *Zeitgeist*. The other half will look in vain for the flatulent giantism which, at the moment, they hold to be the purest vision of America."

Now, with the pretext of reviewing *The Story of a Novel*, De Voto said the same thing all over again, at great length and with variations, and with a vindictive bitterness which made some people remark that his own novels had not been much of a success. He described the supposed subject of his review, *The Story of a Novel*, quite favorably in one initial paragraph, and then announced that he was going "to examine it in relation to Mr. Wolfe's novels, to see what continuities and determinants it may reveal, and to inquire into their bearing on the art of fiction.

"Let us begin with one of many aspects of Mr. Wolfe's novels that impress the reader," he went on with relish, "the frequent recurrence of material to which one must apply the adjective placental. . . . A great part of *Look Homeward, Angel* was just the routine first-novel of the period which many novelists had published and many others had suppressed . . . The rest of it was not so easily catalogued. Parts of it showed intuition, understanding and ecstasy, and an ability to realize all three in character and scene . . . These looked like great talent, . . . but also there were parts that looked very dubious indeed—long, whirling discharges of words, unabsorbed in the novel, unrelated to the proper business of fiction, . . . raw gobs of emotion, aimless and quite meaningless jabber, claptrap, belches, grunts and Tarzan-like screams. . . . It was as if the birth of the novel had been accompanied by a lot of the material that had nourished its gestation. . . . It looked like one of two things, there was no telling which. It looked like the self-consciously literary posturing of a novelist too young and too naive to have learned his trade. Or, from another point of view, it looked like a document in psychic disintegration. And one of the most important questions in contemporary literature was: would the proportion of fiction to placenta increase or decrease in Mr. Wolfe's next book?

"It decreased. . . . The placental material had enormously grown and, what was even more ominous, it now had a rationalization. . . . It had now been retroactively associated with the dark and nameless heaving of the voiceless and unknown womb of Time, and with the unknown and voiceless fury of the dark and lonely and lost America. . . .

Again, a state of mind that had been appropriate to the puberty of Eugene seemed inappropriate as the boy grew older . . . I mean the giantism of the characters. Eugene himself, in *Of Time and the River*, was clearly a borderline manic-depressive: he exhibited the classic cycle in his alternation between 'fury' and 'despair' . . . That was simple enough, but practically every other character in the book also suffered from fury and compulsions, and, what was more suggestive, they were all twenty feet tall, spoke with the voice of trumpets and the thunder, ate like Pantagruel, wept like Niobe, laughed like Falstaff, and bellowed like the bulls of Bashan. . . . To a child all adults are giants: their voices are thunderous, their actions are portentous and grotesquely magnified, and all their exhibited emotions are seismic. It looked as if part of Eugene's condition was an infantile regression. . . .

"Well, *The Story of a Novel* puts an end to speculation and supplies some unexpected but very welcome light. To think of these matters as contempt of the medium, regression and infantilism is to be too complex and subtle. The truth shows up in two much simpler facts: that Mr. Wolfe is still astonishingly immature, and that he has mastered neither the psychic material out of which a novel is made nor the technique of writing fiction. . . ."

Then came the criticism which hurt Wolfe most—the criticism which Perkins had always dreaded:

"The most flagrant evidence of his incompleteness is the fact that, so far, one indispensable part of the artist has existed not in Mr. Wolfe but in Maxwell Perkins. Such organizing faculty and such critical intelligence as have been applied to the book have come not from inside the artist, not from the artist's feeling for form and esthetic integrity, but from the office of Charles Scribner's Sons. For five years the artist pours out words 'like burning lava from a volcano'—with little or no idea what their purpose is, which book they belong in, what the relation of part to part is, what is organic and what irrelevant, or what emphasis or coloration in the completed work of art is being served by the job at hand. Then Mr. Perkins decides these questions—from without, and by a process to which rumor applies the word 'assembly.' . . . The artist writes a hundred thousand words about a train: Mr. Perkins decides that the train is worth only five thousand words. But such a decision as this is properly not within Mr. Perkins's power; it must be made by the highly conscious self-criticism of the artist in relation to the pulse of the book itself. Worse still, the artist goes on writing till Mr. Perkins tells him that the novel is finished. But the end of a novel is, properly, dictated by the internal pressure, osmosis, metabolism—what you will

—of the novel itself, of which only the novelist can have a first-hand knowledge. There comes a point where the necessities of a book are satisfied, where its organic processes have reached completion. It is hard to see how awareness of that point can manifest itself at an editor's desk—and harder still to trust the integrity of a work of art in which not the artist but the publisher has determined where the true ends and the false begins. . . .

"The placental passages are now explained. They consist of psychic material which the novelist has proved unable to shape into fiction. . . . The principle is very simple. . . . A novel *is*—it cannot be asserted, ranted or even detonated. A novelist represents life. When he does anything else, no matter how beautiful or furious or ecstatic the way in which he does it, he is not writing fiction. Mr. Wolfe can write fiction—has written some of the finest fiction of our day. But a great part of what he writes is not fiction at all; it is only material with which the novelist has struggled but which has defeated him. The most important question in American fiction to-day, probably, is whether he can win that encounter in his next book. . . . If he does win it, he must do so inside himself. Mr. Perkins and the assembly-line at Scribners can do nothing to help him. . . ."

Publicly at any rate, Wolfe took De Voto's attack very well. He did not "take on" about it at Scribners, and although it would seem that he must have done so privately to Perkins, none of the latter's close associates have any recollection of it. Meanwhile a number of people, most of whom were perfect strangers to Wolfe, were writing to him and to the *Saturday Review* to protest against De Voto's article, and to these he was able to reply with both humor and forbearance. "As to Mr. De Voto, I think I feel equal to all the De Voto's in the world—and I guess there are a good many—after reading your letter," he wrote to Kent Roberts Greenfield.[1] ". . . My hide is by no means as tough

---

[1] Greenfield was at this time chairman of the Department of History at Johns Hopkins University and is now chief historian of the Department of the Army and general editor of *The U. S. Army in World War II*. He was a stranger to Wolfe but had written to him saying: ". . . I am perfectly willing that you should be criticized for the faults of integration that deprive your book of its full effectiveness, but it annoys me that this criticism should be delivered with such a wallop by anyone who so clearly fails to estimate at its precious value what you have accomplished. Nor can I find any justification either in the book or in my code of personal integrity for the easy assumptions with which he has chosen to stigmatize your personality. They have no basis except in the jargon of a half-baked psychiatrist, and I must confess that in reading De Voto's article, I could not avoid the disturbing sensation that I was witnessing an unconscious exposure on his part of motives and feelings that had better be kept in the darkness of

as it should be, . . . but I have been pounded enough . . . to find out that these matters are not as desperate as I thought them, and what has been most valuable, I think I have really found out for myself that it is the truth that hurts. So usually when something gets in under my hide and hurts, I have found there is a measure of truth in it, and in the end have usually managed to derive some profit from it. The De Voto thing didn't hurt me—it just made me mad. I am not pretending to laugh it off, nor to dismiss utterly everything the man says as false, but I am grateful to you for thinking that the total amount of what he said was false because, even though I do say so myself, I thought so too. . . .

"I suppose the only thing I had a right to get mad over in the De Voto piece, if I had a right to get mad at all, was the fact . . . that when a man's book is published he has a right to expect that his book will be reviewed and not used as a pivot, a thread, a stalking horse, or an excuse by means of which the reviewer may express his dislike, his hostility, or his prejudice against everything the man has ever written. I suppose the excuse in this case might be that the book in question which provided the opportunity for De Voto's onslaught was a little piece of ninety-three pages called *The Story of a Novel*, and that the book did tell something about my other books and the way I wrote them. Well, it seems to me this is a pretty flimsy excuse. I think I have a right to expect a review of *The Story of a Novel* . . . , and I think that what I got was—well, it was what I got. . . .

"Well, what is there to say? I don't think I have been through all of it, but I have been through a good deal of it, and . . . I am prepared for almost anything, and if some reviewer uses his remarks on a book concerning the use of central heating by the Eskimos as a basis for an assault upon everything I write, I don't think I will be very much astonished. It seems to be a favorite occupation of a good many people to shoot down a whole regiment of wooden soldiers, or stick a straw man of one's own concoction full of bayonet holes and then to return bravely from the wars, saying: 'We have met the enemy and they are ours'; but this is no way to kill a living man—it doesn't seem to me to be a very substantial victory, and in the end I think it means nothing.

"I still take it hard; I still get mad about it; but if there is anything true in what they say, I have got a good memory and I don't forget it; and if what they say is not true, then how can a man be hurt by it? I have had some pretty bad times when I didn't think what I did was any good, I was inclined to agree with almost anyone who felt the same

case-books. This feeling may do him a grave injustice, but I have not been able to explain by any other theory the truculence of his onslaught."

way, but I have held on to this conviction, and in fact the conviction grows stronger as I go along—I genuinely believe that if a thing has something good in it, the good in it is indestructible and will be saved, no matter what anyone says or does; and if a thing has no good in it, it cannot be saved, no matter what anyone says or does, and if it is no good, the man who did it ought not to want it to be saved, anyway. Furthermore, if what a man does is good, and another man is false about it and goes on record with his falseness, then it seems to me there is no need of doing anything to him. He has done the job himself. Usually I find when our hides get nailed up to the wall, we not only supply the hide but we also supply the hammer and the nails. It is our own job. Well, I am not going on record myself as saying what I do is either good or bad. I suppose if I didn't really feel there was some good in it, it would be hard to keep on working as I do, in hope of betterment, and I think that the conviction that I have just expressed to you is something more than a mere desire to believe. I believe it is a fact that the good thing can't be hurt, and that knowledge helps me a lot as I go on writing. As you can see from this letter, I don't pretend that I didn't take the De Voto thing seriously, that I am not trying to laugh it off, but it didn't hurt me, it doesn't rankle, I have no vengeful feelings; and in the end I may even get some good from it. The main thing is I am working like a horse and I don't see how anyone, not even Mr. De Voto, is going to do anything about that.

"The other thing is that I think I learn a little, slowly, all the time; that I hope to profit by my own mistakes and errors of the past and grow in wisdom, in power, in maturity; and that whenever I get a letter like the one you wrote me, it makes me want to exert every energy of my life and talent to do so. So thanks again. Your letter meant a lot to me, and I want you to know that it did and that I am deeply and sincerely grateful. Please forgive me for writing you such a long one in return—as you may have heard, brevity is not one of my most noticeable gifts; but maybe I can do something about that too. Anyway, I'm going to try."

But no matter how brave a front Wolfe managed to put up, he was badly shaken by De Voto's article, and in a way which would affect the course of his entire life. For the accusation that he was dependent upon "Mr. Perkins and the assembly-line at Scribners" would rankle deep inside him till it poisoned his entire relationship with them, and it came to a head in his ultimate decision that he must break away from them in order to prove that he could write his books without their help. There were other deep and complex reasons for Wolfe's final break with Perkins, but the necessity to disprove De Voto's accusation was, as Perkins said, "the basic one," "at the very root of our trouble."[2]

During the winter of 1935–36, before the appearance of De Voto's article, Wolfe had had two quarrels with Scribners, but both had been patched up and virtually forgotten. The first had occurred in December, when after two years or more of trying to get his courage up, Wolfe had finally announced that he was going to have his money in a bank account, instead of having it held in "protective custody" for him by Scribners. "I had a big row with Tom, but it is all smoothed out now," Perkins wrote on December 14, 1935, to Wheelock, who was out on sick leave. "I would tell you about it if there were time, because it was amusing in the end, but one result is that he demanded a thousand and fifty dollars in cash, which was delivered to him yesterday morning at eleven. It was for a bank account. I saw him at about seven last night. He had overslept, so had not deposited the money, and he dared not to leave it in the apartment, so it was in his pocket. I am sure he did not wake up to-day in time to deposit it, and to-morrow is Sunday. He had some plan of delivering it to Mrs. Bernstein in the Gotham, where they have what he regarded as a safe safe. I made him promise to go there direct without stopping for any drinks until it was put away. But what he did, I do not know."

However, Perkins' anxieties on this score were totally unfounded. Wolfe had enough of his mother's blood in him to make him hang on to his money with great tenacity, and what he actually did was deposit it in a checking account with the Chase National Bank, together with an additional $11,740.13, which he withdrew from Scribners three weeks later. He seldom filled in his checkbook stubs or balanced his account; he never remembered that he needed cash; and he never could tear himself away from work to get to the bank before it closed, but invariably ended up by cashing a check at the Hilltop Liquor Store at the corner of First Avenue and Forty-ninth Street, which was open in the evening. However, he had taken an important step toward his independence from Scribners: from now on he could go there or not, according to his mood, instead of having to go and "beg Bert Cross" for every cent he spent.

Wolfe's second quarrel with Scribners had been about the royalties on The Story of a Novel—not, as he made clear, about the actual amount of money which he would receive, but about what he considered Scribners' breach of the good faith that existed between himself and them. When Wolfe and Perkins first discussed the possibility

[2] From Perkins' letter of November 13, 1945, to John S. Terry.

of publishing *The Story of a Novel*, they agreed that the price of it should be as low as seventy-five cents or a dollar, both because it was so small a book and because it would then be within the means of students, beginning writers, and other people possessed of more literary appreciation than ready cash. For the sake of this low price Wolfe agreed to waive his regular 15 per cent straight royalty and accept a sliding scale of 10 per cent on the first 3000 copies sold, 12½ per cent on copies 3000 to 7500, and 15 per cent on all copies sold thereafter. The contract was accordingly drawn on the basis of these royalties, but it did not specify the price of the book, as it should have under the circumstances. Almost immediately upon hearing of Perkins' plan to publish *The Story of a Novel*, the sales department began to criticize it. "The sales department could not see the sense in publishing such a little trifle, as it seemed to them," Perkins wrote later, "in the face of the fact that booksellers did not like little books, especially when they seemed priced too high. I could not tell Tom that I was trying to win over the full support of the sales department. He would not have understood that, and would have been enraged by the idea."[3]

Finally the book was priced at $1.50, without Wolfe's knowledge or consent, and when he discovered it on the eve of publication, he accused Perkins and Scribners of deceiving him. "I do not question your legal and contractual right to do this," he wrote to Perkins on April 21, the day of publication. "I agreed to the reduction at the time and for the reason I have mentioned. . . . But just because you have been generous and devoted friends, and because my feeling toward you has been one of devotion and loyalty, I do not want to see you do this thing now which may be legally and technically all right, but is to my mind a sharp business practice. . . . You know very well that I am not a business man and . . . that in matters of this sort, I am not able to cope with people who are skilled at it; but where it concerned you and Scribners, I have never thought for one moment that I would have to cope with it. The thing I really feel and believe is that at the bottom of your heart, . . . you agree with me . . . in this matter and know that I am right, as I know you agreed with me in the matter of almost $1,200, which I was charged for corrections in the proof of *Of Time and the River*. . . . You said at the time . . . that in view of . . . the way the corrections were made . . . , you didn't think I ought to have to pay as much money as that, and I understood you even to say that if I felt too strongly that . . . the bill was unfair, I would not have to pay it. Well,

[3] From Perkins' letter of October 29, 1945, to John S. Terry.

I don't feel that strongly about it . . . But I do feel that the bill of almost $1,200 is excessive and that I am being made to pay too much for corrections which I'll admit helped me and the book, but which were partly done with your collaboration. . . .

"I want to ask you this; if your refusal in this matter is final and you insist on holding me to the terms of the contract I signed for *The Story of a Novel*, don't you think that I . . . would be justified henceforth . . . in making use of a business advantage too if one came my way? Or do you think it works only one way? . . . As you know, I never gave a moment's serious consideration to any offers or persuasions that were made to me by other people and I think that you know . . . that in one case at least, a very large sum of money was mentioned at a time when I, myself, had nothing.[4] . . . You told me . . . I had a right to meet the man and. . . . even consider what he had to offer. Well, I suppose that's business practice . . . , but it has not been my practice. . . . What do you think about this anyway? If people are going to get hard-boiled and business-like, should it all be on one side, or doesn't the other fellow have a right to get hard-boiled and business-like too? . . .

"I don't expect my relations with my publisher to be a perpetual love feast, into which the vile question of money never enters, but I do say that you cannot command the loyalty and devotion of a man on the one hand and then take a business advantage on the other. . . . You may think I am kicking up a hell of a row over nothing, but I do think it is something, a great deal, not in a money way but in the matter of fair dealing, and I am writing to tell you so."

To this, Perkins immediately answered: "I am giving directions to reckon your royalties on 'The Story of a Novel' at 15% from the start. . . . I would rather simply agree to do this and say nothing further, but I should not have the right to do it without telling you that the terms, as proposed, on the $1.50 price are just, and that if the matter were to be looked upon merely as business we should not be justified as business men in making this concession. You are under a misapprehension if you think that when we suggested a reduction of royalty . . . we were basing the suggestion on the question of price. . . . We could not, at that time, know what the price would have to be. We found that the price had to be higher because of the question of basic costs which come into every phase of the handling, advertising, promoting, and making of a book. . . . The terms we proposed were therefore, in my opinion, just.

"You return to the question of the excess corrections . . . I once said

[4] Wolfe is referring to the offer made him by another publisher in 1934.

to you in Charles Scribner's presence that you had a good technical argument for not paying these corrections, because you did not make them, . . . since you did not read your proof, but, if you had done so, is there any doubt but what these corrections would have been much larger? . . . They were . . . rightly author's corrections, and why should the author not pay for them? . . .

"As to the other matter you speak of, . . . I certainly would not wish you to make what you thought was a sacrifice, on my account, and I would know that whatever you did would be sincerely believed to be right by you, as I know that you sincerely believe the contentions you make in this letter to me to be right. I have never doubted your sincerity, and never will. I wish you could have felt that way toward us."[5]

Before this letter could even reach him, Wolfe had begun to regret the necessity of quarreling with Perkins and had gone to make his peace with him. Then, when he received his letter, he answered it with a burst of penitence and affection that was very typical of him: "I got your letter this morning and I just want to write you back now to tell you that everything is settled so far as I am concerned, so let's forget about it. Now that you have told me that you would restore my old royalty of 15%, I want to tell you that I don't want it and want to stick to the contract I signed. That goes for all my other obligations as well. I really made up my mind to this yesterday, and that was the reason I . . . went around to see you. I wanted to tell you and I am afraid I didn't succeed in telling you very well that all the damn contracts in the world don't mean as much to me as your friendship means, and it suddenly occurred to me yesterday that life is too short to quarrel this way with a friend over something that matters so little. But I do want to tell you again just how genuinely and deeply sorry I am for boiling over the way I did the other night. We have had fireworks of this sort before and I am afraid they may occur again. But every time they do, I say something to a friend that is unjust and wrong, and sweat blood about it later. So just help me along with this by forgetting all about it, and let's look forward to the future. . . . I am now started on another book. I need your friendship and support more than I ever did, so please forget the worst mistakes I have made in the past and let's see if I can't do somewhat better in the future."

Wolfe wrote this on April 23. He did not know then that the immediate future, only two days hence, would bring the publication of De Voto's virulent attack upon him, and the planting of the seed of severance from Scribners. It is true that he would have rebelled against

[5] From *Editor to Author: The Letters of Maxwell E. Perkins.*

Perkins' help eventually anyway. Writers always do resent such help, and those who receive the most of it can be counted on to turn against their helpers in the end. Wolfe had been in desperate need of Perkins' help: without it, he could never have "surmounted the accursed barrier of the second book." But he now had won a great success: his expressions of resentment against Perkins' interference had been growing steadily for several years: the time was getting ripe for him to proclaim his independence, for better or for worse. But De Voto had put his finger on the sore spot, and with his bitter accusation that Wolfe could not write his books alone, he had forced the latter's rebellion so that it was sudden, violent, and well-nigh incomprehensible. Within a few weeks' time of the appearance of De Voto's article, Wolfe had begun to brood over the necessity of leaving Scribners; he began to discuss the possibility with his friends, most of whom reacted with amazement and dismay, if not with downright incredulity. "It became evident to me that he was trying to find pretexts for quarrels," Perkins wrote later. "I don't mean that Tom was deliberately and consciously inventing reasons for leaving us, but the underlying reasons were working so strongly in him, and yet were not consciously acknowledged, that he thought the pretexts were true reasons."[6] For the next year and a half he continued to brood about the necessity of leaving Scribners, with successive fits of truculence, desperation, grief, indecision, reconciliation, penitence, and then truculence again. It seemed as if everything that happened to him within that time was somehow transformed into an added reason for his leaving, and slowly, inexorably, he drew nearer to the final break.

One of these things was the series of lawsuits and legal difficulties in which he found himself involved and which he was inclined to blame on Perkins. The first suit, the one brought against him by Mrs. Boyd, he accused Perkins of having made possible by being "foolish, benevolent, soft-hearted, weak"[7] and by failing to obtain a written release from her at the time of the trouble between them and her in January 1931. The second was the threat of a libel suit from Mrs. Bernstein if *The October Fair* was published with a representation of her in it. Wolfe blamed Perkins for being too easily intimidated by her, insisting that she was

[6] From Perkins' letter of December 18, 1945, to John S. Terry.
[7] In his letter of May 23, 1935, Wolfe applied these adjectives to both himself and Perkins, but he obviously meant the latter. It was a sort of editorial "we" in reverse, which he often used in reference to Perkins, since the latter was the arbiter in all of his affairs.

"inwardly praying for nothing better than to be a leading character in a book of mine." Moreover, by a strange process of reasoning, he also blamed Perkins for thus exposing him to other libel suits, saying that "because of our weakness and irresolution, the news got around that we were afraid of publication for this reason," and that this led to the libel suit filed against him and Scribners by the Dorman family, from whom he had rented his apartment at 40 Verandah Place in 1931. This suit was the third—and the most ruinously costly—of those in which Wolfe found himself involved. It was his dissatisfaction with Scribners' conduct of this case which finally impelled him to ask Perkins for formal confirmation that he was bound by "no further agreement or obligation of any sort" to Scribners. The fourth suit was the one which Wolfe himself was forced to bring against a young manuscript agent with whom he had had legal difficulties. This affair dragged on for two entire years: it drove Wolfe wild with anxiety and exasperation, and when Perkins tried to help him with advice, he accused him of being contradictory and pusillanimous, and even of "trying to destroy" him.

There was no real reason why Perkins should have been involved in these affairs, with the exception of the Dorman suit, which named Scribners as a codefendant. However, Wolfe had made him his arbiter in every detail of his life, and he attributed to him, as to a god, not only his good fortunes but his bad ones. The "heroic figure stronger and wiser than himself" had proved unable to "give an answer" for all his "vexation and grief," and in his disillusionment, he turned against him, as a savage might turn against a fetish which had failed to bring him luck.

Another reason for Wolfe's disillusionment with Scribners was his gradual realization that publishers were in business for the sake of their own profit, and not, as he had at first almost believed, for the pure, aesthetic sake of publishing works of talent like his own. Scribners, during the benevolent reign of Charles Scribner III and Perkins, was generous and unmercenary to a fault, but their viewpoint and Wolfe's occasionally differed, as is inevitable in any business relationship between a buyer and a seller. When this happened, Wolfe always felt a bitter disillusionment and sense of personal betrayal which was exaggerated in direct proportion to the intensity of his devotion to Perkins and the firm. "Maybe for me the editor and the friend got too close together and perhaps I got the two relations mixed," he wrote in explanation of this to Perkins two months after his final break with Scribners. ". . . Maybe something like this happened to you too, I don't know. If this is true, it is a fault in both of us, but it is a fault that I would consider more on the side of the angels than the devil's side. I think, however, that what is even more likely to be a fault in modern life is when the elements of friendship and of business get confused, and when there is likely to be a misapprehension on the part of one or both of the parties as to which is which. . . . The artist is not a child where business is concerned but he may seem to be so to business men, because he is playing the game with only one set of chips, and the other people are sometimes playing the game with two sets of chips. I don't want you to understand by this that playing the game with two sets of chips is always wrong and wicked, and playing the game with one set of chips is always right. I do not think so. But I do think that when the players sit down to play, each of them ought to know what kind of game is being played—with one set of chips or two. I think this is important, because I think most of the misunderstanding comes from this."

Another and more cogent reason for Wolfe's break with Perkins was the latter's opposition to his writing about Scribners. Wolfe had always been fascinated by the workings of the publishing house, and during the course of many conversations, Perkins had not only told him about the history of the firm but about the personalities and private lives of many of the people working there. And when, in the spring of 1936, Wolfe began writing about a publishing firm called James Rodney & Co., Perkins suddenly realized that these intimate and highly confidential details concerning his associates at Scribners were in danger of being "written up" by Wolfe and published. He made no objection to being written about himself. Moreover, he knew that he could no more prevent Wolfe's writing what he felt impelled to write than he could prevent the operation of an elemental force. However, he insisted, with a stubbornness which came from moral rectitude, that if Wolfe published anything derogatory about Scribners or the people working there, it would be his, Perkins', duty to hand in his resignation from the firm and go into retirement. It was a case of an immovable object confronting an irresistible force, and it thwarted Wolfe in his creative plan for his new book, and drove him wild. The only possible solution seemed to him to break away entirely from Perkins and from Scribners, so that, as he put it, "if there is ever any necessity for anyone to resign anything on my account, that situation will never arise, simply because I won't be there to be resigned about."

This impasse between Wolfe and Perkins led to another reason for Wolfe's feeling that he must leave Scribners. A year had now elapsed since the publication of *Of Time and the River* and, although Perkins had expressed enthusiastic interest in Wolfe's idea for his new satiric book, *The Vision of Spangler's Paul*, he had done nothing to urge him to work upon it, nor had he offered him a contract for its publication. His failure to do this had undoubtedly come from a variety of reasons. In the first place, Scribners seldom offered a writer a contract until his book was ready to be published or until he needed a sizable advance and definite agreement to sustain him during the writing of it. Wolfe now did not need either: it would be years before his book was finished and ready for publication, and in the meanwhile he had approximately $12,000 in earned royalties from the sale of *Of Time and the River*. Moreover, Perkins undoubtedly felt some hesitation about giving him a contract, for fear that the material which he might write about Scribners might make the book impossible for them to publish; and also because he was beginning to have an intimation that Wolfe might be compelled to break away from Scribners, contract or no contract.

Wolfe was conscious of this hesitation and was constantly upset and puzzled about it. "The reason that I am so earnestly and seriously concerned with this is that in former years, before the publication of 'Of Time and the River,' you did show the greatest anxiety on this score," he wrote finally to Perkins in December 1936. "You were constant in your efforts to spur me on, to get me to complete and finish something for publication. Now, although almost two years have gone by since the publication of my last long book, you no longer show any anxiety whatever and, so far as I can judge, no immediate interest." The truth was that he felt the lack of the "dauntless and unshaken" encouragement with which Perkins had sustained him through the dark days of work upon *Of Time and the River*: he did not stop to realize that, because of his success, this was no longer necessary: and as he brooded over this, he became convinced that it meant that "Scribners no longer wants to publish me" and that he therefore would be justified in going elsewhere.

Still another reason, and one which had been steadily increasing since 1933 or 1934, was the bitter disagreement between Wolfe and Perkins about politics and economics. Wolfe had begun life as a small-town southern reactionary, but gradually, as he had witnessed the widespread suffering of the depression in America and the evils of fascism in Germany, he had become a liberal: in one of his letters of severance to Perkins he even described himself as a "revolutionary," although he made it clear that he used this word in its original sense, not with the modern connotation of "radical" or "communist." Perkins, on the other hand, with his New England and Harvard background, was a conservative. He feared that if Wolfe let himself be influenced by any of the left-wing doctrines which were so prevalent in New York literary circles at that time, his writing would suffer irreparable harm, and he stubbornly opposed Wolfe's growing liberalism till the latter felt that his "whole natural impulse of creation" was being "checked and hampered at every place." It is significant that in his literary apologia for his severance from Perkins, "Ecclesiasticus," in *You Can't Go Home Again*, Wolfe gave this ideological difference between them as the only reason for the break—"the root of our whole trouble, the mystery of our eventual cleavage and our final severance"—saying: "The little tongues will wag . . . will propose a thousand quick and ready explanations . . . but really, Fox, the root of the whole thing is here."

But still deeper than any of these reasons was the basic psychological pattern of Wolfe's life, his endless search to find a father, with its inevitable disillusionment and ultimate rejection of each "superior being" whom he idolized. Perkins had come nearer to fulfilling Wolfe's ideal than anyone: he had enabled him to realize himself as a writer and to win wide recognition for his talent; he had for seven years beneficently guided him in every detail of his life; and in the face of his keen and constant scrutiny, he had proved to be, as Wolfe had admitted, "in very many ways the best person I have ever known." But Wolfe at last had found a flaw in him—too great caution and conservatism—and, as always, he felt an exaggerated disillusionment and sense of having been betrayed. Now, inevitably, the cycle of his childhood pattern was drawing to a close, and just as he had broken away from the too constricting ties with his own mother, or with Mrs. Bernstein, so was he now impelled to break away from these with Perkins and Scribners. As Mrs. Jelliffe pointed out, "The iron bars which held him prisoner were within him, not in Scribners or anybody else."[8] But, unrealizing, he could only follow his blind compulsion to be free. There was, therefore, a deep, ironic truth in his favorite words from Martin Luther, which he often quoted at this time: "*Ich kann nicht anders*"—I can't do otherwise: there is no other way.

[8] From Belinda Jelliffe's unpublished reminiscences of Wolfe.

XXII

T HE early part of 1936 was nothing but a series of confusions and catastrophes for Wolfe. Some were ludicrous, some tragic, and some both, but they all were grimly serious to him because they never left him any peace in which to work. "When 'Of Time and the River' was published . . . , I thought that my troubles were over," he wrote later to his brother Fred. "But it seems now as if they were just beginning. . . . I returned to America feeling sure that now, at last, I had a secure position, a very modest income, the independence and, for the first time in my life, the peace and comfort that would enable me to continue my work hereafter in tranquility. I found instead that I had been thrown into a whirlpool. I was set upon by every kind of parasite, every kind of harpy, every kind of vulture, every kind of female egotist that had a string to pull, or that thought they could get something out of me—whether money, manuscript, royalties, percentages, or simply a sop to their vanity. Since I was—and this is the truth —a more or less unsuspecting and believing person who responds very quickly to people and to apparent overtures of friendship and good will, I was taken for quite a ride." It was not enough for him to be obsessed with brooding about the necessity of leaving Scribners: he had to be assailed by legal difficulties, one by one, in ruinously close succession: and these, in turn, because of his complex relationship with Perkins, only added fuel to his smoldering conviction that he must break free.

His quarrel with his manuscript agent was one of the lengthiest and most fantastic of all his legal difficulties. This agent was a young man, and because of his youth at the time, he shall not be identified by name. Wolfe had often gone to the house of this young man's family, and one Sunday afternoon in February 1935, had shown them his prepublication copy of *Of Time and the River*, which had just come off the press. "It was a very pleasant occasion," he said later in his legal deposition about this case. "The family were delighted that I had at last finished a piece of work which had required years to accomplish. Everyone showed a most friendly interest in the book. I was about to go to Europe and . . . humorously referred to the great bulk of my manuscript which

filled two enormous crates. . . . I think I probably said something like
this: 'I wish I knew what I could do with it: I wish somebody I knew
would keep it for me.' ——. . . then informed me . . . that the manuscript had considerable potential value among collectors . . . and I
probably said that I would be delighted if it was worth money and
would be glad to get something for it. I think —— probably said that he
would like to 'try the market' with portions of it. I think I probably
said, in complete good faith, that I should be glad to have him try."

The upshot of it was that, after consulting with Perkins, Wolfe gave
the young man the manuscript of "A Portrait of Bascom Hawke" so
that he could "try the market" with it while Wolfe was abroad. Later
Wolfe recalled this, since it was a portion of *Of Time and the River*
and he thought it better to offer the entire book manuscript for sale as
a whole. However, in December 1935 he gave the young man several
other things to sell: his own marked copy of *Of Time and the River*,
several short manuscripts, and a bulky one which had been wrapped up
in the Scribner safe and was believed by both himself and Perkins to
be the complete typed manuscript of *Of Time and the River*, but
which finally turned out to be only the material which had been omitted
from that book. The young man's first attempt to sell these in one lot
misfired, and Wolfe summarily demanded the return of them all to
him, but later, after again consulting with Perkins, he let the young
man offer them for sale one at a time. "I suggested good-naturedly
to —— that it seemed to me to be unwise to conduct these transactions
as if he were a member of a secret society, and that it would be better
if he took us, meaning myself and Mr. Perkins, more into his confidence," Wolfe said later in his deposition. ". . . At the same time I
suggested that he may have bitten off a little more than he could chew
in this first transaction, and that it seemed to me it would be wise if he
should make a more modest start the next time." Accordingly, the
young man sold, first, the marked copy of *Of Time and the River* to a
rare-book dealer for $125, from which he was paid a 20 per cent com-
mission: he next sold three short manuscripts for a similar price and
again received his commission: then he undertook to sell what they all
believed to be the typed manuscript of *Of Time and the River*.

Meanwhile the young man had persuaded Wolfe to let him take five
other manuscripts, one of which was a notebook containing early notes
and outlines for *Look Homeward, Angel*. However, friction was steadily
increasing between the two. "He had . . . become steadily more im-
portunate and demanding," Wolfe said later in his deposition. ". . .

He now wanted to get his hands on anything he could sell and . . . he . . . also tried to get hold of notebooks that I had kept in Europe years ago, unpublished manuscripts and anything else which he thought might be of value. I explained to him that I could not let him have these . . . because I had not myself used them yet. His reply was that he thought it extremely doubtful if I ever would make use of them, and that, besides, it did not matter anyway because I wrote so prolifically that I would always have plenty of manuscript. I pointed out to him that this was very faulty reasoning and . . . would also 'kill the goose that laid the golden eggs.' . . . And . . . I told him very kindly that although I was delighted to get something out of these manuscripts, delighted to get paid for them, I could not let this thing eat up my time the way it was beginning to do."

It was at this point, in early February 1936, that the rare-book dealer, who had been collating the supposed typed manuscript of *Of Time and the River* before buying it, announced that it was not that at all, but a great hodgepodge of unidentified material, both typed and longhand. Wolfe became terribly apprehensive, as he always did when unpublished manuscript seemed in danger of escaping from his grasp. He rushed to consult with Perkins and then told his agent that the entire manuscript must be recalled, so that he could see what it actually was and could make sure that he had copies of everything that it contained. The young man protested angrily that doing this would spoil his sale, but he was overruled by both Wolfe and Perkins. He went and got the manuscript from the dealer and brought it back to Scribners.

Wolfe next told the young man to come to his apartment on Monday, February 10, so that they could examine the manuscript and find out if he had duplicates of everything that was in it. He then forgot that he had made this date, and made another to have lunch with Mrs. Jelliffe. He was just leaving with her when the young man arrived, so he gave him two files of carbon copy manuscripts and told him to take them over to Scribners and to start comparing them with the manuscript which had been recalled from the dealer. However, when he himself arrived at Scribners in the middle of the afternoon, he found the young man sitting disconsolately in the fifth-floor library, surrounded by manuscripts but apparently doing nothing to compare them.

At this point Perkins further complicated matters by asking Wolfe to come out and have cocktails with him at the Chatham. "In this matter . . . I have always felt somewhat guilty," Perkins wrote later.

"Frere had just turned up from London, and I knew him very slightly, and was to meet him at the Chatham at five o'clock. I went in where Tom was talking to —— and asked him if he couldn't come over while —— was sorting over the material, and have a drink with us, since he was a firm friend of Frere's. I ought to have known better than that because Tom was not a one-drink man. Frere got to telling us about flying in the World War in those flimsy planes with almost no training, and he talked most eloquently, and the result was that —— waited for an hour, or perhaps two. Tom had had a number of drinks and neither he nor —— was in any state of mind to discuss anything reasonably."[1]

When Wolfe finally returned to Scribners and found the young man still sitting in the library, making no apparent effort to collate the manuscripts, he lost his temper. "I then told him that this whole business had begun to take up too much of my time," he said later in his deposition. "That I was spending a good part of my time fooling around with these manuscripts when I ought to be at work writing, and I told him that we would either have to find a way in which he could do his work without taking up so much of my time and energy or that we would have to call the whole matter off. It was at this point that the fight started. —— remarked that if I took the manuscript away from the dealer after he had gone to considerable labor to collate it and had practically agreed to pay the sum of $275, it was 'one of the skunkiest tricks' that he had ever heard of. I told —— that I did not think this was true. . . ."

Up to this point the whole affair seemed just a tempest in a teapot. However, during the next two months the young man sent Wolfe a series of letters which were a combination of youthful bravado and legalistic threats. In them he claimed that Wolfe could not dismiss him as his manuscript agent since "the contract we entered into can be nullified only by mutual consent," that his "authority was unrestricted, and no autograph was subject to recall" by Wolfe, and that Wolfe was not only "guilty of breach of contract" but had caused him "much mental anguish" and had, "by broken pledges, interference, erratic conduct, and in divers other ways . . . gravely damaged" his "career as a rare book and autograph agent." On March 13 Wolfe went and talked with the young man's family in the hope that they would convince him of the error of his ways. The interview, however, only served to confuse things even more. Finally, on March 24, the young man sent Wolfe a bill for $1900 for services rendered as his agent and

[1] From Perkins' letter of January 3, 1946, to John S. Terry.

for the commission on the "appraised value" of the unsold manuscript of *Of Time and the River*, and threatened to take legal action if this was not paid. In desperation, Wolfe turned the whole fantastic business over to his attorney, Cornelius Mitchell.

Just when Wolfe's troubles with his manuscript agent were at their height, he became involved in the disagreement with Perkins over the material which he was writing about Scribners. Since beginning work upon *The Vision of Spangler's Paul*, he had written several pieces of this material: a story called "Old Man Rivers," which was a bitter portrayal of Robert Bridges, the retired editor of *Scribner's Magazine*; one called "The Lion at Morning," which portrayed Charles Scribner II and told a well-known anecdote about him; and one called "No More Rivers," which supposedly was based upon the character of an editor who was junior to Perkins. Now Wolfe took "No More Rivers," and working nights upon it with Miss Nowell, shaped it into a short story in the hope that she could sell it to some magazine. It contained brief vignettes of various characters at James Rodney & Co.: one showed Perkins expressing his first determination to publish an unknown work of genius very similar to *Look Homeward, Angel*, and others unfavorably portrayed various associates of his who had at first been somewhat in doubt about the book.

Wolfe worked long and hard on this story. He had decided to make a test case of it, and when it was finally revised to his satisfaction, he asked Miss Nowell to take it into Scribners and "sound out" Perkins about it. She took it to Perkins and asked him to read it. After reading it, he became quite disturbed. At first he sat bolt upright at his desk, with unusually pink cheeks and blazing eyes, and refused to discuss the story, but soon he relented enough to take Miss Nowell to the Chatham for a drink, and there he finally began to talk.

He admitted that for years he had known that Wolfe would write about Scribners at some time and that he had often laughingly exclaimed, "When Tom gets around to writing about all of us, *look out!*" He readily agreed that nobody could stop Wolfe from writing what he felt impelled to, and that nobody had any right to try. He also made it clear that he had no objection to Wolfe's writing about him personally. However, he insisted that, although Wolfe must be left in utter freedom, he, Perkins, must assume the responsibility and take upon himself the punishment for what Wolfe wrote concerning Scribners, since he had given him the information in the first place. "I should have *known better*," he ruefully exclaimed, "but I've told Tom all kinds of

highly confidential things about the firm and about the people there."
Thereupon he poured out to Miss Nowell the things which he had
told Wolfe and about which he was now in a state of great anxiety.
For instance, he had once, under point-blank questioning by Wolfe,
admitted that he thought one Scribner executive "never was much
good," and he now put the entire blame for Wolfe's unfavorable
portrayal of the man on this remark. Also, he had once, after closing
hours, surprised a venerable dignitary of the firm and his equally
venerable secretary in a fond embrace, and he had been so astonished
at the sight that he had exclaimed about it afterward to Wolfe. "Can't
you see," he cried in anguish, "if Tom writes those things up and
publishes them, it'll ruin those people's lives, and it'll be *my fault!*"
He paused for a minute and then went on. "Well, don't tell Tom I
said so, but if that happens, I'll hand in my resignation from Scribners
and go live in the country. It's my duty—there's nothing else for me
to do." In vain did Miss Nowell tell him that he was making a mountain out of a molehill: that Wolfe's knowledge of Scribners came
chiefly from his own seven years' intimacy with the firm and its employees. When Perkins once made up his mind that something was
his duty, he would cling to it with unalterable stubbornness, and he
only kept repeating: "I'll hand my resignation in to Charlie. I'll *have*
to, if Tom writes up those things."

To Miss Nowell, the idea of Perkins' resigning from Scribners was
as unthinkable as that of God's resigning from heaven. In her perturbation she entirely forgot to keep in confidence what he had told her,
and she rushed to Wolfe, thinking wildly that surely he would do something to prevent this terrible catastrophe. However, when she told him,
Wolfe only stuck out his lower lip belligerently. "So he's going to resign, is he!" he growled. "Well, I've heard all that before. He needn't
try to make a martyr of himself on my account!" Angrily, he started
pacing up and down the room. "Look here, Miss Nowell, seven years
ago, when we published *Look Homeward, Angel,* Max thought it was
all right, fine, for me to write about those people, and that the only
thing that mattered was for me to do the best job possible on the
writing of the book. But now it's getting close to home, and his attitude
has changed. He seems to think that while it was all right to write about
those humble people down in North Carolina—*my own people in my
native town*—his own fine friends at Scribners are a special race, and
that I mustn't dare to say a word about them. Well, if that's going to
be his attitude, it's just too bad. Because I'm going to write what I
please, and as I please, and nobody is going to stop me!"

Finally Wolfe accepted Miss Nowell's suggestion to revise "No More Rivers" by making the hero a concert pianist rather than an editor and by omitting the short vignettes of the various people at James Rodney & Co. However, this was only a temporary stopgap for the sake of magazine publication. In spite of his avowed intention of making *The Vision of Spangler's Paul* "the most objective book I have ever written," Wolfe had, after a few false starts,[2] lapsed into his old vein of autobiography: the hero of his book was a writer very similar to Wolfe himself, and the hero's publishers, James Rodney & Co., by the same token were very similar to Scribners. As Wolfe kept saying, "You can't make something out of nothing": Scribners was the only publishing house about which he knew anything, and he knew a great deal about it, partially from Perkins' confidences to him but chiefly because he had virtually lived there for seven years and had had interminable conversations with all of the employees, from the boys in the basement shipping department to Charles Scribner III and the other executives on the fifth floor. As Wolfe had said for years, it was "wonderful material," and nobody could prevent his writing it any more than one could prevent a bird from singing. But Perkins, with his stubborn conviction of his own duty, seemed to Wolfe to be doing just exactly that. Wolfe brooded constantly about this suppression of his creative instinct and his disillusionment, because of it, with Perkins. He took to drinking heavily and to phoning to Miss Nowell around 3 A.M. to say lugubriously, "Well, I've done it now." When she would ask what it was that he had done, he'd say, "Why, don't you know! I've left Scribners." To this she angrily would answer that he had done no such thing and never would, that he was only drunk and had better go on home and go to bed. But a few nights later her phone again would ring, and again his deep and drunken voice would say, "I've done it now."

What he had actually done was to compose a letter approaching other publishers:

"To All Publishers:

"Gentlemen: I am the author of four published works, of which two are novels, one a volume of stories, and one a very short book about the experiences a writer has in beginning to write.

"All of these books have been published by the same publishing house, with whom my relations have been satisfactory.

---

[2] Most of these appeared later as the title piece of the book *The Hills Beyond*. The last two chapters of this material also appeared in the August 1936 issue of the *American Mercury* as "The Bell Remembered," under the general title of "Work in Progress."

"At the present time, I am engaged upon the composition of a long book, and since I have no obligation, whether personal, financial, contractual, moral, or of any kind soever to any firm of publishers, I am writing to inquire if you are interested in this book, and if so, upon what conditions, terms, proposals, and contractual alliances you are so interested. . . .

"In all fairness, I should here state that I think my physical resources, which have been generous, are at the present moment depleted; that the kind of vital concentration which has at times in the past attended the act of creation, is diffused. But I think these things may come back, and that there is a possibility I will do better work than I have yet done. That, of course, is my hope: and despite this present depletion of my energies, I am of cheerful and resolute temper, and I have strong hopes that the energy and power of such talents as I have will return.

"Frankly—with no disparagement of any connection I have had—I feel the need of a new beginning in my creative life."

At that point Wolfe broke off short in the writing of the letter. Probably he realized that it would not be exactly the best way in which to make a favorable "new beginning in" his "creative life." But he kept on trying different versions of it—long or short, in pencil, ink, or typewritten, on paper of all kinds, or in his pocket diaries, or on the back of old used envelopes from time to time—for an entire year. He made a list of publishers to whom he thought of sending it: "Macmillan, Harper, Viking, W. W. Norton, Little Brown, Houghton Mifflin, Longmans Green, Dodd Mead, Doubleday Doran, Harcourt Brace." He even wrote an advertisement which said the whole thing in a nutshell: "An author, Thomas Wolfe, being now without a publisher, would like to have a publisher." However, he never sent out any of these communications, but left them lying on his table till they were finally engulfed in the tide of manuscripts and miscellaneous papers which always filled his rooms. But again and again, for the next year and a half, he would phone Miss Nowell in the middle of the night, and in his deepest, drunkest, blandest, and most southern voice, would say, "I've done it now."

XXIII

THE summer of 1936 arrived, and Wolfe began thinking longingly of the scene of his greatest popularity, Berlin. *Of Time and the River* had been published there in April, and had had perhaps the greatest critical success of any of his books in any country, but because of the Nazi restrictions against exporting money, he could not obtain his royalties unless he went to Germany and spent them there. In July he wistfully followed the tryouts at Randalls Island for the Olympic games, which were to be held in Berlin in August: then, when the North German Lloyd magazine, *The Seven Seas*, offered him $150 worth of free passage on the *Europa* in return for a short article or two about Germany, the temptation was too great for him to resist. He sailed on July 23, went directly to Berlin, and launched upon the enjoyable occupation of spending his German royalties as fast as possible. He renewed his friendship with the Dodds, who were still at the American embassy, with Ernst Rowohlt and his son, Heinz Ledig-Rowohlt, with the "beautiful women who filled his hotel room with flowers," and with all the other people who had made his previous visit to Berlin so pleasant. He was wined and dined and interviewed, and he even received an invitation to confer with one of Hitler's officials, who reportedly wanted him to tour the Nazi work camps. This would have been quite understandable, since Wolfe had naïvely promised to do articles on Germany for *The Seven Seas*. However, he was amazed and rather frightened by the invitation, and thanks to warning in advance from some of his close friends, was able tactfully to decline.

The Olympic games took place during the first two weeks of August, and Wolfe attended them religiously. He loved all sports with the boyish and uncomplicated enjoyment of the average American: moreover, he was now intent on examining both the games and Nazi Germany, and "getting it all right" from firsthand observation. As he said later in *You Can't Go Home Again*, "I could never learn anything except the hard way. I must experience it for myself before I knew." During the year which had elapsed since his first triumph in Berlin, he had become increasingly aware of the evils of Nazism, but he had steadfastly refused to accept what he called the "slot-machine" condemnation of it which was urged upon him by the left-wing intellectuals of New York. For, as he wrote in *You Can't Go Home Again,* "about Hitler's Germany he felt that one must be very true. And the reason one needed to be very true was that the thing in it which every decent person must be against was false. You could not turn the other cheek to wrong, but also, it seemed to him, you could not be wrong about wrong. You had to be right about it. You could not meet lies and trickery with lies and trickery, although there were some people who argued that you should." And so, every day, Wolfe sat at the Olympic stadium or prowled the Berlin streets, with his powers of perception keyed up to their highest pitch. His impression, as recorded in his Purdue speech and *You Can't Go Home Again,* seemed somewhat inconclusive at that crucial time, when Hitler was holding Europe and America upon the brink of World War II, but today it remains one of the few living representations of Nazi Germany:

"Almost every day George . . . went to the stadium in Berlin. George observed that the organizing genius of the German people, which has been used so often to such noble purpose, was now more thrillingly displayed than he had ever seen it before. The sheer pageantry of the occasion was overwhelming, so much so that he began to feel oppressed by it. There seemed to be something ominous in it. One sensed a stupendous concentration of effort, a tremendous drawing together and ordering in the vast collective power of the whole land. And the thing that made it seem ominous was that it so evidently went beyond what the games themselves demanded. The games were overshadowed, and were no longer merely sporting competitions to which other nations had sent their chosen teams. They became, day after day, an orderly and overwhelming demonstration in which the whole of Germany had been schooled and disciplined. It was as if the games had been chosen as a symbol of the new collective might, a means of showing to the world in concrete terms what this new power had come to be.

"With no past experience in such affairs, the Germans had constructed a mighty stadium which was the most beautiful and most perfect in its design that had ever been built. And all the accessories of this monstrous plant—the swimming pools, the enormous halls, the lesser stadia—had been laid out and designed with this same cohesion of beauty and of use. The organization was superb. Not only were the events themselves, down to the minutest detail of each competition, staged and run off like clockwork, but the crowds—such crowds as no other great city has ever had to cope with, and the like of which would certainly have snarled and maddened the traffic of New York beyond hope of untangling—were handled with a quietness, order, and speed that was astounding.

"The daily spectacle was breath-taking in its beauty and magnificence. The stadium was a tournament of color that caught the throat; the massed splendor of the banners made the gaudy decorations of America's great parades, presidential inaugurations, and World's Fairs seem like shoddy carnivals in comparison. And for the duration of the Olympics, Berlin itself was transformed into a kind of annex to the stadium. From one end of the city to the other, from the Lustgarten to the Brandenburger Tor, along the whole broad sweep of Unter den Linden, through the vast avenues of the faëry Tiergarten, and out through the western part of Berlin to the very portals of the stadium, the whole town was a thrilling pageantry of royal banners—not merely endless miles of looped-up bunting, but banners fifty feet in height, such as might have graced the battle tent of some great emperor.

"And all through the day, from morning on, Berlin became a mighty Ear, attuned, attentive, focused on the stadium. Everywhere the air was filled with a single voice. The green trees along the Kurfürstendamm began to talk: from loud-speakers concealed in their branches an announcer in the stadium spoke to the whole city—and for George Webber it was a strange experience to hear the familiar terms of track and field translated into the tongue that Goethe used. He would be informed now that the *Vorlauf* was about to be run—and then the *Zwischenlauf*—and at length the *Endlauf*—and the winner: 'Owens— Oo Ess Ah!'

"Meanwhile, through those tremendous banner-laden ways, the crowds thronged ceaselessly all day long. The wide promenade of Unter den Linden was solid with patient, tramping German feet. Fathers, mothers, children, young folks, old—the whole material of the nation was there, from every corner of the land. From morn to night they trudged, wide-eyed, full of wonder, past the marvel of those banner-laden ways. And among them one saw the bright stabs of color of Olympic jackets and the glint of foreign faces: the dark features of Frenchmen and Italians, the ivory grimace of the Japanese, the straw hair and blue eyes of the Swedes, and the big Americans, natty in straw hats, white flannels, and blue coats crested with the Olympic seal.

"And there were great displays of marching men, sometimes ungunned but rhythmic as regiments of brown shirts went swinging through the streets. By noon each day all the main approaches to the games, the embannered streets and avenues of the route which the Leader would take to the stadium, miles away, were walled in by the troops. They stood at ease, young men, laughing and talking with each other—the Leader's bodyguards, the Schutz Staffel units, the Storm Troopers, all the ranks and divisions in their different uniforms—and they stretched in two unbroken lines from the Wilhelm-strasse up to the arches of the Brandenburger Tor. Then, suddenly, the sharp command, and instantly there would be the solid smack of ten thousand leather boots as they came together with the sound of war.

"It seemed as if everything had been planned for this moment, shaped to this triumphant purpose. But the people—they had not been planned. Day after day, behind the unbroken wall of soldiers, they stood and waited in a dense and patient throng. These were the masses of the nation, the poor ones of the earth, the humble ones of life, the workers and the wives, the mothers and the children—and day after day they came and stood and waited. They were there because they did not have money enough to buy the little cardboard squares that would have given them places within the magic ring. From noon till night they waited for just two brief and golden moments of the day: the moment when the Leader went out to the stadium, and the moment when he returned.

"At last he came—and something like a wind across a field of grass was shaken through that crowd, and from afar the tide rolled up with him, and in it was the voice, the hope, the prayer of the land. The Leader came by slowly in a shining car, a little dark man with a comic-opera mustache, erect and standing, moveless and unsmiling, with his hand upraised, palm outward, not in Nazi-wise salute, but straight up, in a gesture of blessing such as the Buddha or Messiahs use."

Wolfe himself had no direct contact with Hitler, although he once came perilously close to it at the Olympic games, in what might have been a difficult diplomatic incident. Martha Dodd describes this in her book of reminiscences, *Through Embassy Eyes*: "Once Tom Wolfe sat in the diplomatic box. When Owens won a particularly conspicuous victory, Tom let out a war whoop. Hitler twisted in his seat, looked down, attempting to locate the miscreant, and frowned angrily. It was the Nazi attitude . . . to consider Negroes as animals and utterly unqualified to enter the Games."[1] The ironic thing was that Wolfe, who in his youth had had an attitude toward Negroes not very different from the Nazi one, should now be carried away with admiration for the great Negro track star Jesse Owens. Gone now were the days when

[1] From Martha Dodd's *Through Embassy Eyes*, Harcourt, Brace, 1939.

he had got into a brawl with the police of Greenville, South Carolina, not because they had arrested him for drunkenness, but because they had put him in the same cell with a Negro; or the days when he had walked up and down seven flights of stairs from his classroom at New York University, swearing never again to use "any elevator operated by that blankety-blank nigger," who had the brashness to "tell off" white people, even white women. Wolfe's sociological education had been progressing slowly during the past six or seven years, and now, under the impact of life in Nazi Germany, it was fast coming to a head.

It was just before the Olympic games that Wolfe met and fell in love with Thea Voelcker. She had been commissioned to make a drawing of him to illustrate an interview in the *Berliner Tageblatt*, and he had proudly posed for it at his hotel, but when he saw the finished picture, he objected violently to it, saying that it made him look "pig-like," which it did. However, he could not put Frau Voelcker out of his mind. She was a striking example of the Germanic type of woman he had always admired: almost as tall as he, and strong and pink-cheeked, with a great braid of shining yellow hair wound peasant-fashion round her head: as he said later, she looked like one of the Valkyries. More-over, she had a tragic, mystical, and strongly emotional temperament which appealed greatly to his own. Only a week after he had insulted her about her drawing, he asked Ernst Rowohlt to invite her to a party which was being given in his honor: he talked to almost no one else and left the party early with her, leaving his other woman friends completely in the lurch. That was the beginning of a stormy love affair, of which he soon grew weary but which virtually broke her heart.

At first his passion for her was insatiable, and not content with being with her constantly in Berlin, he insisted that, at the conclusion of the Olympic games, she go on a trip with him to Austria. That got them ensnarled in difficulties with the Nazis, since she was a German citizen and could not leave the country without a special permit, but she finally obtained one and went with him to Alpbach, a picturesque old village high up in the Austrian Tirol. Wolfe's arrival at the four-hundred-year-old Hotel Boglerhof in Alpbach was heralded by a long-distance call from him at Innsbruck, in which he stammeringly announced that he wanted to come to the Boglerhof for a rest and wondered if they could provide him with a bed two meters and twenty centimeters (over seven feet) long. He arrived a few days later and caused a sensation among the other guests, both because of his own appearance and because the girl who accompanied him was so tall, so striking, so German, and so obviously not his wife. He, however, paid no attention to them and settled down to a routine of writing, drinking, quarreling with Frau Voelcker and then making up with her again. For, although Frau Voelcker strongly opposed his tendency to alcoholism, he spent every evening in convivial companionship with the Tirolean farmers who came to the Boglerhof to drink the pale-red native wine. He was still intent on spending all his German royalties before he went back to America, and this was an ideally pleasant way to do it. He insisted on buying drinks for everyone; he kept demanding the Tirolean harp-and-zither music, to which he hummed an accompaniment, blissfully and quite off key; he watched the folk dancing and tapped his size-13 shoe enthusiastically on the floor, although he shyly refused to join the dancing; and he talked endlessly and compulsively to his new-found farmer friends in fluent, if somewhat faulty, German: to this day, there are natives in Alpbach who know the intimate history of Wolfe's family, simply from hearing him talk about them and without ever having read a word of what he wrote. Wolfe was in his element and would have kept this sort of thing up all night, every night: he always protested bitterly when Herr Moser, the Boglerhof proprietor, insisted that the farmers had to rise at dawn and must go home and go to bed.

Finally there came the day when Wolfe got really drunk. He had been quarreling again with Thea Voelcker, and he suddenly walked off and left her standing in the middle of a mountain meadow, saying, "I am sick and tired of this cow." He then began to drink in earnest, got completely and immovably drunk, and had to be carried up to bed by his farmer friends while Frau Voelcker stood by, weeping silently and angrily. Everybody at the Boglerhof was plunged in sorrow, for her, for Wolfe, and for their holiday, which had come to such an ugly end.

When they went to see how Wolfe was feeling the next morning, they were horrified to find that he had disappeared. The bed was rumpled and his personal belongings were still scattered around the room, but he had simply vanished in the night: nowhere in Alpbach was there any trace of him. Then, finally, a rumor came back to the town: early that morning Wolfe had been seen climbing the biggest of the mountains that towered over Alpbach, the Galtenberg, 2400 meters high and very difficult to climb. At eleven o'clock he reappeared at the Boglerhof, tired, dirty, hungry—and triumphant. Ever since his arrival at Alpbach he had been gazing at the Galtenberg, as if "sizing it up" and comparing it to the mountains of his native western North Carolina. He had also had a pair of mountain-climbing boots made to order, since he could not buy any big enough to fit him. At first he had been horrified and enraged at the price of these, but on being assured by the natives that they were wonderful boots, he had grown very proud of them. However, he had never done anything further about climbing the Galtenberg, and now his holiday was coming to an end. Suddenly, that morning, he had waked up at four o'clock, still drunk, but with the fixed idea that he was going to climb that "goddamned mountain" then and there. He was still dressed in the clothes he'd worn the night before, and so he had only to get out of bed, put on his boots, walk downstairs and out the back door of the inn, across the mountain meadows to the Galtenberg, and so on up it— with no guide, no equipment, no real experience, and in no fit condition to do anything, let alone to climb an Alp. As he wrote the following day to Perkins, "It damn near finished me, but I did it." Moreover, he did it in record-breaking time for the trip up and back, thus establishing himself in Alpbach as the legendary hero which he still is there today.[2]

Wolfe and Thea Voelcker left Alpbach together the next day, August 26, but their quarrel soon flared up again, and he went alone to Innsbruck, Munich, and finally back to Berlin, where he went so far as to send a man friend of his to her apartment to ask for a small amount of American currency which he had left with her. She, meanwhile, had also come back to Berlin, heartbroken and on the verge of a nervous breakdown, and Wolfe finally made up with her and continued their affair until he sailed for home. When he first reached New York he announced that he was going to bring her to America and marry her, but he never really seemed to mean it, or to do anything about it. She wrote him several letters which were tragic, humble, infused with mystical religion and with deep emotion, or, as he described them, "almost like the Bible," but he was absorbed in his work on his new book and in the complexities of his life in America, and he seems never to have found time to write her more than two impersonal, hasty letters, which he dictated to his secretary. By 1937 they had ceased to correspond, and he never saw or heard from her again.

[2] The author is indebted for information about Wolfe's stay in Alpbach to Heinz Ledig-Rowohlt, to Alfons Moser and Fräulein Keiler, proprietors of the Boglerhof, and to Janice Davis Warnke, the author of an unpublished article based on what the Mosers told her of Wolfe's stay in Alpbach. Also to Dr. Wolfgang Fenge for translating some of the material.

All this time, Wolfe's ideas about Germany were in a ferment, with the evidences of Nazi oppression working like a yeast against his deep, unthinking love for the country which was both "his father's land" and the place where he himself had been the happiest and the most admired. The pocket diary which he kept during this trip to Germany is full of arguments about Hitlerism, most of which seem inclined toward its defense. "Horses are happy in Germany," he wrote triumphantly on the flyleaf of the little book, and later, as a kind of a poetical refrain, "Horses are happy in a land I know." This idea undoubtedly came from Ambassador Dodd, who loved horses and often remarked on their sleek, well-fed condition, saying that only horses seemed happy in Germany.[3] In his eagerness to defend the country, Wolfe evidently seized upon this, omitting the word "only" and clutching at the rest of it, as a drowning man clutches at a straw.

In his notebook he tries to rationalize this tendency in a fragment which he called "The Slot Machine": "Nothing good can be said about the Italian or German Dictatorships. If one suggests that benefits from these dictatorships have been considerable, the slot-machine answer is: 'Oh yes, we know—the streets are clean and the trains run on time. But do you think these blessings compensate for the loss of human liberties, freedom of speech, etc. etc.?' It is useless to tell the Slot-machiners that the benefits of the Fascist Dictatorships have resulted in far more considerable benefits than 'clean streets and trains on time,' and if we are really going to combat the evil of Fascism we must first begin by understanding its good." On another page of his notebook he tries to list these benefits, as against the evils of the system:

"Fascism

For	Against
Physical clean-ness	Suppression of Free Speech
Healthy people	A Cult of Insular Superiority
Effective relief	With this, a need for insular
A concentration of natural	domination"
energy	

Then, a few pages later, his sardonic sense of humor begins to get the upper hand: "Benefits. Let us consider some of the probable benefits of such a system. I should be suppressed, which would be a natural loss and a loss to art, but the Malcolm Cowleys, the Mike Golds, the V. F. Calvertons, the Bunny Wilsons, etc. etc. would also be suppressed, which would be a gain to everyone and everything."

[3] The author is indebted to Martha Dodd Stern for this information.

Judged solely on the basis of this notebook, Wolfe would seem to have been inclined to defend Hitlerism through sheer emotionalism, ignorance, and wrongheadedness. However, it must be remembered that most of these entries were made after heated arguments with his friends, almost all of whom were strongly anti-Nazi. Wolfe never could accept a thing on anybody's say-so, and attempts to make him do so always drove him to the opposite extreme. He had to form his own conviction through experience, emotion, and trial and error, and even while he was making these entries in his notebook, he was doing just exactly that. In his final and most carefully considered statement about Germany, in *You Can't Go Home Again*, he describes what happened:

"Little by little the world came in. . . . Sometimes it came to me in the desperate pleading of an eye, the naked terror of a startled look, the swift concealment of a sudden fear. Sometimes it just came and went as light comes, just soaked in, just soaked in—in fleeting words and speech and actions. After a while, however, in the midwatches of the night, behind thick walls and bolted doors and shuttered windows, it came to me full flood at last in confessions of unutterable despair. I don't know why it was that people so unburdened themselves to me, a stranger, unless it was because they knew the love I bore them and their land. They seemed to feel a desperate need to talk to someone who would understand. The thing was pent up in them, and my sympathy for all things German had burst the dam of their reserve and caution. Their tales of woe and fear unspeakable gushed forth and beat upon my ears. They told me stories of their friends and relatives who had said unguarded things in public and disappeared without a trace, stories of the Gestapo, stories of neighbors' quarrels and petty personal spite turned into political persecution, stories of concentration camps and pogroms, stories of rich Jews stripped and beaten and robbed of everything they had and then denied the right to earn a pauper's wage, stories of well-bred Jewesses despoiled and turned out of their homes and forced to kneel and scrub off anti-Nazi slogans scribbled on the sidewalks while young barbarians dressed like soldiers formed a ring and prodded them with bayonets and made the quiet places echo with the shameless laughter of their mockery. It was a picture of the Dark Ages come again—shocking beyond belief, but true as the hell that man forever creates for himself. Thus it was that the corruption of man's living faith and inferno of his buried anguish came to me—and I recognized at last, in all its frightful aspects, the spiritual disease which was poisoning unto death a noble and a mighty people."

It was the final episode of Wolfe's stay in Germany that brought home to him most forcibly the cruelty of Nazi oppression. A man who was traveling in the same compartment with him on the train for Paris was arrested at the border for trying to smuggle out more currency than the Nazi law allowed: it was whispered among the other passengers that the man was Jewish and was trying to escape from Germany.

"The three officials came through the door of the compartment with the little man between them," Wolfe wrote later in "I Have a Thing to Tell You." "They stepped down to the platform and marched him along, white as a sheet, grease standing out in beads all over his face, protesting volubly in a voice that had a kind of anguished lilt in it. . . .

"They had him. Far down the platform the passengers heard the shrill, sudden fife of the Belgian engine whistle. The guard cried warning. All up and down the train the doors were slammed. Slowly the train began to move. At a creeping pace it rolled right past the little man. They had him, all right. The officers surrounded him. He stood among them, still protesting, talking with his hands now. And the men in uniform said nothing. They had no need to speak. They had him. They just stood and watched him, each with a faint suggestion of that intolerable slow smile upon his face. They raised their eyes and looked at the passengers as the train rolled past, and the line of travelers standing in the corridors looked back at them and caught the obscene and insolent communication in their glance and in that intolerable slow smile.

"And the little man—he, too, paused once from his feverish effort to explain. As the car in which he had been riding slid by, he lifted his pasty face and terror-stricken eyes, and for a moment his lips were stilled of their anxious pleading. He looked once, directly and steadfastly, at his former companions, and they at him. And in that gaze there was all the unmeasured weight of man's mortal anguish. George and the others felt somehow naked and ashamed, and somehow guilty. They all felt that they were saying farewell, not to a man, but to humanity; not to some pathetic stranger, some chance acquaintance of the voyage, but to mankind; not to some nameless cipher out of life, but to the fading image of a brother's face.

"The train swept out and gathered speed—and so they lost him."

By the time Wolfe's train had reached Paris he had made his mind up. The sight of that one anguished little man had turned him against Hitlerism as no amount of facts or arguments could do: from this day forth he not only was a fervent anti-Fascist but also made considerable sacrifice of his personal happiness and his general reputation for the sake of his belief. Three days after he arrived in Paris he wrote Miss Nowell: "I've written a good piece over here—I'm afraid it may mean that I can't come back to the place where I'm liked best and have the most friends, but I've decided to publish it." The piece was, of course, the story of the little man, "I Have a Thing to Tell You." As Wolfe later said, "The story wrote itself. It was the truth as I could see it, and I decided that a man's own self-respect and integrity is worth more than his comfort or material advantage." It was published in the March 10, 17, and 24, 1937, issues of the *New Republic*, and immediately all Wolfe's books were banned in the Nazi realm, as he had known they would be. At the conclusion of the longer version of the story in *You Can't Go Home Again*, he says farewell to Germany:

"He . . . was 'out' of that great country whose image had been engraved upon his spirit in childhood and youth before he had ever seen it. He . . . was 'out' of that land which had been so much more to him than land, so much more than place. It had been a geography of heart's desire, an unfathomed domain of unknown inheritance. The haunting beauty of that magic land had been his soul's dark wonder. He had known the language of its spirit before he ever came to it, had understood the language of its tongue the moment he had heard it spoken. He had framed the accents of its speech most brokenly from that first hour, yet never with a moment's trouble, strangeness, or lack of comprehension. He had been at home in it, and it in him. It seemed that he had been born with this knowledge.

"He had known wonder in this land, truth and magic in it, sorrow, loneliness, and pain in it. He had known love in it, and for the first time in his life he had tasted there the bright, delusive sacraments of fame. Therefore it was no foreign land to him. It was the other part of his heart's home, a haunted part of dark desire, a magic domain of fulfillment. It was the dark, lost Helen that had been forever burning in his blood—the dark, lost Helen he had found.

"And now it was the dark, found Helen he had lost. And he knew now, as he had never known before, the priceless measure of his loss. He knew also the priceless measure of his gain. For this was the way that henceforth would be forever closed to him—the way of no return. He was 'out.' And being 'out,' he began to see another way, the way that lay before him. He saw now that you can't go home again—not ever. There was no road back. Ended now for him, with the sharp and clean finality of the closing of a door, was the time when his dark roots, like those of a pot-bound plant, could be left to feed upon their own substance and nourish their own little self-absorbed designs. Henceforth they must spread outward—away from the hidden, secret, and un-fathomed past that holds man's spirit prisoner—outward, outward to-ward the rich and life-giving soil of a new freedom in the wide world of all humanity. And there came to him a vision of man's true home, beyond the ominous and cloud-engulfed horizon of the here and now, in the green and hopeful and still-virgin meadows of the future.

" 'Therefore,' he thought, 'old master, wizard Faust, old father of the ancient and swarm-haunted mind of man, old earth, old German land with all the measure of your truth, your glory, beauty, magic, and your ruin; and dark Helen burning in our blood, great queen and mistress, sorceress—dark land, dark land, old ancient earth I love—farewell!' "

XXIV

WOLFE came home with the French Line, on the *Paris*, and was settled down in his First Avenue apartment by the first week in October. One of the first things he did was to write to *The Seven Seas* asking them to release him from his promise to write articles on Germany and to accept his check for the $150 which they had credited against the cost of his passage in July. "May I tell you that I have the deepest and most genuine affection for Germany, where I have spent some of the happiest and most fruitful months of my life, and for the German people, among whom I have some of the best and truest friends I know," he told them. "For that very reason, above all others, I want to be scrupulous now not to abuse your own generosity or to make any commitments that would not be in full accordance with certain deep and earnest convictions of my own or with anything I might write or say hereafter. I cannot go into detailed explanation here, but I leave it to your intuition to understand what is in my mind."

Having got this off his mind, Wolfe plunged into the writing of "I Have a Thing to Tell You." Just before reaching the German-Belgian border, the man who was later arrested had persuaded Wolfe to take a little of his extra money and thus get it past the inspectors for him. Because of the man's arrest, Wolfe had been unable to return it, although, in a moment of intense excitement, he had wanted to do so and had only been prevented by his fellow passengers. He still had the little handful of two-mark pieces when he reached New York. In fact, one of his earliest titles for "I Have a Thing to Tell You" was "I Have Them Yet." He didn't like to touch the coins: he thought that they were "blood money" and that they felt greasy with their owner's agony and sweat: but they lay for a long time upon his table. He would look at them and his mouth would pucker up with pity, and he would shake his head quickly, repeatedly, too moved for words.

Meanwhile, he had no sooner landed in New York than he had become enmeshed in all of the old difficulties of his life at home. The greatest of these was the disagreement between himself and Perkins, which had been smoldering all the time he had been in Germany and which now broke out more violently than ever. Just before he had gone abroad he had asked Miss Nowell to show Perkins the version of "No More Rivers" which he had written so as no longer to portray anyone at Scribners. Perkins, however, now objected to the story on artistic grounds. "I think this story could do no one any harm now—except perhaps Thomas Wolfe," he had written to Miss Nowell on August 26. "I do not think it is up to his usual level." When Wolfe heard of this, he had been enraged and had continued to brood about it all the way back to the United States. "I do not see how we can go on further," he had written on board the *Paris* in a letter to Perkins which he never mailed. "There has been so much disappointment, so much failure, so much unfulfillment—yes, even so much bitter argument and passionate denial—and it seems to me now there is nothing more to say for me, nothing more to do. I am filled with the profoundest melancholy, the most hopeless sense of finality, when I think of the whole thing."

On the first evening which he and Perkins spent together on his arrival in New York, they became embroiled in a bitter quarrel. Wolfe burst out with his long-suppressed resentment at the letter which Perkins had written Miss Nowell about "No More Rivers" and charged him with personal prejudice and attempted suppression. "Maybe that story isn't the best one I've ever written," he said repeatedly, "but it's not the worst one either. No, Max, you just want to suppress it because you think I'm writing about Scribners and of course to you that's a sin against the Holy Ghost." To this, Perkins answered that, after being Wolfe's editor for eight entire years, he certainly understood that he neither could nor should prevent his writing whatever he felt compelled to. However, Perkins then resorted to the announcement that he had made five months earlier to Miss Nowell—that he would publish Wolfe's book, no matter what it said about Scribners, and would then immediately hand in his resignation from the firm. As always, this quixotic notion infuriated Wolfe more than any outright attempt at censorship could have done. He shouted out that Perkins needn't try to make a martyr of himself; that Charlie Scribner would not accept his resignation anyway, because of his irreplaceable value to the firm; and that, in any case, Perkins needn't bother, because he, Wolfe, would leave Scribners first and so "simply not be there to be resigned about."

By this time both men had lost their tempers, and they argued long and loud and furiously about all Wolfe's grievances, both actual and psychological, against Perkins and Scribners. Finally they parted, still

angry and still stubbornly opposed, Perkins to go home to bed and
Wolfe to brood and drink and roam from bar to bar till dawn. Finally
he wrote a note to Perkins' secretary: "Dear Miss Wyckoff: From now
on, will you please address and send any mail that may come for me to
865 First Avenue, New York City?" This seemingly routine little pencil
note marked one more decisive step toward his severance from Scribners. For the past eight years he had come in to Perkins' office almost
every afternoon, to get his mail, to call on everyone at Scribners, and,
finally, to go out and drink and talk with Perkins for as many hours as
he could spare. From now on Wolfe stayed away from Scribners altogether, unless some vitally important matter made it absolutely necessary for him to come in and confer with them.

Wolfe now tried unsuccessfully to draw a line between Perkins his
father-substitute and friend, and Perkins the editor of Scribners. He
continued to frequent Perkins' house on Turtle Bay and to spend long
convivial evenings with him at Cherio's or the Chatham, or other
restaurants or bars, but no matter where they went or what they did,
they always got embroiled in angry arguments. Most of these were
about politics and economics. Wolfe's experiences that summer in Berlin had intensified his left-wing convictions, not only in regard to Nazi
Germany but also to the United States. His fullest and final explanation of the development of this viewpoint, beginning with the years
before publication of *Look Homeward, Angel*, is given in the concluding pages of *You Can't Go Home Again*:

"Up to that time I had been merely the sensitive young fellow in
conflict with his town, his family, the life around him—then the
sensitive young fellow in love, and so concerned with his little Universe
of Love that he thought it the whole universe. But gradually I began
to observe things in life which shocked me out of this complete ab-
sorption with the independent entities of self. I caught glimpses of the
great, the rich, the fortunate ones of all the earth living supinely upon
the very best of everything and taking the very best for granted as their
right. . . . At the same time I began to be conscious of the submerged
and forgotten Helots down below, who with their toil and sweat and
blood and suffering unutterable supported and nourished the mighty
princelings at the top.

"Then came the cataclysm of 1929 and the terrible days that followed. The picture became clearer now—clear enough for all with eyes
to see. Through those years I was living in the jungle depths of Brooklyn, and I saw as I had never seen before the true and terrifying visage of
the disinherited of life. There came to me a vision of man's inhumanity

to man, and as time went on it began to blot out the more personal and self-centered vision of the world which a young man always has. Then it was, I think, that I began to learn humility. My intense and passionate concern for the interests and designs of my own little life were coming to seem petty, trifling, and unworthy, and I was coming more and more to feel an intense and passionate concern for the interests and designs of my fellow men and of all humanity.

"Of course I have vastly oversimplified the process in my telling of it. While it was at work in me I was but dimly aware of it. . . . Those were the years of the greatest doubt and desperation I had ever known. I was wrestling with the problems of my second book, and I could take in what my eyes beheld only in brief glimpses, flashes, snatches, fragments. As I was later to discover, the vision etched itself upon some sensitive film within, but it was not until that later time, when the second book was finished and out of the way, that I saw it whole and knew what the total experience had done to me. . . .

"By then life's weather had soaked in, although I was not fully conscious yet what seepings had begun, or where, in what directions, the channel of my life was flowing. . . . I had gone back for rest, for recreation, for oblivion, to that land which, of all the foreign lands I had visited, I loved the best. . . . And now it seemed to me, who had so often gone a stranger and unknown to the great cities of the world, that Berlin was mine. . . . The weeks passed . . . —and then it happened. Little by little the world came in. At first it sifted in almost unnoticed, like dark down dropped in passing from some avenging angel's wing. Sometimes it came to me in the desperate pleading of an eye, the naked terror of a startled look, the swift concealment of a sudden fear. Sometimes it just came and went as light comes, just soaked in—in fleeting words and speech and actions. . . .

"But even as I saw it and knew it . . . , there came to me, most strangely, another thing as well. For while I sat the night through in the darkened rooms of German friends, behind the bolted doors and shuttered windows—while their whispered voices spoke to me of the anguish in their hearts . . . —while I heard and saw these things, my heart was torn asunder, and from its opened depths came forth into my consciousness a knowledge that I had not fully known was there. For then it was, most curiously, that all the grey weather of unrecorded days in Brooklyn, which had soaked through into my soul, came flooding back to me. Came back, too, the memory of my exploration of the jungle trails of night. I saw again the haggard faces of the homeless men, the wanderers, the disinherited of America, the aged workers who had worked and now could work no more, the callow boys who had never worked and now could find no work to do, and who, both together, had been cast loose by a society that had no need of them and left to shift in any way they could—to find their food in garbage cans, to seek for warmth and fellowship in foul latrines like the one near New York's City Hall, to sleep wrapped up in old newspapers on the concrete floors of subway corridors. . . .

"So it was . . . that I realized fully, for the first time, how sick America was, and saw, too, that the ailment was akin to Germany's— a dread world-sickness of the soul. . . . In Germany it was hopeless: it had already gone too far to be checked now by any measures short of death, destruction, and total ruin. But in America, it seemed to me, it was not mortal, not incurable—not yet. . . . America was young, America was still the New World of mankind's hope, America was not like this old and worn-out Europe which seethed and festered with a thousand deep and uncorrected ancient maladies. America was still resilient, still responsive to a cure—if only—if only—men could somehow cease to be afraid of truth. For the plain and searching light of truth, which had, in Germany, been darkened to extinction, was the remedy, the only one, that could cleanse and heal the suffering soul of man."

To Wolfe this was a wonderful discovery, a philosophy which gave plan and purpose to his life and a whole new inspiration for his work. However, Perkins was opposed to it. Despite Wolfe's repeated assertions that he was not, and never would be, a "radical" or "communist," Perkins was apprehensive lest he be influenced by the left-wing formulas current in the writing of that time, and so impair his work. Moreover, Perkins himself, in almost every way—by background, education, and conviction—was a dyed-in-the-wool conservative. He passionately loved to argue and was one of the stubbornest men on God's green footstool about ever admitting he might be wrong. He seemed oblivious to the fact that he was alienating Wolfe, or perhaps his personal conviction that he was right and Wolfe was wrong was so intense that he simply did not care.

To make this worse, this month of October 1936, when Wolfe had come home full of neophytic fervor for his new-found liberalism, was also the month before the presidential election in the United States, when the entire population of the country was involved in heated arguments. There was a smart saying among some of the New York literati that Wolfe broke off with Perkins because the latter, after fifty years as an independent Democrat, turned against the New Deal and voted for the Republican, Alfred M. Landon. This was, of course, ridiculous and superficial. However, it was true that Wolfe considered that the election of 1936 was "the most important . . . that has been held in this country since 1860" and that Roosevelt's administration, "whatever its errors of commission or omission may have been, had made the only decisive movement . . . in the direction of social progress and social justice since the administrations of Woodrow Wilson."[1] He got, or thought he got, an admission of this importance of the New Deal from Perkins, and he later found bitter irony in the fact that Perkins had, at the last moment, voted for the Republicans. Perkins explained that he had done so because the Democratic landslide was assured, and he wanted to cast a modifying vote lest the New Dealers become overconfident and too highhanded. Wolfe insisted that Perkins had merely shown himself in his true colors—that he was a conservative and even a reactionary and that, as guardian of the fortune which his daughters had inherited from Mrs. Perkins' family, he was anxious to maintain the capitalistic status quo.

All through October and the first half of November, Wolfe and Perkins quarreled unceasingly about one thing or another, until suddenly a new and unexpected legal difficulty brought their severance to a head. This was the suit brought against Wolfe and Scribners by Marjorie Dorman, Wolfe's former landlady at 40 Verandah Place, who claimed that he had libelously depicted her as Mad Maude Whittaker in his story "No Door," which first appeared in *Scribner's Magazine* and then had been reprinted in *From Death to Morning*. The damages demanded in this suit were ruinous: Marjorie Dorman asked for $50,000, and because Wolfe had said that Mad Maude's sisters and her father were "all touched with the same madness," the Dorman sisters, Mary Roberta Dorman and Louise Dorman Leonard, and the father, William Samuel Dorman, joined in the suit and asked for an additional $25,000 damages apiece, making a total of $125,000.

Wolfe was beside himself with anxiety and rage, and, as always, took his feelings out on Perkins and laid the blame on him. He pointed out that "No Door" had first appeared in *Scribner's Magazine* three years earlier, in July 1933, and had been reprinted in *From Death to Morning* one year earlier, in July 1935. From these facts he deduced, by a complicated process of reasoning, that the idea of suing him for libel had been suggested to the Dormans by Walter Winchell's announcement in the New York *Mirror* on September 21, 1936, that "Thomas Wolfe

[1] From his letter to Jonathan Daniels of October 23, 1936.

. . . has held up publication of his latest novel until all the people in it die. His last two slightly autobiographical tomes brought several libel suits." Wolfe tried to blame this on Perkins, saying that if Perkins had not been intimidated by Mrs. Bernstein into postponing publication of *The October Fair*, the gossip never would have got to Winchell and been publicized.

There was no logical reason for blaming this on Perkins, except that Wolfe had got in the habit of making him a scapegoat for all of his misfortunes. In his excitement, he even reverted to the old tirade which he had first delivered when he'd been sued by Madeleine Boyd in 1935. Perkins described this with wry humor in a letter to Ernest Hemingway: "Spent most of yesterday morning downtown at a lawyer's office with Tom Wolfe on account of a $125,000 libel suit he has got us into. That is my way of looking at it. The other night he told me at great length, and overwhelming eloquence, of the injustice done him on all hands in this blank blank country—Germany as white as snow in contrast with it—where the honest men are all robbed and bludgeoned by scoundrels. And it all wound up with 'And now you have got me into a $125,000 libel suit.' So it is all a matter of the point of view."[2]

The thing which drove Wolfe most wild, however, was Scribners' conduct of the libel case. According to the contract for *From Death to Morning*, he had guaranteed to them that the book contained no libel and that he would hold them harmless "from all suits and all manner of claims and proceedings which may be taken" against it. However, Charles Scribner III had suggested that the firm should bear one half of damages and costs, provided that Wolfe would co-operate with them and join them in retaining first-rate legal counsel. In his anxiety to protect the firm and Wolfe, he had then asked the editors of the New York *Times*, who were noted for their protection against libel, to recommend a lawyer for the case. Unfortunately, the man recommended was distinguished, able, but conservative and terribly expensive, or, as Perkins said afterward, "the worst possible sort of man for Tom."[3] When he and Wolfe went to confer with this lawyer, Wolfe stared about suspiciously at the luxurious reception room and offices, then turned to Perkins. "Who pays for all this, Max?" he asked. "I don't know," Perkins answered quietly. "I guess we do."

Once inside the lawyer's private office, Wolfe made a "statement"

[2] From Perkins' letter to Hemingway, December 9, 1936, reprinted in *Editor to Author: The Letters of Maxwell E. Perkins.*

[3] From Perkins' letter of November 21, 1946, to John S. Terry.

concerning the Dorman family which was taken down by a stenographer. It is rambling, inconclusive, and gives no information on which a lawyer could base a strong defense, and the attorney was probably correct in advising that the suit be settled rather than fought out before a jury—and a Brooklyn jury at that! However, Wolfe by now had formed a strong conviction that libel suits of this kind were "a part of a great organized national industry of shaking down . . . and the only way to stop it is to fight it, because it lives by threat and flourishes on submission." As he later wrote about the suit to Charles Scribner III, "I think that in that particular matter we were wrong in not fighting it, and furthermore I think we were licked before we started, because our lawyers cost so much we were practically forced to settle to protect ourselves against our own lawyer's bill if we went on. Frankly, so far as I can see, we would have done as well if we had had —— and paid him fifty bucks. In the end, the three floors of office space, . . . the magnificent private offices, regiments of slick-looking assistants, etchings of Abraham Lincoln, etc., did not mean a damn thing except trouble and money: it was a sorry job."[4]

At any rate, it was during his initial shock and rage at the prospect of this suit that Wolfe took his first decisive step toward a severance from Scribners. Up to this time he had made innumerable false steps toward breaking free from them and had always lost his nerve, but he now hit upon the idea of *asking them* to state that he was under no obligation to them, instead of proclaiming his own independence.

"Dear Max," he wrote to Perkins in a letter dated November 12, 1936, and evidently mailed four days later. "I think you should now write me a letter in which you explicitly state the nature of my relations with Charles Scribner's Sons. I think you ought to say that I have faithfully and honorably discharged all obligations to Charles Scribner's Sons, whether financial, personal or contractual, and that no further agreement or obligation of any sort exists between us.

"I must tell you plainly now what you must know already, that, in view of all that has happened in the last year and a half, the differences of opinion and belief, the fundamental disagreements that we have discussed so openly, so frankly, and so passionately a thousand times, and which have brought about this unmistakable and grievous severance, I think you should have written this letter that I am asking you to write long before this. I am compelled by your failure to do so to ask you, in simple justice, to write it now.

[4] From Wolfe's letter of February 18, 1938, to Charles Scribner III.

"I think it is unfair to put a man in a position where he is forced to deny an obligation that does not exist, to refuse an agreement that was never offered and never made. I think it is also unfair to try to exert, at no expense to oneself, such control of a man's future and his future work as will bring one profit if that man succeeds, and that absolves one from any commitments of any kind should he fail. I also think it is unfair that a man without income, with little money, and with no economic security against the future, who has time and again in the past refused offers and proposals that would have brought him comfort and security, should now, at a time when his reputation has been obscured and when there are no offers and little market for his work, be compelled to this last and sorrowful exercise of his fruitless devotion. And finally, I do not think that life is a game of chess, and if it were, I could not be a player.

"I have nothing more to say here except to tell you that I am your friend and that my feeling toward you is unchanged."

Up to this point Wolfe's quarrels with Scribners might have been mere outbursts of artistic temperament. Now, however, his letter made it unmistakable that he really intended to leave. Perkins' perturbation over this is shown by the fact that he answered it in three separate letters: two personal longhand notes, and a formal letter written for the firm of Scribners after consultation with Charles Scribner III. The first of these, dated November 17, merely promised to answer Wolfe's letter the following day and added: "I never knew a soul with whom I felt I was in such fundamentally complete agreement as you. . . . I don't fully understand your letter, but I'll answer it as best I can. You must surely know, though, that any publisher would leap at the chance to publish you. . . . You have with us at present a balance of over $2000, all but about $500 of which is overdue."

The second was also a personal note, dated November 18, enclosing a more formal business letter and saying in part: "On my part there has been no 'severance.' I can't express certain kinds of feelings very comfortably, but you must realize what my feelings are toward you. . . . Your work has been the foremost interest in my life, and I have never doubted for your future on any grounds except, at times, on those of your being able to control the vast mass of material you have accumulated and have to form into books. You seem to think I have tried to control you. I only did that when you asked my help and then I did the best I could."

The third and more formal letter was also dated November 18, and it said in part: "You have faithfully and honorably discharged all obligations to us, and no further agreement of any sort exists between us with respect to the future. Our relations are simply those of a publisher who profoundly admires the work of an author and takes great pride in publishing whatever he may of that author's writings. . . . We do not wholly understand parts of your letter, where you speak of us as putting you in a position of denying an obligation that does not exist, for we do not know how we have done that; or where you refer to 'exerting control of a man's future,' which we have no intention of doing at all, and would not have the power or right to do. There are other phrases, in that part of your letter, that I do not understand, one of which is that which refers to us as being absolved from any commitments of any kind, 'should the author fail.' If this and these other phrases signify that you think you should have a contract from us if our relations are to continue, you can certainly have one. We should be delighted to have one. You must surely know the faith this house has in you. There are, of course, limits in terms beyond which nobody can go in a contract, but we should expect to make one that would suit you if you told us what was required."[5]

After this exchange of letters Wolfe and Perkins entered into an uneasy truce which lasted for approximately seven weeks. Perkins was hoping against hope that the break between them might still be averted. Wolfe was hoping the same thing—as he had written years ago to Mrs. Bernstein, "It is part of my temper to postpone pain and a final decision as long as possible"—but his compulsion to complete the break was stronger now than ever. During the greater part of December he was tramping agitatedly up and down the length of his apartment, dictating to his typist a continuation of his correspondence with Perkins in the form of a "business letter" and a separate "personal letter." The "business letter" was only an attempt to pin Perkins down to a definite commitment for a new contract: Wolfe was never satisfied with it and never mailed it, probably because he realized that he didn't really want a contract anyway. The "personal letter," however, is one of the most remarkable things he ever wrote—an overwhelmingly thorough and eloquent explanation of all the reasons for his severance from Scribners, which he considered as his official apologia for the break:

". . . First of all, let me tell you that for what you say in your own two personal letters of November 17th and November 18th I shall be

[5] For the full text of these letters see *Editor to Author: The Letters of Maxwell E. Perkins*, pages 115–17.

forever proud and grateful. I shall remember it with the greatest happiness as long as I live. I must tell you again, no matter what embarrassment it may cause you, what I have already publicly acknowledged and what I believe is now somewhat understood and known about in the world, namely, that your faith in me, your friendship for me, during the years of doubt, confusion and distress, was and will always be one of the great things in my life.

"When I did give utterance to this fact in print[6]—when I tried to make some slight acknowledgment of a debt of friendship and of loyalty, which no mere acknowledgment could ever repay—some of my enemies, as you know, tried to seize upon the simple words I had written in an effort to twist and pervert them to their own uses, to indicate that my acknowledgment was for a technical and professional service, which it was not, to assert that I was myself incapable of projecting and accomplishing my own purpose without your own editorial help, which is untrue. But although such statements as these were made to injure me, and perhaps have done me an injury, I believe that injury to be at best only a temporary one. As for the rest, what I had really said, what I had really written about my debt to you, is plain and unmistakable, clearly and definitely understood by people of good will, who have a mind to understand. I would not retract a word of it, except to wish the words were written better. I would not withdraw a line of it, except to hope that I might write another line that would more adequately express the whole meaning and implication of what I feel and want to say.

"As to those statements which were made, it seems to me, malevolently, for what purpose I do not know, by people I have never met—that I had to have your technical and critical assistance 'to help me write my books,' etc.—they are so contemptible, so manifestly false, I have no fear whatever of their ultimate exposure. If refutation were needed, if the artist had time enough or felt it necessary to make an answer to all the curs that snap at him, it would not take me long, I think, to brand these falsehoods for the lies they are. I would only have to point out, I think, that so far from needing any outside aid 'to help me write my books,' the very book which my detractors now eagerly seize on as my best one—the gauge by which the others must be measured, and itself the proof and demonstration of my subsequent decline —had been utterly finished and completed, to the final period, in utter isolation, without a word of criticism or advice from any one, before any publisher ever saw it; and that whatever changes were finally made

[6] In *The Story of a Novel.*

were almost entirely changes in the form of omission and of cuts in view of bringing the book down to a more publishable and condensed form. That book, of course, was 'Look Homeward, Angel,' and I believe that with everything else I ever wrote, the process was much the same, although the finality of completion was not so marked, because in later books I was working in a more experimental, individual fashion and dealing with the problem of how to shape and bring into articulate form a giant mass of raw material, whose proportions almost defeated me.

"The very truth of the matter is that, so far from ever having been unsure of purpose and direction, in the last five years at any rate I have been almost too sure. My sense of purpose and direction is definite and overwhelming. I think, I feel and know what I want to do: the direction in which, if I live and if I am allowed to go on working and fulfill myself, I want to go, is with me more clear and certain than with any one that I have ever known. My difficulty has never been one of purpose or direction. Nothing is more certain than this fact, that I know what I want to do and where I want to go. Nothing is more certain than the fact that I shall finish any book I set out to write, if life and health hold out. My difficulty from the outset, as you know, has never been one of direction, it has only been one of means. As I have already said and written, in language that seems to be so clear and unmistakable that no one could misunderstand it, I have been faced with the problem of discovering for myself my own language, my own pattern, my own structure, my own design, my own universe and creation. That, as I have said before, is a problem that is, I think, by no means unique, by no means special to myself. I believe it may have been the problem of every artist that ever lived. In my own case, however, I believe the difficulties of the problem may have been increased and complicated by the denseness of the fabric, the dimensions of the structure, the variety of the plan. For that reason I have, as you know, at times found myself almost hopelessly enmeshed in my own web.

"In one sense, my whole effort for years might be described as an effort to fathom my own design, to explore my own channels, to discover my own ways. In these respects, in an effort to help me to discover, to better use, these means I was striving to apprehend and make my own, you gave me the most generous, the most painstaking, the most valuable help. But that kind of help might have been given to me by many other skilful people—and of course there are other skilful people in the world who could give such help, although none that I know of who could give it so skilfully as you.

"But what you gave me, what in my acknowledgment I tried to give expression to, was so much more than this technical assistance—an aid of spiritual sustenance, of personal faith, of high purpose, of profound and sensitive understanding, of utter loyalty and staunch support, at a time when many people had no belief at all in me, or when what little belief they had was colored by serious doubt that I would ever be able to continue or achieve my purpose, fulfill my 'promise.' All of this was a help of such priceless and incalculable value, of such spiritual magnitude, that it made any other kind of help seem paltry by comparison. And for that reason mainly I have resented the contemptible insinuations of my enemies that I have to have you 'to help me write my books.' As you know, I don't have to have you or any other man alive to help me write my books. I do not even have to have technical help or advice, although I need it badly, and have been so immensely grateful for it. But if the worst came to the worst—and of course the worst does and will come to the worst—all this I could and will and do learn for myself, as all hard things are learned, with blood-sweat, anguish and despair.

"As for another kind of help—a help that would attempt to shape my purpose or define for me my own direction—I not only do not need that sort of help but if I found that it had in any way invaded the unity of my purpose, or was trying in any fundamental way to modify or alter the direction of my creative life—the way in which it seems to me it ought and has to go—I should repulse it as an enemy, I should fight it and oppose it with every energy of my life, because I feel so strongly that it is the final and unpardonable intrusion upon the one thing in an artist's life that must be held and kept inviolable.

"All this I know you understand and will agree to. As to the final kind of help, the help of friendship, the help of faith, the help and belief and understanding of a fellow creature whom you know and reverence not only as a person of individual genius but as a spirit of incorruptible integrity—that kind of help I do need, that kind of help I think I have been given, that kind of help I shall evermore hope to deserve and pray that I shall have. But if that too should fail—if that too should be taken from me, as so many rare and priceless things are taken from us in this life—that kind of dark and tragic fortitude that grows on us in life as we get older, and which tells us that in the end we can and must endure all things, might make it possible for me to bear even that final and irreparable loss, to agree with Samuel Johnson when he said: 'The shepherd in Vergil grew at last acquainted with Love, and found him a native of the rocks.'

"You say in one of your letters that you never knew a soul with whom you felt that you were in such fundamentally complete agreement as with me. May I tell you that I shall remember these words with proud happiness and with loyal gratefulness as long as I live. For I too on my own part feel that way about you. I know that somehow, in some hard, deep, vexed and troubling way in which all the truth of life is hidden and which, at the cost of so much living, so much perplexity and anguish of the spirit, we have got to try to find and fathom, what you say is true: I believe we are somehow, in this strange, hard way, in this complete and fundamental agreement with each other.

"And yet, were there ever two men since time began who were as completely different as you and I? Have you ever known two other people who were, in almost every respect of temperament, thinking, feeling and acting, as far apart? It seems to me that each of us might almost represent, typify, be the personal embodiment of, two opposite poles of life. How to put it I do not know exactly, but I might say, I think, that you in your essential self are the Conservative and I, in my essential self, am the Revolutionary.

"I use these words, I hope, in what may have been their original and natural meanings. I am not using them with the reference to any of the political, social, economic or religious connotations that are now so often tied up with them. When I say that you are a Conservative, I am not thinking of you as some one who voted for Governor Landon, for I can see how an action of that sort and your own considered reasons for doing it might easily have revolutionary consequences. When I say that I am a Revolutionary, I know that you will never for a moment think of me as some one who is usually referred to in America as a 'radical.' You know that my whole feeling toward life could not be indicated or included under such a category. I am not a party man, I am not a propaganda man, I am not a Union Square or Greenwich Village communist. I not only do not believe in these people: I do not even believe they believe in themselves. I mistrust their sincerity, I mistrust their motives, I do not believe they have any essential capacity for devotion or for belief in the very principles of Revolution, of government, of economics and of life, which they all profess.

"More than that, I believe that these people themselves are parasitic excrescences of the very society which they profess to abhor, whose destruction they prophesy and whose overthrow they urge. I believe that these people would be unable to live without the society which they profess to abhor, and I know that I could live if I had to, not only under this society but under any other one, and that in the end I might probably approve no other one more than I do this.

"I believe further that these very people who talk of the workers with such reverence, and who assert that they are workers and are for the worker's cause, do not reverence the workers, are not themselves workers and in the end are traitors to the worker's cause. I believe that I myself not only know the workers and am a friend of the worker's cause but that I am myself a brother to the workers, because I am myself, as every artist is, a worker, and I am myself, moreover, the son of a working man. I know furthermore that at the bottom there is no difference between the artist and the worker. They both come from the same family, they recognize and understand each other instantly. They speak the same language. They have always stood together. And I know that our enemies, the people who betray us, are these apes and monkeys of the arts, who believe in everything and who believe in nothing, and who hate the artist and who hate the living man no matter what lip service they may pay to us. These people are the enemies to life, the enemies to revolution. Nothing is more certain than that they will betray us in the end.

"I have said these things simply to indicate to you a difference of which I know you must be already well aware. The difference between the revolutionary and the 'radical,' the difference between the artist and the ape of art, the difference between the worker and those who say they are the worker's friend. The same thing could be said, it seems to me, on your own side, about the true conservative and the person who only votes conservative and owns property and has money in the bank.

"Just as in some hard, strange way there is between us probably this fundamentally complete agreement which you speak of, so too, in other hard, strange ways there is this complete and polar difference. It must be so with the South pole and the North pole. I believe that in the end they too must be in fundamentally complete agreement—but the whole earth lies between them. I don't know exactly how to define conservatism or the essential conservative spirit of which I speak here, but I think I might say it is a kind of fatalism of the spirit. Its fundaments, it seems to me, are based upon a kind of unhoping hope, an imperturbable acceptation, a determined resignation, which believes that fundamentally life will never change, but that on this account we must all of us do the best we can.

"The result of all this, it seems to me, is that these differences between us have multiplied in complexity and difficulty. The plain truth of the matter now is that I hardly know where to turn. The whole natural impulse of creation—and with me, creation is a natural impulse, it has got to flow, it has got to realize itself through the process of torrential production—is checked and hampered at every place. In spite of this, I have finally and at last, during these past two months, broken through into the greatest imaginative conquest of my life—the only complete and whole one I have ever had. And now I dare not broach it to you, I dare not bring it to you, I dare not show it to you, for fear that this thing which I cannot trifle with, which may come to a man but once in his whole life, may be killed at its inception by cold caution, by indifference, by the growing apprehensiveness and dogmatism of your own conservatism. You say that you are not aware that there is any severance between us. Will you please tell me what there is in the life around us on which we both agree? We don't agree in politics, we don't agree on economics, we are in entire disagreement on the present system of life around us, the way people live, the changes that should be made.

"Your own idea, evidently, is that life itself is unchangeable, that the abuses I protest against—the greed, the waste, the poverty, the filth, the suffering—are inherent in humanity, and that any other system than the one we have would be just as bad as this one. In this, I find myself in profound and passionate conflict. I hold no brief, as you know, for the present communist system as it is practiced in Russia to-day, but it seems to me to be the most absurd and hollow casuistry to argue seriously that because a good Russian worker is given a thicker slice of beef than a bad one, or because a highly trained mechanic enjoys a slightly better standard of living and is given more privileges and comforts than an inferior mechanic, the class system has been reestablished in Russia and is identical with the one existing in this country, whereby a young girl who inherits the fortune of a five-and-ten-cent-store king is allowed to live a life of useless, vicious idleness and to enjoy an income of five million dollars annually while other young girls work in the very stores that produce her fortune for ten dollars a week.

"It is all very well to say that the artist should not concern himself with these things but with 'life.' What are these things if they are not life—one of the cruelest and most intolerable aspects of it, it is true, but as much a part of the whole human spectacle as a woman producing a child. You, better than any one, have had the chance to observe during the past year how this consciousness of society, of the social elements that govern life to-day, have sunk into my spirit; how my convictions about all these things have grown deeper, wider, more intense at every point. On your own part, it seems to me, there has been a corresponding stiffening, an increasing conservatism that has now, I fear, reached the point of dogged and unyielding inflexibility and obstinate resolve to try to maintain the status quo at any cost.

"Since that is your condition, your considered judgment, I will not try to change it, or to persuade you in any way, because I know your reasons for so thinking and so feeling are honest ones. But neither must you now try to change me, or to persuade me to alter or deny convictions which are the result of no superficial or temporary influence, no Union Square, Greenwich Village cult, but the result of my own deep living, my own deep feeling, my own deep labor and my own deep thought.

"Had I given full expression to these convictions in 'Of Time and the River' I believe it would have been a better book. You do not think so. But I will say that these feelings, these convictions, are becoming deeper and intenser all the time, and so far from feeling that the world cannot be changed, that it cannot be made better, that the evils of life are unremediable, that all the faults and vices at which we protest will always exist, I find myself more passionately convinced than ever in the faith and the belief that the life and the condition of the whole human race can be immeasurably improved. And this is something that grows stronger with me all the time. . . .

"I have gone into all this not because these bases of contention are even fundamental to you and me, but because they are indicative of all the various widening channels of difference that have come up between us in recent years. Just as my own feeling for the necessity for change, for essential revolution in this way of life, has become steadily deeper and more confirmed, so too have you, hardened by the challenge of the depression, deeply alarmed by the menace of the times to the fortune of which you are the custodian—not for yourself, I know, for you yourself I truly believe are not a man who needs material things, but alarmed by the menace of these times to the security and future of five young and tender creatures who, protected as they have been, and unprepared as they are to meet the peril of these coming times, are themselves, it seems to me, the unfortunate victims of this very system you must now try to help maintain—you have accordingly become more set and more confirmed in your own convictions. With these personal affairs, these intimate details of your fine family, I have no intention to intrude save where it seems to me to have resulted in a bias that challenges the essence of my own purpose and direction.

"What I really want to say to you most earnestly now is this: there has never been a time when I've been so determined to write as I please, to say what I intend to say, to publish the books I want to publish, as I am now. I know that you have asserted time and again that you were in entire sympathy with this feeling—that, more than this, you were willing to be the eager promoter and supporter of this intention, that you were willing to publish whatever I wanted you to publish, that you were only waiting for me to give it to you. In this I think you have deceived yourself. I think you are mistaken when you say that all you have waited for was the word from me, that you would publish anything I wanted you to publish. There are many things that I have wanted you to publish which have not been published. Some of them have not been published because they were too long for magazine space, or too short for book space, or too different in their design and quality to fit under the heading of a short story, or too incomplete to be called a novel. All this is true. All this I grant. And yet, admitting all these things, without a word of criticism of you or of the technical and publishing requirements of the present time that make their publication impracticable, I will still say that I think some of them should have been published. I still think that much of the best writing that a man may do is writing that does not follow under the convenient but extremely limited forms of modern publication. It is not your fault. It is not Scribners' fault. It is just the way things are. But as I have been telling you, the way things are is not always the way, it seems to me, that things should be . . .

"Which brings me now to an essential point, a point that bears practically and dangerously on every thing that I have heretofore said to you.

"About fifteen years ago, as you know, an extraordinary book was produced which startled the whole critical and publishing world. This book was the 'Ulysses' of James Joyce. . . . Was it published by Charles Scribner's Sons? No, it was not. Was it published by Harper's, by Macmillan, by Houghton Mifflin, by one of the great English houses? It was not. Who published it then? It was published privately, obscurely, by a woman who ran a book shop in Paris. And at first, as you know, it was treated by most critics as kind of literary curiosity—either as a work of deliberate pornography or as a work of wilfully complicated obscurity, of no genuine value or importance, save to a little group of clique adepts. And as you know, the book was taken up by clique adepts everywhere and used, or rather misused, in their customary way, as a badge of their snobbish superiority. But in addition to both these groups there was also a third group, I think a very small group, composed of those people scattered throughout the world who are able to read and feel and understand and form their own judgment without prejudice of the merits of a powerful and original work. It seems to me that almost the best, the most fortunate thing in life—in a writer's life at least—is that these people do exist. A great book is not lost. It does not get done to death by fools and snobs. It may be misunderstood for years. Its writer may be ridiculed or reviled or betrayed by false idolatry, but the book does not get lost. There are always a few people who will save it. The book will make its way. That is what happened to 'Ulysses.' As time went on, the circle widened. Its public increased. As people overcame their own inertia, mastered the difficulty which every new and original work creates, became familiar with its whole design, they began to understand that the book was neither an obscene book nor an obscure book, certainly it was not a work of wilful dilettante caprice. It was, on the contrary, an orderly, densely constructed creation, whose greatest fault, it seems to me, so far from being a fault of caprice, was rather the fault of an almost Jesuitical logic which is essentially too dry and lifeless in its mechanics for a work of the imagination. At any rate, now, after fifteen years, 'Ulysses' is no longer thought of as a book meant solely for a little group of literary adepts. . . . Moreover, 'Ulysses' can now be published openly in this country, sold over the counter as any other book is sold, without fear of arrest or action by the law. And at the present time, as you know, it is being sold that way, in what is known as 'large quantities,' by one of your fellow publishers. This man told me a year and a half ago that the sale up to that time, I believe, was something like 30,000 copies. 'Ulysses,' therefore, has made its way not only critically but commercially as well. These are the facts. I do not recall them in order to accuse you with them. I know you did not have the opportunity of publishing 'Ulysses.' Perhaps no other well-known publisher, either in England or America, had that opportunity. I suppose furthermore that at that time it would have been impossible for any reputable publisher to have published that book openly. But the fact remains it did get published, didn't it—not by Scribners, not by Houghton, not by any known publisher in England, but privately, by a little obscure bookseller in Paris.

"And the reason your associates, the Modern Library, Inc., can now publish this book in large quantities, openly, and derive a profit from it now, is because some private, obscure person took the chance fifteen years ago—took the chance, I fear, without the profits.

"What then? You say you are waiting eagerly to discover a manuscript of originality and power. You say that you are waiting eagerly to publish a manuscript of mine—that you will publish anything I want you to publish. I know you believe what you say, but I also think you deceive yourself. I am not going to write a 'Ulysses' book. Like many another young man who came under the influence of that remarkable work, I wrote my 'Ulysses' book and got it published too. That book, as you know, was 'Look Homeward, Angel.' And now, I am finished with 'Ulysses' and with Mr. Joyce, save that I am not an ingrate and will always, I hope, be able to remember a work that stirred me, that opened new vistas into writing, and to pay the tribute to a man of genius that is due him.

"However, I am now going to write my own 'Ulysses.' The first volume is now under way. The first volume will be called 'The Hound of Darkness,' and the whole work, when completed, will be called 'The Vision of Spangler's Paul.'[7] Like Mr. Joyce, I am going to write as I please, and this time, no one is going to cut me unless I want them to. Like Mr. Joyce, and like most artists, I believe, I am by nature a Puritan. At any rate, a growing devotion to work, to purpose, to fulfillment, a growing intensity of will, tends to distill one's life into a purer liquor. I shall never hereafter—I hope that I have never heretofore, but I shall never hereafter—write a word for the purpose of arousing sensational surprise, of shocking the prudish, of flaunting the outraged respectabilities of the middle-class mind. But I shall use as precisely, as truthfully, as tellingly as I can every word I have to use; every word, if need be, in my vocabulary; every word, if need be, in the vocabulary of the foulest-mouthed taxi driver, the most prurient-tongued prostitute that ever screamed an obscene epithet. Like Mr. Joyce, I have at last discovered my own America. I believe I have found my language, I think I know my way. And I shall wreak out my vision of this life, this way, this world and this America, to the top of my bent, to the height of my ability, but with an unswerving devotion, integrity and purity of purpose that shall not be menaced, altered or weakened by any one. I will go to jail because of this book if I have to, I will lose my friends because of it, if I will have to. I will be libelled, slandered, blackmailed, threatened, menaced, sneered at, derided and assailed by every parasite, every ape, every blackmailer, every scandalmonger, every

---

[7] By this time Wolfe had decided to include the material and title of *The Hound of Darkness* in *The Vision of Spangler's Paul* (which finally became *The Web and the Rock* and *You Can't Go Home Again*). The title *The Hound of Darkness* is used for Book II of *The Web and the Rock*, but most of the original material was omitted or used elsewhere in that novel or in *You Can't Go Home Again*.

little Saturday-Reviewer of the venomous and corrupt respectabilities. I will be exiled from my country because of it, if I have to. . . . But no matter what happens I am going to write this book.

"You have heard me talk to you before. You have not always been disposed to take seriously what I say to you. I pray most earnestly that you will take this seriously. For seven years now, during this long and for me wonderful association with you, I have been increasingly aware of a certain direction which our lives were taking. Looking back, I can see now that although 'Look Homeward, Angel' gave you pleasure and satisfaction, you were extremely alarmed even then about its publication, and entertained the hope—the sincere and honest hope, directed, I know, to what you considered my own best interests—that the years would temper me to a greater conservatism, a milder intensity, a more decorous moderation. And I think where I have been most wrong, most unsure in these past seven years, has been where I have yielded to this benevolent pressure. Because I think that it is just there that I have allowed myself to falter in my purpose, to be diverted from the direction toward which the whole impulsion of my life and talent is now driving me, to have failed there insofar as I have yielded to the modifications of this restraint. Restraint, discipline—yes, they were needed desperately, they are needed badly still. But let us not get the issues confused, let us not again get into the old confusion between substance and technique, purpose and manner, direction and means, the spirit and the letter. Restrain my adjectives, by all means, discipline my adverbs, moderate the technical extravagances of my incondite exuberance, but don't derail the train, don't take the Pacific Limited and switch it down the siding towards Hogwart Junction. It can't be done. I'm not going to let it happen. If you expected me to grow conservative simply because I got bald and fat and for the first time in life had a few dollars in the bank, you are going to be grievously mistaken. Besides, what is there longer for me to fear? I have been through it all now, I have seen how women can betray you, how friends can sell you out for a few filthy dollars, how the whole set-up of society and of justice in its present form permits the thief, the parasite, the scavenger, the scandalmonger to rob, cheat, outrage and defame you, how even those people who swear they are your sincerest and most enduring friends, who say they value your talent and your work, can sink to the final dishonor of silence and of caution when you are attacked, will not even lift their voices in a word of protest or of indignation when they hear you lied about by scoundrels or maligned by rascals. So what am I now to lose? Even the little money that I had, the greater part of it, has now been taken from me by these thieves and parasites of life. Well, they can take it, they can have it, they have got it. They can take everything I have, but no one henceforth shall take from me my work.

"I am afraid of nothing now. I have nothing more to lose except my life and health. And those I pray and hope to God will stay with me till my work is done. That, it seems to me, is the only tragedy that can now stay me. . . .

"I do not know if you have always been aware of how I felt about these things; of what a naked, fiercely lacerated thing my spirit was; how I have writhed beneath the lies and injuries and, at times, been almost maddened to insanity at the treachery, the injustice and the hatred I have had to experience and endure; at what a frightful cost I have attained even the little fortitude I have attained. At times, particularly during the last year or two, the spectacle of the victim squirming beneath the lash has seemed to amuse you. I know there is no cruelty in your nature. I do suggest to you, however, that when one is secure in life, when one is vested with authority, established in position, surrounded by a little world of his own making, of his own love, he may sometimes be a little unmindful of the lives of people less fortunate than himself. There is an unhappy tendency in all of us to endure with fortitude the anguish of another man. There is also a tendency among people of active and imaginative minds and temperaments, who live themselves conventional and conservative lives, to indulge vicariously their interest in the adventures and experiences of other people whose lives are not so sheltered as their own. And these people, I think, often derive what seems to be a kind of quiet, philosophic amusement at the spectacle of what is so falsely known as the 'human comedy.' But I might suggest to such people that what affords them quiet entertainment is being paid for by another man with blood and agony, and that while we smile at the difficulties and troubles in which an impulsive and generous person gets involved, a man of genius or of talent may be done to death. . . .

"At any rate, in spite of all these things, I shall push forward somehow to the completion of my work. I feel that any more confusion or uncertainty might be ruinous to my purpose. There has been too much indecision already. We postponed the completion and publication of 'The October Fair,' with some intention, I suppose, of showing the critics and the public I could create in a different vein, in a more objective manner than I had yet done. We also deferred completion and publication of 'The Hills Beyond Pentland.' I know you said you were willing to go ahead and publish these books. You have always assured me on that point. But I did feel that your counsel and your caution were against their publication now.

"I believe you may have allowed your apprehensions concerning who and what I might now write about at the period I had now reached in my writing to influence your judgments. I don't like to go into all this again. The thing that happened last summer, your reaction to the manuscript Miss Nowell brought to you while I was in Europe,[8] and your own comment as expressed to her in a note which she sent to me and which said, after she had cut all the parts you objected to in the manuscript out of it, that 'the only person it can now possibly hurt is Thomas Wolfe,' was to me a shocking revelation. I am not of the opinion now that the manuscript in question was one of any great merit. I know that I've done much better work. But the point, as I told you after my return from Europe, the point that we discussed so frankly and so openly, was that your action, if carried to its logical conclusions and applied to everything I write from now on, struck a deadly blow at the very vitals of my whole creative life. The only possible inference that could be drawn from this matter was that from now on, if I wished to continue writing books which Charles Scribner's Sons were going to publish, I must now submit myself to the most rigid censorship, a censorship which would delete from all my writings any episode, any scene, any character, any reference that might seem to have any connection, however remote, with the house of Charles Scribner's Sons and its sisters and its cousins and its aunts. Such a conclusion, if I agreed to it, would result in the total enervation and castration of my work—a work which, as I have told you in this letter, I am now resolved must be more strong and forthright in its fidelity to purpose than ever.

"Again, in this whole situation there is a display of an almost unbelievable vanity and arrogance. It was first of all, the vanity and arrogance that would lead certain people to suppose that I was going to 'write about them,' and then the vanity and arrogance of people who said that, although it was perfectly all right for me to write about other people 'in humble walks of life,' it was an unpardonable affront to all these important high-toned personages to be 'written about' freely and frankly by a low scribbling fellow, who is good enough no doubt to supply a publisher with manuscript, to give employment to his business, to add prestige to the reputation of his firm, but who must be put in his place when he overstepped the bounds of human sanctity.

"Now, in the first place, as I told you before, whoever got the idea

8 "No More Rivers."

that I was going to write about him or her or them anyway? And in the second place, whoever got the idea that I was not going to go ahead and write as I damned pleased, about anything I wished to write about, with the complete freedom to which every artist is entitled, and that no one in the world was going to stand in the way of my doing this? I am certainly at the present time not interested in writing about Charles Scribner's Sons or any one connected with Charles Scribner's Sons. It has at the present time no part of my creative plan or of my writing effort. And as you know very well, I don't 'write about' people: I create living characters of my own—a whole universe of my own creation. And any character that I create is so unmistakably my own that anyone familiar with my work would know instantly it was my own, even if it had no title and no name.

"But, to go back to this simple, fundamental, inescapable necessity of all art, which I have patiently, laboriously, coherently, explained a thousand times, in such language that no one can misunderstand it, to all the people in this country, to all the people who, for some strange and extraordinary reason, in America and nowhere else that I have ever been on earth, keep harping forever, with a kind of idiot pertinacity, upon the word 'autobiography'—you can't make something out of nothing. You can either say that there is no such thing as autobiographical writing, or you can say that all writing is autobiographical, a statement with which I should be inclined to agree. But you cannot say, you must not say, that one man is an autobiographical writer and another man is not an autobiographical writer. You cannot and must not say that one novel is an autobiographical novel and another novel is not an autobiographical novel. Because if you say these things, you are uttering falsehood and palpable nonsense. It has no meaning.

"My books are neither more nor less autobiographical than 'War and Peace.' If anything, I should say that they are less, because a great writer like Tolstoi who achieves his purpose, achieves it because he has made a perfect utilization of all the means, all the materials at his disposal. This Tolstoi did in 'War and Peace.' I have never yet succeeded in doing it completely and perfectly. Accordingly, Tolstoi is a more autobiographical writer than I am, because he has succeeded better in using what he had. But make no mistake about it: both of us, and every other man who ever wrote a book, are autobiographical. You are therefore not to touch my life in this way. When you or any man tries to exert this kind of control, to modify or shape my material in an improper way because of some paltry, personal, social apprehension, you do the unpardonable thing. You try to take from the artist his personal property, to steal his substance, to defraud him of his treasure—the only treasure he has, the only property and wealth which is truly, inexorably, his own.

"You can take it from him, but by so doing you commit a crime. You have stolen what does not belong to you. You have not only taken what belongs to another man, but you have taken what belongs to him in such a way that no one else can possibly claim ownership. No one owns what he has as does the artist. When you try to steal it from him he only laughs at you, because you could take it to the ends of the earth and bury it in a mountain and it would still shine straight through the mountain side like radium. You couldn't hide it. Any one on earth could find it and would know at once who the proper owner was.

"That is what this final argument is about. I'm not going to be interfered with on this score. I get my material, I acquire my wealth, as every artist does, from his own living, from his own experience, from his own observation. And when any outer agency tries to interpose itself between me and any portion of my own property, however small, and says to me 'hands off,' or 'you can't have that particular piece there,' someone is going to get hurt.

"You told me when I discussed these things with you in October, after my return from Europe, that you agreed with me, that in the last analysis you were always with the man of talent, and that if the worst comes to the worst you could resign your executive and editorial functions. Well, don't worry, you'll never have to. In the first place, your executive and editorial functions are so special and valuable that they can not be substituted by any other person on earth. They could not be done without by the business that employs them. It would be like having a house with the lights turned out. Furthermore, no one is going to resign on my account. There are still enough people in the world who value what I do, I believe, to support me freely, heartily and cheerfully, with no sense that they are enduring martyrdom on my account. So if there is ever any situation that might indicate any future necessity for any one to resign anything on my account, that situation will never arise, simply because I won't be there to be resigned about.

"This business about the artist hurting people is for the most part nonsense. The artist is not here in life to hurt it but to illuminate it. He is not here to teach men hatred but to show them beauty. No one in the end ever got hurt by a great book, or if he did, the hurt was paltry and temporary in comparison to the immense good that was conferred.

"Now, at a time when I am more firmly resolved than ever before to exert my full amount, to use my full stroke, to shine my purest and intensest ray, it is distressing to see the very people who published my first efforts with complete equanimity, and with no qualms whatever about the possibility of anybody getting 'hurt,' begin to squirm around uncomfortably and call for calf-rope and whine that their own toes are being stepped upon, even when nothing has been said, nothing written. They have no knowledge or declaration of my own intention except that I intend in my own way to finish my own book. What are you going to do about it? You say you are not aware that there have been any difficulties or any severance. If these things I have been talking about are not difficulties, if this is not a threatened severance of the gravest nature, I should like to know what you consider difficult and what severance is? We can not continue in this irresolute, temporizing 'Well now, you go ahead for the present—we'll wait and see how it all turns out' manner. My life has been ravaged, my energy exhausted, my work confused and aborted long enough by this kind of miserable, time-serving procrastination. I'm not going to endure it any longer. I'm not going to pour my sweat and blood and energy and life and talent into another book now, only to be told two or three years from now that it would be inadvisable to publish it without certain formidable deletions, or that perhaps we'd better wait a few years longer and see 'how everything turns out.'

"We stalled around this way with 'October Fair,' until all the intensity and passion I had put into the book was lost, until I had gone stale on it, until I was no longer interested in it—and to what purpose? Why, because you allowed your fond weakness for the female sex to get the better of your principle, because you were afraid some foolish female, who was inwardly praying for nothing better than to be a leading character in a book of mine, and who was bitterly disappointed when she was not, might get her feelings hurt—or that the pocketbook of the firm might get touched by suits for libel. Well, there would have been no suits for libel. I never libelled anybody in my life. Certainly, there was no remote danger of libel in 'The October Fair,' but because of our weakness and irresolution the news got around that we were afraid of publication for this reason. The rumor was spread around in the column of a . . . gossip-writer, and the result now is that we have a libel suit on our hands from a person who was never libelled, who doesn't have a leg to stand on, but who is willing to take the chance and make the effort to get something because we were not firm and resolute in the beginning.

"Let's make an end of all this devil's business. Let's stand to our guns like men. Let's go ahead and try to do our work without qualification, without fear, without apology. What are you willing to do? My own position is now clear. I have nothing to be afraid of. And my greatest duty, my deepest obligation now is to the completion of my own work. If that can not be done any longer upon the terms that I have stated here, then I must either stand alone or turn to other quarters for support, if I can find it. You yourself must now say plainly what the decision is to be, because the decision now rests with you. You can no longer have any doubt as to how I feel about these matters. I don't see how you can any longer have any doubt that difficulties of a grave and desperate nature do exist.

"I can only repeat here what I have told you before, that the possibility of an irrevocable and permanent severance has caused me the greatest distress and anguish of the mind for months, that if it occurs it will seem to me like death, but that whatever happens, what I have said and written about the way I feel towards you will remain. . . .

"I'm sorry this letter has had to be so long. It seemed to me there had to be some sort of final statement. I hope, now the statement has been made, the problem is more clear. I send all of you now all my best wishes for Christmas and for a New Year which I hope will bring to all of us an accomplishment and fulfillment of some of those things we most desire.

"Meanwhile, with all friendship, all good wishes,

"—Max, this is not a well-written letter, but it is a genuine and honest one. If you still have any interest in me, please attend to what I say here carefully!"

XXV

B Y T H E time Wolfe had got his two long letters of severance from Scribners dictated and "down for the record," it was Christmas time. In addition to brooding over these and worrying about the Dorman suit, he had been pushing ahead on his new book and, according to his own somewhat exaggerated estimate, had written "over 200,000 words since October." He was "desperately tired" and in need of a vacation, and he decided to go to New Orleans for New Year's. Ironically enough, he postponed his departure until December 26 because he had been invited to eat Christmas dinner at the Perkinses'— "and of course I like to see them," he wrote his mother. "They are a nice family."

Meanwhile his letters of severance still lay unmailed upon his table, but when he packed his suitcase for the trip to New Orleans, he picked them up and shoved them into it. From then on, all through his journey South, he kept reading and rereading them and writing postscripts, with the avowed intention of mailing them at once. "I have deferred sending this, and accordingly am sending it from Richmond, Va.," he wrote at the bottom of the "business letter": then, later, added ruefully: "But I deferred that too!" Also: "I am writing you this from Richmond. Frankly, I think we are at the end. I am sending this to you now. I should have sent it to you long ago, in view of the agony, the despair, the utter desolation this thing has cost me—but I must send it to you now. As to the other letter—the enormously long letter I wrote in reply to your two personal ones—I shall hold on to it a day longer— reread it—perhaps make little revisions here and there. Anything! Anything!—to try to temper the sorrow and the grief of the final decision into which I—God knows—have been compelled without even the power of saying whether I wanted it or not. You must answer this *straight!*"

Then, a few days later, he wrote: "Additional P.S. As to your statement that anyone would *want* me—that, as you must *now* know, is not true. I am almost penniless—this suit for libel has appeared with almost sinister immediacy in the last month or two—I have turned down fortunes—$10,000 *is* a fortune to me, and you knew of *that* one at once, the one that was made me two years ago when I was really penniless, and when you asked me to tell you what the offer was. I am broke—I have lost everything—I do not think we can go on. Who, then, are these eager publishers? Answer at New Orleans."

And finally: "P.S. Max: You'd better send the answer air mail to New Orleans. I am afraid you did not take this thing seriously but, as I told you, it is like death to me. You'd better answer by wire. Atlanta, December 29, 1936. You'd better say *precisely* what you can offer. Atlanta, December 29, 1936."

After writing these last two urgent postscripts, Wolfe again failed to mail the letter, carried it to New Orleans, and finally brought it all the way back to New York. For some time it occupied its old place on the table, but at last his secretary put it in his file, where it still remains today.

The "personal letter," however, he actually sent to Perkins, and the story of how he was finally compelled to mail it is both comic and tragic, and confused in a way that is typical of him.

He arrived at New Orleans on January 1 and found that the Roosevelt Hotel, where he had planned to stay, was full to overflowing with spectators for the New Year's Sugar Bowl game. He accordingly spent his first few days at a boardinghouse on Prytania Street: then he moved into the Roosevelt when a room became available. He had asked Hamilton Basso, who was a native of New Orleans, to write him some letters of introduction, especially to the people on the *Times-Picayune*, but he had then, characteristically, forgotten to bring the letters with him. Finally he presented himself, huge and shy and stuttering, at the *Picayune* city room and asked if he could join the late shift when they finished work and went out for a drink. They went to Earl James' place at Toulouse and Royal Streets, where, according to one of the *Picayune* reporters, Wolfe "took on about a quart and had a wonderful time."[1] When one of the habitués of the place refused to believe that Wolfe had been a newspaper boy, he folded a paper and threw it across the barroom and against the wall—as he had thrown copies of the Asheville *Citizen* upon the porches of Niggertown—saying, "I'm the best damn newspaper boy the Asheville *Citizen* ever had: I'll tell you that much!" Later he and two of the younger reporters explored the Quarter and went at dawn to stand on the levee and watch the great sweep of

[1] The author is indebted to Thomas Sancton for information about Wolfe in New Orleans, contained in letters to her and in his article "Time and the River," in the October 26, 1950, issue of the New Orleans *Item*.

the Mississippi behind the willows. Wolfe turned to his new friends in ecstasy. "*This*—this is America!" he said. He pulled up a fistful of the coarse green grass that grew on the levee and watched the wind blow it from his opened fingers and drop it onto the sliding surface of the water.

Within a day or two the news had got around that the author of *Of Time and the River* was in town, and Wolfe was being overwhelmed with hospitality by the New Orleans literati, by some family friends of his from Asheville, the Allen Eldreds, and by William B. Wisdom, the advertising man and bibliophile who was later to buy Wolfe's manuscripts and personal papers and give them to Harvard University.[2] Wolfe was touched and flattered by his popularity, but he was still a very tired man. He drank a great deal more than was good for him and, as always, when under the influence of alcohol, he felt overwhelmed with resentment against Scribners and was constantly on the verge of mailing his two letters of severance to Perkins and making a clean breast of the whole thing.

Meanwhile a whole new mess of legal difficulties was brewing in New York. Wolfe had finally instituted suit against the young man who had been his manuscript agent, and the latter now was threatening to retaliate and help the Dorman family in their suit. Since the manuscript agent was a resident of New Jersey, Wolfe's own lawyer, Cornelius Mitchell, had been obliged to retain attorneys in that state. They now telephoned Mitchell, and he in turn phoned Perkins, to ask where he could get in touch with Wolfe and urge him to come back immediately to New York. Perkins himself did nothing except suggest that Wolfe might be at the Roosevelt in New Orleans, but when Wolfe got Mitchell's letter, he blamed everything—as usual—on Perkins. "How dare you give anyone my address!" he wired him immediately: then he launched into the writing of a series of angry letters which accused Perkins of everything from being "just a good but timid man" to "trying to destroy" him.

Meanwhile Wolfe's new-found friends in New Orleans kept right on overwhelming him with hospitality, in utter ignorance of the crisis in which he was involved. He was drinking very heavily, both because he wanted to be sociable and because he was emotionally upset, and the more he drank, the more bellicose he became. He had already insulted

[2] The author is greatly indebted to William B. Wisdom for letting her read his unpublished memoirs of Wolfe's visit to New Orleans, as well as for making available to her Wolfe's letters, diaries, manuscripts, and other papers in the William B. Wisdom Collection at Houghton Library, Harvard.

the Louisiana literati by announcing that he "hadn't come all the way to New Orleans to see a lot of goddamned aesthetes" and that he would be goddamned if he would go to a shrimp broil being given in his honor at Elva Godchaux's or a party afterward at Tess Crager's bookshop. However, the climax came a few days later, on January 8, when, after drinking a good deal all day, he took it into his head to go, all by himself, to the famous New Orleans Carnival Ball. For the last few days he had had a notion that he "wanted to meet some attractive young unmarried girls," and when he arrived at the ball and saw an entire galaxy of them sitting in chairs around the ballroom floor, he went and sat down in their midst. Unfortunately, he had blundered into the "call-out seats," which were reserved for the debutantes and other ladies who were to take part in the Maskers' Dance. Somebody told him that he couldn't sit there but must join the other spectators upstairs, whereupon he left, and drowned his chagrin by wandering from bar to bar. He ended up by drinking at Tony's until 3 A.M., when he rolled back to his hotel room, promptly fell into the bathtub with all his clothes on, and passed out. He came to about an hour later, with his head and back aching horribly and his trouser leg torn badly at the knee. He evidently began to brood again about his difficulties with Scribners, and he sent Perkins another wire, saying abruptly: "What is your offer?" After that he went to sleep, this time in the proper place, in bed.

The next day he was somewhat the worse for wear, but he shut himself away from everybody in his hotel room, pushed aside all the drafts and fragments of letters which he had been writing to Perkins for the past two days, and doggedly began a whole new letter:

"Dear Max: I'm sorry I telegraphed you as I did. And I don't even know now exactly what I telegraphed you. But maybe you can understand a little when I tell you that all this worry, grief, and disappointment of the last two years has almost broken me, and finally this last letter of Mitchell's was almost the last straw. I was desperately in need of rest and quiet—the letter destroyed it all, ruined all the happiness and joy I had hoped to get from this trip—the horrible injustice of the whole thing has almost maddened me. I can understand none of it any more . . . most of all your own attitude.

"Max, I simply can't understand: you yourself urged—not only urged but indignantly insisted—that I take action against ——. . . . Now, you speak of paying him off—you told me only a few weeks ago that you would pay the $500 and be done with it—this after insisting at first that I take action, recover the manuscripts and that there should be no compromise. In God's name, what is your meaning? Are you—the man

I trusted and reverenced above all else in the world—trying, for some mad reason I can not even guess, to destroy me? How am I going to interpret the events of the past two years? Don't you want me to go on? Don't you want me to write another book? Don't you hope for my life— my growth—the fulfillment of my talent? In Christ's name, what is it, then? My health is well-nigh wrecked—worry, grief, and disillusionment has almost destroyed my talent—is *this* what you wanted? And why? . . .

"And you—where are you, Max? Have you, too, become terrified at these threats of libel suits? Are you going to advise me to yield . . . simply because the interests of Scribners might be involved? What are we going to do? This thing is like death to me. Have we really reached the end? I fear desperately we have—it is all so tragically sad—and as for that powerful and magnificent talent I had two years ago—in the name of God is that to be lost entirely, destroyed under the repeated assaults and criminalities of this blackmail society under which we live? *Now* I know what happens to the artist in America. *Now* I know what must be changed. *Now* truly, henceforth and forever after, I shall work with all my strength for revolution—for the abolition of this vile and rotten system under which we live—for a better world, a better life.

"And you? You are in very many ways the best person I have ever known, the person for whom I have had the greatest reverence and devotion—but in some few ways, perhaps, I am a better man than you. Forgive me these wild telegrams. Even if we have now come to the end of our publishing connection—a connection for which I have sacrificed everything—a connection that is now being severed when I have nothing left, when no one wants me—for God's sake let us try to save our belief and faith in each other—a belief and faith that I still have— that I hope you have not lost. I would to God I were a better man, but I will not cease trying to be a better one—and for you, I cannot bear to see you just a good but timid man. I am in deadly peril, but right or wrong, I want you to go into battle with me—I see you as the noble captain, strong and faithful, and no matter what the cost, right to the end. I have no right to ask it, but you must be the great man that I know you are. Don't give up the ship. I am leaving here tomorrow, I think. Some friends are taking me to the country in an effort to get me some quiet and rest. I hope to be in North Carolina in a few days— although now, feeling as I do, I doubt the approval of my friends. But if you want to write me, you might address the letter in care of Mr. Garland Porter, *The Atlanta Georgian*, Atlanta. But whatever you do

—unless it is something involving the serious sickness or death of a member of my family—don't give my address to anyone. I'm in a wretched state, and I've got to get on my feet before I come back to New York to fight. . . ."

He had hardly finished this letter when a wire arrived from Perkins, in answer to his own asking what Scribners' offer was: "If you refer to book, we shall make it verbally when you return, as arrangements will depend on your requirements. Gave no one your address but suggested two possibilities to your lawyer, who thought it important to communicate." Perkins was obviously in a difficult situation. He knew from Wolfe's wires that he was in an upset state of mind, or drunk, or both, but he did not fully realize that for an entire month Wolfe had been writing him letters of severance and had been trying to screw his courage up to the point of mailing them. If he wired Wolfe a concrete offer for his book, the latter would almost undoubtedly misinterpret it to suit whatever mood he might be in. Moreover, even if Wolfe did receive and accept an offer, his compulsion to break free from Scribners was so deep and so complex that he probably would end up by leaving them anyway. On the other hand, Wolfe had a perfect right to ask Scribners for a definite commitment or a definite release of his new book, or as he succinctly put it, "They ought to fish or cut bait." To him, Perkins' wire was evidence that Scribners did not want to publish his book, never had wanted to publish it, never had made him an offer for it, and never would. He became more firmly convinced than ever that Perkins was being cautious and evasive with him, and to him, this was the final straw.

The next day, Sunday, January 10, he wrote a postscript to his letter of the day before to Perkins: "I was worn out yesterday when I wrote this. To-day I feel a little better—and I am assured of my course. Further words, arguments, entreaties are useless. We are either at the end or we shall go on. I am sending two letters which I wrote some weeks ago and which, hoping against hope, I have withheld. These letters in a general way put the story of my relation to you and Scribners upon the record. There is nothing in either of them that can do you any harm. But, in case anything happens to me, I am sending duplicates to a friend.[3] I think this is proper."

[3] As far as can be determined, Wolfe did not send a copy of this letter to any friend at this time. In the fall of 1937 he gave a copy to Hamilton Basso, after writing the following words in pencil on the bottom of the final page: "To my friend, Hamilton Basso: Dear Ham—I've gone upon the record here—

Then he got out the "personal letter" and "business letter," which he had never mailed, read them through, discarded the latter, and wrote a postscript on the former: "P.S. New Orleans, Jan. 10, 1937: I have withheld this letter as long as possible. I had hoped against hope not to have to send it. But now, after the shocking events of the past two weeks since I left New York— . . . the growing peril of my situation in a mesh of scoundrelism—and your own telegram—the increasing ambiguity and caution of your own statements—I have read the letter through again and decided that *it must be sent*. In spite of its great length there is much more to say—but let this stand now for the record!"

He at last had come to a decision. He put the "personal letter" and his letter of January 9 into an envelope, took them to the mailbox in the Roosevelt lobby, and dropped them in, for better or for worse. The severance from Scribners to all intents and purposes was made, although he postponed the final act—approaching other publishers—for eight more months, or till September 1937.

Wolfe left New Orleans on January 11. The Eldreds had invited him to their home at Ocean Springs for a rest, but after only one night there he told them that he "had to be alone," and he crossed the river to Biloxi, where he went to a hotel and slept for several days. Then, finally refreshed, he started back up North in what turned out to be a triumphal progress. Six months earlier his old friend William Polk had invited him to speak at the meeting of the North Carolina Literary and Historical Society which was to be held in Raleigh in December. Wolfe had been overjoyed by what this signified. "Honestly," he had written to Polk, "it is good to know that at least I have a chance of coming home without being escorted to the outskirts of the town by the local Vigilantes and told never to darken their public square again." For the seven years which had elapsed since the publication of *Look Homeward, Angel,* he had lived in self-imposed exile from the South. But now at last he had been invited not only to come home to North Carolina but to come as the honored guest of its leading cultural society. He finally declined the invitation to address the Literary and Historical Society, but the knowledge that he would be welcome in his native state had been the motivation for his trip through the South to

---

this is not perhaps the whole story—but in a general way it says some of the things I felt had to be said. I am leaving this copy of the letter in your care and, if anything should happen to me, I leave it to your discretion what should be done with it."

New Orleans, and he now headed back toward Chapel Hill for the return to his alma mater which he had postponed for seventeen long years.

For four or five days he was shepherded around the University of North Carolina campus by his classmate Dean "Shorty" Spruill, who was as small and quiet as Wolfe was huge and talkative. He called on his old professor Horace Williams, was entertained by innumerable old friends, and kept most of the faculty up till 4 A.M. while he talked and drank at Phillips Russell's. However, the high point of his visit was the informal speech he made to a group of young Wolfe worshipers, "the Wolverines," and about a hundred other undergraduates who flocked to see him when the news got around that he would visit Phillips Russell's writing class. "He came at last," wrote one of the Wolverines later, in the *Carolina Magazine,* "stumbling down the stairs, a flushed and sweaty face and a hoarse mutter of apology. He fumbled with his coat button, whispered almost pleadingly to Mr. Russell, . . . photographed the assembly in one long stare and then dropped his head and drew circles on the floor with his feet. 'I-I-I thought I was coming to sit in on a class,' he said. 'I-I-I didn't . . . Wh-when I was here th-there weren't any more than th-this in school.' . . . He was scared. The great devourer of ten thousand nights was cowed by a hundred undergraduates. But somehow the restlessness, the squirming embarrassment that usually comes over an audience when someone is tongue-tied with fright, did not come. . . . A quiet, friendly laugh arose. He looked up, smiling, grateful, warming every face with his eyes' glow. 'It's s-s-so good to be back,' he said naïvely, his words beginning to flow more freely now. 'I was just telling Shorty here how much of it all I had forgotten. The color of our Carolina clay. I never remembered it was so red before. And the dogwood and the broom sage. I-I-I-I . . .' He walked up and down in front of the class, three strides and back, coursing his plentiful hair with hands that never seemed to be still. 'I was just telling Shorty here this morning how things have changed. Why, when we were here, all this part down below Old South was nothing but blackberry thicket. Why, God-a-mighty . . .' His voice was thick and Southern still. On he talked then, of the old days, of how good it was to be in one's home state again—sentimentalities full of wordless pleadings for forgiveness. And this pleading was in every gesture, every movement. Somehow he felt he had personally put a great curse upon this state he loved, and now he was humiliating himself, truly penitent. . . . He said he was going back to Asheville to offer up his humility as an appeasement for the blight he had put on that place. Then—for he knew he could never be accepted in Asheville again . . . —he planned to move with his mother out into the hills of Yancey and write of the homely wisdom he found there. Late into the lunch hour we stood around him with our questions, and it was obvious that he was just warming up. He rested his fat haunches on the desk, his feet still flat on the floor, and answered without hesitation. He was eager to be liked: there was no reserve or feeling of importance in his manner, no effort to inspire respect. . . . At thirty-six, he was our eager boy companion. Circled around him, we Wolverines found the man whose spirit had fed our lives no great Apollo but an image of ourselves—multiplied by two in size, by ten in appetites and passions and by a thousand in expressiveness. Yet he was ourselves."[4]

Wolfe finally decided against going to Asheville on this visit. Before leaving New York, he had written to his brother Fred: "I do not feel that I can endure to be pawed over, talked to nineteen hours a day, pulled and tugged and yanked until every separate nerve is screaming with exasperation, and otherwise maddened or exhausted by people who are . . . well-meaning, but whose total effort seems to be to try to kill you with . . . inconsiderate and thoughtless kindness. . . . If and when I do come back, I want to come back my own way, to be exhibited, shown about and exploited by no one." This had evidently caused a misunderstanding, for he wrote later to Fred: "When I called you up from Atlanta, there seemed to be some excitement and confusion about my coming, or whether I wanted to come or not, so I was too tired to argue the point and decided to pass my visit up until some other time." He accordingly came directly back to New York, but already he had begun planning to make a special trip to Asheville in the spring. "I can't tell you how good it was to be back in my own state again," he kept telling everybody, "and just to get my number thirteens down on North Carolina clay."

By the end of January, Wolfe was back in New York and deeply involved once more in his difficulties with Scribners. Upon receiving the long "personal letter" which Wolfe had mailed in New Orleans, Perkins had written him three answers. The first, dated January 13, said in part: "I just got your long letter and have only glanced through it, so that I can't yet properly answer it. . . . I am dashing this off now to make clear two things. My belief is that the one important, supreme object is to advance your work. . . . What impedes it especially is . . . the harassment . . . of outside worries. When you spoke

[4] From "Eugene Returns to Pulpit Hill," by George Stoney, in the October 1938 issue of the *Carolina Magazine*.

to me about the settlement, it was . . . very plain that this suit was such a worry that it was impeding you in your work. It was only because of that that I gave the advice I did. . . . As to my own self: I stand ready to help if I can, whenever you want. You asked my help on 'Time and the River.' . . . No understanding person could believe that it . . . was much more than mechanical help. . . . Apart from physical or legal limitations not within the possibility of change by us, we will publish anything as you write it."

The second letter was only a short note, dated January 14, saying: "I've read your letter carefully. I think it's a wonderful letter. I have no quarrel with any of it, except that you have greatly misunderstood some things I must explain. But what a task you've put me to, to search myself—in whom I'm not so very much interested any more— and give you an adequate answer. Your position is right. I understand and agree with it."

The third letter, written two days later, was Perkins' attempt to "search himself" and give Wolfe an adequate answer: "In the first place, I completely subscribe to what you say a writer should do . . . But there are limitations of time, of space, and of human laws which cannot be treated as if they did not exist. I think that a writer should, of course, be the one to make his book what he wants it to be, and that if . . . it must be cut, he should be the one to cut it . . . It would be better if you could fight it out alone—better for your work, in the end, certainly . . . I believe the writer, anyway, should always be the final judge, and I meant you to be so. . . .

"I certainly do not care—nor does this House—how revolutionary your books are. I did try to keep you from injecting . . . Marxian beliefs into 'Time and the River,' because they were . . . not those of Eugene in the time of the book. . . . It seems as if you must have forgotten how we worked and argued. You were never overruled. . . . I do not want the passage of time to make you cautious or conservative, but I do want it to give you a full control . . . over your great talent. . . .

"Tom, you ought not to say . . . that I find your sufferings amusing . . . I do try to turn your mind from them and to arouse your humor, because to spend dreadful hours brooding over them . . . seems . . . only to aggravate them. . . .

"Then comes the question of your writing about the people here. . . . I agree that you have the same right to make use of them as of anyone else . . . When I spoke of resigning after we published—and the moment I inadvertently said it I told Miss Nowell she must not

repeat it . . . —I did not mean I would be asked . . . to resign. . . .
But it's up to you to write as you think you should. . . .

"There remains the question of whether we are in fundamental agreement. . . . I have always . . . felt that it was so . . . But I believe in
democracy and not in dictators . . . and that violence breeds more
evils than it kills . . . I believe that change really comes from great
deep causes too complex for contemporary men . . . fully to understand, and that when even great men like Lenin try to make over a
whole society suddenly the end is almost sure to be bad, and that the
right end, the natural one, will come from the efforts of innumerable
people trying to do right, and to understand it, because they are a part
of the natural forces that are set at work by changed conditions. . . .
But this is getting to be too much of a philosophy of history or something, and I don't think it has anything to do with fundamental agreement. I had always felt it existed—and I don't feel, because you differ
with me . . . on such things . . . , that it does not . . .

"Anyway, I don't see why you should have hesitated to . . . send
the letter. . . . There were places in it that made me angry, but it
was . . . a fine writer's statement of his beliefs . . . and it gave me
great pleasure too—that which comes from hearing brave and sincere
beliefs uttered with sincerity and nobility."[5]

Wolfe had received these letters in Atlanta, where he had stopped off
to visit an old college friend, Garland Porter, on his way to Chapel
Hill. He could not help but be deeply touched by them, and he was
even more touched by the fact that when he reached New York, Perkins
came and called on him at his apartment to effect a reconciliation.
The interview was inconclusive and ended only with an agreement between the two men that even if Wolfe felt compelled to break away
from Scribners, their own personal friendship must remain unimpaired.
For the remainder of that spring an uneasy truce prevailed between
the two. Perkins simply could not believe that Wolfe would ever leave
Scribners, and he kept hoping against hope that he would "come
around." Wolfe, on the other hand, vacillated between moments of
indecision—when he wrote (but never sent) telegrams to Perkins saying: "Does Scribners want my next book? Please answer immediately"
—and fits of desperation—when he announced that he was no longer
connected in any way with Scribners and that he had a letter from
Charles Scribner III which confirmed that fact.

[5] For the complete text of these three letters see *Editor to Author: The
Letters of Maxwell E. Perkins*, pages 119–26.

This letter was written on February 17, at Wolfe's insistence, when he was infuriated by the attempts of Scribners and their attorney to persuade him to settle the Dorman libel suit. What it actually said was: "You can feel assured that we have no option or moral claim on any of your future books. We should like to continue as your publishers, as we have every faith in your work and feel that you are due to write even finer books than those which we have published. On the other hand, if you find that the connection with us is not to your liking, I certainly do not wish to press you to continue. Personally I am and always will be very fond of you and count you as a friend whether I act as your publisher or not. Whatever you decide, you will always have my best wishes." Wolfe usually described this letter as saying that he was "free to go anywhere I liked," but sometimes, when excited, he misinterpreted it to the point of saying that "Charles Scribner's Sons . . . have severed their relations with me and are no longer my publishers."[6]

Wolfe finally yielded to the persuasions of Charles Scribner and agreed to the settlement of the Dorman suit for $2850, of which he paid one half. In view of the fact that the Dormans had originally sued for $125,000, Scribners and their attorney considered this a victory. Wolfe, however, considered it an outrage, and the fact that his half of the legal fees and court expenses cost him an additional $1320.05 was to him the final straw. His hard-won earnings from *Of Time and the River* were wiped out completely, and his Scribner royalty account was left with a large deficit. In his rage and desperation, he composed a new and better version of his letter approaching "all publishers" other than Scribners, but, as usual, he failed to mail it.

Meanwhile, however, Wolfe was spending more time at the Perkinses' house than ever before. He was sitting for his portrait to Douglas Gorsline, who had married Perkins' next-to-oldest daughter, Elizabeth, and all the time he posed, he kept reciting his grievances against Scribners and against Perkins! He was so obsessed with his desire for freedom that he could talk of nothing else, till Perkins in exasperation once exclaimed, "All right then, if you *must* leave Scribners, go ahead and *leave*, but for heaven's sakes, *don't talk about it any more!*" Moreover, this resentment against Perkins was so deep that it colored everything he did or said, and on one occasion even brought the two men close to blows. This was one night in April 1937, when Jonathan Daniels, Wolfe's old schoolmate, who had given a dinner for him in

[6] As in his letter of November 15, 1937, to Cornelius Mitchell.

Raleigh when he had visited the University of North Carolina, arrived with Mrs. Daniels in New York. Wolfe wanted to entertain them in return, and he invited them, together with Daniels' sister and brother-in-law, the Nobel Cathcarts, and a woman friend of theirs, to the Perkinses' house for cocktails and then to Cherio's for dinner. Wolfe was always a touchingly eager host, and as Perkins said later, "Everything went well at first at Cherio's. . . . Tom was in good spirits until the woman who had come with the Cathcarts said suddenly: 'Oh, now I know who you are. I read an article about you in the *Saturday Review*. It was by Bernard De Voto!' She could have said nothing worse. . . . Tom sat silent and I could see him begin to brood. Then Daniels began to wonder why it was that *Scribner's* was the only magazine that published him. I cannot remember what he said, but then he turned on me and asked what was the matter with *Scribner's* anyway, meaning that he thought it should be a better magazine, I suppose. But to Tom, with his mistrust of his abilities, it seemed to mean that they showed bad judgment in publishing him. Within the next half hour or so, Tom had insulted everybody at the table, although they took it jokingly. His face had grown white, as it did when he drank a great deal, and you knew all of his doubts and his fears were seething up in his mind. He was in a murderous state. A man with a girl in the extreme opposite corner came over and shouted something at him in a friendly way, but I was afraid of a tragedy, and I went over and told the girl she had better keep him at his table. Everybody else got up by that time—I suppose they saw what a state he was in—and slipped out. Tom and I were left alone, and all Tom's emotion was now turned against me. Cherio was worried to death for what seemed to him to impend. I can't remember what Tom said, but the idea was that he was going to knock me down, and he stood there swinging his arm in preparation. I said, 'Tom, I know if that old sledge hammer landed it would do considerable damage, but it might not land.' But he kept looking at me with hate in his eyes, and a white face, so I saw there was no use joking, and I said, partly on Cherio's account: 'Well, if we must fight, let's do it in the fresh air.' Tom said, 'All right,' and walked out into the street, and as I was following, Harrison Smith came in and shook hands, and said, 'I see you are having author trouble.' I waited a moment to speak to him and that was lucky.[7] When I came out, Tom was standing in the street, off the sidewalk, waiting. I thought only a miracle could

[7] Harrison Smith says that when he walked into Cherio's he found Perkins and Wolfe actually fighting on the floor, with Wolfe on top of Perkins belaboring him and shouting, "Let me alone, you damned old woman!"

prevent something dreadful happening that everyone would regret. The miracle occurred: out of the next restaurant came a group of people, one, a very tall, black-haired, handsome girl, who ran straight at Tom as I approached him, and threw her arms around him and said, 'This is what I came to New York to see!' Within the next three or four minutes, this aristocrat was cursing him in the vilest language I ever heard from any woman. I don't know what exactly had happened, but it diverted Tom's attention entirely from me."[8]

It seems shocking and almost unbelievable that Wolfe could come to the point of actual blows with Perkins after literally idolizing him for so many years, but, to use one of his own phrases, "the cycle had gone full swing." Perkins was no longer "the heroic figure stronger and wiser" than himself: instead, he seemed to be an outgrown and repressive force which was "trying to alter the direction of his creative life" and which he therefore must "repulse as an enemy" lest it make "the final and unpardonable intrusion upon the one thing in an artist's life that must be held and kept inviolable."

[8] From Perkins' letter of November 13, 1945, to John S. Terry.

XXVI

IN MARCH 1937 Wolfe had a frightening intimation of the fatal illness which was to overtake him eighteen months later. "I have been down with a touch of the 'flu' for the last week," he wrote to his mother on March 15, "and although I now feel better, it seems to be a slow business getting over it. . . . I had dinner with the Perkinses Saturday night and told them I thought I was all right again, but Mrs. Perkins took my temperature and found I had two degrees of fever, so I probably had more than that a day or two before."[1] The fever persisted as it had often done with him before, and finally he went to a physician. Just who this doctor was, and what his diagnosis was, remains a mystery[2]—Wolfe was evidently so frightened by it that he seldom mentioned it and then only obliquely. Probably X rays were taken of his lungs and revealed the old tubercular scar on his right upper lobe. He blurted out to Miss Nowell that he had been to a doctor and that "there's something the matter with my lung," but then refused to discuss the matter. Instead, he paced in great agitation up and down the room, pursing his lips and shaking his head, so moved that it was impossible for him to talk. Soon after this he executed a new will, which named his mother as his chief beneficiary, and appointed Perkins and Nathan Mobley, a classmate of his at Chapel Hill, as executors. Then, characteristically, he tried to escape from any possibility of death or illness by dismissing the whole thing from his mind. However, the fear was always there. He loved to have his fortune told by Kathleen Hoagland's mother, but he would stand behind her while she was dealing out the cards and would wring his hands with nervousness: then he would start prowling up and down the room. "If you see death there, Mrs. Dooher," he would say. "If you see death there,

[1] In *Thomas Wolfe's Letters to His Mother* this letter is erroneously dated March 15, 1936 instead of 1937.

[2] Inquiries of the doctors whom Wolfe usually consulted and letters published in the *Journal of the American Medical Association* have failed to uncover this doctor's identity.

don't tell me!" Then he'd come back and look over at the cards. "Is death there?" She'd say "No." "Don't tell me if you see it," he again would say.[3] Finally, the following winter, when he again had a cold with persistent fever and a woman friend of his remarked that perhaps he might be tubercular, he exploded into a fit of violent anger which was really fear. A doctor had told him that, he said, the preceding spring, and his friend must *never, never* mention it to him again.

In spite of everything, Wolfe worked hard during the spring of 1937, both on his "Gulliver" book, as he now called *The Vision of Spangler's Paul*, and on a number of short stories[4] which he hoped to sell to magazines, now that his Scribner royalties had been wiped out by the expenses of the Dorman suit. By the middle of April he was again in need of a vacation, and he set out on his long-anticipated trip to Asheville. He now had an added reason for going home. The Wachovia Bank and Trust Company of Asheville had for many years given loans and mortgages to Mrs. Wolfe for her real-estate speculations and had also acted as her trustee in various investments. The bankruptcy of the entire town had put an end to all these speculations, and now the bank had instituted suit against Mrs. Wolfe and all her heirs, and

[3] From Kathleen Hoagland's narration in "Thomas Wolfe: Biography in Sound," first presented as an NBC radio broadcast and later reprinted in the Fall 1956 issue of the *Carolina Quarterly*.

[4] The stories which Wolfe wrote between January 1 and July 1, 1937, were: "Mr. Malone," which was published in the May 29, 1937, issue of the *New Yorker* and appears in *The Web and the Rock* on pages 525–36; " 'E,' " which was published in the July 17, 1937, issue of the *New Yorker* and appears in *You Can't Go Home Again* on pages 513–27; "April, Late April," which was published in the September 1937 issue of the *American Mercury* and appears with many changes and additions in *The Web and the Rock* on pages 441–52; "Katamoto," which was published in the October 1937 issue of *Harper's Bazaar* and appears with many cuts and changes in *You Can't Go Home Again* on pages 28–36; "The Child by Tiger," which was published in the September 11, 1937, issue of the *Saturday Evening Post* and appears in *The Web and the Rock* on pages 132–56; "The Lost Boy," which was published in the November 1937 issue of *Redbook* and appears in *The Hills Beyond*; and "Chickamauga," which was published in the Winter 1938 issue of the *Yale Review* and appears in *The Hills Beyond*. Also, another revision of "No More Rivers," which was never published in any magazine but portions of which are scattered through *The Web and the Rock* and *You Can't Go Home Again*; and a first rough draft of "The Party at Jack's," which finally was published in the May 1939 issue of *Scribner's Magazine* and appears with many changes and additions in *You Can't Go Home Again* on pages 196–322.

against themselves as her trustee, claiming that she owed them large sums of money as principal and interest on the loans which they had made her, and petitioning that her property be foreclosed and sold to settle this indebtedness to them.

Wolfe, who had always been bitterly opposed to his mother's real-estate speculations, now found himself named as party to the suit, and just at the crucial moment when his own legal difficulties had almost "got him down." He wrote his mother and asked her for an explanation of what the suit was all about, and he got back a reply which described at length and with great indignation how a bank had sold certain pieces of real estate for less than she believed them to be worth, but which failed to make clear that she was in arrears in payment of both the interest and principal which was due them. Wolfe finally excluded himself from this suit by signing a waiver to any claim he might have to Mrs. Wolfe's estate. However, he still was much concerned lest the old lady lose her beloved boardinghouse, the Old Kentucky Home, and the small amount of money left for her old age. For her sake as well as for his own, he wanted to find out about the case, and the only way to do it was by talking about it with her and the others face to face.

By the middle of April, Wolfe had left New York and was "loafing down the beautiful Shenandoah Valley." He stopped off first in Winchester, Virginia, where the Westalls had originally settled and where his great-great-grandfather Thomas Westall had been born. Then he went to Roanoke and Bristol, and finally to Burnsville, Yancey County, North Carolina, where his mother's family had lived for many years before moving into Asheville. A year before, he had got a letter from a cousin, William G. Westall, who had come from Burnsville and whose father, John Westall, a half brother of Wolfe's grandfather, still was living there at the age of ninety-five. Wolfe went to call on the old man and was richly rewarded by hearing from his lips the firsthand account of the battle of Chickamauga which he later wrote up in his story of that title.

Wolfe had always loved the mountains of western North Carolina and wanted to learn all he could about them and about the people living there, but he got almost more than he had bargained for when he witnessed a "shooting scrape" on the main street of Burnsville. According to the testimony which he gave later, he went into a Burnsville soda shop around ten-thirty on the night of May 8, 1937, and noticed two men standing out front. When he came back, after having had a soft drink, he saw that the two had got into an altercation with a third man, and he heard the third man say, "Now, Phil, you're going too far. Leave me alone!" Someone tried to separate the two; at this point Phil backed swiftly away with his hand in his pocket and then pulled it out with a pistol in it. The third man shouted, "Go ahead and shoot. I'm not afraid of you!" And at that point Wolfe and all the other witnesses dived for safety behind a car parked by the curb. Three or four shots rang out. There was the sound of air escaping from one of the auto tires which had been punctured by a bullet close by Wolfe. Then silence. The third man was slumped dead in the middle of the street. Phil and the other man were arrested for his murder, and when their case came up for trial in August, Wolfe was subpoenaed as a witness.

Wolfe arrived by bus in his native Asheville, totally unheralded and unknown, and took a taxi to the Old Kentucky Home. He had hardly ridden a few blocks, however, before the taxi driver turned around and asked, "Aren't you one of the Wolfe boys?" And when he said he was, the man went on: "I thought you talked like one of the Wolfe boys. What ever became of your brother who used to sell the *Saturday Evening Post?*" He was home again, in the old familiar pattern of his boyhood, and he had been met "neither by a lynching mob nor by a brass band," but had come as his "own man," his "own master," as he had wanted. By the next morning the news had got around that he was home: the phone was ringing constantly, his sister Mabel was pouring coffee by the gallon for the reporters and other people who had come to see him, and he was bubbling over with joy and relief, bear-hugging his old friends in smothering embraces. "They're not wanting to kill you now, Tom, because you put them in the book," one of his friends yelled out to him, "but there are a number of them who would, because you *didn't* put them in." As he wrote later, "The homecoming of the prodigal was a crashing success. Everything apparently, to my enormous relief, is forgiven. At any rate, they are glad to have me back again and I do not have to tell you how glad I was to be back. . . . I never really knew how homesick I had been until I got back again."[5]

Wolfe stayed in Asheville for about a week: he retraced his old paper route through Niggertown, gave a talk before the American Business Club,[6] had a reconciliation with Mr. and Mrs. Roberts, and ended up

[5] From Wolfe's letter of May 20, 1937, to Corydon P. Spruill.

[6] The author is indebted, for much of the material about Wolfe's return, to Mabel Wolfe Wheaton; also to an interview with him in the Asheville *Times*,

by writing a piece, "Return," for the Asheville *Citizen*, which was a sort of lyrical peace offering to the town: "I have been seven years from home, but now I have come back again. And what is there to say? Time passes and puts halters to debate. . . . For now I have come home again—and what is there to say? I think that there is nothing—save the knowledge of our glance. I think that there is nothing—save the silent and unspoken conscience in us now that needs no speech but silence, because we know what we know, we have what we have, we are what we are. So what is there to say?"[7]

Wolfe left Asheville for New York on May 15. However, he was so delighted with his home-coming that he planned to return to Asheville for the summer—perhaps even to live there permanently if things worked out all right. Before he left, he rented a cabin in Oteen, on the outskirts of Asheville, from Max Whitson, the cartoonist, and by the second week in July he had moved down there and was reveling in the new experience of "belonging to the landed gentry." "It is a cabin completely hidden from sight by tremendous trees," he wrote to Hamilton Basso. "It is really a good place and I hope to do a lot of work here. . . . About the only human sound I hear out here is the wail of the train whistle going by the foot of my hill in the azalea bottoms and occasionally very faint music from the Merry-Go-Around at the Recreation Park. Of course I love the trains and I don't mind the Park a bit. . . . Well, we shall see what we shall see; there are so many things to find out. I do not even know yet whether I can work here. It has been so long since I have really lived at home and almost all of my creative work has been done somewhere else—in New York, or in London, or in France. And already I have encountered certain learned local psychologists, who hint darkly that I will find it impossible to work here: one even said that I would find these surroundings 'allergic'—I believe that is one of the new words, isn't it? At any rate, the sum and substance of it is that a man like myself could write in a room in a city with a Hell of life and traffic roaring along beneath him, but that he could get no work done in the peace and quiet of the country and among people that he knows, and in the place where he was born. All of which I hold to be ridiculous: work, as you yourself know, is a desperate necessity; and if the need is desperate enough, nothing will stop us—not even our own lazy bones or natural indolence

and an article, "Asheville and Thomas Wolfe," by George McCoy, in the April 1953 issue of the *North Carolina Historical Review*.

[7] From "Return," in the May 16, 1937, Asheville *Citizen-Times*.

of which I have so much more than a fair share—not even, by God, allergic conditions. It is going to be an interesting experience. It is the first time in almost twenty years since I left college that I have come back home with the intention of actually staying a while; and I have come back here after so many years of strife and wandering, after so much turbulence and chaos, after so much work and hope and failure and success, after such a packed and crowded life in which I have always dreamed and hoped of achieving a state of serenity and repose without ever having found it.

"I have come back here as the result of a very powerful and deep-rooted instinct, which has grown slowly and steadily for years. No matter what happens or how this experience may turn out, I know the instinct was right. That is to say, this time it was inevitable; it had gathered for years and I was utterly convinced that it was right for me to come home again, to make the old connections and resume myself; and if I had done anything else at this time, this feeling in me was so strong and single I should never have been satisfied. Feeling so, of course, there was nothing else for me to do. I cannot fairly tell you that I am 'through' with New York; but I have realized in recent months that I am 'through' with it at this present period of my life. In other words, with the same powerful and inevitable instinct, I began to realize that I had taken all of it that I could possibly absorb at this period, and to stay there longer now would not only be foolish but barren. . . .

"So I have come back here to 'set a spell and think things over'; to rebuild here in my brain again these past fifteen years or more of youth, of conflict and of wandering. And from this substance, this accumulation of a life worn down—I pray, a little brighter, and freer, I hope, in some substantial measure, from the degrading egotisms all men know in youth—here to strike out, I hope to God, a living word: to do out of the substance of my one life, my single spirit, a better and a truer work than I have ever done."[8]

Alas, Wolfe was to discover all too soon that "a prophet may be without honor in his own country, but he is also without privacy." He hired a typist and set to work rewriting his long story, "The Party at Jack's," but people simply could not leave him alone, and he was constantly interrupted. There was a steak dinner given in his honor by some of his boyhood friends, a trip to visit his sister Effie and her family in Anderson, South Carolina, a trip to Burnsville to testify about the murder he had witnessed, a weekend spent with two young friends

[8] From Wolfe's letter of July 13, 1937, to Hamilton Basso.

of Mrs. Roberts who came all the way from Tennessee just to meet
their literary idol, and a steady stream of visitors who kept dropping in
unannounced. As Wolfe wrote sardonically to Basso, "Except for casual
intrusions—people driving up to demand if I've seen anything of a
stray cocker spaniel, gentlemen appearing through the woods with a
four-pound steak saying their name is McCracken and I met them on
the train four weeks ago and they always bring their own provisions
with them, and the local Police Court judge and the leading hot-dog
merchant, and friends of my shooting scrape in Yancey County with
bevies of wild females—all of which has and is continuing to happen—I
have practically no company at all out here."

There were also other difficulties. Wolfe's life had always been completely urban: he was not used to living in the country, and there
were many things about it which he did not know or could not do. He
knew virtually nothing about nature, and scarcely the names of the
commonest birds or trees or flowers. He could not drive a car and undoubtedly would have killed himself if he had tried. He could not even
build a good fire in a cookstove, or trim a kerosene lamp so that it
would give a good clear light.[9] He tried hiring a succession of colored
boys to cook and keep house for him, but none of them stayed for
more than a few days. As a result, he had to "poison himself with his
own cooking" or persuade some of his relatives or friends to drive him
into Asheville for a decent meal.

There, however, he encountered many of the old emotional conflicts
which sixteen years before had impelled him to leave home. Fred and
Mabel and Mrs. Wolfe were devoted to him, and he to them, but they
all were nervous, high-strung, garrulous, and involved in endless difficulties of their own, and they never failed to upset him and distract
him from his work. Moreover, Frank, his eldest brother, had come
home broken down in health, and he and Wolfe had never got along.
Wolfe accordingly spent more time at his sister Mabel's than he did
at the Old Kentucky Home, and that, in turn, offended Mrs. Wolfe
and stirred up the old jealousy between her and her daughter. In a
letter written to his brother Fred the following November, Wolfe
blurted out his bitterness and disappointment: "About the summer I
spent at home, my first return in seven years or more, the less said the

[9] The author is indebted for these details to Anne W. Armstrong's "As I
Saw Thomas Wolfe," in the Spring 1946 issue of the *Arizona Quarterly*.
"Which is goldenrod?" Wolfe asked her. "Tell me, please. I have never
known."

better. I'd like to forget about it if I could. . . . It's too bad things had to turn out the way they did this summer: I had hoped that things would have changed: I had been away so long that I thought maybe they would be different. But I found out that they were just the same, only worse: so I guess that's the end of me in Asheville. I'm sorry that you felt that I did not go around to the house enough this summer. I went all I could, but the situation there was such that I could not have gone more often than I did. I am sorry for afflicted and unfortunate people and I tried to do what I could to help: I was willing to go to the wall to use what money I have, or to borrow money to help when I was appealed to. But it all turned out as it always has. . . . I'm sorry to have to talk this way, but I have been driven to it. I've felt pretty sick and sore at heart when I left home, as it has all been so sad and so different from what I had hoped it would be. But I'm getting better now, and I know that it will all slip into its true proportion as time goes on. And of course, I have no ill feeling toward anyone. I've just found out a man must stand alone."

Wolfe had been in Oteen for about two weeks when he suddenly got a letter from Scott Fitzgerald. The previous autumn, Fitzgerald had had a nervous breakdown while staying at the Grove Park Inn in Asheville and had blurted out his troubles to a newspaper reporter, Michel Mok, who had promptly published the whole thing as an interview in the New York *Evening Post*. Wolfe had been filled with solicitude for Fitzgerald, and with rage against Mok and the *Post*. Probably Perkins had told Fitzgerald of Wolfe's indignation on his behalf and had also encouraged him to write to Wolfe. The letter Fitzgerald wrote said, in part:

Dear Tom: I think I could make out a good case for your necessity to cultivate an alter ego, a more conscious artist in you. Hasn't it occurred to you that such qualities as pleasantness or grief, exuberance or cynicism can become a plague in others? That often people who live at a high pitch often don't get their way emotionally at the important moment because it doesn't stand out in relief?

Now the more the stronger man's inner tendencies are defined, the more he can be sure they will show, the more necessity to rarefy them, to use them sparingly. The novel of selected incidents has this to be said that the great writer like Flaubert has consciously left out the stuff that Bill or Joe (in his case Zola) will come along and say presently. He will say only the things that he alone sees. So *Mme. Bovary* becomes eternal while Zola already rocks with age. . . .

That, in brief, is my case against you, if it can be called that when I admire you so much and think your talent is unmatchable in this or any other country.

Ever your Friend,
Scott Fitzgerald

All of these things, as Wolfe said, might be true, but "like the celebrated flowers that bloom in the spring, have nothing to do with the case." A few years earlier he would have been offended and upset, but he now could take it all with a sense of humor and even enjoy "a chance of ribbing Scott a little":

"Dear Scott: . . . The unexpected loquaciousness of your letter struck me all of a heap. I was surprised to hear from you but I don't know that I can truthfully say I was delighted. Your bouquet arrived smelling sweetly of roses but cunningly concealing several large-sized brickbats. Not that I resented them. My resenter got pretty tough years ago; like everybody else I have at times been accused of 'resenting criticism' and although I have never been one of those boys who break out in a hearty and delighted laugh when someone tells them everything they write is lousy and agree enthusiastically, I think I have taken as many plain and fancy varieties as any American citizen of my age now living. . . .

"So I'm not sore at you or sore about anything you said in your letter. And if there is any truth in what you say—any truth for me—you can depend upon it I shall probably get it out. It just seems to me that there is not much in what you say. You speak of your 'case' against me, and frankly I don't believe you have much case. You say you write these things because you admire me so much and because you think my talent is unmatchable in this or any other country and because you are ever my friend. Well, Scott, I should not only be proud and happy to think that all these things are true but my own respect and admiration for your own talent and intelligence are such that I should try earnestly to live up to them and to deserve them and to pay the most serious and respectful attention to anything you say about my work.

"I have tried to do so. I have read your letter several times and I've got to admit it doesn't seem to mean much. . . . I may be wrong but all I can get out of it is that you think I'd be a good writer if I were an altogether different writer from the writer that I am. This may be true but I don't see what I'm going to do about it, and I don't think you can show me. And I don't see what Flaubert and Zola have to do with it, or what I have to do with them. I wonder if you really think they have anything to do with it, or if it is just something you heard in college or read in a book somewhere. This either-or kind of criticism seems to me to be so meaningless. It looks so knowing and imposing but there is nothing in it. Why does it follow that if a man writes a book that is not like 'Madame Bovary' it is inevitably like Zola? I may be dumb but I can't see this. You say that 'Madame Bovary' becomes eternal while Zola already rocks with age. Well this may be true—but if it is true isn't it true because 'Madame Bovary' may be a great book and those that Zola wrote may not be great ones? Wouldn't it also be true to say that 'Don Quixote,' or 'Pickwick' or 'Tristram Shandy' 'becomes eternal' while already Mr. Galsworthy 'rocks with age'? I think it is true to say this and it doesn't leave much of your argument, does it? For your argument is based simply upon one *way*, upon one *method* instead of another. And have you ever noticed how often it turns out that what a man is really doing is simply rationalizing his own way of doing something, the way he has to do it, the way given him by his talent and his nature, into the only inevitable and right way of doing everything—a sort of classic and eternal art form handed down by Apollo from Olympus without which and beyond which there is nothing? Now you have your way of doing something and I have mine; there are a lot of ways, but you are honestly mistaken in thinking that there is a 'way.'

"I suppose I would agree with you in what you say about 'the novel of selected incidents' so far as it means anything. I say so far as it means anything because every novel, of course, is a novel of selected incidents. There are no novels of unselected incidents. You couldn't write about the inside of a telephone booth without selecting. You could fill a novel of a thousand pages with a description of a single room and yet your incidents would be selected. And I have mentioned 'Don Quixote' and 'Pickwick' and 'The Brothers Karamazov' and 'Tristram Shandy' to you in contrast to 'The Silver Spoon' or 'The White Monkey' as examples of books that have become 'immortal' and that *boil* and *pour*. Just remember that although 'Madame Bovary' in your opinion may be a great book, 'Tristram Shandy' *is* indubitably a great book, and that it is great for quite different reasons. It is great because it *boils* and *pours* —for the *unselected* quality of its selection. You say that the great writer like Flaubert has consciously left out the stuff that Bill or Joe will come along presently and put in. Well, don't forget, Scott, that a great writer is not only a leaver-outer but also a putter-inner, and that Shakespeare and Cervantes and Dostoievsky were great putter-inners

—greater putter-inners, in fact, than taker-outers—and will be remembered for what they put in—remembered, I venture to say, as long as Monsieur Flaubert will be remembered for what he left out.

"As to the rest of it in your letter about cultivating an alter ego, becoming a more conscious artist, by pleasantness or grief, exuberance or cynicism, and how nothing stands out in relief because everything is keyed at the same emotional pitch—this stuff is worthy of the great minds that review books nowadays—the Fadimans and De Votos—but not of you. For you are an artist and the artist has the only true critical intelligence. You have had to work and sweat blood yourself and you know what it is like to try to write a living word or create a living thing. So don't talk this foolish stuff to me about exuberance or being a conscious artist or not bringing things into emotional relief, or any of the rest of it. . . . You've got too much sense and you know too much. The little fellows who don't know may picture a man as a great 'exuberant' six-foot-six clod-hopper straight out of nature who bites off half a plug of apple tobacco, tilts the corn liquor jug and lets half of it gurgle down his throat, wipes off his mouth with the back of one hairy paw, jumps three feet in the air and clacks his heels together four times before he hits the floor again and yells out 'Whoopee, boys, I'm a rootin, tootin, shootin son of a gun from Buncombe County—out of my way now, here I come!'—and then wads up three hundred thousand words or so, hurls it at a blank page, puts covers on it and says 'Here's my book!'

"Now Scott, the boys who write book-reviews in New York may think it's done that way; but the man who wrote 'Tender Is the Night' knows better. You know you never did it that way, you know I never did, you know no one else who ever wrote a line worth reading ever did. So don't give me any of your guff, young fellow. And don't think I'm sore. But I get tired of guff—I'll take it from a fool or from a book reviewer but I won't take it from a friend who knows a lot better. I want to be a better artist. I want to be a more selective artist. I want to be a more restrained artist. I want to use such talent as I have, control such forces as I may own, direct such energy as I may use more cleanly, more surely and to a better purpose. But Flaubert me no Flauberts, Bovary me no Bovarys, Zola me no Zolas, and exuberance me no exuberances. Leave this stuff for those who huckster in it and give me, I pray you, the benefits of your fine intelligence and your high creative faculties, all of which I so genuinely and profoundly admire. . . .

"I'm down here for the summer living in a cabin in the country and I am enjoying it. Also I'm working. I don't know how long you are going to be in Hollywood or whether you have a job out there but I hope I shall see you before long and that all is going well with you. I still think as I always thought that 'Tender Is the Night' had in it the best work you have ever done. And I believe you will surpass it in the future. Anyway, I send you my best wishes as always for health and work and success. . . . And now this is all for the present—unselective, you see, as usual. Good bye, Scott, and good luck,

Ever yours."

By the end of August, Wolfe was completely disillusioned with both Asheville and Oteen as places where he could live and work. For two weeks he was lost in one of his periods of brooding and indecision. It was not simply the question of where he should live that was bothering him, but his old compulsion to leave Scribners, which now, at last, was coming to a head. During the entire summer he had not written them at all, and he had received from them only two short communications, which he described ironically to Basso: "I got a letter from Max praising a piece I have just written for the *New Yorker*—also a notice from the publishers to the effect that all of my remaining royalties have been wiped out in the settlement of a suit which . . . never should have been settled . . . At any rate, my profits on the books are not only all wiped out but I am also heavily in the red with Scribners." This deficit was actually not too great—it amounted to $1225.40 and was paid off by royalties on Wolfe's books in two years' time[10]—but to him it seemed both enormous and unjust. After the great success of *Of Time and the River*, here he was, two years later, in debt to his publishers and with no income except what he had earned by selling stories to magazines. He totally forgot that his expenses in the Dorman suit would have been twice as large if Scribners had not voluntarily paid one half of them. He only felt that he was the victim of a great injustice, and he laid the blame on Scribners instead of on himself. "As to friendship in the modern business world," he had written to Basso, "well, it exists: they will bleed and die for you in conversation, but they will not lose money. In fact the principle of modern business friendship seems to be not to let the right hand know what the left hand is doing—one hand is warm and open and extended in the clasp of love, but the other is clenched grimly around a handful of accursed papers. This is the way things are, and I suppose we are fools to think it could be different.

[10] As of February 1, 1939, Wolfe's royalty account at Scribners showed a balance in his favor, for the first time since August 1937, of $170.71.

. . . I'm really not bitter about it. I simply know more about it than
I knew or suspected two years ago."

Now he was at the end of his summer's work and felt the need of a
publisher to read what he had written. In spite of all his difficulties and
distractions, he had finished rewriting "The Party at Jack's" at the
cabin in Oteen and had sent a copy of it to Basso, asking him to read
it and then forward it to Miss Nowell in New York. Judging from what
he wrote to her, he was tempted to send a longer version of it to Perkins,
but he never actually did so. "As to the final disposition of it, I do not
know," he wrote Miss Nowell on August 22. "Someone[11] has told me
that the thing is a unit in itself and could be . . . published as a unit
without further addition. I have not made up my mind about this yet.
The whole thing belongs, as you know, to the entire manuscript of
'The October Fair,' of which sections and fragments have been published for years . . . I, therefore, . . . put it all together with some
tentative idea in my mind of making a complete book of all of it—a
book which would occur within the limits of a single twenty-four hours,
beginning with midnight of one day and ending with the midnight of
the next, and bearing probably the title 'The October Fair.' I have not
made my mind up definitely about this yet, but I am sending the manuscript to a friend in New York to get his opinion.

"As you know, the whole thing has been a very vexed and perturbed
part of my writing experience and it has cost me the utmost worry and
difficulty because it seemed to me that so much labor, so much effort,
and so much that I really think is valuable and good and needs to be
saved was in danger of dying the death, of being in so many various
and complicated ways—all of which apparently sprang out of a friend's
desire to help and perhaps some instinctive timidity and caution—suppressed and killed. I cannot say definitely as to all this, but I do know
that a man must not be thwarted in the process of his creation, and I
feel very strongly that this has happened to me with this piece of work."

It was at this crucial moment, when Wolfe was trying to steel himself for a last-ditch submission of the *October Fair* material to Perkins,
that Bernard De Voto chose to take another crack at him in the
Saturday Review. This was in a piece called "English '37: The Novelist
and the Reader," which stated De Voto's strong conviction that
"fiction is fiction and poetry is poetry, and that when the methods of
the two are blended you get something different from both and much
less important than either. Both call on the same psychic resources,

[11] Basso.

the same emotional vitality, but fiction must . . . shape it to its own purposes, or run into disaster. Emotion in the raw can be an attribute only of the characters whose lives are engaged with one another. When it is left undisturbed as an attribute of the author it has not yet become fiction."

The two most flagrant examples of "emotion in the raw" held up for ridicule by De Voto were Sherwood Anderson and Wolfe: "When Thomas Wolfe's *Of Time and the River* appeared, it was sometimes compared to *Moby Dick*. A more exact comparison would have mentioned Melville's *Pierre*, which is also sown with long passages of unshaped emotion. At that period Melville frequently could not complete the process of creative transformation and was content to substitute rhetoric for fiction, which is what Mr. Wolfe does at his worst. Give him a chance at a railroad train roaring through the beautiful dark, the womb of time, the myriad-voiced America, or man's inhumanity to man, and the affairs of the Gant family will go by the board while Mr. Wolfe, in his own person, pulsates with a superhuman ecstasy or pain. What is wrong with such passages is not their intensity . . . but precisely that they are in Mr. Wolfe's own person. That his novel deals with the imaginary Gant family may be something of a legal fiction, but the reader requires that pretense to be maintained. Once he takes up the novel he is concerned exclusively with the Gant family: he is not indifferent but actively hostile to Mr. Wolfe's feelings, however magnificent they might be in a non-fiction context. . . . The reader who is bored by Mr. Anderson's soul or Mr. Wolfe's agony is bored because the projection has not been complete."

In comparison with De Voto's earlier attacks on Wolfe, this was very mild indeed. Moreover, it made no further reference to Wolfe's dependence on "Mr. Perkins and the assembly-line at Scribners." But to Wolfe, in whom the earlier accusations still rankled bitterly, it must have been like pouring salt into the old, deep wounds. It was published in the *Saturday Review* on August 21, the day before Wolfe had written to Miss Nowell of his intention of showing the *October Fair* material to Perkins. There is no record of just when and how he heard that De Voto had again attacked him, but, as he himself ironically said, "some kind friend" could always be depended on to tell him. In all probability he heard of it almost as soon as it was published, and he was influenced by it in his decision not to send the *October Fair* material to Perkins after all, but to make the final break with Scribners then and there before he went back to New York, and to get it over with.

At any rate, one morning late in August 1937 his sixteen months of brooding and indecision suddenly exploded into action. He sat down in his hotel room, took a drink or two to give himself false courage, and began putting in long-distance calls to the various publishers whom he had long considered as possible successors to Scribners. He called Harcourt, Brace; Knopf; Harpers; W. W. Norton—probably others in New York—and Little, Brown in Boston. However, almost every conversation came to nought, because no one could believe that a major writer like Thomas Wolfe would simply telephone and offer them his work point-blank. He did not even make it clear that he *was* Thomas Wolfe, but simply blurted out: "My name is Wolfe. Would you like to publish me?" Some of the publishers were so bewildered that they gave him noncommittal answers: some were sure that the call came from a crackpot, a drunk, or a practical joker and dismissed it altogether.

At Harpers, Wolfe was by mistake connected with Lee Hartman, the editor of *Harper's Magazine,* instead of with Edward Aswell, the junior editor in the book department, whom he later said that he had asked for. Hartman, like the other editors whom Wolfe phoned, doubted that this deep-voiced, seemingly half-intoxicated man on the long-distance phone was actually Thomas Wolfe. In any case, he thought that what he was asking him to publish was short stories for *Harper's Magazine,* so he got out of his embarrassing predicament by saying, "Send me something. I'll be glad to look it over." Wolfe, of course, thought that this was being said about his book, and that it meant that, although Harpers would give his manuscript a reading, they were not very eager to obtain it. Later, when Miss Nowell begged him to let her tell Aswell that he was without a publisher, he refused, saying that he had approached Harpers and found they were not interested in him.

At Knopf he fared a little better. Mrs. Knopf had been extremely cordial to him after the appearance of *Look Homeward, Angel,* but she was now abroad. However, Bernard Smith, the Knopf editor, told him both on the phone and in a letter that they were "tremendously interested" in his work and would be "delighted to talk about" his "future publishing plans." Later, when Mrs. Knopf got back from Europe, she phoned Miss Nowell and left a message for Wolfe to "march right over with his manuscript" to her. By that time, however, he had decided that he did not want to get involved with them, chiefly because they were Mrs. Bernstein's publishers and friends, and he did not get in touch with Mrs. Knopf at all, in spite of her cordial calls. Perhaps this was just as well, since Alfred Knopf was seemingly in ignorance of, or disagreement with, his associates' enthusiasm.

It was Wolfe's call to Harcourt, Brace, however, which really let the cat out of the bag. Harcourt and Scribners had always made a point of the closeness and friendliness of their relationship. Harcourt, Brace was now extremely anxious not to do anything which could be construed as taking Wolfe away from Scribners. Moreover, they knew more fully than some of the other publishers what a responsibility Wolfe had been to Perkins, and they were somewhat reluctant to take on the burden of editing his books on top of all their regular work. They accordingly gave him a noncommittal answer on the phone. Then Alfred Harcourt went immediately to Charlie Scribner and told him of Wolfe's long-distance call.

It is true that everyone at Scribners had known for months that Wolfe had virtually left them, but they had thought that his letters of severance were only temperamental outbursts and that he would surely "come around in time." The truth was that they felt so secure in the conviction of their own benevolence, and in the knowledge of Wolfe's debt to Perkins, that the idea of his leaving them was utterly unthinkable. But now, all of a sudden, they were told—and by a rival publisher! —that he not only was going to leave them but that he had already left! They were thrown into a state of rage and shock. Even the compassionate, self-abnegating Perkins came close to losing his superhuman self-control. Wolfe had been "the foremost interest of his life," his friend, his alter ego, and his son, for eight long years, and now he suddenly had turned against him, and against the house of Scribners, to which he, Perkins, was so utterly devoted. Even though he understood the reasons why Wolfe had been impelled to make the break, Perkins was only human, after all, and could not entirely suppress his grief and outraged indignation. Moreover, Perkins' associates and friends loudly condemned Wolfe for his ingratitude, without stopping to think that his very debt to Perkins might be threatening to suffocate his talent.

By afternoon the news had spread like wildfire through the New York literary world. Wolfe had "gone and done it now," at last, and the break from Scribners was irrevocably made.

XXVII

W<small>OLFE'S</small> break with Scribners caused an incredible amount of bitter feeling. Other writers had left their publishers, and publishers who had done a good deal for them, too, but such changes had always been taken as matters of course. However, Wolfe has been accused of "betraying" Perkins, and even of having broken his heart and caused his death (which actually did not occur till ten years later). The chief reason for all this censure was the widespread legend of the editorial help which he had got from Perkins—the legend which Wolfe himself had created in *The Story of a Novel* and the dedication of *Of Time and the River*. "I don't want any acknowledgment for seeing and understanding that you were a great editor, even when I first met you," he later wrote to Perkins, "but I did see and understand it, and . . . I acknowledged it in words which have been printed by your own house, and of which now there is a public record. The world would have found out anyway that you were a great editor, but now, when people solemnly remind me that you are, with an air of patiently enlightening me on a matter about which I have hitherto been unaware, I find it ironically amusing to reflect that I myself was the first one publicly to point out the fact in such a way that it could not be forgotten—that I, as much as any man alive, was responsible for pulling the light out from underneath the bushel basket, and that it is now a part of my privilege to hear myself quoted on every hand, as who should say to me: 'Have you read Wolfe?'" Thus the legend which Wolfe had created, which had been exaggerated by his enemies, and which had impelled him to leave Scribners, now rose up again to confront him as the chief reason why he should *not* leave them, but should remain forever bound to them in gratitude.

Wolfe left Asheville on September 5, with the disheartening conviction that "you can't go home again." One of the last things he did was to go to the office of a friend high up in the town's modern skyscraper, the Jackson Building, built on the site of Mr. Wolfe's own tombstone shop, and to stride from window to window, gazing at the mountains that encircle Asheville as though he might never set eyes on them again. He still had dreams of finding some place in the South where he could live and work, and he went first to Bristol, Tennessee, where the writer Anne W. Armstrong had offered to rent him a cabin overlooking the Holston River. However, he stayed there only a few days before he was off again, to spend two days with Sherwood Anderson in Trout Dale, Virginia. Mrs. Armstrong drove him over: autumn and harvest time had come and, as always, he went into an ecstasy about America. "Corn," he exclaimed several times in a low voice, looking at the fields of it, which were now in shock. "Corn, the most American thing in America."[1]

Everywhere he went he talked compulsively and endlessly about his grievances against Scribners, but without mentioning the fact that he had telephoned other publishers. "Tom Wolfe took command in the evening with the tail [sic] of his troubles," Anderson wrote in his diary for September 8. And for September 9: "I laid off and gave the day to Tom Wolfe. He is six feet six inches and gigantic in every way. He is like his writing. . . . He is generous and big, in every way, but a good deal the great child."

Finally, after brief stopovers in Roanoke and Baltimore, Wolfe arrived back where he had started from, New York. Then, almost immediately, he was off again, to Boston and Gloucester. He was quite secretive about this trip, but before going on it, he asked Miss Nowell several times what she thought of Little, Brown. He probably had phoned them from Asheville and went to confer about the possibility of their publishing him, but if he did, negotiations struck a snag. He returned almost immediately to New York, and the current rumor that he was about to sign with them evaporated into nothing.

Meanwhile he had given up his First Avenue apartment and was living in various hotels, keeping his whereabouts a secret and merely telling people that they could communicate with him through his agent, Miss Nowell. As he wrote to Perkins later, "I came up here in September and for two full months I saw no one and communicated with no one except Miss Nowell. During all this time, I stayed alone and tried to think this whole thing out. And . . . one reason I now resent these trivialities and this gossip is that this may be a matter which is only important enough to some people to be productive of false and empty rumor of nonsensical statements, but to me it has been a matter of life and death." Gradually, as the weeks dragged by with no offer from any publisher, he became convinced that no one wanted him. He refused to approach any other publishers or to let Miss Nowell do it for

[1] From Anne W. Armstrong's "As I Saw Thomas Wolfe," in the Spring 1946 issue of the *Arizona Quarterly*.

him, and he withdrew into himself with tragic dignity. Moreover, he no longer recited his grievances against Scribners, but now, when he probably should have done so in self-defense, he maintained silence in the face of all the gossip and accusation against him.

Finally, in the middle of October, he got a letter from Robert Linscott of Houghton Mifflin asking if there was any truth in the persistent rumor that he was considering changing publishers and if he would like to discuss the matter with him. Wolfe was immediately filled with hope. "To my great and deep regret, my former publishers and I have separated," he wrote to Linscott. " . . . I want you to know that this severance is not the result of a temperamental explosion on the part of an author who is now trying to make terms with someone else, and get the best terms that he can; but that it is, for me, at any rate, one of the most grievous and sorrowful experiences of my whole life; it involves deep and complicated differences which touch . . . my whole life and work—differences that are by no means recent, but that began two and a half years ago. I know there are people at my former publishers who could tell you that this is true—chiefly, the man who has stood closest to me for eight years now and who knows more about my life and the problem of my work than anyone else, Maxwell Perkins.

"I am telling you all this to let you know that I can honorably talk about these things to other people now, and other people can talk to me about these things. And honestly, Mr. Linscott, what I need most of all right now is someone I can talk to—someone who understands the problems of publishing and of a writer's work. . . . It will take a long talk, a lot of talk, maybe a whole series of talks, but that is what is needed first. And I know I can make the whole thing clear: I am completely certain of my purpose. . . . I don't know if you would care to assume a publishing responsibility of this nature after I have explained it to you, or whether your house is the best one for a problem of this sort. But I do think that it would help a lot if we could talk about it, and if I could say my piece to you."

After calling on Perkins for confirmation of what Wolfe said, Linscott took Wolfe out to dinner and listened to him sympathetically for hours while he "said his piece." Finally, when he could get a word in, he asked Wolfe which of his various books was nearest to completion, and Wolfe answered *The October Fair*.[2] Linscott accordingly suggested that he show that manuscript to Houghton Mifflin, and if they

[2] Linscott says that Wolfe also talked eloquently about a book he'd like to write someday concerning the adventures of a journeyman filling-station attendant wandering from job to job all over America.

liked it, that he go ahead and finish it for them. This was a mistake: Wolfe had always felt that *The October Fair* should have been published and got out of his system, and his work that summer on "The Party at Jack's" had revived and strengthened this conviction. But he had actually lost his first enthusiasm for *The October Fair* when he had stopped work on it in 1934, and the fact that he had yielded to Perkins' anxiety to shelve it and had launched upon a new and different book, *The Vision of Spangler's Paul*, or "Doaks book," as he now called it, had made him very stale on it indeed.

However, he concurred with Linscott's feeling that *The October Fair* was what he should do first, and he agreed to show the manuscript to him. The only trouble, he said, was that he was living in a tiny room in the Prince George Hotel and had his manuscript in various places: some was with him, some was stored in a Brooklyn warehouse, and some was still at Scribners, where he had left it in the spring of 1935. If he got it all out and put it in his hotel room, he would hardly be able to get inside himself, let alone unpack the crates and packages of manuscript and sort it and arrange it. Linscott immediately suggested that he bring all his manuscript to Houghton Mifflin's New York office, where there would be plenty of room for him to work. This seemed a fine idea to Wolfe, and a few days later, in an atmosphere of jubilation, he and one of Linscott's young associates arrived at Houghton Mifflin's office on Fourth Avenue with one tremendous packing case and nine smaller boxes, bales, and suitcases of manuscripts.

However, some of Houghton Mifflin's New York staff objected to the arrival of this huge and indiscriminate collection, pointing out that they had no safe large enough in which to store it and that Wolfe might hold them responsible for it in case of loss or fire. Accordingly, just as Linscott was leaving to catch the train for Boston, he handed Wolfe an envelope which, he said, contained just a routine acknowledgment of having received the manuscript. Wolfe thought nothing of it and went happily back to unpacking manuscript and arranging it in little piles all over Houghton Mifflin's office, but that night, when he was going to bed, he found the letter in his pocket, opened it, and read it. It was, as Linscott had said, a routine little note, acknowledging receipt of "one packing case and nine packages of manuscripts,"[3] but it went on to say: "I am a little worried by the fact that we have no

---

[3] The legend is that Wolfe delivered eleven cases, ten of which contained manuscript and one nothing but toilet paper. When asked about the latter case, he said he had no idea where it had come from.

fireproof safe in which to store material of this value, and I hope you realize that, under the circumstances, it will have to be held entirely at your risk. Let me take this opportunity to tell you how much I enjoyed our evening together, and how greatly I appreciate the chance to read this manuscript."

In all fairness to Houghton Mifflin, it should be pointed out that the general policy of publishers is to disclaim responsibility for all and any manuscripts submitted to them. Linscott, on the insistence of some of his New York associates, was merely being overconscientious in making this clear to Wolfe, but it was regrettable that he was obliged to do so: Wolfe was supersensitive in general, and suspicious of all publishers in particular. Moreover, he had stored his manuscripts for years at Scribners without anyone's ever bothering to mention that the responsibility for them in case of loss or fire was his own. But what upset him most was not the fact that Linscott disclaimed responsibility, but that the letter addressed him as "Dear Wolfe" although Linscott had asked permission to call him Tom and had done so with great warmth and cordiality. As Wolfe said later, in a fictional account of this experience, which described it as having happened to a writer named Jim Smith: ". . . The author cannot help remembering that the publisher asked if he could call him Jim when they were having drinks together over the dinner table, but calls him Smith when he writes a business letter. . . . The publisher did not tell him that it was going to be Jim in friendship and in editing, but Smith in business. He led the author to believe, with his talk of faith and belief and support and the privilege and the honor of publishing the author, that it was going to be Jim all the time. Now . . . I think that much of the misunderstanding between publishers and authors comes from just this fact. I think the trouble comes when one side is playing with one set of chips, and the other side with two. . . . I am not accusing the side that plays with two of dishonesty or of unscrupulous practices. But . . . when Jim finds out that it is always Smith when a question of business advantage, of profit or loss, is concerned . . . —then there is likely to be trouble."

Immediately upon reading Linscott's letter, Wolfe sat down and wrote him an angry answer: "In view of your letter, . . . I am removing the manuscript from your office and shall try to put it in a place where no risk is involved. . . . If you are willing . . . to assume no risk, our agreement concerning this manuscript is ended. . . . If you do not feel you have a responsibility, then I request that you write me to that effect immediately so that I can make further efforts to find people who will assume that responsibility, and will offer me a chance of obtaining the two things I . . . need now more than anything in the world—a good publisher and a decent living." Characteristically, he never mailed this letter but, after a few days, walked into Houghton Mifflin's New York office and took all his manuscripts away. By that time he had his emotions so well under control that the people there thought he was only sardonically amused by Linscott's disclaimer of responsibility. However, the first seed of discord between himself and Houghton Mifflin had been sown, and when he finally decided to sign with Harpers, he showed them his unmailed letter to Linscott as a partial explanation of the difficulties he had had with Houghton Mifflin.

Having taken his manuscript away with him, Wolfe began rewriting it, and he became increasingly reluctant to let Linscott read it in its four-year-old first draft. Linscott, on the other hand, was unable to make any offer for it unless he could actually read it and find it suitable for publication by Houghton Mifflin. This was the general policy of his house, which was not a one-man or one-family firm like Scribners, but was headed by a board of trustees to whom the editors were accountable. Moreover, this policy was made imperative in regard to *The October Fair* by a letter written to Houghton Mifflin by Mrs. Bernstein in which she repeated her old threat to sue for libel if the book depicted her in any way. If Linscott could have come back to New York almost immediately and have had another good long talk with Wolfe, these difficulties would undoubtedly have all been ironed out. Unfortunately, an abscessed tooth made him postpone his visit, and Wolfe became mistrustful. "Goddammit," he kept saying, pacing up and down the suite of rooms which he had taken at the Hotel Chelsea. "Do you think he *really* has an abscessed tooth, or are they giving me the runaround? They say it's years since they 'moved toward a publishing alliance' with greater anticipation: they say I carry on the tradition of indigenous American literature, like Thoreau, but dammit all, they don't 'move toward any publishing alliance' that I can see! I can't see that we're moving toward anything at all!"

It was at this point that Harpers suddenly made Wolfe a very generous offer, for any book he might want them to publish, sight unseen. This was later described by Edward Aswell, who was then the junior editor in Harpers' book department and who made Wolfe the proposal and finally became his editor: "In November of 1937, Bernard De Voto came down to New York from Cambridge and dropped in to see me. He asked whether I had heard the news that Thomas Wolfe had left Scribners. I said that I had not heard it, and furthermore I did not believe it. He insisted that he had it on good authority, so I decided to check up by telephoning Miss Nowell.

"Miss Nowell was an old friend of my wife and myself, and it so happened that she had been a guest at our house only a short time before: she had said nothing about Wolfe, and I couldn't believe that if any such extraordinary event had occurred she wouldn't have mentioned it. When I got her on the phone and reported my news she exclaimed: 'Thank God it's out and I didn't tell you!' I asked her what she meant. She said that Tom had known she was to spend that evening at my house and had asked her not to say anything to me about his publishing problem because of what had happened when he phoned to Harpers from Asheville: he would not truckle to anyone, and he did not want to be put in the position of seeming to repeat his overture. I was completely mystified by this and told Miss Nowell I knew nothing about a call from Asheville. 'Oh yes,' she said, 'he phoned you, and you weren't interested.' I told her there was something wrong, and I didn't know what it was, and I would like to investigate and phone her back. After making inquiries around the Harper office, I then learned for the first time of the call Lee Hartman had taken, and realized that there had been a misunderstanding at both ends. I gave this information to Miss Nowell and asked her to tell Tom, and to say to him that if he were free and looking for a publisher, I should like to talk to him. This she did, and she arranged a meeting.

"I shall never forget my first visit to Tom at the Chelsea. He had a three-room suite, which sounds more magnificent than it was, for the rooms were dark and dingy, but they had the advantage of ceilings high enough so that he ran no risk of bumping his head. The most impressive feature of the suite was the bathroom, which was quite large, with a toilet set on a raised platform: Tom called it 'The Throne Room.' I took him out to dinner and he talked a steady streak. When we returned to the Chelsea, he started pacing the floor. He peeled off his coat, then his tie, unbuttoned his collar, rolled up his sleeves, and went on pacing back and forth for hours while he talked and talked. That night he told me the whole story of his relations with Max Perkins. In everything he said, and in the way he put it, there was devotion, genuine and unmistakable, for Max. And just as he repeated himself in his writing, so he did, too, in his speaking. Over and over that night, recurring like a refrain in everything he said, was the reiteration: 'No matter what happens, I will always be Max's friend, and I know he will always be mine.' He told me of the reasons why he felt he had to leave

Scribners. . . . But coupled with Tom's explanation of all this, and his obvious grief that it had to be, there was also a certain core of resolution in him that night. It had to be, and he would see it through somehow.

"Then he told me of the telephone calls he had made from Asheville that summer to several publishers, and of how they had come to nothing. He told me of the negotiations with Publisher X and the dead-end they had reached. He told me of his plans for future books, and of the reams of manuscript already written. There it all was in several big packing cases, which stood in the middle of the living-room floor so that Tom had to circle them as he paced. This saga of grief, resolution, desperation, and hope went on till five in the morning.

"As I listened to it, the picture came clear. Here was a man of undoubted genius who for reasons of his own had to make a fresh start. Not knowing what I found out later . . . about the fruitless telephone calls to publishers, he had come to the desperate conclusion that nobody wanted him. He felt that he was back where he had been at the beginning, before he had written a living line; and what Max called 'his tremendous faith in his genius as an obligation put upon him to fulfill' was ebbing fast that night. I think I have never been so profoundly moved as I was by this spectacle of a great man momentarily as alone and frightened as a lost child. He said he was running out of money, and felt he was also out of friends to whom he could turn. There was always Max, of course, but Tom couldn't go back. 'You can't go home again' was one of the lessons he had learned from life. That night he needed desperately some immediate and tangible evidence that someone else believed in him, too. Sensing all this, I did something I had no right to do. I was then a junior editor at Harpers, not authorized to make commitments on my own. Throwing caution to the winds, I told Tom how I felt about *Look Homeward, Angel* and *Of Time and the River*; and, to put real meaning in my words, I added that Harpers would pay him $10,000 advance on his next book, sight unseen, if he wanted it.

"Looking back on it, I am still rather amazed that I had the courage to do it, for I am ordinarily a cautious sort of chap, not given to leaping at things. Happily for me, it turned out well. The next day, when, sleepless, I reported to my superiors what had happened the night before, and with no little uneasiness told them of the pledge I had made in Harpers' name, they backed me without hesitation. For this, all praise to two good publishers and great gentlemen, Cass Canfield and the late Eugene F. Saxton. Tom Wolfe never knew I had risked my job for him, but he was never in any doubt that the house of Harper stood behind him."[4]

Obviously the thing for Wolfe to do was to accept the Harper offer. However, he went into one of his spells of indecision, which lasted for five weeks. The trouble was that, although Houghton Mifflin still had not made him any offer, he could not forget the warmth and friendliness of his first talks with Linscott. To add to the confusion, James Poling, who was at that time the managing editor at Doubleday, also began coming to call on Wolfe, and he told him that Doubleday would equal any offer made by any publisher whatsoever. However, Wolfe was so deeply involved in trying to choose between Harpers and Houghton Mifflin that he did not enter into definite negotiations with Doubleday at all.

Meanwhile, one of Linscott's associates, perhaps unknown to him, approached Miss Nowell with a suggestion which came close to ruining Houghton Mifflin's whole relationship with Wolfe. They all wanted very much to have Wolfe on their list, this Houghton Mifflin editor explained, but they were worried about the responsibility of editing Wolfe's books and managing his affairs. They therefore wondered if they couldn't retain Miss Nowell to act as a sort of editorial consultant in charge of Thomas Wolfe. This she immediately declined to do, explaining that she could not serve two masters and that if Wolfe had wanted her to undertake the grave responsibility of editing his books, he would have asked her to, himself. This put the responsibility back on Houghton Mifflin, where it belonged. However, as Wolfe's agent and his chief adviser at this time, Miss Nowell was duty-bound to tell him of her conversation with the Houghton Mifflin editor. Needless to say, he was quite disturbed: as he said later on to Aswell: "Here I had been dealing with them for weeks, only to discover that they were scared of me. I knew then that I was in the wrong church and the wrong pew."[5]

Finally, the first week in December, Linscott was able to come to New York and make Wolfe an offer. The advance of $10,000 against a royalty of 15 per cent which he proposed was the same as that which had been offered by Harpers, although Linscott suggested that it be paid in monthly installments of $500 for twenty months, instead of

---

[4] From "Thomas Wolfe Did Not Kill Maxwell Perkins," by Edward C. Aswell, in the October 6, 1951, issue of the *Saturday Review of Literature*.
[5] Ibid.

outright in one sum. However, Houghton Mifflin's offer was conditional upon their reading and acceptance of *The October Fair*, whereas Harpers stood ready to sign with Wolfe at any time, on pure faith in his genius, without reading a single page of manuscript. By now, Wolfe had come to the inescapable conclusion that the Harper offer was the one he should accept, but he couldn't bring himself to break the news to Linscott. "But dammit all, I *like* Bob Linscott!" he kept exclaiming. "There's something about him—he looks like the young Abe Lincoln: he's a *fine* man and I think he really is my friend. And his wife just died, and I hate to spoil his Christmas." Then he would shake his head, and go to sit morosely in the Chelsea bar and drink and brood, for hours at a time, without ever seeming to come closer to making up his mind.

Finally, on Saturday, December 18, he arrived at a decision. He called up Aswell at his home in Chappaqua, New York, to tell him that he had made up his mind to sign with Harpers. Aswell was not there, but Wolfe told his wife, Mary Louise, of his decision. He hung up biting his lip and shaking his head, as he did when deeply moved. "She was so excited: she began to cry!" he said, and started pacing back and forth, in a transport of happiness and emotion. "I believe somehow it is going to be one of the most fortunate and happy experiences of my life," he wrote to Anne W. Armstrong about his decision to go with Aswell and Harpers. "They are giving me a great advance, if I want it. But really I was playing a personal hunch. They want me so much, they believe in me so utterly, and there is no doubt they meant everything they said. Moreover I will be associated with a young man just exactly my own age, who is second in command. I am playing this hunch, too: I think it is going to turn out to be a wonderful experience—I feel that the man is quiet, but very deep and true: and he thinks that I am the best writer there is. I know he is wrong about this, but if anyone feels that way, you are going to do your utmost to try to live up to it, aren't you?"

Wolfe broke the news to Linscott the next day, and instead of spending Christmas with him in Boston, as he had originally planned, he spent it in Chappaqua with the Aswells. "We had made plans to meet in the early afternoon of Christmas Eve, in the lower level of Grand Central Station," Aswell wrote afterward, "and knowing how Tom felt about trains, . . . I also knew he couldn't catch them. So it was arranged that if by chance he should not be there, I would take the train and then he would be on the next one, which I would meet in Chappaqua. Well, I arrived ahead of time . . . and Grand Central Station was what it's always like on Christmas Eve—just a milling mass of humanity. But I had no trouble at all discovering that Thomas Wolfe was not there, because he stood head and shoulders above anybody else in the crowd. . . . So I took the train and went home, without Tom. . . . I then motored to the station to meet the next train about one hour later. The train came in, I waited for the people to get off, and they got off in droves, but there was no Thomas Wolfe."[6]

Meanwhile Wolfe had started out to do his Christmas shopping and to celebrate by stopping in at various midtown bars. About five o'clock he suddenly appeared at Miss Nowell's office, loaded down with presents and full of holiday cheer that was about 40 per cent alcohol and 60 per cent boyish sentiment for Christmas. At any rate, in reply to any suggestions that he really ought to catch a train for Chappaqua, he answered pleadingly, "I know, I know, but—look—it's *Christmas Eve!* Let's all go out and have a drink." It was not until almost midnight that, singing Christmas carols entirely off key, he let himself be driven in a taxi to Grand Central Station and poured on the last train.

"About one o'clock of a very clear frosty night, Christmas morning, I met the train," Aswell takes up the story. "There weren't many people, it was almost ready to pull out, when Tom finally came down the steps. . . . In one hand he carried an overnight bag, in the other hand he carried what looked like a dead animal, and he was holding it by the tail. . . . He was sort of sheepfaced and he said, 'Sorry to be late, Ed. I hadn't meant to do this, but,' he said, 'I got something here for your boy for Christmas.' And he held out the dead animal. It was the largest and ugliest stuffed dog anybody had ever seen. It had been gift-wrapped when he bought it, but he had used it to wipe up the bars with, the wrappings had come off, the box had disintegrated, the tail of the dog was almost off—it was hanging by a few threads—and it was very much the worse for wear. Nevertheless, the dog went under the tree that night, and the boy got it for Christmas."[7]

After that somewhat inauspicious beginning, Wolfe proceeded to charm completely the houseful of friends who were celebrating Christmas at the Aswells'. The climax of the weekend came the next day at Christmas dinner, when it was announced that he had chosen Aswell to be his editor. "We really did have a swell Christmas . . . ," he wrote a few days later to Miss Nowell. "I think it was the best one I have

[6] From Aswell's narration in "Thomas Wolfe: Biography in Sound," first produced as an NBC radio broadcast and reprinted in the Fall 1956 issue of the *Carolina Quarterly*.

[7] Ibid.

had since I was a kid. There were a lot of nice people and everyone was really very happy and very moved, and as we finished dinner Mary Lou whispered to me and asked me if it was 'all right to tell them' and I said 'yes' so we got out your bottle of champagne and Mary Lou told them, and I tried to say something and Ed tried to say something, and neither could very well, and everyone had tears in their eyes, and I think they meant it, too."

Wolfe had won the battle to break away from Scribners, and now that his compulsion to be free was satisfied, he was overcome with affection for them and with regret. Perhaps the exchange of letters which he had had with Perkins in November had been partially responsible for this. After leaving Asheville in September, he had kept himself incommunicado from his family as well as from everyone else, until both his mother and his brother Fred, not knowing anything about his severance from Scribners, had written to Perkins to ask if he was all right. Perkins had answered that Tom was quite all right but added: "He has . . . turned his back on me, and Scribners, so I have not seen him at all, though I would very much like to." When Wolfe had heard of this, he had begun an angry letter to Perkins, taking him to task for this and other aggrieved things which he had said, rehearsing once more the reasons for the break with Scribners, then digressing into a long "hypothetical" account of his experience with Houghton Mifflin, and finally ending up by saying: "I am your friend, Max, and that is why I wrote this letter—to tell you so. If I wrote so much else here that the main thing was obscured—the only damn one that matters—that I am your friend and want you to be mine—please take this last line as being what I wanted to say the whole way through."

Perkins, in turn, had written Wolfe to reaffirm his friendship, and there the matter had rested. However, the exchange of letters had cleared the air and opened the way for a reconciliation. It would have been unthinkable for Wolfe to go back to having Scribners as his publishers, but now that he was free of them, had had the last word and made his peace with them, his old compulsive bitterness had magically disappeared, leaving him free to feel the nostalgic love for his old friends which had always been there deep down underneath. "I wish I could tell you I felt happy but I don't," he wrote to his brother Fred. "I am worn out, having been torn up about this thing coming to a point for over two months now, and of course there were two or three people interested in me, and all of them I liked. I had to make up my mind between them. If you've ever had to do this, you'll know how hard it is, and I'm still mourning for the dead. I mean for the people that I knew, with whom I worked for so many years. I will see them again some day, but it is a pretty sad business just now."

Partly because of this regret and partly because of his chronic dread of making irrevocable decisions, he postponed signing the Harper contract until December 31, the last possible day for signing it if he wanted to receive part of his advance in the year 1937 and thus divide the income tax on it between two years. On that day, Aswell took the contract, together with a check for $2500, or one quarter of the advance, down to him at the Hotel Chelsea. He wrote his sprawling signature on the bottom of the contract, but as he did so, he quoted his old favorite words from Martin Luther: "*Ich kann nicht anders.* I can't do otherwise: I have no other choice." "Now I am committed utterly, in every way," he wrote that day to Mary Louise Aswell. "It gives me a strangely empty and hollow feeling, and I know the importance of the moment, and feel more than ever the responsibility of the obligation I have assumed. But I guess it is good for a man to get that hollow empty feeling, the sense of absolute loneliness and new beginning at different times throughout his life. It's not the hollowness of death, but a living kind of hollowness: a new world is before me now."

XXVIII

THE spring of 1938 was one of the happiest and most productive periods of Wolfe's entire life. In the course of his talks with Aswell he had come to the realization that the book he wanted to write was not *The October Fair*, but *The Vision of Spangler's Paul*, or, as he now called it, *The Ordeal of the Bondsman Doaks*. Then he had evolved a way to rewrite *The October Fair* and include it in the Doaks book. "As you will remember, when I first met you and we talked together about what I had to do," he wrote to Aswell, "I spoke to you of the book which I had called 'The October Fair,' and told you something of the conflict in my mind between this book and the other book which I have been describing here. I told you, for example, of the time several years ago when all my heart and life and energy were absorbed by 'The October Fair' and how, at that time, I thought this was the book I had to do and framed it in a sequence to follow 'Look Homeward, Angel' and 'Of Time and the River.' I told you how I had written and striven on this book for two or three years, how 'Of Time and the River' finally grew out of it and preceded it, and of how finally I had gone cold on 'The October Fair': that is, it was no longer the burning, all-absorbing thing I had to do.

"But I described the feeling of incompletion and discontent in my mind because of this book which had been projected and never published—the feeling that it had in it some of the best and truest work I had ever done, and the feeling that this work ought to receive the consummation and release of print. I still feel that way except—and that is what I am trying to explain about my whole position here as concerns my book—my position has changed: I no longer wish to write a whole book about a woman and a man in love, and about youth and the city, because it now seems to me that these things, while important, are subordinate to the whole plan of the book I have in mind. In other words, being young and in love and in the city now seem to me to be only a part of the whole experience of apprenticeship and discovery of which I am talking. They are also a part of the knowledge that you can't go home again.

"That plan, as I now see it in my mind, . . . is as follows: . . . The central character . . . is important now because . . . he will be or illustrate, in his own experience, every one of us—not merely the sensitive young fellow in conflict with his town, his family, the little world around him—not merely the sensitive young fellow in love, and so concerned with his little universe of love that he thinks it is the whole universe—but all of these things and much more, insofar as they illustrate . . . any man's progress and discovery of life, and as they illustrate the world itself, not in terms of personal and self-centered conflict with the world, but in terms of ever-increasing discovery of life and the world, with a consequent diminution of the more personal and self-centered vision of the world which a young man has."

In other words, Wolfe had finally emerged with a new, maturer point of view. As Harry Emerson Fosdick said: "The great day comes when a man begins to get himself off his hands. He has lived in a mind like a room surrounded by mirrors. Every way he turned he saw himself. Now, however, some of the mirrors changed to windows."[1] Or, as Wolfe himself described it: "I began to write with an intense and passionate concern with the designs and purposes of my own youth; and, like many other men, that preoccupation has now changed to an intense and passionate concern with the designs and purposes of life." Or, more simply: "I think my interests have turned more and more from the person who is writing the book to the book the person is writing."

Wolfe's new viewpoint was one of broad humanitarianism which could not be labeled as belonging to any of the political and economic categories of that time: "I had derived . . . a new sense of life, a newer and, it seemed to me, a better hope," he wrote in the speech he delivered at Purdue in 1938. "For . . . I had begun to see and understand and feel the common heart of man, and finally, I had come to see that this, no matter how much it gets corrupted, is the thing that finally can never be corrupted; no matter how much it gets defeated, is the thing that can never be defeated—the thing that is rock bottom at the end. . . ."

Part of Wolfe's new viewpoint was his realization that "you can't go home again." He had been groping toward this ever since his trip to Asheville the previous summer, but it was Ella Winter, Lincoln Steffens' widow, who actually put it into words for him, after a wildly disputatious party at the Sherwood Andersons'. The Andersons had come up

---

[1] The author is indebted to Anne W. Armstrong for this quotation as applied to Wolfe's new point of view.

to New York to visit Mrs. Mary Emmett and had invited Wolfe to
dinner at her apartment with Miss Winter, Max Eastman, and some
other people. He, however, still had his old phobia of literary parties,
and he arrived at the dinner very late, with a chip of suspicion on his
shoulder and a large amount of alcohol beneath his belt. The conversation was of the liberal kind so popular in literary circles of that time:
everyone was talking about the South, and someone finally had remarked that if one was a liberal, southern people never attacked him
for his liberalism, but on entirely different and often spurious grounds.
As an example of this, Mrs. Anderson said to Wolfe that she had been
in North Carolina the week before and had heard it said that he was
Jewish.

To Wolfe, this was the sort of "venomous attack" which he had
come to expect at literary parties, and on a very sore point, too. For
some time, the rumor that his father's family was partly Jewish had
been circulated, probably as an attempt to get even with him by people
who considered that his books were anti-Semitic. There seems to be
no reason to believe that the Wolf family was anything other than good
old "Pennsylvania Dutch," or German, as was true of his paternal grandmother and the other members of the family, whose genealogy has
now been traced back to the eighteenth century. However, Wolfe could
not assert this unequivocally because he never had been able to trace
the genealogy of his grandfather Jacob Wolf. His sporadic attempts to
find these missing ancestors were partly due to filial sentiment and
partly to angry desperation in the face of the rumor that he was Jewish.

Hardly was the word "Jewish" out of Mrs. Anderson's mouth when
he leaped to his feet, beside himself with rage. He was going to catch
the first train back to North Carolina, he shouted, to consult his mother.
The whole thing was an outrage—how dared Mrs. Anderson make such
an accusation against his family! His family name was just as good as
hers (which was also Pennsylvania Dutch), and nobody was going to
cast mud on it and get away with it! His outburst was so violent that
everybody stopped and listened to him, openmouthed. Then Sherwood
Anderson and the other men sprang to Mrs. Anderson's defense. Wolfe
had no business speaking to her that way, they shouted back at him.
Furthermore, he was revealing a dangerous anti-Semitism by taking
such offense at the suggestion that he might be partly Jewish. If *they*
were Jewish, they righteously insisted, they'd be proud of it and would
proclaim it to the world. Undoubtedly their fervor came from the realization that Ella Winter was of Jewish blood and that she might be

offended by Wolfe's outburst. Actually, she was astonished at the accusatory virulence of the men's attack on Wolfe and was more sympathetic to him than anybody else there.

When finally the party ended, Wolfe took her home, walking all the way from the Andersons' in Washington Mews to her hotel in the East Forties, and pouring out a compulsive flood of confidences all the way: about his trip to Germany and publication of "I Have a Thing to Tell You"; about his severance from Perkins and his "grieving for the dead." As she said later, "He was changing much of his outlook: he was very troubled and kind of lost . . . He wanted someone to listen to him and since I was very unhappy myself and alone in New York [Steffens had died only a short time before] we used to have dinner and he would talk. . . . He started telling me about his horror at going back to his home and what he found there, and I just said, 'But don't you know you can't go home again?' He stopped dead and then said: 'Can I have that? I mean for a title? I'm writing a piece . . . and I'd like to call it that. It says exactly what I mean. Would you mind if I used it?' I laughed and told him that I didn't 'own' it any more than I'd own any other thought. . . . But he was violently excited. Later he . . . asked if I'd have any objection, any objection whatever, if he used it for the title of a book."[2]

From that time on Wolfe was so delighted with the phrase "you can't go home again" that he seemed almost obsessed by it. He chanted it over and over to himself, and proclaimed it to his friends as a new, all-revolutionizing discovery which applied to almost every aspect of his life and work, and soon began to consider it as a title for his book. "The whole book might almost be called 'You Can't Go Home Again,'" he wrote to Aswell in a long letter which he never mailed, "which means back home to one's family, back home to one's childhood, back home to the father one has lost, back home to romantic love, to a young man's dreams of glory and of fame, back home to exile, to escape to 'Europe' and some foreign land, back home to lyricism, singing just for singing's sake, back home to aestheticism, to one's youthful ideas of the 'artist,' and the all-sufficiency of 'art and beauty and love,' back home to the ivory tower, back home to places in the country, the cottage in Bermuda away from all the strife and conflict of the world, back home to the father one is looking for—to someone who can help one, save one, ease the burden for one—back home to the old forms and systems of things that once seemed everlasting, but that are changing all the time—back

[2] From a letter from Ella Winter to Elizabeth Nowell.

home to the escapes of Time and Memory. Each of these discoveries, sad and hard as they are to make and accept, are described in the book almost in the order in which they are named here. But the conclusion is not sad: this is a hopeful book—the conclusion is that although you can't go home again, the home of every one of us is in the future: there is no other way." Wolfe did not actually call his book *You Can't Go Home Again*, but chose the title *The Web and the Rock* as being more poetic and more characteristic of himself. However, when Aswell found that it was so long that it must be published as two books instead of one, the obvious title for the second was *You Can't Go Home Again*.

When Wolfe left the Andersons' at the conclusion of their party, he had given Mrs. Anderson one of his bear hugs and had assured her that her unfortunate remark had been forgiven. However, the memory of it and of the violent argument which followed it still rankled in his mind until he happened to run into Anderson at the Brevoort two and a half weeks later. Anderson himself had evidently been worried lest Wolfe had had injured feelings and had written to him on that very morning, saying: "I do hope you didn't take seriously the queer row we seemed to have gotten into that night at Mary's house," and asking him to come to a cocktail party for the benefit of the Spanish Loyalists and to have dinner with him afterward. However, Wolfe had not received this letter when he went into the Brevoort for lunch and found Anderson there, being interviewed by a French newspaperwoman.

This was on December 17, when Wolfe was at the climax of his struggle to choose between Harpers and Houghton Mifflin, and of his grief at the necessity of this final and irrevocable step to break away from Scribners. For at least a week he had done nothing but drink and brood and pace the streets, and, as he later wrote to Anderson, "a good deal of what happened and what was said was just accidental. I wasn't thinking about it or you so much when it happened as about something else—a matter to the conclusion of which I have been working slowly for the past two years, and which involved one of the most grievous and painful decisions of my life. . . . Anyway, . . . the immediate thing that happened—the flare-up, the explosion, or whatever it was— was really not about you at all, but about something else. You just happened to be present when it happened."

This undoubtedly was true, and Wolfe was undoubtedly half drunk, or the "explosion" would never have occurred. However, he was also motivated by that strange moral compunction which, again and again throughout his life, made him explain to people whom he had admired the causes of his disillusionment with them. At any rate, he called

Anderson out into the Brevoort lobby and "told him off," saying that
Winesburg, Ohio had meant something very important to him and his
entire generation of writers, but that Anderson had "failed them" in his
later work[3]—that "this business of sitting around and talking, naked, on
parlor sofas" was "no good," that he was "ruined by the female company
he kept," by parties and all that sort of thing, and that he was now
"washed up." Having got this off his chest, he wrung Anderson's hand
in his great paw, told him that he had done the best writing that had
been done in America in the twentieth century, and assured him with
great emotional sincerity that he was his friend and that they must
"stick together" and never let anything come between them. Then he
went rolling out of the Brevoort and up Fifth Avenue.

Now it was Anderson's turn to have hurt feelings rankling within
him. He went back to the dining room and finished his luncheon interview with the French newspaperwoman, but the next day he wrote
Wolfe an angry note:

Dear Tom: When I wrote you yesterday, suggesting that you have
dinner with me Tuesday evening, I had no notion how you felt. As you
have expressed such a hearty desire to chuck our acquaintance—why not.

Upon receiving this, Wolfe wrote Anderson a letter of apology, in
various drafts; then said to hell with it and never mailed it. For a while
he was quite conscience-stricken at having "told old Sherwood off" in
such thoroughly outspoken style, but he had told what seemed to him
to be the truth, and his final judgment of Anderson, written a few
months later to Hamilton Basso, was almost the same: "The Squire of
Marion is, beneath his guise of ambling folksiness, an embittered and
defeated man."

By the first of February 1936 Wolfe had launched into intensive
work on his book. His cratefuls of manuscripts were all unpacked and
scattered around his three big high-ceilinged rooms at the old Chelsea;
he hired a typist, Gwen Jassinoff, one of the best he'd ever had; and
day after day, page after page, the book took form. "It is an immense
undertaking that I have embarked on," he wrote to Mrs. Roberts.
". . . I have about reached the conclusion that when a man gives himself completely to a tremendous piece of work, there is just no such
thing as rest, and he had better reconcile himself to it. . . . It is

---

[3] As in *Many Marriages* and Anderson's other later work under the influence
of D. H. Lawrence.

curious how many hard and thorny things we find out about life, and how strangely palatable they become to us. It is all so different from what we imagined it was going to be when we were children, and curiously in so many ways it is so much better. I suppose, like so many other boys, I pictured a future life of brilliant works crowned by success and fame and ease, and surcease from labor; but it does not work out that way at all. Work gets harder all the time because as one digs deeper one goes into the rock. And there is no rest—those periods of delightful relaxation as a kind of reward for work accomplished that I used to look forward to with such eagerness simply do not exist. . . .

"It sounds pretty grim, but like so many other grim discoveries, it is not so grim once you recognize it, accept it, and make up your mind on it. In fact, when I think of all the dreams I had as a boy—my idea of 'happiness,' 'fame,' and so on—I do not know that I would have them back again, even if I could recapture them; and as for this thing I used to call happiness, I am not so sure but that it, too, is a very hard and thorny thing, and not the smooth and palatable thing I thought it was. And I am perfectly sure that whatever it is, if it exists at all, it cannot exist without work—which would have been a strange doctrine indeed when I was twelve years old. As far as I am concerned, there is no life without work—at least, looking back over my own, everything I can remember of any value is somehow tied up with work."

The only serious distraction which bothered Wolfe that winter was the case which he had instituted against the young man who had acted as his manuscript agent, and which now, finally, was coming up in court. After being so upset about the conduct of his case in January 1937, when he was in New Orleans, Wolfe had dismissed the New Jersey lawyer who had been handling it for him and had got another, who proved to be a lucky choice. As Wolfe wrote to Perkins, "I am glad to say that it looks at last as if something is going to get done, and that I have a man on the job who knows how to do it." The new lawyer had paid no attention to the young agent's threats, but had resolutely pushed Wolfe's case until it now was scheduled for a hearing on February 8 before Vice-Chancellor Kays in Jersey City.

The most important witness for Wolfe's case was Mr. Perkins, who had acted as adviser in almost all his dealings with the manuscript agent. Accordingly, Wolfe wrote and asked him if he would testify, saying: "I am just as sorry as I can be to have to trouble you again about this thing, or about anything else. But I do believe we are beginnng to see the light at last, and I know you have always wanted me to get this thing settled and thought I ought to see it through. . . . And honestly, Max, I hate like hell to bother you, but I do think this is one of those cases where people ought to stand together if they can, not only for personal or friendly reasons, but just because it's taking a stand in favor of the human race. But anyway, I am your friend, and I know that whatever you do will be all right."

Perkins immediately answered that he would be glad to testify and suggested that Wolfe meet him on the afternoon of February 1, so that they could discuss the case together. This was the first time the two had met face to face since Wolfe's break with Scribners, and he went to it in a highly emotional state of mind: "I have . . . found out that although you can't go home again, there are certain things you do not lose, but that grow and flourish as the years go on, and one of them is the love and belief of a friend," he wrote that day to Mrs. Jelliffe. "And that is why it means so much more to me than I can ever utter here to know that in another hour I shall meet again and hear the voice again of the wonderful and noble man who has been, I think, the greatest, best, and most devoted friend that I have ever had; of whose friendship and belief I hope I may be forever worthy. Great bridges may be burned, and there is a path which we can never take, a road down which we never shall go back again; but there is also a fire that once lighted will always burn, and that never while life lasts can be put out." Thus it was that the lawsuit which had had so much to do with Wolfe's disillusionment with Perkins was, finally, the cause of their being reconciled again.

The case was heard on February 8, and was won hands down by Wolfe.

Wolfe took the stand and, as Perkins noted with surprise, "conducted himself admirably all through the trial" and "gave an overwhelming impression of sincerity and dignity."[4] Mrs. Jelliffe also testified, and the rare-book dealer who had purchased Wolfe's manuscripts from the young agent appeared in readiness to testify, although he was not called. But the high point of the trial, and the thing which moved Wolfe almost to tears, was Perkins' appearance on the stand with a hearing aid in his deaf ear for the first time, and the last, that he ever wore it. He had been embarrassed about his ears ever since being teased about them as a boy, and he had steadfastly refused to admit that he was deaf, but he felt it was his duty to Wolfe to wear the hearing aid lest he might fail to understand the lawyers' questions.

Thus it was that Wolfe emerged from the series of lawsuits in which

[4] From Perkins' letter of January 3, 1946, to John S. Terry.

he'd been enmeshed for three entire years—and emerged with a victory which bore out his contention that the only way to deal with such suits was to fight them. He, Perkins, Mrs. Jelliffe, and the rare-book dealer took the ferry and rode in triumph back from Jersey City, with Wolfe standing tall and hatless in the bow, against the skyline of New York. He was flushed with victory and talking a blue streak, pouring out the fruits of his three years' experience with lawyers and insisting that "Dickens only scratched the surface" when it came to writing of the law. Suddenly he stopped and blurted out, amazed, "What do you suppose was on those pages that my erstwhile agent said he burned because of 'their filthy and obscene character'?" His sardonic grin began to spread across his face. "I must have used some absolutely new word! How I wish I could see them now: I fear I'll never sink low enough to achieve such heights of obscenity again! What a loss to the field of belles lettres!"[5]

They went to Cherio's for lunch; then Wolfe, Perkins, and Mrs. Jelliffe embarked on one of those celebrative rounds that he so loved, ending up that night at Lüchow's for dinner. All the time Wolfe talked endlessly and brilliantly, pouring out to Perkins the history of his every act and thought since their estrangement. Perkins had heard and loved this flood of talk for nine entire years, and tragically missed it when Wolfe had left him. Now Wolfe was pouring it all out to him again, but with the greater philosophical detachment and pervasive sense of humor which had come to him with his new, less egotistic attitude toward life and his conviction that "you can't go home again." Both Perkins and Mrs. Jelliffe sat spellbound, listening to him, and both noted that they had never heard him talk so brilliantly or with such humor. They could not know that this was the last time they would ever see and hear him.

Except for this brief interruption, Wolfe kept right on working steadily on his book. "I work every day from about ten in the morning until about six at night," he wrote in March to Mrs. Roberts, "but after that I can't stop thinking about it: it goes rumbling and roaring around in my head, or what serves me for a head. The result is there is usually no sleep until long after midnight. I don't know what to do about all this, it has always been the same—at least every time I start to work. The only satisfaction I get from it is the rather gloomy one that I must be really at work again." As always, this terrible insomnia began to undermine his health. No matter where he went or how much

[5] The author is indebted to Belinda Jelliffe for this information.

he drank, or how many endless miles he tramped the city's streets, he could not sleep till dawn. Then he would fall into a troubled sleep from which he would drag himself, half drugged with exhaustion, the next morning, when his secretary came to work; then he would drink black coffee by the gallon till he finally "got going" again upon the book, and so would add the tension of that day's work upon the insomnia of the night before. By May he was on the verge of complete exhaustion, and when he was invited to speak at a literary banquet at Purdue University, for a fee of $300, he seized upon the chance for a vacation with all expenses paid. "But, Tom, you're not a public speaker!" one of his friends exclaimed. "No," he answered happily, "but I can d-d-do a hell of a lot of stammering for th-th-three hundred dollars."

He left New York on May 17 a tired but happy man. "I have not felt such hope and confidence in many years," he wrote to Miss Nowell a few days before. "It may be that I have come through a kind of transition period in my life—I believe this is the truth—and have now, after a lot of blood-sweat and anguish, found a kind of belief and hope and faith I have never had before. . . . This is packing-up day—I approach with considerable fear and trembling the job of assembling a good part of the manuscript I have done for the last three or four years. . . . Aswell is going to keep it for me until I get back, but I don't know whether it would be a good idea to let him read it now or not. I know where I stand, but it is like presenting someone with the bones of some great prehistoric animal he has never seen before—he might be bewildered. . . . I have an idea I've got something roughly similar—so far as state of completion is concerned—to the first rough draft of 'Of Time and the River' which Perkins saw at the end of December, 1933. . . . But I have a very strong hunch that I know where I am going a lot more clearly than I ever did before."

It was only four hours before Wolfe left for Purdue that Aswell arrived at the Chelsea to get the manuscript. "The day was May 17, 1938," he wrote later. "Tom had been spending his last days in New York packing his voluminous papers and notebooks and checking over the new manuscripts to see that it was all in order. He phoned that morning to say he was catching a train for Indiana at 9 o'clock that night and he asked if I could come down to his room at 5 in the afternoon to talk over several points about the novel and take delivery of the manuscript. I arrived on the hour, to find Tom still busy checking through the pages of the manuscript. He had two or three days' growth of beard, his hair was wildly dishevelled, he was in his shirt sleeves with the sleeves rolled up, no collar, and the neck band open, seated at a table in the middle of his big room. Before him was a pile of manuscript which he was running through rapidly to see that all the pages were in order and that nothing had been omitted. Now and then he would come on some page or an entire chapter which he decided didn't belong in the book, and he would yank it out and throw it on the floor. All around him the floor was littered ankle deep with these discards. His secretary bustled about, gathering up the pages and putting them in neat stacks after Tom had swept through them chapter by chapter like a tornado.

"One of the bartenders of the Chelsea bar was also on hand, but not in official capacity. Tom had brought him upstairs and had entrusted to him the job of packing his clothes for the trip, but all of his suits had been sent to the tailor for pressing and had not come back, so there was nothing for the bartender to do but sit around and wait. About 7 o'clock the tailor arrived with the suits, and the bartender began packing them, using his own judgment about what shirts, ties, and socks to put in and what to leave behind. Tom didn't care what he wore and couldn't be bothered. The pile of manuscript on the table was rapidly diminishing under Tom's swift scrutiny, but it was not until 8:30, half an hour before train time, that the last page was turned and the job done.

"While I busied myself wrapping up the manuscript in two enormous bundles and tying it so it could be carried, Tom at last began to face the problem of getting ready to catch his train. He had not yet dressed for the trip, had not yet checked out of the hotel, and had made no arrangements about the storage of his books and other personal effects which he was not going to take with him. These last, in characteristic fashion, he entrusted to the bartender to take care of until he returned, and at 20 minutes to nine, I said goodbye and left him, limping under the weight of the manuscript which ran to more than 4000 typewritten pages and to well over 1,200,000 words in length. I fully expected to have a call from Tom the next morning saying that he had missed his train, for though he loved trains like a small boy, he was almost never able to catch them. But in some miraculous last burst of speed, he did catch that one."[6]

How Wolfe ever caught that train, God only knows, but catch it he did, in typical last-second style. Thus it was that he left New York for what he intended to be a brief "two or three weeks' vacation" exploring his beloved America and riding on a streamlined train.

[6] From a publicity release written for Harpers by Edward C. Aswell at the time of the publication of *The Web and the Rock*.

"Did I sleep last night?" he wrote the following day to Arthur Mann. "Say—I haven't missed a house, a barn, a horse, a cow, or a plowed field since we left Buffalo. I'm dog tired but I feel swell. I put through a big job and completed it—and feel completed. I'm going a few thousand miles further and raise hell. Whee!"

He could not foretell the disastrous ending of this journey; nor his death in Baltimore only four months later.

XXIX

Wolfe's Purdue speech was a great success. After saying that it was "perhaps a little premature to start summing up one's life at the age of thirty-seven," he proceeded to do exactly that, tracing the various stages of his development with insight, frankness, and disarming humor. He stayed at Lafayette for two days and then insisted that his hosts, the Herbert Mullers, together with the rest of the Purdue English Department, come with him to Chicago and let him give them "a big party." "I've just made th-three hundred dollars," he kept exclaiming, "and you've g-g-got to help me spend it!" Finally, on Friday night, a group of them piled into one car and drove him the hundred and twenty-five miles to Chicago. All the way he was in a state of boyish anticipation, and when the others sang to pass the time away, he joined in with great gusto, even when he knew neither words nor tune. The songs he knew and loved most were the old ones that Mabel had sung and played on the old upright back at Woodfin Street, and soon he insisted on rendering a solo of "one of Poppa's favorites," "I Wonder Who's Kissing Her Now." However, the song that he sang all weekend was the "Heigh-ho" song from Walt Disney's *Snow White and the Seven Dwarfs*. He sang it constantly, on the streets of Chicago, at his hotel, and everywhere he went, till his companions could quite cheerfully have gagged him had he not been so blissfully unaware that he was off key.

He insisted on staying at the Auditorium Hotel because, as he wrote Miss Nowell, "we had a book when I was a child called 'Wonders of Science' or 'The Marvels of the Modern Age' with a picture of the hotel," and here, on Saturday, he began his party by serving drinks to his companions from Purdue and some friends of theirs from the University of Chicago. Wolfe always was an ideal host, touchingly anxious for his guests to enjoy themselves, and he insisted on paying for everything when the party went to a restaurant for dinner and, later, to a night club. Sunday they went to the Brookfield Zoo, where he fed box after box of Crackerjack to a coyly gesticulating polar bear; then to the Red Star Inn for dinner; and then back to the hotel, where his friends said good-by before driving back to Lafayette. Monday he started on his journey West on the *Burlington Zephyr*, the first streamlined train in which he'd ever ridden. His expansive mood was as strong as ever, and he bought a lower berth though it would be too short for him. "By God," he exclaimed naïvely, "I m-m-might as well go the whole hog!"[1]

He stopped off for a day in Denver, to see the friends he'd made there three years earlier when he had lectured at the University of Colorado Writers' Conference, and he was given such a royal welcome that he stayed a week. However, by the second week in June he had reached his goal of Portland, Oregon, and had been invited by Edward M. Miller, Sunday editor of the *Oregonian*,[2] and Ray Conway, manager of the Oregon State Motor Association, to go on the trip which later became famous as "The Western Journey." "I'm . . . leaving . . . Sunday morning on what promises to be one of the most remarkable trips of my life," he wrote to Miss Nowell on June 15. "It means I'll be away about two weeks longer than I intended, but it is the chance of a lifetime and after long battlings with my conscience, I have decided I'd be foolish not to take it. Here's the program: a young fellow I know on one of the local papers is starting out Sunday morning . . . on a tour of the entire West, and he has asked me to come with him. We leave here Sunday and head south for California stopping at Crater Lake on the way down; we go down the whole length of California taking in Yosemite, the Sequoias and any other national parks they have; then we swing east across the desert into Arizona to the Grand Canyon, etc., north through Utah, Zion and Bryce Canyons, Salt Lake, etc., then to the Yellowstone, then north to the Canadian Border, Montana, Glacier Park, etc., then west again across Montana, Idaho, Washington, then Rainier Park, etc.—in other words a complete swing around the West from the Rocky Mountains on, and every big national park in the West. . . . My conscience hurts me about this extra two weeks, but I believe I'd always regret it if I passed it up. When I get through I shall really have seen America (except Texas)."

[1] For the account of Wolfe's weekend in Chicago the author is greatly indebted to William Braswell's article "Thomas Wolfe Lectures and Takes a Holiday," in the October 1939 issue of *College English*. Also to Herbert J. Muller for his correspondence with her and for his evaluation of Wolfe as a writer in *Thomas Wolfe*, in The Makers of Modern Literature series, published by New Directions in 1947.

[2] Miller is now assistant managing editor of the *Oregonian*. His two articles on the trip, "Gulping the Great West," appeared in the July 31 and August 7, 1938, issues of the *Oregonian Magazine*.

This chance to see the West with a speed and scope which outdid his wildest expectations was a perfect climax for Wolfe's trip. However, before he could actually start on it, he had to go through another period of brooding about his breach with Perkins. He had met several people from the book department of the J. K. Gill Company of Portland, including its manager, Warren Wright, who had invited him to spend a few days at his cabin on the Washougal River. It was probably from Wright that he heard of the derogatory things about himself which had been said by some of the Scribner salesmen. The old bitterness flared up again, and while he was still brooding over it, he got a letter from Miss Nowell saying that Perkins had invited her to lunch, had asked repeatedly and wistfully about him, and had seemed old, tired, sad, and deeply depressed by the spread of fascism in Europe. That brought the whole thing to a head, and he sat right down and wrote Miss Nowell: "I'm sorry about M.P. Everything you tell me about him touches and grieves and hurts me like hell. Please—*please* don't tell him about me, or anything about me, if you can avoid it. For six years he was my friend—I thought the best one I ever had—and then, a little over two years ago he turned against me. . . . It's almost as if he were praying for my failure. I can't understand or fathom it, but it is a sad strange thing. Max still tells people that he is my friend, and then he runs me down; and out here in the West I have run on one or two stories that the Scribner salesmen apparently have been instructed to pass around that sicken me. It's like a nightmare, but I won't let it get me down. What is this thing in life anyway that causes people to do things like this? The hell of it is, the people who say they love you are often the ones who do the most to injure you. . . . I can't make it out, and now Perkins, under this mask of friendship, is doing the same thing. I don't think I'll ever change in the way I feel about him—the funny thing is I'm always supposed to be the one who changes, but at the bottom I'm the most solid of the lot.

"I don't think he *consciously* wants me to fail or come to grief, but it's almost as if *unconsciously*, by some kind of *wishful* desire, he wants me to come to grief, as a kind of sop to his pride and his unyielding conviction that he is right in everything—the tragic flaw in his character that keeps him from admitting that he has wronged anybody or made a mistake. That is really his great weakness, and I believe it is at the root of his failure—his growing reaction, his sense of defeat. . . . I shall always remember him as one of the most wonderful people I ever knew —but I have neither time nor energy to cope with this thing in him now;

all that I know is that it is against me, and against my work and I can't give it any sort of break. As much as I can, I want to sever the connection entirely. Someday, perhaps, if he is willing, I'll take it up again—but meanwhile, let's not play with fire. Tell him nothing about me or what I'm doing: that's the only way, believe me, to avoid trouble. Anyway, it's not a matter of personalities any more: if I'm wrong it will show in my work: if he's wrong it's going to show in his life."[3]

Having come to this conclusion, Wolfe put the whole thing from his mind and plunged into preparations for his trip with Miller and Conway. On Monday morning, June 21, they left Portland punctually at eight-fifteen and started driving south in Conway's white Ford sedan with the official AAA and Oregon State Motor Association insignia on its sides. Wolfe had not met Conway until now, and so for that first morning he sat in front beside him, wearing a broad grin and a new brown gabardine suit, with which he was inordinately pleased, and exclaiming with stuttering sincerity that it "s-s-sure was s-s-swell" of Miller and Conway to take him on this trip. For the greater part of the trip, however, he sat alone in the back seat, with his knees spread wide apart and his arms akimbo, drinking in the sights that flowed so swiftly past him. He had always loved the land, but on this trip he was especially interested in the people, too: the rangers and the waitresses in the parks, the young people at Yosemite, the older tourists at Grand Canyon, the four small Indian girls beside the road, the dour-faced schoolteacher who wept when sung good-by to at Bryce Canyon, and all the rest.

The trip as conceived by Conway was a grueling endurance test. It called for driving 4632 miles in thirteen days: that meant an average of about 356 miles daily, but because the parks were not spaced evenly along the route, the actual daily distances varied from a minimum 192 miles to a maximum of 693. On the third day, after driving 693 miles from Yosemite to Mojave, California, Wolfe and Miller were all in and

[3]When Perkins saw this letter for the first time in August 1945, he wrote Miss Nowell saying: "Were you capable of believing—I know Tom could believe anything when his imagination got working—that we would instruct our salesmen to damage him? Besides, we should betray our profession, and everything we believe in, if we tried to injure a great talent. It's incredible that even Tom could believe that. It is possible that some of the men were so aggrieved at Tom's leaving us, that they expressed derogatory opinions of him as a man. Very likely they did, because many salesmen haven't the faintest understanding of literature, or of writers, and they might have interpreted Tom's decision in the most obvious way. But you must know that I never said much of anything about the whole matter, and that when pressed, I spoke in Tom's defense."

told Conway that the whole trip was insane. To this he answered imperturbably: "If you two would spend more time sleeping and less time drinking beer, you'd feel better in the mornings."[4] After that, the three of them settled down to an amicable and somewhat less hectic trip, with Conway and Miller taking turns at driving, a hundred miles apiece. Wolfe, who knew nothing about driving, didn't even have the strain of watching the road. However, the mere act of riding all those miles, sixteen hours a day, day after day, was a physical ordeal. During the two weeks' trip he pounded through two good pairs of pants; his beloved new brown gabardines wore through on the eighth day, and another pair, into which he hastily changed, gave out on the next-to-last day of the trip. Day after day the white Ford sped along; night after night Wolfe sat up for hours, pouring out his endless stream of talk to Miller or writing in a gray cloth ledger hasty impressionistic notes of what he'd seen; and morning after morning Miller and Conway had to wake him up, after having been dressed and ready to start for a long time. Sometimes, after a grueling long day, the nerves of all three got as frayed as the seat of Wolfe's brown pants, but they knew and understood each other now and through it all they became increasingly good friends.

The trip came to a successful end at Rainier on July 1. They spent the night at Sunrise Lodge and, next morning, drove to Olympia, where Wolfe took a bus for Seattle. He had already spent three days there before starting on the trip and had looked up his cousins there, descendants of his great-uncle Bacchus, who had gone West in the 1890s. Now he wanted to go back and "get the whole history of the Pentlands out West for a future book," but even more than this he wanted to go to a good hotel and catch up on his sleep, and then to write up the rough notes for his *Western Journey*.

He checked in at the New Washington Hotel late in the afternoon of the second and found waiting for him there a wire from Aswell, who all this time had been reading the great stack of manuscript which he had given him. "Dear Tom," the wire said. "Your new book is magnificent in scope and design, with some of the best writing you have ever done. I am still absorbing it, confident that when you finish you will have written your greatest novel so far." He was greatly moved by this reaction to the book. "I'm going back and try to live up to it," he wrote,

[4] For this quote and for much of the information about the trip, the author is indebted to Miller's articles "Gulping the Great West"; also to letters written her by both Miller and Conway and to Wolfe's *A Western Journey*.

"until it's finished as I want it." In his first elation he forgot how much he needed sleep and conceived the notion of going to British Columbia to celebrate Independence Day. Accordingly, on July 4, he embarked for Vancouver on the Canadian Pacific steamship *Princess Kathleen*, on the ill-fated voyage which indirectly caused his death.

With his zest for voyages and his new-found love for all his fellow men, Wolfe had soon made friends with almost everybody on the ship. Among these was a man who, after going out on deck in the cold winds of Juan de Fuca Strait, contracted such a chill that Wolfe always referred to him afterward as "a poor shivering wretch."[5] Wolfe had bought a bottle of whisky in celebration of the Fourth, and he offered it to the sick man, who took a drink and handed back the bottle, whereupon, with a characteristic disregard of hygiene, Wolfe merely wiped off the mouth of it with one swipe of a great palm and drank from it himself. Evidently the man was coming down with pneumonia or a virulent form of influenza and passed it on to Wolfe. By the next day Wolfe had chills and fever, and he stayed in bed in his Vancouver hotel till afternoon. Later, after he had died, Mrs. Bernstein said that he had telephoned her from there and told her he was sick and dying, but that, thinking he was only drunk, she had paid no attention. It was quite characteristic of him to have said this to her, but it was also characteristic of him not to have consulted a doctor and not even to have stayed in bed. If he had got good medical attention when his illness was just beginning, he probably could have prevented it from developing into pneumonia and would still be alive today.

He decided to go back to Seattle by the train that left around seven o'clock that evening, but with his old hunger to explore the North American continent still strong within him, he could not bear to leave Vancouver without having seen more of it than his room in the hotel. He accordingly got up and dressed around three o'clock and went down to the street, where he engaged a quaint old cabby with a horse and carriage to drive him around for two hours and show him the important sights. By the time he got on board the train, he was shaking from head to foot with chills and had "an awful retching pain in his chest and back."[6] He appealed to an old Negro Pullman porter, saying,

[5] This quote is taken from what Wolfe later told his doctor, E. C. Ruge, James Stevens, and his sister Mabel. James Stevens thinks the sick man may have shared a stateroom on the ship with Wolfe, but he is not sure.

[6] For the material on Wolfe's final illness, including the direct quotations from the various people involved, the author is heavily indebted to Mabel Wolfe Wheaton's letters to her and the records which she made for the Library of

"John, can you get me a blanket and comfortable seat? I'm very sick."
The porter took him to the club car, put him on a leather sofa there,
and wrapped him in a blanket, and so, late that night, he arrived back
in Seattle, only to find that there was a convention of Sunday-school
teachers at the New Washington Hotel and not a room available. Somehow, finally, they found a room for him, and he fell into bed, where he
remained, desperately sick but still with no medical attention, for six
more days.

Wolfe had met James Stevens, the author of the Paul Bunyan stories,
and his wife Theresa during his first short visit to Seattle. They had
given a party to introduce him to some of the literary people there, and
now the Sophus Winthers of the English Department of the University
of Washington had asked him to a party in return. Saturday, July 9,
the night of the party, came, and he was still sick, but since he was the
guest of honor, he felt that he could not decline. He finally arrived at
the party at ten o'clock, after they had telephoned to ask if he was coming. He was wild-looking and obviously had an awful cold, but they
didn't realize how dangerously ill he was and kept him happy with food
and drink and admiration until late that night, when the Stevenses
drove him back to his hotel. On the way, he insisted on having both
front windows of the car wide open, despite their protests that he might
catch more cold: he was actually burning up with fever, but he didn't
seem to realize it, or if he did, he didn't tell them so.

Finally, on Monday, July 11, an entire week after the inception of
his illness, he phoned Theresa Stevens and asked her for the Winthers'
phone number, saying that Mrs. Winther had promised to give him
some cough medicine and that his cough was now a great deal worse.
Then, in reply to Mrs. Stevens' urging that he see a doctor, he let James
Stevens take him to their own physician, Dr. E. C. Ruge, who found
him to be suffering from pneumonia, with a fever of 102, a terrific
cough, and accompanying slight infections of the kidneys and the
muscles around the heart. He obviously needed hospitalization, but he
had a dread of hospitals and protested wildly that he did not want to go
to one. "I don't want to die out here," he said in terror to James Stevens.
"Don't let me be kept out here to die!" As it happened, Dr. Ruge, after

Congress: "Mrs. Wheaton, Sister of Thomas Wolfe, Chronologically Telling
His Life History, ✕1302, February 23, 1947." Also to James and Theresa
Stevens, Annie Laurie Crawford, Dr. and Mrs. E. C. Ruge, Dr. Charles E.
Watts, and Bessie Y. Fisk.

being a well-known surgeon and diagnostician and superintendent of the Northern State Hospital for some years, had begun to specialize in psychiatry and had established a private sanitarium, Firlawns, twelve miles from Seattle at Kenmore. The Stevenses had the greatest admiration for him as a doctor and a man, and they felt that he would be the ideal physician to treat Wolfe's respiratory illness; they also knew that Firlawns, which consisted of two former private houses, would be less frightening to Wolfe than a big Seattle hospital would be. Wolfe himself agreed with them and went immediately to Firlawns, where Ruge gave him the intensive care which he so badly needed. By Thursday, July 14, the pneumonia crisis had been safely passed, his fever, which at one time had reached 105, had subsided to 100, and by the following week, when his brother Fred arrived to take the responsibility of his illness off the Stevenses, he was well enough to have his bed wheeled out onto the lawn under the magnificent fir trees that gave the place its name.

However, it soon became evident that his convalescence was not progressing as it should. As Dr. Ruge wrote later, "It became increasingly certain that the illness was serious. His low-grade temperature did not respond to rest and good food and the usual medicines. I became worried, for he did not respond to treatment. There seemed to be an underlying condition which I had not discovered. . . . He did not appear very ill, not any more than many others who have had a bronchitis with some unresolved area in the lung. But I could discover no lung pathology other than this. A chronic T.B. could not be ruled out. No T.B. Bacillus."[7] In an effort to combat this lurking infection, Ruge gave him a blood transfusion on July 19. The fever still persisted, and on July 22 he called in consultation Dr. Charles E. Watts, who, however, could find nothing definitely wrong and nothing to indicate pneumonia except occasional basal râles. Finally, on August 8, after two more weeks of intermittent fever, Ruge again called Watts in consultation, and with the urging of Fred Wolfe and Edward Aswell, had Wolfe taken to Providence Hospital in Seattle for a complete course of X rays, blood cultures, and other tests. The tests all came out negative, but the X ray showed a spot on Wolfe's right lung. As Dr. Watts described it, it was "a large area of consolidation in the right upper lobe, involving one-third to one-half of the right lung. This was very dense in the upper portion, and the lower portion was mottled."[8]

Unfortunately, the doctors disagreed about this X ray: Ruge and

[7] From "Tom Wolfe," an unpublished memoir by Dr. E. C. Ruge.
[8] From Watts' letter of September 5, 1938, to Dr. Russel Lee.

the radiologist thought that it showed an old tubercular condition, but Watts and the allergy specialist Dr. Philip Schoenwald insisted that it gave no evidence of tuberculosis and, for lack of a better diagnosis, called it "pneumonia with delayed reaction." Meanwhile, however, Dr. Ruge was so sure of the verdict of tuberculosis that he broke the news to Wolfe, saying that it was "the handwriting on the wall." Wolfe became violently excited. For seventeen years, since he had first coughed blood during his first few weeks at Harvard, he'd been haunted by the specter of tuberculosis of the lung and, like a small boy with a bogey-man, had managed to escape it by pretending that it wasn't there. Now Dr. Ruge, with a few incisive words, had brought him face to face with it and destroyed his whole elaborate defense. In a violent access of fear and anger, Wolfe dismissed Dr. Ruge from his case and put himself in the care of Dr. Watts, in the desperate hope that the latter's diagnosis would prove true.

Wolfe stayed at Providence Hospital under the care of Dr. Watts, and for the first few days, seemed to be progressing nicely. Then, suddenly, on August 12, his fever shot up to 103. On that day he had received a letter from Perkins, a delightful letter which said nothing about publishing that might upset him, but only told about the Perkins family's private life and of Mrs. Perkins' landscape gardening of the place at Silvermine. Wolfe, however, was overcome with love and longing for his old friend, and he insisted on sitting up and writing him an immediate reply. It was the last letter that he ever was to write:

"Dear Max: I'm sneaking this against orders, but 'I've got a hunch' —and I want to write these words to you.

"I've made a long voyage and been to a strange country, and I've seen the dark man very close; and I don't think I was too much afraid of him, but so much of mortality still clings to me—I wanted most desperately to live and still do, and I thought about you all a thousand times, and wanted to see you all again, and there was the impossible anguish and regret of all the work I had not done, of all the work I had to do—and I know now I'm just a grain of dust, and I feel as if a great window has been opened on life I did not know about before—and if I come through this, I hope to God I am a better man, and in some strange way I can't explain, I know I am a deeper and a wiser one. If I get back on my feet and out of here, it will be months before I head back, but if I get on my feet, I'll come back.

"Whatever happens—I had this 'hunch' and wanted to write you and tell you, no matter what happens or has happened, I shall always think of you and feel about you the way it was that Fourth of July day three years ago when you met me at the boat, and we went out on the café on the river and had a drink and later went on top of the tall building, and all the strangeness and the glory and the power of life and of the city was below.

Yours always, Tom"

At first it was thought that the emotional strain of writing this letter to Perkins was responsible for Wolfe's sudden attack of fever, but when it persisted, off and on for several days at a time, it became evident that it was still a symptom of infection. Meanwhile Dr. Watts was continuing to have tests and X rays made. On August 17, a second X ray of Wolfe's lung was taken, and it showed the area of consolidation to be definitely smaller. As Watts said in his report, "Below the right clavicle there was an oval area of increased density with a definite border, about the size of an egg." On August 26, a third film was made, and this one showed the spot to be still smaller, or about the size of a twenty-five-cent piece. Wolfe's fever was decreasing, but he had begun having headaches, which gradually increased in severity until he had to have dilaudid to dim the pain enough for him to sleep. When Mabel Wolfe Wheaton arrived in Seattle on August 19, to relieve Fred Wolfe of the care of Tom, Tom looked at her and blurted out, "Well, what do you think? Have you come out here to tell me I'm going to die?" Then, when Mabel tried to reassure him, he only said, "I have these headaches, Mabel, awful headaches." His "hunch" was growing stronger all the time.

Meanwhile Dr. Watts had gone to a medical convention at Bellingham, on Puget Sound, after telling Wolfe that perhaps, when he got back, he might be able to dismiss him from the hospital and treat him as an outpatient until his recovery was complete. As the day of Watts' return drew near, Wolfe worked himself into a state of great anticipation: in spite of his headaches and his tragic premonitions, he had a touching belief that if he could only leave the hospital, it would prove that he was getting better. He began making plans to rent an apartment with Mabel for a week or two, and then to go to his old friend Dr. Russel Lee of the Palo Alto Clinic to complete his convalescence. He told Mabel to reserve an apartment at the Spring Hotel, where he had planned to go to rewrite his *Western Journal*, because it had a magnificent view of Puget Sound. "Get a nice apartment with plenty of room," he told her. "This is no time to be parsimonious, Mabel. Parsimony

has killed more people than you'll ever know. I can afford it now."
Mabel, accordingly, had rented one with a huge living room for Tom,
a bedroom for herself, and a small electric kitchen and was busy stock-
ing up the larder with provisions. She was planning to cook all of Tom's
favorite things for him, the way she used to do at home. As she said,
tragically, later, "We Wolfes always think that if you can eat, you're
going to live, especially if you eat hearty."

Sunday, September 4, was the long-awaited day on which Tom and
Mabel hoped for his release. Mabel went to the hospital early in the
morning, packed Wolfe's bags, and paid his bill: then, in a fever of
impatience, they sat and waited for Watts to come. However, when he
did appear, he began by saying, "I've been looking at your chart. I see
you still have those headaches: that medicine I gave you didn't do
much good, did it?"

"D-Dr. Watts," said Wolfe earnestly. "I n-notice when I get up and
s-sit on the s-side of the b-bed here and hang my feet over onto this
o-ottoman, that my head stops aching. But when I lie down it aches."

"Well, listen," Watts replied. "I've been meaning to look into your
eyes with an ophthalmoscope. It'll only take a minute."

"Oh my God!" cried Wolfe. "I hope you don't find a tumor!"

Mabel left the room while Watts made his examination, but he soon
came out to her in the sunroom, where she was waiting.

"Mrs. Wheaton," he said, "I want to talk to you. You know this has
not been any ordinary case of pneumonia. I've just looked in Tom's
eyes and it looks to me as if there's a choked disk there. I would almost
bet my life on it. I want to call in a good eye man, and I want to have
another set of X rays taken the first thing tomorrow morning. Try to
get Miss Crawford to come and take Tom down for his X rays."

Wolfe had not had special nurses at Providence Hospital but had
been cared for by the regular floor nurses under the supervision of nuns,
the Sisters of Charity of Providence. However, a young registered nurse
named Annie Laurie Crawford, a native of Asheville and a friend of
some of the Westalls there, happened to be in Seattle, taking special
graduate training at the University of Washington. She had befriended
Tom and Mabel: they were both frightened and a long, long way from
home, and they had great difficulty in understanding what Wolfe's doctors meant: they had seized gratefully upon Miss Crawford's friendship,
and she had begun helping Mabel with Wolfe's care almost as if she
were his private nurse.

Now, in response to Mabel's anxious phone call, she came immediately to the hospital, and together the two of them went into Wolfe's

room. His lunch had been brought in, and the head nurse on his floor
was there. He was staring straight ahead of him with a morose preoccupation, and he hardly spoke to Annie Laurie Crawford though he was
very fond of her. Instead, he looked at Mabel and held up a capsule
which the head nurse had evidently given him. It was grayish blue in
color and almost an inch long, and he said with his wry humor, "I'm
taking horse medicine now. This is a horse pill for my headache." He
took the pill with a great gulp and began to eat his dinner, but nothing that Mabel or Miss Crawford said could dispel his brooding.

Finally Mabel couldn't stand it. "Now look, Tom," she said. "There's
no use in your being morose about this thing because we have to stay
in here until tomorrow morning. Now I'm going to leave Annie Laurie
here with you, and I'm going in town to get some dinner. But I'll come
back and stay with you tonight until they *put* me out—until you go to
sleep—and we're going out of here tomorrow morning if I have to pack
you up and take you out myself!"

He looked at her with childish faith: "You'll get behind 'em, won't
you, Mabel? You'll get behind 'em!" and she promised him she would.

Late that afternoon she was sitting on the mezzanine floor of her
hotel, writing a letter to her brother Fred, when the phone there started
ringing. It was Annie Laurie Crawford calling her. "Mabel," she said,
"I don't think Tom has known a single thing all afternoon: he's been
talking so strangely: he doesn't know what he's talking about."

Mabel went immediately to the hospital, and as she started down
the corridor toward Wolfe's room, she saw him standing in his doorway,
in his blue pajamas, staring up and down the hall. When she saw her
he flipped his hand in greeting and called out, "Hello, Mabel! How
did you get out here? Did you come by plane?" He had greeted her as
if she'd only just got to Seattle, though she'd been with him constantly
for two entire weeks, and he had known that she had come by train.
"Listen, Mabel," he went on. "You know at least fifty people in this
town with automobiles. I don't want you taking that streetcar. Where's
Henry Westall?"

Henry Westall was their cousin back in Asheville. She realized that
Tom's mind was terribly confused, and she took him by the arm and
led him back into his room, saying, "Tom, you're tired—you've been
up too long. Come on, honey, and get in the bed and let me rub your
head with witch hazel." She had brought him a bottle of Three Star
Hennessy with which to make hot toddies, and she noticed that some
of it had been poured out into two glasses that were standing on his

bureau. "Good," she said, "you've had a drink. Who had one with you?" He answered wearily, "Oh, I don't know. I don't know. I don't know, Mabel. So many of them have been passing in front of me all afternoon—so many of them have been here."

She rubbed his head till he seemed half asleep; then she went out to the floor nurse and asked her who had called on him that afternoon, only to find that no one had been with him except Miss Crawford. For some time Mabel had been convinced that he'd been getting too much medication, and she now burst out wildly, saying, "What in the name of heaven has he been taking? What have you people been giving him!" The floor nurse then realized that his mind had become affected: she called several of the other nurses, and they all went in to him, but he only lay with his eyes half closed, saying nothing, and remained that way all evening. True to her promise, Mabel stayed until they "put her out" at eleven, and she only left then after extracting a promise from the night nurse that she would watch him constantly. "I was afraid he might go through that window," Mabel said.

The next day he didn't even recognize Miss Crawford when she came to take him for his X rays. He came back from them in a wheel chair, totally exhausted, fell into bed, and slept and slept while his doctors gathered solemnly to break the news to Mabel. He had either a tumor or an abscess of the brain,[9] they said, and should be taken as soon as possible to the best brain surgeon in the country, Dr. Walter Dandy of Johns Hopkins Hospital.

They suggested that Mabel had better take Miss Crawford to care for Wolfe on the train and give him injections of morphine for his headache, and they also gave her a list of doctors in various cities across the continent in case his illness reached a crucial stage. However, they were evidently careful not to frighten her, because her first reaction was not one of shock, but of relief: "I was glad to know that I could take him back East," she said later. "That was what I'd been trying to do." Moreover, since Wolfe was going to Johns Hopkins, Watts now released him from the hospital. This was what he and Mabel had been longing for, and when they left around one o'clock that afternoon, they

[9] Dr. Watts' report to Russel Lee, written on this day, September 5, 1938, said: "Bronchogenic carcinoma seems to me most likely to explain the whole picture. . . . In any case, whether this be bronchogenic carcinoma with metastasis or pulmonary suppuration with metastatic brain abscess, the situation is a serious one." The report sent to Edward Aswell on September 6, 1938, by Dr. George Swift said: "Condition serious. Has either brain abscess . . . or possible metastasis from cancer bronchus."

left in a mood of jubilation. One of their Seattle cousins, Lonnie Harris, came to get them in his car, and Wolfe walked out of the hospital on his cousin's arm, with his battered old felt hat upon his head and a smile upon his face. Mabel followed them and found him sitting in the back seat of the car. "We're out, Mabel!" he exclaimed. "We're *out* at last!"

However, when they reached the Spring Hotel Apartments, he barely had the strength to walk inside the back door and along the hall. He almost collapsed when he got in the elevator, and when finally inside the apartment, he fell upon his bed; but later he was up and looking out the windows at the superb view of Puget Sound. He was fascinated by a little boat that kept plying back and forth between Seattle and the Navy Yard, and he kept exclaiming, "You picked well this time, Mabel. You picked a nice place!" Meanwhile she and Miss Crawford were cooking a tremendous meal of all the things he liked to eat: one of his favorite porterhouse steaks, creamed corn, baked potatoes, string beans cooked the southern way with a piece of pork, pickled peaches, sliced tomatoes, homemade buttermilk biscuits, and tea brewed in the brown earthenware teapot that he had insisted Mabel buy. "I hate those damned little tea bags," he had said.

He ate his supper, laughing and excited, though he was so tired that Mabel had to feed him toward the end. He had showed no signs of mental aberration since he'd left the hospital, and in spite of the doctors' diagnosis, everything seemed fine. It was not till Dr. George Swift came and examined Wolfe that evening, and virtually repeated the diagnosis of Watts and the other doctors at Providence Hospital, that they came to a final realization of how critical his condition really was.

Dr. Swift was a brain surgeon who was a friend of the head of Harpers' medical-book department and who had been asked by Aswell to find out about Wolfe's illness when he had first gone to Firlawns with pneumonia. He had conferred with Dr. Ruge several times but had no official connection with Wolfe's case, and until the sudden development of the past two days, Wolfe's illness had not been in his field. Now, in reply to a call from Mabel, he came to the Spring Hotel Apartments and said, "Mr. Wolfe, with your permission, I'm going to examine you." He looked into his eyes with an ophthalmoscope, tested his reflexes, and then said, "Where's your mother?" "I want to talk to you, man to man," he continued. "You're very ill. You owe it to yourself to do everything possible to get well. You must leave on the first train I can get you on for Johns Hopkins Hospital."

In sudden panic, Mabel ran out of the room: she said later that she couldn't get control of herself enough to go back and face Tom for three entire hours. Swift came out to her and said, "Now keep your chin up, girl. He's either got a tumor or an abscess there—and I want the biggest man in the country to do Tom Wolfe." But now all her energy and courage had deserted her. It was Dr. Swift who had to phone Mrs. Wolfe to break the news and who got reservations for Wolfe, Mabel, and Miss Crawford on the train.

They left Seattle on the *Olympian* at ten-thirty the following night. Wolfe was pushed through the lobby of the Spring Hotel in a wheel chair: he hardly noticed the little group of adoring students from the University of Washington who had been standing vigil in the lobby. His eyes seemed glazed, but he said good-by affectionately to the Stevenses, who had come to see him off. Dr. Swift was at the station, and Dr. Watts, with his wife's well-worn copy of *Look Homeward, Angel* for Wolfe to autograph. He wrote her name and his on the fly-leaf and announced that when his next book was published he'd come back out to Seattle and give "a big autographing party." But he was whistling in the dark, and everybody knew it. As Dr. Swift wrote to Aswell, "He looked pretty rocky, and I hated to see him go. However, under the circumstances there was nothing else to do."

Dr. Swift and Dr. Watts had warned Mabel and Miss Crawford that Wolfe might go into convulsions, and had told them that if his illness seemed to be getting to such a crucial stage, they must get off the train at St. Paul, Minnesota, and take an ambulance to Rochester, to the Mayo Clinic.

However, Wolfe stood the trip quite well. He had occasional shots of morphine for his headache, but he ate great plates of food and showed only a little mental aberration. They had two staterooms opening together and, the first night, after he had gone to sleep, Mabel and Miss Crawford piled all the luggage up against the door leading from his stateroom to the outside corridor, and went to bed in the adjoining room. Around 2 A.M. they were suddenly awakened by the opening of their stateroom door: the light from the corridor shone in upon their faces and they heard Tom saying, "Hello, Mabel!" There ꜱd in his blue pajamas, with a porter and a conductor. He had got ꜱlked through seven entire cars until he'd reached the observa- ꜱ wanted to send a telegram, he'd told the trainmen who had him, but he had quite willingly let them lead him back, and the exact letter and number of his staterooms and the

number of the car that they were in. After that, Mabel and Miss Crawford tried to stay awake in shifts. He did not like to take morphine,
although the pain and pressure in his head were very bad: he thought
that putting cold towels on his head, rubbing his forehead, and massag-
ing the back of his neck helped more, and they did those things for him
hours at a time.

For three long days and nights they endured the trip across the continent that Wolfe had made in the opposite direction so eagerly three
months before. Mabel, fearing that he might rebel against going to
Johns Hopkins, had told him they were on their way to Russel Lee's at
Palo Alto, but he probably knew where they were really going all along.
His fits of high-strung emotionalism and of black despondency seemed
to have almost vanished: perhaps it was because of his illness or because
of his premonition of his death: he was childish and appealing, with
heart-rending attempts at humor, and when she finally told him that
they were getting to Chicago and that Mrs. Wolfe was going to meet
them there, he only smiled and winked, and said, "Well, if she looks too
bad, we just won't speak to her." Then, when the train pulled in and
little Mrs. Wolfe came hurrying down the platform, calling out "Yoo-
hoo, I'm here!" he kissed her, laughing, and using the words of a family
joke, said, "Mrs. Julia E. Wolfe of the Old Kentucky Home!"[10]

They changed trains at Chicago and started on the last leg of the
trip, with Mrs. Wolfe feeding Tom the Georgia peaches which she had
brought with her all the way from Asheville. In spite of what Dr. Swift
had told her on the phone, she had a strong conviction that Tom
would "be all right" if she could take him home and nurse him, and
she clung to it, blindly, until the very end. Finally, on Saturday, September 10, they arrived at Baltimore, where they were met by an ambulance
sent by Dr. Dandy. Tom looked up at Mabel from the stretcher on
which they'd put him and asked, "Where are you taking me now,
Mabel?" "Tom," she said, "you're going to Johns Hopkins Hospital
and we're going to find out where these headaches come from." "Well,
Mabel," he replied, "your ideas of Johns Hopkins may be all right,
I've got ideas of my own. I need a rest. I need a rest, Mabel. I
fully tired." They put him in the ambulance, and Mrs. Wolfe
Crawford got in beside him, while Mabel collected all their
a taxi and took it to the boardinghouse where they were goi

[10] When Mrs. Wolfe and Mabel had gone to the Centur
Exposition in Chicago in 1933, she had got the hotel manager to
bill by introducing herself as a rival manager, Mrs. Julia E. W
Kentucky Home, and saying that *she* always made *her* bills out

They had all been here at Johns Hopkins many times with Mr. Wolfe, when he was having the radium treatments which had retarded the growth of his cancer for seven years.

Wolfe had come to dread and hate the place. "The great engine of the hospital, with all its secret, sinister, and inhuman perfections, together with its clean and sterile smells which seemed to blot out the smell of rotting death around one, became a hateful presage of man's destined end," he had written prophetically in *Of Time and the River*. "Suddenly, one got an image of his own death in such a place as this— of all that death had come to be—and the image of that death was somehow shameful. It was an image of death without man's ancient pains and old gaunt aging—an image of death drugged and stupefied out of its ancient terror and stern dignities—of a shameful death that went out softly, dully in anesthetized oblivion, with the fading smell of chemicals on man's final breath. And the image of that death was hateful."

Now he was being taken to that very hospital. The image of his death there had become sickeningly close.

For the next five days the final chapter of Wolfe's life moved to its inexorable end. For several hours after being admitted to Johns Hopkins, he was lost in deep despondency: he felt that Mabel had somehow tricked him into coming here, and when she came into his room and said she had good news, he looked at her sardonically and said, "Now, Mabel, is it *really* good this time?" But when she told him that Aswell had come from New York to see him, his whole mood changed, and all his spirit and intelligence came back. "Tom was lying in the bed," Aswell wrote later. "He half lifted himself into a sitting position, resting on his elbows, put out an immense hand and shook mine and said: 'Ed, it's wonderful to see you. Glad to see you. How are you, how are you?' I told him that I was all right, but how was he? 'Oh,' he said, 'these terrible headaches. I don't know what causes it, maybe they'll find out.' And I said 'I hope so.' And I sat down beside the bed and we began to talk. I knew what he wanted from me was reassurance about the manuscript which he had left with me and which by then I had the was the manuscript from which three books[11] were edited and he published posthumously. I gave him complete reassurance about those up and w tion car. He three books, edited by Aswell and published by Harpers, were *The* questioned *Rock, You Can't Go Home Again*, and *The Hills Beyond*. Their he had known reception helped tremendously to establish Wolfe's reputation as greatest writers.

books, how wonderful they were. And he began talking to me very lucidly, very clearly, and suddenly he stopped in the middle of a sentence, and it was as though a shade had been drawn on a scene you'd been looking at. The shade came down, everything went blank. He sat there for a moment, not looking around wildly or anything, just blank. The shade then went up. He resumed the sentence in the middle, exactly where it was. That was the only evidence I saw of the effect on his mind of what later turned out to be the cause of his death, which was tuberculosis of the brain."[12]

Wolfe and Aswell were still talking when Dr. Dandy and his assistants came to examine him for the first time. Aswell, Mabel, and Mrs. Wolfe waited in the corridor outside till finally Dandy came and beckoned to them. Mabel was suddenly overcome by her old mistrust of doctors: she seized Aswell by the arm and cried: "Oh, Mr. Aswell, will you *please* try to get to the bottom of this thing and find out what is wrong with him? I'm afraid Dr. Dandy won't tell me—I'm awfully tired and upset, and he knows I am!" Aswell, accordingly, went alone to speak to Dandy, but Mabel and Mrs. Wolfe could hear what Dandy said: "He's desperately ill. I doubt if there's a single thing that can be done for him." Then Aswell turned and ushered Mrs. Wolfe and Mabel forward, and Dandy took them all into an empty room, where they could talk undisturbed. "I want to tell you about your son and brother," he began. "He's a desperately sick man. I doubt if there's a thing that can be done for him. I've just examined him—there's so much pressure in his head, it's hard as a rock. Now if it's cancer, the case is hopeless. And if it's multiple tuberculosis, it's hopeless—there's absolutely nothing we can do. There's only one chance: if it's an abscess or a tumor—and it depends a great deal on where it is—if it's right here"—he pointed to the back of his own head—"there may be some hope."[13]

"Dr. Dandy," Mabel said. "What are his chances?"

"They're ninety-five per cent against him," Dandy said. "But if he had only one chance in a million, we ought to try to save him: he has that right."

"Mama," said Mabel, turning almost roughly in her panic upon Mrs. Wolfe. "What are we going to do!"

[12] From "Thomas Wolfe: Biography in Sound," first produced as an NBC radio broadcast and reprinted in the Fall 1956 issue of the *Carolina Quarterly*.

[13] For correcting the material concerning Dr. Walter E. Dandy the author is indebted to his son, Dr. Walter E. Dandy, Jr., who, as a boy of twelve, watched his father operate on Wolfe. The author is also indebted for preliminary advice to her own surgeon, Dr. Edward Ryan.

"Let's wait until Fred gets here," said Mrs. Wolfe, who shared her children's fear of surgery and doctors.

But Mabel had a sudden new burst of courage. "No," she said. "Let's put him in the hands of Dr. Dandy, and let him do whatever he thinks best."

It was then agreed that Dandy was to operate in an attempt to save Wolfe's life. In the meanwhile he recommended immediate trephining to decrease the pressure in his brain: it would make him much more comfortable, he said, and would also make it possible for them to put air in the brain for X-ray diagnosis. They all went back into Wolfe's room, and Dandy said, "I want, with your permission, to do a little work on you this afternoon. I just want to bore a little hole in your head, right back here. You won't even feel it, but it'll relieve that headache."

Wolfe looked up at him in fear. "You're not going to bore clean through, are you?"

"No, no," Dandy said. "Just through the bony shell."

The trephining was done that afternoon. Mrs. Wolfe and Aswell stood beside Wolfe's stretcher as it was taken up to the operating room in the elevator, and he clung to their hands like a frightened child. The pressure in his skull was so great that the intercranial fluid spurted out like a little geyser when the hole was bored, and for a while, his headache went away. "They've fixed it, Ed, they've fixed it," he told Aswell jubilantly when he was taken back to his own room, but the relief was only temporary. As Dandy said, he was a desperately sick man. Moreover, now, after the trephining, Dandy knew exactly what that sickness was: it was not an abscess or a tumor, but tuberculosis of the brain. The only remaining hope was that instead of many tubercles there might be only one, a tuberculoma, which could be removed. It was with this last shred of hope that the major operation was performed.

All that weekend Wolfe lay half comatose in his room in the Marburg Building, while his family sat in the sitting room just down the hall and talked as only Wolfes and Westalls can, seesawing between hysteria and panic and blind hope and heroic courage. Aswell went back to New York to break the tragic news to Harpers, and his place in Baltimore was taken by Miss Nowell. Fred Wolfe flew up from South Carolina and arrived at 4 A.M. on Sunday morning. And Sunday night, in reply to an urgent wire from Fred, Mr. Perkins came. Mrs. Bernstein wanted to come, too, but was dissuaded by Mr. Perkins. The sight of her was always very upsetting to Mrs. Wolfe, and it was vitally important that Wolfe rest undisturbed and not become involved in any great emotional crises until the crucial operation. Because of this, Perkins did not even go to talk with him or even let him know that he was there in Baltimore, but stayed quietly in the sitting room with the frantic family, the "dauntless and unshaken friend" until the very end.

The crucial operation was scheduled for Monday morning, September 12. Wolfe's friends and family saw him wheeled along the corridor upon a stretcher, motionless and swathed in white from head to foot. Then they sat and waited for what seemed forever in a tiny waiting room close by the operating room. Annie Laurie Crawford had been replaced by Dandy's specially trained surgical nurses, but at the Wolfe family's insistence, she had stayed on with them as a friend. Dandy had given her permission to watch the operation, and the family, still distrustful of doctors and of surgery, had persuaded her to do it so that she could tell them everything that happened. Now, suddenly, she came running down the corridor to the little waiting room. Her face was as white as her operating-room gown, and she was weeping. "He didn't operate," she said. "They opened up Tom's skull, and Dr. Dandy took one look and laid the scalpel down."

Dandy himself came right behind her, still in the white suit and skullcap of the operating room. "The case is hopeless," he said grimly. "He has miliary tuberculosis of the brain. His brain is simply covered with tubercles—there must be millions of them there." Later, after the family's first outburst of shock and grief, he explained the case more fully. At some time in his youth, Wolfe had had tuberculosis of the lung, but it had cured itself, and the lesion had healed over, sealing up the tubercles inside. Then, when he had contracted pneumonia in Seattle in July, the lesion had reopened, the tubercles had gone into his blood stream and finally had been carried to his brain. "He may live for six weeks more," said Dandy, "and we can keep him fairly comfortable. But it's absolutely hopeless. If he can die now, without recovering from the operation—as he may within the next three days— it will be much better."

Wolfe lay in a semicoma for three days and nights. His head was swathed in great white bandages, his eyes were shut, his breath came stertorously through half-opened mouth, but perhaps a spark of consciousness still was in him. Again and again, the nurses would say to the members of his family: "See if you can call him back," and they would lean down over him and call his name. Mabel, with her ringing voice, could do it best. "Tom!" she'd say. "Tom! Can you hear me?

Answer me! Tom! Tom!" Finally, she says, he spoke, with infinite weariness, infinite patience, as if from a different world. "All right, Mabel. I'm coming. . ." Then he lapsed into unconsciousness again.[14] They gave him a blood transfusion, but it did no good: he was slowly sinking, sinking, to his death, and early on the morning of September 15, he died, so peacefully that there wasn't even time to call his family to his bedside.

There wasn't a coffin big enough to hold him in the whole of Baltimore, but finally the undertaker had one made to order in New York and laid him out upon its pale pink-satin padding, embalmed and rouged, and with an ill-fitting black toupee upon his head to hide his shaved skull with its terrible incision. Then his exhausted family took him back to Asheville, and he lay in his reopened coffin in the parlor of the Old Kentucky Home, while Fred ushered in his friends and relatives to take their final look at him. Mrs. Wolfe stood by the coffin all day long, tearless and untiring, talking, talking of Tom's illness and his death with the awful matter-of-factness of a woman who has had a long, hard life and seen death many times. However, Mabel had reached the limit of her endurance: she didn't even attend the funeral held at the Presbyterian church where he had gone to Sunday school as a small boy, but, as she described it, "went out with a bang."

One of the callers at the Old Kentucky Home was Perkins, who, together with Mrs. Perkins, had come down for the funeral. "It was a most horrible day to me," he said later. "It is probably better to be emotional on occasions like that, but it is wholly contrary to our Yankee and Episcopal ways. I had to go in and look at Tom, who, thank God, did not look in the least like Tom, so I didn't much mind what I had dreaded. But Fred was all the time imploring me to say something to Tom. I couldn't do that. The funeral service was very impressive. At the burial I didn't see much. I kept as far in the background as I could. I hated the whole business."[15] Under the terms of the will which Wolfe had made in the spring of 1937, Perkins was executor of his estate and administrator of all his literary affairs. Thus it was that, in death, Wolfe went back under Perkins' benevolent control, even though the posthumous novels were published by Harpers instead of Scribners.

[14] From Mrs. Wheaton's recorded interview made for the Library of Congress. According to what Dr. Dandy told Edward Aswell, Wolfe never regained consciousness after the second operation. If he answered Mrs. Wheaton, it was probably almost automatic.

[15] From Perkins' letter of November 13, 1945, to John S. Terry.

Wolfe is buried in Riverside Cemetery, Asheville, which had been the scene of his prophetic youthful vision:

"Around them in the cemetery the air brooded with a lazy drowsy warmth. There was the cry of the sweet-singing birds again, the sudden thrumming bullet noises in undergrowth and leaf, and the sharp cricket-ing stitch of afternoon, the broken, lazy sounds from far away, a voice in the wind, a boy's shout, a cry, the sound of a bell, as well as all the drowsy fragrance of a thousand warm intoxicating odors—the resinous smell of pine, and the smells of grass and warm sweet clover. It was all as it had always been. . . . And now he heard his mother's voice again: 'And you'll come back!' he heard her saying. 'There's no better or more beautiful place than in these mountains, boy—and someday you'll come back again,' she cried with all the invincible faith and hopefulness of her strong heart.

"An old and tragic light was shining faintly on the incredible, time-enchanted hills. It was shining like the light of dreams on the rocky little river which he had seen somewhere, somehow, from the windows of a train long, long ago, in his childhood, somewhere before memory began, and which had wound its deathless magic in his heart forever. And the old and tragic light of fading day shone faintly on their faces, and suddenly they were fixed there like a prophecy with the hills and river all around them—and there was something lost, intolerable, fore-told and come to pass, and like old time and destiny—some magic that he could not say.

"Down by the river's edge in darkness now he heard the bell, the whistle and the pounding wheel. It brought to him, as it had done ten thousand times in childhood, its great promise of morning, new lands, and a shining city.

"And now, receding, far and faint, he heard again the whistle of the great train pounding on the rails across the river. It swept away from them, leaving the lost and lonely thunder of its echoes in the hills, the flame-flare of its terrific furnace for a moment, and then just the heavy wheels and rumbling, loaded cars—and, finally, nothing but the silence it had left behind it.

"Now, even farther off and almost lost, he heard for the last time its wailing and receding cry, bringing to him again all its wild and secret prophecy, its pain of going, and its triumphant promise of new lands. He saw them fixed forever in his vision, and the lonely light was shin-ing on their faces, and he felt an intolerable pain, an unutterable joy and triumph as he knew that he would leave them."

The prophecy had all come true. He had escaped from home and the encircling hills, and gone out in the world: he had made his life and work prevail with a strength that even cheated death, and now he had come home again to stay. His tombstone, on the crest of the hill beside Ben's and Grover's and his father's, reads:

TOM

SON OF

W. O. AND JULIA E. WOLFE

A BELOVED AMERICAN AUTHOR

OCT. 3, 1900—SEPT. 15, 1938

"THE LAST VOYAGE, THE LONGEST, THE BEST."

—LOOK HOMEWARD, ANGEL

"DEATH BENT TO TOUCH HIS CHOSEN SON WITH MERCY, LOVE AND PITY, AND PUT THE SEAL OF HONOR ON HIM WHEN HE DIED."

—THE WEB AND THE ROCK

Perhaps an even better epitaph is the final lines of *You Can't Go Home Again:*

"Something has spoken to me in the night, burning the tapers of the waning year; something has spoken in the night, and told me I shall die, I know not where. Saying:

" 'To lose the earth you know, for greater knowing; to lose the life you have, for greater life; to leave the friends you loved, for greater loving; to find a land more kind than home, more large than earth——

" '—Whereon the pillars of this earth are founded, toward which the conscience of the world is tending—a wind is rising, and the rivers flow.' "

INDEX

Adams, Agatha Boyd, 38n.
Adams, Walter S., 151
"Adoration of the Kings," 266
Agassiz Theatre, 62
Aldington, England, 252
Aldington, Richard, 168, 178
Alpbach, Austria, 329–31
American Business Club, 381
American Express, 93, 251
American Mercury, 25n., 86n., 233, 234, 323n., 379n.
Anatomy of Melancholy, The, 40
Anderson, S.C., 71
Anderson, Sherwood, 28, 282, 391, 395, 408, 409, 411, 412
Anderson, Mrs. Sherwood, 408, 409, 411
Andover, Mass., 213
"Angel on the Porch, An," 132n., 140
Appleton, D., & Company, 82
"April, Late April," 379n.
Arizona Quarterly, 287n., 384n., 395n.
Arlen, Michael, 168
Armstrong, Anne W., 384n., 395, 403, 408n.
Asheville, N.C., 21, 23, 24, 26, 65, 101, 118, 143, 249, 372, 379–82, 389, 394, 439, 440
  financial collapse of, 186, 379
  and *Look Homeward, Angel*, 137–39, 141, 150ff., 165, 167, 209
  memorial at, 26
Asheville *Citizen*, 31, 91, 138, 141, 142, 150, 249, 365, 382
Asheville *Daily Mail*, 186
Asheville *Times*, 151, 167
"As I Saw Thomas Wolfe," 384n., 395n.
Astors, the, 139
Aswell, Edward C., 117n., 392, 399ff., 407, 416, 417, 423, 426, 431n., 435–37, 439n.

Aswell, Mary Louise, 403, 405, 406
Atlanta, Ga., 374
Atlantic City, N.J., 165, 169
Atlantic Monthly, 233, 301, 302
Auditorium Hotel, Chicago, 419
Austin, J. B., 21
Austin, Steven, 21
Austria, 329–31

Baker, George Pierce, 27, 48, 51–60 passim, 62ff., 81, 214
Baltimore, Md., 22, 48, 61, 434
Barber, Philip W., 69n.
Basso, Hamilton, 293, 297, 298, 365, 369n., 382–84, 389–90, 412
Bath, England, 91
Beer, Thomas, 156, 194, 216n.
Beethoven, Ludwig van, 120, 121
Belgium, 104
"Bell Remembered, The," 323n.
Belmont Prize, 64
Berengaria, S.S., 103
Berlin, 267, 268, 269–78, 325ff.
Berliner Tageblatt, 329
Bermuda, 213
Bernstein, Aline, 24, 28, 82, 96, 98–129 passim, 140, 162, 166, 167, 171, 186, 250, 283, 308, 392, 424, 437
  quarrel with Wolfe, 162ff., 171, 177ff., 188ff., 195, 196
  reconciliation with Wolfe, 283–84, 293
  threatens to prevent publication of *The October Fair*, 279, 295, 312, 343, 399
  see also Wolfe, Thomas, letters to Aline Bernstein
Big Basin, Cal., 289
"Big Short Trip, The," 212
Bingham School, Asheville, 47
Bishop, Don, 38n., 41n.

Black Forest, 181
Blythe, LeGette, 38n.
Boni & Liveright, 112
Bonn, Germany, 120, 121
Bonnier, A., 208
Bookman, 155
Booloo Club, 34
"Boom Town," 234
Boothbay Harbor, Me., 139
Boston, Mass., 51, 300
Bottomley, Hilda Westall, 22n., 51, 210
Boulder, Col., 285, 295
Bowman, William Clayton, 23
Boyd, Ernest, 113
Boyd, James, 156, 161, 165, 302, 303
Boyd, Madeleine, 113, 126, 127, 130–35, 150, 177, 208, 233, 277, 286, 287, 312, 343
Braswell, William, 420n.
Bremen, S.S., 277
Brett, Catherine, 236, 239
Brett School, Dingmans Ferry, Pa., 236
Breughel, Pieter, 266
Bridges, Robert, 321
Bristol, England, 91
Bristol, Tenn., 395
Brookfield Zoo, Chicago, 419
Brooklyn, N.Y., 194, 195, 198, 208, 209, 213, 219, 237, 243, 269, 270, 279, 280, 291, 313, 339–44 passim
Brooklyn Bridge, 200
Brooks, Van Wyck, 233
Brothers Karamazov, The, 156
Brown, Curtis, 233
Brussels, 119
Buckham, Waldo, 101n.
Budapest, 127
"Bums at Sunset, The," 173
Burdick, Edmund, 42
Burlington Zephyr, 420
Burnsville, N.C., 380, 383
Burton, Robert, 40

Calverton, V. F., 332
Canby, Henry Seidel, 256–58, 261, 302
Cane, Melville, 113

Canfield, Cass, 401
Cargill, Oscar, 76n., 78n., 85, 101n.
Carlton, Henry Fisk, 53, 71, 100, 114
Carolina Folk Plays, 83
Carolina Magazine, 34, 38n., 39, 41n., 45, 47, 198, 228, 231, 237, 283, 371–72
  quotations from articles on Wolfe, 38n., 198, 206, 228, 231, 237, 283, 290
Carolina Playbook, 46n.
Carolina Playmakers, 46, 47
Carolina Quarterly, 297n., 404n.
Carroll, D. D., 93, 95
Carswell, Catherine, 266
Cathcart, Nobel, 302, 376
Cattelle, Elizabeth, 62n.
Chamberlain, John, 155
Chapel Hill, 33, 37ff., 371
Chappaqua, N.Y., 403
Chase National Bank, 308
Chatterton, Thomas, 91
Cherbourg, France, 96
Cherio's, New York, 376, 415
Chicago, Ill., 238, 241, 419, 434
"Chickamauga," 379n.
Chickamauga, battle of, 380
"Child by Tiger, The," 175n., 379n.
Coates, Albert, 50
Cocke, William, 105
Coleridge, Samuel Taylor, 54, 63
College English, 420n.
Colmar, Alsace-Lorraine, 183
Cologne, 119, 120
Colorado, University of, 284, 285, 301, 420
Colorado State College of Education, 285
Concerning Honest Bob, 47
Cone, Benjamin, 34, 90, 92
Conway, Ray, 420, 422ff.
Cooper, Lee, 167
Copenhagen, 277
Covici, Friede, 113
Cowley, Malcolm, 265n., 332
Crager, Tess, 367
Crawford, Annie Laurie, 425n., 429–34, 438

Crockett, David, 21
Cross, Robert, 266, 308

Dandy, Dr. Walter, 431–39 passim
Dandy, Dr. Walter E., Jr., 436n.
Daniels, Jonathan, 151, 152, 342, 376
Daniels, Mrs. Jonathan, 376
Daniels, Josephus, 39
"Dark in the Forest, Strange as Time," 233
Darrow, Whitney, 261n., 294
Dashiell, Alfred, 13, 185, 203, 217, 233, 287
Davenport, Basil, 155
"Death the Proud Brother," 202, 214
Deferred Payment, 46
de Forests, the L. Effingham, 240
Denver, Col., 285, 287, 420
De Voto, Bernard, 14, 242, 247, 302ff., 311, 312, 376, 390, 391, 399
Dialectic Literary Society, 34
Diaries, *see* Journals, Notebooks, and Diaries
Dingmans Ferry, Pa., 236
Disney, Walt, 419
Dodd, Martha, 272–75, 282, 328, 332
Dodd, William E., 272, 273, 325, 332
Dodd, William E., Jr., 273
Donne, John, 40, 140
Dooher, Mrs., 378
Dorman, Marjorie, 342
Dorman, Mary Roberta, 342
Dorman, William Samuel, 342
Dorman family, 313, 342, 344, 366, 375, 379, 389
Doubleday & Company, 402
Dow, Robert Bruce, 72
Dowden, Hester, 266
Dows, Olin, 83, 87, 88, 139
Doyle, A. Gerald, 77, 78
Du Bois, Dr. Eugene F., 125
du Mauriers, the, 265
Dybbuk, The, 103

" 'E," 379n.
Eastman, Max, 409

Editor to Author: The Letters of Maxwell E. Perkins, 198, 231n., 244n., 246n., 311, 343n., 346n., 374n.
Ehrsam, Theodore G., 78
Eldreds, the Allen, 366, 370
Emmett, Mrs. Mary, 409
Emrich, Duncan, 26n.
England, 103ff., 252, 268
"English '37: The Novelist and the Reader," 390
"Eugene Returns to Pulpit Hill," 372n.
Europa, S.S., 191, 325
Exiles, 104

Fadiman, Clifton, 262, 264
Farewell to Arms, A, 156
Fast Express, The, 135, 181, 211
Fenge, Wolfgang, 331n.
Ficke, Arthur Davison, 158
Firlawns, 426
Fisher, Vardis, 84, 116
Fisk, Bessie Y., 425n.
Fitzgerald, F. Scott, 134, 170, 171, 177, 179, 181, 238, 280, 385–89
Folger, William, 71
Forays and Rebuttals, 242n.
Forty-seven Workshop, Harvard University, 48, 50ff., 62ff., 244
Forum, 233
Fosdick, Harry Emerson, 408
"Four Lost Men, The," 233
Frankau, Joseph, 98
Frankfurt, Germany, 104, 121
French, the, 166
Frere, A. S., 168–71, 178, 183, 188, 211, 236, 241, 242, 246, 252, 265–67, 320
Frings, Ketti, 156
From Death to Morning, 173n., 194, 202, 214, 229n., 286, 287, 293, 294, 342, 343
"Further Memories of Thomas Wolfe," 25n.

Galtenberg, the, 330, 331
Gambrell, Effie Wolfe (Mrs. Fred W Gambrell), 43, 71, 383

Gambrell, Fred W., 28
Gant, Eugene, 24n., 30, 33, 34
Gant, W. O., death of, 236, 237
Gardners Church, Pa., 22
Geneva, Switzerland, 177, 181
"Genius Is Not Enough," 242n., 247, 302ff.
Germany, 120ff., 267, 269–78, 325–36, 337, 340–41
Gettysburg, 22, 218
Gill, J. K., Company, 421
Glasgow, Scotland, 103
Godchaux, Elva, 367
Goethe, Johann Wolfgang von, 274, 275
Gold, Mike, 332
Gooch's Café, 41
Good Child's River, The, 181, 202
Gorsline, Douglas, 375
Gorsline, Elizabeth (Perkins), 375
Gould, Elaine Westall, 51, 68, 210, 213
Gould, Gerald, 179
Graham, Frank P., 92
Graham Memorial, 71
Grand Canyon, 287
Grand Central Station, New York, 16, 208, 209, 232n., 262, 403, 404
Grandmothers, The, 156
Greeley, Col., 285
Green, Paul, 46
Greenfield, Kent Roberts, 305
Greenlaw, Edwin, 37–40, 54
Greenough, Chester, 54
Greenville, S.C., 329
Grove Park Inn, Asheville, 385
Guaranty Trust Company, Paris, 167
Guggenheim Foundation fellowship, 161–63, 235
"Gulping the Great West," 420n., 423n.

Hale, Nancy, 14, 300
Hamburg, Germany, 277, 278
Hampstead Heath, England, 266
Hanford, James Holly, 37
Hansen, Harry, 148
Harcourt, Alfred, 393
Harcourt, Brace & Co., 392, 393

Harlow, Jean, 288
Harper & Brothers, 392, 399ff.
Harper's Bazaar, 379n.
Harper's Magazine, 69n., 233, 392
Harris, Lonnie, 432
Harris, William E., 67
Harrisburg, Pa., 22
Hartman, Lee, 392, 400
Harvard Club, 109
Harvard Library Bulletin, 50n.
   Perkins' article on Wolfe, 33n., 130ff., 135, 138, 210, 239, 246, 250n.
Harvard Library Bulletin, 50n.
   62ff., 244, 366
"Heigh-ho" song, 419
Heikes, Eleanor Jane, 22
Heinemann, William, Ltd., 168, 177, 208, 235
Heirs, The, 58, 64
Hellman, Geoffrey T., 155
Hemingway, Ernest, 132, 187, 208, 231, 244, 343
Herndon, Richard, 64, 69, 70
Heyward, Dorothy, see Kuhns
Hill, Cynthia, 22
Hills Beyond, The, 218, 323n., 358, 379n., 435n.
Hilltop Farm, Oxford, 105
Hilltop Liquor Store, New York, 308
Hinkson, Mr., 284
Hitler, Adolf, 271, 273, 328
Hoagland, Clayton, 296
Hoagland, Kathleen, 296, 297, 378, 379n.
Hogarth, William, 266
Holland, 268
Hollywood, 214, 215, 288, 289
Holt, Henry, & Company, 83
Hotel Albert, New York, 83
Hotel Am Zoo, Berlin, 271
Hotel Boglerhof, Alpbach, Austria, 329–31
Hotel Brevoort, New York, 411, 412
Hotel Chatham, New York, 11, 16, 200, 232, 235, 283, 319, 321
Hotel Chelsea, New York, 399, 400, 403, 412, 416, 417

Hôtel d'Alsace, Paris, 92, 93
Hotel Lafayette, New York, 280
Houghton Mifflin Company, 396–99, 402, 403
Hound of Darkness, The, 295, 297, 356
House, The, 58, 82, 83, 90, 92
"House of the Far and Lost, The," 235
Hunger, 181
Hunter, Louis C., 60
Hyde, Robert, 169
Hyde, Susan, 169

"I Have a Thing to Tell You," 277, 334, 335, 337, 410
"I Knew Thomas Wolfe," 78
Ile de France, S.S., 248, 250, 283
Ilkley, England, 103
Independent Magazine, 31, 32
"In the Park," 286n.
Italy, 95, 128

Jack, Peter Munro, 258–59
Jackson Building, Asheville, 394
Jacobson, Dr. Arthur C., 209n.
James, Earl, 365
James, Laura, 35, 36
Jassinoff, Gwen, 412
Jelliffe, Belinda (Mrs. Smith Ely Jelliffe), 214, 249, 250, 291, 293, 316, 319, 414, 415
Jelliffe, Smith Ely, 249
Jersey City, N.J., 413, 415
Jews, 86, 98, 333, 334, 409
Johns Hopkins Hospital, 36, 48, 215, 431–35
Johnson, William Perry, 22n.
Journals, Notebooks, and Diaries, Wolfe's, 90, 91, 107, 108, 114, 118, 120, 121, 129, 133, 138–39, 164ff., 180, 182, 184, 202, 207, 217, 252, 266, 267, 279, 295, 297, 298, 318, 319, 332
Journey Down, The, 99, 103
Joyce, James, 104, 105, 108, 121, 354, 356

K 19, 211ff., 234

"Katamoto," 379n.
Kays, Vice-Chancellor, 413
Keiler, Fräulein, 331n.
Kennedy, Richard S., 50n., 113n., 211n.
Kittredge, G. L., 54
Knopf, Alfred A., 392
Knopf, Mrs. Alfred A., 392
Koch, Frederick H., 46, 48, 51, 52, 83
Kuhns, Dorothy, 70

Lancaster, Pa., 165
Lancastria, S.S., 89
Landon, Alfred M., 342
Lang, Anton, 126
Langley Flying Field, Hampton, Va., 42
Langner, Lawrence, 71
Latimer, Margery, 149
Lavin, Patrick, 46
Lawrence, D. H., 412n.
Ledig-Rowohlt, Heinz, 272, 298, 325, 331n.
Lee, Dr. Russel, 289, 426n., 428, 434
Lemmon, Elizabeth, 241, 291
Lemon, Courtenay, 71, 82
Lentz, Jacob, 22
Leonard, Louise Dorman, 342
Letters of Thomas Wolfe, The, 17
Lewis, Sinclair, 156, 187, 188, 208, 249
Lewisohn, Alice, 82
Library of Congress, Mabel Wheaton's recorded interview at, 26n., 150n., 425n., 439n.
Lieber, Maxim, 234
Linscott, Robert, 396–99, 402, 403
"Lion at Morning, The," 321
Little, Brown & Co., 392, 395
London, 91, 103, 104, 105, 183ff., 252, 265, 266
London Evening News, 178
London Observer, 179
Look Homeward, Angel, 24n., 35, 56, 60, 78, 80, 82, 98, 102–8, 111, 176, 222, 280, 318, 357
dedication for, 140, 166n.
earnings, 162

Look Homeward, Angel (contd.)
    foreign publication of, 177ff., 208,
        271
    lawsuit over, 277, 286, 287, 312,
        343
    manuscript of, presented to Aline
        Bernstein, 166
    publication of, 126–29, 130ff.,
        148ff., 158
    quotations from, 24–30, 34, 37, 43–
        45, 47, 48
    reviews of, 148ff., 158, 177ff.
    Sinclair Lewis' praise of, 187
    suggested titles for, 111
Look Homeward, Angel (play), 156
"Lost Boy, The," 26, 379n.
Love, Lola, 150
Lowes, John Livingston, 54, 62, 63
Lüchow's, New York, 415
Luhan, Mabel Dodge, 287
Luther, Martin, 316, 406
"Lycidas," 111
Lyons, France, 180

McCoy, George, 90, 91, 298
McCoy, Mrs. George (Lola Love),
    150
McCrady, Louisa, 64, 67
MacDonald, Ann, 82
McGreevy, Thomas, 168
Mainz, Germany, 121
Majestic, S.S., 107
Malines, Belgium, 119
Mandel, James, 78–79, 110
Mann, Arthur, 418
Mannerhouse, 58, 92, 95, 102
"Man on the Wheel, The," 212
Many Marriages, 412n.
Marble Man's Wife, The, 36
Marinus, 266
Marseilles, France, 180
Marx, Sam, 288
Mayo Clinic, Rochester, Minn., 433
"Men of Old Catawba, The," 229n.
Meredith, Lacey, 71
Metro-Goldwyn-Mayer, 288
Meyer, Wallace, 130
Mezö-Kövesd, Hungary, 127
Middlebrook, L. Ruth, 25n., 86

Miller, Edward M., 420, 422ff.
Milton, John, 111, 140
Mitchell, Cornelius, 321, 366, 367,
    375n.
Mobley, Nathan, 378
Modern Library, Inc., 235, 355
Moe, Henry Allen, 192n., 212
Mok, Michel, 385
Montreal, Canada, 213
Montreux, Switzerland, 171, 177
Moser, Alfons, 330, 331n.
Mountains, The, 52, 57, 60, 62, 63,
    64
"Mr. Malone," 379n.
Muench, Irma Wyckoff, 245
Mullers, the Herbert, 419, 420n.
Munich, Germany, 107, 110, 115,
    121ff.
Munn, James B., 76, 112, 113, 119
Murray, A. N., 62
"My Experiences with Thomas
    Wolfe," 84n., 116n.
"My Record as a Writer," Wolfe's,
    136

Nancy Ann, 70
Nation, 264n.
National Broadcasting Company,
    297n, 379n., 404n., 436n.
National Gallery, London, 266
Nazism, 267, 273ff., 325ff.
Negroes, 328, 329
Neighborhood Playhouse, 82, 95, 98,
    104
New Canaan, Conn., 232, 233
New Orleans, La., 364ff.
New Orleans Carnival Ball, 367
New Orleans *Item*, 365n.
New Orleans *Times-Picayune*, 365
Newport News, Va., 42
New Republic, 155, 265n., 335
New Washington Hotel, Seattle, 423–
    25
New York City, 71, 72, 107ff., 129,
    202, 232, 279ff., 291ff., 326,
    337ff., 372, 383, 395, 416, 417
    literary circles of, 243, 316, 325–26,
        341, 409

New York Drama Critics Circle Award, 156
New Yorker, 262, 379n.
New York *Evening Post,* 385
New York *Herald Tribune,* 248, 301
  Books section, 149, 249, 258ff.
New York *Mirror,* 342
New York, New Haven & Hartford Railroad, 209
New York Public Library, 84
New York *Times,* 187, 189, 197, 343
  Book Review, 148, 258
New York University, 64, 72, 74ff., 89, 95, 101, 103, 107, 108, 114, 139, 161, 162, 329
New York *World,* 148
Niggertown, 68
Noble, Marcus, 92
"No Door," 214, 342
"No More Rivers," 291, 321, 338, 359, 379n.
Norfolk, Va., 42
North American Review, 229n.
North Carolina, 370ff., 380
North Carolina, The, St. Louis, 26
North Carolina, University of, *see* University of North Carolina
North Carolina Literary and Historical Society, 370
North German Lloyd, 325
North State School, Asheville, 29–32
Northwestern University, 64, 67
Norton, W. W., & Company, 392
Norwood, Robert, 156, 161
Notebooks, *see* Journals, Notebooks, and Diaries
"Note for the Publisher's Reader," Wolfe's, 111–12, 142
Nowell, Elizabeth, 239, 250, 321, 323, 324, 378, 422n., 437
  Martha Dodd's letter to, describing Wolfe, 275
  as Wolfe's agent, 234, 285, 301, 321, 338, 359, 390–92, 395, 400, 402, 404
  see also Wolfe, Thomas, letters to Elizabeth Nowell
Nuremberg, 110

Oberammergau, 126
October Fair, the, Munich, 101n., 115, 123–25
October Fair, The, 135, 174, 175, 181, 194, 211, 224, 227, 279, 287, 295, 298, 312, 343, 358, 362, 390, 391, 396, 397, 399, 403, 407
"Of Thomas Wolfe," 121n., 287n.
Of Time and the River, 13, 27, 65, 86, 119, 135, 136, 168n., 173–76, 194, 208, 214, 217, 218, 229n., 245, 256, 257, 279, 295, 318ff., 407, 416
  acclaimed by press, 251–55, 256ff., 282
  death of Gant in, 236, 237
  dedication for, 245, 246, 394
  foreign publication of, 235, 236, 271, 325
  lawsuits over, 277, 317
  preface for, 246, 247, 285, 301ff.
  promotion of, 261
  proposed introduction to, 246–47
  publication of, 160, 233–42, 245ff.
  quotations from, 28, 48–49, 50–54, 58, 64, 65, 73, 76, 80, 85, 86, 94, 96, 129, 173, 183, 435
  sales of, 291, 294, 315
  success of, 277, 279ff., 294
"Old Catawba," 229n.
Old Kentucky Home, 26, 27, 35, 380, 381, 439
"Old Man Rivers," 321
Olympian, 433
Olympic, S.S., 96, 99, 101
Olympic games, 325ff.
"One of the Girls in Our Party," 173
Oppenheimer, George, 288
Orange Street School, Asheville, 29
Ordeal of the Bondsman Doaks, The, 407
Oregonian (Portland, Ore.), 420
Oregonian Magazine, 420n.
Oregon State Motor Association, 420, 422
"Orestes: Flight before Fury," 219
Orrs Island, Me., 202
Oteen, N.C., 382, 385, 389, 390

Owens, Jesse, 328
Oxford, England, 105

Palo Alto Clinic, 289
Paris, 91ff., 103, 107, 110, 119, 166ff., 251
Paris, S.S., 337, 338
Parker, Dorothy, 288
"Party at Jack's, The," 173n., 379n., 383, 390
"Passage to England, A," 90
Paterson, Isabel M., 261, 264
Patmore, Mrs. Brigit, 168
Patton, Aaron, 21
Patton, Elizabeth, 21
Patton, George, 21
Patton, Nancy, 21
Patton, Robert, 21
Patton, Wendell L., 22n.
Paul, Clara, 35, 36, 42
Penland, Leander, 21
Penland, Marilda (Patton), 21
Penland, Martha Anne, 21
Penland, Peter, 21
Pennsylvania, 165, 213, 236
Perkins, Louise S. (Mrs. Maxwell E.), 243, 292, 364, 378, 427, 439
Perkins, Maxwell E., 11–17 passim, 109, 126, 128, 135ff., 150, 160, 161, 170, 186, 199, 212, 218, 279ff., 286, 364, 439
  and Aline Bernstein affair, 162–63, 189ff., 279, 295
  appointed Wolfe's executor, 378, 439
  dedication of *Of Time and the River* to, 245, 246
  father-friend to Wolfe, 24, 28, 98, 196–98, 205, 215, 232ff., 265, 277, 279ff., 292, 298–300, 311, 339, 347, 364, 375–78, 391, 393, 396, 400, 401, 405, 414, 427, 428, 437–38
  as Foxhall Edwards, 196, 197
  gave Wolfe faith in himself, 197, 298–300, 315, 347ff.
  and publication of *Of Time and the River*, 248–55 passim
  quotations from his articles on

Wolfe, 33, 130ff., 135, 138, 198, 206, 228, 231, 237, 239, 246, 250, 283, 290, 292–93
  quotations from letters of, to:
    Thomas Beer, 194–95, 216
    A. S. Frere, 236, 241, 242, 246
    Ernest Hemingway, 231, 244, 343
    Elizabeth Nowell, 422n.
    Marjorie Kinnan Rawlings, 233
    Charles Scribner III, 217
    John S. Terry, 137, 162, 223, 227, 232, 233, 295, 308, 309
    John Hall Wheelock, 308
    Thomas Wolfe, 127, 148, 162, 198, 203, 206, 223, 245–47, 252, 286, 310–12, 345–46, 369, 372–74
  Wolfe's gratitude to, 205, 206, 281, 347ff., 394, 400, 405, 414
  and Wolfe's lawsuits, 277, 312, 313, 317ff., 342ff., 366, 367, 413
  and Wolfe's Marxian views, 244, 245
  Wolfe's quarrel with, 243ff., 307–16, 321ff., 337–39, 341–63, 366, 372–77, 390–93
  Wolfe's reconciliation with, 405, 406, 414, 415
  Wolfe's resentment of, 231, 234, 236, 246, 312, 375
  and Wolfe's writing about Scribners, 314, 315, 321–23, 338
  his work on *Of Time and the River*, 207ff., 222–26, 227–42 passim, 373
  see also Wolfe, Thomas, letters to Maxwell E. Perkins
Plymouth, Mass., 60
Poling, James, 402
Polk, William, 50, 69, 285, 370
Pollock, Thomas Clark, 76n., 85
"Polyphemus," 229n.
Porter, Garland, 368, 374
Portland, Ore., 420
"Portrait of Bascom Hawke, A," 210, 212, 318
Pound, Ezra, 182
Powell, Desmond, 84, 121, 213, 287

Prague, 110
Prince George Hotel, Brooklyn, 279, 280
Princess Kathleen, S.S., 424
Princeton University, 33, 35, 36
"Prologue of America," 297
Proust, Marcel, 140
Providence Hospital, Seattle, 426, 427, 429
Provincetown Theatre, 82, 95
Puget Sound, 432
Pulitzer Prize, 156
Purdue University, Wolfe's speech delivered at, 16, 17, 39, 45, 53, 74, 102, 103, 145–48, 154, 155, 166, 171, 186, 194, 243, 244, 269, 288, 326, 408, 416, 419

Rackety Rax, 288
Radcliffe College, 62
Rainier, Ore., 423
Raisbeck, Kenneth, 53, 93, 207
Raleigh, N.C., 22, 376
Raleigh *News and Observer*, 39, 151
Randalls Island, 325
Rascoe, Burton, 212, 249, 259–61, 264
Rawlings, Marjorie Kinnan, 231, 233
Raynolds, Robert, 155, 212, 218, 219, 232, 234, 237, 242, 277
Redbook, 234, 379n.
Red Star Inn, Chicago, 419
"Reminiscences of Thomas Wolfe," 86n.
Resor, Helen, 114
"Return," 382
Return of Buck Gavin, a Tragedy of the Mountain People, The, 46, 52, 83
Rhinebeck, N.Y., 87, 88, 139
"River of Youth, The," 256
River People, The, 119, 120, 134, 181
Riverside Cemetery, Asheville, 440, 441
Road to Xanadu, The, 54
Roberts, Henry, 266
Roberts, J. M., 29, 154, 381
Roberts, Margaret (Mrs. J. M.), 24, 27, 29–32, 33, 101, 127, 141–43, 381

her reaction to *Look Homeward, Angel*, 153, 154
see also Wolfe, Thomas, letters to Margaret Roberts
Robinson Crusoe, 297
Roll River, 302
Romanisches Café, 274
Roosevelt, Franklin D., 218, 342
Rouen, France, 168
Rowohlt, Ernst, 208, 271, 272, 325, 329
Ruge, Dr. E. C., 424n., 425, 426, 427, 432
Ruggles of Red Gap, 265
Russell, Phillips, 371
Russia, 277
Ryan, Dr. Edward, 436

St. Louis, Mo., 26, 290
St. Raphaël, France, 93, 95
Sancton, Thomas, 365n.
San Francisco, Cal., 288, 289
Santa Fe, N.M., 287
Saturday Evening Post, 28, 175n., 379n., 381
Saturday Review of Literature, 38n., 155, 242n., 256, 258, 302, 376, 390, 391, 402n.
Saxton, Eugene F., 402
Sayre, Joel, 288
Schiebelhuth, Hans, 271n.
Schiller, Johann Christoph Friedrich von, 275
Schoenwald, Dr. Philip, 427
Scribner, Charles II, 321
Scribner, Charles III, 131, 161, 217, 235, 266, 313, 343–45, 374
"Scribner's and Tom Wolfe," 198, 206, 228n., 231n., 237n., 283, 290
Scribner's Magazine, 132, 140, 155, 173n., 208, 209, 210, 212–14, 233–35, 342, 376, 379n.
Scribner's Sons, Charles, 111, 137, 197, 210, 211, 215, 279, 280, 283, 284, 294, 302, 389, 390
  acceptance of Wolfe's first book, 128, 129
  Wolfe's discontent with, 234, 367ff., 391–93, 394ff., 421

Scribner's Sons, Charles (*contd.*)
  and Wolfe's finances, 139, 161–62,
    308ff., 389
  and Wolfe's lawsuits, 186, 319ff.,
    342ff., 389
  Wolfe's manuscripts stored at, 249,
    250, 397, 398
  and Wolfe's publicity, 247, 248, 261
  Wolfe's writing about, 321, 338,
    359, 360
Seattle, Wash., 423–33
Seeman's Printing Shop, 41
"Servants," 266
Seven Seas, The, 325, 337
Shakespeare, William, 31, 40
Shakespeare Tercentenary, 31
"Shakespeare the Man," 31, 32
Silvermine, Conn., 427
Sisters of Charity of Providence, 429
"Slot Machine, The," 332
Smith, Abe, 198
Smith, Bernard, 392
Smith, Harrison, 376
Smith, Marian, 169
Snow White and the Seven Dwarfs,
  419
Soskin, William, 212
Spring Hotel, Seattle, 428, 432, 433
Spruill, Corydon P., 41, 371, 381n.
Steffens, Lincoln, 408, 410
Stern, Martha Dodd, *see* Martha Dodd
Stevens, George, 92
Stevens, Henry, 83
Stevens, James, 424n., 425, 433
Stevens, Theresa (Mrs. James), 425,
  433
Stoney, George, 372n.
Story of a Novel, The, 17, 247, 285,
  347, 394
  publication of, 301ff.
  quotations from, 25, 27, 39, 91–92,
    96, 103, 105, 133, 142, 148, 152,
    156, 159, 160–61, 167, 169–70,
    172, 183–85, 192, 195, 200, 201,
    205, 207, 219–22, 224, 225, 227,
    228–30, 238–39, 243–44, 250–52
Strasbourg, Alsace-Lorraine, 107, 110,
  183

"Streets of Durham, or Dirty Work at
  the Crossroads; A Tragedy in
  Three Muddy Acts, The," 39
Stuart, Gloria, 288
Stuttgart, Germany, 107
"Sun and the Rain, The," 235
Sunday Referee (London), 178
Sunrise Lodge, Rainier, Ore., 423
Swannanoa, 21, 22
Swift, Dr. George, 431n., 432–34
Swinnerton, Frank, 178, 179
Switzerland, 171, 172

Tamerlane, 280, 281
Tannhäuser, 276
Taos, N.M., 287
Tar Baby, 39
Tar Heel, 38, 41, 42, 45
"Telemachus," 229n., 234
"Tender Is the Night," 389
Ten Eyck, Oswald, 50
Terry, John S., 11, 23, 131n., 137n.,
  162, 199n., 223, 227n., 232n.,
  233n., 280n., 295, 308n., 309n.,
  312n., 320n., 343n., 377n., 414n.,
  439n.
Thalberg, Irving, 288
Theatre Guild, 70, 71, 82, 95
Third Night, The, 47, 52, 83
Thomas Wolfe (by Herbert J. Muller),
  420n.
"Thomas Wolfe" (by Maxwell E. Per-
  kins), 33n., 130n., 135, 138,
  210n., 239, 246n., 247n., 250n.
"Thomas Wolfe, a Reminiscence,"
  79n.
"Thomas Wolfe at Harvard, 1920–
  1923," 50
Thomas Wolfe at Washington Square,
  76–78, 101n.
"Thomas Wolfe: Biography in
  Sound," 297n., 379n., 404n.,
  436n.
Thomas Wolfe: Carolina Student,
  38n.
"Thomas Wolfe Did Not Kill Max-
  well Perkins," 402n.
"Thomas Wolfe I Knew, The," 38n.

"Thomas Wolfe Lectures and Takes a Holiday," 420n.

"Thomas Wolfe—Maxwell Perkins," 116

"Thomas Wolfe: Playmaker," 46

Thomas Wolfe's Letters to His Mother, 23

Thompson, J. Walter, 114

Three Blue Suits, 163–64

Through Embassy Eyes, 273, 328

Tiergarten, Berlin, 269, 270, 271

Time, 265n.

"Time and the River," 365n.

Times Literary Supplement (London), 178

Tolstoi, Leo, 360

Tomorrow, 84, 116n.

"Tom Wolfe," 426n.

"Tom Wolfe as a Student," 38n., 41n.

"Tom Wolfe, Teacher," 76n.

"Tom Wolfe Writes a Play," 69n.

"To the Reader" (in *Look Homeward, Angel*), 142

Tours, France, 94

"Train and the City, The," 214

Twain, Mark, 12

Ulysses, 105, 108, 354–56

University of North Carolina, 33, 37ff., 371

"Usurers, The," 266

Vancouver, B.C., 424

Vanderbilt, Sanderson, 248, 249, 301

Van Doren, Carl, 155

Van Doren, Mark, 264

Vanity Fair, 173n.

Vermont, 219

Vevey, Switzerland, 177

Vienna, 110, 126–28

Virginia Quarterly Review, 229n.

Vision of Spangler's Paul, The, 299, 315, 321, 323, 356, 379, 397, 407

Voelcker, Thea, 329–31

Vogue, 297

Volendam, S.S., 166

Volkening, Henry T., 84, 178n.
    see also Wolfe, Thomas, letters to Henry T. Volkening

Vulcania, S.S., 129

Wachovia Bank and Trust Company of Asheville, 379

Wagner, Richard, 276

Walker, N. A., 50, 59

Wallace, George, 53, 83, 213, 215, 217

Wallace, Margaret, 148–49

Wall Street, 186

Walpole, Hugh, 156, 266

War and Peace, 360

Warnke, Janice Davis, 331n.

Wartburg, 274, 275, 276

Washington, D.C., 215

Waterloo, 104

Watson, Hattie, 23

Watt, Homer A., 72, 75, 76, 86n., 89, 93, 95, 161
    see also Wolfe, Thomas, letters to Homer A. Watt

Watts, Dr. Charles E., 425–33

Web and the Rock, The, 119, 135, 136, 175n., 176, 194, 209, 214, 297, 356n., 379n., 411, 435n.
    quotations from, 108, 110, 121–23

"Web of Earth, The," 209, 210, 233, 294n.

Webster, Daniel, 297

Weimar, Germany, 274, 275

Welbourne, Middleburg, Va., 241

Welcome to Our City, 58, 68ff., 82, 83, 95, 102

Wescott, Glenway, 156

Westall, Eliza (Mrs. J. B. Austin), 21

Westall, Henry A., 22n., 33, 48, 51, 210, 430

Westall, John, 380

Westall, Thomas, 21, 380

Westall, Thomas Casey, 21, 23

Westall, William G., 380

"Western Journey, The," 420ff.

Westport, Conn., 207

Wheaton, Mabel Wolfe (Mrs. Ralph H.), 24, 26, 33, 35, 65, 215, 216, 381, 384, 414, 424n., 428–39
    quoted, 26, 35, 143, 150, 439
    reaction of, to *Look Homeward, Angel*, 150, 153

Wheaton, Mabel Wolfe (*contd.*)
  see also Wolfe, Thomas, letters to
    Mabel Wolfe Wheaton
"Wheaton, Mrs., Sister of Thomas
    Wolfe, Chronologically Telling
    His Life History," 26n., 150n.,
    425n. 439n.
Wheaton, Ralph H., 35, 66, 143
Wheelock, John Hall, 13, 130, 133,
    136n., 139, 198, 225n., 239, 241,
    242, 245, 246, 261n., 308
  see also Wolfe, Thomas, letters to
    John Hall Wheelock
White, Hal, 84
Whitman, Walt, 257
Whitson, Max, 382
Widener Library, 60
Wierman, Gertrude, 22
Wierman, William, 22
Wiesbaden, Germany, 121
Wilde, Oscar, 92
William and Sarah, 22
William B. Wisdom Collection, 211n.,
    366n.
Williams, Horace, 45, 48, 371
Wilson, Edmund, 212, 332
Wilson, Woodrow, 29
Winchell, Walter, 342, 343
Winchester, Tenn., 21
Winchester, Va., 21, 380
Winesburg, Ohio, 412
Wings, 155
Winter, Ella, 408, 409, 410
Winthers, the Sophus, 425
Wisdom, William B., 366
"With Apologies to Pepys," 38
Wolf, Edgar, 213
Wolf, Eleanor Jane (Heikes), 22
Wolf, George, 22
Wolf, Gilbert, 213
Wolf, Jacob, 22, 409
Wolf, Wesley, 22
Wolfe, Benjamin Harrison, 23, 26, 31,
    33, 35, 42–44, 441
Wolfe, Effie, 23, 26
  see also Gambrell, Effie
Wolfe, Frank, 23, 384

Wolfe, Fred, 23, 28, 35, 67, 93, 167,
    186, 213, 218, 405, 426, 437, 439
  see also Wolfe, Thomas, letters to
    Fred Wolfe
Wolfe, Grover Cleveland, 23, 26, 288,
    290, 441
Wolfe, Julia E., 21–26, 47, 48, 89, 213,
    214, 218, 384, 405
  and Aline Bernstein, 195, 196
  her boardinghouses, 26, 33, 35, 61,
    384
  her possessiveness, 23–26, 29, 89,
    102
  quoted, 23, 32, 36
  her reaction to *Look Homeward,
    Angel*, 150, 153
  her real-estate speculations, 118,
    119, 379ff.
  and Tom's finances, 66, 89, 93
  and Tom's last illness, 433–39
  visits Tom in New York, 209
  see also Wolfe, Thomas, letters to
    Julia E. Wolfe
Wolfe, Leslie, 23
Wolfe, Mabel, 23, 35
  see also Wheaton, Mabel Wolfe
Wolfe, Thomas:
  appearance, 13, 40, 52, 86
  "black moods," 12, 113, 158, 167,
    170, 179ff., 213, 215, 217, 232,
    250, 251, 262ff., 435
  conflicts in, 12, 25, 203–5, 217, 230–
    31, 237, 242, 253, 312
  death of, 224, 418, 435–41
  did not want to be autobiographical,
    216, 296–99, 360
  difficulty in cutting manuscripts,
    134, 139, 227–29, 237, 238
  difficulty in making decisions, 12, 16,
    64, 108, 180, 402, 405, 406, 411
  as a dramatist, 46–48, 50ff., 62, 102
  drinking, 109, 170, 200, 232, 252,
    265, 330, 366, 367, 376
  eating, 15, 41, 109, 122, 289, 296
  finances, 57, 66, 67, 89, 93, 94, 105,
    110, 161–62, 166, 167, 186, 187,
    208, 213, 214, 233–35, 288, 291,
    308, 315, 364, 375, 389

Wolfe, Thomas, (*contd.*)

health, 56, 57, 95, 223, 224, 378, 379, 415, 424ff.

humor, 12, 37, 38, 41, 182, 231, 332, 415

hunger for knowledge, 28, 31, 54–56, 121–23, 220

lawsuits, 51, 92, 167, 185, 277, 286, 287, 312, 313, 317ff., 342, 364ff., 375, 380ff., 389, 413–15

letters of, to:

Sherwood Anderson, 28

Edward C. Aswell, 407–8

Hamilton Basso, 293, 297, 298, 382–84, 389–90, 412

Aline Bernstein, 99, 101, 102, 106, 123–27, 139, 283, 346

James Boyd, 165

Catherine Brett, 239

Benjamin Cone, 34

Alfred Dashiell, 13, 185, 203, 217

the L. Effingham de Forests, 240

Martha Dodd, 282

Arthur Davison Ficke, 158

F. Scott Fitzgerald, 386–89

Elaine Gould, 68, 213

Kent Roberts Greenfield, 305–7

Heinz Ledig-Rowohlt, 298–300

Elizabeth Lemmon, 241, 291

George McCoy, 90, 298

Arthur Mann, 418

Henry Allen Moe, 212

James B. Munn, 119

Elizabeth Nowell, 35, 99, 100, 103, 117, 143, 335, 416, 420, 421

Maxwell E. Perkins, 101, 116–17, 127, 128, 143, 156–57, 172–75, 177, 179, 182, 185–87, 189–91, 203–5, 218, 224–25, 252–55, 262–65, 267, 272–77, 285–90, 295, 309–11, 313–15, 331, 344–63, 364, 367–69, 395, 405, 413, 427–28

Desmond Powell, 213

Robert Raynolds, 212, 218, 219, 234, 237, 242

Margaret Roberts, 30, 36, 61, 68, 82, 91, 95, 101–2, 109, 131–33, 137, 141–42, 412–13, 415

Charles Scribner III, 344

Corydon P. Spruill, 381

Henry T. Volkening, 140, 170, 171, 177, 180–82, 187, 293

George Wallace, 215, 217

Homer A. Watt, 75, 81, 92, 114

Mabel Wolfe Wheaton, 112, 136, 216, 218, 249

John Hall Wheelock, 168, 173, 174, 179–80, 182

Fred Wolfe, 66, 207, 209, 219, 317, 372, 384–85

Julia E. Wolfe, 56, 57, 61, 71, 72, 80, 82, 89, 94, 96, 111, 165, 182, 213, 215, 239, 364, 378

loneliness, 27, 34, 35, 60, 84, 93, 96, 169, 173, 196, 268, 406

lost manuscript, 302

love affairs, 35, 36, 42, 93–97, 98ff., 116ff., 159, 162ff., 177, 179, 182, 188ff., 195, 196, 285, 329–31

love of spending, 12, 214

love of trains, 16, 33, 165, 172, 232, 297, 382

loyalty, 12, 235, 309, 310

maturity, 16, 24, 90, 98, 408

naïveté and trustfulness, 12, 113, 317

need for approval, 15, 42, 197

need to write, 13, 14, 25, 80, 81, 96, 105, 106, 108, 168, 194, 199, 202, 289

"nothing cut ever lost," 136, 173n., 214, 215

periods of hope and joy, 12, 133, 158, 225, 269ff.

prolonged infantile relationships, 23–26, 29, 89, 102

search for a father, 16, 27, 28, 157, 162, 175, 196, 201, 316

sense of time, 12, 39, 41, 60, 69, 202, 209, 220, 232, 241

social consciousness and political

Wolfe, Thomas, (*contd.*)
    views, 243ff., 315, 316, 329, 332, 333, 339ff.,
    stammering, 34, 52, 285
    suspicion of people, 12, 109, 166, 200, 398, 399, 409, 421
    walks, 199, 200, 219, 268
    see also Perkins, Maxwell E., letters to Thomas Wolfe
Wolfe, William Oliver, 21, 22, 24, 25, 33, 36, 47, 48, 61, 64–66, 214, 435, 441
Wolff, Hans Bernhard, 22
Wolff, Hans Georg, 22
"Wolverines," 371, 372
"Work in Progress," 323n.

World's Fair, Chicago, 241
Worth Prize, 45
Wright, Warren, 421
Writers' Conference, University of Colorado, 11, 285, 301, 420

Yale Review, 379n.
York Springs, Pa., 22, 165, 213, 218
You Can't Go Home Again, 42n., 126, 136, 176, 209, 214, 255, 297, 356n., 379n., 410, 411, 435n.
    quotations from, 126, 158, 188, 193ff., 222, 316, 325–28, 333, 339–41, 441
Young Men's Christian Association, 41, 42

DATE DUE